YALE LAW LIBRARY SERIES IN LEGAL HISTORY AND REFERENCE

THE INTERBELLUM CONSTITUTION

UNION, COMMERCE, AND SLAVERY IN THE AGE OF FEDERALISMS

Alison L. LaCroix

Yale
UNIVERSITY PRESS
New Haven and London

Published with support from the Lillian Goldman Law
Library, Yale Law School, and with assistance from the
Mary Cady Tew Memorial Fund and from the income
of the Frederick John Kingsbury Memorial Fund.

Yale University Press books may be purchased in quantity
for educational, business, or promotional use. For information, please e-mail sales.press@yale.edu (U.S. office) or
sales@yaleup.co.uk (U.K. office).

Set in Scala type by IDS Infotech Ltd.
Printed in the United States of America.

Library of Congress Control Number: 2023939000
ISBN 978-0-300-22321-7 (hardcover : alk. paper)

A catalogue record for this book is available
from the British Library.

This paper meets the requirements of ANSI/NISO Z39.48-
1992 (Permanence of Paper).

10 9 8 7 6 5 4 3 2 1

To Elspeth, Isolde, and Alana

Contents

The Interbellum Constitution

Introduction: The Age of Federalisms

The subject of this book is the nature of the American union between 1815 and 1861. The central argument is that we must change our view of those decades, and in particular of the legal and political debates that took place within them. The book offers a new framework for this forty-six-year period, which is best understood as the era of the Interbellum Constitution.

On each side, the period was bordered by war: the War of 1812, which ended in 1815, and the Civil War, which began in 1861. Debates about American law and politics during this period focused unceasingly on the question of what union meant—in particular, what the proper structure of governmental authority was in the adolescent American union. The puzzle was how the system should respond to conflicts among local interests and collisions among federal, state, municipal, and other authorities. Such friction might be inevitable in a federal republic. Or it might be the duty of the national government to harmonize where it could, encourage what it chose, and coerce where it must.

Many of the most contested issues in interbellum constitutional discourse were relational and structural. The problem that bedeviled contemporaries was how to fit together the pieces of the various governments that constituted the Union. Today, we would term this a problem of federalism. But, as this book shows, the word "federalism" in its modern sense does not accurately capture the landscape of constitutional debate in the early nineteenth century.

The Constitution of 1787 established a system of multilayered powers with roughly defined zones of authority. But what happened when those zones overlapped? At the core of constitutional contestation in the early nineteenth century was the question of how to divide governmental power among rival claimants. These rivals were numerous, many more than merely the states versus the federal government. They included local governments and actors, the states, the federal government, and the amorphous entity called "the people." The fundamental relationship was not one of binary federalism; that arrangement coalesced later, during the Civil War, and was produced by the debates of this period. The messy norm of the early nineteenth century was concurrence and overlap and conflict. The claimants included cities, towns, and assemblies of private citizens. The argument mattered because these questions were not only theoretical. On the contrary, they had practical consequences for the most pressing concerns of their day and the nation's future: commerce, migration, and slavery.

The period between 1815 and 1861 witnessed a transformation in American constitutional law and politics. *The Interbellum Constitution* argues that these decades were a foundational era of both constitutional crisis and self-conscious creativity. The book thus upends the conventional story of the period as a hiatus between the "real" constitutional moments of the founding and Reconstruction.

Scholars of constitutional law, especially those who like to use history, tend to speak in terms of shocks and moments. The focus of such accounts is the singular event: the convention, the lawsuit, the amendment. In these special moments, we are told, constitutional law is made. Between these peaks are periods of quotidian legal and political time. During these in-between spells, law and politics operate in a "normal" register.[1] In these everyday stretches, which form the bulk of American constitutional history, no real constitutional law is being made, according to this view. Rather, normal politics is presented as a period of mulling, talking, and debating, but not actually *producing* anything constitutionally significant.

"We the people" are not creating during these times. The people are presumably mindful of their constrained capabilities, humbly accepting of their mere normality. They have a "constitutional conversation" that is limited in scope and bounded by the terms of the text of the Constitution that they have passively inherited. They discuss "whether and how to amend" the "document" and "how to interpret and implement" it. They know they are not worthy of the title "founders." They implement, they put into practice, but they do not create. If they are clever, they know that they should look to the founders for the "right legal answers to the burning issues" of their normal moment.[2] They understand that they are lucky to be aboard the ship of the republic. But they know their limits. They are mere passengers, borne along between the ports of constitutional moments, meekly liquidating the text as they go.

As this book shows, however, this account is wrong in both a specific and a general sense. It is specifically incorrect because it fails to account for the actual historical reality of American constitutional debate between the founding era and the Civil War. It is generally erroneous because it misunderstands the process of constitutional change.

The Interbellum Constitution was a set of widely shared legal and political principles, combined with a thoroughgoing commitment to investing meaning in those principles through debate. The shared principles were commerce, concurrent power, and jurisdictional multiplicity, all of which contemporaries grouped under the heading of "commercial union." The debates took place in many arenas: newspapers, private letters, legislative chambers, and the special forum of the courtroom, compassing lawyers' arguments as well as judges' opinions.

Each of these issues concerned what might now be termed "federalism," insofar as they pertained to the relationships among multiple levels of government with varying degrees of autonomy. A core claim of this book, however, is that there existed many more *federalisms*, plural, in the early nineteenth century than today's constitutional debates admit. This book does not offer a genealogy of a static concept. The narrative that follows seeks to witness and interpret debates in which meaning was being created, not to engage in retrospective diagnoses of discovery.

Understanding the Interbellum Constitution requires attending to the contexts in which specific historical actors defined that concept through their speeches, writings, and arguments. Situating familiar legal and political contests in their broader intellectual, social, and indeed personal milieux shows interbellum federalism to have been far more intellectually and legally generative than standard accounts suggest. This method also demonstrates the existence of distinct species of federalism that vary from our familiar modern ones. Simply put, the range of plausible constitutional arguments in the early nineteenth century was different from and richer than the modern array. Claims that would not be colorable under modern constitutional doctrine were recognized as legitimate then. To give just one example, exclusive federal power over interstate commerce was a plausible construction of the Constitution for at least three decades. Even more surprising, perhaps, was the pervasiveness of arguments for nonbinary federalism—a view of the federal-state relationship as one of concurrence and negotiation, rather than as a stark, all-or-nothing contest between federal and state power.

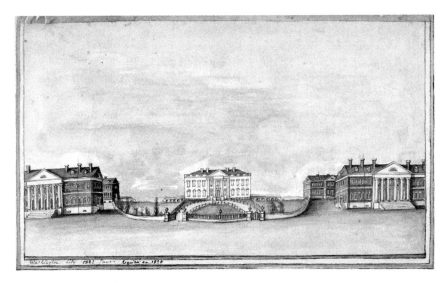

Anne Marguérite Joséphine Henriette Rouillé de Marigny, Baroness Hyde de
Neuville, *Washington City,* 1821. The White House is shown at center, viewed from
the north, with the Departments of State and Treasury at left (State in front),
and Departments of War and Navy at right (War in front). (Miriam and
Ira D. Wallach Division of Art, Prints and Photographs: Print Collection,
The New York Public Library.)

What was the nature of the American union between 1815 and 1861? Early-
nineteenth-century Americans had not yet decided what every provision of the
Constitution signified. But they believed that the only way of determining that
meaning was to distill potential interpretations into words, to argue about
those words, and to accept that the arguments of the day would set the parameters for the rounds to come.

Later generations have come to regard early-nineteenth-century constitutional debates as either quaint set pieces of high-flown declamation by gentlemen in fussy cravats and puffy shirts, or as masques performed to conceal
ugly truths of partisan, regional, racial, or economic interests. To be sure,
there were neckcloths and perorations, and there were unsavory deals struck
in back rooms of taverns while a majority of the population looked silently on,
ironing those lengths of linen and hushing the children.

But to see the era solely through such generalizations is to miss important
transformations in constitutional law. Interbellum Americans were not people who knew their limits. They were not mere passengers. They were produc-

ers of constitutional discourse whose arguments charted the maps of the American constitutional sea.

Let us travel for a moment to the heart of the interbellum period. As the United States expanded, and roads unfurled from the Potomac to the Ohio and beyond, so too did law. Layers of law, in fact: local regulations governing the placement of distilleries and piggeries; state legislation concerning banks, lotteries, devises, immigrants, and ports; and, increasingly, federal law, in the form of international treaties, coasting statutes, enforcement actions, and import duties. The nation was busy, its people quarrelsome yet desirous of order.

In July 1830, before an audience of several hundred people, many of whom had traveled by steamboat from New York City to New Brunswick, New Jersey, to attend this signal event of the Rutgers College commencement exercises, the former attorney general of the United States took the stage to deliver an oration. This speaker was William Wirt, described by a chronicler as "the distinguished jurist and statesman and scholar, perhaps the preeminent man of his day in public address."[3]

The ostensible subject of the lecture was "the cause of education." But Wirt's central theme quickly became clear: the condition of the American union. The Union was nothing less than a "political phenomenon," in Wirt's words. It was a "national government" comprising a confederacy of states, with each state "being, in itself, a separate sovereignty." The confederacy was continental in scale, stretching from north to south "through several degrees of latitude," as well as from east to west "from the Atlantic to the Pacific Ocean." Wirt, who in his long career as a member of the Supreme Court bar was famed for his ability to conjure pictures in the minds of his listeners, did not stint in his imagery that day in the overflowing Old Queens Hall. He described the Union in terms that suggested a pyramid: at the top, a national government constituted by a confederacy (the middle layer), and that confederacy in turn constituted by another layer of states.[4]

Up to this point, a modern reader of Wirt's address might be tempted to assume that the attorney general was offering a familiar refrain of the early-nineteenth-century American union. The tune sounds familiar at first: the Union was both a nation and a confederacy. It contained a national government and a set of states, each with its own status as a distinct sovereign. The paradox of such a structure seems ineluctable—a nation comprising separate sovereigns? The potential for conflict seems unavoidable—a federal government lacking coercive power, a group of states resisting central authority? The

Union appears to have been constituted by two equal and opposing forces: the federal government and the states. Or, really, the federal government *versus* the states—a binary and zero-sum relationship.[5]

Twenty-eight years after Wirt's speech, in 1858, Senator William H. Seward warned of an impending "irrepressible conflict" between the "antagonistic systems" of free and enslaved labor that "existed in different States, but side by side within the American Union."[6] But, one might think, Wirt got there first. One might read Wirt's 1830 Rutgers speech as two things: first, a recognition of the instability of the nineteenth-century Union; and second, evidence that this instability inhered in the nature of a federal republic, which necessarily pitted the nation against the states. One can all too easily read Wirt as a prophet of war, and to assume that 1830 was but a way station along the normal-politics turnpike, between the tollgates of the founding and the Civil War.[7]

Except that it was not. For the bottom of Wirt's pyramid was not the states, and the states were not monolithic. The states were "various in their soil and climate, and necessarily various in their productions" and "in the pursuits of their citizens." The states were also various in "their local interests."[8] In other words, the Union was not only a union of states; it was a union of productions, citizens, and local interests.

Wirt was not simply laying out a scheme, familiar to modern eyes, of federal versus state power. He was allowing for the possibility that the structure of the Union reached around, above, and below the states, to their people and to their localities. Wirt's praise for the "political phenomenon" of the Union was indeed tempered with a warning. But it was not simply a warning about a conflict between the federal government and the states. It was an even graver message. For Wirt contemplated a much wider confrontation that would sweep in every level of government, every type of affiliation—even those below the level of the state—and possibly end in an unmappable war of unraveling institutions all the way down the multilayered pyramid of the republic's governments.

"These institutions are beautiful in theory, but they are complex," Wirt cautioned his audience. One danger was that "the people should not sufficiently understand them, and, not understanding them, should fall into the hands of corrupt and ambitious leaders who will contrive to make a job out of these governments for themselves." The other danger was that "the conflicts of local interest in this widely extended empire, and the collisions between so many separate sovereignties, operating at the same time, over the same territory, should produce a concussion which may bring down the whole fabric in ruins about your ears."[9] This second danger, Wirt argued, was the more likely to transpire because it was "seated too deeply in the theory of our institutions." In all their variousness, these institutions stoked "the conflict of local interest, and the collisions between the Federal and State authorities."[10]

Note the phrasing: the "conflict of local interest" was distinct from the "collisions between the Federal and State authorities." Wirt clearly envisioned a domain of "the local" as something distinct from the federal-state binary but no less important—or hazardous—to the Union as a whole. The Union comprised "many separate sovereignties" operating at the same time over the same territory. Many layers of government touched the same object, person, or land at once. But the result was not a neat scheme of divided authority or a negotiated concurrence. The prospect for Wirt was far more worrisome: conflict at every level of government, and between all institutions. His fear was that jurisdictional multiplicity would collapse, leading to "a rupture of the union."[11]

Wirt was not foretelling a war thirty-one years in the future. The 1830s were not simply a rehearsal for the 1860s. The Civil War was a profound break in American political and constitutional time; it has been called a "second founding," the meaning and consequences of which continue to be fought over in the twenty-first century.[12] But the violent and transformational nature of that rupture should not lead us to believe that everything that preceded it was mere prologue. One duty of a historian is to resist teleology—to warn against reading historical events as though they proceeded toward some (to them) future goal. The first five decades of the nineteenth century were not experienced by people living in them as "the coming of the civil war." To be sure, the war that eventually came was causally related to the events that had preceded it. But causation runs in only one direction. The events of the early nineteenth century caused the Civil War. But the fact of the Civil War should not necessarily dictate how historians interpret the years prior. The interbellum period was legally and politically distinct.

Interbellum Americans were not the first generation to encounter the puzzle of governmental multiplicity. The American founders had discarded one canonical version of sovereignty, that offered by William Blackstone, who insisted that a government could contain only a single sovereign, and that any system that contemplated multiple sources of governmental authority was definitionally impossible.[13] In the 1770s and 1780s, Americans came to reject this view that a government within a government, or an *imperium in imperio*, was necessarily a "solecism." Instead, they turned to Continental theorists and their own experience under the British Empire to argue that multiple, multi-layered sovereignty was not only possible, it was the optimal structure for a republic on the scale of the United States. Many members of the founding generation argued that the specter of the *imperium in imperio* could be banished by building a structure that allocated sovereignty, along with functions, to particular spheres of government. This subject-matter vision of sovereignty, which aimed to de-pathologize a system of multiple sovereigns, was the paramount innovation of the American federal republic.[14]

The ideological origins of American federalism lay in answering the following question: What was the status of subpolities within the American federal union? One provisional answer, reached in 1787, was that the division of power based on subject matter (treaties, money, war, post offices) allowed a multiplicity of governments to exist within a single, overarching union. The Constitution not only rejected the solecism view of *imperium in imperio*; it embraced the possibility of multiple, overlapping governments, reframing *imperium in imperio* as a virtue and a source of strength.[15]

The central question of the interbellum period, however, was a different one: How far down (or out) should the rejection of *imperium in imperio* go? How many levels of multiple government were permitted before the system crumbled into a mess of shards, decentralized but with no claim to their own particular spheres of authority? The new theories supporting the Constitution established that layering a general government on top of the states did not necessarily raise *imperium in imperio* problems. But it was not at all clear how sovereign the states were permitted to be with respect to each other, to the general government, or to the governments of other nations.

Early-nineteenth-century Americans found themselves consumed by arguments about concurrent power—the areas in which the Constitution had left the line between federal and state authority unclear. The scope of specific concurrent powers became increasingly important, and controversial, in the early nineteenth century. In 1815, the most pressing political and legal issues increasingly concerned situations in which multiple layers of governmental power overlapped—and the Constitution provided no clear delineation. Moreover, the choice of which level of government regulated each subject had dramatic consequences for the policy that resulted.

The interbellum economy was alternately booming and busting, as the market revolution and the empire of cotton expanded their reach. Turnpikes and canals transported goods from producers to consumers; the global cotton trade devoured raw materials and human lives on all sides of the Atlantic; and a communications revolution fed the public's growing hunger for news.[16] Americans—both free and enslaved—were moving, sometimes between states and sometimes between states and federal territories. The tidy but vague boxes that the founders had created to contain the different sources of government power were collapsing.

Amid these upheavals, interbellum Americans exhibited an adolescent mix of bravado and anxiety. They viewed themselves as abandoned when the members of the founding generation died in the 1820s and 1830s. They worried that the meaning of the Constitution might be impossible for them to comprehend without their elders as guides and absent a mass of authorities to elucidate it. At the same time, the creativity of interbellum lawyers such as William Wirt lay in their ability to generate legal precedents, and to do so with a flourish that carried their words to a broad popular audience. In an era in which Supreme Court arguments extended for days, providing some of Washington's finest entertainment and celebrity sightings, the courtroom offered legal theater and public spectacle. These arguments were speech acts and moments in which meaning was created. The arena was public, and the stakes—both professional and social—were high.

Wirt and his contemporaries believed themselves to be living in what this book calls a "long founding moment." They frequently invoked Revolutionary figures and ideals, which for many interbellum Americans were both a gift and a burden. In his 1838 address to the Young Men's Lyceum of Springfield, Illinois, the twenty-nine-year-old Abraham Lincoln argued that the task before his generation was nothing less than "the perpetuation of our political institutions."[17] Lincoln exhorted his audience, "We find ourselves under the government of a system of political institutions, conducing more essentially to the ends of civil and religious liberty, than any of which the history of former times tells us." Those institutions depended on "reverence for the laws." Indeed, Lincoln urged, law—which he specifically identified as the Declaration of Independence and the Constitution—ought to become "the political religion" of the United States.[18]

Duty obliged early-nineteenth-century Americans to be faithful heirs of the Revolutionary generation. Fulfilling this charge required reverence for the political religion of the nation's founding charters. Yet interbellum constitutional thinkers rarely appeared to feel confined by the actual text of these documents. William Wirt, Maria Henrietta Pinckney, Frederick Douglass, John Marshall, John Ross, Elias Boudinot, Daniel Webster, William Johnson, John C. Calhoun— these producers of constitutional discourse understood themselves as working within the structure of the Constitution, even as they offered innovative arguments about its application to what they viewed as novel situations in a nation roiled by political, economic, and social upheaval. They sometimes discussed potential amendments to the Constitution. But they did not conceive of themselves as limited by text. Indeed, their commitment to constitutional interpretation through argumentation—oral as well as written—suggests that they understood fidelity to the Constitution to include far more than text alone. In order to understand the Interbellum Constitution, one must spend time embedded among these producers of constitutional discourse, listening to their words and situating those words in their context.

In 1830, when James Madison was asked to explain a veto he had issued thirteen years earlier during his presidency, he wrote, "[W]hether the language employed duly conveyed the meaning of which J. M. retains the consciousness, is a question on which he does not presume to judge for others." Still pondering the issue a month later, Madison added, "I am aware that the document must speak for itself, and that intention cannot be substituted for the established rules of interpretation."[19] Once the text—in this case, a presidential veto—had left its author's pen, it had to speak for itself, and it was subject to interpretation. Interbellum constitutional law was understood by contemporaries to be an ongoing process of writing, speaking, and interpreting.

This book makes five central claims about the nature of the Interbellum Constitution.

First, the interbellum period was a distinct period. For too long, the early nineteenth century has been treated as the flyover country of constitutional history.[20] But, as this book demonstrates, the period was not a gap between the constitutional landmarks of the founding era and the Civil War.

Second, the book rejects two conventional stories about constitutional debates in the period between 1815 and 1861. One of these stories is the binary federalism account, which frames all disputes about the structure of the American union as contests about the power of the general government versus the states. The second of these stories follows from the first. It concerns the valence of each power in the federal-state dyad. According to this view, the substantive tendency of federal power was toward liberty. The exercise of federal power— and the embrace of federal power through the ideology of nationalism—is thus associated with freedom, and specifically with limits on slavery. State power, meanwhile, in its many incarnations (states' rights, state sovereignty, localism) is seen as tending toward—perhaps even necessarily tied to—protections for slavery and limits on freedom, in particular the freedom of Black people.[21]

As the book discusses, however, the valence of federal power in the inter-bellum period did not necessarily run toward freedom, and the embrace of state authority did not always serve racial subordination. Because the era has typically been viewed through the lens of the Civil War, the federal-state align-ments of the 1860s have frequently been projected in reverse, onto the early nineteenth century. A foundational tenet of intellectual history, however, is that one must beware of reading later arguments and ideas back onto earlier debates.[22] The lesson has particular applicability to the study of constitutional law. Interbellum federalism should not be reduced to a federal-state dichot-omy. Nor were the directions of federal and state power in this period neces-sarily what they later became. The book delineates many instances in which the roles were reversed.

Third, the book argues that ideas of concurrent power were uniquely cen-tral to interbellum constitutional discourse, setting the period apart from both the founding era and the post–Civil War regime. Concurrent power had been one of the principal questions left unresolved by the Constitution as drafted in 1787. Were the enumerated powers of the federal government exclusive? Or did the states share regulatory authority in certain domains? Alexander Ham-ilton had theorized about this question in *The Federalist* No. 32, but a regime in which the federal government and the states consented to a future of con-stant negotiation rather than sharp line-drawing was a different matter.[23] Con-current power might be possible in the fevered abstractions of the *Federalist*, but whether it could exist in the wild was a question that the founding genera-tion had been happy to leave unsettled.

After 1815, however, many of the most pressing legal and political questions concerned areas in which either exclusive or concurrent power might be plau-sible. These domains included commerce, migration, and slavery. Impor-tantly, arguments for concurrent power were not necessarily the same as arguments for state authority. Nor were they merely cover for the substantive policies sometimes associated with states' rights claims. In a series of signifi-cant but now largely, and wrongly, overlooked cases, the U.S. Supreme Court wrestled with the practical meaning of concurrent power. These cases, many of which involved years of litigation and rallied the argumentative talents of the leading lawyers of the era, were not necessarily rearguard actions in favor of state sovereignty. Nor were they tidy doctrine-generating vehicles. They were disorderly sites of constitutional creativity that took seriously a version of federalism that has since largely disappeared from the realm of possibility.[24] These debates provide powerful evidence of what concurrent power looked like in practice to Americans of the interbellum period. This book's extensive archival investigation into the tangled procedural posture of these cases, which sometimes involved sheaves of handwritten pleadings replete with surprising gaps and carefully crafted factual stipulations, offers a unique window into the contestation that went into bringing these cases to trial.

The fourth claim is related to the issue of concurrent power. But unlike concurrent power, which modern commentators tend to treat as either impossible or dubious, this point concerns a core element of twentieth- and twenty-first-century constitutional law: the federal commerce power. In practical terms, commerce was the crucible in which interbellum battles over federalism boiled. In terms of constitutional structure, the Commerce Clause of Article I was the doctrinal vessel into which these conflicts were poured, and which in turn shaped their resolution. The interbellum period witnessed a burst of intellectual ferment—and conflict—over the nature and scope of Congress's power to regulate commerce among the states, with foreign nations, and with Native nations.

Debates about commerce were also about apportioning control among multiple overlapping jurisdictions.[25] In addition to an existential question— "What is a commercial union?"—lawyers and jurists struggled with a jurisdictional one—"Which governments will regulate in any particular domain?" The controversy accepted jurisdictional multiplicity as a given. It then asked which among many contesting levels of authority should do the governing.

The Marshall Court's Commerce Clause cases have been widely studied, so much that they might seem at this point to offer only truisms and bromides. But such a view is mistaken. Today, these cases are regarded as foundational (perhaps even founding) interpretations of constitutional questions. Certainly, the Marshall Court laid down the precedents that shaped future adjudication on these questions; such a dynamic is characteristic in our system of common law constitutionalism, and all the more so when the precedents come from a court both close in time to the founding and led by a chief justice of Marshall's intellect and political nous.[26] Nevertheless, the uses to which these cases are often put in the modern era is a modern gloss, not a true representation of what the speakers intended their statements to mean when they uttered them two centuries ago. To understand what was constitutionally possible in 1824, for example, one must read deeply in 1824, not look to 1937 or 2012 to explain what 1824 meant.

What, then, was the constitutional law of commerce between 1815 and 1861? Where should one look to comprehend the outer boundaries of what could and could not plausibly be claimed?

This book's answer includes not only the justices' decisions but also the lawyers' arguments. For lawyers, too, were producers of constitutional discourse. The actual holdings in the cases provide only a partial view of the landscape. Judicial decisions display merely some arguments that did prevail, not all the arguments that might have been plausible, or—perhaps even more valuable—the arguments that clearly failed. As a matter of litigation strategy, the arguments of counsel in those cases sketch the outlines of the reasoning that a cadre of expert, economically and socially invested attorneys believed might convince the justices. Attending to the lawyers' speeches and writings therefore gives a more textured analytical map than does a workaday march through the Court's opinions. As a matter of intellectual history, these cases offer rich evidence of the full array of arguments that contemporaries viewed as the most compelling ones. But in order to extract this meaning from the lawyers, we must read their words not simply as efforts to mold some preexisting thing called "law" in favor of their own clients, but rather as attempts to order their increasingly messy political and legal world. We must, in other words, take the arguments made in the courtroom and aerate them in the currents of their own moment, rather than lining them up in a path leading toward our own.

Arguments in, and around, the Supreme Court on the question of commerce are where one can perceive the true significance and novelty of interbellum constitutional thought. The courtroom was where mercantile, "shoppy" reality encountered the aspiration toward (if not the achievement of) Ciceronian eloquence.[27] The widely felt imperative to create the commercial republic seemed to elevate disputes about competing ferry monopolies or the tortious destruction of a dam into questions of constitutional significance. Everyday commerce created the conflicts, and the language of the Constitution gave parties and lawyers the rhetorical tools to escalate those arguments. It was an era of constitutional maximalism: questions of commerce became issues of the Commerce Clause; questions of which law governed raised fundamental questions of federalism and the Supremacy Clause.

The early Commerce Clause cases of the Marshall Court era display a much richer array of approaches to the federal-state relationship than has generally been recognized. Many studies of the Marshall Court assume that federalism was always based on conflict, with federal legislative power opposing state power. This conflict-centered strain has been familiar to twentieth- and twenty-first-century students of constitutional law. It posits that the states and the federal government stand in opposition to each other, competing for power and hawkishly defending their respective spheres of authority, a portion of which is constitutionally granted and other areas of which have been zoned by the action of case law, legislation, or practice.

Interbellum lawyers and judges were clearly familiar with the conflict scenario. Indeed, the preeminent Marshall Court precedent on the commerce power sounds in the conflict mode: *Gibbons v. Ogden*, the steamboat case of 1824, which is understood primarily as pitting a state-granted monopoly against a federal coasting statute. Yet, a chapter on this case will show, even the canonical *Gibbons* is more complex than the hornbook picture conveys.

The fifth claim concerns union—both "the Union," as in the American federal republic, as well as "union" in a more general and theoretical sense. The book highlights the many and varied meanings of the concept of "union" in this period. Sometimes commentators invoked a substantive vision of the Union—for example, the argument that the commerce power was a tool to foster the "Commerce of the Union," which was central to some of the lawyers' arguments and the Supreme Court's decision in *Gibbons v. Ogden*. Sometimes theorists called upon the Union as a talisman of national unity and purpose, to rebut claims of local and particular power. In other instances, "the Union" was more of a stand-in notion, an agreement to defer difficult and divisive political choices in favor of compromise. This use of "union" concepts was thinner, and it was felt to be so by some contemporaries. By the 1850s, critics of the rhetoric of union were demanding more. They asked what the purpose of the Union was, expressing dissatisfaction with what seemed to them tautological views that assumed that the Union existed, that it could be maintained, and that it was worth preserving. The emotional, moral, and constitutional heft of the phrase "the Union" was, like so much else in this period, contested and fragile. For many interbellum observers, the Union was simply inadequate.

The interbellum Union was not the same Union that would end slavery, first by an order from its commander-in-chief and then by constitutional amendment. Nor was it the same Union that would send its army to burn a swath through the South, with special vengeance meted out to South Carolina and Georgia. Nor was it the same Union that would bolster Congress and the federal courts to watch over state governments and reshape the structures of American federalism. The interbellum Union was different.

A word about methodology is in order. This book is a work of both legal and intellectual history. It therefore emphasizes the ways in which ideas develop over time and in the context of argument. Such an approach is particularly fruitful when applied to ostensibly timeless legal and political concepts such as "federalism." Lawyers and legal scholars benefit from constant reminders of the time-bounded nature of such doctrinal lodestars.

The creativity and contestation within interbellum constitutional thought has not been adequately recognized or understood by scholars. Indeed, some prominent commentators dismiss the era as a period in which little happened that was constitutionally noteworthy. Bruce Ackerman calls the years after 1815 "qualitatively different from the previous decade," consigning them to the category of "a period of 'normal politics.' " In contrast to Ackerman's canonical "constitutional moments" of the founding, Reconstruction, and the New Deal, the interbellum period did not witness "great ideological struggles between competing parties."[28] Employing a similar chronology, Akhil Reed Amar's story of constitutional development focuses on four key moments: the founding, Reconstruction, the New Deal, and the civil rights revolution of the 1960s.[29] Yet Ackerman and Amar do each acknowledge the significance of some of the era's major Supreme Court decisions, principally *McCulloch v. Maryland* (1819).[30]

A strange paradox of the interbellum period is visible here: the fact that John Marshall was the Great Chief Justice is a casebook commonplace. The fact that the Marshall Court issued a host of foundational decisions has been established through numerous important works of scholarship.[31] Yet, somehow, the period is held to have been bereft of constitutional creativity or intellectual development. How can this be?

This lacuna cannot be, because events were not so. The conventional story of the interbellum period as a gap between moments of constitutional creativity is long overdue for reexamination. To be sure, the first half of the nineteenth century has been the subject of renowned narrative histories from political and cultural historians, who have offered a number of themes to give coherence to these decades: the age of Jackson; the market revolution; the rise of American democracy; the transportation and communications revolution; and the era of the impending crisis.[32] We also know the period as the prelude to the cataclysm of the Civil War, in anticipation of which these decades are often referred to as the "antebellum period," the origins of the irrepressible conflict. But these accounts overlook the profound interconnection between law, politics, and history in this period. Our governing narratives of the early nineteenth century are incomplete and in need of updating using new techniques that meld constitutional law with legal and intellectual history.

This book examines the landscape of constitutional possibility in the early nineteenth century. It does not simply march through Supreme Court cases.

It aims to take in the full argumentative panorama—not only the outputs (for example, judicial decisions published in the *U.S. Reports*) but the inputs, broadly construed. This landscape therefore includes arguments plausible enough to be aired by lawyers making hours-long arguments before the justices, as well as newspaper essays, lower-court decisions, speeches, letters, and political tracts. The cases, in this view, can function for us as they did for contemporaries: as anchoring positions around which arguments eddied, collided, and sometimes coalesced. The cases were not isolated tableaux. They were collection points for intellectual creativity, opportunities to use legal discourse to shape reality, and arenas in which to lay claim to power.

Capturing these varied imperatives requires curating a substantial amount of social and cultural material in the narrative, including histories of families, houses, cities, and physical space. Constitutional debates in the period were conducted far outside the chamber of the Supreme Court, and by a far wider array of commentators than the standard histories of the Marshall and Taney courts compass. My focus upon producers of constitutional discourse allows for explorations of the important contributions made by Maria Henrietta Pinckney, Elias Boudinot, John Ross, and Frederick Douglass, among others, none of whom was an elite white man. Broadening the range of interlocutors also requires broadening the lenses of place, territory, and family, all of which were integral to the ways in which these producers of constitutional discourse, and their contemporaries, understood the stakes of their arguments.

Pinckney may provide the most striking example of this point. A daughter of one of the wealthiest and most influential families of the eighteenth- and nineteenth-century United States, she exists in the archival record in her writings, and in a piece of material culture (a gown), but not in a portrait. Her writings on nullification and her financial and reputational contributions to the cause of states' rights in South Carolina have hitherto received almost no attention from historians. In order to situate her writings and to understand her political activities, it is essential to understand the Pinckney family, as well as the social and political ecosystem of early-nineteenth-century Charleston. The Supreme Court was but one center of interbellum federalism. Other centers revealed themselves in the geographic peripheries of South Carolina, Georgia, Cherokee Nation, Indian Territory (modern-day Oklahoma), the Chesapeake, Boston, New York, and Wisconsin.

Pinckney's writings also shed new light on the story of South Carolina in the 1820s and 1830s. This account illustrates the variegated nature of constitutional thought even within a single, self-consciously insular society. It also suggests that courts were by no means the only voices in establishing what counted as constitutional argumentation. The justices of the Supreme Court were embedded in local debates thanks to their circuit-riding duties, and their correspondence with each other spread news and legal arguments across the states. But equally important for our understanding of the landscape of constitutional possibility in this period are other primary sources: newspaper essays, political tracts, accounts of parades, and protest petitions. A Jeffersonian justice endorsed broad federal power; the daughter of one of the leading members of the postwar Federalist Party supported nullification; and the congressman who urged a national program of roads, canals, and banks insisted that the states had the ultimate power to decide the validity of federal law.

Interbellum producers of constitutional discourse understood the federalist project to be one of constant negotiation among competing, and sometimes overlapping, powers. They believed that multiple sources of authority could extend over a given activity. One of the most important of these was the police power. Held by a state or a municipality, the police power was sometimes a companion to the commerce power and sometimes its opponent. Questions of how these various powers mapped onto political boundaries arose in gritty fact patterns involving money, trade, migration, race, and slavery.

Issues of race and slavery were constantly present in early-nineteenth-century constitutional debates, even when they were not squarely at stake in a given situation. The question of slavery's expansion into new states gained particular salience in the debates surrounding the Missouri Compromise of 1820. Sectional ideology acquired new converts by raising the specter of a federal government flush with expanded national power and moving to outlaw slavery in the territories, the District of Columbia, or even the slaveholding states.

The federal government was in fact structurally tilted toward the slaveholding states by constitutional provisions such as the Three-Fifths Clause, the Fugitive Slave Clause, and even the Senate and the Electoral College. Antislavery and abolitionist activists often exhorted their audiences to beware the machinations of the "Slave Power," their phrase for the structural boons that the Constitution granted to the slaveholding South. The question whether the Constitution was fundamentally proslavery, antislavery, or agnostic was pervasive in public debate during this period.[33] Nevertheless, the most effective conspiracy theorists were the slaveholders themselves, who managed to convince many of their contemporaries that any increase in federal power would necessarily be hostile toward slavery. A crucial component of the federal versus state binary was born in this era. Even though the slaveholding states controlled at least two branches of the federal government throughout the interbellum period, somehow "federal power" could serve as a shorthand for "antislavery," and "states' rights" for "proslavery."

Yet states' rights arguments did not necessarily tend only in a proslavery direction. On the contrary: the content of states' rights depended on the particular state—and on the wishes of its legislature, courts, and voters. In the 1830s and 1840s, a number of states—including Massachusetts and Pennsylvania—passed anti-kidnapping statutes that were specifically aimed at protecting Black persons, whether fugitive or free, from being seized and forcibly carried out of the state. Other states, most notably Wisconsin, went so far as to adopt the language of nullification, arguing that federal officials and even the Supreme Court lacked the power to overturn state-court decisions or to compel state officials to enforce the federal fugitive slave laws. Shouts of "states' rights" might have come more frequently and forcefully from slaveholding southerners. But Wisconsin officials in 1859 had as robust a theory of nullification as had their South Carolinian counterparts in 1832.

The modern view of federalism—dominant among scholars as well as those in public life—assumes a dichotomous relationship between the national (federal) government and the states. This view also tends to take as given a particular orientation of that binary relationship: namely, that the federal government, and thus arguments for national power, tend in a liberal, emancipatory direction, while arguments for state power are either inherently liberty-constraining or else are simply a cover for reactionary policies. This view of federalism may be a largely accurate description of U.S. constitutional law and politics for much of the twentieth and twenty-first centuries, and indeed since Reconstruction. But it does not accurately describe federalism as it existed before the Civil War, in theory or in practice.

One aim of this book is to challenge this backward-projecting conception of American federalism. This goal is important as a matter of historical methodology and analysis. The post-Reconstruction view of federalism simply does not apply to constitutional debates in the interbellum period. The single term "federalism" does not capture the era's many competing, sometimes conflicting views about how the relationship among multiple overlapping governmental authorities ought to operate. Examination of the interbellum period shows that the apparent timelessness of today's stable notion of federalism obscures the heterogeneous nature of these relationships through much of the nineteenth century. Given the current ascendancy of "originalist" models of constitutional interpretation, many of which assume the fixity of constitutional meaning since the founding era and are therefore fundamentally unhistorical, telling the rich story of America's deeply grounded and long-standing federalisms becomes all the more imperative.

In order to understand what the Interbellum Constitution was, one must listen to these producers of constitutional discourse. Their statements not only provide evidence of meaning; they were speech acts in which meaning was created. Examining the archive of the judges' decisions, the lawyers' arguments, the editors' columns, the observers' letters, and the commentators' pamphlets affords a broad view of the landscape of constitutional possibility at a particular moment in time. Only through such analysis can one begin to answer the question of what constitutional law was, is—or, indeed, could be.

1 • The Constitutional Lawyer in the Long Founding Moment

A Practice of Federalism

Wherever there is much commerce, & that too sustained by a bank, there will always be plenty of law & money too.

—William Wirt, 1804

The first time the future attorney general appeared on the court rolls, he was a parentless twelve-year-old whose claims to the tavern, billiards room, and smith shop owned by his late father—dead for eleven years—were dispatched by the Prince George's County Orphans Court in six lines of the register. He was not even named in that entry of October 8, 1785. The clerk's flowing script clumped him with his five elder siblings before recording the judge's order for a valuation of their Swiss emigrant father's real property, most of it located in Bladensburg, Maryland, a port town just across the Anacostia River from what in a few years' time would become Washington, D.C.[1]

The second time he appeared in the official records, in 1791, he was nineteen years old. Now he was before the state legislature, and his name was at the head of the record. The intervening six years had yielded a series of disputes about the ownership of the largest of the buildings, a brick structure that, during his father's lifetime, had been rented out as a store. After his father's death in 1774, a family friend had taken over the operation of the store, in contravention of the deceased father's will. That friend—a tobacco planter and lawyer, as well the impresario responsible for the first hot air balloon ascent in America—had also become his stepfather. Sometime after his mother's death in 1779, the stepfather married the boy's eldest sister. The boy's uncle, acting as his guardian, brought an action against the planter-balloonist for rent owed. When the latter failed to appear in court, the circuit court ordered a seizure of assets to satisfy the claims.[2]

Amid these tangled lines of family and property, the boy kept moving—from one school to another, from relatives' house to boardinghouse, throughout central Maryland—and studying. First, he studied the classics. Later, sitting in on county-court trials with his classmates as part of their study of rhetoric and oratory and admiring the arguments he saw, he developed an enthusiasm for the law. He took a position as a tutor in the home of a prominent landowner who had recently served in the state convention that ratified the U.S. Constitution, and who permitted him the use of the family's large library. (His student, Ninian Edwards, later became the governor of the Illinois Territory and, post-statehood, a U.S. senator and governor.) He read and he taught, but his lack of funds made his future uncertain, and he was frequently ill with what he feared was consumption. In late 1789, around the time he turned seventeen, he traveled five hundred miles on horseback to Augusta, Georgia, to recover his health and to visit his sister and her husband, the planter-balloonist. According to rumors that circulated during and after his lifetime, the young man was actually the illegitimate son of the planter-balloonist.[3] At roughly the same time, the First U.S. Congress was adopting the Judiciary Act of 1789, establishing the federal judiciary and the office of the attorney general.

The young man returned to Maryland in the spring of 1790. Soon after that, he introduced himself into the legal record under his own name. He petitioned the state legislature for assistance in converting his interest in his late father's store into funds to pay for his legal education. His request noted "that he has received a classical education, and is now engaged in the study of the law, but his personal estate, with the annual value of his real estate, are insufficient to enable him to prosecute his studies with any advantage." Still a minor at eighteen, he asked that trustees be appointed "to sell and dispose" his "one moiety of a house and lot in Bladensburgh, in Prince-George's county, known by the name of the Brick Store" and to "apply the same to the finishing his education." In December 1791, the Maryland General Assembly granted his request, passing a private bill titled "An Act for the Benefit of William Wirt."[4]

In October 1792, pursuant to the act, the Brick Store was sold. The act's beneficiary, William Wirt, was already reading law with one of the trustees, William Pitt Hunt, the son of the teacher who had introduced Wirt to the drama of the courtroom. Later that year, at the age of nineteen, Wirt was admitted to the bar of Virginia.

By the time he died forty-two years later, in 1834, Wirt was one of the nation's most renowned lawyers, orators, and men of letters even among a generation well supplied with those talents. His twelve years of service as U.S. attorney general, from 1817 to 1829, made him the longest-serving holder of that post to date. He revolutionized the chaotic office through heretofore novel practices such as keeping records and hiring clerks. Wirt also transformed the attorney generalship into a full Cabinet-level position, in an era when the Cabinet comprised only a small handful of the president's closest advisors. Moreover, Wirt held the office under three presidents: James Monroe, John Quincy Adams, and—for twenty-seven days—Andrew Jackson. He argued approximately 170 cases in the Supreme Court of the United States between 1816 and 1834, all during John Marshall's tenure as chief justice. In forty-one of those cases, Wirt appeared on behalf of the government; in 129 of them, he represented private clients (some of whom included government entities such as the Bank of the United States).⁵ The cases he argued generated some of the landmark decisions of the Marshall Court: *McCulloch v. Maryland* (1819); *Dartmouth College v. Woodward* (1819); *Cohens v. Virginia* (1821); *Gibbons v. Ogden* (1824); *Ogden v. Saunders* (1827); *Cherokee Nation v. Georgia* (1831) *Worcester v. Georgia* (1832); and *Charles River Bridge v. Warren Bridge* (1837).

Even in an era in which courtrooms drew crowds of spectators, with celebrity lawyers delivering speeches that extended over hours or even days, Mr. Wirt arguing a cause was a major event, drawing the ladies of Washington as well as fellow members of the bar. "In logical precision of mind, clearness of statement, full investigation of complicated points, and close comparison of precedents, he had no superior at the bar of the Supreme Court," observed his biographer John Pendleton Kennedy, who witnessed many of Wirt's arguments. Another contemporary praised "the blaze of his reasoning and declamation": "The march of his mind is direct to its object, the evolutions by which he attains it, are so new and beautiful, and apparently necessary to the occasion, that your admiration is kept alive, your fancy delighted, and your judgment convinced, through every stage of the process." And, unlike many of his fellow orators, Wirt was entertaining: "His key was that of earnest and animated argument, frequently alternated with that of a playful and sprightly humor."⁶

Everywhere one looks in the world of early-nineteenth-century American law and politics, Wirt is there. He first gained national renown as a prosecutor in the 1807 treason trial of Aaron Burr. Wirt was not the most senior member of the prosecution team, but his soaring courtroom poetics portrayed Burr as the diabolical mastermind behind a conspiracy to establish an independent nation in the southwestern United States. The speech was a staple of school-room recitation into the twentieth century, thrilling speakers and audiences with its combination of rhetorical flash and morality play.

Wirt's own writing capped his reputation as the era's leading man of law and letters. He wrote the best-selling *Sketches of the Life and Character of Patrick Henry* (1817), which memorialized—and, perhaps, embellished—such phrases as "Give me liberty or give me death!" and "If this be treason, make the most of it." He also produced two popular series of humorous essays on the American character: *The Letters of the British Spy* (1803) and *The Old Bachelor* (1812).

Wirt's combination of legal and literary fame extended beyond the courtroom, and indeed beyond his lifetime. In cities such as Baltimore and Philadelphia, one could find meetings of "William Wirt Societies" and "William Wirt Literary Institutes" in the 1830s and 1840s, including one in 1843 at which Wirt's old Baltimore acquaintance Edgar Allan Poe presented a lecture on American poetry.[7] Didactic children's texts of the period offered salutary life lessons based on his progress from dissolute youth to republican statesman. He and his family served as the models for at least two popular novels during and after his lifetime.

Late in his career, Wirt feared that his early successes had marked him as an ornamental rather than an analytical lawyer—a "florid declaimer," as he fretted in 1829.[8] He need not have worried. Yet it was precisely this worry that spurred him. He was a tavern-born, orphaned son of an immigrant, a striver who married into the Virginia gentry, a proud and ambitious lawyer, and an anxious father of ten surviving children.

He also shaped constitutional ideas through a uniquely interbellum combination of channels: the chamber of the Supreme Court, the president's Cabinet, and the public sphere of politics and letters. Wirt ran unsuccessfully for the presidency in 1832, as the candidate of the newly formed Anti-Masonic Party—which, more saliently for Wirt, was an anti–Andrew Jackson party. In addition to the attorney generalship, his posts included clerk of the Virginia House of Delegates; chancellor of the Eastern District of Virginia; member of the Virginia House of Delegates; and U.S. attorney for the District of Virginia. During the War of 1812, he commanded a flying artillery company that spent the summer of 1813 encamped on the James River, waiting (and, in Wirt's case, hoping) to defend Richmond against a British attack that never came.

Even the offices that Wirt refused testify to his prominence. He declined two offers from Thomas Jefferson, despite long ties of personal and political friendship: an 1808 invitation from then-president Jefferson for Wirt to "come into Congress"; and an 1826 proposal from Jefferson, on behalf of the board of the University of Virginia, that Wirt become the school's first president and its first professor of law. Upon Wirt's death in February 1834, Congress and the Supreme Court adjourned; John Quincy Adams delivered a eulogy on the floor of the House of Representatives; and President Jackson and the entire Cabinet attended the funeral.

Even Bladensburg, where Wirt was born in November 1772, became freighted during his lifetime with cultural and political significance. In the late eighteenth and early nineteenth centuries, the town was a bustling commercial port. But after 1800, it was also infamous as the location of the dueling ground for the new capital: across the Anacostia River, thus outside the jurisdiction of the federal city; clandestine, but openly so. One of the most notorious duels of the period, in which Captain Stephen Decatur (the "hero of Tripoli") was mortally wounded by his fellow commodore James Barron, occurred in Bladensburg in March 1820. The night before the duel, Barron stayed at the Indian Queen Tavern—next door to the Brick Store, and also formerly owned by Wirt's family.9

Aside from its unsavory association with the settlement of affairs of honor, Bladensburg's location on the perimeter of the capital gave it an additional claim to disrepute. It was the site of the "Bladensburg Races," the rout of American troops by British forces in August 1814. The Americans' flight opened a path for Major General Robert Ross and his brigade of veterans—fresh from their Continental defeat of Napoleon—to push into Washington and burn the White House, the Capitol, and many other government buildings while the retreating Americans fled, at a run, through the streets of the city. Bladensburg managed to cling to respectability for a few decades, helped by its natural spring, which drew fashionable Washingtonians—including the attorney general and his family—who sought the healthful benefits of taking the waters. By the late nineteenth century, however, it had declined to what one commentator termed a "cross-roads Sodom."10

As a natal location for a statesman of the young republic, Bladensburg occupied a distinctly lower rank than Jefferson's Monticello, James Madison's Montpelier, or even the sturdy Braintree saltbox in which John Quincy Adams was born. Bladensburg was not a theater of operations for an ambitious young man; it was a place to be escaped. It was a town that owed its existence to commerce; its prosperity to a river (already silting when the trustees sold off Wirt's interest in the Brick Store, and impassable to large ships a few decades later);

William Wirt at around age 35, by Charles Balthazar
Julien Févret de Saint-Mémin, engraved in Richmond ca.
1807–8, at the time of the Burr trial. (Library of
Congress.)

and its fame to its location on a border between a state and the capital city. In these respects, Wirt never would escape Bladensburg. For the attorney general would, in the end, owe his profession, prosperity, and fame to the same factors: commerce, mobility, and the tension—sometimes productive, sometimes destructive—created by competing government powers operating in overlapping physical space. In contrast to unhappy Bladensburg, however, on whom these forces acted, Wirt had the power to shape them, at least some of the time.

The Interbellum Constitutionalist

But why begin a history of antebellum American constitutional thought with William Wirt?

Wirt's life, from 1772 to 1834, illustrates the themes of this book. His career both embodied and created the Interbellum Constitution. He was a producer of constitutional discourse across a range of realms, institutions, and levels and branches of government. Wirt was not a Supreme Court justice, but he was at the center of many of the most important moments of debate concerning Union, commerce, concurrent power, and slavery between 1815 and 1834. He was a writer, attorney, public servant, reformer, and slaveholder. Like the interbellum period itself, he was there in plain sight. Also like the interbellum period, though, he has been left out of the standard narrative of American constitutional thought.

Interbellum constitutional thought did not reside in constitutional text; no amendments were added to the Constitution between the Twelfth Amendment in 1804 and the Thirteenth Amendment in 1865. Yet, as Wirt's career demonstrates, the landscape of constitutional possibility nonetheless shifted dramatically over the course of his own life, and over the longer interbellum era. The decades between 1815 and 1861 were neither a lull between the founding and Reconstruction, nor a mundane domain of what Bruce Ackerman calls "ordinary politics" filling the space between "constitutional moments."[11] During this immensely creative and conflict-filled period, the stuff of constitutional thought did not reside in constitutional amendments. It came in other forms: judicial decisions; opinions of attorneys general; lawyers' arguments in federal, state, county, and city courtrooms; the letters of state-crafters; and political speeches and essays.

Commerce, mobility, and concurrent power were the defining elements of Wirt's life. They were also the defining elements of American constitutional thought and debate in the early nineteenth century, between approximately 1815 and 1861. As a matter of biography, Wirt's story illustrates the foundational themes of his era. He entered public life as a member of Virginia's Republican Party, a protégé of Jefferson and Madison. When he died, he was a public and avowed foe of Jackson, a critic of the states' rights claims made by South Carolina and Georgia, and a defender of the rights of Native nations. He had witnessed—and sometimes shaped—the Janus-faced nature of federal power: at one time resisting the nullifiers of Charleston, at another time enabling the capture of runaway slaves. He understood and operated within the many layers of governmental power that interacted to shape interbellum federalisms.

For modern constitutional scholars, one striking aspect of Wirt's oeuvre is the degree to which it scrambles received understandings of who was on which side of debates about federal power. Wirt was born in Maryland, became a Virginian, and owned slaves, but he was a strong supporter of federal power—even when federal power appeared to run contrary to slave-owning interests. He identified himself as a Jeffersonian and a Republican, but he endorsed broad congressional authority over commerce—even over realms touching on the state's police powers. His official attorney general's memoranda on the international slave trade elicited angry responses from the governor of Georgia and the legislature of South Carolina, but John Quincy Adams was nevertheless suspicious of his Cabinet colleague's "Virginian" constitutional principles.

The causal chain runs still deeper, however. Wirt not only embodied the legal and political debates of these decades. He played a crucial role in setting the terms of those debates, and in establishing the legal frameworks through which questions not only of law but of politics, economics, and morality were channeled. Wirt was an indispensable agent of the Interbellum Constitution. He was a member of the uneasy generation born during the Revolution and saddled with ensuring the survival of the republic. For lawyers of the era, the task was even more formidable: to lay the fragile skein of the Constitution atop the messy conflicts that were already shifting beyond what the document's drafters envisioned, in the hope of providing answers that would both respond to novel problems and remain true to a founding spirit that was rapidly vanishing into the past. The mania for writing biographies of the Revolutionary generation, which Wirt joined with his *Life of Patrick Henry*, was but one piece of this broader effort to hold onto the long founding moment, even as it quickly receded. Wirt spent his career struggling with problems the founders had had to gloss over in order for the republic ever to have been created.

Moreover, these new interbellum disputes forced contemporaries to grapple with a set of complex and divisive questions that had deviled the founders, but that lay submerged beneath the smooth text of the Constitution. The theory of American government as laid out in the Constitution proceeded from the premise that power could legitimately be divided among different levels of government—the general government on one hand, the states on the other. This was the central contribution of American federal theory. Some types of power belonged in the hands of the general government, while others resided in the states. Externally focused powers, such as the powers to declare war, conduct international affairs, sign treaties, establish a post office, and raise armies, were properly allocated to the nation. Exercises of authority that were more local, such as the traditional "police" powers to regulate health, safety, morals, and general welfare, belonged in the hands of the states. The innovation of 1787 was the claim that divided authority was structurally legitimate.

By 1815, however, the most pressing political and legal issues concerned situations in which federal and state power overlapped, intermixed with a thicket of local power, and overlaid by the tendrils of foreign affairs. To these questions, the Constitution provided no clear answers.

Wirt was omnipresent in those debates between 1815 and 1834. Wirt's government posts; his busy private practice; and his restless ambitions across the realms of law, politics, and letters placed him at the center of the controversies over commerce and concurrent power. In some ways, he was typical of a certain type of rising young lawyer at that time: trained at the elbow of a practicing lawyer, rather than through systematic study; always striving for business, elbowing his way into the county courtroom to plead "a cause"; and inspired by a diffuse sense that attorneys were particularly important in a republic. Moreover, like many other sons of the Upper South who styled themselves as the republican heirs to Jefferson and Madison, Wirt owned slaves.

But Wirt was also atypical among interbellum lawyers. Unlike his many affluent contemporaries at the bar of Virginia, and later Maryland, Wirt's income derived entirely from his professional earnings. There was no family plantation underwriting his expenses or buffering him with credit. Wirt consequently directed his career toward earning enough money to support his wife and children, spending most of his life consciously suppressing or at least sidelining his desire for a life of letters, public service, and fame. The essays and satirical sketches came, but they were produced after hours, and sometimes—as with the *Life of Patrick Henry*—they issued forth in the hope of both literary renown and a stream of royalty income.

Most significantly, Wirt was unique because of where he was and what he did while he was there. He was, first and foremost, a lawyer—indeed, one of the preeminent advocates of his era. He held both federal and state offices, and he served in the executive, legislative, and judicial branches. In contrast to contemporaries whose names are more famous to twenty-first-century Americans, Wirt is not associated with a single idea—no Jacksonian Democracy (a Jackson–Martin Van Buren joint effort), American System (Henry Clay), or nullification (John C. Calhoun). Wirt argued more cases before the Supreme Court than Daniel Webster, but Webster lived eighteen years after Wirt—until 1852, by which time the politician Webster's views of the nature of the Union took on a new salience amid the breakdown of national politics over the issue of slavery. Wirt had more of an impact on federal law, the practice of the executive branch, and constitutional doctrine than did John Quincy Adams, but Adams was the scion of a founding dynasty and took the unprecedented and uncopied step of following his single presidential term with seventeen years in Congress.

Wirt is difficult to categorize because his contributions lay across many different realms of government service, and they can be traced only by reading his writing and following the trail of his work. This body of writing and practice is the measure of Wirt's contribution to the Interbellum Constitution. From the historian's vantage point, Wirt's attorney general opinions and his arguments before the Court defined what constitutional law meant in the early decades of the nineteenth century. But unlike the efforts of his more famed contemporaries, many of whom aired their theories on the floor of Congress or from the bench, Wirt's views emerged from practice—daily, and often nightly, labors in the courtroom, in the office, and at his writing desk. Yet his legal practice was far from a quiet and solitary effort; on the contrary, the analytical and rhetorical work began with his pen, but it was completed only when it confronted the arguments of his opponents. Wirt's skills as a constitutional lawyer were constantly being tested in the adversarial arena, which compassed both arguments before the Supreme Court and meetings with the president and Cabinet.

For interbellum Americans, feeling themselves cast adrift as the founding generation died off, the meaning of the Constitution was impossible to comprehend without a mass of precedents to elucidate it. Solutions to the problem of concurrent power were especially barren of content when viewed in the abstract. Wirt's creativity lay in his ability to generate those precedents, and to do so with a flourish that made them speak to a broad popular audience.

The Rising Young Lawyer: Maryland to Virginia

When the nineteen-year-old Marylander was admitted to the Virginia bar in 1792, Wirt later recalled, his library consisted of a copy of William Blackstone's *Commentaries*, two volumes of Miguel de Cervantes's *Don Quixote*, and a volume of Laurence Sterne's *Tristram Shandy*. Despite this meager estate, however, the young lawyer quickly proved himself able in the courtroom. He had traveled to Virginia because friends had advised him that it was a promising place to launch his legal career, but he first had to satisfy a residency requirement, thereby transforming himself, in the eyes of the venerable bar of the Commonwealth, into a Virginian. He somehow did so. As Wirt wrote to his brother-in-law Peter Carnes (the quondam balloonist) in Georgia, "I applied to the judges for a license; by a manoeuvre, removed the objection of non-residence, and, after a minute scrutiny into my information, obtained the signature of three of their Honours to my license."[12] The nature of the "manoeuvre," which Wirt described with the lighthearted sauciness that came to mark his epistolary style, is impossible to determine. But it succeeded, to the delight of the newly admitted attorney.

Wirt returned briefly to Maryland to attend to the sale of the Brick Store, but his presence in Bladensburg was only transient. "I have disposed of my property, and am now over . . . for the purpose of receiving the money," he wrote to Carnes from Prince George's County. "Immediately upon the reception of this, I commence the practice of the law."[13] By selling off his moiety in his father's building, Wirt purchased an interest in his future profession. Sale triggered law.

Having established himself as a member of the Virginia bar by disposing of his Maryland property, Wirt—in the company of Blackstone, Cervantes, and Sterne—did what young lawyers did in late-eighteenth-century America: he bent himself to the project of hustling for business. He obtained a case of joint assault and battery in Culpeper County, in which he and his co-counsel convinced the justices of the peace to grant summary relief on a motion rather than the customary writ, a novel procedural gambit the young attorneys gleaned from their Blackstone.[14] Wirt spent the years between 1792 and 1800 traversing the muddy roads of the Piedmont, riding the circuit and extending his practice into nearby Fluvanna and Albemarle counties. Albemarle was the home county of Thomas Jefferson and James Monroe, and it bordered Orange County, in which James Madison's plantation, Montpelier, was located.

As Wirt's courtroom successes mounted, his name became known, and his practice expanded. In 1795, he married Mildred Gilmer, the daughter of Dr. George Gilmer and Lucy Walker Gilmer. Dr. Gilmer was Jefferson's physician and close friend; Pen Park, the Gilmer family's seat near Charlottesville, became the young couple's home. Joining in the Gilmers' frequent visits to Monticello, Wirt was soon on friendly terms with Jefferson, who took an interest in young lawyers in his broader circle. Wirt also expanded his literary knowledge, reading widely in Dr. Gilmer's library, where he encountered the works of Richard Hooker, Robert Boyle, John Locke, Francis Bacon, and John Milton.

After Dr. Gilmer's death in December 1795, Wirt assisted his mother-in-law, Lucy Walker Gilmer, in running Pen Park. These duties included such quotidian items as writing to Jefferson to inquire about purchasing a substantial quantity of nails—30,200—from the Monticello nailery. Jefferson had established the nail-making operation as part of the blacksmith shop on Mulberry Row, the "principal plantation street" of Monticello, in 1794.[15] His aim was twofold: to establish a stream of cash income and to perfect his control over the people he enslaved, whose efforts enabled that income stream: "I determined to set up some work which might furnish my current expences, in aid of my farms. [T]he making of nails was what peculiarly suited me, because it would employ a parcel of boys who would otherwise be idle."[16] Within a year, the nailery was producing from eight thousand to ten thousand nails per day.[17] As suggested by Wirt's 1797 order on behalf of Mrs. Gilmer, however, Jefferson's hopes for cash might have been frustrated by the widespread reliance of Virginia planters on credit. After querying, "In what time they can be got ready?," Wirt added, "Or, if they be now ready, whether it would suit you to take a draught for the amount on Mr. James Brown of Richmond payable on sight, or to wait for the money until the post from Richmond to Charlott[e]s-ville gets again in motion?" Jefferson's notes on the letter indicated that for at least some portion of the price of the nails, he settled for payment not by money but "by order on James Brown."[18]

Having attained this relatively comfortable position in Charlottesville planter society, Wirt continued to expand his legal practice. The nature of county-level lawyering at the time was such that attorneys traveled extensively, riding from town to town as the courts held session, staying in inns and engaging in a certain amount of outstation frolics. As one commentator, writing a few decades later, put it, the "gentlemen of the bar . . . indulged in a license of free-living, which habitually approached the confines of excess, and often overstepped them." With "something of the light-heartedness and improvidence of the old-fashioned strolling theatrical companies," they rode the circuit. "Every dinner-party was a revel; every ordinary visit was a temptation."[19]

Newly arrived among the sons of the gentry, Wirt seems to have relished this festive atmosphere. But he was ill-equipped to withstand its excesses. He was, as his biographer Kennedy dryly notes, "not the most sedate of all who rode the circuits." An "admired object in the court-house during the day, a leading spirit in the evening coterie," Wirt indulged in revelry that certainly included heavy drinking. Reports of Wirt's behavior during these years would continue to circulate throughout his lifetime and beyond, to such an extent that Kennedy, writing in 1849, took pains to rebut them as "gross calumny" and "utterly groundless."[20]

During the same period, Wirt made several close friendships that deepened his connections with the Virginia elite. With manners "highly engaging and prepossessing," conversation "very polished, gay, and witty," and a "figure . . . strikingly elegant and commanding," Wirt appears to have charmed his new acquaintances.[21] Many of them evidently regarded Wirt's appearance as bearing the marks of his German heritage. According to his biographer, Wirt's "face and figure"—"his height rather above six feet, his broad shoulders, capacious chest, and general fullness of development"—were "characteristic" of "his

Teutonic origin." Indeed, with "light hair falling in crisp and numerous curls upon a broad forehead," a "high arching eyebrow," a "large nose" and "ample chin," Wirt reminded some contemporaries of "the portrait of Goethe."[22]

The young Wirt's regular companions on the circuit included Dabney Carr and James Barbour. Carr was the son of Dabney Carr the elder, the best friend of Jefferson; the husband of Jefferson's sister, Martha; and a leader of Virginia's Revolutionary movement. Dabney Jr.'s older brother Peter Carr was Jefferson's protégé, and was later erroneously rumored to be the father of Sally Hemings's children, who were in fact the children of Jefferson.[23] Barbour was also a member of one of Virginia's oldest planter families.

Dabney Carr quickly became Wirt's closest friend. They were lifelong correspondents, and their letters display an intimacy that is striking to modern eyes but that was not unusual among men of their milieu.[24] In one particularly effusive letter written shortly before Carr married in 1802, Wirt expostulated, "How your transport kindles me. Yes—at this moment I have the very swelling of the heart which you describe. O! it is a delicious pain. I wish I had hold of your hand. You should be electrified with a vengeance."[25]

As young lawyers, the trio frequently traveled throughout Albemarle and the nearby counties. One such journey, to Fluvanna County—" 'the State of Flu,' as that county was called in their jocular terms," achieved near-mythic status in the lore of Wirt's life. Wirt's biographer John Pendleton Kennedy wrote:

> They had been amusing each other with the usual prankishness which characterized their intercourse. Wirt was noted for making clever speeches, as they rode together. . . . During this visit, whilst indulging in their customary merriment, Barbour entertained them with a discourse upon the merits of himself and his companions, in the course of which he undertook to point out their respective destinies in after life. "You, Dabney," said he, "have indulged a vision of judicial eminence. You shall be gratified, and shall hold a seat on the Bench of the Court of Appeals of Virginia. Your fortune, William," he continued, addressing himself to Wirt, "shall conduct you to the Attorney Generalship of the United States, where you shall have harder work to do than making bombastic speeches in the woods of Albemarle. As for myself, I shall be content to take my seat in the Senate of the United States."[26]

Wirt's biographer then noted the accuracy of Barbour's prophecy. Carr became a leading Virginia judge and spent the last thirteen years of his career on the Court of Appeals, the state's highest court, to which he was elected in 1824. Barbour held several political posts, including serving as governor of Virginia and as a U.S. senator. In 1825, having been named secretary of war by President John Quincy Adams, he joined Wirt in the Cabinet.

Wirt's early success, both professional and social, received a shock in 1799, when his wife, Mildred, died. Records for this period of Wirt's life are sparse, but he appears to have been deeply affected by her apparently sudden death. He sought a change of scene, and his loneliness ushered in a period of wild behavior. He moved to Richmond and was elected clerk of the Virginia House of Delegates, the lower house of the Virginia General Assembly. The post "was one of sufficient consideration to be regarded by a young man, to whom all public station was new, as an advancement in the career of life," noted Kennedy.[27] Previous holders of the position had included such luminaries as Chancellor George Wythe and U.S. attorney general Edmund Randolph. Importantly for Wirt, the position came with a salary, and its duties permitted him to continue his legal practice. Most significantly for his career, the office of clerk gave Wirt a seat—indeed, a desk—from which he witnessed firsthand one of the most crucial debates of the early republic concerning the relationship between federal and state power.

Virginian Constitutionalism: Richmond

During the three years he held the clerkship, Wirt gained increasing prominence in the state's legal and political circles. In the winter of 1799–1800, his role as clerk of the House meant that he recorded the debate on the Report of 1800. The report was a forceful statement of what had emerged during the politically polarized 1790s as the Republican theory of American constitutional law and politics.[28] The view was associated with Virginia, and in particular with two leading Virginians: Jefferson and Madison.

Wirt, by virtue of his Gilmer connections, was a junior member of these founders' social and political circle. Even after Mildred's death, Wirt appears to have been seen as a loyal insider. He was also a rising young lawyer with a name to make for himself. As such, Wirt was well situated to benefit from the patronage of his Virginian political elders.

Not everyone in Virginia ascribed to Republican beliefs, however. The Federalist Party counted among its ranks a number of prominent Virginian political figures, including Secretary of State (later Chief Justice) John Marshall, Attorney General Randolph, and Governor Henry "Light-Horse Harry" Lee.[29]

Debates in the state legislature were contentious, with each of the nascent parties fighting to claim the Revolutionary mantle and to shape the future of state and national politics.

The Report of 1800 was written by James Madison after his election to the Virginia House of Delegates in 1799. In the report, Madison took up the arguments that he and Jefferson had put forth in their anonymously authored Virginia and Kentucky Resolutions of 1798.[30] The resolutions were protests against the Alien and Sedition Acts, which the administration of President John Adams had sponsored and the Federalist-controlled Congress had passed in the summer of 1798 as part of an effort to squelch dissent and monitor foreign nationals during the Quasi-War with France. Federalists feared that radical movements were stirring within the United States and that Jacobinical tendencies had migrated from France. Critics of the laws, including Jefferson and Madison, charged that the Adams administration was using the undeclared war as an opportunity to silence its political opponents.[31]

Jefferson and Madison anonymously authored a pair of resolutions that were subsequently adopted by the legislatures of Kentucky and Virginia, respectively, in late 1798. The resolutions rejected the Alien and Sedition Acts as unconstitutional.[32] Both resolutions referred to the Union as a "compact" to which the states were parties. The powers of the federal government derived entirely from this compact, which was, in the words of Jefferson's Kentucky Resolution, "a General Government for special purposes."[33] The states therefore retained the authority to opine independently on the actions of the federal government. Consequently, the resolutions maintained, the states were acting entirely within constitutional parameters when they objected to federal laws such as the acts and declared them "unauthoritative, void, and of no force."[34]

Both resolutions left unsettled the specific form that these state protests should take. Jefferson's first draft of the Kentucky Resolution had referred to "nullification" of the offending laws as "the rightful remedy" for the injury they did to the states and the constitutional structure.[35] The final draft, the product of debate in the Kentucky legislature, was more tempered. It urged Kentucky's congressional delegation to carry the resolutions to Washington and there urge their "Co-states" to "to procure at the next session of Congress, a repeal of the aforesaid unconstitutional and obnoxious acts."[36] Nullifying the federal law outright was a bold measure; it would mean that the state was declaring void a lawfully passed act of Congress, and thereby arguably violating the Supremacy Clause of the Constitution. Working through the state's congressional delegation to repeal the law, by contrast, was a fairly moderate recommendation.

Madison's Virginia Resolution was more vague in its proposed remedy. Referring to the compact that formed the Union, Madison wrote, "[T]he states, who are the parties thereto, have the right, and are in duty bound, to interpose, for arresting the progress of the evil, and for maintaining within their respective limits, the authorities, rights, and liberties appertaining to them."[37] States had a duty to "interpose" against the "evil" of a federal government exceeding its powers under the constitutional compact. In such a situation, the states should "protest" the federal government's overreach—such as the passage of the Alien and Sedition Acts. But Madison did not specify what, if any, concrete effect such protest ought to have. Should Virginia's congressional delegation also seek a repeal of the statute? Or did Madison have a more aggressive response in mind, such as state judges refusing to enforce the federal laws? The resolutions ignited a spirited debate on the relative powers of the states and the federal government, and on the nature of the Union. The legislatures of the two authoring states circulated the resolutions to the other fourteen states.[38]

From the Gilmer family seat in Charlottesville, Wirt was watching the political storm closely. In December 1798, a month after Kentucky had passed its resolution and while Virginia was formulating its own, he assessed the crisis in a letter to Carr. Addressing his friend as "Citizen Chevalier"—an indication of both young lawyers' strong ties to the Francophilic Jeffersonians—Wirt mused about the possible consequences of Kentucky's declaration. "I know not whether we ought to rejoice or mourn over this event," he wrote. He praised Kentucky for taking a stand against what he viewed as a concerted power grab by Congress, which had passed the "offensive" Alien and Sedition Acts, and the "ambitious views of the man at the helm," President Adams:

> [I]f Kentucky be left alone, or feebly supported we go to the devil headlong. John the first will have what he has long been laboring at, a pretext for a standing army, and when he gets a standing army at his back— Rome and England will tell us the rest. In every event this Kentucky resolution has brought the cause to issue, and the balance of the States are obliged to decide it—They must positively declare either for the Constitution or the general government; or else, by a dastardly silence, sneak under the yoke.[39]

The final sentence is telling. Wirt was explicitly framing the other states' responses to the Kentucky Resolution as a choice between the Constitution on one hand, and the general government on the other. The executive and Congress, he suggested, had taken control of the national level of government and were using it to undermine the Constitution itself. Only the states remained, then, to defend the constitutional structure. Within a few months, after Mildred's death and his election as clerk of the House of Delegates, Wirt found himself in the midst of the battle against "John the first."

The controversy continued for much of 1799, with the presidential election of 1800 looming. Madison took his seat in the Virginia General Assembly in December 1799, arriving in Richmond determined to defend both resolutions. He was particularly eager to respond to the criticisms of several states that had objected to the resolutions' insistence that state legislatures possessed the power to declare federal laws unconstitutional. The authority to judge the constitutionality of federal laws was the domain of the Supreme Court, not the states, these critics argued. (Notably, *Marbury v. Madison*, the first Supreme Court decision formally to recognize such a power, was still four years in the future—a fact that confirms the important point that *Marbury* recognized but did not create judicial review.[40])

As Madison was taking up his pen to write what would become the Report of 1800, the Kentucky legislature was passing a second resolution. The author of this Kentucky Resolution of 1799 remains unknown, but the resolution included the word "nullification," which Jefferson had removed from his 1798 version. The 1799 resolution described the states as "sovereign and independent." Therefore, they had "the unquestionable right to judge" potential violations of the Constitution. The "rightful remedy" for such infractions was a "nullification, by those sovereignties, of all unauthorized acts done under color of that instrument."[41]

In his report, Madison took a seemingly more conciliatory tone while nevertheless continuing to insist that the states possessed the power to interpret the Constitution. Reiterating that "the federal powers are derived from the Constitution," and that the Constitution was "a compact to which the states are parties," Madison asserted that Virginia and Kentucky were well within their domain when they challenged the Alien and Sedition Acts: "Where resort can be had to no tribunal superior to the authority of the parties, the parties themselves must be the rightful judges in the last resort, whether the bargain made, has been pursued or violated." The states, he maintained, were the only umpire that the Constitution provided to oversee the federal structure.[42] They were therefore not only permitted but obliged to speak. And these speech acts, in the form of resolutions, were simply "expressions of opinion

[and] unaccompanied with any other effect, than what they may produce on opinion, by exciting reflection."[43] The report won approval from the Virginia legislature in January 1800, passing the House by a vote of sixty to forty and the Senate by a vote of fifteen to six.[44]

The debates surrounding the Virginia and Kentucky Resolutions thrust ideas of nullification and interposition into the center of public debate, both in their own moment and for decades to come.[45] By insisting forcefully and publicly on the role of state consent in establishing the federal government, the resolutions offered a set of foundational texts for future commentators seeking to challenge federal authority. The open secret of their authorship by Jefferson and Madison made them even more rhetorically powerful.

The resolutions began as challenges to the authority of Congress, as in the Alien and Sedition Acts and later in the context of federal tariffs. Yet the resolutions also functioned as a rejoinder to the Supreme Court's increasingly vocal assertions of interpretive supremacy. Madison's language in the Report of 1800 had spoken in judicial terms. The "parties" were the states, and there was no "tribunal" superior to them; therefore, they were entitled to act as "rightful judges" of possible violations of the constitutional bargain. Throughout the interbellum period, the "Resolutions of '98" echoed down the constitutional debates. They were perpetually invoked in the name of state or local autonomy, and against manifestations of federal power. But the valence of the views for which they were cited was always shifting.

Commerce: The Tidewater

Wirt's public connection to the Virginia Republicans yielded additional benefits, especially following Jefferson's election to the presidency in 1800. In 1800, Wirt represented the Jeffersonian editor James T. Callender in Callender's sensational prosecution for violating the Sedition Act with his printed attacks on the Adams administration.[46] In addition to cementing his affiliation with Virginia and Jefferson, Wirt's political prominence brought with it a new degree of social and economic status. In the spring of 1801, he purchased a two-wheeled chair to be drawn by one horse, and he also acquired a slave to serve as his valet and coachman.[47]

Wirt's service to the legislature, and his efforts on behalf of the Jeffersonians, earned him a further mark of regard from the legislature: an appointment to the newly created position of chancellor for the Eastern District of Virginia. After consulting with another of his Albemarle friends, Governor

James Monroe, who urged him to accept the position, Wirt did so. Shortly thereafter, in 1802, he moved to Williamsburg to take up his new duties. The old city on the James River had lost its capital status when Richmond became the center of state government in 1780, but it was still the leading city of the tidewater region and a center of trade, law, and intellectual life. The move to Williamsburg marked a professional transition for Wirt. Having worked in the legislative branch of the state's government as clerk of the House of Delegates, he would now become a member of its judiciary.

The chancellorship marked a shift in other ways, too. Wirt was again pursuing a wife: Elizabeth Washington Gamble, daughter of Colonel Robert Gamble and Catharine Grattan Gamble. Colonel Gamble was a veteran of the Revolution, a wealthy Richmond merchant, and a Federalist who regularly played whist with Chief Justice John Marshall. Wirt proposed to Elizabeth twice and was rebuffed both times. The Gambles evidently had doubts about Wirt's habits, and stories circulated about his dissolute revels—chiefly gambling and drinking—with the fast young set in the capital. Now that he was established in quieter Williamsburg, Wirt hoped that he would be able to press his suit with more success. "I wished to leave Richmond on many accounts," he confided to Carr. "I was dissipating my health, my time, my money and my reputation. This conviction dwelt so strongly, so incessantly on my mind that all my cheerfulness forsook me, and I awoke many a morning with the feelings of a madman."[48]

The strategy succeeded: Elizabeth accepted his third proposal. In September 1802, they were married at the Gambles' Richmond home, Grey Castle, a stately mansion atop Gamble's Hill designed by Benjamin Henry Latrobe, architect of the U.S. Capitol.[49] Shortly thereafter, Elizabeth became pregnant. In September 1803, the Wirts were back at Grey Castle for the birth of their first child, Laura Henrietta.[50]

Impending fatherhood sent Wirt, whose own father had died before the young William turned two, into a frenzy of financial anxiety. He briefly considered moving to Kentucky, where many Virginians were seeking their fortunes. The "iron hand of want" compelled him to consider resigning the chancellorship in order to pursue his career in what was then considered the remote west. "This honour of being a Chancellor is a very empty thing, stomachically speaking," he wrote to Carr. "[H]onour will not go to market and buy a peck of potatoes." The chancellor's salary no longer seemed sufficient to the needs of a growing family. "On fifteen hundred dollars a year, I can live, but if death comes how will my wife and family live?," he asked. Mortality and the desire to make a name for himself seemed to require action: "Entre nous, I was thirty years old the eighth day of last November—Have I any time to lose?"[51] But the mania for Kentucky soon subsided, cooled by Elizabeth's opposition to moving so far away from her family, which manifested itself in nighttime bouts of weeping.

The family's need for Wirt to earn money at his profession continued to press, however. The ebullient spirit that counseled movement to the frontier soon redirected itself toward a new target: the commercial maritime mecca of Norfolk, some fifty miles southeast of Williamsburg at the mouth of Chesapeake Bay.

Settled in Norfolk, where he joined the practice of the prominent Tidewater lawyer Littleton Waller Tazewell, Wirt described his thinking in a letter to Carr (whom he here addressed, in the cod Latin the two often employed, as "My dear Aminadab"). The move to Norfolk, prompted by his professional ambition and his family's need for cash, was clearly linked in Wirt's mind with the territorial and commercial expansion of the United States:

> It was the scarcity of l'argent in Kentucky which induced me to renounce the project of removing thither. How will the Louisiana acquisition affect the trade & consequently the cash of that country? The Kentuckians, I should think, would find a market at Orleans, and consequently draw specie from that source; which specie, as they deal but little in imports, would remain in their own country. . . . It is sufficient for me to know that there is cash enough in Norfolk, if I know how to come at it.[52]

Practicing his profession in Norfolk presented richer prospects for the thirty-one-year-old lawyer than had the judgeship in Williamsburg. Perhaps as a consequence of his own unstable childhood, Wirt constantly evaluated his professional opportunities in terms of their economic consequences for his family.[53] Calculations of streams of income, prosaic references to household consumption, and wistful remarks about a future of "more prosperous days" filled his letters. In Norfolk, Wirt anticipated an annual income of twelve hundred pounds (in Virginia currency). He hoped to "retire from business in ten or fifteen years, with such a fortune as will place my family, at least, above want."[54]

Meanwhile, Wirt reported himself pleased by his prospects and invigorated by the challenges of mastering a new body of law. "Yes I am settled in Norfolk: and, for what I can see to the contrary, for life. How little did I expect this when you & I used to be bush whacking it to Fluvanna & Amherst!" he wrote in a double-length letter to Carr, who was practicing law in Charlottesville. Norfolk was "a famous place—Her commerce, population & wealth increase in an incalculable degree. Wherever there is much commerce, & that too sustained by a bank, there will always be plenty of law & money too."[55]

Elizabeth's father, Colonel Robert Gamble, provided financial assistance to aid the Wirts in "Necessaries to wards housekeeping," a category in which he included enslaved people. When they moved to Norfolk, Gamble urged his son-in-law "to look out . . . for a Boy & a girl fit for Betsys chamber & a driver of her carriage & waiter—and if possible a good Cook also—& I will endeavor to remit you the needful or honor your drafts." By 1806, the Wirts' household included five enslaved adults and some number of enslaved children.[56]

Even as he planned for what he hoped would be a long and profitable career in private practice, Wirt continued to feel the tug of ambition and the desire to exert his energies on a broader stage. Bladensburg was a river town, but Norfolk was a seaport city. Its character was decidedly more cosmopolitan, linked as it was with the wider Atlantic world of national and international trade. "The people here have such an intercourse with the West Indies as with Europe that they talk of the islands, the towns, the particular inhabitants, their houses & every recent foreign anecdote as familiarly as they do of the morning occurrences at the market house," Wirt marveled to Carr.

> They talk of their wharves, of commerce, of the best articles either for *ex-* or *im*portation, of the foreign ports which furnish them of the best quality and on the best terms, of the merits of this or that ship, of the mismanagement of the particular sail which occasioned the wreck of such a vessel, of the quality of such a man's Burgundy or Champaigne, &c. &c. . . . As yet I make no figure either in their conversations or their commercial controversies; but as my fortune & fame are at stake, it shall go hard with me but I get all these themes at my finger ends, before the year goes round.[57]

A world of "fortune & fame" beckoned, and commerce was its language. Norfolk would be "the ladder by which we are to climb the hills of Richmond advantageously," William wrote to Elizabeth. "Norfolk is the cradle of our fortune."[58]

But another avenue to fame opened itself to William at the same time that he was setting about his toils in Norfolk and adjusting to fatherhood. In August 1803, while he and Elizabeth were at her parents' home awaiting Laura's birth, he began writing a series of humorous sketches of life in Virginia, which were subsequently published in Richmond's *Virginia Argus*. Collected under the title *The Letters of the British Spy*, the pieces were styled as letters "written by a young Englishman of rank, during a tour through the United States, in 1803, to a member of the British parliament." Although no author was identified, the fact that they had come from Wirt's pen became an open secret throughout Richmond and the Tidewater. The "letters" included thinly disguised, occasionally barbed portraits of some of the leading statesmen of the era. The Spy's subjects included Chief Justice Marshall ("as far removed from the idolized graces of lord Chesterfield, as any other gentleman on earth," but with eyes that "possess an irradiating spirit, which proclaims the imperial powers of the mind that sits enthroned within"); Governor Monroe ("Nature has given him a mind neither rapid nor rich; and therefore, he cannot shine on a subject which is entirely new to him"); and former U.S. attorney general Randolph ("if there be a blemish in the mind of this amiable gentleman, it is the want of a strong and masculine judgment").[59]

In addition to appearing in the newspaper, the essays were published in a pamphlet that quickly ran into several editions; the tenth edition appeared in 1832. Well-suited to the contemporary tastes for cultural commentary with a frisson of scandal, the *Spy* established Wirt as a man of letters. Moreover, it gave him standing as a social critic, for the Spy lamented Virginia's "most deplorable destitution of public spirit," its citizens' "fatal apathy," and their consuming goal: *"to grow rich."*[60] Such sentiments sounded in a long tradition of republican political rhetoric, which focused on the need for virtue and devotion to the public good.[61]

Wirt had certainly imbibed these principles through his association with Jefferson and his friendships with the Carrs. His stint as clerk to the House of Delegates had further steeped him in republican political theory, as well as Republican Party orthodoxy. But letters, and specifically nonlegal writing, also beckoned to Wirt as a means of achieving distinction. "The idea has always been very dismal to me, of dropping into the grave like a stone into the water, and letting the waves of Time close over me, so as to leave no trace of the spot on which I fall," he confided to Elizabeth. "[I]f a man wishes his memory to live forever on the earth, he must either *write* something worthy of being always read, or *do* something worthy of being written and immortalized by history."[62]

Evidently taking his own words to heart, Wirt threw himself into both writing and doing. His continued loyalty to Jeffersonian Republicanism soon brought him two rewards. First, in 1807, he was tapped to serve as a prosecutor in the treason trial of Vice President Aaron Burr. Second, in 1808, he was elected to the Virginia House of Delegates, the lower house of the state assembly and the successor to the colonial House of Burgesses, in which the storied Patrick Henry had served.

Speeches, Serpents, and Fame: Richmond and the Burr Trial

The Burr trial, held in Richmond during the summer of 1807, was a spectacle that riveted the entire nation.[63] The alleged conspiracy also fed fears of insurrection and internal warfare stoked by the ongoing Napoleonic Wars in Europe. In 1805, less than a year after his fatal duel with Alexander Hamilton, Burr stepped down from the vice presidency and headed west, traveling down the Ohio River and into Louisiana Territory, which the Jefferson administration had acquired from France in 1803. Burr's plans and activities were difficult to unravel; he had either intended to lead a military expedition against Spain to gain territory in the southwestern United States, or else he had intended to establish a separate confederation of southwestern states, extending into Mexico, with himself at its head. After Jefferson learned of Burr's activities, Burr was arrested in the Mississippi Territory on suspicion of committing treason and brought to Richmond to stand trial in federal circuit court before Chief Justice Marshall and U.S. district judge Cyrus Griffin.

In August 1807, the court convened in the chamber of the House of Delegates in the Capitol at Richmond. It had been outfitted with sandboxes to absorb the unusually heavy rain of tobacco juice expected in the packed courtroom. The Jeffersonian *Virginia Argus* reported archly that the "Drama . . . first reported to be a *Farce*, is now said to be of the new species of *Melo Drama*."[64] One report noted that Richmond's population of approximately six thousand people had almost doubled as spectators poured into the city in the hope of glimpsing the infamous defendant, the chief justice, and the team of celebrity lawyers employed in his defense as well as those selected by Jefferson for the prosecution.[65] "So great was the number of distinguished persons claiming seats within the bar," wrote Burr's biographer, "that the lawyers of twenty years' standing were excluded from their accustomed places, and thought themselves fortunate to get within the walls."[66]

Burr's six-member defense team included Luther Martin, a longtime Anti-Federalist, opponent of Jefferson, and one of the nation's leading trial lawyers; former U.S. attorneys general Edmund Randolph and Charles Lee; the prominent Virginia attorney John Wickham; and Burr himself. The prosecution was led by the competent but dull George Hay, born a cabinetmaker's son in Williamsburg and now U.S. attorney for the District of Virginia (as well as James Monroe's son-in-law).[67] U.S. attorney Caesar Rodney participated briefly as well. Wirt's star was on the rise: his practice was flourishing, and his reputation for eloquence was firmly established by his authorship of the *British Spy*.

Burr's defense lawyers had in fact sought to retain Wirt, but Wirt had already agreed to join the prosecution. Wirt wrote to his friend and former brother-in-law Peachy Gilmer that the lure of "the glory & the cash" drew him to take on the daunting assignment. Wirt's association with Jefferson also impelled him to join the prosecution. The president, who had already taken the unprecedented step of declaring his former vice president guilty of treason in an address to Congress in January 1807, was known to be closely involved in the management of the case against Burr. Wirt had no illusions about the hard work that lay ahead of him in Richmond. As he wrote to Gilmer, the job promised "the heat of dog days, in a room filled chuckful, of hearers respiring in air, which has been poisoned & filled with abominations, by bugs of every sort." The prospect was "enough to make a man sweat to think of it."[68] The public, however, was keen to see Wirt perform. As one observer, Bishop James Madison (cousin to the future president), wrote, the trial would provide "a fine Field for Wirt" and an "opp[ortunity] to display a Store of Talents, as rare as rich."[69]

As the trial wore on, and the prosecution team struggled against the difficult burden of proving the case against Burr and producing clear evidence of his participation in the alleged conspiracy, Wirt unleashed his oratorical skills. The climax of the proceedings came on August 25, when Wirt rose to argue against Burr's motion to exclude certain key evidence of the conspiracy. Marshall had indicated that he was disinclined to admit as evidence reports of conversations that had occurred in December 1806 among the alleged conspirators at the home of one Harman Blennerhassett, an Irish émigré whose manorial establishment on an island in the Ohio River was said to have served as the situs of the plot.[70] Burr was not alleged to have been present on Blennerhassett's Island, and Marshall instructed the jury that evidence of such conversations was therefore inadmissible because it was irrelevant to proving the charge that Burr had levied war against the United States. Moreover, Marshall had rebuked the assembled counsel for playing to the gallery, noting that "the court thought it proper to declare that the gentlemen on both sides had acted improperly in the style and spirit of their remarks; that they had been to blame in endeavouring to excite the prejudices of the people; and had repeatedly accused each other of doing what they forget they have done themselves."[71]

Wirt began his seven-hour speech with a nod to the bench, promising to "keep no flounces or furbelows ready manufactured and hung up for use in the millinery of my fancy." And just to prove that he did not intend to volley prose at his listeners, he disavowed any literary leanings—with a literary reference to his old companion Sterne: "I cannot promise to interest you by any classical and elegant allusions to the pure pages of Tristram Shandy. I cannot give you a squib or a rocket in every period."[72] But then Wirt did precisely what he had promised not to do. He launched a fusillade of ornate rhetorical artillery aimed not at Blennerhassett, whom he painted as a guileless dupe, but directly at Burr:

> Who is Blennerhassett? A native of Ireland, a man of letters, who fled from the storms of his own country to find quiet in ours. Possessing himself of a beautiful island in the Ohio, he rears upon it a palace, and decorates it with every romantic embellishment of fancy. . . . Music that might have charmed Calypso and her nymphs, is his. An extensive library spreads its treasures before him. A philosophical apparatus offers to him all the secrets and mysteries of nature. Peace, tranquility, and innocence shed their mingled delights around him.

But then, into this arcadia, this "innocent simplicity," this "pure banquet of the heart," crept Burr—the "destroyer" who came "to change this paradise into a hell." Drawing on what the lettered among his audience would have recognized as Milton's *Paradise Lost*, and what the rest of his hearers knew as the biblical story of Adam and Eve, Wirt hammered away at Burr: "Such was the state of Eden when the serpent entered its bowers." Burr filled the hapless Blennerhassett with "the poison of his own ambition," his "daring and desperate thirst for glory," and his "ardor panting for great enterprises, for all the storm and bustle and hurricane of life." Finally, Wirt appealed to the sensibilities of his audience: "Is this reason? Is it law? Is it humanity? Sir, neither the human heart nor the human understanding will bear a perversion so monstrous and absurd! so shocking to the soul! so revolting to reason!" Burr must not be permitted to "finish the tragedy by thrusting that ill-fated man"—Blennerhassett—"between himself and punishment."[73]

Despite Wirt's theatrics, Marshall ruled in favor of Burr's motion to exclude the evidence. The jury then returned a lawyerly verdict stating that Burr was "not proved to be guilty under this indictment by any evidence submitted to us." The scandal surrounding the trial, and the widespread belief that Burr had in fact contemplated raising his own army and installing himself as emperor of a breakaway nation, decisively ended whatever had remained of Burr's political career. Meanwhile, Wirt's "Who Is Blennerhassett?" speech quickly became famous. It was printed as a standalone pamphlet, and it was memorized and declaimed by generations of schoolchildren who studied it as a model of classic American oratory.[74]

Wirt's highly public, widely celebrated performance in the Burr trial opened further doors of opportunity, both professional and political. Elizabeth Wirt had never warmed to Norfolk, and both William and Elizabeth feared the unhealthy Tidewater climate, with its annual waves of fever. Elizabeth was also in frail health, enduring three pregnancies in fewer than three years. Two more children had arrived to join Laura Henrietta: a son, Robert, and a daughter, Emily, who died shortly after birth. In 1806 the family moved back to Richmond. Another impetus to return to the capital was the recent marriage of Elizabeth's sister Agnes (called Nancy by the family) to William H. Cabell, a prominent lawyer who was elected governor in 1805.

As confirmation of this new stature, Wirt was invited by President Jefferson in January 1808 to "come into Congress" in the upcoming election.[75] Jefferson's concern for the future of the nation, as well as for Wirt's future prospects, impelled him to "frankness." His respect and affection for Wirt were clear from the "sacredly secret" letter. The president professed "an ardent zeal to see this government (the idol of my soul) continue in good hands, and from a sincere desire to see you whatever you wish to be." Congress is "the great commanding theatre of this nation and the threshold to whatever department of office a man is qualified to enter."

> [W]ith your reputation, talents, & correct views, used with the necessary prudence, you will at once be placed at the head of the republican body in the H. of R. and after obtaining the standing which a little time will ensure you, you may look at your own will into the military, the judiciary, diplomatic or other civil departments, with a certainty of being in either whatever you please; and in the present state of what may be called the eminent talents of our country you may be assured of being engaged through life in the most honorable emploiments.[76]

The letter was nothing less than a professional and personal benediction from Jefferson. Yet Wirt declined, citing his duties to his family—by which he meant the need to continue earning legal fees. Jefferson had attempted to preempt this counterargument, citing the intangible benefits that would accrue to Wirt's children should their father take high public office. "I will not say that public life is the line for making a fortune. [B]ut it furnishes a decent and honorable support, and places one's children on good grounds for public favor. [T]he family of a beloved father will stand with the public on the most favorable ground of competition," Jefferson urged.[77]

The invitation to dedicate himself to high public office, which combined honor and fame, clearly appealed to Wirt. "[W]ere my fortune other than it is, there is not in life a course on which I would enter with more spirit and ardor than that to which you invite me," Wirt assured Jefferson.[78] Like his alter ego, the British Spy, Wirt feared for the future of the republic—"most dear to my affections"—as the Revolutionary spirit receded into the past. He planned to write a biography of Patrick Henry in the hope of rekindling that spirit.

Nevertheless, the need to continue earning was paramount. In his letters to friends, Wirt expressed his fears about his family's fate in the event of his early death. He had grown up parentless; his mission now was to ply his hard-won profession into a stream of income for them. At least for the moment, worry for the future of his family outweighed worry for the future of his country. The three imperatives that drove Wirt were literary fame, political benisons, and his family's welfare. The biography of Henry offered an avenue to combine the three, such that the glories of the Revolutionary past might be harnessed to build the reputation of the current generation and ensure the prosperity of the next one. Nevertheless, with two children under the age of five and another baby on the way, Wirt could not afford to give up his legal practice just as the notoriety he had won in the Burr trial was increasing his book of business. And so he rejected Jefferson's offer.

Unlike a congressional seat, state office seemed conducive to continuing his law practice. In April 1808, Wirt was elected to represent Richmond in the House of Delegates, the body in which he had previously served as clerk. He was informally retained as Jefferson's personal lawyer.[79] Wirt was a fixture on the civic and legal circuit, leading Fourth of July celebrations and organizing gala dinners at Richmond's Eagle Tavern, a center of Republican politics. The Eagle Tavern was also a center of the city's busy trade in slaves.[80]

Another set of essays, *The Old Bachelor*, mainly written by Wirt with occasional additions by Carr, St. George Tucker, and other members of the elite Virginia bar, began appearing in the Richmond *Enquirer* in 1810. The family spent summers with Elizabeth's sister Agnes and her husband, William Cabell—now a judge on the Court of Appeals, Virginia's highest court—at the Cabells' Buckingham County plantation, which Wirt and Cabell had named Montevideo. More children were born: Catharine in 1811; twins Ellen and Rosa in 1812; Elizabeth in 1813; and Agnes in 1814. ("Cabell, his wife and Co., are here. Would you were with us! I am in a storm of children," Wirt wrote to Carr.[81]) The family moved several times, finally settling in a large house with several outbuildings (including a brick office from which Wirt ran his practice) at the fashionable corner of Fifth and Main streets, a few blocks from the capitol. Another brother of Wirt's first wife, Francis Walker Gilmer, read law with Wirt while also serving as "eldest son, tutor, and steward."[82] As of 1815, their household included eight slaves, as well as a few hired white servants.[83] At the age of forty-two, Wirt had risen far from his Bladensburg days.

The summer of 1813 found Wirt in a third-story room at the Cabells' plantation, Montevideo, windows open to the eponymous view of the Blue Ridge Mountains, surrounded by his children. ("Laura is reading Virgil," he proudly reported to Carr of his nine-year-old daughter.[84]) But he was not content. He found it difficult to write: "Writing requires a solitude & self possession which my children will not allow me."[85] He asked Carr if he should continue writing the play he had recently begun. But he worried that such endeavors would make him the target of "the dirty ... water spouts of the federal presses."[86]

A few months later, Wirt wrote to Carr that he had just received word that he had been defeated in his bid for a seat in the U.S. Senate. Instead of Wirt, the Virginia state legislature had elected Wirt's old county-court-circuit-riding comrade James Barbour. Wirt took an ironic tone toward the news, but it clearly smarted: "I am exceedingly obliged to the assembly of Virginia for this warm effusion of friendship," he wrote. The legislature had "taught my vanity a salutary lesson, in shewing me that my true rate is among the minor characters of the state."[87]

It was the last time Wirt would seek legislative office. For the rest of his career, with one important exception, he devoted himself to the practice of law. But that dedication should not make one think that Wirt quit the constitutional field. On the contrary, for the next twenty years, Wirt's unstinting labors as a lawyer representing both the government of the United States and his private clients gave him a forum in which to develop a robust theory of the Constitution and the federal system. Wirt's views derived from his unique combination of roles: a public servant, courtroom advocate, and peerless rhetorician. In addition, his lived experience in the Mid-Atlantic urban world of commerce, trade, and borders—and, indeed, as a striving member of the professional bourgeoisie—gave him a nuanced understanding of the complex nature of interbellum federalism.

The Search for an Umpire: *Martin v. Hunter's Lessee*

When Wirt failed to win election to the Senate in December 1814, he commented darkly that by its choice of Barbour, the Virginia legislature had shown him his "true rate" among "the minor characters of the state." He could not have known it then, but his loss at the state hustings coincided with the beginning of a steady rise to the top of the nation's bar.

In 1814, questions that the Virginia and Kentucky Resolutions had raised about the nature of the Union returned to the center of American law and politics. The United States was again at war with Britain, the conflict so unpopular that it was derided by critics as "Mr. Madison's War." In December, while Wirt was brooding over his defeat, delegates from five New England states met in a convention at Hartford to discuss proposals ranging from negotiations for a separate peace (despite the Constitution's explicit ban, in Article I, section 10, on such activities by states) to secession.[88] Republicans excoriated Federalists for disloyalty, while Federalists accused Madison of "military despotism" and praised New England for emulating doughty Holland, which "threw off the yoke of Spain (our Virginia)."[89] Barbed political commentary, cartoons, and poems jeered New Englanders for treachery.

Neither talk of disunion nor the general animosity adhered strictly to regional lines. Justice Joseph Story, a proud son of the coastal town of Marblehead, lambasted his fellow Massachusettsians for their noisy dissidence. "I am thoroughly convinced that the leading Federalists meditate a severance of the Union, and that if the public opinion can be brought to support them, they will hazard a public avowal of it," he wrote to a friend in Baltimore. The proposal from Massachusetts to convene a New England convention "is unquestionably designed to pave the way." Story, who had been appointed to the Court by Madison in 1811, could hardly believe his home state capable of such behavior. "I abhor their conduct!" Story pronounced. "Gracious God! that the people who led the van in the Revolution, should be the first to sell their liberties to a few designing, ambitious men, who hate even the name of patriotism!"[90] Yet again, the long shadow of the founding era lay over the thoughts and actions of interbellum Americans.

The functional structure of American federalism was still unsettled. Two important questions pressed with particular urgency. First, Americans believed in something called "the Union"; invocations of that talismanic phrase could be found on all sides of the debates in the 1810s. But what *was* the Union? Was it synonymous with the Constitution? Was it embodied in the general government? Or was the Union something distinct from the general government, a balanced and aspirational entity to be guarded from the power-grabbing tendencies of the temporary occupants of the executive and legislative branches? In his 1798 letter on the Kentucky Resolution, Wirt had portrayed the Constitution and the general government as opposed to each other. Other states "must positively declare either for the Constitution or the general government; or else, by a dastardly silence, sneak under the yoke," he had written to Carr. Wirt offered an either/or: either the Constitution, or the general government. (Or, even less attractively, silence and the yoke.)

Second, did the constitutional system provide an arbiter, an umpire, to oversee this balance? Or was the constant struggle in fact the goal? Was the Supreme Court the arbiter, or was it merely another branch of the general government, jostling and grasping for power? In the Report of 1800, Madison had seemed to reject the claim that any branch of the general government, including the Court, was the umpire. Recall his analysis of the constitutional compact: "Where resort can be had to no tribunal superior to the authority of the parties, the parties themselves must be the rightful judges in the last resort, whether the bargain made, has been pursued or violated." As with Wirt's "either/or" proposition, Madison was asking less about actual substantive legal rules, and instead about decisional authority.

Both Wirt and Madison believed that the states had the better of the merits in the debate over the Virginia and Kentucky Resolutions. They objected to the Alien and Sedition Acts, and they feared that the Adams administration was improperly entrenching itself against political checks by silencing critics and ejecting foreigners. Would they hold the same views if and when their partisan and ideological comrades were in control of the general government? Or did their answers to the question of decisional authority obtain only for a particular arrangement of substantive views?

At the same time that Wirt was making his unwished-for exit from state legislative politics, his career took a turn that plunged him fully into another forum in which these vital debates about federalism, interpretive supremacy, and the nature of the Union were raging. In 1814, Wirt was indirectly before the Supreme Court in a case that traveled up and down between the state court and the Supreme Court twice. The case raised deep and unresolved questions of decisional authority that lay at the heart of the American system of federalism. It touched on the politically charged issue of the Supreme Court's power to review the decisions of state high courts. It was also a turning point in Wirt's career, and in interbellum constitutional debates.

The case was the long, tortured dispute over the ownership of the three-hundred-thousand-acre Fairfax estate in the Northern Neck of Virginia. The complex facts turned on the question whether the title to the lands had vested in David Hunter by virtue of a Virginia patent, or whether the lands remained in the hands of the Fairfax heir, Denny Martin Fairfax, and later of his devisee, Philip Martin.[91] The posture of the case was further complicated by the fact that Chief Justice Marshall had a substantial personal interest in the issues at stake. In 1793, he and his brother James, along with a few others, had formed a syndicate to purchase certain tracts within the Fairfax lands. The commonwealth of Virginia, however, asserted ownership over the lands. The cloud over title to the lands hampered the Marshall syndicate's efforts to sell land, and therefore jeopardized the entire venture. The Marshalls spent more than a decade litigating the ownership of the lands in Virginia state courts. The rights over one particular piece of land, a one-thousand-acre parcel along Cedar Creek in northern Shenandoah County, proved especially vexing. James Marshall claimed ownership of the tract, which he intended to sell, under a 1797 grant from Denny Fairfax to the syndicate. But another claimant, David Hunter, argued that a patent he had received from Virginia in 1789 gave him title to 739 acres that lay within James Marshall's thousand acres.[92]

After twenty-one years of litigation, during which the central case concerning the property had chivvied its way through the Virginia courts, from the district court at Winchester to the Court of Appeals, the case came before the U.S. Supreme Court in 1812. The issue was whether the anti-confiscation provisions of the 1783 peace treaty with Britain controlled the disposition of the case, in which the Fairfax heirs properly claimed title, or whether title had vested in Hunter by the actions of the Virginia legislature, including a patent and an act of compromise (proposed by assembly member John Marshall) from 1796.

The case, *Fairfax's Devisee v. Hunter's Lessee*, came before the Court in large part due to the efforts of John Marshall—land speculator and chief justice. Marshall apparently hoped that a judgment from the Court would settle the disputed title over the Cedar Creek lands, ideally by confirming his brother's ownership. The chief justice routinely withdrew himself from the many cases involving the Fairfax lands that came to his circuit court or to the Supreme Court.[93] Now, Marshall helped bring the dispute over the Cedar Creek tract before the Court, on the narrow question whether the treaty of 1783 (under which Denny Fairfax, and therefore Marshall, claimed the land) superseded the state's claims over the lands (under which Hunter claimed).[94]

Marshall's primary objective appears to have been to "form a precedent" concerning the effect of the treaty, which he believed the state courts would likely follow. At a minimum, a ruling from the Court would help to clarify the snarl of competing claims, even if it did not vindicate the Marshalls' claims. "The decision of the supreme court if against us will save the expence of further litigation on the points decided; if in our favor it will I presume be respected by the state courts or if not, it will ascertain the points on which we may rely on an ultimate determination in favor of our title," Marshall wrote to Charles Lee, the attorney for the Fairfax interests.[95]

The chief justice was hoping for a ruling on a point of law that might be persuasive to state courts. He was likely not seeking an explosive confrontation between state and federal jurisdiction concerning the existential nature of the Supreme Court's power.[96] But in the end, the latter was what Marshall— watching the case from off the bench but not offstage—got.

The Court decided *Fairfax's Devisee v. Hunter's Lessee* in March 1813. The decision was supported by a three-justice plurality: Justices Henry Brockholst Livingston, Gabriel Duvall, and Joseph Story, who wrote for the Court. Marshall did not participate, as has been noted, and Justices Bushrod Washington and Thomas Todd were also absent from some of the argument and deliberations.[97] Justice William Johnson dissented.[98] Story held that title had not been divested from the Fairfax heirs, and therefore the Virginia grant to Hunter was invalid.[99]

The case then went back to the Virginia Court of Appeals—by Story's order, to reverse its previous judgment in favor of Hunter and to assess costs; by the lights of the judges of the Virginia Court of Appeals, however, to consider whether the Supreme Court in fact had the power to overturn the decisions of state courts.

When the case came back before the Court of Appeals in August 1813, the bitter and complicated issue of the enormous land grant was subsumed by an even more controversial, albeit less fact-bound, dispute: whether the U.S. Supreme Court could reverse a state's highest court on a question of constitutional law. The Virginia judges, meeting as usual in Richmond's colonial era Henrico County Courthouse, took particular offense at the wording of the mandate that accompanied the judgment from the Supreme Court. The mandate, which was directed to "the Honorable the Judges of the Court of Appeals in and for the Commonwealth and Virginia," stated that the previous judgment of the Court of Appeals in favor of Hunter was "reversed and annulled." The mandate then set forth a series of directives to the Virginia high court:

"[I]t is further ordered, that the said cause be remanded to the said Court of Appeals ... with instructions to enter judgment for the appellant. ... You therefore are hereby commanded that such proceedings be had in said cause, as according to right and justice, and the laws of the United States, and agreeable to said judgment and instructions of said Supreme Court ought to be had."[100]

The question now before the Virginia Court of Appeals was whether to obey the mandate. With such momentous issues before them, the Virginia judges reopened the case, under the caption *Hunter v. Martin, Devisee of Fairfax*—a pointed reversal of the order of the parties from the caption in the Supreme Court, and a subtle statement of their skepticism about the validity of the Court's order. According to a report of the case published three years later, the Virginia court, "after much reflection, informed the bar" of a series of "*doubts*" "whether it ought to register and enforce the mandate? whether this was a case in which jurisdiction was given to the Supreme court of the *United States* by the judicial act of congress? whether it was shown of record that any decision was given by this court against the validity or application of any treaty? and whether the jurisdiction exercised in this case by the Supreme court of the *United States* be justified by the constitution?"[101]

To resolve these doubts, the Court of Appeals invited the parties' lawyers and "any other gentleman who was disposed" to "express [their] sentiments, the questions being of great delicacy, and of public concernment."[102]

Arguments unfolded over six days in late March and early April 1814. Five lawyers appeared. Fairfax's devisee (Philip Martin) was represented by Benjamin Watkins Leigh and William Wirt. David Hunter, claiming under the grant from the Virginia legislature, was represented by William C. Williams. Appearing as amici curiae were Philip Norborne Nicholas, the attorney general of Virginia; and George Hay, still serving as U.S. attorney. Although Nicholas and Hay technically represented neither party, the published report of the case listed them among the counsel for Hunter, giving some indication of which side their arguments favored.[103] Thus, the array of lawyers in the Court of Appeals was Leigh and Wirt for the Fairfax claimants under one or another treaty, versus Williams, Nicholas, and Hay for Hunter's claim under Virginia law.

Wirt was the third lawyer to speak. In contrast to the Virginia claimant Hunter's argument that the Supreme Court lacked jurisdiction to review the case at all, much less to overrule the decision of the Virginia court, Wirt's arguments sounded themes of nationalism, congressional power, and strong judicial review. But he began quietly.

First, Wirt reminded his audience of the advantage his client brought with him to the Richmond courtroom. "As one of the counsel of Mr. *Martin*, in favour of whom the decision of the Supreme court of the *United States* has been pronounced, I . . . claim the registration of the mandate."[104] After working through the intricacies of Section 25 of the Judiciary Act of 1789, under which the Fairfax claimants had carried their case to the Supreme Court, Wirt turned to the treaty, the ostensible hook between a Virginia land dispute and the jurisdiction of the Supreme Court. The treaty was not merely an ancillary fact, he insisted; it was "a material link in the chain of the defendant's title." Therefore, the construction of the treaty was clearly drawn into question, and thus the case fit within the ambit of Section 25.

Up to this point, Wirt's argument was solid and fairly incremental. But when he turned to the more difficult question of the constitutionality of Section 25, he began to invoke different values of state, and national, identity. The constitutional question was one of "such extreme delicacy, of such awful moment, and, withal, lies so wide of the ordinary track of forensic investigation in Virginia, that I feel much difficulty and reluctance in approaching it," he stated.

> It has not been, I think, until within the last year or two, that the constitutionality of an act of congress has been made a question, in any court of any grade, within this commonwealth. I mention it to the honour of the state; for I think it a proof that our courts have none of that baleful spirit of jealousy which would excite them to be prompt and forward in endangering the peace of the union, by raising needless contests for power with the general government.[105]

Wirt's point was clear: challenging the constitutionality of an act of Congress was not an assertion of long-established rights but a new phenomenon, motivated by a "baleful spirit of jealousy" that could only reflect poorly on the state raising the challenge.

Contrary to the Hunter claimants' assertion that the Constitution was a compact between the states, and that therefore the Court—a mere agent of that compact—could not impose its will on the states, Wirt argued that the Constitution was intended as "a remedy" for "the weakness of the old confederation." Moreover, the Constitution was "composed of powers made up of concessions of certain powers from the state sovereignties, for certain purposes of general good."[106] Producing this "general good," not protecting the specific sovereignties of the state, was the purpose of the new structure.

Indeed, Wirt insisted, polemics against "state prostration" misconceived what had actually occurred in 1787. The states themselves "have agreed to this prostration, in certain respects; and the only question is whether this be one of the respects in which they have so agreed to lower the flag of the state."

Wirt thus turned compact theory back on both Hunter and the Virginia judges, pointing to the states' ratification of the Constitution as "consent to yield their sovereignty *over the subjects ceded*, and in those respects to bow to the sovereignty of the federal government."[107] By its terms, in particular the enumeration of powers in Article I, the Constitution manifested the states' agreement to yield their authority over certain domains to the general government.

Finally, Wirt addressed the question of concurrent judicial power. The judges of the Court of Appeals, especially the court's fiery intellectual leader, Spencer Roane, maintained that Article III's grant of jurisdiction to the federal courts over certain categories of cases did not also strip the state courts of jurisdiction over those cases.[108] The state courts possessed concurrent jurisdiction to interpret federal law, and therefore they could not be overruled by the Supreme Court. On this view, the state courts and the Supreme Court existed in parallel planes, with the Court perhaps persuading, but not necessarily overriding, the state courts. Wirt rejected this conception of concurrent jurisdiction. "[I]t is very clear that both the terms and the reason of the grant, certainly exclude the *final* jurisdiction of the state courts. For how can the judicial power of the United States extend to *all* cases arising under treaties, if the state courts decide *finally* all cases brought before them?" This structural, theoretical argument was followed immediately by the insight of a seasoned courtroom lawyer: consider the plaintiffs. He argued: "For if plaintiffs choose to institute all such suits in the courts of their respective states, then the jurisdiction of the United States, instead of extending to *all* such cases, will extend to *none* of them." The consequence? A "disorganized, disjointed, jarring and clashing chaos of jurisprudence."[109]

Wirt ended with a final fillip: a citation of the records of the convention that had ratified the Constitution in one particular state—Virginia. He particularly emphasized Madison's argument that a single supreme court with the power to decide treaty disputes consistently was necessary to carry out the nation's foreign policy. "The establishment of one revisionary, superintending power can alone secure such uniformity," Wirt declared, quoting from Madison's remarks at the Virginia ratification convention.[110] His co-counsel Leigh had "already cited several passages of the Federalist to this effect," but their oppo-

nent Williams "puts aside the authority of the Federalist with a high and indignant hand—'it is a party work,' he says, 'written merely to persuade the people
to adopt the constitution.' "

Wirt appeared at first to demur on the question of the probative value of the
Federalist essays, stating, "It is not for me to pronounce the eulogy of that
work." But then he continued, offering not a eulogy to a relic but a tribute to a
still-useful guide: "[W]ho they were that wrote it—how eminent in point of
abilities—and what their opportunities of understanding the true design and
meaning of the constitution, is well known to this court."[111] The argument
over the power of the Supreme Court to override the judgment of a state court
was also a fight to claim the authority of the founders. Even as Mr. Madison's
war raged around them, the lawyers and judges in Richmond and Washington
battled to claim the imprimatur of founding father Madison's writings. Post-
founding Madison also had a place in the debate, for Roane cited the "Report,
commonly called *Madison's* Report," to support his own theory of the constitutional compact.[112]

But, one must ask, how seriously should we take Wirt's arguments? He
was, after all, representing a client. Yet the scope of his arguments about concurrent power, coupled with his understanding of the complex Virginian
psyche and his subtle rechanneling of Virginian arguments from the drafting
and ratification of the Constitution, suggest that he was motivated by something more than zealous advocacy for the Fairfax heirs. Wirt was now a Virginian, but he had spent the first twenty years of his life as a Marylander, and a
highly mobile one at that. His own peripatetic upbringing might have given
Wirt some appreciation for the simple fact that multiple jurisdictions did exist,
and that those jurisdictions might have different legal regimes that could
come into conflict, warranting the oversight of a revisionary, superintending
power.

Wirt failed to convince the judges of the Virginia Court of Appeals, however. From the moment the Supreme Court's mandate arrived in Richmond,
the Virginia judges took umbrage at both its tone and content. In the order
from the Supreme Court, they heard an attack not only on the independence
of their own court, but on the autonomy of their state. The judiciary of one
government seemed to them to be reaching into the sphere of another government's judiciary.

Even worse, the invading justices were dictating terms to the state judges.
To the Virginia judges, the mandate amounted to a forced ventriloquization.
The Supreme Court had seized hold of the Fairfax lands case, reversed the

Virginia Court of Appeals's previous decision in favor of Hunter, and now presumed to order—indeed, "commanded"—the Virginia court to "enter and execute a judgment different from that which it had previously rendered."[113] It was an affront to state judicial power, to the federal compact, and to the Constitution. Each of the four judges who issued an opinion in *Hunter v. Martin* insisted that the Constitution permitted them the final word on the construction of the Fairfax land grants, and that Section 25 was unconstitutional to the extent it conflicted with this proposition. The insult lay in the command.

And here lies another reason to think that Wirt's arguments reflected his own views. One of the judges before whom Wirt argued was William H. Cabell—husband of Agnes Gamble Cabell, proprietor of Montevideo, and Wirt's brother-in-law. Cabell and Wirt were longtime friends and colleagues, as the two families' summer visits demonstrated. Indeed, it was only eight months before the argument before the Court of Appeals that the Wirt family had been guests at Montevideo, with Wirt rhapsodizing about his daughter's grasp of Virgil.[114] Moreover, Wirt's friendship with Dabney Carr, and the fact that Carr and Cabell were fellow judges in the Virginia courts, created additional ties of friendship and collegiality between the brothers-in-law.[115]

When the Court of Appeals handed down its decision in December 1815, Cabell's led the quartet of seriatim opinions. In it, he insisted that the layered and concurrent nature of the American federal republic required strict delineation of authority. The fact that multiple governments "embrac[ed] the same territory, and operat[ed] on the same persons and frequently on the same subjects" made imperative the maxim that "each government must act by *its own* organs." Thus, "from no other can it expect, command, or enforce obedience, even as to objects coming within the range of its powers." The arrangement was paradoxical: because any given space, person, or subject might be regulated by multiple sources of governmental authority, each of those governments had to exist in hermetic isolation from the others. Yet such was the constitutional structure, in Cabell's view. The alternative—a scenario in which "the Federal Court can act directly on this Court, by obliging it to enter a judgment not its own"—was unthinkable.[116]

And what of border skirmishes? If more than one governmental authority claimed power over a given space, person, or subject, but each authority had to remain in its own sphere and none had the right to check another, how would the conflict be resolved? Cabell recognized the issue, which one might think of as a problem of "who decides who decides."[117] But he offered no clear solution. The Constitution "contemplates the independence of both governments," he wrote. "It must have been foreseen that controversies would some-times arise as to the boundaries of the two jurisdictions. Yet the constitution has provided no umpire, has erected no tribunal by which they shall be set-tled."[118] Cabell's colleague Roane was even more emphatic in his denial of the Supreme Court's authority. Indeed, existing scholarship on the Fairfax lands case has portrayed Roane as the dominant voice among the Virginia judges.[119] But Cabell's rejection of the "umpire" idea was a direct refutation of Wirt's call for a superintending power. The U.S. Supreme Court was just another branch of the general government—a mere department of the agent created by the parties to the constitutional compact.

Even as the bench and bar of Virginia argued over whether there was any judicial glue holding the federal republic together, New Englanders were con-templating splintering themselves off from the Union. In their arguments for Martin's claim under the Fairfax grant, Wirt and Leigh had emphasized the political volatility of the moment, urging the judges to be mindful of the grave threats the nation faced, from both within and without, as they deliberated over the case. This line of argument presumably represented a strategic choice. By reminding the Virginia court of "the anarchical principles prevalent" in "a particular section of the union," Wirt and Leigh might convince some of the judges that moderation, not defiance, was the prudent course of action.[120]

But, as Roane's opinion made clear, the strategy might instead have alien-ated the Virginia judges, or even pushed them to take a strong stance. Roane chided "the appellee's counsel": the court did not control the timing of the case, and it did not "regard political consequences, in rendering it's [sic] judg-ments." More substantively, Roane highlighted the dangers that might result from failing to recognize that "a centripetal, as well as a centrifugal principle, exists" in the federal republic: "[N]o calamity would be more to be deplored by the American people, than a vortex in the general government, which should ingulph and sweep away, every vestige of the state constitutions."[121]

In one important way, however, Wirt and Leigh's strategy had succeeded. Arguments in the case had taken place over six days in late March and early April 1814. Yet the court did not issue its decision until December 1815—twenty months later. By that time, the war had ended, and the immediate threat posed by the Hartford Convention had receded. Roane alluded to the delay in a foot-note to his opinion: "This opinion was prepared, and ready to be delivered, shortly after the argument. The crisis alluded to by the appellee's counsel, has now, happily passed away."[122] Roane's own opinion might have been complete in the spring of 1814, but the fact was that the court had refrained from issuing its decision for more than a year and a half, well after the emergency had passed. Roane and his colleagues clearly sought to distance themselves from the New Englanders, whose separatist project the Virginia judges viewed as categorically different from their own claim of interpretive autonomy. Even bold Virginia cared enough about the Union, or was confident enough in its own power, to know when to bide its time. And then it would speak, loudly.

The Virginia judges' defiance meant that the case returned to the Supreme Court in 1816, with the aid of Marshall, whose continued interests in the Fairfax lands caused him to recuse himself but did not stop him from participating behind the scenes.[123] The case, now titled *Martin v. Hunter's Lessee*, was argued over three days in March 1816. Six days later, on March 20, Justice Story delivered a unanimous opinion for the Court.

Story's opinion endorsed Wirt's reading of Article III. "It is the case, then, and not the court, that gives the jurisdiction," Story wrote. "If the judicial power extends to the case, it will be in vain to search in the letter of the Constitution for any qualification as to the tribunal where it depends."[124] Indeed, even the Articles of Confederation, "an instrument framed with infinitely more deference to State rights and State jealousies," had granted the Congress the power to establish courts with a "revising" power over certain types of state-court decisions, such as prize cases. "This was, undoubtedly, so far a surrender of State sovereignty, but it never was supposed to be a power fraught with public danger or destructive of the independence of State judges," Story observed. "On the contrary, it was supposed to be a power indispensable to the public safety, inasmuch as our national rights might otherwise be compromitted and our national peace been dangered."

In the final sentence of the opinion, Story delivered the Court's rejoinder to the Virginia Court of Appeals. "It is the opinion of the whole court, that the judgment of the court of appeals of Virginia, rendered on the mandate in this cause, be reversed, and the judgment of the district court, held at Winchester, be, and the same is hereby affirmed," Story pronounced.[125] The Supreme Court was no longer ordering the Virginia court to execute a mandate. It was entering judgment itself.[126] This was a full-throated defense of national judicial power and a rebuttal of compact theory. It was the declaration of an umpire, not a mere agent.

Unusually for the Marshall Court, which typically issued per curiam opinions in a unified voice, one of Story's fellow justices took up the pen to add a separate concurrence. "I acquiesce in their opinion, but not altogether in the reasoning, or opinion, of my brother who delivered it," wrote Justice William Johnson, Jr.

Johnson, a native of Charleston, South Carolina, had joined the Court in 1804, when he was thirty-two years old. He was the first of President Jefferson's three appointments to the Court. Johnson had previously served in South Carolina's state legislature, including as speaker, and then on the state's high court.

Johnson has been called "the first dissenter."[127] Jefferson nominated Johnson in part to provide a Republican bulwark against the consolidating Federalist tendencies that were already evident on the Court under John Marshall.[128] But in the thirty years that Johnson served on the Court before his death in 1834, he increasingly confounded and disappointed Jefferson's expectations. Johnson did fulfill Jefferson's expectations in two ways: he was outspoken, and he was comfortable writing separate opinions from Marshall's. Johnson wrote more than 160 opinions during his time on the Court, thirty-eight of which were dissents and ten of which were concurrences.[129] Sometimes Johnson styled his opinions as concurrences but wrote them as dissents, and sometimes he explicitly dissented from Marshall and the majority.

But, to Jefferson's frustration, Johnson often split with Marshall for the wrong reasons. Despite his impeccable Republican upbringing and credentials, Johnson did not always hew to the Jeffersonian credo of decentralization and narrow constitutional construction. Instead, Johnson developed his own distinctive view of federal power, one that frequently took a more nuanced, historically informed view of the federal structure than did those of Marshall or Story. The South Carolinian was independent-minded and irascible. He also possessed keen powers of analysis, which he had honed in his twenties while rising to the top of his state's government. In contrast to Story, whose majority opinion in *Martin v. Hunter's Lessee* invoked constitutional text and trumpeted national supremacy with a zeal that outstripped even his mentor, Marshall, Johnson declined to accept the premise that the federal government and the states were locked in a fixed binary of perpetual struggle.

In his concurrence, Johnson laid out a vision of the Union that was refreshingly different from the federal-state dichotomy upon which many of his contemporaries relied. On one hand, Johnson argued that "free government" was impossible if "the State sovereignties" were to be "prostrated at the feet of the General Government." Quoting "a celebrated orator" (Patrick Henry, who was not coincidentally also the father-in-law of Virginia judge Spencer Roane), Johnson declared, "I rejoice that Virginia has resisted."[130]

But then Johnson changed tone. First, he chided the Virginia judges for not stating their views "with a little more moderation." Then he reframed the central issue in the case—not as a battle between total federal domination and abject state submission, as Roane had framed it, but as a question about border disputes between the judiciaries of overlapping governments. Johnson was thus in dialogue with Wirt and Cabell: Wirt, who had argued for a "revisionary, superintending power," and Cabell, who had insisted in his judicial opinion that the Constitution established no "umpire" over the system. The judge and the advocate—brothers-in-law—had disagreed about the answer, but they were asking the same question. And now so was Justice Johnson: "[W]e will inquire whether the Constitution sanctions the exercise of a revising power over the decisions of State tribunals in those cases to which the judicial power of the United States extends."[131] For Johnson, as for Wirt and Cabell, the key inquiry was about the judiciary. All of them viewed it as the hinge that connected the many interlocking pieces of the Union.

Johnson also challenged the by-then orthodox Republican view of the Constitution as a compact. As we have seen, in the Resolutions of 1798, Madison and Jefferson had argued that the Constitution was a compact; the states were the parties; and the general government was merely an agent. But Johnson blasted this theory. The Constitution was not a compact among sovereign states who agreed to create a general government to do their bidding. There was indeed an agreement, but general government was there from the beginning: "To me, the Constitution appears, in every line of it, to be a contract, which, in legal language, may be denominated tripartite. The parties are the people, the states, and the United States."[132]

Johnson's view took the language of compact and contract that were beloved of Jefferson and Madison (in 1798, at any rate—each adopted different views when acting as president) and upended it. The states were parties, but so too was the United States, and so were the people. Johnson thus refused to engage with debates about priority or which came first. All three parties to the "tripartite" contract were present at the beginning, in 1787: the people, the states, and the United States. Acting together, and memorialized in the Constitution, they created the Union.

A vital practical tool of this tripartite contract was the revising power "over cases and parties in the state courts," which was "secured to the United States" and thus validly established by Congress in Section 25 of the Judiciary Act.[133] Such a revising power could not permissibly take the form of "compulsory or restrictive process upon the state tribunals."[134] But short of that limitation, Johnson concluded, "In this act I can see nothing which amounts to an assertion of the inferiority or dependence of the state tribunals."[135]

The debate that the Fairfax land cases ignited between the Virginia Court of Appeals and the U.S. Supreme Court is often treated as a set piece in the history of early-nineteenth-century federalism. As the exchange among Wirt, Cabell, and Johnson shows, however, the views were more variegated than a reductive state-versus-federal template suggests. Johnson, in particular, put forth a different theory of the nature of the Union from the ones offered by the figures who conventionally dominate this history. It was not a compact among the states, but it was also not a unitary national government. The Constitution was a tripartite contract between the people, the several states, and the United States. For Johnson and Wirt, the Supreme Court was the institution that would maintain this three-way balance and manage conflict. In their view of the Fairfax cases, the Court was acting to vindicate the interests of two of the parties to the contract (the people, acting through Congress; and the United States, through its treaty power) against the third party (the state). For Cabell, however, no such umpire was needed; the system was inherently unstable and conflict-ridden. All shared a belief that federalism entailed the Union, but not necessarily a nation.

At the Bar of the Supreme Court: Washington City

The Fairfax land cases can be regarded as Wirt's oblique entry into Supreme Court practice. Indirectly, they were a triumph. The general outlines of his argument before the Virginia court in *Hunter v. Martin* in the dark year of 1814 were reflected in Story's opinion for the Court in *Martin* in 1816. Moreover, the subtleties of Wirt's conception of the revising power were shared by Johnson's forceful concurrence.

Wirt's involvement in the much-bruited Fairfax litigation likely helped him to secure a prize that he had long sought: the opportunity to argue before the Supreme Court, and thus to expand his practice to the most important controversies of the day. In so doing, he would also be able to demand increased fees. Writing to Carr, who was now a Virginia chancery judge, Wirt attempted to downplay the news. But he also asked his friend to meet him in the capital, which had been burned by the British only four months earlier, to mark the occasion: "I shall be opposed to the Attorney General of the U.S. & perhaps to Pinkney—I should like to grapple them—'The blood more stirs, you know, to rouse a lion than to start a hare.' "[136]

Reorienting his practice toward Washington and the Court marked a new epoch in Wirt's life and career. Prior to his appointment as U.S. attorney general in 1817, he argued two cases before the Court. Over the course of his career, he would argue 168 more. In his appearances before the Court, Wirt returned again and again to questions of commerce and concurrent power. His maritime practice in Norfolk had educated him in the web of trade and intercourse that connected the United States to the Caribbean and Europe; his time on the chancellor's bench in Williamsburg had sharpened his equity practice, as well as giving him the judge's perspective; his busy city work in Richmond had immersed him in the workings of merchants; and his stint in the legislature had bathed him in Virginia's rich ideological mix, which combined state sovereignty with a paternal, Jeffersonian pride in the nation.[137]

When Wirt traveled to Washington, he brought all these influences with him. He also carried a practitioner's appreciation for the clarifying powers of argument—for the need to put claims and assertions into collision with each other in order to test their viability. And, in an era that prized words, he had not only mastered the languages of both law and politics; he was producing them, in the *British Spy* as well as in his courtroom exhibitions. The next step was to master the language of the Constitution.

The Supreme Court's practice at that time was ideally suited to Wirt's already-substantial talents. With no requirement of written briefs, the focus of the proceedings was the oral arguments, for which there was no time limit.[138] Consequently, Wirt and his colleagues often referred to their arguments as "speeches," and indeed a single advocate's address to the Court might last as long as four hours at a time, sometimes continuing over two days. Cases not uncommonly stretched over several days. Members of the public occasionally attended; the presence of ladies in the courtroom was often noted by attorneys as a reason to indulge in greater oratorical heights.

While the Capitol was undergoing repairs following the British conflagration of 1814, the Court met in a series of temporary accommodations, including a "large double house" on Pennsylvania Avenue, a "brick dwelling" on New Jersey Avenue that would thereafter become a tavern, and finally a "dungeon"-like room in the Capitol.[139] Only in 1819 did the Court return to its chamber in the basement of the Capitol.[140]

In this period, the justices spent between six weeks and two months in Washington each year; at other times, they were sitting on their circuit courts or else were at home. When the Court was in session, it sat from eleven in the morning until four in the afternoon. The beginning of the proceedings was felt by some onlookers to lack in gravitas. The justices entered "in rear of the bench, and assume their robes, in the same manner as a farmer puts on his frock, or the sportsman his hunting shirt, preparatory to the pursuits of the day," reported a correspondent for a New York paper who was attending the Court's session. Another observer noted that after donning their robes, the justices took their places on the bench and then spent some period of time "receiving from the Marshal their cards of invitation and taking up their pens to answer them before the list of cases is called for hearing."[141]

Once the arguments commenced, the mood changed: "Counsel are heard in silence for hours, without being stopped or interrupted. The Judges of the Court say nothing, but when they are fatigued and worried by a long and pointless argument, displaying a want of logic, a want of acuteness, and a destitution of authorities, their feelings and wishes are sufficiently manifested by their countenances and the manners which are displayed."[142]

As events unfolded, Wirt's longed-for argument before the Court ended up being a different case from the one he had mentioned to Carr, and it did not take place until February 1816. To Wirt's distress, the debut was neither smooth nor momentous. In typical fashion, he channeled his disappointment into writing. In a letter to a friend, Wirt described the lawsuit, a dispute between the representatives of two customs collectors over the distribution of the penalty from a bond issued under the Embargo Act, by saying that "there never was a case more hopeless of eloquence since the world began."[143]

However pedestrian the case, though, Wirt described a harrowing process of preparations hoped for but then foiled, beginning with the loss of his notes and culminating in a near-slapstick series of late nights, surprise interruptions, and disruptive sociability:

> My only hope then was that I should be able to recall the arguments by meditation in the stage [from Richmond to Washington]. . . . My consolation then was, that I should have one day in Washington before the cause came on,—and to effect this, I left Alexandria when the stage arrived, at about ten o'clock on Tuesday night, and went to Washington that night. I got to McQueen's [tavern] about eleven. In two minutes after, Dr. F[lood] came in, so delighted to see me. . . . He thus kept me up till two o'clock. Immediately after breakfast I retired to my room, borrowed the acts of Congress, on which my cause arose, and had just seated myself to study, when several of my warm-hearted friends rushed into my room and held me engaged 'till court hour. So it was again in the evening; and so, on Thursday morning. In this hopeless situation I went to court to try the tug of war with the renowned Pinkney.

"I was never more displeased with any speech I have made since I com-menced practice," Wirt confided after thus unburdening himself, as always, to Carr. But frustration seemed to spur his ambition: "I must somehow or other contrive to get another cause in that court, that I may shew them I can do better."[144]

Wirt's ambition was also fired by this first encounter with William Pinkney. Pinkney was a renowned trial lawyer known for his arrogant demeanor and dandyish dressing. A fellow Marylander and onetime U.S. attorney general, Pinkney had been wounded at the Battle of Bladensburg in August 1814. After the war, Pinkney represented Maryland in Congress and consolidated his posi-tion atop the Baltimore legal market. Wirt both envied and disliked him. The antagonism was productive. Pinkney was later the opponent in the only duel Wirt ever came close to fighting.[145] The stage seemed to be set for Wirt to stir his blood, test his skill against the finest adversaries, and find out what it was like to, in his words, "rouse a lion."

While Wirt was looking for his next opportunity to prove himself in the Supreme Court, in March 1816 he was appointed by President Madison to the position of U.S. attorney for Virginia.[146] More and more, the Virginian-by-adoption was practicing law at the intersection of state and federal power. He was now an agent of the general government—albeit a general government controlled by Virginians.

Another chance came one year later, in February 1817, when Wirt argued a prize case before the Court. "I have been to Washington again and I made a speech, Sir, in the supreme court *four hours and a half long*! Does not this alarm you!" he wrote to Carr. But the subject matter was exceedingly dull, Wirt noted. "It was, therefore, matter of surprize [*sic*] to me, that the ladies stuck to us 'till dinner time."[147]

Despite the narrow scope for imagination these first two cases presented, Wirt clearly enjoyed his new arena. "You cannot conceive . . . what a rejuvenes-cence this change of theatre and audiences gives to a man's emulation," he wrote. "It makes me feel young again, and touches on nerves that have been asleep ever since 1807."[148] Not since the Burr trial ten years earlier had the forty-four-year-old Wirt felt so invigorated. He reveled in the case across two letters to Carr that spanned a month. His opponents had visited him to com-pliment him on his argument, he recounted. He relayed that Henry Wheaton, editor of the reports of the Court, told him that "the judges expressed the greatest satisfaction with my argument." Naval hero Captain Stephen Decatur, who was in the process of building his grand brick home on President's Park (today's Lafayette Square), hallooed Wirt in the street to tender his regards: "Decatur, whom I met afterwards in the street, I in a hack, he on foot, came to the door of the hack. 'Why,' said he, in his rough sailor way, 'they tell me you have been playing the devil at the Capitol.' "

Even president-elect Monroe had broken through his customary reserve to congratulate Wirt. Monroe "said to me, with the most beaming pleasure, that he had been told I had covered myself *with reputation and glory*. These were his words; and when I looked a little distrustful, he added, 'Upon my honour, it is a fact, and I was told so, too, by a person who had no political prejudices in your favour.' "[149] For Wirt, reporting to Carr on the *éclat* he had wrought from a dry prize case assumed priority even over the news that Elizabeth had just given birth to a son, named Dabney Carr Wirt.[150]

The Attorney General in the Court and the Cabinet

The year 1817 brought Wirt within sight of the pinnacle of success. His *Life of Patrick Henry*, on which he had been working intermittently for twelve years, was finally published in November. Within a few weeks of the *Life's* appearance in print, Wirt became attorney general of the United States.

The publication of the *Life of Patrick Henry* caused Wirt great anxiety. Having spent years collecting tales of Henry's life and accounts of his many speeches during and after the Revolution, Wirt had difficulty assembling the various fragments he had culled into a readable narrative. He had never met the great Virginian orator, who died in 1799. Wirt had had extensive correspondence with Jefferson about the project, and the ex-president sent along recollections and offered suggestions from Monticello. While Wirt was preparing the *Life*, he circulated drafts among his friends; the distribution list included members of the founding generation who had known Henry as well as Wirt's own contemporaries. Wirt found the task of writing the *Life* more difficult than his previous projects, such as *The Letters of the British Spy* and *The Old Bachelor*. In part this was because those works had been published anonymously. As he confided to Carr, "[T]his is the first work I have ever offered to the public, *with my name to it*—and I confess the novelty of the situation gives me some unpleasant throbs."[151]

But the principal challenge for Wirt was the process of researching and gathering facts, which his essays and commentary had never required of him. Wirt found a new sympathy for James Boswell, whom he had previously viewed as larding his *Life of Samuel Johnson* with unnecessary complaints. "I now know by woful experience that Bozzy was right. . . . I found, at every turn of Henry's life, that I had to stop and let fly a volley of letters over the State, in all directions, to collect dates and explanations, and try to reconcile contradictions." Writing was nearly impossible when one had to keep halting to find out what had actually happened. Moreover, Wirt found it difficult to balance his taste for literary style with both the awkward reality of facts and the need to keep propelling the narrative forward, writing, "My pen wants perpetually to career and frolic it away. But it must not be." He paused at page 107 to dash off a lament to Carr: "[A]fter I have gotten the facts accurately, they are then to be narrated happily; and the style of narrative, fettered by a scrupulous regard to real facts, is to me the most difficult in the world. It is like attempting to run, tied up in a bag."[152]

Declaring the *Life* "the most oppressive literary enterprise that ever I embarked in," Wirt nevertheless managed to govern himself to produce a 427-page biography of Henry. The *Life* sold well, although some critics faulted Wirt for what they viewed as a too-glowing portrayal of Henry. Wirt himself had worried about this, asking Jefferson repeatedly for reassurance. The former president's conclusion was lukewarmly encouraging: "It constitutes perhaps the distinction between panegyric and history. On this opinions are much divided, and perhaps may be so on this feature of your work. On the whole however, you have nothing to fear."[153] Wirt's concern about the tone of the book manifested itself in his preface, which craved his readers' pardon for the contents: "crude sketches" based on "scanty and meagre" materials and composed by a "practicing lawyer" amid "incessant professional annoyance."[154]

Far away in Quincy, Massachusetts, eighty-two-year-old John Adams read the *Life* and was moved to take up his pen to write to Wirt. Adams praised the book but then raised a quibble: the Revolution, he insisted, had in fact begun in Massachusetts in the 1760s, not Virginia in the 1770s. "I envy none of the well-merited glories of Virginia, or any of her sages or heroes, but I am jealous, very jealous, of the honour of Massachusetts," the former president wrote. Wirt, perhaps sensing that he had stepped into an old quarrel, responded smoothly: "I have not the honour to boast of my nativity in either of those States, and therefore feel none of that local, and I will add, honourable pride and jealousy which naturally grow out of our attachment to the *natale solum*." Instead, Wirt noted, he had always regarded Virginia and Massachusetts as "twin sisters in this race of glory, and as running pretty fairly abreast through the whole course of it." Adams seemed satisfied with Wirt's response, although he sent a follow-up letter with page references and notes for Wirt's perusal. But Adams did "congratulate the nation on the acquisition of an Attorney General of such talents and industry as your Sketches demonstrate."[155]

Indeed, just as the *Life of Patrick Henry* was appearing in bookshops, and while Wirt was in Norfolk attending court in his capacity as U.S. attorney for Virginia, a letter marked "Private" arrived at the Wirts' home in Richmond. The letter, dated October 29, 1817, was from President Monroe. In it, Monroe invited Wirt to become attorney general of the United States. "Highly respecting your talents, and having long entertained a sincere friendship for you, I need not add that it would be very gratifying to me to find that this proposition accorded with your interest and views. Should this be the case, I hope that it will be convenient to you to join us at an early day, as there are many subjects of great importance requiring early attention."[156]

Fifteen days later, on November 13, less than a week after he turned forty-five, Wirt received a recess appointment from President Monroe. The incumbent attorney general, Richard Rush, had already taken up his new duties as ambassador to Great Britain. The day of the appointment, William wrote from Washington to Elizabeth, who was at home in Richmond, "The die is cast,—I have accepted the office."[157]

The Senate confirmed the appointment on December 15, and the appointment was dated as of December 16. Wirt had secured Monroe's assurance that he need not divest his part ownership of a foundry on the James River that occasionally contracted with the federal government. Wirt had also informed the president of his intention to carry on his private practice, which was already a long-standing norm for the attorney general: "They all assure me that there is nothing in the duties of the office to prevent the general practice of my profession in this place, and attending occasional calls to Baltimore, Philadelphia, or elsewhere."[158] With those matters settled, Wirt immediately began making the "round of official and ceremonious visits" and attending to the subjects of great importance to which Monroe's letter had alluded.

Wirt was, by and large, a popular choice for attorney general. Wirt's renown was sufficient that he had been rumored as a possible attorney general as far back as 1811, during the Madison administration. One newspaper noted that in addition to his qualifications as "a profound lawyer, a fine speaker, and a classical and elegant writer," Wirt had risen "from obscurity and indigence, by the superiority of his mind, and by his own unaided and individual exertions."[159]

Between November and January, the Wirts searched for and purchased a home in Washington and arranged to move their sprawling household—which now included ten children—to the capital city. They settled on a large brick house on the south side of G Street between Seventeenth and Eighteenth streets, which they bought from the widow of Tobias Lear, George Washington's personal secretary, for twelve thousand dollars. At the same time they also acquired the two lots that constituted the rest of the block, for an additional eighteen hundred dollars. Elizabeth would be "the mistress of a whole square," William wrote—and that square just a block from the recently rebuilt White House. He paid for the property with cash, much of which he borrowed. The intention was to mark the family's arrival in Washington, where lavish entertaining was expected of high officials and politics took place in the drawing room as well as the Capitol.[160]

The Wirts also made changes in the household's staff, selling three of their six slaves and hiring paid white servants in their place. Elizabeth, who frequently reported difficulty managing both enslaved and free workers when William was away, continued to write often to him that both the slaves and the servants disobeyed her or subverted her authority.[161]

New duties immediately pressed upon Wirt. In January 1818, he wrote to his friend William Pope, "[S]ince I have been here I have had to work 'till midnight, every night, to keep the channel of my office from being blocked up by drift-wood." Wirt's pace was partly fueled by the six pipes he smoked each day.[162]

The first order of business was defining what the office actually was, and what it was not. The position of attorney general had been established by the First Congress in the Judiciary Act of 1789, but the outlines of the post were sketchy. Absent clear statutory guidelines, norm and practice governed.[163] The first attorney general, Edmund Randolph, described the office as "a sort of mongrel between the State and the U.S.; called an officer of some rank under the latter, and yet thrust out to get a livelihood in the former."[164] Under Wirt's predecessors, the attorney general had functioned as a federal prosecutor and a legal adviser to the president, the heads of departments, and a variety of other federal officers, sometimes including members of Congress. During Wirt's tenure, from 1817 to 1829, the remit of the office shrank, yet its influence grew. The attorney general became a full-fledged member of the Cabinet, a counselor to the president, and the chief attorney representing the interests of the United States before the courts. Wirt's duties thus combined those of the modern-day attorney general, solicitor general, and Office of Legal Counsel.[165]

Wirt, the loquacious writer and careful arguer of precedents, was immediately dismayed by the office's dearth of records. One of the chief duties of the attorney general was to produce opinions—memoranda containing legal analysis in response to particular questions put to him by the president and heads of departments. But Wirt was horrified to discover that there were no records of his predecessors' opinions. He alerted the chair of the House Judiciary Committee, a fellow Virginian, to the parlous state of affairs in the office:

[W]hen I had the honour of receiving the appointment, my first inquiry was for the books containing the acts of advice and opinions of my predecessors: I was told there were none such. I asked for the letter-books, containing their official correspondence: the answer was, that there were no such books. I asked for the documents belonging to the office; presuming that, at least, the statements of cases which had been submitted for the opinion of the law-officer had been filed, and that I should find, endorsed on them, some note of their advice in each case; but my inquiries resulted in the discovery that there was not to be found, in connection with this office, any trace of a pen indicating, in the slightest manner, any one act of advice or opinion which had been given by any one of my predecessors, from the first foundation of the federal government to the moment of my inquiry.[166]

Wirt hastened to add that he did not consider these problems to be the result of lapses by previous attorneys general, "for no law had enjoined it on them as a duty," and "the plan which I suggest could not have been executed, without an expense, in clerk-hire, office-fuel, stationery, &c., for which there is no provision by law." But now he urged Congress to take up appropriate legislation. The attorney general's office required at least one full-time clerk, a library of "the local laws of the several States," and a system for preserving in the office "a record of the opinions and official correspondence of the Attorney-General" and "the documents submitted for his advice."[167] Such modernization was necessary for two reasons: first, because the inefficient organization of the office was "injurious to the public," yet not widely known; second, so that the attorney general could maintain "the individual pursuits of his profession, and rest, for the support of his family, on the salary attached to the office."[168] Congress responded to Wirt's pleas, increasing his salary and appropriating funds to purchase a library for the office.[169]

Nevertheless, a prominent lawyer was taking a risk by accepting the post of attorney general, given the office's time demands coupled with its relatively low pay ($1,500 per year when Wirt took office in 1817, or roughly $35,000 today).[170] During Wirt's time in office, the annual salary was increased to $3,500. To this he added the fees for his private practice: $500 per case (around

$16,000 today) in the Supreme Court (of which he argued approximately twelve each year) or the appellate courts; between $50 and $100 for a written opinion; and $1,000 each for a single term of the federal district or circuit courts at Baltimore, or for the Maryland Court of Appeals at Annapolis. One estimate suggests that his total annual earnings amounted to around $10,000.[171] As he took up his new position, Wirt felt the press of debt and the responsibilities of providing for his family. "I am really laughing to keep myself from crying, as cowards whistle in the dark," he wrote to Pope. "Whether I shall find the practice of the law profitable here I do not know, as yet."[172] Assistance from Congress and a clarification of the duties of his office were therefore necessary to maintaining the precarious balance of his private and public responsibilities.

In his first two published opinions, Wirt undertook to delineate the boundaries of his new office. Responding to a query from a major of the U.S. Marines, Wirt replied crisply that complying with the request for an opinion was beyond the scope of the attorney general's power and duty. "I have no legal authority to answer it officially," Wirt wrote. Citing the Judiciary Act of 1789, "the law which creates this office," he explained that he lacked the power "to give an *official opinion* in any case, except on the call of the President, or some one of the heads of departments." A major of the Marines qualified as neither. To do otherwise would improperly "attach the weight of *my office*" to an unauthorized opinion.[173] Permissible topics for opinions in his first few months included advice to President Monroe on the president's power to grant bail, to issue warrants for the execution of mail-robbers, and to order an arrest; to Treasury Secretary William H. Crawford on the liability of stockholders of the Saline Bank of Virginia for notes issued by the bank (in which he observed that the issue was one "which I had occasion to consider very elaborately previous to my appointment to this office," when the case was "before the chancellor of the Winchester district"—viz., Dabney Carr).[174] Some opinions called for constitutional analysis, many others for statutory construction. Questions of international law frequently presented themselves. Other recurring topics included the scope of the president's authority over criminal prosecutions, as well as military regulations, pensions, land warrants, customs, and prizes.

Wirt found himself busier than he had anticipated. "As to the office I find it is no *sinecure*—I have been up 'till midnight, at work, every night, & find, still, my hands full," he wrote to Carr. But he assured his friend that he had no ambition beyond his current office, and that he did not intend to serve beyond the end of Monroe's administration: "My single motive for accepting the office was the calculation of being able to pursue my profession on a more advantageous ground—i.e. more money for less work."[175] Wirt disclaimed any goal other than "the single object of bettering the fortunes of my children, by pursuing my profession on more advantageous ground." And yet he clearly felt proud of what he had accomplished and how far he had come: "I am already higher than I had any reason to expect."[176]

The notoriety attached to his office made even Wirt's frequent travels slightly less onerous. At the conclusion of yet another uncomfortable coach trip from Washington to Baltimore, he wrote to Elizabeth that the other passengers had thanked him for the unusually rapid journey. "[T]hey had observed, what I had not, an indorsement on the way bill to carry the Attorney General through to Baltimore with all possible dispatch as he was on public business." Upon reaching his Baltimore inn, Wirt went upstairs to talk with his fellow guest, Justice Gabriel Duvall, who was riding circuit. Bespeaking both the informal atmosphere of the inns frequented by judges and lawyers as well as the cordial relationship between bench and bar, Duvall later came into Wirt's room "while I was shaving" to discuss the schedule for an upcoming trial in which they were both participating. Following "a few minutes parley" in Duvall's room "after I had dressed," Wirt evidently felt sufficiently relaxed to visit one of the city's milliners on the instructions of his daughters at home in Washington: "then to Madam Gouge's on the hat topic."[177]

Wirt came to take great satisfaction in his official opinions. They called upon his decades of lawyerly craft, as well as his facility for composition. They also immersed him in the most important federal questions of the era, many of which were entirely novel to him. "The official questions which are propounded to me, too, are all out of the usual walks of my profession, and call upon me to explore new paths, and frequently to chop out an original trace, with my own hands, through the wilderness," he observed. "My opinion books are full of this labour, and will save much trouble to my successor. If they were published they would do me more honour than anything else I have ever done."[178] In slightly more than eleven years as attorney general, Wirt would produce more than 370 official opinions—an average of more than thirty-three each year. The opinions fill more than seven hundred pages in the first two volumes of the official reports.

Although some commentators have criticized Wirt for what they view as his putting his personal interests ahead of his duties as attorney general, such claims are difficult to sustain based on the sheer scale of the official writing he produced.[179] Clearly, the president and Wirt's fellow Cabinet members relied on his judgment, as demonstrated by their incessant queries. Non-lawyers might view with skepticism Wirt's early clarifications of his duty, on the assumption that his sole motive in limiting the ambit of the office was to leave more room for his private practice. To clarify duty was not to avoid it, however, especially in the early decades of the nineteenth century. Asserting that the duty of the attorney general was to advise the president and heads of department, and refusing to provide casual legal analysis to any and all federal or state officials, were necessary steps to elevate the office from a taxpayer-funded law office to a crucial organ of the federal governmental structure.

Moreover, by producing such a relentless flow of opinions on urgent legal questions facing the executive branch, Wirt transformed the office into a source and arbiter of substantive federal law. In his opinions, the attorney general sounded less like an advocate than a judge. Indeed, Wirt sometimes told his client what that client surely did not want to hear, as when he advised the president to wait for a clearer statement from Congress before taking a particular action.

Two years into his attorney generalship, Wirt appeared to have weathered the initial shock of the workload. He decided to test a new routine that he hoped would allow him to wring still more work out of each day. Rather than staying up until midnight to answer queries from President Monroe and his fellow Cabinet members, work up those answers into official opinions, attend to his private practice, and attack his omnipresent pile of correspondence, Wirt embarked on another of his many plans for self-discipline. He would start the day's toils in the morning, when solitude might help him find the focus he could never seem to maintain once business, with its inspiriting buzz of crisis and raillery, seized hold of him. At forty-seven, Wirt knew himself well enough to realize that his lively wit and ability to hold in thrall an audience—whether in the jury box or the drawing room—could garner easy victories, but not the ones about which he cared most. Wirt viewed himself as undisciplined, a lucky dabbler whom "over-ruling Providence" had seen fit to reward handsomely.[180] Yet this harsh judgment of himself, his constant self-measuring against his contemporaries, always impelled Wirt to action. Wirt may have lacked discipline, but his consciousness of that deficiency served as a perpetual spur to strengthen his government of himself.

Early on a Wednesday morning a few days after Christmas in 1819, that impetus propelled Wirt to closet himself in an upstairs room of the house on G Street. Wirt had held the attorney generalship long enough to know that the holiday provided little reprieve from the crush of official duties. He set to work in darkness, at five o'clock in the morning, nearly burning through two candles before pausing to open the window. Snow had begun to fall. Wirt's spirits rose at the sight, for reasons both poetic and practical. Not only was snow "always a cheering spectacle to me," but the precipitation bespoke an end to a drought that had slowed operations at his cannon foundry on the James River. With snow falling, labors begun, and breakfast still ahead, Wirt permitted himself the luxury of a personal letter to Carr. Writing to Carr frequently provoked Wirt to contemplation. Some letters ended on a melancholy note, but most moved from reflection to a mood of vigorous action.[181]

On this day, the snow worked its cheering effect. Wirt's letter took up a theme that he and Carr had begun earlier: the relationship between free will and providential intervention. Wirt expressed one of his periodic regrets: that his own lack of discipline had prevented him from rising higher in life. Wirt had not possessed Carr's connections or advantages; he had worked since his youth, always conscious of the need to build his practice and bring in fees because, lacking Carr's gentry status and property, his family had to live on his earnings. Sometimes Wirt expressed frustration that his need to devote himself to his legal practice had kept him from his literary pursuits. Here, however, he blamed himself: "It is the reflection of what I might have been and what I am that stings and shames me," he wrote to Carr. Instead of "a professional man merely," Wirt might have achieved the status of "a gentleman and scholar." In the end, however, Wirt's optimism and competitive nature—perhaps the distinguishing marks of a professional man after all— won. Contemplation of the eternal gave way to the race for this-worldly fame: "If I had a twenty years' lease of my life, I might be fit to live, by the time I come to die. But I will give these fellows a hustle for their eminence yet, if I am spared in health for a few years. So, you see the modest fit is going off."[182]

Wirt's surviving papers do not reveal how long he was able to adhere to his new five o'clock schedule. By 1820, however, debates within the Cabinet were taking on new urgency as the Monroe administration worked through several controversies, all of which involved complex issues of concurrent state and federal power.

The Attorney General and the Practice of Federalism

As with the Fairfax lands case, one overarching, unanswered question was whether the federal government had the authority not only to impose its laws on the states, but also to act as a superintending power—an "umpire," to borrow Judge Cabell's term—over when federal law could supplant state law. As Secretary of State John Quincy Adams confided to his diary:

> There are several Subjects upon which the public mind in this Country is taking a turn which alarms me greatly for the continuance of this Union—The Bank—the Currency, the internal improvement Question—The extension or repression of Slavery [—] The conflicting ambition of the great States of New-York and Virginia; and the workings of individual ambition mingling with all these controversial topics. It seems to me that we are at the eve of a great crisis of which scarcely any one is yet aware.[183]

Each of the issues in Adams's list raised difficult questions of the boundary between federal and state power. Each of them eventually found its way to the attorney general's office on the second floor of the War Department at Seventeenth Street and Pennsylvania Avenue.

One such issue was the Bank of the United States. The Second Bank of the United States had been under constant attack since its establishment in 1816. In 1819, in *McCulloch v. Maryland*, the Marshall Court upheld the constitutionality of the bank and invalidated Maryland's attempts to tax the bank as exceeding the state's power to tax. Wirt had appeared on behalf of the bank in both his capacity as attorney general and as the bank's own attorney (for which he received a two-thousand-dollar fee). Even after the Court handed down the *McCulloch* decision, however, other states challenged the validity of the bank itself and the jurisdiction of the federal courts to hear cases brought by the bank.[184] The internal improvements debates raised the related question whether Congress had the power to fund (or, even more controversial, to build or operate) public works projects such as roads, canals, and turnpikes within the states.[185] President Monroe had initially supported congressionally funded internal improvements, but he then modified his view and maintained that internal improvements, while desirable, likely required a constitutional amendment to be valid.[186]

Another looming question concerned Missouri's admission to the Union. The Missouri Territory was part of the 828,000-square-mile parcel of land acquired through the Louisiana Purchase of 1803, which had doubled the size of the United States. In 1819, Congress began debating a Missouri statehood bill. The expectation was that Missouri would permit slavery, as significant numbers of its white population were slaveholders, and 15 percent of the population was enslaved by 1820. They, of course, were not permitted to vote on the question. But during the debate on the floor of the House, Representative James Tallmadge, Jr., of New York introduced an amendment to the bill providing that "the further introduction of slavery or involuntary servitude be prohibited, except for the punishment of crimes, whereof the party shall have been fully convicted; and that all children born within the said State, after the admission thereof into the Union, shall be free at the age of twenty-five years."[187]

After months of angry debate in Congress and among the broader public, the "Missouri Compromise" was passed in March 1820. Under the compromise, Missouri would be admitted to the Union as a slave state; Maine would be admitted as a free state; and slavery would be prohibited in the rest of the Louisiana cession north of latitude 36°30'. The compromise proved immediately unsatisfactory. Supporters of slavery rejected both the dividing line and the underlying premise that Congress could outlaw slavery in the territories, much less in any new states. Opponents of slavery viewed the line as, in Adams's words, "a Law perpetuating Slavery in Missouri, and perhaps in North-America" that "has been smuggled through both houses of Congress."[188] On one view, federal power had impermissibly interfered with slaveholders' rights to property in their chattel, and with states' plenary power to regulate internal affairs. But another view held that federal power had legitimated slavery and committed the authority of the United States not only to the support of slavery but to its extension.

When the Missouri bill had passed both houses of Congress and was presented to Monroe, he solicited his Cabinet members' views while he considered whether to sign it. On March 4, 1820, the president presented them with two questions: first, "Has Congress a right under the powers vested in it by the Constitution to make a regulation prohibiting Slavery in a territory?"; second, "Is the eighth section of the act . . . for the admission of Missouri into the Union consistent with the Constitution?" The five Cabinet officers agreed unanimously that Congress did indeed have the power to prohibit slavery in the territories, and that the provision admitting Missouri into the Union was constitutional. In a sign of how portentous the Missouri debates had become, they produced a trio of written opinions in response to Monroe's query.[189]

Close reading of the opinions reveals subtle but important distinctions among them. To both questions, Secretary of State Adams responded with a simple affirmative. The members of the Cabinet who owned slaves— Secretary of War Calhoun, Treasury Secretary Crawford, and Wirt—also answered affirmatively. They did note, however, that their response assumed that congressional power to ban slavery extended only to territories and not to states:

> We are of opinion that Congress has a right, under the powers vested in it by the Constitution, to make a regulation prohibiting Slavery in a territory.
>
> We are, also, of opinion that the 8 section of the act . . . for the admission of Missouri into the union, is consistent with the constitution, because we consider the prohibition as applying to territories, only, and not to states.[190]

Two decades later, however, congressional power even over the territories would be denied by a majority of southern supporters of slavery.

Secretary of the Navy Smith Thompson, a New Yorker (and future Supreme Court justice), wrote separately, saying, "My answer to the within questions is in the affirmative, and would add that in my opinion the 8th section of the act applies only to Territories." Thompson's fine-grained wording reached the same conclusion as Calhoun, Crawford, and Wirt, but he did not join them in explicitly excluding the states.[191]

All three opinions were careful statements that took seriously the boundaries between the powers of the general government and those of the states. But it would be a mistake to read them as simply statements of a zero-sum relationship of federal versus state power. The complex layers of authority debated by the participants in the Fairfax land litigation were canvassed here as well. The tripartite contract of Justice Johnson's *Martin* concurrence was evident: the people (through Congress), the states, and the United States. The fact that the debate concerned the territories, which were placed within Congress's power by Article IV of the Constitution, added another domain within which federal power operated.

As these multifaceted debates about concurrent power played out in Monroe's Cabinet, they necessarily required both the official opinions and the informal views of the attorney general. Wirt's increasingly numerous appearances before the Court and his involvement in constitutional litigation such as the Fairfax land case gave him a practicing lawyer's insight into the technical, legal arguments on all sides. In addition, his commitment to the role of the attorney general as an officer of both the U.S. government and the Constitution gave him an appreciation for the interests of the Union. His affiliation with a long tradition of Virginian republican ideology added to this sense of stewardship for the nation. But his identity as a member of the Virginia slave-owning elite, which was wrapped up in his own rise from obscurity, also meant that he had a stake in recognizing the states' power to regulate slavery.

Wirt's interactions with Adams are particularly revealing of the ways in which the attorney general approached these difficult questions of concurrent power. Adams had once referred in his diary to a view of Wirt's as "a natural County Court objection," a characterization that suggested a degree of disdain for such parochial qualms. (One can only imagine what Adams's reaction would have been had he learned of Wirt's jibes against his father, "John the first," back in 1798.) Adams's "County Court" comment came in the context of the Adams–Onís Treaty with Spain, signed in 1819. Wirt objected that there was no precedent for Congress to execute the unratified treaty as though it had been ratified.[192] Adams was correct: a lack of precedent was precisely the sort of objection that a county-court lawyer would raise. But, as he learned in his subsequent dealings with Wirt, the attorney general had long service in courts more exalted than those of the old State of Flu. Their intellectual styles were very different, but when Adams was elected president in 1824, he asked Wirt to remain as attorney general.

One noteworthy exchange between Wirt and Adams began in November 1821, when the attorney general asked to borrow some books from the secretary of state. Wirt was drafting an opinion for President Monroe on the case of the "Newfoundland pirates." The question was whether the United States was obligated to deliver up to Great Britain a British subject, Daniel Sullivan, who had feloniously taken a British ship (the *Maria*) and her cargo into a Maine port, in violation of U.S. law. Wirt asked Adams to lend him several books on the law of nations, including works by Jean-Jacques Burlamaqui, Emmerich de Vattel, Hugo Grotius, and Jean Barbeyrac. When Adams personally delivered a volume of Burlamaqui to Wirt, the two fell into a discussion that began with the case but quickly moved to the law of nations and theories of constitutional interpretation. Adams wrote, "Mr. Wirt had the English translation of Grotius with a part of Barbeyrac's Notes, and I had sent him the French Edition of Barbeyrac; which we compared together." But Wirt "did not seem to be satisfied with the authorities—He wanted a Latin Grotius; but finally came to the denial of the President's authority to deliver up" Sullivan to British authorities.[193] Adams told Wirt that he had articulated the same view in his discussions with British officials.

Adams then began putting hypotheticals to Wirt: if the law of nations clearly required that fugitives charged with heinous crimes such as piracy should be delivered up, would it not be the duty of the president to take care that the law of nations should be faithfully executed, and would he not therefore have the power to discharge the duty? Wirt was unwilling to go along with such an expansive view of the president's authority. Adams wrote: "He said that doctrine was too bold for him: he was too much of a Virginian for that. I told him that Virginian Constitutional scruples were accommodating things. Whenever the exercise of a power did not happen to suit them, they would allow of nothing but powers expressly written; but when it did, they had no aversion to implied powers."[194]

Wirt's identification with Virginia here is interesting. As we have seen, he became a Virginian only in 1792, with the "manoeuvre" that gained him admission to the state's bar. After he became attorney general in 1817, he never again lived in Virginia. Upon leaving the attorney generalship in 1829, he and Elizabeth chose to move their family to Baltimore rather than returning to Richmond.

Adams then offered the case of President Jefferson's Louisiana Purchase of 1803: Did Wirt think it was constitutional? Wirt cited the treaty power as one basis for the acquisition. Adams countered that the purchase had effectively dissolved and recomposed the Union, "and all this done by an Administration which came in, blowing a Trumpet against implied powers. After this, to nibble at a Bank, a Road, a Canal, the mere mint and cummin of the Law, was but glorious inconsistency." Wirt replied "that the People had sanctioned it." Adams's response: "How the People?—By their Representatives in Congress; they were the People—Oh! said I, *that doctrine is too bold for ME*." Wirt had declared himself "too much of a Virginian" to support a broad view of the president's power under the Take Care Clause. But he was willing to endorse the notion that acts of Congress, in this case treaty ratification by the Senate and an appropriation by the House, amounted to a "sanction" by "the People." In Wirt's view, such a sanction proceeded not from an implied power claimed by an arm of the government, but from the people's affirmative approval, acting through their representatives. In the end, Adams reported, "We both agreed that it was a subject deserving the attention of Congress."[195]

Adams did not record in his diary whether this exchange, with its citation of Continental theorists and tone of intellectual banter, changed his view of the attorney general's "county court" tendencies. Nearly a year later, in October 1822, however, Wirt and Adams returned to the issue of the president's duty to hand over a person sought by another jurisdiction. In this case, the issue was whether the United States was obliged to deliver up a slave who had hidden aboard an American ship on a voyage from St. Croix to New York. The slave, James Barry, belonged to a Mrs. Johnson, a Danish subject who lived in St. Croix, a Danish colony in which slavery was legal. The Danish government demanded restoration of the slave. During a Cabinet meeting at the White House, Wirt presented his written opinion on the case: the president had the power to deliver up Barry to Danish authorities. Adams wrote, "I asked [Wirt] where he found the grant of the Power in the Constitution. He said it was in the general instruction to take care that the Laws should be faithfully executed. I said that in his opinion that the President could *not* deliver up a Pirate, he did not admit that doctrine—where did he find it now? He said, laughing, that he took it from me."[196]

Adams, evidently not amused, asked Monroe to excuse him from drafting the order to the federal marshal or the governor directing Barry's rendition. Wirt, meanwhile, seemed less than fully committed to his conclusion. He said in the meeting "that this subject was quite as much political as legal," and he urged the president to "take other opinions as well as his." Adams excoriated Wirt's analysis in his diary: "The truth is that between his Virginian aversion to constructive powers, his Virginian devotion to State-Rights, and his Virginian *autocracy* against Slaves, his two opinions form the most absurd jumble of self-contradictions that could be imagined." Noting that Secretary of War Calhoun had agreed with Wirt that Barry should be handed over to Danish authorities, Adams commented, "Calhoun has no petty scruples about constructive Powers, and State-Rights—His opinions are at least consistent."[197] As events in the following decade showed, however, Adams's assessment of Calhoun's political beliefs—and those beliefs themselves—were soon to undergo a dramatic shift.

Perhaps the problem lay as much in Adams's expectations of what a "Virginian" should believe as in Wirt's ostensible inconsistency. Wirt's views on Barry's case were consistent in one way with his views on the case of the Newfoundland pirates: in both, he looked to practice, especially when a question seemed to be "political as well as legal." In the case of the pirates, he had rested his conclusion that Sullivan should not be delivered up to British authorities on "practice," not "precept." The practice was that nations typically disavowed responsibility for fugitives or else required that the fugitive have been convicted before turning him over to the nation making the demand. In the case of the enslaved Barry, however, Wirt held that the relevant practice was how the United States had customarily treated property, such as ships, improperly taken from a foreign subject. In such cases, he found the question "settled long since by the practice of the government, sanctioned by the acquiescence of the people."[198] The analogy of slaves to property did not appear to trouble Wirt, but his opinion did suggest some discomfort with the legal authorities, perhaps especially in light of Adams's charge of inconsistency between the two cases. The opinion (which was addressed to Adams) ended by recommending that the secretary consult "the archives of state" to determine the most appropriate course of action.[199]

Wirt's own position as a slaveowner played a role in forming his views on the constellation of legal rules surrounding slavery. But Adams might have been too quick to adopt his father's assumptions about "Virginian Constitutional scruples" in general, and about this Virginian's views on broad federal power and states' rights in particular.

A Federalism of Competing Umpires

Wirt was one of the most important producers of constitutional discourse in an era in which the authority of the Supreme Court was an open question, and in which constant collisions between multiple sources of governmental authority spawned multiple competing American federalisms. Even as Wirt and his contemporaries worried like anxious adolescents about measuring up to their Revolutionary forbears, by dint of their constitutional creativity, they became the grown-ups.

The search for a revising power to oversee the tripartite contract of the people, the states, and the United States was paramount in the 1810s and early 1820s. The revising power was different from the one upon which Wirt as lawyer and Johnson as judge had insisted in the Fairfax cases, and it was also distinct from the one that Virginia judge Cabell had warned against. But contemporaries sought it nonetheless. And it was present, in the difficult work of parsing what it meant to have a Union with governmental multiplicity. Perhaps the debate itself was the revising power.

2 • The Many Directions of Federal Power

A Federalism of Commerce and Migration

The U.S. government's power over interstate commerce was summoned to its first important action by an unlikely agent: a fourteen-gun Spanish brig named the *Arrogante Barcelones*, which sailed into the island port of Margarita, off the coast of Venezuela, in the summer of 1819. Following proceedings in the local prize court, the brig became the property of its captor, Joseph Almeida of Baltimore, a Portuguese-born merchant and privateer who had served his adopted country during the War of 1812 by launching a series of bold raids on British ships. ("Brilliant Cruize!" a Philadelphia newspaper in 1815 hailed Almeida's wartime sorties.) Now, four years after the end of the war, Almeida's thriving predation extended from his home in Baltimore throughout the Caribbean and across the Atlantic, from the new revolutionary republics of South America to the seat of the Spanish Empire.

Following nautical custom, Almeida rechristened the brig upon taking ownership of it. Following Almeida's own custom, he selected a name that would produce utmost confusion among the revenue officials of nations up and down the Atlantic seaboard. The *Arrogante Barcelones* became the *Wilson*. The appellation borrowed the surname of George Wilson, who commanded one of Almeida's other ships (a schooner Almeida cannily named the *Almeida*). Although Almeida was present aboard the *Wilson*, the brig was commanded by Ivory Huntress of Berwick, of the province of Maine in the U.S. state of Massachusetts.

On August 12, 1819, the brig *Wilson* (Huntress in command, Almeida aboard) and the schooner *Almeida* (Wilson in command) set sail from Margarita. Four days earlier, Captain Huntress's wife, Ann, had died in Boston; the cause was listed in town records as "childbed." In September, while the brig continued its voyage, one-month-old John Huntress followed his mother.[1] Presumably, Huntress did not learn of their deaths until more than two months later.

The *Wilson* put in at the Danish Caribbean island of St. Thomas to take on supplies and eighteen additional crew members, most of whom would have been identified in the categories of the day as people of color. Then the *Wilson* continued north, bound for Norfolk, Virginia.

Both brig and schooner caused occasional havoc in their search for ships traveling under the flag of Spain, with which the republic of Colombia (of which Venezuela was a part) was at war. Both the *Wilson* and the *Almeida* sought to claim Spanish vessels as prizes. The unfortunate schooner *Emily*, out of Alexandria, Virginia, and under the command of one Captain Spilman, was first boarded by the *Wilson* and "suffered to proceed"; a few days later, the *Emily* encountered the *Almeida*, with less happy results. Spilman's schooner was "robbed of sugar, coffee, hides, &c." by a vessel the crew identified as a "felucca under Spanish colors."

The thieving ship in question was not in fact a Mediterranean sailboat; it was the schooner *Almeida*, captained by Wilson. The beleaguered crew were likely correct about the flag, however. The enterprising Wilson, who elsewhere derided the ships of the "moronic Spanish government," routinely flew the flag of the Catholic Monarchy in order to lull prey through a *ruse de guerre*. Perhaps it was some comfort, however, that Captain Wilson was "civil" to the *Emily*'s crew.[2]

The brig *Wilson*, with Huntress commanding, arrived in Norfolk after a less eventful journey. After a preliminary round of customs inspections and the requisite powder discharge while the brig lay in Hampton Roads, just outside the port, the *Wilson* sailed into Norfolk on October 27, 1819. The cargo included thirty-one demijohns of brandy, thirteen cases of gin, and divers other merchandise, all of which had been taken as prize from a Spanish schooner. The crew numbered eighty or ninety sailors, among them at least three free people of color.

Over the next few days, the *Wilson* was visited by the port's customs inspector and deputy collector. Both of these were federal posts under the aegis of the U.S. Treasury Department. On October 29, Captain Huntress made out prize tickets for his crew, "a number of whom were persons of colour." That same day, while searching the ward room, customs inspector William Bush noted several demijohns of Spanish brandy and cases of gin that were not listed on the manifest Huntress subsequently submitted to port officials. On November 1, when Bush returned to the brig as it lay abreast Fort Norfolk, he "found a great part of the crew discharged that morning, of different colors and nations."[3]

Here began the brig *Wilson*'s legal travails.[4] On November 4, the *Wilson* was taken into custody by order of the collector of the port of Norfolk for an "informality in her entry at the Custom-House—requiring investigation."[5] An order issued that same day from the U.S. District Court for the Eastern District of Virginia directing the federal marshal to "arrest and safely keep the Brig Wilson, her guns, stores, tackle, apparel and furniture" as well as "sundry Demijohns of distilled spirits and cases of Gin brought in the said Vessel," pending admiralty proceedings against the brig for violating federal revenue laws.[6] Huntress as master and Almeida as owner were required to answer a "libel"— a forfeiture proceeding by the federal government that was styled as an action against the ship itself, even though any penalty would in reality be borne by the ship's owner and any investors.[7]

The November 1819 order was signed by the clerk, Seth Foster, on behalf of the Honorable St. George Tucker, U.S. district court judge for the Eastern District of Virginia. Tucker was one of the young nation's preeminent jurists and the author of an influential edition of William Blackstone's *Commentaries*, in which Tucker supplemented the English common lawyer's treatise with essays based on his own lectures as professor of law and police at the College of William and Mary. Tucker also gained renown for his sedulous note-taking, producing a series of notebooks in which he recorded judicial decisions from state and federal courts in Virginia, as well as the U.S. Supreme Court. Tucker used the notebooks in his law teaching and permitted colleagues to consult them for precedents relevant to their own cases.[8] In an era without regular, professional law reporting, even Tucker had to keep abreast of new cases by culling reports of opinions from the newspapers, which he then copied into his notebooks.[9] The suit *United States v. Brig Wilson* was thus first heard in the courtroom of the most-cited American legal scholar of the era.[10]

And here also began the brig *Wilson*'s vital role in shaping the constitutional law of commerce. For not only did Huntress and Almeida face possible forfeiture of the brandy, gin, and other merchandise for allegedly flouting the federal revenue laws, as the first four counts of the libel charged. They also faced the more grievous accusation of violating state and federal laws governing the categories of persons who were and were not welcome in Virginia. The fifth count of the libel claimed forfeiture of the brig itself on the ground that it had brought in and landed "three persons of Colour" in violation of both federal and state law.

A Virginia statute of 1793 prohibited "the migration of free negroes and mulattoes into this commonwealth." An 1803 act of Congress supplemented such state laws with federal enforcement. Hence, when three members of the crew of the *Wilson* debarked in Norfolk at the end of a sixty-five-day voyage from the Caribbean, the brig's owner and master became susceptible to penalties imposed by two levels of lawmaking authority: the state of Virginia and the U.S. government.

Judge Tucker eventually determined that Huntress and Almeida had violated the Virginia statute as well as the act of Congress, and in December 1819 he ordered the forfeiture of both brig and cargo. The indefatigable Almeida promptly appealed Tucker's decision.[11] The case of the brig *Wilson* then went up to the federal appeals court that covered Tucker's district court: the U.S. Circuit Court for the Fifth Circuit, sitting in Richmond. The appeal, now captioned *The Brig Wilson (Ivory Huntress, Claimant) v. United States*, was decided in 1820 by Chief Justice John Marshall, making his twice-yearly rounds of his assigned circuit.

This obscure case of *The Brig Wilson* warrants incorporation into the intellectual history of American constitutional law. It was Marshall's initial foray into interpreting the Commerce Clause of the Constitution. The Marshall Court later became famous for issuing the nation's first decisions on the subject of the commerce power. But the true "first" came earlier, in this case, which shaped Marshall's views on the commerce power in a context far different from the ones he faced four years later, in the company of his colleagues on the Supreme Court.

The Brig Wilson was a constitutional case that was decided not in Washington, but in Richmond, in an appeal from a federal trial-court judge who was considered one of the leading legal thinkers and teachers of his day. The case thus provides a crucial glimpse into Marshall's conception of the federal commerce power in a case that was far less renowned than the marquee commerce decisions that issued from the Court between 1824 and Marshall's death in 1835, such as *Gibbons v. Ogden* in 1824 and *Brown v. Maryland* in 1827. *The Brig Wilson* is a window into alternative interpretations of the Commerce Clause. Even more important, examining the political and intellectual context in which the case arose enriches our understanding of the many federalisms of the interbellum United States. The chronicle of *The Brig Wilson* depicts an ambivalent federalism with respect to commerce, overlapping powers, and slavery and the status of Black people.

Federalism, Supremacy, and Commerce

If one seeks monuments to federalism from the 1810s and 1820s, one must look into the pages of the reports by William Cranch, Henry Wheaton, Richard Peters, and John W. Brockenbrough of decisions in the federal courts. In 1815, just twenty-seven years had elapsed since the ratification of the Constitution. Already, the fragile and underspecified agreements about the distribution of power between the nation and the states that underpinned the document and made its passage possible were proving inadequate to the formidable task of mediating among the eighteen states and the general government at Washington. By 1835, the number of states had climbed to twenty-four. In January 1861, on the eve of the Civil War, the Union—including the state of South Carolina, despite the secession ordinance it had passed a month before—comprised thirty-four states. What James Madison had referred to as the "centrifugal tendency of the States" was only becoming a more and more powerful force as the states increased in number, and their geographic and affiliative bonds with the center began to fray.[12]

The founders had purposely designed a structure of government that divided power between two levels of authority: the national government and the states. Courts were at the center of this structure. The founders relied on courts at each level of government to carry out two functions: first, to decide cases and controversies that originated in each court's respective body of substantive law; and second, to be able to orbit outside this ambit in order to maintain the boundaries between the distinct levels of government. No less a founder than Madison himself had urged a legislative solution to this problem of boundary policing. The centerpiece of Madison's plan at the Constitutional Convention was to vest Congress with a "negative" on state lawmaking, such that no proposed state legislation could become law without gaining the approval of Congress.[13] Madison viewed the negative as the essential joint that would hold together the new federation, saving it from the fissiparous forces that he believed had riven every one of history's prior confederal structures.

But Madison lost. The negative was defeated in the convention. For the rest of his life, Madison counted the defeat of the negative as one of the greatest regrets of his political career.[14] In its place, the Constitution's drafters turned from an exclusively legislative solution to the problem of multilayered government toward a more complex, judiciary-centered system. The Constitution granted a set of enumerated powers to Congress; forbade a smaller set to the states; decreed that all other powers remained with the states or the people;

and assigned courts at both levels of government the duty of policing the whole arrangement. Instead of the negative, the Constitution as drafted and ratified included the Supremacy Clause: "This Constitution, and the Laws of the United States which shall be made in Pursuance thereof; and all Treaties made, or which shall be made, under the Authority of the United States, shall be the supreme Law of the Land; and the Judges in every State shall be bound thereby, any Thing in the Constitution or Laws of any State to the Contrary notwithstanding."[15]

The Supremacy Clause is the Constitution's most explicit statement concerning how the mechanics of American federalism are designed to work.[16] Federal laws and treaties are the supreme law of the land; the Constitution itself (which sets forth the domains in which Congress and the states may regulate) is the supreme law of the land; and judges are required to ensure that the supremacy is preserved. Moreover, every judge in the United States is charged with this duty: clearly those of the Supreme Court; clearly also those of any inferior federal courts that Congress establishes; and, by the text of the Supremacy Clause, state-court judges as well. In this way, the Supremacy Clause steps outside the Constitution itself, setting forth a supervening rule of interpretation about how the structures, rights, and guarantees set forth in the document are to be understood and enforced. The Supremacy Clause is therefore both a clause in the Constitution as a document and a precept that governs the operation of the Constitution as a working system.

By 1816, as the previous chapter demonstrated, the practical meaning of the Supremacy Clause had occupied the courts of both the United States and Virginia in the course of the decades-long dispute over ownership of the Fairfax lands, culminating in the case of *Martin v. Hunter's Lessee*.[17] The conflict began as a contest between competing landowners, but by the time it reached the Supreme Court—not once, but twice—it had transformed into a battle between the judges of the Virginia Court of Appeals and the justices of the Marshall Court. As David Hunter's (fictitious) lessee and Lord Fairfax's devisee altercated over who owned the parcel of land along Cedar Creek, the pressure between their warring property claims ballooned when each side obtained a favorable judgment from a different level of the judicial system. The Virginia high court found for Hunter's lessee, while the U.S. Supreme Court held for Fairfax's devisee. By the time the case had gone up to the Supreme Court, back down to the Virginia court, and back up to the Supreme Court, one could not have found a more perfectly pitched instrument to breathe life into the written phrases of the Supremacy Clause. Much was at stake, and so the parties, their lawyers, and the courts found it worthwhile to throw their entire energies into the fight. Argument forged law—and even the arguments that were dismissed as outside the ambit of what "law" meant now offer insight into the widest possible version of the constitutional universe at that time.

Yet the Supremacy Clause was not the only textual ground on which federalism battles were fought in the years between 1815 and 1861. Nor did early-nineteenth-century Americans have to ponder meta-principles of interpretation in order to find ways to argue about the distribution of national versus state authority. The primary terrain on which interbellum struggles over federalism unfolded was the field of commerce. Its text was the federal commerce power of Article I, section 8, of the Constitution.

Since 1787, many Americans had held the conviction that they had a collective special destiny as the world's only federal republic. "Preparation for War to defend Commerce" trumpeted handbills depicting the building of American frigates before the War of 1812. The war ended in 1815: Washington burnt, Britain defeated, commerce defended. In public discourse between 1815 and 1837, the adjective "commercial" joined "federal" to describe the nation's essence. Defining what a federal republic was and how it should operate had been difficult enough. In these years, however, the central question in American public debate became: How can a nation be committed to both the structural principle of federalism and the material goal of expanding commerce? To be sure, both "federal" and "commercial" were often used as talismans, almost-mystical signifiers of what the nation hoped to become. But given that federalism meant multilayered government, it guaranteed some degree of friction among the levels of law-producing authorities. Commerce—not markets, but *commerce*—was the true end of American government. In the Enlightenment sense in which the drafters of the Constitution used the term, "commerce" entailed a rich web of connections, interactions, and even emotions that were civic and social as well as economic.[18] But how was it to be promoted amid this congeries of sovereigns, quasi-sovereigns, and demi-sovereigns?

The multiplicity of law-producing entities in interbellum America required lawyers constantly to engage in conflict of laws analysis. The primary legal domain in which such analysis took place was with respect to questions of commerce. For interbellum lawyers, questions of where federal power began and ended, and how that boundary mapped onto the amorphous terrain of broad state powers, were questions that emerged from gritty fact patterns involving money, trade, ships, merchandise, and—sometimes—people, both free and enslaved.

As this chapter will demonstrate, interbellum debates about the commerce power were a veritable hothouse of federalism species. The early Commerce Clause cases of the Marshall Court era display a much richer array of approaches to the federal-state relationship than has generally been recognized. The arguments of the advocates as well as the opinions of the justices suggest that there was not just one mode of interbellum federalism, but several credible versions that were recognized by the Court and commentators. "Interbellum federalism" thus should more properly be pluralized as "interbellum federalisms."

Placing *The Brig Wilson* in its broader political and legal context demonstrates that interbellum federalism was far more intellectually and legally generative than standard accounts suggest. Excavating the arguments surrounding the cases not only reveals multiple distinct species of federalism. It also reveals the existence of unfamiliar species of federalism from the modern ones. The landscape of possible constitutional arguments in the early nineteenth century was different from the modern landscape.

The Brig: Interlocking Statutes

In December 1819, while the unlucky brig *Wilson* remained in the custody of U.S. marshals in Norfolk, judicial proceedings on the libel began fifty miles up the Virginia Peninsula in Williamsburg. The pre-Revolutionary "Town Court House" on Market Square was not the customary forum in which St. George Tucker convened his federal district court. Ordinarily, the *Wilson*'s suit would have been heard at the June session in Norfolk. But the brig's master, Ivory Huntress—presumably following instructions from the vessel's owner, Joseph Almeida—had petitioned Judge Tucker for a special, accelerated hearing, citing "great injury to your Petitioner by the Deteriorations of the Vessel, the interruption of her Employment, the Dispersion of her Crew, and by the Loss of the personal Evidence which at this time he is able to offer."[19] The sixty-seven-year-old Tucker, who suffered from poor health and whose rambling white-frame home, with its "Spanish red" roof and "Chocolate colour" trim, stood less than a block from the courthouse, granted Huntress's petition.[20] At the same time, Huntress appears to have come into a sizable amount of money: he paid off a debt of $881.50 on December 14, just two days before the trial began.[21]

On Thursday, December 16, the trial commenced with the presentation of the charges. The libel, drawn up by Robert Stanard, U.S. attorney for the

District of Virginia, comprised five counts. Four of the counts charged the *Wilson* and its master with unlawfully importing, concealing, and avoiding the payment of duties on "thirty one demijohns of Brandy, thirteen Cases of Gin, and sundry other Goods as per Schedule annext," in violation of a 1799 act of Congress.[22] These were the items that customs officer William Bush had found aboard, and that Captain Huntress had not declared on the manifest. The penalty for these crimes was forfeiture of the goods in question.[23]

The fifth count of the libel compassed a graver charge and consequently threatened a more severe punishment: "That the said Brig Wilson arrived &c. having on board three *persons of Colour*, not being natives, Citizens, or registered Seamen of the U:S: or Seamen natives of Countries beyond the Cape of Good Hope, the Admission or importation of which is prohibited by the Laws of Virga. and were afterwards landed from on board the said Brig, contrary to the act of Congress &c. whereby the said Brig Wilson her Tackle &c have become forfeited and lost."[24]

According to the record, at the time the *Wilson* departed Margarita its crew had numbered around eighty or ninety sailors. During the cruise from Margarita (between present-day Aruba and Trinidad and Tobago), the crew added "some eighteen seamen, principally people of colour, and all free."[25] By the time the brig put into Norfolk more than two months later, it had undergone some personnel shifts owing to the need to dispatch prize crews to captured ships, as well as an abortive mutiny. At that point, a significant number of crew members were described as persons of color. "The proof that a large part of the crew of the Brig Wilson was composed of these Persons, is unquestionable," Tucker noted in his opinion.[26]

The presence of these crew members on board the *Wilson* was not in itself unusual or even legally noteworthy. Significant numbers of sailors working on ships in the late eighteenth and early nineteenth centuries were African or of African American or Afro-Caribbean ancestry; others hailed from the Barbary States of North Africa, or from India or Southeast Asia (often referred to as "lascars" and "Malays"). As the case of the *Wilson* shows, contemporary usage differed as to whether these individuals were classified as "persons of color."[27]

The problem for the *Wilson's* captain and owner was the fact that three of these crew members had disembarked while the brig lay in Norfolk Harbor. The consequences of these three individuals' departure became the central issue in the trial before Judge Tucker in Williamsburg and then before Chief Justice Marshall in the federal circuit court at Richmond. According to the testimony of Andrew Johnson, Huntress's clerk, "[O]n the 29th of October, the people of colour received their prize tickets, went on shore, and, of course, took their own discharge."[28] When the three crew members—whose names have not survived in the record—debarked from the *Wilson* and set foot on Virginian soil, an array of entwined state and federal statutes was summoned into action. The penalty for flouting these laws, which ran against the ship's master, was forfeiture of the vessel.

The fifth count of the libel charged Huntress, as master of the brig, with violating a pair of interlocking laws: a Virginia statute from 1793 and an act of Congress from 1803.

The 1793 Virginia statute, titled "An Act to Prevent the Migration of Free Negroes and Mulattoes into This Commonwealth," provided that "it shall not be lawful for any free negro or mulatto to migrate into this commonwealth." Any such individual who entered Virginia contrary to the act was to be "apprehended and carried by any citizen before some justice of the peace," who in turn was authorized to "examine, send and remove every such free negro or mulatto out of this commonwealth, into that state or island from whence it shall appear he or she last came." The act extended to masters of vessels, who faced a hundred-pound fine for every such person they brought into the state. An exception provided that the act would not apply to "masters of vessels bringing into this state any free negro or mulatto employed on board and belonging to such vessel, and who shall therewith depart," nor to "any person travelling into this state, having any free negro or mulatto as a servant."[29]

The act of Congress that Huntress was charged with violating was structurally more complex than the Virginia statute. It was a hybrid creature: a projection of federal power, with its scope defined by state law. This dual nature—both derivative of, and superintending to, state law—is evident in the title of the statute: "An Act to Prevent the Importation of Certain Persons into Certain States, Where, by the Laws Thereof, Their Admission Is Prohibited."[30]

Passed by Congress in 1803, the act provided that

no master or captain of any ship or vessel, or any other person, shall import or bring, or cause to be imported or brought, any negro, mulatto, or other person of colour, not being a native, a citizen, or registered seaman of the United States, or seamen natives of countries beyond the Cape of Good Hope, into any port or place of the United States, which port or place shall be situated in any state which by law has prohibited or shall prohibit the admission or importation of such negro, mulatto, or other person of colour.[31]

Vessels carrying such persons were to be denied entry into states that prohibited their admission. The provision carried a penalty of one thousand dollars, to be paid by the ship's master or captain, "for each and every negro, mulatto, or other person of colour" brought or imported into a state in violation of that state's law. Suits to enforce the law could be brought in federal court, and the amount recovered was to be split equally between the person bringing suit and the federal government. The vessel's owner, too, was subject to penalty: the forfeiture of the vessel, its tackle, apparel, and furniture, with half the proceeds of the sale to be paid to "such person or persons on whose information the seizure on such forfeiture shall be made."[32]

The final section of the 1803 act placed the enforcement power of the federal government in the service of state law. Section 3 stated:

> That it shall be the duty of the collectors and other officers of the customs, and all other officers of the revenue of the United States, in the several ports or places situated as aforesaid, to notice and be governed by the provision of the laws now existing, of the several states prohibiting the admission or importation of any negro, mulatto, or other person of colour, as aforesaid. And they are hereby enjoined vigilantly to carry into effect the said laws of said states, conformably to the provisions of this act; any law of the United States to the contrary notwithstanding.[33]

With this provision, Congress instructed federal customs and revenue officials to "be governed by" the laws of the states in which they were stationed, and to "carry into effect" those laws. Federal officials were therefore ordered to enforce state laws prohibiting the admission or importation of persons of color, with the precise scope of the prohibition—as well as the definition of "persons of color"—to be determined by state law.

By its terms, the 1803 act of Congress was to be overlaid on top of the Virginia law of 1793. The 1803 act added federal enforcement to state bans on the "importation" of "certain persons," but the 1803 act itself appeared to be agnostic as to the nature of the state prohibition. Yet the 1803 federal law contained subtle differences from the 1793 state law.

First, the Virginia act targeted free Black individuals, while the federal statute applied to "any negro, mulatto, or other person of colour" who was neither "a native, a citizen, or registered seaman of the United States" nor a seaman who was a "native" of a "countr[y] beyond the Cape of Good Hope." Slavery was legal in Virginia, protected by a range of state laws. While the 1793 statute was aimed at free, not enslaved, people, it was part of that larger legal regime.

As part of entrenching the racially delineated system of slavery, and as the title of the act made explicit, the legislature sought to block free persons of color from migrating to the state.[34] The federal law, in contrast, provided federal enforcement for any state laws barring the admission or importation of Black persons, whether free or enslaved.

In addition, the goal of the Virginia law was to prevent "migration," while that of the 1803 federal law was to prevent "importation." The federal law was thus directed at masters and captains of vessels, who were assumed to be responsible for the importation; the fines and forfeitures applied to them. The 1803 act did not specify any penalties for the "imported" individuals. The Virginia statute, meanwhile, punished free Black migrants as well as the shipmasters who transported them. The migrants could be "apprehended and carried by any citizen" before a justice of the peace, who would then "send and remove" them from the state.

The timing of the 1803 act of Congress was significant, for it was passed during the period in which Congress was forbidden from halting the international slave trade. Article I, section 9, of the Constitution unamendably barred Congress from prohibiting the "migration or importation" of "such persons as any of the states now existing shall think proper to admit" prior to the year 1808.[35] The 1808 Clause did permit Congress to impose a "tax or duty" on "such importation," which presumably did not include "migration."

The meaning of the 1808 Clause's prohibition was contested from the moment of its drafting in 1787. The terms "migration" and "importation" had been used throughout the eighteenth century to refer to both indentured servants and enslaved persons, both of whom were regarded as "articles of commerce" and were often regulated as such by the colonial legislatures.[36]

By the time of the Constitutional Convention, however, the connotations of the terms "migration" and "importation" were less clear and sometimes disputed. As Mary Sarah Bilder notes, "To some, 'importation,' and perhaps 'commerce,' referred to immigrants, indentured servants, and slaves. To others, 'imported' could refer only to slaves—or, at the most, involuntary imported convicts."[37]

Some members of the founding generation worried that the phrase "migration or importation" implied that Congress possessed the power to ban immigration by white Europeans, and that such power was in a state of only temporary abeyance until 1808. Others, including the South Carolina, North Carolina, and Georgia delegations to the Constitutional Convention, rejected the notion that the clause had any relevance to white migrants.[38] Instead, they claimed it as a protection for their own states' prerogative to permit the international trade in enslaved people and a shield against any federal intervention other than taxation. They also ensured that the shield would be fixed well into the next century. In combination with three New England states and Maryland, the trio of the Carolinas and Georgia approved South Carolina delegate Charles Cotesworth Pinckney's motion to make 1808 the expiration date for the curb on Congress—eight years longer than initially proposed, and a full twenty years after ratification.[39]

Congress regulated elements of the international slave trade via statute in 1794 and 1800, but the 1808 Clause effectively put the issue of the nation's participation in the international slave trade into the hands of the states. In 1787, when the Constitution was drafted, only one state—Georgia—permitted the importation of slaves from abroad.[40] In December 1803, however, South Carolina reopened its international trade.[41]

Also in 1803, while the constitutional prohibition on prohibiting the international slave trade was in force, Congress acted to augment states' efforts to block the entry of persons of color from outside the United States. The result was the Act to Prevent the Importation of Certain Persons into Certain States—the federal law at issue in *The Brig Wilson*. The act was passed by Congress in February 1803.

The Act to Prevent the Importation of Certain Persons into Certain States of 1803 was motivated by a variety of impulses. One goal that emerged clearly in the debates was to secure the institution of American slaveholding against threats from without. Southern slaveholders' perpetual fear of slave revolt increased after the bloody Haitian Revolution began in August 1791.[42] The largest successful slave revolution in the Americas, the Haitian Revolution shocked many U.S. observers and caused them to worry that admitting more free people of color into the country or reopening the international slave trade—especially the trade from the Caribbean—would bring in radical Black leaders who would spread insurrection on American plantations. These voices were present in debates concerning the status of the international slave trade while the 1808 Clause's prohibition was in force.

The Virginia statute of 1793 under which the brig *Wilson* was libeled reflected such sentiments. The Act to Prevent the Migration of Free Negroes and Mulattoes into This Commonwealth was a product of legislators' perception that events in Haiti had emboldened a dangerous and ungovernable population—not only of slaves, but also of free Black people—whose very presence might spark rebellion, and who therefore had to be barred from entering the state.

Congress debated and passed the 1803 Act to Prevent the Importation of Certain Persons into Certain States within the constitutionally mandated pre-1808 limitations period. The legislative history of the act suggests that many members of Congress agreed on "the propriety of the General Government enforcing every legitimate authority it possessed" to prevent "the introduction into the United States of brigands from the French West India islands."[43] Their concern was "the imminent danger of the Southern States."[44] But opinions differed as to how far such a federal backstop ought to go in bolstering state law—and, crucially, which states' laws warranted federal enforcement.

Like so many other federal laws, the act was capable of multiple and conflicting interpretations.[45] To some, as we have seen, it was a means of securing the nation against foreign threats. To others, it was a federal supplement to state laws limiting the freedoms of free Black people already inside the United States who might foment insurrection among the local enslaved population. To still another group, however, the 1803 act was the best available tool to fight the international slave trade, given the ban in the 1808 Clause. Each of these distinct points of view was aired during the congressional debates on the act.

Congressman John Bacon, a Democratic-Republican from Massachusetts, objected to the original draft of the bill, which contained no exception for a situation in which the "certain person" imported was a Black sailor who was "a native, a citizen, or registered seaman of the United States." Bacon argued that the bill violated the Privileges and Immunities Clause of Article IV of the Constitution because it worked "a discrimination between the citizens of the United States" that was both heretofore "unknown" and "repugnant to the radical principles and general tenor of the Constitution." The "principle of the bill," Bacon stated, "excites my disgust."[46]

Notably, Bacon's comments implied that at least some Black seamen might be U.S. citizens. "A number of persons described in the bill are citizens of the United States" and "were such previous to the time of the forming of the Constitution," he insisted. Yet "[t]hese persons, by the provisions of the bill, are to be deprived of the common rights of citizens; they may not, in a peaceable manner, either for the purpose of commerce, or in the case of distress, enter the ports, or sail along the coast of particular States, without subjecting themselves to severe penalties."[47] Bacon's attack focused on the bill's consequences for seamen who were free persons of color and U.S. citizens.

Bacon assumed that at least some free Black sailors were also citizens of the United States. Fifty-four years later, in his opinion in *Dred Scott v. Sandford*,

Chief Justice Roger Brooke Taney erroneously asserted that such a contention had never been possible in American history.[48]

The citizenship of free Black people was a deeply contested issue in inter-bellum law and politics.[49] From retirement at Monticello, Thomas Jefferson continued to urge Virginia statesmen to adopt a scheme that coupled emancipation with mandatory colonization—or "deportation"—of freed people, a plan he had proposed forty years earlier, in his *Notes on the State of Virginia*.[50] Distinctions between state and national citizenship often lay at the core of these debates. Bacon's argument proceeded from the premise that some Black seamen were citizens of the United States. Other commentators, however, regarded national citizenship as derivative of state citizenship. In an 1821 opinion, U.S. attorney general William Wirt concluded that "free people of color in Virginia are not citizens of the United States, in the sense of our shipping laws, or any other laws, passed under the authority of the Federal constitution; for such people have very few of the privileges of the citizens of Virginia."[51] This view placed state law at the center of the analysis. Different states varied widely in how they addressed citizenship and migration, with little agreement as to what protections even state citizenship entailed.[52]

In addition to raising concerns about the privileges and immunities of free Black sailors, Bacon criticized the bill as an effort by certain states—in particular, Virginia—to commandeer the national legislative power:

> Should that sacrifice be made of the interests and the Constitutional rights of the citizens, of a certain description, in some of the States, to gratify the wishes of the citizens of some other States . . . this conduct of the Legislature would be represented by some, and believed by too many, to furnish ample proof of the sovereign and despotic sway of the "Ancient Dominion" over most of the other States in the Union.[53]

Another Democratic-Republican critic, Samuel L. Mitchill of New York, explicitly linked the proposed act with the international slave trade. According to the *Annals of Congress*, which were compiled a few decades later from contemporaneous accounts, Mitchill stated during the debates that he was "very desirous of guarding the States of the nation from the introduction of the negroes, mulattoes, and persons of color, comprised in the bill; he would add his wish to guard the country from all other mischievous and evil-disposed people." But he expressed concerns about the "heavy punishment" the bill imposed "upon any captain, or master of a vessel, that shall bring in any negro, mulatto, or person of color, into any port of the United States, lying within a State which has prohibited the same." The *Annals* continue: "As far as this respected the trade in human beings, carried on to the rivers Senegal or Gambia, or other parts of the slave coast of Africa, it met with his most hearty approbation. He was desirous of putting an end to this detestable traffic, and of punishing in an exemplary manner such citizens of the United States as could be convicted of the crime of being engaged in it."[54]

To the extent that the act was employed as a federal weapon against the transatlantic slave trade, Mitchill supported it wholeheartedly. He worried, however, about a potential scenario in which "persons of color from the French West Indies"—that is, Haiti—were "forcibly put on board an American vessel" without the consent of the ship's captain. "In these instances the master of a United States ship, engaged in lawful trade, is compelled to receive on board some of the banditti or brigands of the islands. They are crowded upon him contrary to his inclination. He receives them at his peril." Subsequently, upon arrival in a U.S. port, "this innocent man is made the object of prosecution."[55] Mitchill's critique of the bill thus embraced its ostensible national security purpose but also sought to bolster its potential as a wedge against the overseas slave trade.

In addition, Mitchill argued, if "importation" was the ill that the act aimed to remedy, then the importers—not only the shipowner and shipmaster—should also be penalized. Mitchill proposed a five-hundred-dollar fine on importers for each violation of the statute, an amendment that ultimately failed.[56] Importation was the focus of the act, and the customshouse was the locus of federal authority. Congress might call upon revenue officers and customs officials to enforce state law against ship captains and owners; federal officials routinely dealt with those individuals when ships carrying goods arrived in the nation's ports.[57] Mobilizing federal power against importers of persons who were not themselves present at the dockside was an entirely different matter.

As the title of the 1803 act demonstrates, the activity that Congress sought to prevent was the "importation" of persons. This aim was subtly but importantly different from the Virginia act's focus on preventing the "migration" of persons. The federal act's penalty provisions and explicit instructions to U.S. customs and revenue officials provided an additional, federal layer of enforcement of state law—whatever valence that state law had. Congress was constitutionally forbidden from withdrawing the United States from the international slave trade. With the 1803 act, Congress vested federal officials with a duty to carry into effect state anti-slave-trade laws.[58] But the act was also consistent with federal enforcement for state laws that curtailed the movements of free

Black people in order further to entrench slavery. The ambiguous effects of the 1803 act were precisely what made it palatable to a wide array of viewpoints among members of Congress. The 1803 act did not mention the words "free" or "slave." Therefore, it was theoretically available to reinforce both state laws attacking the slave trade and state laws barring migration by free Black people. The Janus-faced nature of the act renders it an apt synecdoche for the larger regime of interbellum regulation of commerce, slavery, and migration.

The 1803 act emerged in the same political and legal context in which the nation doubled in territorial size by the addition of the 828,000-square-mile Louisiana Purchase.[59] The 1803 act was signed into law on February 28, 1803, the same day that President Thomas Jefferson also approved an appropriation of $2,500 for the Lewis and Clark expedition. The Louisiana Purchase was formally completed by treaty on April 30, 1803. The acquisition of lands formerly held by France and Spain also brought into the United States several thousand slaves of African descent and approximately fifteen hundred free persons of color—all of whom, the treaty stated, would be "incorporated into the Union of the United States." At the same time that Congress was putting federal power behind states that banned the importation of slaves, therefore, the nation was gaining a massive amount of territory (with the legality of slavery in that territory yet to be determined), thousands of enslaved residents, and a sizable increase in the percentage of the population of free persons of color, many of them in the culturally distinctive environs of New Orleans. Finally, 1803 was also the twelfth (and, as it turned out, penultimate) year of the Haitian Revolution. In short, the act of 1803 was passed at a time of collision among several distinct international legal regimes governing slavery. It was also a moment in which the legal categories of "free person of color" and "slave" gained increased salience because those categories had different meanings in different jurisdictions. Yet those jurisdictions were now to be joined into a single union.

The Brig on Trial

This interconnected pair of state and federal laws was conjured into action when the *Wilson* put into the port of Norfolk in October 1819. Over the course of the few days in which the brig lay in the harbor, Captain Huntress had dealings with three federal officials: customs inspector William Bush; deputy collector Alexander Tunstall; and Francis Benson, commander of a revenue cutter. Each of these officers represented the U.S. government, exercising constitutionally prescribed federal power over imports into and exports from the nation as a whole. At the same time, each of these federally commissioned officers was physically present in the specific local vicinage of Norfolk. Because they were operating within Virginia, Bush, Tunstall, and Benson were bound by federal law to enforce the laws of Virginia that barred certain persons of color from entering the commonwealth. The 1803 act of Congress obliged these federal officers to carry out state law.

But was the seizure of the *Wilson* and its cargo lawful under this complex of laws? This question was the central issue in the proceeding before Judge Tucker. After hearing testimony over several days, Judge Tucker issued his opinion and decree on December 22, 1819. Tucker found the charges in the libel to be substantiated, and he was unpersuaded by the defenses Huntress offered in his answer and claim. In his decree, Tucker condemned the brandy, gin, and other undeclared merchandise, finding that the items had been concealed and that Huntress had failed to make a true report of them.[60]

Tucker then turned to the fifth count of the libel, charging that the *Wilson* violated Virginia law by arriving in Norfolk with *"three persons of Colour*, not being native Citizens, or register'd Seamen of the U: S: or *Seamen* natives of Countries beyond the Cape of Good-hope" and landing those persons.[61] Tucker held that the congressional act of 1803 applied to the case of the *Wilson*, insofar as it "expressly prohibit[ed] the importing, or *bringing in*, of such persons" and required that such vessels be denied entry. The federal prohibition, of course, was derivative of the Virginia prohibition on such importation. Not only had the *Wilson* entered the port of Norfolk, it had discharged three persons of color. "[I]f any such negroe, Mulattoe, or other person of Colour shall be *landed* from on board any ship or Vessel, in any such port, the Ship &c. shall be forfeited to the United States," Tucker held. Moreover, Huntress could reasonably be held liable for the landing of the three persons of color: they "received their prize tickets (from the Captain I presume) and then went on Shore." Therefore, "[i]t was in the Captain's power to have prevented this; by not doing it, he has brought the Case within the words of the second section of the Act." Tucker therefore ordered the forfeiture of the brig, along with its chandlery.

Tucker's notes suggest that either Huntress or General Robert B. Taylor, who represented Almeida in the litigation, challenged the constitutionality of the act of 1803 as part of their effort to fend off the forfeiture action. Tucker dismissed this argument, but not without stating his view that the act was in fact constitutional: "My infirm state of health will not permit me to enter into an elaborate discussion of the *Constitutionality* of this Law: suffice it to say, I do not recollect ever to have doubted of its *constitutionality*, and I have ever approved of its policy; the object of which is to prevent the introduction, not only of Slaves, but of a Description of persons of whom we have already more, than the principles of our Government, and the Moral Improvement of our population renders eligible."[62]

Tucker's statement requires careful parsing, for it points to certain important ambiguities surrounding the interaction between federal and state law on the issue of migration by persons of color—both free and unfree—in this period.

First, the issue of constitutionality: Tucker's malarial ague prevented him from including a disquisition on the act of 1803 in his *Wilson* opinion. But in a case one month before, *United States v. Schooner Louisa*, he had offered a more substantial treatment of the subject. The *Louisa*, a Dutch ship, had arrived in Norfolk "having onboard four Negroes or people of Colour, not natives &c.," who were brought onshore and sold as slaves by the schooner's captain, Christoffel Rasmyne. The four captives were young Spanish-speaking West Indians: John Joseph, age eighteen, John Lewis, age twenty-three, John Rose, age twenty-two, and Peter Martin, age "about 20."[63] The four young men had worked as crew members before Rasmyne "landed" them in Norfolk and sold them in nearby Portsmouth for $1,200. They were then "clandestinely carried into the State of North Carolina."[64] The libel, brought here as in the *Wilson* by U.S. attorney Robert Stanard, charged Rasmyne with breach of both the act of 1803 and the 1807 Act to Prohibit the Importation of Slaves, under which Congress had outlawed the international importation of slaves into the United States.[65]

Captain Rasmyne's attorney objected that both acts were unconstitutional. Challenging the 1803 act, he argued that Congress "have no power to prohibit the *Migration* or *Importation* of any *free* persons, of any description whatsoever, whatever power they might have under the Constitution to prohibit the Importation of Slaves." Rasmyne's lawyer also asserted that Congress also lacked the power to "pass any Act to aid or enforce any Act of the Legislature of any State."[66]

In the case of the *Louisa*, as in that of the *Wilson*, Tucker was evidently unmoved by arguments against the constitutionality of the federal statutes. "My own Impressions are very different," he noted with disarming mildness. He then launched into a full-throated endorsement of the two species of congressional authority at issue in the case: the power to reinforce state law, and the power to regulate the migration and importation of persons. On the first point,

Tucker quickly dispatched the argument that Congress lacked the power to pass legislation supplementing state law. Clearly, he wrote, Congress was "competent" to "pass acts which may contribute to prevent any Evasion of a state Law (as in the present Case)."

On the second point, Tucker was no less emphatic but a great deal more expansive. In attempting to fend off the libel of the *Louisa*, Rasmyne argued that even if Congress had the power post-1808 to prohibit the importation of slaves, that power did not extend to prohibiting migration by free persons. (This contention was offered, to say the least, in bad faith, given the evidence that Rasmyne had then sold those same free individuals into bondage.) But Tucker rejected this argument outright and found that the *Louisa* had violated both acts of Congress. Congress did indeed have the authority to prohibit the migration or importation of free persons, Tucker wrote. Moreover, such power was clearly granted by the Constitution—specifically, by the 1808 Clause itself: "[U]nder the true Construction of the ninth section of the first Article of the C: U: S: Congress *now* possess, and ever since the year 1808 have possess'd the power and right to prohibit the Migration or Importation of such persons, as the Wisdom of the federal Congress may think it proper to exclude."

Tucker's language was unequivocal here: the "true Construction" of the 1808 Clause required the conclusion that Congress held—and had always held—the power to regulate both migration and importation, of both free persons of color and slaves. Why had the drafters of the Constitution "stiled" the power as "a *negative pregnant*" rather than an affirmative grant of power? Because of the intransigence of some members—"the opposition of a few States to such a Measure." But, Tucker suggested, that resistance was but a fleeting phenomenon, confined to the peculiar dynamics of the Philadelphia Convention of 1787. Now, with the tolling of the 1808 Clause, Congress came into possession of its full "absolute, and irrevocable" power. The negative pregnant of the 1808 Clause marked the scope of Congress's power, which covered the "migration or importation of such persons as any of the states now existing shall think proper to admit." Therefore, under the combined weight of the 1803 and 1807 acts, and "in consequence of the nefarious Conduct of the Master Christopher Rasmyne," the *Louisa* and her tackle, apparel, and furniture were forfeited to the United States.[67]

As a consequence of his holding that "the Case falls fully within both Acts of Congress," Tucker penalized Rasmyne and the schooner's owner for kidnapping John Joseph, John Lewis, Peter Martin, and John Rose and selling them into slavery. Federal law and state law thus worked together to punish perpetrators of activity that was illegal under the laws of the day. Yet the forfeiture remedy did nothing to aid the four victims: they were seized by North Carolina authorities acting under municipal ordinances, and sold into slavery.[68]

Given that the case unfolded within a legal regime that protected chattel slavery, Tucker's decision might be seen as an instance in which federal power landed a small but meaningful blow against one element of state-sanctioned bondage. In the *Louisa*, by action of Congress and the federal judiciary, a slaving captain lost his livelihood (at least temporarily), and his employer lost his ship. This aspect of the outcome in the *Louisa* aligns the case with Congress's 1807 ban on the importation of slaves, which sought to withdraw the American republic from an inhumane traffic that many contemporaries believed contravened the law of nature and nations.[69]

Can such a reading be drawn from Tucker's opinion in *The Brig Wilson*, though? Did the direction of federal law point toward at least some amount of freedom? Some aspects are similar: in both cases, Tucker held that the act of 1803 applied, and he consequently ordered the forfeiture of the vessel. But important differences between the cases also exist. If the case of the *Wilson* had ended with Tucker's decision, the result would have been that by action of Congress and the federal judiciary, a captain who had taken on free persons of color as crew members and allowed them to leave the ship lost his livelihood (at least temporarily), and his employer lost his ship.

And what of the three persons of color whose debarkation had amounted to a violation of Virginia law? That element of the case seems to fit more clearly within the purpose of the act of 1793 than did the facts of the *Louisa*. The three persons of color who stepped off the *Wilson*, prize tickets in hand, "took their own Discharge" and departed the pages of Tucker's notebook for unknown fates in Norfolk. By any reasonable interpretation, they clearly did "migrate"— the key word of the Virginia statute—into the commonwealth. Free persons of color left a vessel and joined the population of Virginia. As a result, Tucker held, Huntress ought to lose his captaincy, and Almeida should lose his brig. This result defies a reading of federal power as liberatory. Rather, it affirms federal reinforcement of a state regime of slavery so robust that it also extended to prohibitions on the movement of persons of color.

Within the space of five weeks in late 1819, Tucker had found that the 1803 act of Congress required forfeiture of a vessel in two scenarios: first, when a captain had sold four crew members who were apparently free "Negroes or people of Colour" into slavery; and second, when a captain had signed prize tickets and allowed three crew members who were free "persons of Colour" to leave the ship.

In both cases, the seamen at the center of the events were non-U.S. residents; all appear to have hailed from the West Indies. In both cases, the constitutionality of the statute was explicitly challenged, and in both Tucker held that the statute was a proper exercise of Congress's power. The first case, *The Schooner Louisa*, appears consistent with the purpose of some congressional advocates of the 1803 act, who hoped that the act might operate as a placeholder for an outright ban on the international slave trade. The second case, *The Brig Wilson*, is difficult to square with that reading of the statute's purpose. But it does comport with the view held by a different set of supporters of the 1803 act. This group "vindicated the constitutionality of the law, by observing that it only prevented the importation of negroes and persons of color into those States which had already prohibited their admission."[70] In other words, they hoped to secure federal assistance in preventing "importation," but their real goal was in preventing "migration."

But the outcomes become more congruent when viewed in light of their timing: 1819. By the time Tucker was deciding the cases of the *Louisa* and the *Wilson*, the 1808 Clause no longer applied, and Congress had acted to outlaw the international slave trade. Federal law now prohibited any person from "import[ing] or bring[ing] into the United States or the territories thereof from any foreign kingdom, place, or country, any negro, mulatto, or person of colour, with intent to hold, sell, or dispose of such negro, mulatto, or person of colour, as a slave, or to be held to service or labour."[71]

In 1819, the federal ban that could not have been passed in 1803 was in place. Yet the act of 1803—providing federal enforcement for "certain states" that prohibited the admission of "any negro, mulatto, or person of colour" from outside the United States—still stood. The federal government still had the power to enforce not only state bans on the slave trade, but also state bans on migration by free persons of color. The power of Congress extended to both species of enforcement, regardless of the valence of the state law in question.

Tucker's complex views on the connections between federal power, state authority, and slavery, which manifested themselves in his decisions in the cases of the *Louisa* and the *Wilson*, were not anomalous. A Bermuda-born slaveholder who owned several of the largest plantations in northern Virginia, Tucker was nonetheless convinced that slavery was incompatible with the republican ideals of the United States.[72] In 1796, he published *A Dissertation*

John Marshall, by James Reid Lambdin, 1832. (Virginia Museum of History and Culture [1988.8].)

on Slavery: With a Proposal for the Gradual Abolition of It, in the State of Virginia, in which he called for abolition over the course of a century.[73] Although the state legislature rejected Tucker's plan, critiques of slavery and calls for reform—ranging from gradual abolition to immediate emancipation—circulated among some early interbellum Virginian commentators, even those who later came to be associated with the states' rights views cited by secessionists.[74]

Whether or not Huntress and Almeida were aware of Tucker's views on slavery, they immediately appealed his forfeiture order to the federal circuit court in Richmond. Under the Judiciary Act of 1802, this circuit court was staffed by two judges: the district court judge of the district in which the court was sitting, and the chief justice of the Supreme Court of the United States.[75] The former was of course Tucker, whose health did not allow him to travel to

Richmond for the spring session.[76] The latter was Chief Justice John Marshall, who took up the appeal in late May 1820.

The Chief Justice and the Commerce Power

The Fifth Circuit, also known as the U.S. Circuit Court for the District of Virginia and North Carolina, held its sessions in the Virginia State Capitol. Thomas Jefferson had designed the white, columned edifice in the 1780s in an effort to bring the Roman splendors of the Maison Carrée in Nîmes, France, to the republican elevations of Shockoe Hill.[77] In August 1807, the sensational trial of Aaron Burr for treason, over which Marshall had presided and at which William Wirt had soared to fame, packed the Capitol with lawyers and spectators. Less than a quarter mile from the Capitol, in the elegant Court End neighborhood, Marshall's imposing brick house sat comfortably on a block-sized curtilage—including a two-story law office, a stable, an orchard, and gardens both ornamental and vegetable.[78] Marshall's Richmond household also included around twelve enslaved people, who constituted a small percentage of the hundreds of slaves he owned over the course of his life.[79]

Marshall's nine-page, handwritten opinion in *The Brig Wilson*, issued sometime between May 22 and June 8, 1820, reversed Tucker's forfeiture decree and ordered restoration of the *Wilson* and cargo to its owner, Almeida.[80] Marshall rested his decision on two grounds. First, he held that federal laws regulating the collection of duties on imports did not apply to privateers, "unless they take up the character of merchant-men, by attempting to import goods." The brandy and gin in question were "designed for the crew, to be used as stores," Marshall found after examining the evidence, and were not intended to be landed or sold. Thus, the *Wilson* had not fraudulently attempted "under the garb of [its] military character, to conceal real commercial transactions." The *Wilson* had entered the port of Norfolk openly and lawfully: as a military vessel engaged in privateering against Spain, with which the nascent South American republic under which it was commissioned was at war.[81]

Like Tucker, Marshall appears to have viewed the fifth count of the libel—charging the *Wilson* with violating the congressional act of 1803, which added federal enforcement to the Virginia anti-migration law of 1793—as presenting the most important and difficult issues in the case. Unlike his colleague in Williamsburg, however, Marshall hastened directly to the question of the constitutionality of the 1803 statute—"the act of congress, under which this condemnation has been made." This ground was the second on which Marshall overruled Tucker.

Indeed, Marshall's emendations to his handwritten opinion suggest that he initially considered starting the opinion by tackling the question of the constitutionality of the 1803 act of Congress. Marshall began this section of the opinion at the top of a fresh page, and he included the caption "Huntress v. The U.S.," which he did not do on other continuous pages. The first line as Marshall wrote it read, "The first question which will be considered in this case is the constitutionality of the act of Congress under which this condemnation has been made." He appears later to have revised the sentence, adding a line in the top margin of the page and a carat. In so doing, he changed the passage from an opening of the decision to a later section, before which he added two additional pages on the question whether the revenue laws extended to privateers. With the additions, the sentence reads, "I proceed now to the 5th count in the libel. The first question which will be considered in this part of the case is the constitutionality of the act of Congress under which this condemnation has been made."[82] A reader of the finished opinion would be greeted by several paragraphs discussing the classification of vessels and the status of imported goods before being confronted by the issue of the constitutionality of a federal law.

Marshall agreed with Tucker that the act of 1803 was constitutional. Unlike Tucker, however, Marshall did not base this conclusion on the 1808 Clause. Tucker had read the 1808 Clause of Article I, section 9, as a negative pregnant through which an affirmative grant of authority to regulate the migration and importation of persons could be implied. Marshall, by contrast, grounded the constitutionality of the 1803 act on an affirmative power set forth in the text of the Constitution: the Commerce Clause of Article I, section 8.

Sitting on circuit in the spring of 1820, in Jefferson's temple to the ideals of classical liberty, Marshall reframed the case of the *Wilson*. In order to decide this controversy arising out of war, revolution, trade in goods, and trade in humans, the chief justice chose to apply the constitutional provision that enabled Congress "to regulate commerce with foreign nations, and among the several states, and with the Indian tribes."[83] The Capitol looked over the Falls of the James River; the principal events of the saga of the *Wilson* had occurred in Hampton Roads and at the Norfolk quayside; the brig that had brought the three persons of color to Virginia had begun life in the service of the Spanish Crown. The movement of persons and things over water was fundamentally connected with the exercise of national authority to regulate and protect that movement across boundaries.

Marshall's opinion in *The Brig Wilson* (*Huntress v. The U.S.*), page 3, beginning: "I proceed now to the 5th count in the libel." (American Philosophical Society.)

The *Wilson* opinion is the earliest reported case in which Marshall construed the Commerce Clause. It was not the first time the federal judiciary had grappled with the commerce power, however. In the 1808 case of *The William*, John Davis, U.S. district judge for the District of Massachusetts, upheld the Embargo Act of 1807 as a valid exercise of Congress's commerce power. From his Boston courtroom, Judge Davis wrote that the power to regulate commerce could permissibly be used as "an instrument for other purposes of general policy and interest."[84] The policy purpose of the Embargo Act was clear, Davis wrote: to cut off Great Britain and France from American trade during the Napoleonic Wars. "The capacity and power of managing and directing" commerce was "an important ingredient of sovereignty." Moreover, the commerce power was sufficiently robust to serve as the basis for even a prohibition on commerce, such as the embargo. In support of this proposition, Davis cited the 1808 Clause of the Constitution, which he—like Tucker—regarded as setting a temporary hiatus on Congress's exercise of its full powers. "It was perceived, that, under the power of regulating commerce, congress would be authorized to abridge it, in favour of the great principles of humanity and justice," Davis noted. "Hence the introduction of a clause, in the constitution, so framed, as to interdict a prohibition of the slave trade, until 1808."[85] Here again, the 1808 Clause and the Commerce Clause appeared to contemporaries to be analytically connected.[86] Even after the 1808 Clause had expired, it continued to demarcate the scope of one of Congress's most important powers.

In *The Brig Wilson* Marshall began his discussion of the commerce power with a volley of definitions and assertions. As in some of his more famous decisions, such as *McCulloch v. Maryland* from the year before, the force of this rhetorical fusillade was unsullied by citations.[87] The pronouncements came in the form of a series of questions and answers—a constitutional catechism of commerce.

What, Marshall asked, was the activity that Congress sought to regulate in its 1803 Act to Prevent the Importation of Certain Persons into Certain States? That activity was "navigation," which Marshall defined as "power over vessels." Did this power over vessels reside in Congress? And if so, what was the textual basis for the grant of that power? Here Marshall broke through his own dialogic structure to provide an unequivocal answer:

> There is not, in the Constitution, one syllable on the subject of navigation. And yet, every power that pertains to navigation has been uniformly exercised, and, in the opinion of all, been rightfully exercised, by congress. From the adoption of the Constitution, till this time, the universal

sense of America has been, that the word commerce, as used in that instrument, is to be considered a generic term, comprehending navigation, or, that a control over navigation is necessarily incidental to the power to regulate commerce.[88]

Marshall's reasoning here is striking: the Constitution was silent on "navigation," the activity at issue in the case of the *Wilson*. But since 1788 (and, indeed, since 1777, under the Articles of Confederation), Congress had been routinely regulating vessels through port bills, confiscation statutes, and other acts governing ships' cargoes.[89] Moreover, such regulation had, in Marshall's view, been accepted as lawful by the American people—evidently an important criterion. The "universal sense of America" over the past four decades was that the commerce power necessarily encompassed the power to regulate navigation. And even if "commerce" was not a "generic term comprehending navigation," the ability to control navigation was a necessary tool for Congress to carry out its core commerce power.[90] In summary, Marshall observed, "the power to regulate commerce, clearly comprehended" the case of the *Wilson*.

To quell any lingering doubts among his audience, Marshall followed Judge Tucker below and Judge Davis from *The William* in pointing to the 1808 Clause of Article I, section 9. "This has been truly said to be a limitation of the power of congress to regulate commerce, and it will not be pretended, that a limitation of a power is to be construed into a grant of power," Marshall wrote. Nonetheless, "though such a limitation be not a grant, it is certainly evidence of the extent which those who made both the grant and limitation, attributed to the grant." The 1808 Clause was a temporary carve-out from a preexisting domain of authority: "[T]he power of congress over vessels, which might bring in persons of any description, whatever, was complete before the year 1808, except that it could not be so exercised, as to prohibit the importation or migration of any persons, whom any state, in existence at the formation of the Constitution, might think proper to admit."[91]

Amplifying Davis's and Tucker's analyses, Marshall turned the 1808 Clause—a bar on congressional action in the realm of the international slave trade—into a mandate directly from the founders for Congress to regulate trade in general, and the slave trade after 1808. A limitation of power might not be able to be construed into a grant of power. But an explicitly temporary withholding of power did imply the existence of that power at any point that was not within the relevant time period (namely, 1789 to 1808). Paradoxically, the restraint of the 1808 Clause had become a guide to the broad sweep of the Commerce Clause.

Having demonstrated the constitutionality of the 1803 act of Congress un-der which federal officials had confiscated the *Wilson*, Marshall then turned to the business of statutory construction. He first addressed the 1803 federal stat-ute, and then the Virginia act of 1793—the state law that the federal act was enforcing.

Parsing the language of the act of 1803, Marshall questioned whether its second section applied to the three crew members who had debarked the *Wil-son* at Norfolk. "The second section enacts, 'that no ship or vessel, arriving in any of the said ports or places of the United States, and *having on board* any negro, mulatto, or other person of colour, not being a native, a citizen, or reg-istered seaman of the United States; or seamen, natives of countries beyond the Cape of Good Hope . . . shall be admitted to an entry.' "[92]

"It is obvious," Marshall continued, "that this clause was intended to refuse an entry to every vessel, which had violated the prohibition contained in the first section; and that the words 'having on board' were used, as co-extensive with the words 'import' or 'bring.' " But could such language reasonably be read to apply to anyone aboard the vessel who was regarded as a "person of color," whatever their nation of origin, and even if they were crew members? Marshall was skeptical that the statute extended this far:

> We had, at that time, a treaty with the Emperor of Morocco, and with several other Barbary powers. Their subjects are all people of colour. . . . [C]an it be believed, that this law was intended to refuse an entry to such a vessel? . . . [T]here are many nations, with whom we have regular com-merce, who employ coloured seamen. Could it be intended by congress, to refuse an entry to a French, a Spanish, an English, or a Portuguese merchant vessel, in whose crew there was a man of colour? I think this construction could never be given to the act.[93]

Moreover, Marshall noted, the statute's use of the phrase "shall be landed" suggested that it was meant to apply to "a person, or thing, which is imported, or *brought in* . . . not by its own act, but by the authority of the importer," and thus would not cover "a mariner, going on shore voluntarily, or on the business of the ship." Knowing that the crews of international ships comprised many "persons of colour," Congress could not have intended to sweep all those individuals within the ambit of the 1803 statute. Therefore, Marshall found, "the forfeiture is not incurred by a person of colour, coming in as part of a ship's crew, and go-ing on shore." Indeed, to permit Congress to grant such broad enforcement power to U.S. revenue and customs officers would be "an attempt to regulate the manner in which a foreign vessel should be navigated in order to be admitted into our ports." Such a regulation would exceed even Marshall's capacious view of the commerce power.[94]

With this initial construction of the act of 1803, Marshall began to call into question Tucker's decree of forfeiture for the *Wilson*. But the final six paragraphs of the opinion demonstrated the Möbius-strip complexity of the intertwined set of federal and state statutes at issue in the case. This section of Marshall's analysis also suggests that by 1820, the federal enforcement mechanism set forth in the congressional act of 1803 was aiding a different set of policies from some of those that had motivated the 1803 act.

The third section of the 1803 act, Marshall reminded his audience, enjoined "the officers of the United States, in the states having laws containing such prohibition, 'to notice and be governed by the provisions of the laws, now existing, of the several states, prohibiting the admission or importation of any negro, mulatto, or any person of colour." Federal officials were thus to follow state law. But observers in 1820 should not mistakenly think that the 1803 act was Congress's way of "inflicting a penalty for the violation of a state law," Marshall cautioned. In so warning, Marshall implied that a federal penalty for the violation of a state law might raise constitutional problems. Instead, he stated, Congress in the 1803 act was "limiting the operation of the penal law of the United States, by a temporary demarcation given in the Constitution." Given the background fact of the 1808 Clause, the 1803 act was "proper" insofar as it made "the prohibitory act of the state, the limit of its own operation."[95]

Marshall's analysis is difficult to penetrate here. What he appears to have been suggesting, however, was that prior to 1808, the "penal law of the United States," which he implied might otherwise prohibit the importation of slaves, was temporarily suspended by operation of the 1808 Clause. During that time, however, the states were free to prohibit such importation, and Congress could direct federal officers to be governed by those state laws, as it did in the 1803 act. By so directing, Congress was not aggrandizing its power; on the contrary, it was acting in an appropriately constrained manner, given the constitutional limits on the operation of its "penal law." Presumably, had the penal law of the United States been unlimited, Congress could have passed its own legislation prohibiting the migration or importation of persons, rather than merely bolstering states' prohibitions. (Recall that the source of the limitation was the 1808 Clause, which was specifically addressed to prohibitions on migration or importation.) Marshall therefore appears to have viewed the 1803 act as primarily motivated by hostility to the slave trade. Congress was doing through additive regulation what it could not do outright: supporting states that sought to prevent the migration or importation of slaves. Furthermore, this trade might have included domestic as well as international trafficking in enslaved people.[96]

But the Virginia act of 1793 was, as we have seen, motivated by different concerns. Its aim was not to halt the international slave trade using the means available to it while the 1808 Clause was in effect. Rather, as its title made clear, its goal was to prevent "free negroes and mulattoes" from migrating into the state. Virginia's policy tended to maintain slavery by stopping free persons of color from entering the state, further entrenching slavery and creating a presumption that all persons of apparent African descent were enslaved.

The chief justice owned enslaved people on a large scale.[97] Whatever Marshall's views on the merits of the Virginia law of 1793, his decision in *The Brig Wilson* put federal power in the service of state law—up to a point. Marshall deemed it "proper" that "the act of congress should make the prohibitory act of the state, the limit of its own operation." The 1803 act of Congress was not coextensive with state law—it "does not, necessarily, extend to every object comprehended in the state law, but neither its terms, nor the Constitution, will permit it to be extended farther than the state law."[98] The federal government was not simply carrying out the will of the states. Nor was it acting as an unfettered leviathan, despite the broad commerce power that Marshall held that it wielded. In this domain, state law set the substantive limits of federal enforcement. The relationships among levels of government were complex and overlapping, and they did not operate according to a neat dichotomy between federal and state power.

What did these analytical arabesques mean for the brig *Wilson*? Having determined that the act of Congress made state law "the limit of its own operation," Marshall held that the facts of the case did not support finding a violation of Virginia law. "The act of assembly [of 1793] prohibits the admission of free negroes and mulattos only, not of other persons of colour," Marshall found. Indeed, "[o]ther persons of colour were admissible into Virginia." To be sure, the act of Congress of 1803 applied to "persons of colour." But given that the Virginia statute did not bar such individuals from migrating into the state, there was no basis for federal action. State law was the measure of federal law's operation. No state prohibition had been violated, and therefore the forfeiture procedures of the 1803 act of Congress had not been triggered.

Marshall ended his opinion by referring again to the testimony of the U.S. customs inspector and the clerk of the *Wilson*, respectively:

If, under this libel, it were allowable to prove, that the sailors landed, were, in fact, negroes or mulattos, it is not proved. Mr. Bush does not prove, that any were landed, but says, that those discharged were "of different colours and nations." Andrew Johnson says, "that on the 29th of October, *the people of colour* received their prize tickets, went on shore, and, of course, took their own discharge. There is, then, no evidence, that these people were negroes or mulattos."[99]

In the end, then, the derivative nature of the federal law of 1803 meant that the forfeiture of the brig could not stand. The relevant terms were to be supplied by state law, and state law did not clearly bar the category of persons to which the record showed the three discharged crew members belonged. The record described them as "persons of colour"; the statute's bar applied to "negroes or mulattos." The category denominated by the facts of the case was broader than the category covered by the statute. The narrowness of the state law's category—a law whose entire purpose was to prevent free Black individuals from entering the state—ultimately led to the brig's release.

Discharged from federal custody, the brig *Wilson* promptly resumed its depredations—a fact Tucker dryly observed in the notebook entry following his own, overruled, opinion: "This Decree was reversed by Judge Marshal, in toto. & the Brigantine released & restored.—She has since been cruizing off our Coast, from Virginia to South Carolina & Georgia, as appears by the papers.—I am not inform'd of the Grounds upon which the Decree was revers'd, as none are assigned in the record."[100]

The *Wilson*, now occasionally operating under the name *Bolivar* in a patriotic tribute to the hero of Venezuela's independence movement, continued to figure in the columns of U.S. newspapers. Baltimore's *Niles' Weekly Register* carried the following report of the brig's pursuits—again involving privateering, revolution, and the slave trade:

> The brig Wilson, *alias* Bolivar, &c. commanded by capt. Almeida, *et alias*, and apparently having several flags, Buenos Ayrean, Artigan, Venezuelian, *et alias*—by which a Spanish ship bound to Baltimore was recently captured on our coast, was lately off Charleston waiting for men. Information of the fact being given, lieutenant McClunie, of the United States schooner Revenge, happily arrested a sloop load of her intended crew, and they were lodged in jail.[101]

The next edition of Hezekiah Niles's magazine provided additional details about the *Wilson*'s activities. The "Spanish ship bound to Baltimore" that the

Wilson had captured was the *Santiago*, lately from Cuba, and reportedly on its way to Baltimore "to be fitted to proceed to the coast of Africa for slaves, from whence she had just returned with 450 human beings." The editor noted that this account of the *Wilson's* conduct made "a very different story of the matter; and, if true, rendering the capture estimable in our eyes."[102] Despite the paper's general opposition to privateering, the *Wilson's* seizure of a ship that was unlawfully engaged in the international slave trade redeemed Almeida somewhat in Niles's eyes.

Within weeks of Marshall's decision, the *Wilson's* activities brought it back before Tucker and the chief justice on charges that "a number of persons had been unlawfully enlisted and taken onboard." Tucker issued a warrant for the arrest of approximately thirty persons, some of whom escaped, and others of whom were brought to Richmond for examination before Marshall. A grand jury of the U.S. circuit court indicted a handful of the crew; all were eventually acquitted.[103] *Niles' Weekly Register* applauded Marshall's "nobleness of mind and character" in his handling of the case. The chief justice "dispensed with all unessential formality on this occasion, and held his court for the examination of the prisoners on board the steam boat, which lay at Rockets [Landing], and to which place he repaired on foot, a distance of about two miles from his residence."[104]

Cross-Circuit Commerce Conversations

Two of Marshall's colleagues on the Supreme Court clearly regarded the chief justice's reasoning in *The Brig Wilson* as a sword that could be wielded against both the international slave trade and state restrictions on free Black sailors. Within three years of the *Wilson* decision, when each was riding circuit, Justices Joseph Story and William Johnson invoked the Commerce Clause as the source of federal power in these domains. *United States v. La Jeune Eugenie* (1822) arose when the U.S. schooner *Alligator* apprehended *La Jeune Eugenie*, a schooner flying the French flag, off the western coast of Africa on suspicion that it was in fact an American ship unlawfully engaged in the slave trade. Adjudicating the libel on circuit in Boston in the fall of 1821, Story wrote that "the power over slaves was referred to the authority which congress had, to regulate commerce." He also found that the slave trade violated the law of nations.[105]

In *Elkison v. Deliesseline* (1823), Justice Johnson held that South Carolina's Negro Seamen Act of 1822 (also known as the South Carolina Police Bill), which mandated that free Black sailors be jailed while their vessels lay in port, violated Congress's commerce power. In *Elkison*, unlike the case of the *Wilson*, federal power stood in opposition to state law. "[T]he right of the general government to regulate commerce with the sister states and foreign nations is a paramount and exclusive right," Johnson held.[106] The justice, who was a Charlestonian and a slaveholder, was vilified in the South Carolina press, and the decision—as well as the executive branch's endorsement of it, via the opinion of U.S. attorney general William Wirt—were condemned in the state house at Columbia.

Elkison and its context will be explored more fully in Chapter 4. For now, the important point about the case is that it prompted Marshall to further reflections on his decision in the case of the *Wilson* three years earlier. In a letter to Story in 1823, Marshall drew a line connecting his 1820 decision in *The Brig Wilson* to "our brother" Johnson's recent decision in *Elkison* and the controversy it had unleashed. Marshall also offered some insight into his own reasoning:

> Thus you see fuel is continually adding to the fire at which the *exaltées* are about to roast the judicial department. You have, it is said, some law in Massachusetts not very unlike in principle to that which our brother has declared unconstit[utional]. We have its twin brother in Virginia, and a ca[se was] brought before me in which I might have considered its constitutionality had I chosen to do so; but it was not absolutely necessary, &, as I am not fond of butting against a wall in sport, I escaped on the construction of the act.[107]

The "twin brother" of the South Carolina Police Bill was, of course, Virginia's 1793 Act to Prevent the Migration of Free Negroes and Mulattoes. The case in which Marshall "might have considered" the constitutionality of the Virginia law was *The Brig Wilson*.

As we have seen, in *The Brig Wilson*, Marshall had plunged directly into one constitutional issue: the validity of Congress's act of 1803. That question was his opportunity to adumbrate the scope of the federal commerce power. But he had chosen not to take up the other constitutional issue presented by the case: the validity of Virginia's ban on migration into the state by "free negroes and mulattoes." Marshall's letter to Story three years later makes clear that Marshall deliberately chose not to address the question of the Virginia law. The case could be disposed of, and the forfeiture of the brig lifted, by means of statutory construction alone. Marshall thus consciously avoided finding a conflict between state law and the Constitution.

Nonetheless, Marshall's opinion in *The Brig Wilson* contains some hints that he might have doubted the constitutionality of the state's restrictions on the migration of free Black people. The reason for this doubt was the commerce power. Commerce included navigation, Marshall wrote in *The Brig Wilson*, and navigation included vessels. Congress clearly possessed "an unlimited power over the cargoes." Moreover, Marshall observed, "No man has been wild enough to maintain" that "while the whole power of commerce is vested in congress, the state legislatures may confiscate every vessel which enters their ports, and congress is unable to prevent their entry."[108]

In Marshall's view, Congress possessed the entire power to regulate commerce among the states and with other nations. The exclusive nature of that authority necessarily limited the states' powers in that realm. A federal commerce power would be meaningless if a state could confiscate vessels for violating state laws. A similar argument underpinned Johnson's decision in *Elkison*: the South Carolina Police Bill was a regulation of commerce, but the regulation of commerce was a "paramount and exclusive right" of the federal government. Finally, Marshall suggested that even this expansive federal power over commerce could not support a ban on the movement of *persons*, as opposed to the movement of *vessels*. "Let it be admitted, for the sake of argument, that a law, forbidding a free man of any colour, to come into the United States, would be void, and that no penalty, imposed on him by Congress, could be enforced: still, the vessel, which should bring him into the United States, might be forfeited," Marshall wrote.[109]

A Federalism of Commerce and Migration

Marshall's earliest decision on the Commerce Clause brought together several vital issues of interbellum constitutional debate: the definition of "commerce"; federal enforcement of state law; international relations; and migration. The case also concerned the status of persons of color—not slaves, on the particular facts of *The Brig Wilson*, but free individuals who might well have been of African descent, and thus the target of the Virginia law. Tucker and Marshall—two slaveowners—both upheld the constitutionality of the congressional act of 1803, and in so doing, enacted and expanded federal power. But both judges read the federal law as merely additive to state law, which in turn gave controlling power to the words of the Virginia statute. Interlocking layers of law were at work, and Tucker and Marshall each took it as his duty to pick them apart. The federalism at work in *The Brig Wilson*, like so many other regulatory schemes of the era, was one of overlap, not separately demarcated state and federal spheres.

The difference between Tucker's and Marshall's approaches lay in their respective interpretations of the state law. Tucker read the Virginia act's "free negroes and mulattoes" language expansively, so that it included these "persons of colour." Tucker's construction put Congress more firmly in the position of enforcing Virginia's increasingly entrenched protections for slavery and racial hierarchy. Marshall read the state law narrowly, concluding that the statute's specification of "free negroes and mulattoes" meant that "persons of colour" were not clearly covered, and therefore were not barred.

It is too simple a reading of the case to say that it stood for a notion of federal power as humanitarian and liberating, in contrast to state power as necessarily protecting slavery. Such a view is unduly blunt and projects the dynamics of the twentieth and twenty-first centuries back onto the early nineteenth century. To be sure, federal power in the interbellum period sometimes stood against slavery and racial subordination, and contemporaries—both critics and supporters of slavery—often attributed this stance to it.

Nevertheless, as the outcome in *The Brig Wilson* demonstrates, federal power was also employed during the period to uphold restrictions on the movement and liberty of Black individuals, both free and enslaved. The result of the case ultimately reinforced the regime of slavery, insofar as Marshall interpreted the commerce power to permit Congress to bolster state laws regarding persons of color aboard ships. This outcome was the effect of Marshall's capacious interpretation of the federal commerce power. Had the text of the Virginia statute referred to "persons of colour," or had the testimony of the customs officers or the brig's clerk included further detail on the origins and appearances of the three crew members, the outcome of the case would likely have been very different. The crew members still would have been able to melt into the Norfolk waterfront if they so chose, but Captain Huntress and his privateering chief, Almeida, would have lost their brig as forfeit to the U.S. government.

Yet Marshall's approach to the complex case also cabined the effect of the Virginia law, the undoubted purpose of which was to stop free Black people from migrating into the state. The Virginia law was not before the Court, as Marshall noted with relief in his letter to Story. Nevertheless, the chief justice managed to construe it. And in that construction, he limited its reach. Marshall's roomy interpretation of the 1803 act of Congress sat atop his narrow, text-bound reading of the 1793 Virginia law. Because the scope of the federal law depended upon the specific terms of the state law, the result of Marshall's analysis was that the brig escaped federal forfeiture, just as its onetime crew members were held to have eluded the state's prohibition on their entry. Both levels of law were necessary to the interpretive machinery of the court's opinion.[110] The result was thus not amenable to simple description—it stood for neither broad nor narrow federal power, neither broad nor narrow state control. It contained all these strands.

This interpretation of *The Brig Wilson* presents a challenge to one influential account of early-nineteenth-century federalism. According to this account, as advanced by the constitutional historian Charles Warren in his Pulitzer Prize–winning work, *The Supreme Court in United States History*, "[T]he long-continued controversy as to whether Congress had exclusive or concurrent jurisdiction over commerce was not a conflict between theories of government, or between Nationalism and State-Rights, or between differing legal construction of the Constitution, but was simply the naked issue of State or Federal control of slavery."[111]

The assumption that interbellum debates about the commerce power simply mirrored sectional views about slavery is incomplete, and in many cases incorrect. So, too, is the view that federal power was always synonymous with antislavery views, and state sovereignty with proslavery sentiment. A binary understanding of federalism that posits a perpetual opposition between state and federal power misconceives much of the actual content of interbellum constitutional debates.

3 • The Steamboat and the Commerce of the Union

A Federalism of Beneficent Exchange

Generations of influential commentators have taken for granted a certain view of the Marshall Court's Commerce Clause cases, according to which the Court faced a choice between state and federal power and chose federal power. Key to this view are three assumptions: first, that the Court was put to this choice; second, that the Court chose federal power; and third, that this choice eliminated the possibility of any other modes of organizing the federal union.

These post hoc characterizations of the early-nineteenth-century commerce power gained particular salience in the early twentieth century, during the debates over the constitutionality of the New Deal. Two years before he joined the Court, Felix Frankfurter pointed to the 1824 decision in *Gibbons v. Ogden* as the moment of inception for the "actual operation" of the "process by which the conflicting claims of the nation and the states, in this profoundly important phase of the distribution of power under our federal system, are mediated through the Supreme Court."[1] Political scientist Edward S. Corwin framed the issue even more starkly, titling his 1936 book *The Commerce Power versus States' Rights.*[2]

The debates surrounding *Gibbons* illustrate another fundamental yet overlooked feature of interbellum constitutional thought: the viability of concurrent power. Interbellum lawyers and judges held a range of views about where the commerce power resided. For some, it lay exclusively in the federal government; for others, it was shared—not only between the federal government and the states, but sometimes with localities such as cities and even local officials, some of whom acted upon their own interpretations of the Constitution. Concurrent power was a real and meaningful alternative to binary federalism. Rather than Corwin's choice between "the commerce power versus states' rights," the possibilities for interbellum Americans included zones of shared power; distinctions among different types of commerce; and a competitor to the commerce power called the "police power." On this view, concurrent power theory was not merely "a doctrine designed to resurrect state sovereignty."[3]

As the previous chapter's exploration of the progress of *The Brig Wilson* through the federal courts makes clear, the Commerce Clause had a substantial doctrinal history by the time the Supreme Court explicitly took up the issue for the first time, in 1824. Reading the opinions by St. George Tucker and John Marshall in the case of the *Wilson* illuminates the intellectual context in which judges were operating when they addressed the "Steam-Boat Cause," as the case of *Gibbons v. Ogden* became known in the extensive coverage it received in the nation's newspapers.[4]

The Brig Wilson asked whether Congress could deploy its commerce power to bolster states' efforts in domains in which Congress was not able to act directly. Chief Justice Marshall's circuit-court decision in the case worked to present a relatively harmonious picture of state and federal power—albeit a somewhat forced harmony. As Marshall's 1823 letter to Justice Joseph Story demonstrates, the chief justice had striven to avoid conflict by deciding the case on statutory grounds rather than on the issue of the constitutionality of the Virginia statute.[5] Marshall's decision arguably frustrated the intention of the Virginia legislature—to bar free African Americans from migrating into the state—insofar as his decision ratified the entry of three individuals described in the record as "persons of colour." By declining to consider the question of the state law's constitutionality, however, Marshall left intact the interwoven structure of the 1793 state law and the 1803 congressional act.

Gibbons presented the justices with a very different question: whether the fact that Congress had acted, or even might at some future point act, prevented a state from legislating in the same realm. *Gibbons* conjured existential federal-state struggle out of a decades-long squabble between rival business owners. Its array of issues compassed state monopolies, patents, the commerce power, international trade and shipping, and the Supremacy Clause. The esteem in which the decision is held is captured by the historian Albert J. Beveridge's 1919 characterization of the case: "On March 2, 1824, Marshall delivered that opinion which has done more to knit the American people into an indivisible Nation than any other one force in our history, excepting only war."[6] Subsequent scholars have endorsed, albeit less breathlessly, this view of the case's iconic status, even while some have critiqued the uses to which the case has been put.[7] Unlike *The Brig Wilson*, which earns only occasional and passing reference in the scholarship, *Gibbons* occupies the highest levels in the pantheon of landmark cases.

The authority of *Gibbons* stems in part from the scale of the issues it involved. But the case's preeminence is also the result of its location in time, both historical and precedential. Some modern commentators regard *Gibbons* as an utterance from the founding era, while others wonder why the Court waited so long to tackle such an important provision as the Commerce Clause. *Gibbons* was the first case in which the Supreme Court construed the meaning and scope of the commerce power; it was decided by the Great Chief Justice and his confrères, some of whom had fought in the Revolution and participated in the drafting and ratification of the Constitution; and it was decided several decades before the Civil War.

Gibbons might thus appear to be a simple application of settled principles—a case study in setting the abstract tenets of the Constitution into action, its authority virtually equal to that of utterances by the founders despite the passage of thirty-seven years between the drafting of the Constitution and the issuing of the decision.[8] From another perspective, however, the Court took its time, and "Supreme Court attention to the commerce clause" was "long delayed."[9] Although at first glance these views might appear to conflict, with one treating *Gibbons* as a product of the 1780s and the other viewing it as issuing decades later than it ought to have, they have much in common. Both characterizations share the premise that the case contained a set of fundamental questions that were immanent in the Constitution from the moment it was drafted. Marshall's 1824 opinion, according to both views, is a timeless statement about American constitutional law that in some sense "needed" to be issued.

But the case was not timeless, any more than any piece of legal doctrine can be dissociated from the facts and the context in which it arises. First, the case concerned the quintessential early-nineteenth-century technology: the steamboat. Steamboats began to be developed in the 1790s and were not proved commercially successful until 1807.[10] Moreover, the judges and justices who heard *Gibbons* as it traveled from the New York state courts to the Supreme Court came to it cognizant of the rapidly changing political structures, economic conditions, and world events around them. *The Brig Wilson*, as we have seen, touched on the Haitian Revolution, the sovereignty of the South American republics, the 1808 Clause and its tolling, and the thriving privateering trade that operated out of Norfolk and Baltimore.

The intellectual and doctrinal landscape in which *Gibbons* was fought and decided looked radically different from the one that had obtained three decades earlier. Causes that invoked the commerce power were percolating through the lower federal courts, and as the justices rode their circuits, they were the conduits between those geographically peripheral cases and the jurisprudential center of Washington. The Court that took up the steamboat case in 1824 included several justices who had already encountered the Commerce Clause in cases they heard on circuit: Marshall, who had decided *The Brig Wilson* four years before; Story, who had gone out of his way to condemn the slave trade two years earlier; William Johnson, who had struck down the South Carolina Police Bill one year before; and Bushrod Washington, who was in the process of drafting a circuit-court decision concerning competing state and federal regulation of oyster fisheries.[11] (And of course this roster of experiences does not include the lawyers in the case, each of whom was a seasoned advocate with years of practice to his credit.)

All these circuit-court actions hinged in some way on the Commerce Clause, and they in turn shaped the meaning of that provision. The Court would not—indeed, could not—have decided the abstract question of the scope of the Commerce Clause in the way it did in *Gibbons* without its members having come to the case with the ideas about the federal-state relationship that they developed in those circuit cases. Four of the seven justices—a majority of the Court—had experience interpreting the commerce power when the steamboat case arrived before them in Washington City in February 1824. They, like the lawyers, came to the case with a set of ideas and practical examples of how the commerce power functioned.

In the standard view of American constitutional history, *Gibbons* looms large in the corpus of notable decisions that the Court issued between the Revolution and the Civil War. But the case is often presented as though it simply put a punctuation mark on a few constitutional truisms—a just-so story about how Marshall's dominance of the Court led to a predetermined outcome in line with his Federalist preferences.[12] Other accounts tend to treat the case as the starting point for a highly dichotomized view of federalism—"the commerce power versus states' rights," in Corwin's titular phrase.[13]

But *Gibbons* contains more strands of argument and offers more possible visions of the federal-state relationship than such views suggest. This chapter recovers the creativity of the ideas that were circulating in *Gibbons*, and the ways in which they collided with each other as they were aired by lawyers and judges at various stages of the lengthy litigation over New York's steamboat monopoly. As in *The Brig Wilson*, the federal-state relationship was a work in progress in the 1820s, not a rigid choice between federal power and states' rights. Moreover, concurrent power was a real possibility, an idea with meaningful content, not simply a cover for an ideology of states' rights. Even *Gibbons v. Ogden*, the preeminent case establishing Congress's commerce power and the supposed nationalism of the Marshall Court, contained more varied strands of federalisms than previous accounts have acknowledged.

The Steamboats: Federalism and Conflict

The creativity of the arguments offered in *Gibbons* can be seen by examining three themes that recurred throughout the dispute. These themes included two possibilities and a vision: the possibility of concurrent power over commerce; the possibility that the commerce power was exclusively held by Congress; and an affirmative vision of what became known as the "Commerce of the Union." Together, these disparate strands made up commerce's federalisms.

First, some background. The *Gibbons* litigation was the product of a decades-long series of disputes about navigation between New York City and Elizabethtown (now Elizabeth), New Jersey. The first American steamboats were developed by John Fitch and James Rumsey, in Pennsylvania and Virginia, respectively. Fitch's *Perseverance* made a trial run in the summer of 1787 on the Delaware River, which was witnessed by several of the delegates to the Constitutional Convention.[14] In 1791, Fitch triumphed over Rumsey by winning a patent on his steamboat, and in 1798, Fitch obtained a grant of monopoly rights from the New York legislature. But although Fitch and Rumsey were able inventors, and Rumsey also ran a thriving Philadelphia inn and tavern that catered to government officials, each of them was unable to find sufficient political backing and investment to develop his creation into a fully realized business.

That step came a decade and a half later, and was taken by a different pair of entrepreneurs: former New York chancellor Robert R. Livingston and engineer Robert Fulton, the latter of whom had been studying steam propulsion in Europe. In August 1807, twenty years after the *Perseverance*'s trip on the Delaware, Fulton's *North River Steamboat* made a successful trial run up the Hudson (known then as the "North River") from New York to Albany, covering one hundred fifty miles in the then-astonishingly brief span of thirty-two hours. In 1808, Fulton secured a transfer of Fitch's 1798 New York monopoly to himself and Livingston. In February 1809, despite ongoing murmurs questioning the originality of his design, Fulton received a patent for his steamboat, now called the *North River*.

Not surprisingly, competitors emerged, among them Aaron Ogden, a Revolutionary War veteran and New Jersey assemblyman, who began running a steam-powered ferry between Elizabethtown and New York City in 1812. Equally unsurprisingly, litigation with the Livingston-Fulton concern ensued, culminating in settlement and a license to Ogden to continue his ferry service. Meanwhile, in 1810, Georgia native Thomas Gibbons arrived in Elizabethtown, where he soon after acquired a private dock and entered into partnership with Ogden. But that partnership soured, its nadir occurring with the issuance of a dueling challenge from Gibbons to Ogden in 1816. This rencontre did not end in a dawn meeting on Weehawken Heights. It did, however, impel Gibbons to further provocation: in 1817, he began running his own small steam ferry, the *Stoudinger* (also known as the *Mouse*), between Elizabethtown and New York City. A year later, he acquired a larger steamboat, the *Bellona*, and hired the twenty-four-year-old Cornelius Vanderbilt to pilot it. Knowing that he was courting a lawsuit from Ogden, Gibbons sought legal advice, including from Aaron Burr, recently returned from a European sojourn following his acquittal of treason in the sensational trial of 1807.[15]

As Gibbons had anticipated, Ogden took the battle from the field of honor to the courts of law. In October 1818, Ogden brought a bill in equity in New York's Court of Chancery, where he prayed for an injunction against Gibbons "to restrain the defendant, his agents, &c., from using, employing, and navigating the said two steam-boats, or either of them, or any other steam-boat by him purchased or built . . . on the waters of this state lying between *Elizabeth-town*, or any place within the bounds of the township, and the city of *New-York*, &c."[16]

The chancellor immediately granted a preliminary injunction against Gibbons. Nearly a year later, in October 1819, the chancellor confirmed the injunction. Gibbons was prohibited from running his steamboats in "the whole of the waters in the bay of *New-York*, on the passage or route between the city of *New-York* and *Elizabeth-town Point*, or *Elizabeth-town*," not including the waters of Long Island Sound between Staten Island and the New Jersey coastline.[17]

The chancellor who issued the injunction halting Gibbons's steamboats was the renowned jurist James Kent. At this point in his career, Kent was a highly respected lawyer who had served three terms in the New York Assembly and delivered a widely cited set of law lectures at Columbia College. From

1798 to 1814, he had served on the New York Supreme Court of Judicature (the state's principal common law court), including ten years as chief justice. In 1814, four years before Ogden filed his bill, Kent was appointed chancellor of New York, putting him at the helm of the New York Court of Chancery, one of the leading state courts in the nation. In 1826, Kent published his four-volume *Commentaries on American Law*, which joined St. George Tucker's edition of Blackstone's *Commentaries* on the shelves of lawyers seeking to master the burgeoning field of American law.[18] One year after their publication, Kent's *Commentaries* edged out Tucker's *Blackstone* to become the most frequently cited American legal authority in the United States.[19]

Kent's opinion in *Ogden v. Gibbons* framed the conceptual architecture that accompanied the case all the way to the Supreme Court five years later. As had been the case in *The Brig Wilson*, when Chief Justice Marshall took possession of the steamboat litigation, he had the luxury of building upon a legal and intellectual foundation laid by another titan of the interbellum bench—there, Tucker of Virginia; here, Kent of New York. Unlike *The Brig Wilson*, however, the dialogue between the judges ended not in disagreement about the meaning of a phrase in a statute, but rather in clashing views as to whether a constitutional collision had taken place.

Kent began his opinion by listing the chain of deeds, licenses, and rights that underpinned the respective claims. The most complex was Ogden's, which required tracing back to John Fitch's 1787 grant, and then focused on the legislature's grant to Livingston and Fulton. Kent quickly began referring to the various parties by initials ("*R. R. L.*" and "*F.*" for Robert R. Livingston and Robert Fulton, respectively). By virtue of this complex lineage of deeds, tracing back to the New York legislature's grant of 1808, Ogden claimed "the exclusive right of navigating the waters of the state of *New-York*, by boats moved by steam or fire, between *New-York* and *Elizabethtown*." Ogden, who had recently begun running a new steamboat, the *Atalanta*, claimed that Gibbons's operation of the *Stoudinger* and the *Bellona* in those same waters of New York Harbor violated his exclusive right.[20]

In response to Ogden's claim, Gibbons asserted his own right to navigate his steamboats across the Hudson based on two grounds: a license from the representatives of Livingston and Fulton, and "a license to carry on the coasting trade, granted under the laws of the *United States*." The latter claim, that the *Stoudinger* and the *Bellona* were authorized by federal law to ply the waters of New York Harbor, was supported with concrete details. Gibbons averred that both ships were

> enrolled at *Perth Amboy*, in *New-Jersey* ... and licensed for one year,
> which license was renewed on the 20th of *October*, 1818, for one year, by
> the collector of the port of *Perth Amboy*, in the form prescribed by law, in
> pursuance of an act of congress, entitled, "an act for enrolling and li-
> censing ships and vessels to be employed in the coasting trade and fish-
> eries, and for regulating the same."[21]

Gibbons argued that the consequence of this federal license, derived from
a 1793 act of Congress, was that his ships "may be lawfully employed and
navigated in the coasting trade between parts of the same state, or of different
states, and cannot be excluded or restricted therein, by any law or grant of any
particular state, on any pretence to an exclusive right to navigate the waters of
any particular state by steam-boats, &c."[22]

The congressional act of 1793 on which Gibbons relied was titled "An Act
for Enrolling and Licensing Ships or Vessels to Be Employed in the Coasting
Trade and Fisheries, and for Regulating the Same."[23] The act set forth the procedures by which vessels would be authorized to engage in either the coasting
trade (that is, running between ports) or the fishing trade. The authorization
came in the form of a license, valid for one year, that was issued by the collector
of customs for the vessel's home district. Vessels of twenty tons or more were
also required to obtain a document called an "enrolment certificate." The 1793
licensing regime was a key component of the federal customs system; that
customs system was central to Treasury Secretary Alexander Hamilton's plan
for establishing the fiscal-military structure of the new nation.[24] Fees for the
licenses ranged from twenty-five cents (for vessels weighing less than twenty
tons) to one dollar (for those of more than one hundred tons).[25] Pursuant to the
act, vessels carrying their proper coasting or fishing papers, and only those vessels, would be "deemed ships or vessels of the United States, entitled to the
privileges of ships or vessels employed in the coasting trade or fisheries."[26]

According to Gibbons, the touch of federal authority endowed the vessels with
an affirmative right to engage in the coasting trade and shielded them from the
effect of state law, even state laws governing steamboats. Moreover, Gibbons's
argument suggested that the ships' activity did not have to be designated as interstate in order to be protected from state regulation. The coasting trade included
navigation "between parts of the same state, or of different states." A vessel carrying such a license was thus protected from a state's effort to restrict the vessel's
operations—for example, by granting a monopoly to a competitor.

Chancellor Kent was unpersuaded by Gibbons's efforts to cloak his ships in their federal coasting licenses. He therefore issued the injunction against Gibbons's steamboat enterprise.

Kent offered two related rationales for rejecting Gibbons's claims. First, the federal coasting statute did not invest Gibbons with the type of right that he claimed: "The act of congress referred to, never meant to determine the right of property, or the use or enjoyment of it, under the laws of the states." What, then, did the coasting statute do? "The license only gives to the vessel an *American* character, while the right of the individual procuring the license to use the vessel, as against another individual setting up a distinct and exclusive right, remains precisely as it did before," Kent wrote. "It is neither enlarged nor diminished by means of the license: the act of the collector does not decide the right of property."[27] A mere brush with an emanation of congressional power did not automatically convert the *Stoudinger* and *Bellona* into vessels of federal rights cloaked with immunity from state regulation. On the contrary: state law controlled. Even a "duly patented vehicle, or machine, or vessel, or medicine, or book" must be "held, used, and enjoyed, subject to the general laws of the land," Kent stated. By "general laws of the land," Kent meant local, or "police" laws, the traditional purview of the states, such as "laws establishing turnpike roads and toll bridges, or the exclusive right to a ferry, or laws for preventing and removing nuisances."[28]

Second, Kent held, because the federal license did not create a property right, it did not conflict with New York's monopoly grant to Ogden: "I do not perceive that this act confers any right incompatible with an exclusive right in *Livingston* and *Fulton* to navigate steam-boats upon the waters of this state." The federal coasting license, "which was to be obtained as a matter of course, and with as much facility as the flag of the *United States* could be procured and hoisted," was not "sufficient to interpose and annihilate the force and authority" of state law. Moreover, both laws could coexist without doing violence to each other, as demonstrated by the fact that the state had granted a monopoly to Livingston and Fulton (later transferred to Ogden) years after the enactment of the coasting statute. Consequently, Kent held, the "suggestion that the laws of the two governments are repugnant to each other" was "new, and without any foundation." In other words, "[t]here is no collision between the act of congress and the acts of this state, creating the steam-boat monopoly." Absent such a conflict, the Supremacy Clause of the Constitution was not triggered; consequently, there was no basis for striking down the state law.[29] In Kent's view, both the specific state grant and the overarching federal coasting statute could coexist. Ogden's monopoly was therefore valid, and the coasting license was largely irrelevant to the controversy.

Lest his audience mistake this endorsement of state regulatory power for a denial of federal authority, however, Kent—a Federalist of long standing—described when, in his view, the Supremacy Clause would require a state law to give way to federal law. If, for example, Ogden's New York monopoly was pitted against an act of Congress mandating that "all vessels, duly licensed, should be at liberty to navigate . . . bays, harbors, rivers and lakes within the several states, any law of the states, creating particular privileges . . . to the contrary notwithstanding," then "the only question that could arise in such a case, would be, whether the law was constitutional." If the federal law was constitutional, it would "overrule and set aside the state grant." That situation, Kent explained, would clearly present "a collision."[30]

In issuing the injunction against Gibbons, Kent sketched a theory of concurrent power, according to which both the states and Congress could regulate activities that fell within the constitutionally salient category of "commerce among the states." Notably, Kent did not attempt to parse whether steamboat navigation was properly categorized under the heading of "commerce." Nor did he spend much time discussing whether the specific navigation of Gibbons's steamboats took place within a single state or among several states. Instead, he began from the premise that the federal government possessed certain powers over commerce, that the states also held a body of related powers, and that those powers were certain to overlap. Kent took his task to be defining the contours of a dynamic relationship, not defining the static meaning of a term.

Indeed, in a previous case involving the Fulton-Livingston steamboat monopoly, Kent had taken a similar view of the Commerce Clause. In 1812, in his capacity as chief justice of the New York Supreme Court of Judicature, Kent sat on a panel of the Court for the Trial of Impeachments and Correction of Errors—the state's highest appeals court—and issued an opinion in *Livingston v. Van Ingen*, another case involving a dispute over steamboat navigation on the Hudson River. But *Van Ingen* differed from *Gibbons* in that the travel at issue was entirely within New York State, between New York City and Albany.[31] The principal issue in the case was whether Fulton's 1809 patent limited the state monopoly. But the wide-ranging argument touched on the scope of congressional power in general, including the power to regulate commerce among the states.

Thomas Addis Emmet, representing the Livingston-Fulton interests, argued that the apparent conflict between the New York grant and federal power was not in fact a collision, "which necessarily implies an absolute contradiction and repugnancy to the power given to congress," but merely an instance of the operation of "an accidental or occasional interference in the policy of a branch of the administration of the union." In short, Emmet contended, the dispute was really a natural outgrowth of the concurrent nature of commerce power in the federal union. The states, having long wielded an array of police powers governing the health, safety, and welfare of the people, also possessed the authority to regulate commerce.[32] In some cases, where those powers trenched on Congress's realm, the states would give way. But the conflict had to be proved, not simply gestured toward. "[I]t is not denied, that where there is an actual collision with the law of congress, the state law must yield. But this interference must be pointed out," Emmet argued.[33]

Kent adopted much of Emmet's argument in his opinion upholding the New York grant. He embraced the theory of concurrent state and federal power over commerce. Citing "the authority of Mr. Hamilton" in "the thirty-second number of the *Federalist*," Kent attempted to limn the boundary where state power ended and federal power began. Therefore,

> the states are under no other constitutional restriction, and are, consequently, left in possession of a vast field of commercial regulation; all the internal commerce of the state by land and water remains entirely, and I may say exclusively, within the scope of its original sovereignty. The congressional power relates to external not to internal commerce, and it is confined to the *regulation* of that commerce.[34]

Kent acknowledged that delineating between internal and external commerce was a difficult task, "for every regulation of the one will, directly, or indirectly, affect the other." He thus advised adhering to Hamilton's tripartite analysis: (1) Was there an express and exclusive grant of power to the federal government?; (2) Was the power expressly prohibited to the states?; or (3) Would the states' exercise of the power be "absolutely and totally contradictory and repugnant to one granted to the union"?[35]

The case did not involve either of the first sets of facts, Kent maintained. The federal power to regulate commerce "is not, in express terms, exclusive," and the grant to the Fulton-Livingston steamboat concern lay squarely within the "vast field of commercial regulation" possessed by New York. As for the third scenario, while Kent insisted that in cases of repugnancy "the laws of the union" must be supported, he adopted Hamilton's view that the conflict must be "immediate" and "constitutional" in terms of significance. But this case did not involve such repugnancy:

[W]hen there is no existing regulation which interferes with the grant, nor any pretence of a constitutional interdict, it would be most extraordinary for us to adjudge it void, on the mere contingency of a collision with some future exercise of congressional power. Such a doctrine is a monstrous heresy. It would go, in a great degree, to annihilate the legislative power of the states.[36]

In other words, an actual collision, not merely a potential one, was required in order to find that a state grant was repugnant to the laws of the union. Indeed, Kent added, he had difficulty envisioning an act of Congress under its commerce power that would present such an immediate, constitutional-level collision: "I can hardly conceive of such a case, because I do not, at present, perceive any power which congress can lawfully carry to that extent."[37]

Seven years later, when Kent heard *Ogden v. Gibbons* in his role as chancellor, he found that Gibbons had taken a cue from Kent's earlier *Van Ingen* decision. Gibbons argued that the federal coasting statute of 1793 created an actual, immediate collision with the state monopoly. But Kent was still not convinced. On Kent's view, the commerce power was robustly concurrent, shared between the states and the federal government, and almost always capable of being divided rather than allocated entirely to one level of government or another.

Gibbons appealed Kent's 1819 decision in *Ogden v. Gibbons* to the New York Court of Errors. In January 1820, the court affirmed the chancellor's injunction against Gibbons's operation of steamboats in New York Harbor. Justice Jonas Platt cited *Van Ingen* as binding precedent, despite differences in the facts: the bodies of water being navigated were not the same (up and down the Hudson River between New York City and Albany in *Van Ingen*, versus across the harbor to New Jersey in *Ogden*), and the federal acts under which the challengers claimed were also different (the patent power in *Van Ingen* versus the coasting statute in *Ogden*). The Court of Errors had little to add to Kent's analysis: the decision reprinted the entirety of the chancellor's opinion, followed by a two-and-a-half page opinion from Platt.[38]

The Gibbons-Ogden dispute worked its way through the New York courts between 1818 and 1820. Kent issued his chancery decision in October 1819, and the Court of Errors affirmed in January 1820. The timing of the steamboat case thus overlapped with the progress of the case of the brig *Wilson* through the federal courts: Tucker issued his district-court opinion in December 1819, and Marshall his circuit decision in May or June 1820. One note in the argument of the Gibbons-Ogden dispute in the Court of Errors resounded with *The*

Brig Wilson. In his argument in favor of upholding Kent's injunction, Ogden's attorney Josiah Ogden Hoffman, a former attorney general of New York, offered what he clearly viewed as a compelling illustration of the strength of a state's police powers, even in a zone in which federal law also operated: "Congress may give to authors and proprietors of books, an exclusive right of publication and sale. But would a state in which slaves exist, allow an author, though he had taken out a copy right, to vend a book exciting slaves to insurrection and murder? The patent right must be subject to such laws as a state may pass for its own security."[39]

According to Hoffman, the touch of the federal patent power could not by itself displace a state's authority to maintain its security. In contrast to *The Brig Wilson*, where federal power (the 1803 act of congress) reinforced state law (Virginia's 1793 bar on migration), here the state's police power and congressional authority were pitted against each other.

Hoffman's allusion to slavery, and the response from Gibbons's lawyer citing Congress's power over the slave trade, reflected the case's particular context in another way. Between February 1819 and March 1820, congressional debates were dominated by the issue of Missouri's admission to the Union, and the question whether slavery would be permitted or prohibited in the new state.[40]

The Steamboat Case in the Supreme Court

By the time *Gibbons* arrived at the Supreme Court in February 1824, it had accumulated an even denser and more complex history, including an abortive initial appearance on the Court's docket. Gibbons first took the appeal to the Court on a writ of error in October 1820, but the Court dismissed the case in March 1821 for lack of a final decree from the New York Court of Errors, which was required under Section 25 of the Judiciary Act of 1789.[41] The case was put off until the 1824 term.

In the meantime, Supreme Court justice Henry Brockholst Livingston—a cousin of Fulton's steamboat partner, Robert R. Livingston—died in March 1823, setting off a round of speculation and jockeying for the newly vacant seat on the Court. The norms of appointment at the time suggested that the post ought to go to another representative of the middle states, and preferably to another New Yorker. One leading candidate was Smith Thompson, secretary of the navy. Thompson had come to the Monroe Cabinet in 1818 from the chief justiceship of New York, which he had assumed upon Kent's appointment as chancellor. During his tenure as a state judge, Thompson served on the panel that heard *Livingston v. Van Ingen* in 1812; in that case, he joined Kent in upholding the New York monopoly grant to Livingston and Fulton.

Thompson's chief rival for the New York seat on the Court was the state's leading jurist, who, as we have seen, also had a long history with the steamboat litigation: Chancellor Kent. In the spring of 1823, while rumors eddied and the steamboat case was making its way back to the Court, Kent was the subject of a letter from Attorney General William Wirt to President James Monroe. Wirt had already been retained by Gibbons to argue in favor of the competing steamboat enterprise. Kent had upheld the New York monopoly not once but twice, in *Van Ingen* and *Ogden*. Kent's arguments thus formed the chief obstacle to Wirt's prevailing for his client. In addition, Thompson was Wirt's colleague in the Cabinet.

Nevertheless, on May 5, 1823, while Wirt was making one of his frequent trips to Baltimore for his nonofficial practice, he composed a letter to Monroe that he marked with the heading "private." In the letter, Wirt urged Monroe to appoint Kent to the vacant seat on the Court in the event that Thompson, who was rumored to be considering accepting the appointment, declined.[42] Wirt was candid: Kent's appointment might upset Republicans—Monroe's and Wirt's own party—in New York, as well as in their mutual home state of Virginia. But Wirt cautioned Monroe not to allow the pressure of "faction" to outweigh more profound imperatives. "The appointment of a judge of the supreme court is a *national* and not a *local* concern," he wrote.

> The importance of that court in the administration of the federal government begins to be generally understood, felt and acknowledged. The local irritations at some of their decisions in particular quarters (as in Virginia and Kentucky for instance) are greatly overbalanced by the general approbation with which those same decisions have been received throughout the Union. . . . The Constitution is the public property of the United States. They have a right to expect that the best means will be adopted to preserve it entire which can be no otherwise ensured but by organizing each department under it in such a manner as to enable it to perform its functions with the fullest effect.[43]

True, Wirt acknowledged, Kent was a Federalist. Therefore, "some of the fire-hot republicans and interested radicals who seize every handle for cavil may, in every quarter of the Union, harp a little for a time." But Kent was not a "federal partizan [sic]." Indeed, as the chancellor's record in the steamboat litigation demonstrated, he could be dogged in his defense of state power:

With regard to the great subject of state rights, which has produced so much excitement in Virginia and Kentucky, it happens that if he has any leaning it is in favor of state rights. This has been shewn by his decisions in the steam boat cases, where he has uniformly upheld the state laws of New-York against all the objections which could be raised of their repugnance to the Constitution and laws of the United States.[44]

Wirt's praise for Kent's intellect and integrity illustrates the esteem in which the chancellor's jurisprudence of concurrent power was held, even by his opponents of party and region. The letter also conveys the ferment of creative thinking about federalism that was taking place among leading jurists and lawyers in the early interbellum period. The steamboat trade unleashed not only a transportation revolution, but also a revolution in understandings of the federal-state relationship.

Despite Wirt's urging, however, Monroe did not appoint Kent to the Court. In September 1823, Thompson received a recess appointment to the justiceship, which was confirmed by the Senate three months later. Speaker of the House Henry Clay, who as a candidate in the election of 1824 was well aware of the presidential ambitions that had led Thompson to regard a justiceship as a fallback option, echoed Wirt's sentiments when he observed that Thompson joined the Court "in the place Chancellor Kent should have filled."[45]

The Arguments: Commerce and Concurrent Power

On February 4, 1824, the Court took up the case. Attorney General Wirt and Daniel Webster appeared on behalf of Gibbons, and Thomas Addis Emmet and Thomas Oakley represented Ogden.

As Wirt's correspondence urging President Monroe to appoint Chancellor Kent to the Court suggests, the attorney general was deeply invested in the politics—both partisan and constitutional—of the capital. At the time of *Gibbons*, Wirt was at the height of his powers: a fifty-one-year-old father of ten, the possessor of a demanding private legal practice, and a famed man of letters based on his *Old Bachelor* serial and his more sober, but equally quotable, *Life of Patrick Henry.*

Ever since his early adulthood, Wirt had displayed a zeal for trade, markets, and commerce, participation in which seemed to energize him. As he was embarking on his service as attorney general in 1817, he predicted to Francis Walker Gilmer that in ten years' time, "you will have discovered that we are not an agricultural people merely, for we shall have a fleet of thirty sail, and

William Wirt, by Charles Bird King, 1820. (Redwood Library
and Athenaeum, Newport, Rhode Island. Gift of Charles
Bird King.)

our commerce will cover every sea. The spirit of manufactures, too, will have
spread from the north to the south, and our country will be a pretty large
epitome of all the pursuits of human life."[46] In many of his attorney general's
opinions, Wirt depicted commerce among the states and with foreign nations
as a salutary American imperative, a necessary component of existence as a
nation. Congress's power over these types of commerce, then, served both to
encourage such intercourse and to remove barriers. Wirt's most compelling
arguments for a broad conception of the Commerce of the Union came, appropriately, in an argument before the Supreme Court.

As he prepared for the case, Wirt was in high spirits. He urged his dear
friend Dabney Carr, who was about to take a long-hoped-for seat on the Virginia Court of Appeals, to make the trip to Washington to watch what Wirt

promised would be a spectacular clash of orators: "Tomorrow begin my toils in the supreme court, and about tomorrow week will come on the great steam boat question from New York. Emmett [sic] and Oakley on one side, Webster and myself on the other. Come down and hear it." Of his co-counsel, Wirt wrote, "Webster is ambitious as Lucifer. He will not be outdone by any man, if it is within the compass of his power to avoid it. It will be a combat worth witnessing." Wirt planned on having several more days to prepare the case. "I have the last speech, and have yet to study the cause, but I know the facts and have only to weave the argument," he reported breezily to Carr.[47] Wirt soon discovered, however, that the justices had a different schedule in mind.

The other lawyers were equally illustrious. Representing Ogden were Thomas Addis Emmet and Thomas Oakley. Emmet had successfully represented the claimants under the New York grant in *Van Ingen*. He was an Irish émigré from "Rebel Cork" who had fled his home country to avoid prosecution for his membership in the revolutionary Society of United Irishmen. His younger brother, Robert Emmet, had been executed for high treason. In 1812, Emmet was named attorney general of New York State, a post he held for two years before returning to his busy private practice. His "winning Corkonian brogue" and his "great nervous energy and mental control" struck observers as "persuasive and convincing, rather than strictly eloquent, but eminently graceful in gesture and pose."[48] Emmet's co-counsel, Oakley, had also served as New York's attorney general and represented the state in Congress. Following *Gibbons*, he returned to Congress before becoming a judge of the newly established superior court of the city of New York.

Wirt's co-counsel, Webster, was famed for his oratorical skill and his darkly brooding genius, which complemented his political savvy. At the time of *Gibbons*, Webster was a Massachusetts (previously New Hampshire) congressman and chairman of the House Judiciary Committee. He had appeared before the Court in several important cases, including *McCulloch v. Maryland* and *Dartmouth College v. Woodward*. In *Dartmouth College*, Webster and Wirt were on opposing sides. In *McCulloch*, they served as co-counsel to the Second Bank of the United States.

The *Dartmouth College* case, argued from March 10 to 12, 1818, was the first time that Webster and Wirt met. They clearly took the measure of each other. Webster's peroration on behalf of his alma mater, ending with a famous emotional appeal—"It is, Sir, as I have said, a small college. And yet *there are those who love it!*"—drew the most plaudits from contemporaries.[49] But Webster found himself impressed with Attorney General Wirt's skills during the course

The "Black Dan" portrait: Daniel Webster, by Francis Alexander,
1835. (National Portrait Gallery, Smithsonian Institution;
bequest of Mrs. John Hay Whitney.)

of the trial. Perhaps Webster anticipated flowery declamation along the lines of Wirt's "Who Is Blennerhassett?" speech from the Burr trial eleven years earlier. The rhetorical flights of youth still stirred Wirt's courtroom performances. (Responding to Webster's peroration, Wirt invoked the spirit of the college's founder: "The Ghost of Wheelock was introduced exclaiming to Webster 'Et tu, Brute!' " reported one of Wirt's clients with glee.)[50] But now they were supplemented by a depth of experience and knowledge. In March 1818, Wirt was in his fourth month as attorney general. So far that year, he had already argued eight cases before the Court, all of them in February.[51] He was working past midnight and rising before five o'clock in the morning to prepare cases and review Cabinet business. "Wirt is a man of a good deal of ability. He is rather more of a lawyer than I expected," Webster admitted to a friend.[52]

A few months after *McCulloch* and *Dartmouth College* were decided in March 1819, and while the steamboat case was pending in the New York Court of Errors, Thomas Gibbons had written to Webster to retain him and Wirt as his lawyers in the event that he lost in state court and appealed to the Supreme Court. Gibbons's letter began with a description of the case, the issue of which he described as "the constitutionality of the Laws of the State of New York granting an exclusive right to Messrs. Livingston and Fulton to navigate the waters of the state of New York with steamboats." The case was "now under consideration in the Court of Errors." Gibbons was already strategizing about what action he would take next. "If that Court should decide against me and in favour of the law I shall carry it before the Supreme Court of the United States at Washington where I shall wish your services associated with Mr Wirt the Attorney General."[53]

Webster and Wirt agreed to represent Gibbons. Shortly before the case made its abruptly truncated first trip to the Supreme Court in March 1821, they each received a retainer in the amount of five hundred dollars, which Gibbons delivered via his business manager and steamboat captain, Cornelius Vanderbilt.[54] Following the oral arguments, but before the Court issued its decision, the two lawyers wrote jointly to Gibbons's son William, who was assisting his father, in which they politely but firmly requested an additional payment of one thousand dollars each, to which the Gibbonses agreed:

> Agreeably to your suggestion we have conferred together on the subject of fees, in the case Gibbons vs Ogden. We have recd, thro the hands of Mr Vanderbilt five hundred Dollars each; & we think that a thousand dollars more, for each of us, is not an unreasonable compensation, especially if success should attend our efforts to reverse the Judgment of the N York Court of Errors. You are doubtless sufficiently authorized to arrange this part of the business on behalf of the Plf in error.
> Yrs with regard
> W. Wirt   Danl. Webster.[55]

Arguments opened on Wednesday, February 4, and continued for four days, through Monday, February 9. (The case does not appear to have been called on February 6, and the Court was not in session on Sundays.) Webster, representing Gibbons, opened the contest. He was followed by Oakley and then Emmet, appearing on behalf of Ogden and the New York monopoly. Wirt, for Gibbons, rounded out the arguments.

Through their oratory, the lawyers presented an array of distinct approaches to the problem of fixing the boundary between the state's broad regulatory powers and the federal government's constitutionally defined realm of authority. They did not present written briefs, and their arguments—which enjoyed, and surely sometimes abused, the privilege of unlimited time—were not contemporaneously recorded. As the previous chapter discussed, the best evidence of what the attorneys actually said over those days in the Court's chamber in the basement of the Capitol comes from a patchwork of sources: the reports of Henry Wheaton, which were assembled after the fact; newspaper accounts; and occasional references in contemporary correspondence. Based on these sources, we know that the lawyers regarded their arguments as a combination of performance and rhetorical combat, benefiting not only their clients but their own reputations.[56]

Despite the stakes of argument, experienced members of the bar of the Court might find ways to be relatively comfortable in the chamber. The space was both grand and intimate. The vaulted masonry ceiling, a bravura element of design by architect Benjamin Henry Latrobe, domed over the semicircular chamber, which measured seventy-five feet wide and fifty feet deep. Red, lozenged carpeting covered the floors. The focal point of the courtroom was the bench—actually a row of mahogany desks, so closely fitted as to appear as one continuous burnished surface, set side by side in front of the east-facing windows. There were seven such desks from 1807 until 1837, when President Andrew Jackson, on his last day in office, signed legislation expanding the Court to nine seats.[57]

The attorney general, a regular attendee when the Court was in session, had a designated desk next to the bench, at the right hand of the justices, just outside the bar surrounding the bench. Also on the right, inside the bar, was a desk for the clerk and deputy clerk of the Court. On the justices' left were desks for the marshal, deputy marshal, and court reporter. In the well of the chamber were four green baize-topped counsel's tables. Red velvet settees sat between the lawyers' tables and the bar surrounding the justices' bench. The settees faced, and were nearly in front of, the counselors' desks. When the lawyers stood to deliver their multi-hour arguments, a spectator on the settee would have been within a few feet of the performance—seated and therefore looking up at the declaiming, gesturing, often perspiring orator. Former first lady Dolley Madison was a frequent attendee at arguments, often bringing with her "a train of ladies."[58] The lawyers often held objects during their speeches, sometimes brandishing books (Wirt) or holding a quill pen behind the back while nervously stripping it of barbs (Emmet). Glossy wooden benches for observers ranged along the outer perimeter of the room, forming the gallery to which the attorneys accused each other of playing, even while each of them constantly attended to the reactions from those precincts of the chamber.

A lawyer who had completed his own oratorical efforts might find time to catch up on correspondence while partially listening to his opponent's remarks. In February 1830, Wirt—at that point the former attorney general, and appearing before the Court in private practice—took up his pen to write to his fifteen-year-old daughter, Agnes, who was at home in Baltimore. The letter, headed "Hall of the Supreme Court—1/2 after 2'o'clock," began, "I have just finished my argument in the great Aster cause; to *my entire satisfaction*— and Mr. Webster is replying also to my entire satisfaction." As he was no longer the attorney general, Wirt was likely seated at one of the counsel's tables, and so nearly within arm's reach of his opponent, Webster. After reporting various items of news, Wirt concluded, "Webster is getting warm—I must stop to hear what he is in a rage about—and so good by my sweet little mouse."[59]

When the arguments in *Gibbons* commenced that Wednesday morning in February 1824, Chief Justice Marshall sat flanked by Johnson on his left and Washington on his right. Justice Thomas Todd sat on Washington's right, and Story to Todd's right. Justice Gabriel Duvall sat to the left of Johnson.[60] Justice Thompson, the newly appointed New Yorker, did not take part in the arguments or deliberations of *Gibbons* when it finally came before the Court in early 1824; his daughter had recently died, and he did not take his seat until the day after arguments finished.[61]

Daniel Webster later described the start of the proceedings, in typically self-referential mode:

> Chief Justice Marshall always wrote with a quill. He never adopted the barbarous invention of steel pens. That abomination had not been introduced. And always, before counsel began to argue, the Chief Justice would nib his pen; and then, when everything was ready, pulling up the sleeves of his gown, he would nod to the counsel who was to address him, as much as to say, "I am ready; now you may go on."[62]

And Webster, true to form, went on.

Many accounts of *Gibbons* suggest that Marshall and his colleagues greeted the steamboat case with a blank precedent book. The case was the first time the Supreme Court interpreted the commerce power, so the justices must have come to it empty-handed—and, as a result, the decision they produced was an entirely novel piece of handiwork. Or so the story goes. This picture emerges from a series of lectures titled "The Commerce Clause" given by then-professor Felix Frankfurter in 1936, which were published in book form the following year:

> Marshall had, as it were, the duty of creation to a degree greater than falls to the lot of even most great judges. When he was called upon to apply the commerce clause, he had available no fund of mature or coherent speculation regarding its implications. . . . The influential early commentators on the Constitution—*The Federalist* and Tucker's *Blackstone*—shed most flickering and ambiguous light on the reach of the commerce clause. Nor had lower court decisions built a coral reef of doctrine, although two of the Justices on circuit, William Johnson and Bushrod Washington, had indulged in suggestive observations regarding the interaction of state and national powers. And so, when first confronted with the commerce clause, the Supreme Court had to evolve doctrines without substantial guidance or restriction by previous discussion and analysis.[63]

But such an approach is similar to asking, "Why did it take the Court so long to hear a Commerce Clause case?" It reads the history of the doctrine backwards. Marshall took up his quill with the experience of having decided *The Brig Wilson*, and as we have seen, Johnson and Washington had also had occasion during their circuit duties to rule on the scope of the commerce power. These efforts were more than "suggestive observations." They were, in fact, utterances with the force of law.

When Webster, Oakley, Emmet, and Wirt commenced their speeches on February 4, they launched them forth within an existing legal and conceptual framework. As soon as the arguments began, that framework began to change. The match was not merely one between debaters deploying tricks and winning points. It was a contest that sought to harness abstract ideas and give them meaning by applying them to a specific set of facts. In the end, Marshall and his colleagues had to decide the narrow but important question of how many companies could run steamboats between New York City and Elizabethtown. But in order to reach a conclusion on that cause of action, the justices would listen to arguments about the nature of federal relationships that would stretch all the way to the edge of credulity while staying just inside that boundary. The lawyers were well aware that this was their task. Not to push would be to fail in zealous advocacy. But not to attend to the available portents—the judges' remarks, the hints from precedent—would be to fail to grasp the realist necessities of strategy. The imperatives that propelled the lawyers also yield evidence of the scope of possible meaning at the time.

Webster's Exclusive Federal Power

Over the course of the four days, the lawyers' greatest creativity came in their efforts to map the boundaries of federal and state power, and to clarify where the border between the two lay. Four competing approaches emerged:

(1) federal power over commerce among the states was exclusive, and states could not regulate any activity that amounted to commerce, even in the absence of federal regulation (the strong exclusive-power view);

(2) federal power over commerce among the states was supreme but not necessarily exclusive, and states could not regulate any activity that amounted to commerce if such regulation conflicted with actual federal regulation (the collision view);

(3) federal power over commerce among the states was exclusive, but states could regulate other types of commercial activity under their police powers (the police-power view);

(4) federal power over commerce among the states was neither exclusive nor supreme, and states were free to regulate interstate commerce as well (the concurrent-power view).

The first approach, the strong exclusive power view, formed the core of Webster's argument. It was adopted by Johnson in his concurring opinion. Webster began by reminding his audience that Connecticut and New Jersey had passed legislation retaliating against New York's monopoly grant to Livingston and Fulton. Under the terms of the New York grant, a steamboat that traveled between Elizabethtown and New York without a license from Livingston and Fulton was susceptible to forfeiture to Livingston and Fulton's representatives. New Jersey, in response, had created a cause of action for costs and treble damages that could be brought by New Jersey plaintiffs against representatives of Livingston and Fulton who attempted to carry out the forfeiture provision against that New Jersey citizen. Connecticut, meanwhile, had passed a law prohibiting any vessel with a New York license from entering its waters.[64]

All these acts, Webster contended, were beyond the power of the state leg-islatures because they interfered with rights under the laws of the United States. As Henry Wheaton paraphrased the argument in the ninth volume of his reports, "He [Webster] should contend, that the power of Congress to regu-late commerce, was complete and entire, and, to a certain extent, necessarily exclusive; that the acts in question were regulations of commerce, in a most important particular; and affecting it in those respects, in which it was under the exclusive authority of Congress."[65]

Webster appeared to hedge on the scope of this exclusive power, stating this proposition "guardedly." He did not intend to suggest that "*all* regulations, which might, in their operation, affect commerce, were exclusively in the power of Congress; but that *such power* as had been exercised in this case, did not remain with the States."[66] Nevertheless, Webster was making a bold state-ment. To establish a steamboat monopoly was to regulate commerce. The au-thority to regulate commerce was "complete and entire" in Congress. That authority extended to both "foreign and domestic trade."[67] Therefore, New York's grant to Ogden of a monopoly was invalid.

At this point in his argument, Webster had not yet mentioned the federal coasting statute of 1793—the source of the putative conflict between state and federal law. Rather, in his conception, the power that New York had exercised in granting the monopoly was itself beyond New York's capacity, regardless of Congress's action. Even if Congress did not act to regulate commerce, the state had to stay out of that domain. Beginning with the New York law and as-sessing whether it was a valid exercise of the state's powers, irrespective of federal action in the domain, was tantamount to an endorsement of the exclu-sive-power thesis. Indeed, a power could be held exclusively by Congress even if that exclusivity was neither explicit in Article I of the Constitution nor im-plied from a textual prohibition on the states. "Some powers are holden to be exclusive in Congress . . . from the nature of the powers themselves," Webster maintained.[68]

When Webster confronted arguments for concurrent power over com-merce—shared between the states and Congress—his belief in federal exclu-sivity became evident. The history and structure of the Constitution demonstrated that the commerce power had been "transfer[red] . . . from the several States to a general government." The very nature of the power required exclusivity. From the founding onward, "the commerce of the States was to be an *unit*; and the system by which it was to exist and be governed, must neces-sarily be complete, entire, and uniform."[69] The commerce of the states was a "unit," and so also was the power to regulate that commerce. The unitary power to oversee the unitary system lay entirely with the general government.

Moreover, attempts at concurrent power would end in "confusion" and "perpetual hostility."[70] Webster professed not even to understand what such an approach would mean: "[C]an more than one power, in cases of this sort, give the rule, establish the system, or exercise the control?" No, he answered. In an argument that hearkened back to late-eighteenth-century warnings against an *imperium in imperio*, or a government within a government, Webster in effect argued that multiple controlling powers could not exist within a single polity: "A power in the States to do any thing, and every thing, in regard to commerce, till Congress shall undo it, would suppose a state of things, at least as bad as that which existed before the present constitution. It is the true wisdom of these governments to keep their action as distinct as possible."[71]

And what of the vast array of state acts that looked as though they regulated commerce—"pilot laws, the health laws, or quarantine laws"? Ogden's lawyers cited these laws to support their contention that the commerce power was divided between the states and the federal government, Webster noted. If the domain of commerce was thus shared, then New York could validly regulate in that domain, and so it could issue the monopoly to Ogden.

But such arguments rested on a misapprehension of these laws, Webster insisted. Such acts were not properly deemed "commercial regulations." This was not because they touched purely internal activity, as later doctrine might suggest. Webster was clear on this point: the difference was not where the regulation was aimed, or where its effects were felt, but the nature of the regulation itself. As Wheaton reported, "The truth was, he thought, that all these things were, in their general character, rather regulations of police than of commerce, in the constitutional understanding of that term." For Webster, the universe of laws was divided into two categories: commerce and police. Acts governing "roads, and bridges, and ferries" clearly "affect commerce and intercourse," but they lacked "that importance and elevation, as to be deemed *commercial regulations*." So, too, with quarantine laws, which were "in their nature, *health laws*."[72] Laws that lacked importance and elevation, laws that were health laws: these were separate categories from the special realm of the Commerce of the Union. "Commerce" and "police" were separate boxes, not points on a spectrum.

At least as glossed by Wheaton, who generally reprinted the arguments from versions that the lawyers delivered to him afterward, Webster's argument canvassed all four of the approaches to the relationship between federal and state regulation.[73] The bulk of the argument hovered between the strong exclusive power view and the police power view. He briefly discussed the inter-mediate, collision-based approach.[74] And he rejected the concurrent power approach altogether.

As when the steamboat case was before the state courts four years earlier, the issue of slavery surfaced in the lawyers' arguments. Webster noted that in the New York proceedings, "no small reliance was placed on the law of that State prohibiting the importation of slaves, as an example of a commercial regulation, enacted by State authority." The lawyers for Ogden had contended that if the state could ban the importation of slaves, which it had, then it clearly possessed the power to oversee commerce. (Their claim assumed that the trade in enslaved people was appropriately categorized as "commerce," a premise to which the Supreme Court returned in the 1830s and 1840s, as later chapters will discuss.) Counsel for Gibbons had countered with a species of preemption argument. If Congress expressly authorized the slave trade, no single state would have the power to prohibit the importation of enslaved persons.[75] What the states could and could not do in the realm of commerce depended at least in part on whether Congress had chosen to act in the same area.

Now, before the Supreme Court, Webster refrained from stating definitively on which side of the police-commerce line the steamboat monopoly fell. More significantly, Webster declined to state his view on the constitutionality of New York's ban on the importation of enslaved people into the state. "That law may or may not be constitutional and valid," he observed. "It has been referred to generally, but its particular provisions have not been stated. When they are more clearly seen, its character may be better determined." Such was the ex-tent of his comment.[76]

The statement was an odd one. Congress had not acted to authorize the inter-state slave trade. Nor, to the regret of many, had it banned it. The issue of Con-gress's power to ban the interstate slave trade was a recurrent and controversial one throughout the interbellum era.[77] With his obscure statement, Webster ap-peared to go out of his way to raise doubts about the constitutionality of New York's bar on the importation of slaves into the state. It was the opposite ap-proach from that of Chief Justice Marshall in *The Brig Wilson*, when Marshall was confronted with Virginia's ban on the migration of free Black people into that state. As Marshall had written to Story in September 1823, he might have addressed the Virginia law's constitutionality, but "it was not absolutely neces-sary, &, as I am not fond of butting against a wall in sport, I escaped on the construction of the act."[78] Webster, in contrast, was openly, and unnecessarily, speculating from the well of the Court's chamber about the constitutionality of a statute that was not even at issue in *Gibbons*.

But there was a difference between *The Brig Wilson* and *Gibbons*. While the result that Marshall reached in *The Brig Wilson* depended on the fact that the individuals who had debarked at Norfolk were specified in the record as "free persons of colour," the hypotheticals being offered four years later in *Gibbons* concerned the movement of persons who were held in bondage. As a host of cases over the coming decades would illustrate, the movement of African American people across state lines increasingly implicated the supremacy of federal law. By 1850, if not before, Congress and the Court placed their power firmly behind enforcement of state regimes of slavery. This effort, manifested through case law as well as statutes, maintained the additive mode of federalism that informed *The Brig Wilson*. But the valence of the interlocking federal and state laws had shifted and solidified.

The Case for the New York Monopoly

In order for Ogden to prevail in his claim of a valid monopoly over steamboat travel in New York Harbor, he and his lawyers had both to rebut Webster's exclusive-power theory and to fend off the argument that the state law collided with some valid federal law.

Both Oakley and Emmet resisted Webster's characterization of concurrent power as impossible and undesirable. Oakley's argument sounded themes of state sovereignty, citing the Tenth Amendment, which he interpreted to mean that in order for the national government to exercise a power, that power must be "expressly granted."[79] Oakley also focused on the distinction between commerce among the states and internal commerce, "that which is wholly carried on within the limits of a State."[80] Congress's commerce power, he maintained, could not reach internal commerce, even if that activity had some effect on trade with other states. The vast powers of the state legislature, in contrast, compassed any trade, whether internal or external, including "turnpike roads, toll bridges, exclusive rights to run stage wagons, auction licenses, licenses to retailers, and to hawkers and pedlers [*sic*], ferries over navigable rivers and lakes, and all exclusive rights to carry goods and passengers, by land or water." The New York monopoly was therefore valid, "considered either as a regulation of intercourse and trade among the several States, or as a regulation of the internal navigation of the State."[81]

Oakley characterized his view as one based on concurrent power, but it might more accurately be seen as endorsing not shared authority but state authority. "The States no where derive any powers from the constitution," Oakley maintained. "All its provisions are in restraint of their authority." For Oakley, the Union was an entity limited in scope that did not disturb "the original inherent power of the State."[82] The federal system established in 1789 postdated this power, and its array of enumerated federal powers were therefore subordinate to it. As part of this original inherent power, a state might regulate commerce. There was, Oakley insisted, "no necessary repugnancy between the acts of the two governments under this power." On the contrary, "a great variety of regulations" might "operate together, without direct interference."[83]

Emmet's argument in favor of the New York grant offered a more robust theory of concurrent power that was qualitatively different from Oakley's reliance on the original inherent powers of the states. Emmet began with a precise definition:

> The expression, *concurrent powers*, is objected to, as if it implied equality in the rights vested in Congress and the States. It is only a verbal criticism, that it would be more correct if the term used was *co-ordinate*. The term, concurrent, is adopted by the *Federalist*, and has constantly been used to express those powers. It is always understood, when so applied, that the exercise by the States must be subordinate, and never can be in collision with that by Congress.[84]

Absent such a collision, states were free to regulate navigation and trade within their borders, as well as non-commerce activities, such as transportation of passengers, that reached beyond the state. Moreover, Emmet expressed impatience with the justifications offered by Webster and others who supported exclusive federal power. He suggested that they were more poetical than legal: "[T]here is no grant in the constitution giving the navigable waters peculiarly to the Federal government, and not to the States within which they may be." Nor, contra his opponents, could the power over navigation be "traced to any grant." Rather, he noted satirically, it seemed to derive from "some mystical consequence of the Union itself."[85]

Finally, Emmet offered what Oakley had not attempted: a discussion of how concurrent power might work in practice. Emmet acknowledged that such a system might be difficult to comprehend; no less an authority than Judge Tucker, in his *Blackstone*, had stated that the commerce power was "not susceptible of a concurrent exercise."[86] But Emmet thought otherwise, citing

Kent's opinion in *Livingston v. Van Ingen* for the proposition that concurrent power was "the only safe and practicable rule of conduct, and the true constitutional rule, arising from the federal system."[87]

To be sure, Emmet admitted, the contours of shared power over commerce were difficult to define ex ante. But he offered examples. One was a proposal that Madison had made in 1785, prior to the Constitutional Convention. The plan would have granted states the power to ban imports of certain types of goods, but it would also have prohibited the states from imposing duties on imports. States would thus have been able to outlaw specific imports but not to tax imports generally. In this distinction, "it was clearly contemplated, that the individual States should at least retain the power of *absolutely prohibiting* the importation of any article they thought fit, within their own respective limits." Moreover, Emmet contended, the Constitution had preserved this distinction: the states are "qualifiedly restrained from laying imposts or duties on exports or imports, but not from entirely prohibiting their exportation or importation."[88] That arrangement, he suggested, amounted to concurrent power in action: concurrent power still obtained in a system that permitted Congress to override the state's prohibitory legislation, as long as the state law was "valid until Congress shall have made regulations inconsistent" with the state law.[89]

Indeed, Emmet argued, a canvass of state laws would reveal that "they have always exercised the power of making very material regulations respecting commerce." In Emmet's view, this "immense mass of State laws" were regulations of *commerce*, not exercise of police power. Here was another point on which Emmet's view differed from Webster's; indeed, as we have seen, Webster had temporized on this point with respect to slavery. If the power of Congress was determined to be exclusive, the necessary result would be "declaring to be unconstitutional, an appalling body of State legislation."[90]

Chief among this immense mass of state laws that would be disrupted should the Court adopt exclusivity were "the laws respecting slaves." Emmet cited state laws restricting trade in imported slaves dating back to the 1780s. He also pointed to Congress's 1803 Act Preventing the Importation of Certain Persons into Certain States, at issue in *The Brig Wilson*, as evidence that Congress had long "recognised and acted on the power of the States to prohibit this trade." Moreover, he contended, the 1803 act was based on Congress's power over commerce—just as Tucker and Marshall had held in *The Brig Wilson*. Thus, Emmet argued, the Constitution contemplated that both Congress and the states would have power over the trade in enslaved human beings. The power was asymmetrical, however: Emmet noted that states were constitutionally permitted to legislate on the question "unless Congress should prohibit the trade."[91]

Emmet's theory of concurrent power was far more theoretically rich than Oakley's vision of the Union as a compact of the states. It was also truly a theory of *concurrent* power, insofar as it allocated power over a single subject—commerce—to both Congress and the states. Both levels of government would share regulatory authority over commerce, and they would have to negotiate the scope of their respective zones. The division was not self-executing; one could not simply read Article I to understand where the lines of concurrence lay. Norms, practice, and judicial intervention would be required. In contrast to the delineation that Kent and Webster made between "commerce" and "police," Emmet proposed a system more functional than categorical. In this way, Emmet's concurrent power was conceptually distinct from states' rights arguments. Emmet's arguments suggest that concurrent-power theory had real content and was different in important ways from compact theory's focus on state sovereignty and the chronological and legal priority of the states. Many aspects of concurrent-power theory in *Gibbons*—as well as some of its most vexing challenges—could be traced back to *The Brig Wilson*.

The Attorney General's Middle Path

It fell to Wirt to complete the *Gibbons* tetralogy. The attorney general "rose at two o'clock on Saturday, February 7 to unravel the arguments of his opponents," one newspaper reported.[92] The reports do not indicate whether Wirt rose from the attorney general's desk or from one of the counsel's tables.

Wirt's speech that day lasted for two hours, and he then spoke for four more hours on Monday. The Richmond *Enquirer* reported with pride on its adopted son, lauding Wirt's argument as "the finest effort of human genius . . . ever exhibited in a court of justice," a "powerful and splendid effusion, grand, tender, picturesque, and pathetic":

> The manner was lofty and touching—the fall of his voice toward the conclusion, was truly thrilling and affecting—and I never witnessed such an effect from any burst of eloquence—every face was filled with the fine transport and prophetic fury of the orator, and all united in applauding the peroration, as affording for matter, diction, manner, happy application and striking effect, the most powerful display of real oratory that they ever witnessed.[93]

A New York paper whose reporter had an eye for detail noted that Wirt's efforts at picking apart "the knotty points" of Oakley's argument "literally caused the attorney general to perspire freely. The hall was crowded, and in the heat of the discussion, large drops of sweat started from his forehead and ran down his face."[94]

Wirt's argument emphasized the epochal nature of the dispute, leaving his audience in no doubt of the stakes. *Gibbons* was the first case in which the Court had explicitly taken up the question of the scope of the commerce power. The case also raised related issues of concurrent power that had lain just beneath the surface of many other controversies. The attorneys for Ogden made the affirmative argument that regulations governing the steamboat trade were properly understood as exercises of the police power that governed health, safety, and welfare, and were therefore entirely within the state's purview. On this view, the case did not raise any issue associated with the federal commerce power; rather, the source of the regulatory power in dispute was the qualitatively distinct police power, which everyone understood resided with the states.

Wirt eschewed these category-driven arguments in favor of a more dramatic line of rhetoric: the prospect of war among the states. Wirt capitalized on this scene of strife to paint a picture of destruction. As Webster had noted, New York, New Jersey, and Connecticut were already locked in a cycle of legislation and retaliation. New York had passed a law requiring a license from the state for all steamboats navigating the waters in or around the state. Connecticut had responded by passing a similar law. New Jersey, perhaps feeling threatened by these unneighborly actions, had passed an "act of retortion" against New York, pursuant to which any New Jersey citizen who was restrained under the New York law from operating a steamboat between the two states would have a cause of action for damages in the New Jersey courts, with treble costs against the party who so restrained him.[95] Wirt capitalized on this scene of strife to paint a picture of destruction. The conflict would not only pit the states against the federal government, as had been the case in the Fairfax land disputes. It would lead to war among the states themselves—that is, in Wirt's view, civil war.[96] "[S]ir, if you do not interpose your friendly hand, and extirpate the seeds of anarchy which New York has sown, you *will* have civil war," Wirt exhorted Marshall.[97]

How could such a conflict be avoided? Nine years earlier, in *Hunter v. Martin*, Judge William H. Cabell of the Virginia Court of Appeals had insisted that the Constitution had established "no umpire" to superintend disputes among

different levels of government. Wirt had disagreed then, when he had appeared before the Virginia high court among the phalanx of the state's leading
lawyers, even though Cabell was his brother-in-law and close friend. Now Wirt
elaborated on his earlier argument: "Here are three States almost on the eve of
war. It is the high province of this Court to interpose its benign and mediato-
rial influence. The framers of our admirable Constitution . . . establish[ed] this
guardian tribunal, to harmonize the jarring elements in our system."[98]

The Constitution has given us an umpire, Wirt argued: the Supreme Court.

In addition to his structural argument that the Court was the necessary
hinge of the multilayered federal system, Wirt provided a refinement of Webster's argument from a few days earlier. He contended that one need not believe that the federal commerce power was exclusive in order to conclude that
Gibbons's *Stoudinger* and *Bellona* could lawfully operate in New York waters.
Some commercial powers were exclusive, and others were not. But even assuming that the states retained some concurrent power to regulate commerce,
they could not do so in a way that obstructed the exercise of congressional
power. "[W]here Congress has legislated concerning a subject, on which it is
authorized to act, all State legislation which interferes with it, is absolutely
void," Wirt maintained.[99] Three months later, carrying out another part of his
remit as attorney general, Wirt went even further. In an official opinion, Wirt
stated that the South Carolina Police Bill unconstitutionally interfered with
Congress's exclusive authority over both interstate and foreign commerce.[100]

In his *Gibbons* argument, however, Wirt offered a mediating solution between Webster's flirtation with exclusivity and Oakley's version of concurrent
power. In so doing, Wirt combined the second and third of the approaches to
the federal-state relationship sketched above. Citing both Hamilton's *Federalist*
No. 32 and his own close friend Tucker's *Blackstone*, Wirt suggested a different
formulation. Perhaps, he suggested, the field of commerce was itself so broad
that it comprised two domains: one that was exclusively allocated to Congress,
and another that belonged to the states in their capacity as guardians of the
public welfare.

> [I]f these police regulations of the States are to be considered as a part of
> the immense mass of commercial powers, is not the subject susceptible
> of division, and may not some portions of it be exclusively vested in Con-
> gress? It was viewing the subject in this light, that induced his learned
> associate to assume the position which had been misconceived on the
> other side. This proposition was, not that all the commercial powers
> are exclusive, but that those powers being separated, there are some

which are exclusive in their nature; and among them, is that power which concerns navigation, and which prescribes the vehicles in which commerce shall be carried on.[101]

With this synthesis, Wirt clarified Webster's argument as well as providing a framework that avoided an all-or-nothing choice between the commerce/police and federal/state dichotomies.

Wirt also offered a useful interpretive avenue to the Court: here, the distinction between the exclusive and concurrent species of power was immaterial because the New York grant to Ogden clearly interfered with Gibbons's federal coasting license. "To say that Congress shall regulate it, and yet to say that the States shall alter these regulations at pleasure, or disregard them altogether, would be to say, in the same breath, that Congress shall regulate it, and shall not regulate it; to give the power with one hand, and to take it back with the other."[102] The Constitution created the special "national powers" listed in Article I, and the "whole United States" was their "theatre of action."[103] The powers were therefore not simply the negative space left over by the state police powers, but rather an entirely different type of tool to be used by the people of the United States. "The whole subject," Wirt maintained, "is regulated by the general commercial law" issued by Congress.[104]

Finally, Wirt offered a linguistic and textual flourish, refashioning a favorite term of his opponents into a new definition. When *Gibbons* and *Van Ingen* were making their way through the New York courts, the advocates for the monopoly continually offered a litany of state commercial regulations in order to demonstrate New York's long history of regulating commerce. These activities were invariably grouped under the heading of "intercourse." The usage made its way into Kent's opinions. For example, in *Van Ingen*, Kent itemized "the code of our statute laws," including "our Sunday laws, our rights of ferriage over navigable rivers and lakes, our auction licenses, our licenses to retail spirituous liquors," and others. He asked, "[W]hat are all these provisions but regulations of internal commerce, affecting as well the intercourse between citizens of this and other states, as between our own citizens?"[105]

Just before closing his argument before the Court, Wirt borrowed Kent's term but reoriented it. "Intercourse" was not the stuff of workaday state law. It was synonymous with commerce, in the constitutional sense:

> That the regulation of commerce and navigation, includes the authority
> of regulating passenger vessels as well as others, would appear from the
> most approved definitions of the term *commerce*. It always implies inter-

communication and intercourse. This is the sense in which the constitution uses it; and the great national object was, to regulate the terms on which intercourse between foreigners and this country, and between the different States of the Union, should be carried on.[106]

Meaning was being created here. To be sure, commentators had used "commerce" and "intercourse" synonymously for decades. Samuel Johnson's *Dictionary*, first published in 1755, had defined commerce as "intercourse; exchange of one thing for another; interchange of any thing; trade; traffick."[107] Beginning in 1790, Congress had passed a series of Trade and Intercourse Acts that aimed to prohibit the sale of Native nations' lands to U.S. states or citizens. The general concepts of "commerce," "trade," and "intercourse" had long been related.

What was new in 1824, however, was Wirt's repurposing of the word "intercourse" in a way that elevated it and gave it special constitutional salience. A few days earlier, "intercourse" had not had this meaning. The Commerce of the Union was something distinct from the quotidian buying and selling that went on every day within America's busy marketplaces. That was commerce *in* the Union. But this commerce was constitutive *of* the Union. The Union depended on this unique mode of exchange, transportation, and communication. Without the Commerce of the Union, protected and encouraged by Congress, the Union might crumble into acts of retortion and civil war.

The audience in the courtroom seems to have perceived that a legal and conceptual change had occurred. Henry Seawell, a lawyer and state legislator from North Carolina who was present in the courtroom, offered the following waggish commentary:

> [A]ccording to the construction now contended for, and what is more than probable will be supported by the Supreme Court, the States can do nothing, [that] is not in the power of Congress to *regulate*; and there is scarcely anything they can act upon at all—the trade or commerce, being subject to the regulation of Congress, is supposed to draw after it almost all power of regulation, and according to a definition given to the word "commerce" by the Attorney-General that it means "*intercourse*." I shall soon expect to learn that our fornication laws are unconstitutional.[108]

Indeed, when Marshall issued his opinion for the Court a few weeks later, on March 2, 1824, Seawell's quip proved accurate: "Commerce, undoubtedly, is traffic, but it is something more: it is intercourse. It describes the commercial intercourse between nations, and parts of nations, in all its branches, and is regulated by prescribing rules for carrying on that intercourse."[109] In February, asserting that commerce was intercourse was a lawyer's gambit. In March, commerce had become intercourse, as a matter of law.

The rhetorical climax of the *Gibbons* argument came at the end of Wirt's speech on Monday, February 9. The finale was a classic Wirt flourish: a learned turn of phrase applied with humor, even while pointedly aimed at an opponent. At the culmination of Ogden's attorneys' case on Saturday afternoon, Emmet had closed his remarks with a peroration out of the rhetoric books. As the newspapers reported it, he delivered an encomium to the state that had licensed the original steamboat monopoly, under which Ogden was now claiming:

> The state of N[ew] York by its liberality and munificence, generously seconding the active exertions of Messrs. Fulton and Livingston, has called into existence one of the greatest and most useful inventions of modern times—that of navigation by steam. . . . Its benefits, and the signal services of its author, were not confined to New-York: They had extended to every part of the Union. The waters of the Ohio, of the Mississippi, of the Lakes, nay more, of the Ocean itself, bear on their bosoms this trophy of genius. . . . They were the means of speeding the intercourse between different states, affording commercial facilities, and strengthening the bands of the Union.[110]

New York's generosity and foresight had given the steamboat not only to the United States, but to the world. The ties of commerce and affiliation that followed were consequences of this virtuous action by the state. Emmet's language soared to its conclusion:

> New-York might proudly lift her head, and survey the blessings, which her munificence had scattered over the whole earth. Appropriating to herself the language of Æneas, she might very properly exclaim,
>   "Quæ regio in terris nostri non plena laboris."[111]

Many of Emmet's listeners would have recognized the quotation from Virgil's *Aeneid*. The full version reads:

> constitit et lacrimans, "quis iam locus," inquit, "Achate, quae regio in terris nostri non plena laboris?"

Or, in English,

He stopped and weeping cried: "Is there any place, Achates, any land on earth not full of our sorrow?"[112]

Thanks to his boyhood lessons from the Reverend Hunt of Montgomery County, Maryland, Wirt knew his Latin. Now, rising to address the Court, the ladies, and the press, he deployed it—against Emmet and, indirectly, against any other members of the bar who attempted to compete with his own command of language. Wirt laid out his argument for the necessity of a national commerce power as a bulwark against the naked animosity that New York, New Jersey, and Connecticut had displayed toward each other.

Then Wirt took Emmet's invitation to return to the classics. He observed "that his learned friend had eloquently personified the State of New York casting her eyes over the ocean, witnessing everywhere this triumph of her genius, and exclaiming in the language of Æneas." Wirt, however, begged to correct Emmet's translation:

[I]t was not in the moment of triumph, nor with the feelings of triumph, that Æneas uttered that exclamation. It was when, with his faithful Achates by his side, he was surveying the works of art with which the palace of Carthage was adorned, and his attention had been caught by a representation of the battles of Troy. . . . The whole extent of his misfortunes, the loss and desolation of his friends, the fall of his beloved country, rushed upon his recollection.[113]

The passage from Virgil recounted the aftermath of sadness and destruction, not a moment of victorious celebration. Emmet had unwittingly helped Wirt make his case. Wirt's conclusion was "remarkable," reported a correspondent for the *Richmond Enquirer*, because the attorney general "turn[ed] this quotation upon his adversary, and terminat[ed] his speech with the same line, and with an exactly opposite effect."[114] Upholding the New York steamboat monopoly would allow the state to look out across the waters of the nation and survey not the fruits of her labors, but rather the "loss and desolation" of her fellow states and, perhaps, the fall of her country: "The war of legislation which has already commenced, will, according to its usual course, become a war of blows. Your country will be shaken with civil strife. Your republican institutions will perish in the conflict. Your constitution will fall. The last hope of nations will be gone."

Wirt therefore urged the Court to prevent this disastrous result. All it had to do, Wirt said, was "interpose [its] friendly hand."[115]

The Court Decides: Commerce, Collision, and Supremacy

Less than a month later, on March 2, 1824, the Court made a friendly inter-position on behalf of national commerce. The "sole question" in the case, as Marshall framed it, was "[C]an a State regulate commerce with foreign nations and among the States, while Congress is regulating it?"

In his opinion for the Court, Marshall briefly entertained Webster's sugges-tion that federal power over commerce was exclusive. In a pair of delphic para-graphs that would haunt American constitutional law for three decades, Marshall aired his thoughts:

> It has been contended by the counsel for the appellant, that, as the word "to regulate" implies in its nature, full power over the thing to be regu-lated, it excludes, necessarily, the action of all others that would perform the same operation on the same thing. That regulation is designed for the entire result, applying to those parts which remain as they were, as well as to those which are altered. It produces a uniform whole, which is as much disturbed and deranged by changing what the regulating power designs to leave untouched, as that on which it has operated.
>
> There is great force in this argument, and the Court is not satisfied that it has been refuted.[116]

Justice Johnson, concurring, fully endorsed this proposition, which had un-derpinned his circuit-court decision in *Elkison v. Deliesseline* one year before. "[T]he language which grants the power as to one description of commerce, grants it as to all," Johnson wrote. "[I]f ever the exercise of a right, or acquies-cence in a construction, could be inferred from contemporaneous and contin-ued assent, it is that of the exclusive effect of this grant."[117] Marshall's and Johnson's fascination with exclusivity meant that federal commerce power re-mained unsettled until the early 1850s. Over that time, the issue came before the Court in cases involving state licenses on imports and local regulations of ship passengers and pilots—that is, cases in which commerce occurred across state and sometimes national boundaries.[118]

But Marshall's decision ultimately relied on the more moderate analysis Wirt had offered. The New York law and the federal coasting statute were in "collision," and acts of Congress were "supreme." Therefore, "the law of the State, though enacted in the exercise of powers not controverted, must yield to it."[119] The state monopoly grant and the federal coasting license were both regulations of commerce, Marshall suggested. Unlike the patent analogy that

Chancellor Kent and Ogden's lawyers had insisted upon in the New York litigation, the two powers both focused on the same subject. The coasting license was therefore unlike a federal patent, insofar as the license was a touch of federal authority to regulate commerce, and hence occupied the same domain as the state monopoly. Thus, state and federal law were clearly in collision. In such a situation, the Supremacy Clause governed, and federal law must prevail.

Marshall's analysis in *Gibbons* was connected to his reasoning in *The Brig Wilson*, but with a different result. In *The Brig Wilson*, he had also asked what the subject of the two potentially competing powers was. There, the candidates were the 1793 Virginia act prohibiting migration into the state by free Black people, and the 1803 congressional statute adding federal enforcement to state bans on the importation of foreign Black people. What were the two laws about? They were both about the movement of persons of African descent. But they were not in conflict, according to Marshall's reading. They failed to intersect because of the mismatch between the facts of the case, as they came before Marshall, and the language of the Virginia statute, which defined the terms of the state prohibition. The federal and state laws had the same subject, but they were not in conflict. Therefore they could operate concurrently, and therefore Marshall was not compelled to invoke the Supremacy Clause and compel the state to give way.

In *Gibbons*, however, once Marshall decided that the state monopoly and the federal coasting license were both regulations of the key category of "commerce," he had committed to a different path from the one he had taken in *The Brig Wilson*. With both laws trained on the same subject, the next step was to find "collision."[120] Commerce led to collision; collision led to the Supremacy Clause; and the Supremacy Clause led to the repugnancy of the state law.

Marshall's view was not the only plausible one. As Johnson argued in his concurrence, collision was omnipresent given the jurisdictional multiplicity embedded in the federal union: "It would be in vain to deny the possibility of a clashing and collision between the measures of the two governments. The line cannot be drawn with sufficient distinctness between the municipal powers of the one, and the commercial powers of the other." Yet Johnson did not rely on "clashing and collision" to trigger federal power. Navigation, including "[s]hip building, the carrying trade, and propagation of seamen," clearly amounted to the Commerce of the Union, even absent a coasting license. Such commerce was the exclusive province of Congress. But Congress might decide to respect the claims of competing governments—as when it directed federal officials to uphold state inspection and health laws. The "only remedy" to preserve harmony among the overlapping powers, in Johnson's view, was "a frank and candid co-operation for the general good."[121]

The view of national power that Wirt and Webster had propounded had triumphed. The nation had been treated to "a most brilliant passage at arms in a forensic tourney," in the words of Wirt's biographer John Pendleton Kennedy. "It is said by the bar, that no cause, up to that date, in the Supreme Court, had ever excited a greater degree of interest and expectation in the country than this: that none was ever argued with greater ability."[122] On the evening that the arguments concluded, Wirt indulged in a crowing letter to his wife, Elizabeth: "The steam boat case is finished—and we are triumphant, I hope—not as to the decision of the cause for that is not yet settled, [b]ut as to the argument."[123]

Aftermath

On March 9, 1824—exactly one week after the Court handed down its decision in *Gibbons*—the Wirts threw open their house on G Street to celebrate the attorney general's great victory. Secretary of State John Quincy Adams noted in his diary that Tuesday night that he had attended an "evening party and dance at Mr. Wirt's."[124] One can only hope that the bills for the festivities were not presented until sometime later, when the additional one-thousand-dollar payment from the Gibbonses had made its way from New York to Washington City.[125]

Wirt was subsequently piqued to learn that Henry Wheaton had permitted Emmet to provide an amended version of his speech for publication. In Wheaton's version, which became the official report of the case, Emmet introduces the quotation from Virgil with the following characterization of New York: "[A]nd, conscious of the value of her own good works, she may turn the mournful exclamation of Æneas into an expression of triumph, and exultingly ask." The result of this emendation was to diminish the force and drama of Wirt's peroration. As Kennedy observed, the change "takes away the chief point of the reply, and to a certain extent renders that reply unintelligible."[126] Wirt had won the moment in the courtroom, as well as the contest over the meaning of the Commerce Clause, but the power of his words was diminished. He was victorious in law and in words, but he could not control the historical record. The record was, however, supplemented when Kennedy reprinted the original version of the *Aeneid* speech in his *Memoirs of the Life of William Wirt*.[127]

Wirt also suffered at the hand of his frenemy Webster, whose later account of their collaborations managed to achieve that difficult combination of ostensibly ingenuous admiration veneering over subtle slight. "[T]he opinion of the court [in *Gibbons*], as rendered by the chief justice, was little else than a recital of my argument," Webster told his biographer a few decades later. "And, which was a little curious, he never referred to the fact that Mr. Wirt had made an argument. . . . It was an accident, I think. Mr. Wirt was a great lawyer, and a great man. But sometimes a man gets a kink, and doesn't hit right. . . . But that was nothing against Mr. Wirt."[128]

Webster spoke too soon, however. His exclusive-power theory, and Marshall's apparent fascination with it, did much to shape the subsequent decades of Commerce Clause doctrine. But then, after lingering and causing confusion in the *U.S. Reports* for twenty-eight years, in 1852 it died—at the hands of Webster's friend, political ally, and fellow Bostonian, Justice Benjamin Robbins Curtis.[129] Wirt's conception of the Commerce of the Union, meanwhile, along with the robust role that it envisioned for Congress and its focus on actual collision between state and federal law, survived to become the core of modern Commerce Clause jurisprudence.

Chancellor Kent, for his part, found little to savor in Marshall's opinion. In his copy of Wheaton's ninth volume of reports, Kent pasted a memorandum discussing the cases from that term. He approved heartily of the Court's decision in *Osborn v. Bank of the United States*. But he was less impressed with Marshall's opinion in *Gibbons*, which he described as "involved & perplexed & contradictory & arrogant."[130] Like Judge Tucker reading in the newspaper of Marshall's overruling of his decision in *The Brig Wilson*, Kent was dissatisfied from afar with what the Court had done with his case. Neither of the eminent jurists agreed with the Court's disposition of the Commerce Clause issue, although each would have settled it differently from the other.

A Federalism of Beneficent Commerce

Neither Wirt nor Webster cited *The Brig Wilson* in their arguments in *Gibbons*. At one level, this absence is puzzling. *The Brig Wilson* was decided in 1820, one year before *Gibbons* made its first trip to the Supreme Court. Wirt was a Virginian, and Tucker and Wirt were friends of long standing. But most of Wirt's nonofficial practice after he became attorney general took place in Baltimore, not Richmond, and Webster was a New Englander. Still, it is difficult to believe that they did not know about the case, even given the lack of systematic reporting, especially for circuit-court cases. Wirt maintained an extensive practice in admiralty and prize cases for which he would have needed to keep abreast of recent important precedents.

Yet perhaps one should put the question differently: Why would Wirt or Webster have cited *The Brig Wilson* in their *Gibbons* arguments? The cases are certainly related in the *longue durée* of constitutional history, but a lawyer in 1824 might not have taken the same view regarding their connection. In both cases, Chief Justice Marshall endorsed a robust view of the federal commerce power. It is not at all clear, however, that Wirt and Webster would have regarded *The Brig Wilson* as a useful case for their argument on behalf of Gibbons. Wirt, whose official practice involved aiding the U.S. attorney in Baltimore in bringing piracy prosecutions against ship owners including Joseph Almeida, might have viewed *The Brig Wilson* as too entwined with those issues. The case was also tainted by bad facts, given that Marshall's opinion freed a brig that then proceeded to maraud along the southeastern coast of the United States. And perhaps Marshall's strategy in *The Brig Wilson* of avoiding a difficult and unnecessary constitutional question—"I escaped on the construction of the act"—simply worked.

Marshall did not cite *The Brig Wilson* in his decision in *Gibbons*. This fact seems to require less explanation, however, since Marshall did not cite a single case in his *Gibbons* decision.

Can some element of the *Gibbons* debates nonetheless be traced back to *The Brig Wilson*? One common thread is the less adversarial vision of the relationship between federal and state power that the cases share, if one attends to the arguments of the lawyers in *Gibbons*. The concurrent-power interpretation offered by Kent, Emmet, and, to a lesser degree, Oakley, points to the existence of a mode of early-nineteenth-century federalism that has not been adequately appreciated. Constitutional thinkers of the period did not understand themselves to be making an all-or-nothing choice between federal and state power. The additive version of federalism in *The Brig Wilson* was a viable possibility, as was the concurrent power view offered in *Gibbons* and endorsed in subsequent Commerce Clause cases. As the highly creative interbellum period demonstrates, a binary state-federal opposition need not be the only style of American federalism. Yes, *Gibbons v. Ogden* defined the federal commerce power. But the decision left many important questions unsettled, in particular the relative merits of the distinct interpretations of the Commerce Clause that the lawyers had sketched through their exhaustive oratory.

4 • The Justice, the Sailors, and the Founders' Legacy

A Federalism of the Tripartite Contract

This chapter and the following one tell the story of two South Carolinians, their contributions to early-nineteenth-century constitutional thought, and the house in Charleston that connected them.

We have no record of the two individuals being in a room together, although the archives suggest that they might well have met. But Maria Henrietta Pinckney and William Johnson, Jr., lived intersecting lives and participated in a shared constitutional conversation. They learned political theory from the same teacher, who linked both of them directly to the founding era. Yet they took diametrically opposing lessons from their shared Revolutionary heritage. Each of them developed a distinct theory of the federal-state relationship during the critical decades of the 1820s and 1830s. They were both arguers, writers, and producers of constitutional discourse, albeit in different arenas. They lived and worked in the heart of Charleston, the city that they and their forbears had long belonged to, that defined their own legacies, and that still today bears tangible markers of their presence.

The earliest surviving image of the Pinckney Mansion can be found in a five-foot-long panoramic oil painting from 1774, in which the white columns striping the red-brick structure are just visible across the oceanic waves of the Cooper River. The house appears to be floating atop the water, along with the other prominent buildings of Charles Town, in His Majesty's colony of South-Carolina. Two other recognizable structures are Anglican churches, St. Michael's and St. Philip's, in whose churchyards Pinckney rests, and Johnson is commemorated, today. The third building is the Exchange, the city's principal public and commercial building as well as its customshouse. Those structures embodied the identity of the colonial city, which in 1774 was already nearly a century old: British Atlantic, cosmopolitan, and commercial.

Thomas Leitch, *A View of Charles-Town*, 1774. (Collection of the Museum of Early Southern Decorative Arts [MESDA], Old Salem Museums & Gardens.)

In the middle distance, looming above the town while making for port, is a Royal Navy frigate, visibly bedecked with guns and peopled by naval officers, marines, and sailors. In the immediate foreground, on the edge of a small island known as Shute's Folly, stand an assortment of figures, including a white man with a spyglass and four individuals, several of them apparently dark-skinned, hauling ashore a small boat. Contemporary viewers of the painting might have associated the frigate with the "Charles Town tea party" of November 3, 1774; on that day, seven chests of East Indian tea, on which duty was owed under Parliament's controversial Tea Act of 1773, were dumped into the harbor, in what one newspaper described as "an Oblation . . . made to Neptune."[1] The ship and the figures suggest additional important elements of Charles Town's identity in 1774: maritime, racially diverse, and politically vigorous.

Important events were also occurring inside the Pinckney Mansion in 1774. Sometime that year, the owners of the house welcomed their first child, a daughter. The parents were Charles Cotesworth Pinckney and Sarah (known as "Sally") Middleton Pinckney; they named their daughter Maria Henrietta Pinckney. The Pinckneys and the Middletons were among the wealthiest and most well-established planter families in South Carolina. The Pinckneys were especially renowned. Charles Cotesworth Pinckney's mother, Eliza Lucas Pinckney, had gained fame when, as a teenager left by her army-officer father and sickly mother to manage three plantations, she became the first planter in South Carolina to grow and process indigo, which developed into the colony's second-most-profitable cash crop.[2] By the time she was twenty, the redoubtable Eliza Lucas had become "a model eighteenth-century planter patriarch."[3] Charles Cotesworth Pinckney's father, Charles Pinckney, was a leading attorney—the first member of the South Carolina bar to have been born in the colony—and held several important government posts, including speaker of the assembly and chief justice.

Charles and Eliza Pinckney began planning the building of the brick mansion on East Bay Street shortly after their marriage in 1744. Much of the actual construction was carried out by John "Quash" Williams, a Black master carpenter who was enslaved by the Pinckneys.[4] The house—"the earliest house in the United States known to have a temple front superimposed on its façade"—was likely completed in 1749.[5] In 1750, the Pinckneys manumitted Williams, who immediately established his own business as a "carpenter and joyner."[6] With two main stories—in addition to paneled wainscoting and mantelpieces carved with figures of shepherds and cupids, cellars and garrets with eight-foot ceilings, and landscaped grounds extending to the water's edge—it was accounted one of the finest properties in the city.[7] Charles Cotesworth, born in 1746, lived there as a boy. Twenty-eight years later, in 1774, Maria Henrietta was born to Charles Cotesworth and Sally Middleton Pinckney, perhaps in the Charles Town house or at their plantation, Belmont, a few miles upriver. By October 1774, the infant Maria Henrietta and her parents were living in their mansion.[8]

Maria Henrietta Pinckney, who was born in 1774 and died in 1836, was a member of one of South Carolina's oldest and most elite founding families. The Pinckney family's roots stretched across the British Empire from the Carolina Lowcountry to Antigua to England and back. In 1830, she wrote and published a tract that marshaled constitutional arguments in support of the nullification movement, in which South Carolina claimed the power to declare acts of Congress null and void within the state. She discussed politics with the leading gentlemen of city, state, and national government. She plotted with the governor to violate federal revenue laws in order to lay the groundwork for a legal challenge to those laws. Throughout her adult life, she received visits from foreign dignitaries, including the Marquis de Lafayette and the English social theorist Harriet Martineau. She and her sister, neither of whom married, inherited the Pinckney Mansion, one of the grandest, most famous houses in Charleston, from their founding-father father.[9] She was a human bridge connecting the Revolutionary and antebellum generations of her storied family.

A more voluble, and volatile, participant in the constitutional debates that roiled Charleston in the 1820s and 1830s also had reason to visit the Pinckney Mansion—albeit not to parse the nuances of sovereignty with the eldest daughter of the house. This personage was William Johnson, Jr., born in Charles Town in 1771 to radical blacksmith William Johnson, Sr., and his wife, Sarah Nightingale Johnson.[10] (As this chapter will illustrate, repeating family names were a particular custom of eighteenth- and nineteenth-century South Carolinians, and thus are a special affliction to their historians.) After graduating first in his class from the College of New Jersey at Princeton, the younger William Johnson returned to Charleston in 1790 to begin his preparation for the bar.[11] William Johnson the elder had risen in the postwar political order, serving first in South Carolina's convention to ratify the Constitution, and then in the state legislature. He was therefore able to arrange for his clever son William to begin reading law with one of the city's most illustrious and successful lawyers: Charles Cotesworth Pinckney, the father of Maria Henrietta.

General C. C. Pinckney, as he was known (to distinguish him from his brother, General Thomas Pinckney), had served with distinction in the southern theater of the war, then represented South Carolina at the Constitutional Convention of 1787. In 1790, C. C. Pinckney was in the middle of a twelve-year period of service in the state legislature (which moved that year to the new state capital, Columbia) while also maintaining a thriving and lucrative legal practice. Between 1789 and 1795, President George Washington offered C. C. Pinckney various high government posts, including the secretaryships of state and war, as well as an associate justiceship on the Supreme Court and command of the Army. But Charles Cotesworth Pinckney declined them all, citing the need to rebuild his family's fortunes by focusing on his legal practice and his rice and indigo plantations. Those labors in town and on the family's plantations relied on the general's enslaved workers, who numbered around 319 in 1801.[12] As part of his expanding legal practice, C. C. Pinckney took on fee-paying students, one of whom was the eighteen-year-old William Johnson, Jr., whose parents lived just across East Bay Street from the Pinckneys. Johnson's father's blacksmith shop was on the other side of the Pinckney Mansion. The Johnsons and the Pinckneys were neighbors.[13]

Beginning in 1790, Johnson read law with C. C. Pinckney for more than two years. During that time, Johnson would have been a regular visitor to the mansion. C. C. Pinckney's grandfather had designed the house with an unusual feature: the kitchen and several storerooms, called "offices," were in the basement. The specifications of the carpenters' and joiners' work from 1746 called for the "cellar Story" to be "7 & 1/2 or 8 feet high" with fifteen windows and two "four pannel [sic] outside doors." Access to the main floor of the house, which was elevated and reached from outside by a "high flight of stone steps with a small canopied porch," was possible inside the house via a "flight of stairs, under the great stairs with plain hand rail to go up to the first floor."[14]

When Johnson arrived at the house each day to set about his studies, he likely spent much of his time in the library, which the mansion's original owner, Charles Pinckney, had used as an office, and which his son, C. C. Pinckney, likely did as well.[15] The library occupied the northeast corner of the main floor of the house, with windows facing east over the street and the Cooper River just beyond.[16] There, at Pinckney's direction, Johnson would have drafted pleas and read the four volumes of notes that C. C. Pinckney had taken while personally attending William Blackstone's law lectures at Oxford in the early 1760s.[17] Perhaps Johnson sometimes encountered the family—which, depending on the time of year, included Maria Henrietta, her two younger sisters, and her stepmother—in the dining room. He may even have occasionally climbed the stairs to one of two second-floor drawing rooms. On his way, Johnson would have passed the triple-arched window, with its deep window seat. Everywhere, the house displayed the fine work of John Williams. The interior was "wainscoted in the heaviest panelling, the windows and doors with deep projecting pediments and mouldings," the mantelpieces "very high and narrow, with fronts carved in processions of shepherds and shepherdesses, cupids, etc." and "square frames in the panelling above, to be filled with pictures."[18]

In 1793, Johnson was admitted to the South Carolina bar. His subsequent rise in state politics was swift. After serving as speaker of the state legislature and as a judge on the state high court, he was appointed to the U.S. Supreme Court by President Thomas Jefferson in 1804. Johnson was thirty-two years old when he joined the Court. He and Justice Joseph Story, who was appointed to the Court by President James Madison in 1811, also at age thirty-two, share the distinction of being the two youngest justices in the history of the Court to date.

Johnson has been called "the first dissenter."[19] But his most notable achievements on the bench were those that earned him even greater notoriety, and on occasion infamy, than his moments of disagreement with Marshall. Johnson's views on the federal-state relationship, and in particular on the scope of Congress's power to regulate commerce, diverged sharply from those of many of his fellow South Carolinians. In a case that reached his circuit court in 1823, Johnson took on some of the mightiest forces of the planter aristocracy (including multiple Pinckneys), issuing a decision that rejected South Carolina's assertion of its powers to regulate free Black seamen in its ports. Evidently constitutionally incapable of resisting a fight, Johnson threw himself into a public debate over his ruling, taking to the pages of newspapers and pamphlets in a series of essays that were reprinted throughout the nation. A few years later, when the controversy over the Tariff of 1828 erupted, Johnson again put himself at the center of the rhetorical melee, publicly announcing himself to be "altogether opposed to the doctrine of nullification."[20] Denounced as a traitor to his state by legislators and governors in South Carolina, Georgia, and elsewhere, Johnson died in New York in 1834 at the age of sixty-three.

Johnson and Pinckney embody the breadth and variety of ideas about the federal-state relationship that were being debated in the 1820s and 1830s in the notorious firebrand state of South Carolina. After 1832, South Carolinians were widely considered to be the most extreme proponents of the theory that the Constitution had not divested the states of their sovereignty. Yet close examination of the writings of Johnson and Pinckney demonstrates a marked divergence of views on the nature of federalism—even among these members of the state's slaveholding elite.

This chapter and the one that follows examine debates in a variety of arenas, including private correspondence, newspapers, pamphlets, legislative debates, executive-branch opinions, and courtrooms. It demonstrates that not all South Carolinians or slaveholders supported states' rights; on the contrary, many were fervent Unionists.[21] Indeed, many South Carolinians, including some slaveholders, endorsed a broad federal commerce power. It was not obvious to them that broad federal power necessarily translated into antagonism toward their local or state regimes of slavery and racial subordination.

Moreover, the lines of disagreement and conflict did not fall along what one might think of as the obvious state-versus-federal lines. For example, the battle over South Carolina's so-called Negro Seamen Acts in the early 1820s involved numerous levels of governmental and nongovernmental actors, each with its own views concerning the constitutionality of the state regulations. Some of those participants included British diplomats, the U.S. secretary of state, the U.S. attorney general, the U.S. attorney for South Carolina, the federal circuit judge for the Sixth Circuit (Justice Johnson), the state attorney general, the South Carolina legislature, the sheriff of Charleston, the sailors who were seized and jailed under the act, city officials, and a newly formed group of planter vigilantes who called themselves the "South Carolina Association."

The story of South Carolina in the 1820s and 1830s illustrates the variegated nature of constitutional thought even within a single and self-consciously insular society. It also suggests that courts were one but by no means the only voice in establishing what counted as constitutional argumentation. The justices of the Supreme Court were embedded in local debates thanks to their circuit-riding duties, and their correspondence with each other spread news and legal arguments across the states.

But equally important for our understanding of the landscape of constitutional possibility in this period are other sources: Johnson's newspaper essays, Pinckney's dialogic tract, and John C. Calhoun's "Exposition and Protest." The Jeffersonian justice endorsed broad federal power; the daughter of one of the leading Federalists of the postwar period supported nullification; and the congressman who urged a national program of roads, canals, and banks insisted that the states had ultimate power to decide the validity of federal law.

As the 1774 painting of Charleston suggested, the city had always been the creature of its harbor. By the 1820s and 1830s, the waters were still the highway connecting the port to trade and commerce. But in the eyes of some South Carolinians, the harbor was increasingly a moat of autonomy surrounding what they wanted to see as a bastion of untrammeled state power. They hoped that the tidal rivers surrounding Charleston, with their littoral of "pluff" (plough) mud, would serve as a buffer that protected, not a road to be traveled.[22] Given the city's long history as a center of first imperial, then national, exchange, however, claims that local authority should control not only the city but the waters around it collided with equally powerful assertions of power by the federal government. An urge to spoil for that conflict led many South Carolinians to increasingly forceful and punctilious avowals of their sovereignty. Others aimed their bellicosity in the opposite direction, delivering passionate, sometimes intemperate, defenses of the supremacy of the Union.

Examining Charleston in the 1820s and 1830s illustrates the variety of interbellum federalisms in at least three ways. First, this chapter tells a story of local power and local connections in a period in which local dominance was itself contested. Who was the "real" Charlestonian who could speak for the city, William Johnson or Maria Henrietta Pinckney? Charleston was a city obsessed with connections; how did local power, both formal and informal, interact with the many layers above it—state, national, and international? Second, the chapter delineates the multiple strands of the long founding moment, which both Johnson and Pinckney explicitly claimed for themselves. Finally, by focusing on the early 1820s rather than the tariff controversy of 1828 through 1833, the chapter argues that the nullification crisis began earlier, encompassed broader claims, and had more surprising and lasting consequences than existing scholarship has recognized.

Let us begin with William Johnson.

The Vesey Conspiracy and the South Carolina Association

The 1826 edition of *Miller's Planters' and Merchants' Almanac*, printed in Charleston, was similar to the five previous years' editions that Archibald Edward Miller's printing office at 4 Broad Street had produced. It contained dates for solar and lunar eclipses and moveable feasts, lists of federal and state officers, names and hours of banks, rates for harbor pilotage, and toll schedules for the state road that ran between Charleston and Columbia.

But the 1826 almanac also featured a new item. Immediately following the roster of city constables and before the list of members of the "Free Mason's Hall," the almanac included an entry for an entity called the "South-Carolina Association." The brief record enumerated the officers of this association and the members of its "standing committee." Among the names listed were some of the leading members of Charleston's planter aristocracy, including General Thomas Pinckney, Joseph Manigault, and John Middleton. A number of prominent lawyers and politicians were also present: Isaac E. Holmes (specified as the association's "solicitor"), Benjamin Faneuil Hunt, and Robert J. Turnbull.[23] What was this association, and why were the names of its officers included among lists of government officials, public utilities, fee schedules, and all the other ordinary civic minutiae of the nineteenth-century almanac, that ephemeral monument to antebellum print culture?

The association appeared in the pages of the almanac in 1826 because it had by that point become one of Charleston's leading regulatory agents. It was not an arm of the government and enjoyed no official status. It did, however, count among its members some of the city's most wealthy and prominent gentlemen, including former governor Thomas Pinckney, younger brother of C. C. Pinckney and uncle to Maria Henrietta Pinckney.

Formed in the summer of 1823, the association was an organization of slaveholders who made it their mission "to aid the execution of the laws founded upon the *local and peculiar policy of South Carolina*."[24] In essence, it was a vigilante group, well funded and well connected, that pressed for enforcement of the state's laws restricting the manumission of slaves and, even more critically, the movement of free Black people and persons of color.[25] By 1826, after only three years of existence, the association had managed to exert its will over the objections of a variety of federal and state officials, all the while engaging in a highly public legal duel with another of Charleston's native sons, Justice William Johnson.

In 1820, Charleston was the sixth-largest city in the United States, with a total population of 25,356 people. Nearly 56 percent of Charlestonians (or

14,127 people) were designated as Black, of whom 12,652 were enslaved and 1,475 were free.[26]

The association was formed in response to the events of June 1822, when residents of Charleston were reeling from the news of an alleged conspiracy among the city's enslaved population, led by a freedman named Denmark Vesey. Contemporary accounts of the planned rebellion were contradictory, inflammatory, and unreliable, and scholars today continue to debate Vesey's role and how extensive and well formed the plans were.[27] Vesey, who was in his fifties at the time of the alleged conspiracy, had been born into slavery in West Africa or on the Danish Caribbean island of St. Thomas and had been brought to the French colony of Saint-Domingue before arriving in Charleston in 1783. He won the city lottery in 1799 and purchased his freedom for six hundred dollars. Over the following two decades, Vesey married, had children, worked as a carpenter, and participated in the political and religious life of the city's free Black community.

The scope of the alleged rebellion of 1822 was and continues to be disputed, but the general outline that emerged from most reports was that Vesey intended to lead a rebellion of Charleston's enslaved population while the bells of St. Michael's Church tolled midnight. The leaders of the revolt would set fire to the city, kill white residents, and escape by ship to Haiti, which had thrown off French rule—and with it the name "Saint-Domingue"—in 1804.

"My Reputation Is the Property of the United States": William Johnson, 1822–24

Word of the plot began spreading throughout the city on June 16, 1822, a Sunday. Fifty-year-old Justice Johnson and his family were at home in their two-and-a-half-story white clapboard house on the newly renamed Pinckney Street (now Rutledge Avenue) in Cannonborough, a district in the area known as the "Neck" of Charlestown.[28] Cannonborough was outside the city boundaries and was undergoing a transition from rural farmland to a more developed, densely populated suburb. The Johnsons were part of this transition. They had built the house sometime around 1812, perhaps with the assistance of Sarah Johnson's father, Thomas Bennett, who was an architect and lumberman. Before the name of their street became "Pinckney Street," it was called "Cannon Bridge Road," a descriptive label that remained apt for decades owing to the causeway crossing over the sizable and meandering mill pond that bordered the edge of the borough.[29] The Johnsons' house sat a block and a half up the Neck from the bridge, and the rear of the property abutted the pond.[30]

The Johnson house was not a mansion on the grand scale of the Pinckneys' establishment, but it was a roomy and gracious example of the distinctive Charleston "single house."[31] The house's narrow gable end fronted the street, and its longer side, along which stretched two levels of balconies ("piazzas," in the local argot), faced a side garden and outbuildings. Despite its relatively simple white frame exterior, the house's interior featured extensive neoclassical detailing: cornices with friezes of garlands, urns, griffins, and eagles; fireplaces with carved and stuccoed panels featuring "two girls in classic costume" holding a festoon of leaves and a "gracefully draped woman accompanied by a child."[32] Each of the two main floors had two rooms. The first floor comprised a front room and a dining room. The west-facing front room, which looked out to the street, may have been an informal drawing room as well as Johnson's study. The second floor had two more rooms: a front room that likely served as the Johnsons' formal drawing room, given that it contained the most elaborate cornicework in the house, and another room with a finely worked but less ornate cornice and mantelpiece. A dormered attic ran atop the length of the house.

At the time of the Vesey conspiracy, the U.S. Supreme Court was not in session; its term was held in February and March. The news touched the Johnsons personally. Two of Vesey's alleged co-conspirators were Rolla Bennett and Ned Bennett, the trusted household slaves of Governor Thomas Bennett, Jr.—brother of Johnson's wife, Sarah Bennett Johnson. The Johnsons, too, were slaveholders. Ten slaves worked and lived in the house in Charleston, and some number of additional slaves labored on the family's plantation at Goose Creek, seventeen miles north.[33] Sarah Johnson gave birth to eight children, only two of whom survived past childhood—daughters Anna and Margaret. The household also included two adopted white children who had fled the Haitian Revolution, John and Madeleine L'Engle.[34]

Despite this proximity to a bloody local sequel to the Haitian Revolution, which most white Charlestonians regarded as their most terrifying nightmare come to life, Johnson took up his pen amid the eagles and draped females to urge moderation and some degree of judicial process. On June 21, an unsigned essay headed "Communication: Melancholy Effect of Popular Excitement" appeared in the *Charleston Courier*. In it, the author—Johnson—described a series of events "which actually occurred within the recollection of thousands" in "the year 1810 or 1811" in the Edgefield district of western South Carolina, near the border with Georgia. The narrative, as Johnson presented it, involved a trumped-up claim of an imminent slave revolt; the immediate mobilization of armed patrols; a Georgia governor who "could not brook the mortifying discov-

William Johnson, by an unknown artist. (Collection of the
Supreme Court of the United States.)

ery of his having been duped" and who therefore stoked the white public's
hysteria; failed interventions by a local judge who "interfered only to prevent a
legal murder"; and, in the end, the hanging of an innocent enslaved man
named Billy. "[S]uch appeared to be the popular demand for a victim," Johnson
concluded, "that it is not certain a pardon could have saved him."[35]

The Vesey plot was discovered when one of the alleged conspirators confessed a few days before the rebellion was supposedly planned to take place.
The intendant (Charleston's term for "mayor"), James Hamilton, Jr., responded by calling out the militia and assembling a court of magistrates and
freeholders to investigate the alleged conspiracy.[36] The proceedings were conducted in secret, and the defendants were not permitted to confront their ac-
cusers or hear the testimony offered against them. Some were tortured or
threatened with death if they refused to give evidence.[37] Vesey and thirty-four

other men were hanged. Forty-two others, including one of Vesey's sons, were sold into slavery outside the United States, many to Spanish Cuba.[38] The African Methodist Episcopal Church, which had included Vesey among its congregants, was destroyed, and its leader was driven out of the state. Rumors flew around the city; the entire population was gripped with terror.

Johnson's words of caution appeared in print the same day that Vesey was arrested. The essay enraged the members of the Charleston court of magistrates and freeholders, who were busy conducting their secret process of investigation and punishment. Declaring themselves "injured and defamed," the court sent two representatives to the offices of the *Courier* to demand the name of the author of the piece. Members of the court wrote to Johnson to demand that he publish an apology. One publication—the *Charleston Southern Patriot*—refused to print a reply (not an apology) that Johnson had written. Finally, on June 29, the *Courier* published a statement from the court reiterating its own victimhood and charging Johnson with stirring up prejudice and suspicions against the court. On the same page was a response from Johnson, in which he called the court's statement "one of the most groundless and unprovoked attacks ever made upon the feelings of an individual" and promised that a more comprehensive reply would follow shortly.[39]

That rejoinder was a sixteen-page pamphlet titled "To the Public of Charleston" and signed "William Johnson."[40] The essay was a paragon of the Johnsonian rhetorical style. It began mildly, rebutting the inflammatory construction that his opponents had put on his statements. But then it cycled through a mix of protest, hauteur, defensiveness, attack, and gallery-playing declamation.

First, Johnson described how his "Melancholy Effect" essay had come to be printed. He had written it as a mere anecdote a few days after the Vesey plot had come to light: "The anecdote when written was thrown on my table before me, not deemed of sufficient importance to be sent by a servant." The next day, he had put it into his pocket, gone into town, and left it in the care of the publisher of the *Courier* with the direction "that he could do what he pleased with it, or words to that effect." Insisting that he had not meant the piece as an attack on the court of magistrates and freeholders, Johnson engaged in some lawyerly caviling: "I neither put a signature to it, nor requested that it should be printed."[41]

Then flowed forth the outrage. Perhaps no aspect of Johnson's personality demonstrated his membership in the Carolina planter elite more than his lifelong sensitivity to perceived affronts. "I feel sensible, that I am the injured man," Johnson wrote. The court's demand that he explain and retract his statement touched his honor.[42] Charging them with speaking "not in the language of my natural political and social equals, but that of dictators," Johnson objected to what he viewed as the court's highhandedness in demanding an apology. "Your address to me . . . is that of men, on whom my misconduct had conferred a right to command me."[43]

Johnson then turned to the court's attack on him in the June 29 edition of the *Courier*. There, the court had suggested that Johnson's conduct was not "that which ought to influence a gentleman" and that he had failed to be "sensible of the obligations of decency and propriety."[44] These allegations were clearly intended to damage Johnson's standing in the community, insofar as they portrayed him as attacking a legally constituted court that viewed itself as a bulwark against a full-scale slave insurrection. The court had addressed him in the tones of "dictators," and they had cast aspersions on his dignity and character. Such slings always nettled Johnson. He responded in magisterial tones:

> My reputation is the property of the United States. It is in safe hands and defies scrutiny. But I wish to live in harmony with those who surround me. The smiles of my fellow citizens are dear to me. They will read and consider my defence; and though for a time a cloud may intercept the beams of their favour, I fear nothing.[45]

The Charleston court officials had portrayed Johnson's criticisms of their tribunal as disloyalty to his community. With his statement, however, Johnson demurred—aggressively. As a justice of the U.S. Supreme Court, he suggested, his professional honor and standing were no longer susceptible to damage from local controversies. His phrasing contrasted the wider arena of the United States with "those who surround me"—the local community. By describing his reputation as "the property of the United States," Johnson aligned himself with the Union rather than South Carolina. It was in the Union, the Episcopalian Johnson might have thought, where he lived and moved and had his being.[46] Yet, sensible also of his deep local ties, he did not wish to antagonize his neighbors. On the contrary, he wished "to live in harmony with those who surround me."

The editions of the Charleston city directory published at that time contained two consecutive entries for Johnson. One read "Johnson, William, Judge, U.S. Supreme Court"; the other, directly below, "Johnson, William, Planter." For each, the directory listed the Cannonborough address.[47] The dual directory listings demonstrate how deeply embedded Johnson was in the history and society of Charleston. He had been a state legislator and a state-court judge; he was a planter. Justice Johnson's brother Joseph was a prominent doctor who served as intendant of Charleston from 1825 to 1827, following a stint as president of the Charleston branch of the Bank of the United States.

Moreover, Johnson's Charleston origins were deeply connected with the city's Revolutionary history. Johnson seems to have felt keenly the responsibility of inheriting the mantle of the founding generation. His father, who had rallied around Charleston's Liberty Tree in 1766 to protest Parliament's Declaratory Act, captained a South Carolina artillery unit and was captured by the British during the siege of the city in 1780. His mother was said to have sewn cartridges into her petticoats in order to smuggle them to his father in the trenches.[48] After the war, Johnson, Sr., had served in the South Carolina convention that ratified the Constitution. The ratification convention met in the Exchange, the large cupolaed building visible in the 1774 panorama of the city. In 1822, Justice Johnson wrote a two-volume biography of General Nathanael Greene, one of Washington's most trusted major-generals, who had commanded the southern theater of the war and later became a South Carolina planter.[49]

The justice gained additional notoriety in Charleston through his efforts to locate and save the roots of the Liberty Tree, which had been reduced to a stump. In 1817, he sent former president Jefferson, who had nominated him to the Court, a specially made cane. The head of the cane was "taken from the root of an oak" under which assembled "the first little band of conspirators that convened in our country," Johnson wrote. "The tree was cut down by the British but I took up the root and have made use of it in various ways to keep alive the sacred flame of '76."[50]

Johnson was therefore unlike many of his fellow justices, who established households and legal practices later in life and in places other than where they had been raised. Johnson was profoundly *of* Charleston, in ways that Marshall was not of Richmond, nor Story of Cambridge. He lived in Charleston as a lifelong Charlestonian, not as a recent arrival whom federal office or his own enterprise happened to place there.

Yet the Vesey plot and the ensuing weeks of panic and controversy left their mark on Johnson. They also estranged him from many of his fellow Charlestonians. Writing to a cousin a few weeks after the height of the crisis, Johnson's twenty-one-year-old daughter, Anna, observed that her father "has been most unkindly and unhumanely treated—But the fact is that you would be surprised to see the low petty jealousy of my father—exercised and maintained" by many "men in this state."[51]

Johnson's bold statement—"My reputation is the property of the United States"—was both a rebuttal of his critics and a declaration of independence from what he likely viewed as the low, petty jealousies of many of his fellow South Carolinians. He was a man of deep and complex allegiances. The declaration echoed his concurrence in *Martin v. Hunter's Lessee* six years earlier, in 1816. There, he had argued that the Constitution had established a "tripartite" contract among "the people, the states, and the United States."[52] Johnson's sometimes-tense relationship with his home city was a manifestation of the difficulties involved in a three-party pact. The Johnsonian tension was to feel keenly the pull of the local—the state, the city, the borough—even as he allied his reputation, something so close to his core, with the general government.

Johnson's judicial opinions suggest a similarly anti-parochial sensibility. Despite Johnson's embeddedness in Charleston, his position on the Court required him to travel to Washington for the February term and to make the rounds of his circuit. The Sixth Circuit sat in Charleston as well as Columbia, 120 miles to the northwest; in North Carolina, at Raleigh; and in Georgia, at Savannah and Milledgeville, the capital.

By 1823, after nineteen years on the Court, Jefferson's first justice was showing decidedly un-Jeffersonian tendencies with respect to his relationship with his brethren and his disposition toward some aspects of substantive law. On the Court, Johnson often thwarted Marshall's efforts at issuing a single, unanimous opinion.[53] But this independence came more from a willingness to disagree with the chief justice on the merits, and Johnson's own contrarian streak, than it did from political motives of fighting the good Republican fight against the Federalist Marshall. Moreover, Johnson was more often aligned with the majority than the "dissenter" sobriquet would suggest. Johnson served on the Court for nearly thirty years, from 1804 to 1834; during that time, he wrote 172 opinions in cases before the Court, placing him third behind Marshall and Story. Of these, only thirty-four were dissents.[54]

Johnson's occasional correspondence with Jefferson during this period demonstrates that Johnson felt himself duty bound to affiliate with neither the states nor the national government. In his view, there was a third entity to which allegiance was due: the Constitution, an indivisible whole that subsumed both the several states and the national government, and that stood for the people. In April 1823, Johnson described his conception of what he thought was his and Jefferson's shared commitment to Republicanism: "[T]he distinguishing Characteristic of the Republican Party was, to check the Intemperance of both Democrats and Federalists and administer the Government agreeable to the true Views of the Constitution, *equally uninfluenced by the Pretensions of the States or the United States.* Pray give me an explicit Opinion on the Correctness of my general Proposition."[55]

This was a bold statement. Johnson equated Republicanism—by which he meant both a party and a political philosophy—with a middle position between the extremisms of the Democrats (perhaps referring to the heirs of the Anti-Federalists) and the Federalists (Hamilton, Adams, Sr.). Republicanism required one to reject the "pretensions" of both the states and the national government and instead to focus on administering the government according to the true view of the Constitution. In his reply, the eighty-year-old former president expressed what one can only imagine was his profound disapproval of Johnson's views. Jefferson insisted on "the barriers of the state governments as co-ordinate powers."[56] But Johnson's view rejected this dichotomy between state and federal. Administering the government properly required listening to the Constitution, not choosing sides between its constituent parts.

The Seamen Act

While Johnson and Jefferson were exchanging these letters in 1822 and 1823, the South Carolina Association was cementing its grip on the state's machinery in order to ensure that there would be no sequel to the Vesey plot. The private group explicitly styled its purpose as "to aid in the execution of the laws founded upon the *local and peculiar policy of South Carolina.*"[57] But the association was not alone in this crusade.

In December 1822, six months after the conspiracy had been discovered and its alleged ringleaders executed or enslaved and banished, the South Carolina legislature passed a law titled "An Act for the Better Regulation and Government of Free Negroes and Persons of Colour, and for Other Purposes."[58] The act, which was commonly referred to as the "Negro Seamen Act" and sometimes as the "Police Bill," provided that any "free negro or person of colour" debarking from his vessel in any South Carolina port would be immediately jailed for the duration of his vessel's stay in port. The captain of the vessel was required to pay the cost of the sailor's imprisonment, and the captain was liable for a one-thousand-dollar fee and two months' jail time if he did not collect the sailor. In such situations, the sailors were to be "deemed and taken as absolute slaves" and sold by the sheriff, who was then entitled to half the proceeds of the sale. This portion of the act was drafted by Robert J. Turnbull, a planter and lawyer who had served on the court of magistrates and freehold-ers during the Vesey proceedings.[59]

The law focused on free Black sailors because they were extremely numer-ous in the world of transatlantic commerce, and because they were presumed to be outside agitators—foreign agents of radicalism and insurrection, as Vesey's background was thought to demonstrate.[60] In this way, the purpose of the act echoed that of the Virginia anti-migration law at issue in *The Brig Wil-son*, discussed in Chapter 2.

But the South Carolina law also laid heavy restrictions on free Black persons already residing in South Carolina. They were forbidden to leave the state and then return. In addition, "every male negro, mulatto, or mestizo, in this State, above the age of fifteen years" was required to have a "guardian, who shall be a respectable freeholder" and who would certify to the local court that the indi-vidual in question was "of good character and correct habits." Finally, the act levied an annual head tax of fifty dollars (roughly $1,300 in today's dollars) on each "free male negro or person of colour" between the ages of fifteen and fifty. The penalty for nonpayment of the tax was, again, to be sold into slavery.[61]

As the Seamen Act demonstrates, South Carolinians in general, and white Charlestonians in particular, were panicking in 1822. General Thomas Pinck-ney, the brother of General Charles Cotesworth Pinckney (as well as a wealthy planter, former governor, minister to Britain and Spain, congressman, and president of the South Carolina ratification convention in which William John-son, Sr., had sat as a delegate in 1788), penned a pseudonymous pamphlet on the subject. Writing under the name "Achates," he catalogued a number of recent developments that in his view had brought the state to a dangerous precipice. Among other factors, Pinckney pointed to the example of Haiti; "the indiscreet zeal in favor of universal liberty, expressed by many of our fellow-citizens in the States north and east of Maryland; aided by the black population of those States"; and the "disparity in numbers between the white and black inhabitants of the City," for which he gave a ratio of fourteen to twenty-two (or 64 percent; the actual figure, per the 1820 census, was closer to 56 percent). Finally, Pinckney cited "the most dangerous of those indulgencies" permitted among Charleston's Black population: "their being taught to read and write."[62] Pinckney did not mention the fact that eight decades previously, his mother, Eliza Lucas Pinckney, had as a young woman taught some of the slaves on her Wappoo Plantation to read precisely so that they could teach other enslaved children.[63] He did, however, propose that the state expel Black tradesmen and mechanics and replace them with "free white men" from such places as the "ill-fated Island" of Ireland.[64]

The Seamen Act was erratically enforced in its first few months, in part owing to resistance by local officials who objected to the additional tasks that it imposed. A halt in proceedings occurred in March 1823 because the harbormaster had not received his statutory fees and therefore had ceased making reports of vessels manned by free Black sailors to the sheriff, whose duty it was to carry out the law's provisions.[65] The harbormaster was an official of the city of Charleston; the sheriff, of Charleston County. A report from the harbormaster was the necessary predicate for "all free Negroes & Coloured People that were Imployed on board of any vessel arriving & coming into the Port of Charleston from any other Country or State" to be "taken out" and "confined in Prison" by the sheriff.[66]

Disputes over the execution of the act continued for several months, echoing from the Charleston portside to the state capital in Columbia. In November 1823, harbormaster Thomas Paine petitioned the state legislature in Columbia, praying to be "remunerated for services performed & to be relieved from exercising them in future." Paine complained that the harbormaster's duties were already "so grate that it Imploy's his whole time," frequently keeping him "on the wharfs in the Winter until Eight or Nine oclock in the Evening to attend to getting vessels safe mo[o]red," after which he "hath his writing to do for the day which keeps him up until Eleven oclock at Night before he can go to Rest." Adding to those obligations the new tasks imposed by the Seamen Act—gathering information on "the arrivals of vessels having those free Negroes & People of Colour on board" and preparing a report for the sheriff—was "Impossable [sic]," Paine argued. He therefore requested payment for performing "the two offices" over the past eleven months. In the future, Paine suggested, the sheriff should be permitted to enforce the act "immediately," without waiting for a report from the harbormaster. Indeed, he noted, in several recent instances, "the Deputy Sheriffs have gon[e] on board and taken Them out without there being Reported by the Harbour Master."[67]

The legislature's committee of claims recommended against granting the harbormaster's prayer; the senate accordingly rejected Paine's petition.[68] No explanation was recorded. Clearly, however, the harbormaster's intransigence frustrated the intention of the state legislature. Even within a single state, layers of governmental authority operated—and sometimes clashed.

Rumors also circulated that Justice Johnson had urged local officials not to enforce the act.[69] Johnson had indeed lambasted the statute, which he argued had been passed "without due consideration," in a letter to Jefferson:

Incalculable are the Evils which have resulted from the exaggerated Accounts circulated respecting that [Vesey] Affair. Our Property is reduced
to nothing. Strangers are alarmed at coming near us; our Slaves rendered uneasy; the Confidence between us and our Domestics destroyed—and all this because of a trifling Cabal of a few ignorant
pennyless unarmed uncombined Fanatics, and which certainly would
have blown over without an Explosion had it never come to light.[70]

South Carolina's newly elected U.S. senator, Robert Y. Hayne, offered feeble
criticism of the Seamen Act as "certainly not very acceptable" and wished that
its supporters had employed "a tone at least of more moderation."[71] Just a decade later, in 1832, however, Hayne would chair the state's nullification convention, where he defended the state's authority to invalidate federal laws that
it deemed unconstitutional.

In late July 1823, the South Carolina Association announced itself in the
pages of the *Charleston Courier*. A few days later came another notice, this time
listing the names of the association's officers: a president, five vice presidents
(including General Thomas Pinckney), two secretaries (including the same
Robert J. Turnbull who had sat on the Vesey court and drafted the Seamen Act),
a treasurer, and a solicitor.[72] A standing committee would monitor the com-
ings and goings of ships in the harbor and the activities of the free Black population to ensure that the laws were being enforced. Writing in the *Courier*, "A
Member" described the group as "not an association of individuals combining
for party purposes or political influence—not of men who under the plea of
expediency or necessity would usurp the functions of the civil Magistrate—but
instead a society of well informed citizens, most of them owners of the soil,
and all of them ready to bow with reverence to the supremacy of the laws."[73]

The broad array of Charleston politics was evident in the varied responses
to the Vesey crisis. Johnson had counseled soberness and a measure of due
process. Other members of the city's elite, however, had banded together to
form the association, while the legislature in Columbia had passed the Seamen Act.

Other writers offered further justifications for why a private organization
was needed when the legislature already showed such enthusiasm for passing
stringent new laws such as the Seamen Act. The objective was merely to supplement enforcement of "the many wholesome statutes in force relative to our
colored population, and *nothing else*," one advocate stated.[74] Indeed, the
"wholesome" nature of the laws, and thus the need for their zealous enforcement, was a recurring note sounded by the association and its defenders.

Moreover, they emphasized the group's ample coffers—which any reader of the newspapers would have perceived from the monied names listed among the officers. Many of the act's provisions depended on individual informants coming forward, but some might hesitate to do so if they could not expect compensation or if they might face "the odium which attaches to the character of an informer." The association could fill this enforcement gap by "undertaking prosecutions at its own expense." Indeed, the group's wealth and willingness to accuse were touted as precisely its strengths, as this chilling passage demonstrated: "With ample means and with permanent funds; with the eyes of *Argus* and the hands of *Briareus*, it is difficult to conceive, how a violation of the laws, can occur in our community, without the offender being instantly known, and almost as instantly finding himself in the grasp of the Association."[75]

The association's efforts at self-promotion worked. The Charleston organization spawned branches in other parts of the state; members gathered each summer in Charleston for the annual meeting, which became an important locus of socializing as well as information sharing. A petition from the association to the state legislature in November 1823, urging stricter enforcement of the Seamen Act, bore 334 names.[76]

The Seamen Act also attracted notice outside South Carolina, much of it critical. In Washington, two months after the passage of the act, British Envoy Extraordinary and Minister Plenipotentiary Stratford Canning lodged an official remonstrance with Secretary of State John Quincy Adams. Given Charleston's long-standing connections to the Caribbean and its ongoing importance in Britain's West Indian trade, many vessels flying the British flag employed sailors who fell under the act's categories of free Black people or persons of color. Canning specifically complained to Adams of an instance in January 1823 in which the mate and four seamen of a British ship out of Nassau had been seized and jailed when the ship docked in Charleston. Terming the treatment of these Black British subjects "a most reprehensible act of authority" and an "outrage," Canning demanded the secretary of state's intercession.[77] In June 1823, Adams replied to Canning that the federal government had taken "measures" to ensure that such offenses would be halted.[78] But Adams's assurances ultimately proved ineffectual.

Behind the scenes, Adams discussed the act's enforcement with two of South Carolina's nine congressmen, Joel R. Poinsett and James Hamilton. Poinsett, a lifelong friend of Justice Johnson, had been the Madison administration's special agent to Latin America; Hamilton had been the intendant of

Charleston during the Vesey crisis six months earlier.[79] Both Poinsett and Hamilton were Charlestonians with deep connections to the city and its power structures. They therefore could, at least in theory, provide the secretary of state with a channel between the federal executive branch's conduct of foreign relations and the activities of the local harbormaster and sheriff in Charleston. In his dealings with the British minister, Adams appeared confident that this international-to-municipal conduit would work, and that the message of non-enforcement would be carried down from the diplomatic heights to the gritty wharves.[80]

But Adams had not reckoned on the disruptive power of the owners of the soil amassed in the South Carolina Association.

Elkison's Case: Beginnings

The brief hiatus in the enforcement of the Seamen Act in Charleston ended in the summer of 1823, even as Adams was making overtures to South Carolina's congressional delegation in Washington. The influence of the association was growing. That fall, the association trumpeted that its "incessant informations and prosecutions" had "Caused the Act . . . to be executed against *one hundred and fifty-four* colored persons."[81]

One of those persons was Henry Elkison, a Jamaican-born British subject, a free man, and apparently a person of color. Elkison had made his way from the Caribbean to Liverpool, where he lived for a number of years before joining the crew of the *Homer*, a "fine coppered" British trading ship.[82] The *Homer* was captained by Robert Kerr, who hailed from Greenock, a busy port town on the southern shore of the Firth of Clyde some twenty-five miles west of Glasgow.[83] The *Homer* made multiple trips to Charleston in 1823. In late March of that year, it arrived in Charleston after a thirty-six-day trip from Greenock, carrying ballast; within a fortnight, it had sailed for Liverpool, carrying a cargo of "691 bales Upland, 155 bales Sea Island cotton."[84]

A few months later, in July, Kerr and the *Homer* returned to Charleston. The *Charleston Courier* reported on July 11 that the *Homer* had been sighted "in the Offing" the evening before from J. M. Elford's observatory, located at 149 East Bay Street.[85] Elford was a noted mathematician and man of science, as well as the inventor of a new maritime signal code, or "marine telegraph," that was widely used in American ports through the late 1850s.[86] Captain Kerr of the *Homer* was one of the first shipmasters to adopt Elford's code.[87] Kerr was notable enough in the Charleston maritime community that Elford's signal book carried his endorsement: "the best and most simple and practical method of holding a conversation between Vessels at Sea, and of making communications from Vessels to the Shore."[88]

When Kerr brought the *Homer* into port in Charleston on Wednesday, July 23, after a sixty-three-day voyage from Liverpool, the ship docked at Chisolm's Wharf on the southwestern tip of the peninsula, where the Ashley River opened into the harbor, and where the counting-house of James Calder was located.[89] Calder, a prosperous Liverpudlian cotton merchant, was the consignee, or agent for sale, for the *Homer*.[90] As such, his name was listed in the shipping columns of the city's newspapers along with reports of the ship. While the *Homer* was in port, Calder also placed notices in the newspaper advertising "freight or passage" aboard the ship for its return trip to Scotland.[91]

Aside from its captain's interest in maritime telegraphy, the *Homer* might appear to have been just another British ship transporting cotton and the occasional passenger across the Atlantic Ocean between the cotton metropolis of Liverpool, the factory town of Greenock, and Charleston. In many ways, the *Homer* was a typical vessel of its time and place. While the *Homer* was docked at Chisolm's Wharf, however, it became famous—or infamous, depending on whom one asked. For when the *Homer* arrived in Charleston in July 1823, just as the Charleston Association was mobilizing for "incessant informations and prosecutions" under the Seamen Act, its crew included one Henry Elkison.

The *Homer* immediately encountered the newly robust enforcement of the Seamen Act. Elkison was apprehended, "taken by the sheriff under this act out of the ship Homer, a British ship trading from Liverpool to this place," and jailed.[92] Captain Kerr apparently complained to the British consul in Charleston, Benjamin Moodie.[93] Moodie, likely on alert for such renewed aggression against British seamen, engaged a lawyer, Mitchell King, to bring a claim on Elkison's behalf—and, in a larger sense, to press the claims of the British government against South Carolina. King was also a British subject, a Scot from Fife.[94] By the end of the proceedings, the case came to involve not only the rights of Great Britain, but also the power of the U.S. government.

The structure of the case was notable. It was not a criminal prosecution brought against Elkison by the state. Rather, it was a petition brought on behalf of Elkison against the sheriff of Charleston, Francis Gottier Deliesseline, who had seized Elkison and jailed him. The petition comprised two motions. The first motion sought the writ of habeas corpus, "regarding the prisoner in a criminal . . . aspect" and "having for its object his discharge from confinement absolutely." If Elkison succeeded on this claim, he would be immediately released from jail. In the alternative, Elkison's lawyer requested the writ *de homine replegiando*, which concerned the prisoner "in a civil aspect" and sought "his discharge on bail, with a view to try the question of the validity of the law under which he is held in confinement."[95] Securing this writ would free Elkison from detention upon giving security to the sheriff that Elkison would answer the charges against him. The case was formally captioned *Ex parte Henry Elkison, A Subject of His Britannic Majesty, vs. Francis G. Deliesseline, Sheriff of Charleston District.*[96]

Here the procedural posture of the case becomes somewhat murky, at least to modern eyes. But some of that obscurity might have been a deliberate strategy by Elkison and his advocates. Elkison's lawyer, Mitchell King, brought suit in the U.S. circuit court in Charleston. The judge of that court was Justice Johnson, sitting in his capacity as a judge of the Sixth Circuit.[97] King applied directly to Johnson for the writs on behalf of Elkison. As the case unfolded, these choices of court and judge proved to be the most important strategic decisions that Elkison's advocates could have made.

Elkison's case was not a fluke or a coincidence. One sailor from one British ship was arrested by local authorities—these were not on their own novel facts in Charleston in 1823. Ship captains had been criticizing the Seamen Act since it was passed, especially as enforcement increased. In February 1823, forty-one masters of American vessels petitioned Congress, arguing that the South Carolina law was "in *violation of the constitution of the United States*, and of the authority of the federal head."[98] Elkison's arrest was unusual, however, because of the individuals whose attention it captured. The British consul in Charleston engaged a lawyer to petition a federal court for the sailor's release. King's client was nominally Elkison, but his fees were being paid by Consul Moodie.

The records suggest that Elkison's case was a special one, and the individuals involved in it understood it as such. A key player was James Calder, merchant, of Chisolm's Wharf, Charleston. Calder, as we have seen, was the consignee of the *Homer* for at least two of its voyages in 1823, including the one that brought Elkison to Charleston. The ship docked at Chisolm's Wharf, which is likely to have been the place where Elkison was taken into custody by Sheriff Deliesseline. Calder had emigrated from Liverpool to Charleston sometime before 1817, where built a successful business, married, and started a family that would ultimately number eleven children.[99]

Calder, as consignee and agent for both freight and passage, was well acquainted with both the *Homer* and its captain, Kerr. As a British merchant,

Calder also had a substantial stake in Charleston's viability as a port for the transatlantic trade in cotton. As city officials, under pressure from the South Carolina Association, increased enforcement of the Seamen Act, Calder would have witnessed Black British sailors being dragged from ships for which he was consignee. The growing frequency of the jailing of crew members in Charleston made shipping more unpredictable and expensive. Many British merchants were critical of American slavery on moral grounds, but even those who were not objected to this economic injury.[100] In Washington, Secretary of State Adams was fielding complaints from British diplomats and conducting meetings with South Carolina's congressmen. In Charleston, Calder was using more local avenues to challenge the Seamen Act.

Even before Elkison arrived in Charleston aboard the *Homer*, Calder had had dealings with Sheriff Deliesseline regarding enforcement of the Seamen Act. Indeed, Calder had been at the center of the events that Ambassador Canning cited in his remonstrance to Secretary of State Adams. In January 1823, a different vessel of which Calder was consignee—the sloop *Bob* out of Nassau, New Providence, in the Bahamas—had been searched by the sheriff's officers as it was preparing to go to sea, while the captain was not aboard.[101] Deliesseline's deputies "arrested the mate and seamen, and carried them to gaol," without even summary judicial process.[102] Crucially, all five men—the entire crew of the sloop—swore to the sheriff's officers that they were "British subjects."[103] Deliesseline and the others took this statement to mean that the men were free men of color.

Upon learning of the arrest, Calder and the captain informed Consul Moodie and consulted with a lawyer.[104] They also took direct action, confronting Deliesseline and demanding the release of the crew. Deliesseline, "so soon as he became satisfied that they were immediately about to depart," discharged the men "upon payment of the accruing fees"—$18.21—which Calder paid.[105] The men returned to the *Bob*, which continued on its voyage.

Calder, however, sued, bringing an action against Deliesseline to recover the fees. Calder lost. At trial and on appeal, he apparently argued that the jailed men "were considered as British subjects," and therefore that "they were protected from seizure, under the treaty of commerce between the United States and Great Britain." But the court was unmoved. Sometime in late 1823, he appealed again, to the South Carolina Constitutional Court. There, he argued that although the mate was "a free man of color," the four seamen were enslaved. Therefore, Calder argued, they were not subject to seizure under the Seamen Act, which "has reference to free negroes or persons of color, and not to slaves."[106] Indeed, Calder noted in a letter to Moodie, if the Seamen Act was enforced, it would mean the imprisonment of substantial numbers of the crew members manning British ships: "[C]onsidering that colonial vessels generally are navigated by coloured people, it will in effect amount to a prohibition of the West India trade with this port, unless relief is speedily granted."[107]

In January 1824, after Elkison's case had been decided, the constitutional court found in favor of Calder in his suit against Deliesseline and ordered a new trial. Calder was awarded damages in the amount of the jail fees he had paid for the four seamen, but not those for the mate, who was a free man.[108] The case established a cruelly ironic principle for Black seamen in Charleston: enslaved sailors, and only enslaved sailors (or those who claimed to be enslaved), could escape imprisonment and possible sale into slavery.[109] Free Black sailors could be jailed, and possibly sold. Their claim to be "British subjects" was unavailing. They were not entitled to protection, despite the commercial treaties that existed between the United States and Britain.

Calder's suit against Deliesseline in the case of the *Bob* was still working its way through the state appeals courts when Elkison's petitions were filed in the summer of 1823. It was another dispute with city officials regarding enforcement of the Seamen Act, involving some of the same Charlestonian dramatis personae: the merchant, Calder; the consul, Moodie; and the sheriff, Deliesseline. Based on the decisions of the state trial and appeals courts in the case of the *Bob*, it was likely already clear to observers by July 1823, when Elkison was jailed, that the state courts were unmoved by arguments that the Seamen Act was unconstitutional.[110] With the state courts essentially closed to facial challenges to the Seamen Act and pressure mounting from British officials both at home and in the United States, the contest moved to a new stage: the federal circuit court in Charleston, where Justice Johnson presided.

Elkison's Case: In Court and in Print

On August 7, 1823, just two weeks after the *Homer* arrived at Chisolm's Wharf and Henry Elkison was seized, the case commenced. A crowd numbering in the "hundreds" packed the federal courtroom of the neoclassical courthouse on the northwest corner of Broad and Meeting streets.[111] Given Johnson's outspoken critiques of the Vesey proceedings just one year previously, the high-profile activities of the association, and the controversial enforcement of the Seamen Act, many Charlestonians expected to witness satisfying theater in the circuit justice's courtroom. Otherwise, it is difficult to imagine what would have induced so many people to pack themselves into what was likely a suffocatingly hot chamber that Thursday.

The outer structure of the courthouse had been built beginning in 1790, framed around the remains of what had been the colonial statehouse, which dated from 1753. In 1788, the statehouse was partially destroyed by fire. That same year, South Carolina's convention to ratify the Constitution, in which Justice Johnson's father served, had convened two blocks down Broad Street in the Exchange, the colony's principal center of civic and market life.

In 1823, when Justice Johnson alighted from his carriage or horse at the courthouse's front door after the one-mile trip from his Cannonborough home, had he glanced eastward he would have been able to spy the cupola on top of the Exchange. Catercorner across the street from the courthouse was St. Michael's Church, with its stepped Christopher Wren–style steeple already a seven-decade-old landmark.[112] The Revolutionary past was always close at hand, for Johnson as for his city.

Passing through the pedimented front door of the courthouse, Johnson would have ascended the broad flight of stairs that turned at a massive three-part Palladian window and split into a pair of flanking flights. The climb to the courtroom bore some resemblance to the ascent to the second floor in the Pinckney Mansion, which featured a similar "Venetian" window overlooking the house's principal stair landing.[113] The second floor of the courthouse had been the top floor of the colonial statehouse. There, in the southeast corner, was the federal courtroom—occupying essentially the same footprint as had the chamber in which the council, the upper house of the colonial legislature, had met.[114] The bench from which Johnson presided was located at the south end of the room, between two windows that looked down onto Broad Street. The crowd was crammed into the remainder of the room, some perhaps on chairs and some standing, some fanning themselves, some trying to dispose themselves favorably to whatever breeze reached in through the deep-paneled windows that ran along the east side of the room, overlooking Meeting Street.

If the onlookers came to the courtroom anticipating a fracas, they were not disappointed. The reports of the proceedings come from three sources. The most comprehensive of these was Johnson's opinion, which included a notable amount of exposition and commentary. Johnson had it published as a pamphlet when the city's newspapers refused to print it. A competing account of the proceedings issued from Benjamin Faneuil Hunt, one of the association's lawyers, who published a post-trial pamphlet. Johnson's opinion also found its way into a compilation of reports of criminal cases from around the country, edited by New York lawyer Jacob D. Wheeler, that was published in Albany and New York in 1824.

Elkison v. Deliesseline became a public spectacle in sweltering late-summer Charleston. King, representing the jailed Elkison, argued that the Seamen Act was invalid on two grounds. First, King contended that the act conflicted with Congress's power to regulate commerce among the states and with foreign nations. He also argued that the act conflicted with the Anglo-American Convention of 1818, a treaty governing fisheries, boundaries, and the restoration of American slaves under a previous treaty. Therefore, King concluded, Elkison's detention was unlawful.[115]

The state of South Carolina did not make an official appearance in the case, and no counsel represented it. The obvious candidate, state attorney general James L. Petigru, did not argue the case. Observers as well as Johnson speculated that Petigru declined to participate in the case because he opposed the Seamen Act.[116] The result was that the state declined to defend its law in an action brought by a state prisoner to challenge his detention under that law. Instead, the arrest and imprisonment of Elkison were defended by the association.

Two lawyers represented the association, both of whom were also its officers: Isaac E. Holmes (the association's solicitor) and Benjamin Faneuil Hunt (a member of its standing committee). They rejected King's arguments entirely, insisting that the Seamen Act was a valid exercise of the state's power. Holmes compassed the possibility of dissolving the Union, although just how seriously he had intended these comments became the subject of dispute. Hunt, for his part, took the opportunity to adumbrate at length theories of state sovereignty drawn from political theory and international law.

Despite its relative underreporting, *Elkison* was a watershed confrontation, as its contemporaries perceived. Because of the context in which it arose—one year after the Vesey crisis, scrutinized by the secretary of state and the British ministry—it became an arena for the assertion and elaboration of what were at that moment state-of-the-art arguments about the relationship between federal and state authority. Its unusual posture gave it an element of anomalousness that appears to have spurred the participants to riskier strategies than if it had arisen as a straightforward litigation—for instance, if it had arisen as an appeal from a criminal conviction, as was the posture of some of the era's highest-profile Supreme Court cases dealing with questions of federalism.[117] The named parties in the case were not the only real parties in interest, as demonstrated by the identities of the counsel who actually appeared in court.

To be sure, Elkison had the most to lose, insofar as the outcome of the case determined whether he would remain in jail or not. But Elkison was functionally represented by the British government, while the authority of South Carolina was being openly ventriloquized by a wealthy vigilante organization. Consequently, the arguments ranged more widely than might have been the case in a typical proceeding. In one of the opening acts of South Carolina's states' rights drama, the state itself was a silent party.

Moreover, the fact that the presiding judge in the case had also publicly questioned the wisdom of the law at issue, and that he was known for his outspokenness, contributed to contemporaries' sense that *Elkison* was a momentous case in which not only Elkison's freedom but South Carolina's self-rule was at stake. The case came before Johnson—and Johnson on circuit, not on the bench of the Court, where he was constantly resisting Marshall's efforts to build unanimity. Three years earlier, as Chapter 2 discussed, Marshall had suggested in a case on his own circuit, *The Brig Wilson v. the United States*, that the federal commerce power might be relevant to assessing the states' power to control migration—specifically, the migration of Black persons and free people of color.[118] But because Marshall had ultimately resolved the case on grounds of statutory construction, he had managed to avoid committing himself to any particular view of the Commerce Clause. He had, in classic Marshall fashion, offered suggestive dicta but then decided the case on narrower grounds. Not so with Johnson, who swamped his disposition of Elkison's claim in ringing pronouncements concerning not only the Commerce Clause but the nature of the Union itself.

Representing the association, B. F. Hunt's argument—at least as he presented it in his subsequent pamphlet—proceeded along the following lines: he dealt briefly with the jurisdictional issues raised by Elkison's suit, and he then devoted the bulk of his energy to defending the constitutionality of the Seamen Act. Hunt, like Johnson and the other participants, blended jurisdiction with remedy in a mode of analysis that appears foreign to modern eyes. His argument was that neither writ—habeas corpus nor *de homine replegiando*—was available to Elkison. Habeas could not issue because a federal court lacked authority to grant habeas against a state official. In order for Elkison to challenge his detention by the sheriff, he would have to seek habeas relief from a state court. "The confinement, complained of, is by virtue of a law of the State," Hunt noted. "It is by a state officer, in the name of the State." If Elkison sought to challenge the constitutionality of his detention under state law, his remedy was to do so in the course of a state prosecution, and then to appeal to the Supreme Court of the United States: "Where a defendant to a criminal prosecution, relies upon the Laws and Constitution of the United States, he must plead them before the State Court, and if the decision be against the defence, a *writ of error* lies to the Supreme Court of the United States."[119]

The writ *de homine replegiando* was also inapplicable, Hunt argued, because it would have to lie against the state, insofar as Elkison was in state custody. But such an action was barred by the shield the Eleventh Amendment placed around the state's sovereign immunity. "[T]he writ cannot issue," Hunt contended, "unless, in violation of this article of the Constitution, this Court shall presume to serve a writ upon the State of South-Carolina." The fact that Deliesseline was the named defendant was immaterial, according to Hunt, because the sheriff "*is the minister of the state.*"[120]

The nature of the defendant was but one bar to the suit. In addition, Hunt pointed to what he characterized as deficiencies in the plaintiff. Elkison was not a British subject—at least not in any meaningful sense that would allow him to claim protection against the state law, whether as a matter of international law or of U.S. alienage jurisdiction. Elkison was merely a "person claiming to be a British seaman" and "claiming to be a subject of His Britannic Majesty."[121] Finally, and fatally as far as Hunt was concerned, as a free Black person, Elkison was without capacity to bring an action challenging his detention by the state: "Henry Elkinson [*sic*] is a person of the class of those who *cannot sue at all*, except by Guardian in the State Court." Those state-court rules also applied in federal court, according to Hunt: "[H]e cannot surely then issue a writ to compel the State of South-Carolina to answer him in the Circuit Court. It shocks all our ideas of the relative rights of the parties."[122]

Then Hunt turned to the constitutional question: Was the Seamen Act in conflict with the federal government's commerce or treaty powers? As an initial matter, he argued that South Carolina was a sovereign state, and thus had authority under the law of nations to pass the Seamen Act. To support this proposition, Hunt cited Emmerich de Vattel, whose 1758 treatise *The Law of Nations* had been the subject of debate between Attorney General William Wirt and Secretary of State John Quincy Adams in the context of a piracy case involving the United States and Britain in 1821. Vattel was a key source for all who sought to claim nationhood in the early nineteenth century.

Under the terms of the "Federal Compact," Hunt argued, the state had not ceded its power to pass such a law to the federal government, given "the peculiar circumstances of her slave population." Here was his most pointed rebuttal to the notion that the Seamen Act violated the federal commerce or treaty powers. He characterized the law as "a mere police regulation," a category of regulation governing the state's own "peculiar circumstances"—namely, "having a large slave population" susceptible to "the moral contagion which the intercourse with foreign negroes produces."[123] Hunt repeatedly likened "foreign negroes" to an alien infection that would ravage the state's slave population by contaminating them with ideas of liberty and revolution. Just as nations possessed the well-established power to protect themselves against "pestilence, famine, and what they choose to term moral corruption" by imposing quarantines or other police regulations, so too could South Carolina protect itself against external, existential threats to its polity. "[A] State cannot lawfully commit suicide," Hunt proclaimed.[124] Without explicitly referring to the Vesey conspiracy, Hunt summoned images that resonated with white Charlestonians' continuing fears. South Carolina was "not bound to wait until her citizens behold their habitations in flames and are driven to seek a refuge by the glare of the conflagration."[125]

Critically, Hunt claimed to accept the proposition that the power to regulate commerce was vested exclusively in Congress. This point might have been asserted by Elkison's attorney, Mitchell King, or else by Justice Johnson during the course of the proceeding.[126] A broad commerce power might seem to bolster Elkison's claim, insofar as it raised the possibility that the Seamen Act interfered with federal authority, and therefore had to give way, in accordance with the command of the Constitution's Supremacy Clause. An exclusive commerce power might be even worse for South Carolina, in that it would leave little room for the state to regulate interstate or foreign commerce. On the other hand, an exclusively federal commerce power could be better for the state, insofar as South Carolina and like-minded states held control of Congress and the presidency. An exclusively federal commerce power in the hands of slaveholders bent on preserving their political and economic power had the potential to be a more formidable weapon than even the boldest states' rights argument.

Hunt did not appear to feel that his argument had to bear the burden of defining the boundaries of the federal commerce power. The Seamen Act, he maintained, was not a regulation of commerce; it "merely effects [sic] the mode and prescribes the manner in which the commerce regulated by the Congress shall be carried on." The mode and manner of carrying on an activity was distinct from the activity itself. And the state was free to regulate mode and manner. Hunt elaborated:

I admit the right to regulate commerce, is an exclusive right, but I deny that the enactment of police laws infringes that exclusive right. Were Great-Britain to send her *convicts* or her *incurables* to our shores, the prohibition of their entry, would be no regulation of commerce. . . . New-York, subjects our vessels to quarantine, and confines our citizens to her hospitals, although we have no faith in contagion. Yet, if we confine *her* negro cooks to a particular spot in Charleston, we are told it is a violation of the Constitution! We have much more reason to believe in the moral contagion they introduce, than in the importation of yellow-fever.[127]

By citing New York's quarantine laws, Hunt raised the salience of the dispute. In August 1823, *Gibbons v. Ogden* had not yet been decided, although it was known to be in the offing and indeed had been on the Court's docket in 1820. But as we have seen, police regulations proliferated in early-nineteenth-century America.[128] If states and municipalities were not permitted to pass such laws because they affected the residents of other states, then a host of laws would necessarily fall—not only those that collided with acts of Congress, but also those that arguably interfered with other states' policy choices. Regulation of persons was necessarily concurrent across state borders, Hunt suggested, given the enormous degree of movement and interchange taking place in the nation. British seamen sailed to the United States; New Yorkers voyaged to South Carolina; South Carolinians traveled to New York. Could it really be the case that a state was not permitted to pass laws for public safety and welfare if those laws happened to affect people who had traveled from elsewhere? Hunt portrayed such a suggestion as both untenable and unfair to South Carolina. His argument was a cynical reframing of the reality of commercial union into a mandate for parochial insularity.

Hunt then described the law's effect in terms that at least some in the audience must have recognized as disingenuous: "All that South-Carolina has done in the provission [*sic*] under discussion, is to require free persons of colour, when they arrive, to take up their abode in a very airy and healthy part of the city, until the vessel in which they came is ready to depart."[129]

Justice Johnson Decides

Johnson delivered his decision at the end of the hearing on August 7, 1823. Speaking from the bench at the southern end of the courtroom to the assembled throng, the justice rejected virtually every aspect of the association's arguments in support of the Seamen Act.

Again, as in his written rebuttals of his critics during the Vesey crisis, Johnson scorned a modest or conciliatory rhetorical style. The justice was clearly appalled by the association's lawyers' arguments in defense of the statute, and by the legislature's ill-advised decision to pass the law in the first place. One modern commentator calls the decision "a tactically clever maneuver worthy of Marshall in *Marbury v. Madison*," and indeed in some ways it was.[130] The decision bore other similarities to *Marbury*, most notably the lack of a remedy it ultimately afforded to the petitioner.

Before reaching the merits or the remedial issues, Johnson began by situating the case in its broader political and diplomatic context. Clearly, he was determined to educate his audience on the many levels of power that were interested in this case, extending far up into the reaches of governmental hierarchy, well beyond the petty power struggles of the harbormaster, the sheriff, or the association. He described Britain's efforts to demand protection for its sailors, providing an unusual degree of detail about diplomatic correspondence between Secretary of State Adams and Minister Canning. He alluded to the seizure of the crew members that had led to the contemporaneous case of *Calder v. Deliesseline*. Then Johnson moved from the diplomatic realm to the judicial arena:

> Applications were immediately made to me . . . for the protection of the United States authority, in consequence of which I called upon the district attorney for his official services. Several reasons concurred to induce me to instruct him to bring the subject before the state judiciary. I felt confident that the act had been passed hastily, and without due consideration, and knowing the unfavorable feeling that it was calculated to excite abroad, it was obviously best that relief should come from the quarter from which proceeded the act complained of.[131]

This was remarkable candor—especially given that it was delivered in the middle of a judicial opinion read from the bench and then published in a pamphlet. The "district attorney" referred to the U.S. attorney for South Carolina, John Gadsden. Johnson was telling his audience that he had called upon the U.S. attorney to "bring the subject before the state judiciary"—presumably by means of correspondence or conversation, since the federal prosecutor could hardly initiate a suit in state court. Johnson seems to have hoped that his insider status in Charleston might help him bring about another cessation in enforcement of the Seamen Act—to convince his onetime colleagues on the state bench to allow the statute at least to lie dormant. Moreover, despite Johnson's experience in the Vesey crisis, he still had enough local political acumen to believe that the most palatable resolution would be for state officials quietly to draw down enforcement, rather than setting up a conflict between the state and the federal government.

In Johnson's telling, this strategy had succeeded—for a time. U.S. attorney Gadsden followed Johnson's suggestion and spoke with the state judges; Johnson met with the British consul in Charleston, Benjamin Moodie; Johnson also contacted the group of northern ship captains who then petitioned Congress to protest the treatment of their sailors and urged restraint. Secretary of State Adams spoke with members of South Carolina's congressional delegation.[132] An informal agreement was reached, and prosecutions under the act dwindled. The niceties had been observed, and all was reasonably under control.

But then the association came onto the scene. Johnson noted that Attorney General Petigru had not appeared in defense of the application of the Seamen Act. Naming Holmes and Hunt as the association's lawyers who were at that moment in court, Johnson observed that "pressing the execution of the law at this time is rather a private than a state act."[133]

Johnson unleashed a fusillade of structural, textual, and pragmatic arguments against the Seamen Act. He castigated his home state for its imprudence and mocked the statute's efforts at racial exclusion. He identified the statute's classifications as particularly nonsensical and overbroad: "[I]f this state can prohibit Great Britain from employing her colored subjects (and she has them of all colors on the globe), or if at liberty to prohibit the employment of her subjects of the African race, why not prohibit her from using those of Irish or of Scottish nativity?" Or, he added, Massachusetts might "expedite to this port a vessel with her officers black, and her crew composed of Nantucket Indians, known to be among the best seamen in our service. These might all become slaves under this act."[134] Echoing Chief Justice Marshall's circuit-court opinion in *The Brig Wilson* two years earlier, Johnson pressed the logic of the Seamen Act in order to show how far it might potentially reach.

Turning to the constitutional issues, Johnson deemed the Seamen Act a violation of both the federal commerce power and the treaty power. He rejected the association's argument that the statute represented a valid exercise of South Carolina's power to regulate foreign and interstate commerce. First, Johnson noted, Elkison's case did not raise issues of concurrent power. The Seamen Act actually conflicted with the laws and treaties of the United States that made it "lawful for this seaman to come into this port, in this vessel, and for the captain to bring him in the capacity of a seaman." These, he maintained, "are the very acts for which the state law imposes these heavy penalties. Is there no clashing in this? It is in effect a repeal of the laws of the United States, pro tanto, converting a right into a crime." Johnson thus rejected Hunt's argument that the Seamen Act represented an unexceptionable use of the state's police powers. On the contrary, Johnson held, it was an effort "to divest a right conferred by the general government."[135]

Johnson's repetition of the term "right" here is important. It was not only the states that had rights, contra the arguments of Hunt and Holmes. In Johnson's view, the federal government also had rights—not only powers, but *rights*. Thus, he insisted that "the right of the general government to regulate commerce with the sister states and foreign nations is a paramount and exclusive right"—not a power that was shared with the states. Congress, acting for the United States, had a "paramount and exclusive" right to legislate in the sphere of interstate and foreign commerce. This right came from the Constitution itself, "the most wonderful instrument ever drawn by the hand of man," Johnson said. "I still daily find in it some new excellence."[136]

As in his letter to Jefferson five months previously, Johnson again suggested that the Constitution was a lodestar that was distinct from either the "Pretensions of the States or the United States." As in his concurrence in *Martin v. Hunter's Lessee* in 1816, Johnson continued to view the Constitution as a "tripartite contract" between the people, the states, and the nation. His fellow Charlestonians were simply wrong to frame the issue as a choice between state or federal power. Johnson rejected that binary. Instead, he sought to follow a third path: embracing the overall system established by the Constitution, which required a more dynamic system of balancing competing interests and negotiating with various levels of government.

It was not an accident that Johnson began his *Elkison* opinion by sketching the many exchanges he had had with other officers: the secretary of state, members of the British diplomatic corps, the U.S. attorney, the state judges, the northern ship captains. The commands of the Constitution were paramount and exclusive, but they nevertheless allowed—indeed, required—negotiation and good faith discussion among public officials. But such discourse was impossible once a private entity such as the association seized the machinery of government.

Finally, Johnson observed that the claims of the association amounted to a fundamental attack on the Union that the Revolutionary generation—his father, his mother, his mentor, Charles Cotesworth Pinckney—had built.[137] His own state of South Carolina was claiming to be a sovereign state, and yet such claims were "altogether irreconcilable with the powers of the general government." Worse, such a view "leads to a dissolution of the Union, and implies a direct attack upon the sovereignty of the United States." Johnson then noted (again, all this was part of his opinion) that Holmes, the association's solicitor, had "concluded his argument with the declaration, that, if a dissolution of the Union must be the alternative, he was ready to meet it."[138]

In the battle of newspaper essays that followed the decision, Holmes denied this report, clearly recognizing that it was a serious accusation of his having engaged in what were at that time still shocking and inflammatory polemics. But Johnson insisted that Holmes had said just what Johnson had reported— and he had said it "before the hundreds" who were in the courtroom that day: "All who were present know better. Every one saw me lay down my pen, raise my eyes from my notes, and fix them on the speaker's face. He still proceeded, and in a style which bore evidence of preparation and study."[139] Holmes had attempted to win over the crowd with emotional appeals to the nation-state of South Carolina. But Johnson was more than equal to such histrionics.

These, then, were Johnson's views on the merits of the Seamen Act. But what of Elkison's claim? Johnson concluded his opinion in a different tone. With apparent regret, Johnson held that the federal court lacked the power to grant Elkison's habeas petition because Elkison was being held in state custody. In such circumstances, according to Section 14 of the Judiciary Act of 1789, a writ could issue only from a state court.[140] Johnson delivered this portion of his opinion in acerbic tones that were unmistakably critical of the South Carolina legislature. "Either I misapprehend its purport," he wrote, or the act "is studiously calculated to hurry through its own execution, so as to leave the objects of it remediless." In other words, Johnson suggested that the law had been deliberately constructed to frustrate any attempt to challenge it:

> By giving it the form of a state prosecution the prisoner is to be deprived of the summary interference of the United States authority; and by passing it through the sheriff's hands without the intervention of any court of justice, he is to be deprived of the benefit of the twenty-fifth section of the judiciary act, by which an appeal might be had to the supreme court. Thus circumstanced, it is impossible to conceal the hardships of his case, or deny his claim to some remedy.[141]

And yet, Johnson concluded, unless Congress amended the Judiciary Act, as a federal judge he was "not vested" with the power to grant habeas corpus in Elkison's case.[142]

Having denied Elkison's habeas corpus petition, Johnson then took up the motion for the writ *de homine replegiando*. Here the justice's response was more complex. First, he framed the issue in a manner that distinguished this writ from the habeas writ: "[H]ere the question appears to me to be 'what right I have to refuse it.' " Citing Sir Anthony Fitzherbert's famed and frequently cited sixteenth-century English treatise *New Natura Brevium*, Johnson observed that while the writ *de homine replegiando* might not ultimately prove to be the proper remedy against the sheriff, that question was not currently before the court.[143] The lawyers for the association had argued that the writ was clearly unavailable to Elkison, and that Johnson should therefore deny it unequivocally. With this Johnson disagreed. "I have no right to refuse it," Johnson wrote, "but although it will unquestionably lie to a vendee under the sheriff, I doubt whether it can avail the party against the sheriff himself. The counsel will then consider whether he will sue it out."[144]

In the final paragraphs of the opinion, Johnson restated his conclusion about remedies and reiterated that the Seamen Act was "unconstitutional and void." Thus, he held, "the party petitioner, as well as the ship-master, is entitled to actions as in ordinary cases."[145]

Johnson's equivocal treatment of the writ *de homine replegiando* suggests a note of realism about the limits on the court's power. It may also provide a clue to the details of Elkison's situation. Perhaps Johnson was willing to leave the case in this apparently inconclusive state because he had learned through his back-channel communications with the British consul that Elkison was soon to be redeemed from imprisonment. Presumably, Elkison and his lawyers had little intention of allowing Elkison to be sold into slavery by Sheriff Deliesseline so that they could then bring the writ *de homine replegiando* against that putative buyer (the "vendee"). Or perhaps Johnson reasoned that if he issued the writ to the sheriff, it would be flouted, and therefore his decision represented a rejection of the act's constitutionality paired with a recognition of the limits of federal judicial power.

Elkison's fate is difficult to discern. According to one account, he and his supporters in the British consulate were eventually able to secure his freedom—not through judicial action, but through "informal diplomatic and political pressures."[146] On August 15, 1823, eight days after the trial before Justice Johnson, the *City Gazette and Commercial Daily Advertiser* announced the following departure: "Exports from Charleston—Thursday, August 14. Ship *Homer*, Kerr, for Greenock." According to the notice, the *Homer* was carrying 477 bales of upland cotton, 111 bales of Sea Island cotton, some number of bales of New Orleans cotton, and more than 268 tierces (casks) of rice.[147]

Again, the consignee of the goods was listed as "J. & J. Calder." The four-line entry did not mention whether Elkison was also aboard the ship.

Elkison was a turning point in interbellum constitutional debates. Johnson's decision appears to have been the first instance in which a federal judge found that a state law violated the Commerce Clause of the Constitution.[148] Holmes and Hunt, meanwhile, aired states' rights doctrine in such a way as to both expand its claims and tie it more closely to states' power to regulate their free Black populations.[149] By 1823, it was possible to see the progression of increasingly bold claims about state authority and independence. The timeline ran thus: the Virginia and Kentucky Resolutions of 1798–99, with their fairly mild assertions of states' power to interpret the Constitution; to the Hartford Convention of 1815, with its suggestion that a handful of New England states could withdraw from the Union; to *Martin v. Hunter's Lessee* of 1816, in which the Court had beaten back—barely—the Virginia judges' assertion that they were not bound by the Court's interpretations of federal law. By the time *Elkison* came before Johnson, a related branch of this chronology came from the Missouri Compromise of 1820, in which Congress delineated certain portions of the nation as off-limits to slavery, whatever their white inhabitants might prefer.[150]

Over the two decades following *Elkison*, congressional committees launched investigations into the Seamen Act, and individual states such as Massachusetts sent commissioners to South Carolina in order to mount legal challenges to the act.[151] Repeated efforts to bring the act before the Supreme Court failed. The last and most prominent of these fruitless efforts was brought in 1853 in the federal circuit court in Charleston by James L. Petigru (the state attorney general who had declined to defend the Seamen Act in *Elkison*) and his partner, Benjamin Campbell King (the son of Elkison's lawyer, Mitchell King).[152] The case, *Roberts v. Yates*, was a copy of *Elkison*, thirty years later: a free Black cook on a British ship was jailed and, with the support of the British consul, sued the sheriff of Charleston.[153] But there was one key difference: the judge on the bench in the second-floor courtroom at Broad and Meeting was not Johnson. Johnson had died in 1834. Now, in 1853, the challenge to the Seamen Act was heard by U.S. district judge Robert Budd Gilchrist, a Jacksonian Democrat who had been appointed to the post by President Martin Van Buren. After a brisk proceeding and both parties' stipulation to the facts, Gilchrist held that the Seamen Act was "valid and constitutional."[154]

An appeal to the U.S. Supreme Court was a foregone conclusion, as Gilchrist's opinion explicitly noted. But the judge seemed confident that a reversal was unlikely: "Of the final result we need not say that we entertain no doubt."[155] The case never reached the Supreme Court, however. A combination of fear on the part of South Carolina Unionists, who worried that the Court would uphold the state law and thus enshrine the Seamen Act in high-court precedent, and a change of policy in the British Foreign Office led to the suspension of the appeal.[156] As Chapter 9 will demonstrate, critics of the Seamen Act were likely correct in their apprehensions about placing their case before the Supreme Court under Chief Justice Roger Taney. A lack of resolution was preferable to a bad precedent.

Reactions in Washington

In the immediate aftermath of the *Elkison* case, the association carried on its campaign, and state officials resumed their aggressive enforcement of the Seamen Act. Merchants from Britain and the northern states continued to besiege the State Department with complaints about South Carolina's treatment of their sailors.

Secretary of State Adams learned of the *Elkison* result within a fortnight of the Charleston hearing, when he received a letter from Johnson in which the justice enclosed the pamphlet version of his decision in the case.[157] Adams noted in his diary that British officials had "remonstrated against this Act" the previous winter, and that the administration had been "assured" that "it should sleep." But now, evidently, the act had been roused. Adams sent Johnson's letter on to President Monroe. Three weeks later, while Adams was in Boston visiting his elderly father, former president John Adams, the younger Adams attended a dinner party at which South Carolina U.S. senator Robert Y. Hayne was present. During the meal, the conversation turned to Johnson's opinion in *Elkison*. It became heated, particularly between George Blake, who was U.S. attorney for Massachusetts, and Hayne. Hayne "discovered [displayed] so much excitement and temper that it became painful, and necessary to change the topic," Adams confided to his diary.[158]

Adams hoped that South Carolina would moderate its stance, but enforcement of the act continued. In the spring of 1824, the British chargé d'affaires in Washington, Henry Unwin Addington, visited Adams to press for action against South Carolina. "Mr. Addington said he had received a new express instruction from his Government to make a new complaint in the case of a British vessel from which three men had been taken, to the great injury of the captain," Adams noted. "He asked what had been done in the case of which he had complained last summer."[159] Two weeks later, Addington was again demanding action from the administration. The "papers concerning it"—possibly a reference to Johnson's letter—were "before the President," Adams commented in his diary.[160]

Finally, on April 20, Monroe took action. Adams noted: "The President directed that the opinion of the Attorney-General should be taken upon the constitutionality of the South Carolina Statute."[161] Adams, who clearly had already formed his views upon the act's unconstitutionality, advocated even stronger measures. He urged Monroe to "lay the subject before Congress" or, short of that step, to investigate whether "the South Carolina delegation, could devise any other way of getting rid of that law."[162] Meanwhile, Adams sent a request for an official opinion to Attorney General Wirt's office.

Wirt, who was spending much of his time that spring traveling between Washington and Baltimore, where his private practice was booming, delivered his opinion on May 8. After reciting the relevant provisions of the South Carolina act, Wirt put the question: "Whether it is compatible with the rights of nations in amity with the United States, or with the national constitution?" His answer to each was an unequivocal "no." Like Johnson, Wirt maintained that the state simply had no power to regulate "commerce with foreign nations and among the States." This power is "given to Congress; and this power is, from its nature, exclusive."[163] A state had no valid claim to any competing power that would limit Congress's power in this realm.

In drafting his opinion, Wirt was clearly drawing on his and Daniel Webster's arguments in *Gibbons v. Ogden* three months earlier. If federal power over interstate and foreign commerce was exclusive, then the state was entirely barred from regulating in those domains. This had been Webster's argument against New York's grant of the steamboat monopoly. Here, Wirt applied that logic to the Seamen Act and concluded that the state law was invalid because it sought to regulate with "the terms on which the intercourse between foreign nations and the United States, and between the several States of the Union, shall be carried on."[164] South Carolina's law was not an exercise of the state's police power; it was an incursion into the waterborne trade among the states and foreign nations. "Intercourse" was, of course, the concept that Wirt had offered during his argument in *Gibbons*, and that the Supreme Court had adopted in its opinion, as the definition of commerce. Here it was again, now being adopted by the executive branch in its work of constitutional interpretation.

In addition to the exclusive-power argument, Wirt offered another basis for his conclusion that the Seamen Act was invalid. Congress had in fact acted in the same sphere, which was an even clearer bar to state action—and might convince those who were skeptical of the exclusive-power argument. "Congress has exercised this power," Wirt wrote, "and among those terms there is no requisition that the vessels which are permitted to enter the ports of the several States shall be navigated wholly by white men." Congress had already acted in the domain of interstate and international commerce—presumably, although Wirt did not cite it, through the 1793 coasting statute that had done so much analytical work for both Wirt and the Court in *Gibbons.* One did not need to subscribe to exclusivity in all cases in order to accept supremacy in this instance. Congress had acted, and its action was supreme. "For the regulations of Congress on this subject being both supreme and exclusive, no State can add to them, vary them, obstruct them, or touch the subject in any shape whatever, without the concurrence and sanction of Congress," Wirt wrote. The South Carolina provision, "a regulation of commerce, of a highly penal character, by a State," was "incompatible with the national constitution and the laws passed under it." It was also "incompatible with the rights of all nations which are in amity with the United States." Therefore, it was "void."[165]

Adams, evidently pleased with Wirt's conclusions, sent the attorney general's opinion along with copies of protests from the British government to the governor of South Carolina, John L. Wilson. Adams asked Wilson if, given Wirt's opinion, the state might stay its enforcement of the Seamen Act. Wilson conveyed the opinion and remonstrances to the state legislature.[166] The response from both governor and legislature was unequivocal, bellicose, and loud. Wilson denounced "the opinion of Mr. Wirt" as "sophistry and error" and an "unconstitutional interference" with slavery, which they insisted was guaranteed by the Constitution (specifically, the Three-Fifths Clause of Article I, section 2).[167] The state legislature then passed a concurrent resolution stating that slavery was "inseparably connected with their social and political existence," and denying the federal government's power "to interfere in any manner whatever, with the domestic regulations and preservatory measures in respect to that part of their property."[168]

Despite South Carolina's intransigence, Wirt's opinion remained the official view of the executive branch, until it was reversed by Andrew Jackson's attorney general, John Macpherson Berrien, a Georgia native, in 1831.[169] Adams, by then a member of Congress, continued the fight against the South Carolina act until his death in 1848.

One must ask: In the standoff with South Carolina, was Wirt representing a client, or did his opinion reflect his own views? The answer is difficult to ascertain with certainty. But clearly, having witnessed the hostile responses to Johnson's *Elkison* decision, Wirt knew that his opinion would earn him infamy in many quarters. Yet nothing about the opinion suggests that he was merely providing legal support for Monroe's or Adams's plans. On the contrary, as his opinion in the case of the St. Croix slave James Barry demonstrated, Wirt knew how to draft opinions in such a way as to leave open certain questions about their scope. Nowhere in his opinion on the South Carolina Seamen Act, however, did he warn his interlocutor against giving the opinion more weight "than it fairly deserves"; nor did he describe the question as a political one suited to the statesman rather than to the lawyer.

When Wirt wrote as attorney general, he viewed himself as writing on behalf of the United States—"the Government whose officer I am," as he put it on more than one occasion.[170] In that capacity, he understood himself to be obliged to offer his own best analysis of the Constitution and laws of the United States. "I do not consider myself as the advocate of the government . . . but as a judge, called to decide a question of law with the impartiality and integrity which characterizes the judician," he wrote to Secretary of War Calhoun. "I should consider myself as dishonoring the high-minded government, whose officer I am, in permitting my judgment to be warped in deciding any question officially by the one sided artifice of the professional advocate."[171]

For this reason, it is significant that Wirt's theory of the federal commerce power in his opinion on the Seamen Act reached even farther than had his description of the power three months earlier, when he had argued *Gibbons v. Ogden*. As attorney general, Wirt rested his opinion on the bold proposition that federal power over interstate and foreign commerce was exclusive, and therefore that a state law that trenched on the domain of that power was invalid. His opinion began with the exclusive-power thesis. Additional support came from the fact that Congress had in fact legislated in the arena of foreign and interstate commerce, by virtue of the 1793 coasting statute, thus preempting conflicting state legislation. The commerce power was robust and extensive enough to defeat a state's effort to "add to, vary, or obstruct" its exercise, or even to "touch the subject" of federal commercial regulation. In the arena of commerce among the states and with other nations, Wirt's deep-seated commitment to a superintending federal authority apparently outweighed his "Virginian" affinities for concurrent power and even, in some cases, for slavery.

Justice Johnson and the Press

And what of Johnson? True to form, in the months following his decision in *Elkison*, he engaged in a protracted debate in the pages of the Charleston newspapers defending his opinion on the constitutionality of the South Carolina statute. Under the pen names of "Philonimus" and "Hamilton," he battled with "Caroliniensis," the collective nom de plume of Isaac Holmes, who had represented the association in *Elkison*, and Robert Turnbull, author of the Seamen Act and an officer of the association. Another pseudonymous author, "Philo-Caroliniensis," also joined the fray, attacking Johnson's "Philonimus" essays.[172] In 1827, Turnbull, now writing under the name "Brutus," published a set of essays titled "The Crisis."[173]

The tone of these pieces was unmistakably sectional, although the sections were more varied than a strict north-south delineation. "People in the four great divisions of the United States are divided in sentiment," Turnbull wrote. "[W]e are a united people it is true—but we are a family united only for external objects."[174] Much of the argument took the form of pointed attacks on Johnson himself, for the supposed perfidy he displayed in holding the Seamen Act invalid. "Caroliniensis" repeatedly sounded this theme; one particularly sharp example came in the emotion-laden conclusion to the sixth essay:

> Was there nothing due to the people of Charleston, among whom Judge Johnson was born, and to whom he is indebted for many honors? Would it not at least have been respectful to the people of South-Carolina, and to its Legislature, to have passed *sub silentio* a question, which was not necessary to the performance of his duty, but which must necessarily inflict a severe wound upon their sensibilities? Or are we to understand, that when a citizen becomes a servant of the General Government, he is to disregard the views, opinions, and feelings of those among whom he was bred, and from whose early notice of him, he perhaps derives the exalted honor of being a Judge of the Supreme Court of the United States?[175]

Johnson responded with his customary pungent flair. Under his own name, as we have seen, he described the polemics that the association's lawyers had deployed in the courtroom. Reporting Holmes's invocation of "dissolution of the Union," Johnson wrote, "Every one saw me lay down my pen, raise my eyes from my notes, and fix them on the speaker's face. He still proceeded, and in a style which bore evidence of preparation and study."[176]

In his "Philonimus" essays, Johnson parried his opponents' legal arguments with his own doctrinal analysis. One crux of the dispute concerned the 1803 act of Congress that was at the center of *The Brig Wilson*, which Marshall had heard on his circuit in 1820, and which Chapter 2 examined. Neither party appears to have raised the 1803 act in the *Elkison* proceeding, however. Johnson's critics argued that the 1803 act—which was titled "An Act to Prevent the Importation of Certain Persons into Certain States, Where, by the Laws Thereof, Their Admission Is Prohibited"—insulated South Carolina's Seamen Act from attacks on its constitutionality.[177] By putting federal enforcement behind state laws that prohibited the "admission or importation" of Black seamen, "Philo-Caroliniensis" argued, Congress had implicitly endorsed laws such as South Carolina's. Indeed, the author claimed, the Seamen Act "is, by act of Congress, made an United States law."[178]

Johnson rejected this argument altogether. First, he noted, the 1803 act had not federalized any state laws; it had merely offered federal enforcement to state laws touching on the migration or importation of Black persons. Second, while he acknowledged that "by virtue of the Act of Congress of 1803, the State Act of 1822 is a valid Act as far as an Act of Congress can give validity to it," the qualification in the final clause raised more questions than it answered. Most important, that clause was limited by the Supremacy Clause of the Constitution: "That is, as far as it does not violate existing treaty stipulations."[179] Given the United States' treaties with Britain and the increasing pressure from the Foreign Office as well as British officials in the United States, Johnson contended, the Seamen Act could not be valid. The parties to a treaty could not "pass navigation laws which will convert the treaty into a nullity," he insisted.[180]

The essays were as forceful as ever, but Johnson's correspondence suggested that the events of August had left him in a somber mood. Johnson sent copies of his *Elkison* opinion—which the newspapers still refused to publish, so he had had it printed in pamphlet form—to his confidants around the nation. Writing to Jefferson four days after he rendered his decision in the case, a copy of which he enclosed, Johnson wrote,

> I acknowledge to you my dear Sir, that I have sometimes some gloomy Doubts crossing my Mind respecting the Destiny of our beloved Country. . . . That greatest of Evils Disunion, appears to be losing its Terrors. My Ears are shocked at Times by Expressions that I hear on the subject. I enclose you a Copy of an Opinion which I had to deliver a few Days ago which will excite some Surprise.

Johnson ended by noting that he his decision had earned him enmity from many of his fellow Charlestonians. "I have received a Warning to quit this City. I fear nothing so much as the Effects of the persecuting Spirit that is abroad in this Place."[181]

A few weeks later, Johnson sent a copy of his opinion to Secretary of State Adams, which, as we have seen, Adams forwarded to President Monroe.[182] In another letter to Adams nearly a year later, in July 1824, Johnson observed that the association was continuing its campaign of legalized persecution of Black sailors. Despite his own *Elkison* decision and Attorney General Wirt's opinion, the federal government appeared utterly impotent to effect any change in the state's enforcement of the Seamen Act. "I am wholly destitute of the power of arresting those measures," Johnson wrote to Adams:

> Both the writs of habeas corpus and injunction I am precluded from using, because the cases assume the form of State prosecutions; and, if I could issue them, I have nobody to call upon, since the district attorney is himself a member of the association; and they have, further, the countenance of five other officers of the United States in their measures. To this I attribute much of the confidence with which these measures are prosecuted.[183]

At home in Richmond, Chief Justice Marshall learned of Johnson's *Elkison* decision, and the ensuing contretemps in Charleston, from the newspapers. "Our brother Johnson, I perc[ei]ve, has hung himself on a democratic snag in a hedge composed entirely of thorny state rights in South Carolina, and will find some difficulty, I fear, in getting off into smooth open ground," Marshall wrote to Story.[184] "You have I presume seen his opinion in the national Intelligencer, & could scarcely have supposed that it would have excited so much irritation as it seems to have produced." The issue in the case "is one of much feeling in the south," Marshall observed. "Of this I was apprized, but did not think it would have shown itself in such strength as it has." The chief justice then contrasted Johnson's approach with his own in *The Brig Wilson*. Marshall characterized the state law at issue there—Virginia's 1793 law barring the migration into the state of "free Negroes and Mulattoes"—as the "twin brother" of South Carolina's Seamen Act. "I might have considered its constitutionality had I chosen to do so," Marshall mused. "[B]ut it was not absolutely necessary, &, as I am not fond of butting against a wall in sport, I escaped on the construction of the act."

Marshall appeared to pride himself on his ability to escape on construction of the act. By so doing, he believed that he had avoided adding "fuel" to "the fire at which the *exaltées* are about to roast the judicial department."[185] He was likely correct in that assessment, as events in Charleston demonstrated. But unlike Marshall, Johnson could never resist adding fuel to a fire when he believed himself to be in the right.

Johnson's opinion in *Elkison* endured, albeit perversely. The case's immediate significance lay in its inability to be put into action. It was a constitutional decision by a federal court, in which the intended force of federal judicial power was utterly stymied. In the view of some of Johnson's fellow South Carolinians, the case stood as proof of the state's power to ignore, or indeed nullify, federal law.

At a Fourth of July celebration held by the State Rights and Free Trade Party in Charleston in 1831, South Carolina U.S. senator Robert Y. Hayne told his audience that a state's right of nullification was protected by the Constitution, despite critics who charted that it was tantamount to endorsing disunion. In contrast to Hayne's attack on Johnson eight years earlier, which had so embarrassed Hayne's Boston dinner-party companions, the senator's remarks now found friendly listeners. Hayne's evidence for this proposition was *Elkison* and its sequelae:

> [H]as not South Carolina, by an act of her Legislature in relation to persons of colour coming into this State on board of foreign ships, *Nullified a treaty* according to the opinion of the late Attorney General, of the President of the United States, and the Federal Judiciary? It becomes a *grave* question therefore, whether we are not out of the Union *now*, or are we "in the Union and out of the Union at the same time?"[186]

For Hayne, as for others who identified themselves with the newly formed State Rights and Free Trade Party, the outcome of *Elkison* was a victory. South Carolina's Seamen Act was still being enforced. The state's legislative will, which in Hayne's view represented the constitutional judgment of the state's people, had triumphed not only over some abstract notion of the federal commerce power, but over a formal treaty of the United States. The state's interpretation of the Constitution effectively canceled out those of the president, the U.S. attorney general, and the federal courts. If a state could thus release itself from the obligations of a treaty, surely it could annul a mere piece of domestic legislation passed by Congress.

In 1832, Johnson again drew the ire of his fellow Charlestonians when he refused to allow the issue of the constitutionality of the federal tariff of 1828, the so-called Tariff of Abominations, to be put to the jury.[187] Because the case had been conjured into existence by opponents of the tariff who wished to challenge its validity in court, they viewed Johnson's decision as a political act depriving them of their chosen arena—which, indeed, it was.

Johnson continued to perform his duties as a justice, including riding circuit, although he began to spend summers outside Charleston. In the summer of 1834, feeling himself exiled from his native state and in pain from "a serious indisposition"—cancer of the jaw—Johnson traveled to New York to seek treatment. On August 4, in Brooklyn, Johnson underwent "the most painful surgical operation," which he bore "without the aid of friends, or being bound." Prior to the surgery, the doctor had "expressed his opinion of the inability of the Judge to survive the operation," but Johnson nevertheless decided to proceed. Within half an hour of the end of the procedure, Johnson died, at the age of sixty-two.[188]

Johnson's marker stands in the graveyard of St. Philip's Church in Charleston, three blocks from the courthouse where he presided, and where he won himself local infamy.[189] The marble obelisk, placed by "His Children who loved and valued him most dearly," bears a lengthy inscription concluding, "His virtue pure his integrity stern his justice exact his patriotism warm and his fortitude not to be shaken in the hour of Death. Conscia Mens recti famae mendacia ridet."

The final Latin phrase can be translated as "The mind conscious of what is right scorns the falsehoods of rumor."[190] In 1822, when Johnson was being attacked for urging calm and moderation at the height of white Charlestonians' panic over the Vesey conspiracy, he had stated in print, "My reputation is the property of the United States." And yet, he noted, "I wish to live in harmony with those who surround me."[191] With a hint of Johnsonian pugnacity, the marker celebrates upright reputation, even as it stands peacefully in the quiet verdancy of the churchyard, among neighbors whose headstones bear storied Charleston names.

A few yards away from Johnson's obelisk is the grave of John C. Calhoun. The conflict between Johnson's vision of the Union—as a tripartite contract among the people, the states, and the United States—and what became known as Calhoun's theory of nullification effectively damned Johnson to exile.

Despite the volume of Johnson's writings, no major collection of his papers currently resides in any publicly accessible archive. The substantial trove of documents that survived him likely found their way to the state capital at Columbia, where they are believed by his descendants to have been destroyed during the burning of the city in February 1865, when it was captured by the Union Army under the command of General William T. Sherman.[192]

5 • The Revolutionary Daughter

A Federalism of Inheritance

When William Johnson dug up the roots of Charleston's Liberty Tree and sent a fragment to Thomas Jefferson in 1817, the justice was asserting a claim to the Revolutionary heritage of the city as well as the nation. Johnson researched the tree's whereabouts, took physical possession of its remains, and dispatched a piece of it to the Virginia radical who had appointed him to the Supreme Court.

Johnson's sense of connection to the founding era was both intellectual and emotional. It was also deeply personal, having come to him through his parents' stories of the great events of the Revolution and the South Carolina ratification convention. As a young man, he was further steeped in living history when he began reading law with General Charles Cotesworth Pinckney. As we have seen, the Pinckney Mansion on East Bay Street was a carefully constructed monument—complete with a temple front on its façade—to the ideals of Anglo-American culture, politics, and law. Those ideals formed a crucial underpinning of eighteenth- and nineteenth-century South Carolinian constitutional ideology.

Another Charlestonian, nearly an exact contemporary of Johnson, was also imbibing those same principles, in that same house, from the same person. But the house was her house, and the statesman was her father.

Born in 1774 and known in her large and influential family as "a woman of masculine intellect," Maria Henrietta Pinckney was the eldest of three surviving children—all daughters—of General Charles Cotesworth Pinckney.[1] Upon her death in 1836, she was mourned by many of Charleston's most prominent political leaders. An unmarried and childless woman, she was regarded by her family as one of its "great Politicians."[2]

No image survives of Maria Henrietta Pinckney (if indeed any was made in her lifetime). A dress she is said to have worn to meet President George Washington has been preserved. Her true legacy lies in the handful of writings that has endured and come down to us in the record. These writings include manuscripts as well as published pamphlets. The documents she produced, the house whose notoriety she deployed in the service of her political beliefs, and her family connections placed her at the center of the ideological hothouse that was Charleston in the 1820s and early 1830s.

From the perspective of the twenty-first century, Pinckney is a shadowy presence in the background of debates over commerce, union, and slavery in the 1820s and 1830s. But she is nonetheless present. Indeed, her contemporaries would not have needed to look closely to find her. Her political views were well known in Charleston, and she occupied an important, and unique, place in public debates concerning nullification, state sovereignty, and the structure of American federalism.

Unlike the men of the Pinckney family, Maria Henrietta Pinckney did not enjoy a position in government that would have afforded her a public role in shaping legal and political affairs. Yet she was arguably one of the most influential of her generation of Pinckney offspring—the children of the founding generation (Charles Cotesworth, Thomas, and Harriott), and the grandchildren of the estimable Eliza Lucas Pinckney. Two of Maria Henrietta's male first cousins served in the South Carolina nullification convention in 1832. During that crisis, however, it was the Pinckney Mansion—now owned by Maria Henrietta and her sister Harriott—that nullificationist leaders sought for the backdrop of their parades and public ceremonies. It was Maria Henrietta's defense of nullification, titled *A Political Catechism*, that became one of the core documents of the movement.[3] When she died in 1836, at the age of sixty-two, the *Charleston Mercury* carried a notice directed "To the State Rights Men of 1834" that lauded her "heroic patriotism," the "strength of her bright character," and "the tributes of her cultivated intellect."[4]

Examination of Maria Henrietta Pinckney's writings reveals her to be an important, and surprising, producer of constitutional discourse during the South Carolinian crisis of the late 1820s and early 1830s. As with William Johnson, Pinckney's career demonstrates the crucial nature of local power and local connections in the midst of a struggle for political control among city, state, national, and international levels of authority. Also like Johnson, Pinckney was both a product and a producer of the long founding moment. Her access to the world of politics came through her storied family connections, and she used that legacy as a source of rhetorical power. In so doing, she shaped and recast the meaning of her own Revolutionary heritage, as well as that of her city and state.

Yet Pinckney diverged sharply from Johnson in her views of the relationship between federal and local power, the nature of the Union, and the role of the federal courts. Moreover, unlike Johnson, Pinckney was not herself present to witness many of the moments when her ideas were transmitted to the political and legal community. Johnson's opinion in *Elkison v. Deliesseline* began with a lengthy narrative of events that had occurred in his courtroom on Broad Street, in front of hundreds of people. Johnson himself was everywhere in Charleston—in court, as a landlord, as a member of civic organizations, as a planter.

Pinckney, by contrast, operated from the family mansion, which—after her father's death in 1825—belonged to her and her sisters. But the Pinckney manse was no secluded domestic sphere. As the former home of a great statesman, it retained the aura of a landmark edifice, a cachet that Pinckney and her political associates deployed strategically.

Pinckney's arguments came from the house, through her writing. The words likely issued from her pen in the same library on the northeast corner of the first floor that her father and grandfather had used as their offices. From there, the manuscript pages traveled to A. E. Miller's printing office on Broad Street, where they were transformed into pamphlets that made their way into the drawing rooms and onto the streets of the city. Visitors, including congressmen, mayors, and foreign luminaries, discussed political theory with Pinckney in the drawing room. When she did personally take part in the political spectacles of the day, she made careful efforts to structure the terms on which her political participation took place.[5]

Pinckney's views of the relationship between federal, state, and local power helped to shape what became the nullificationist platform. In some respects, her defense of states' rights, and her related attack on federal power, were more vigorous than the views of her more famed contemporaries, such as John C. Calhoun. Pinckney seems to present the picture that one might expect to see from an elite white Charlestonian of the antebellum period. If Johnson's full-throated endorsement of national power was a startling discovery to his contemporaries, it remains so today. Pinckney, by contrast, appears unremarkable—but for the fact that she was a woman, and a woman who managed to claim a public platform. Both Johnson and Pinckney understood themselves to be living in a long founding moment, in dialogue with their Revolutionary forbears.[6] The meaning of that legacy informed each of their lives, at times seeming to compel them to comment on political and legal events unfolding around them. The lessons they drew from this shared inheritance, however, could not have been more different.

What did federalism look like in South Carolina in 1832? It comprised multiple levels of government; it potentially entailed alternatives as diverse as exclusive federal power over commerce or state power to nullify federal law; it was both parochial and nationalistic; and it insisted on every punctilio of respect for the state's Revolutionary heritage. It was at once William Johnson and Maria Henrietta Pinckney.

Maria Henrietta Pinckney and Her Circle

Maria Henrietta Pinckney was born into one of the wealthiest and most prominent families in South Carolina. Her forbears had been renowned since the colonial and Revolutionary eras—especially her paternal grandmother, Eliza Lucas Pinckney, the pioneering indigo planter and mother of two generals who became Revolutionary statesmen, Charles Cotesworth Pinckney and Thomas Pinckney. Eliza Lucas Pinckney left a letterbook that provided her descendants, as well as subsequent historians, with a remarkably detailed window into her daily life from the 1730s to the 1760s.[7]

Maria Henrietta's father, Charles Cotesworth, and her uncle Thomas were both close to their mother, corresponding with her frequently from English schools, Revolutionary battlefields, and later from their diplomatic postings in Europe. Maria Henrietta's aunt Harriott Pinckney Horry resembled her mother, Eliza Lucas Pinckney, in that Harriott was widowed at a relatively young age and then took over management of her own plantations as well as overseeing the business affairs of her brothers, the Generals Pinckney, while they were on campaign or abroad.[8] Maria Henrietta, her sisters, and various cousins spent much of their childhoods with their aunt Harriott and grandmother Eliza, who helped to raise the young Pinckneys—affectionately termed, by Harriott, "all our Children."[9]

The Pinckneys were a founding family with women at the center. The Pinckney women were planters, writers, entrepreneurs, revolutionaries, keepers of records, and "kin specialists" who maintained the "family connection," as it was always termed, among the multitudes of aunts, uncles, cousins, nieces, and nephews (many of whom were named, in iterative tribute, Charles, Thomas, Harriott, or Eliza).[10] As a teenager, Eliza Lucas's formidable energy and intellect had been channeled into many avenues that were typically outside the compass of the young lady of the planter class. When she was not walking the fields and supervising her family's enslaved workers, she spent hours reading works of history, philosophy, and literature; she "japanned" (lacquered) trays, tea chests, and stands and sent them to her acquaintances; and she tried her hand at amateur lawyering, drawing up wills for several neighbors.[11] Her range of activities and her ambition made her a "female planter-patriarch."[12]

Yet the current historical record contains no image of either Maria Henrietta Pinckney or of her famous indigo-planting grandmother. Indeed, despite Maria Henrietta's "masculine intellect," which made her "a woman of unusual force of mind and a student of public questions," precious few of her writings have come down to the modern day.[13] The vast collections of the Pinckney family papers contain letters that mention Pinckney as a daughter, granddaughter, cousin, or niece; a few notes actually address her directly. During her lifetime, she met Washington and Lafayette and was well acquainted with South Carolina's leading politicians, John C. Calhoun, James Hamilton, Jr., and Robert Y. Hayne. Harriet Martineau's tour of America in 1834 and 1835 included a visit to Pinckney, at the mansion. And yet we know comparatively little about Pinckney's life, despite the fact that she lived in the highest echelon of a society that considered itself the nation's most elite and most cultured.

Besides her dress, we have two important sources produced by Pinckney herself—her writings.[14] The most important is titled *The Quintessence of Long Speeches, Arranged as a Political Catechism*, which she published in Charleston in 1830. Pinckney's name was not listed on the title page; instead, the essay was identified as having been written "By a Lady, for Her God-Daughter."

With the *Political Catechism*, Pinckney claimed a place at the center of the developing nullification crisis that began in South Carolina in 1828 and reached its critical point in 1832 and 1833. The second piece, an essay titled *A Notice of the Pinckneys*, was a sketch of the family dating back to colonial times. It was printed in 1860, twenty-four years after Pinckney's death, at the request of her sister Harriott. Although the title page bore no author's name, Pinckney was credited on the third page as its creator.[15]

A Revolutionary Childhood

Throughout Maria Henrietta's Pinckney's early life, her family connections placed her in the midst of many significant moments of the Revolutionary and early national period. During her early childhood, her father (General C. C.

Pinckney) served in the South Carolina Assembly and then as an officer in the Continental Army. When Charleston fell to the British after a long siege in May 1780, C. C. Pinckney was designated a prisoner of war and ordered to leave the city with his family. The family—C. C. Pinckney, his wife, Sally Middleton Pinckney, seven-year-old Maria Henrietta, and her five-year-old sister, Harriott—traveled to Pennsylvania, where they lived in·a state of quasi-exile with the family of C. C. Pinckney's brother Thomas Pinckney. Also among the little group of paroled officers and their families were Edward Rutledge (C. C. Pinckney's law partner) and his wife, Henrietta Middleton Rutledge, the sister of Sally Middleton Pinckney.[16]

By the time the Pinckney family returned to South Carolina in 1782, their main plantation and home, Belmont, five miles up Charleston Neck from the city, had been burned down by British troops. The family's other properties had been damaged or destroyed, and two infant sons had died. In 1784, Maria Henrietta's mother, Sally, died of consumption. Ten-year-old Maria Henrietta, eight-year-old Harriott, and two-year-old Eliza were sent to live with their aunt Harriott Pinckney Horry at her Hampton Plantation, some fifty miles northeast of Charleston, on the Santee River. There the girls' aunt and their grandmother Eliza Lucas Pinckney (of indigo fame) raised them, alongside several cousins.

When their father remarried in 1786, the three sisters returned to the family mansion in Charleston. But the girls spent substantial periods of time at Hampton with their aunt and grandmother, as when their father and stepmother, Mary Stead Pinckney, traveled to Philadelphia for the Constitutional Convention in 1787. In May 1791, George Washington accepted Aunt Harriott's invitation to stop at Hampton as part of his extended tour around the country as president. The widowed Harriott was one of the wealthiest people, and certainly the wealthiest woman, in South Carolina.[17] She was also the fourth-largest slaveowner in the state. At the time of Washington's visit, her human property at Hampton numbered 340 enslaved individuals.[18] "Mrs. Horry" was one of the leading members of the Carolina planter aristocracy. That fact, coupled with her brothers' friendship with Washington, meant that the president's visit was an opportunity to highlight the importance of the Pinckney family to the new republic.

When Washington arrived at Hampton with his sizable entourage, he was greeted on the large, columned veranda by Harriott, her mother, Eliza Lucas Pinckney, and her three nieces—Maria Henrietta Pickney and her sisters. Harriott wore a silk gown of her mother's that had its own unique transatlantic provenance. The silk from which it was made had been grown on the Pinckneys' Belmont plantation decades earlier and then carried to England by Eliza and her husband when they traveled there in 1753. Eliza had presented one length to Princess Augusta when the Pinckneys appeared before the royal court. She brought the remainder of the fabric home to South Carolina and had it made into a gown. Now, in 1791, on the day of Washington's visit to Hampton, it was Eliza's daughter Harriott who wore the silk dress, along with a sash bearing the American coat of arms.[19] After a lavish breakfast, the president discussed agriculture and plantation management with Eliza Lucas Pinckney, and the Revolutionary history of the region with Harriott Pinckney Horry.[20] Harriott's Pinckney nieces were present throughout the visit, witnesses to the great ceremony and the honored positions that their elders—female as well as male—held in the new nation.[21]

The *Notice of the Pinckneys*

Maria Henrietta Pinckney's admiration and affection for her grandmother were evident in her *Notice of the Pinckneys*. Maria Henrietta likely wrote the *Notice* sometime after 1830, as it contains an anecdote of her uncle General Thomas Pinckney, involving a "sportive" note he wrote "when nearly eighty." Her uncle had been born in 1750. But the *Notice* was not published until 1860, when, as a twenty-page pamphlet, it was "privately printed for Harriott Pinckney at Charleston."[22] The subject of the *Notice* was the "early years" of "the Generals Pinckney" as well as "the lives of those who preceded them"—Eliza Lucas Pinckney and Chief Justice Charles Pinckney. "This Notice is, therefore, intended for their descendants," stated the prefatory note, which was signed "Maria Henrietta Pinckney."[23]

The chief part of the *Notice* was devoted to Eliza Lucas Pinckney and Charles Cotesworth Pinckney. Chief Justice Charles Pinckney, Maria Henrietta's grandfather, appeared briefly in its pages. But the key players in the Pinckney lineage were her grandmother and her father. "The Pinckneys" were constituted not only by the male line, but also by the women who earned fame as patriots and founders.

Of her grandmother, Maria Henrietta wrote, "Respected, admired, at the head of society in Carolina, all that she thought, and said, and did, was right."[24] The account emphasized Eliza's independence of thought from a young age: "In compliance with her father's wishes, she never engaged in any of the feminine accomplishments of the needle, but spent the greatest part of her time in reading; and, as there were no reviews in those days, to save the labor of thinking, to be well informed, it was necessary to read deeply and think for oneself."[25] (Here the writer gives a hint of her own views on the subject as well.) But, Maria Henrietta suggested, it was through her piety that Eliza left her deepest impression on her children and grandchildren: "She always obliged the young people of her family to recollect the text of the sermon they had heard at Church, and search for it in the Bible as soon as they came home." The tone of grandmotherly inquiry was not punitive, however: "[S]he explained to them those parts they did not understand, or had forgotten."[26] Nor did Eliza "believe that a moderate participation in the recreations and amusements of civilized society was contrary to the precepts or spirit of the Gospel, that the relinquishing of the ball-room, or the drama, was a proof of the spirituality of any one's state." Indeed, Eliza regaled her young relatives with tales of "the gaities in which she had participated during her second visit to England," noting "that she had never missed a single play when Garrick was to act."[27]

Then Maria turned to her father, General C. C. Pinckney. His parents took "unremitting pains" with his education, such that "he knew his letters before he could speak." After graduating from Christ Church College, Oxford, at the age of eighteen—young even for the time—Charles Cotesworth began to study law in the Middle Temple, where he was "indefatigable in study" to such a degree that his mother wrote worriedly from South Carolina to urge him to attend to his health. Here, in discussing her father's legal studies, Maria Henrietta made a point of noting his distinguished teacher: "It is a matter of too much interest to be forgotten, that General PINCKNEY attended the lectures of Blackstone, and took notes of the whole course. The volume containing these is carefully preserved."[28] Lineage mattered, especially intellectual lineage. The volume of Pinckney's notes was surely on the shelves of the library in the East Bay mansion, perhaps within reach of where Maria Henrietta sat drafting her *Notice*.

Early Adulthood and Loss

In 1793 (the year that Johnson was admitted to the South Carolina bar), the young Maria Henrietta Pinckney journeyed to Pennsylvania. This time, the occasion was a somber one: the family's matriarch, Eliza Lucas Pinckney, was suffering from advanced breast cancer. Maria Henrietta accompanied her seventy-year-old grandmother to Philadelphia to consult a renowned physician and seek what the family hoped would be successful treatment. Eliza had applied leeches to the tumor, on the recommendation of other doctors, but to no avail. Her children urged her to make the journey to Philadelphia to visit Dr. James Tate, whose advanced treatments involved the use of arsenic as well as various pills and tinctures.[29] Also in the traveling party were Maria Henrietta's sister Harriott; their aunt Harriott Pinckney Horry; and their first cousin Harriott Horry. Maria Henrietta was nineteen years old; her sister Harriott was sixteen; and Cousin Harriott was twenty-two.[30] It was Eliza's wish to be thus accompanied by her daughter and three granddaughters. Charles Cotesworth had proposed accompanying them, but his mother refused.[31]

The travelers, three generations of Pinckney women, left Charleston aboard the ship *Delaware* on April 10. They were accompanied by five enslaved people from Harriott's Hampton Plantation: three women, Sibby, Hannah, and Dye; and two men, Ned and Isaac.[32] After a miserably rough ten-day journey, during which all were intensely seasick, they finally reached Philadelphia.

The list of well-wishers who visited the Pinckneys at their lodgings at the corner of Spruce and Third streets reflected the family's prominence in the young republic. Elizabeth Schuyler Hamilton called more than once; other visitors included President Washington, Treasury Secretary Alexander Hamilton (both generals Pinckney were leading Federalists), and Supreme Court justice James Iredell and his wife, Hannah Johnston Iredell.[33]

Despite the treatments, however, after weeks of pain and bouts of "sick stomach," Eliza Lucas Pinckney died on May 26, 1793. Family lore holds that Washington himself served as a pallbearer at her funeral, which was held in Philadelphia.[34] She was buried for some period of time in St. Peter's churchyard in that city, and her daughter Harriott intended to move her remains to St. Michael's at the corner of Broad and Meeting in Charleston.[35] But the yellow fever epidemic that struck Philadelphia in the summer of 1793 prevented Harriott from doing so when she had planned, and surviving records in Philadelphia and Charleston do not reveal whether she succeeded before her own death in 1830.[36]

A Pinckney Lady

The archives afford glimpses of Maria Henrietta Pinckney's activities between roughly 1793 and 1830—that is, the years of her life between the ages of nineteen and fifty-six.

In 1796, sisters Maria Henrietta and Harriott—now twenty-two and nineteen years old, respectively—returned to their aunt Harriott's Hampton Plantation for a period of two years while their father (accompanied by their stepmother and fourteen-year-old sister, Eliza) was in France carrying out his duties as U.S. minister plenipotentiary under the Washington, then Adams, administration. Upon his departure, Charles Cotesworth Pinckney left detailed instructions for his attorneys regarding his property and investments. He also made provision for the expenses of the daughters who were remaining at home: "The net profits of my own Negroes, Interest of Bank Stock & rents, (after my Daughters (Maria & Harriott's) expences are *fully* paid) to be put in Bank, & remitted."[37]

The following year, 1797, gave rise to events for which C. C. Pinckney was to become famous in early American high politics and popular culture. The "XYZ Affair," as it quickly became known, involved an infamous meeting in Paris between three U.S. commissioners and a group of intermediaries acting on behalf of French Foreign Minister Charles Maurice de Talleyrand. The three U.S. envoys were C. C. Pinckney, John Marshall, and Elbridge Gerry.[38] They had been dispatched to France by President John Adams, who charged them with negotiating an amicable resolution to the French Directory's new bellicose habit of seizing U.S. merchant ships. Instead of meeting with Talleyrand himself, as they had been led to expect, Pinckney, Marshall, and Gerry were contacted by three highly placed individuals—"X," "Y," and "Z," as they were identified in published reports—who demanded concessions from the Americans in order to establish formal negotiations with Talleyrand. The demands included a low-interest loan from the United States to the French government and a fifty-thousand-pound bribe to Talleyrand himself.[39] Otherwise, the French intermediaries warned, the Directory might declare war on the United States.

When "X" (Baron Jean-Conrad Hottinguer) pressed for an answer, Pinckney was said to have replied: "No, no, not a sixpence." Pinckney and Marshall then returned to the United States, as did news of their thwarted diplomatic efforts. American newspapers lauded the envoys as honorable republican heroes standing against the corrupt French government. Pinckney's blunt response fit nicely into the speech bubbles of the era's political cartoonists. Soon it was expanded into a ringing motto suitable for roomier banners, broadsides, and placards, especially those of the Federalist Party: "Millions for defense but not one cent for Tribute." The XYZ Affair, and his highly quotable riposte, made C. C. Pinckney into a popular political hero.[40]

At home in South Carolina, his eldest daughter, Maria Henrietta, would have read popular accounts of the XYZ Affair as well as had access to private versions of the story from her father himself. These events carried lessons: about republican honor, public service, Pinckney dignity, and the power of rhetoric in both the elevated realms of diplomacy and the ink-smeared pages of newspapers and pamphlets. Charles Cotesworth Pinckney had no sons to follow him into high federal office, but his eldest daughter—brought up in an atmosphere redolent of family and national pride—was watching these events closely.

In December 1799, her cousin Thomas Pinckney, Jr.—the eldest son of her father's brother—wrote to her from an army encampment at Harpers Ferry, in western Virginia, to inform her of the death of Washington. "Our great, our glorious Commander, is indeed no more," nineteen-year-old Lieutenant Thomas Pinckney, Jr., wrote breathlessly to his twenty-five-year-old cousin. "This event is so momentous, that I can speak of nothing else, it has thrown a general damp on every heart, that beat in unison with the welfare of its Country." He signed the letter "Yours unalterably, T Pinckney."[41] Cousin Thomas and Maria Henrietta appear to have been close, perhaps as a result of long periods spent together as children at their aunt Harriott Horry's Hampton Plantation. Thirty-three years after writing this letter, Cousin Thomas—or "Colonel Thomas," as he became known, suitable to his station as the owner of multiple plantations as well as a massive brick house on Broad Street—served in South Carolina's nullification convention, along with his brother (named, inevitably, Charles Cotesworth Pinckney and called "Cotesworth" by the family).[42]

In another sighting from March 1823, Maria Henrietta is glancingly mentioned ("in consequence of the message from my nieces") in a letter from her uncle, General Thomas Pinckney, the father of Cousin Thomas. Writing from his plantation, Eldorado, to his sister Harriott Pinckney Horry, who was at that moment in Charleston, the elder Thomas Pinckney detailed travel plans, then closed by noting that he was sending his sister "a few asparagus by Mr Rutledge."[43] The Vesey crisis had occurred less than a year before; General Thomas Pinckney's "Achates" pamphlet, urging the forced expulsion of the state's population of Black people and free persons of color, had followed shortly thereafter. The Seamen Act was in its brief period of reduced enforcement. The South Carolina Association—with that same uncle of Maria Henrietta as one of its founding vice presidents—would announce itself in three months.

The Pinckneys and Slavery

One aspect of her father's history that Maria Henrietta did not mention in her *Notice of the Pinckneys* was his personal and political commitment to the institution of slavery. As a member of South Carolina's delegation to the

Constitutional Convention in Philadelphia in 1787, Charles Cotesworth Pinckney was an outspoken advocate of a powerful federal government. He also pressed for constitutional provisions that protected slavery, joining with his South Carolina and Georgia colleagues to form a deep-South bloc.[44]

At the convention, Pinckney was especially vocal on the issue of American participation in the international slave trade. Critics of the trade included delegates from New England and Virginia, many of whom raised moral objections to the "inhuman traffic" and argued that slavery—"a nefarious institution"—had no place in the new republic.[45] In response, "the South Carolinians unapologetically insisted on its necessity for their state and Georgia" and argued that the critics' arguments were made in bad faith: "the Virginians because of their obvious self-interest—with the trade closed, the price of Virginia's slaves would rise—and the New Englanders because so much of their trade had been, and still was, carried in New England bottoms."[46]

South Carolina was particularly dependent on the international trade. Over the forty years leading up to the Revolution, six out of every seven enslaved people imported into the state had been taken from Africa, with the remaining one person taken from the Caribbean colonies. Very few enslaved people were brought to South Carolina from elsewhere on the mainland.[47] Consequently, Pinckney and his fellow delegates (including Charles Pinckney, his first cousin once removed) regarded the overseas trade as vital to the interests of their state. When draft provisions to tax, limit, or shut down the trade were discussed, the South Carolinians threatened disunion—"an exclusion of S. Carola from the Union," as C. C. Pinckney put it.[48] "[W]hile there remained one acre of swampland uncleared of South Carolina," he later proclaimed in the South Carolina legislature during the ratification debates of 1788, "I would raise my voice against restricting the importation of negroes."[49]

In the end, the South Carolinians prevailed, with the support of compromise-minded delegates from Connecticut, who had evidently overcome their New England scruples. In the 1808 Clause of Article I, section 9, the Constitution barred Congress from prohibiting the international slave trade for twenty years.[50] The slave trade issue implicated a host of related controversies, including how the states' population would be counted for purposes of congressional representation. Many delegates clung to the notion that the Constitution was largely silent on the question of slavery, and that it had not disturbed what one scholar terms "the federal consensus," which held that slavery was a local matter, that the states alone could regulate it, and that therefore the U.S. government lacked authority over slavery in the states.[51]

But the 1808 Clause was not neutral. Nor was the provision of Article IV, section 2, that became known as the "Fugitive Slave Clause." That clause required that any "Person held to Service or Labour in one State, under the Laws thereof" who "escap[ed] into another" state be "delivered up on Claim of the Party to whom such Service or Labour may be due."[52] The Fugitive Slave Clause was also the result of the South Carolinians' demands. Two of Pinckney's fellow delegates had moved "to require fugitive slaves and servants to be delivered up like criminals."[53] The insertion of the clause into the Constitution placed federal authority in the service of the ostensibly local institution of slavery, giving extraterritorial effect to state laws holding individuals to service or labor. "We have obtained a right to recover our slaves in whatever part of America they may take refuge, which is a right we had not before," Charles Cotesworth Pinckney told the South Carolina legislature in 1788. "In short, considering all circumstances, we have made the best terms for the security of this species of property it was in our power to make. We would have made them better if we could; but, on the whole, I do not think them bad."[54]

Charles Cotesworth Pinckney and his wife, Mary Stead Pinckney, returned to South Carolina from the Constitutional Convention in 1787. Along with them traveled the three enslaved people whom they had brought with them to Philadelphia: Jenny, George, and Fortune, longtime "body servant" to Charles Cotesworth Pinckney.[55]

Upon arriving at home, C. C. Pinckney set about expanding his law practice and rebuilding the family's fortunes following the destruction that the war had caused. He was extremely successful in these projects, which kept him busy enough that he declined offers from President Washington to serve as commander of the army, associate justice of the Supreme Court, secretary of war, and secretary of state.

Pinckney's efforts relied on the work of enslaved laborers. Over these years, Pinckney expanded the number of individuals whom he enslaved. In an 1801 document listing his property for purposes of taxation, he stated that he owned around 319 people: sixty at Pinckney Island, 127 at Charleywood, 103 at Tippicutlaw, and twenty-nine in Charleston. His 1808 list of holdings included "Twenty Eight Negroes in Town" and "151 Negroes in the Country." In 1810, those numbers grew to thirty-two people in town and 162 in the country.[56]

Between 1787 and 1796, when Maria Henrietta was between the ages of thirteen and twenty-two, the three Pinckney daughters were back in the family mansion for some parts of the year. For some of this period, between 1790 and 1793, the young William Johnson was visiting the mansion to read law with

C. C. Pinckney. Also in the mansion and its sizable garden and work yard were some twenty-five or thirty people who worked and lived there, and who were held in bondage by Maria Henrietta's "jocular" father and William's "profound" yet "amiable and estimable" teacher.[57]

The Pinckney daughters did not only share in the bounty and profits that their family's enslaved laborers produced. They were also slaveowners themselves. In 1807, when he was sixty-one years old and soon to stand as the Federalist Party's presidential candidate, Charles Cotesworth Pinckney transferred ownership of two female slaves to his youngest daughter, Eliza Lucas Pinckney. Eliza, who was twenty-five years old and single at the time, became the owner "forever" of "a Negroe Wench Beck (the Daughter of Cælia) & a Negroe Girl Phyllis the Daughter of Lena & their future issue and encrease."[58] Shortly thereafter, C. C. Pinckney wrote a new will. The will granted his wife, Mary Stead Pinckney, a life estate in the East Bay mansion, "my house Negroes," and the contents of the house, as well as a "one fourth part of the annual net profits arising from the crops which shall be made by my negroes on my plantations," after taxes and expenses had been paid. The remainder in the East Bay property, as well as "all the rest and residue of my Estate real and personal, wheresoever & whatsoever," were given, devised, and bequeathed to "my dear Daughters Maria Henrietta Pinckney, Harriott Pinckney and Eliza Lucas Pinckney," to be "equally divided between them, share and share alike."[59] Their father also named Maria Henrietta, Harriott, and their sister Eliza among the executors and executrixes of his will.[60]

Charles Cotesworth Pinckney's wife, Mary, predeceased him, dying in 1812. When their father died in 1825, the three Pinckney daughters inherited his entire estate.[61] The youngest sister, Eliza, had married in 1822 but had been widowed shortly thereafter. The sisters became the mistresses not only of the Pinckney Mansion, but of several plantations, as well as the owners of some two hundred people. Maria Henrietta and Harriott, neither of whom ever married, lived in the East Bay house together until their deaths (Maria Henrietta in 1836, Harriott in 1866). In 1825, fifty-one-year-old Maria Henrietta Pinckney had become not a female planter-patriarch, but a female planter-political theorist.

The *Political Catechism* and the Pinckneys

We do not know what Maria Henrietta Pinckney thought of the turbulent events that occurred in Charleston in 1822 and 1823. In 1826, she and her sister Harriott traveled north, stopping to visit one of Virginia's spa springs resorts before continuing to Philadelphia.[62] But in 1830, at the age of fifty-six, she appears to have burst onto the South Carolina political stage, in a controlled yet forceful way.

Perhaps she made a conscious decision to begin sharing her political views outside the family. Her father had died in 1825; her uncle General Thomas Pinckney in 1828; and her aunt Harriott Pinckney Horry in December 1830. That year—1830—witnessed Maria Henrietta's debut as a political writer. The formidable sibling trio of the Revolutionary generation above her was gone. Meanwhile, South Carolina was becoming increasingly voluble in its challenges to federal power and insistent on its particular view of the Union. It fell to Maria Henrietta and her cousins to preserve the family's legacy of republican service mixed with aristocratic Lowcountry gentility.

The year 1830 appears to have been a turning point for Maria Henrietta Pinckney. That year, she announced herself as a nullifier, and she wrote and published a closely argued treatise to explain why.

The slim volume—numbering sixteen pages in one edition and twenty-four in another—issued from the mansion on East Bay Street, by way of A. E. Miller's printing office on Broad Street, where so many arguments, broadsides, and screeds were rendered into paper and type. It was titled *The Quintessence of Long Speeches, Arranged as a Political Catechism*. The phrase "quintessence of long speeches" had a certain dry humor to it. The title seemed almost like a wink, leavened with a sigh. Many long speeches had been delivered in the statehouse at Columbia and on the floor of Congress—all of them by men. This "quintessence," however, promised to distill them into a manageable dose of discourse.

The other part of the title was even more significant. The refined essence of these long, windy speeches was here "Arranged as a Political Catechism." The use of the term "catechism" was by no means accidental. In nineteenth-century America, particularly among upper-class, white Protestants, religious instruction was understood as the province of women—in particular, mothers.[63] In one of two surviving handwritten manuscript versions of the essay, the title is *A Political Catechism*; the "Quintessence" phrase appears to have been added later, at the time of publication.[64]

Then, the attribution of authorship—which, in true nineteenth-century style, immediately deflected into a dedication to a supposed listener. The arrangement of this boiled-down set of arguments into a political catechism was being carried out "By a Lady." Not a named man; not a pseudonymous writer traveling

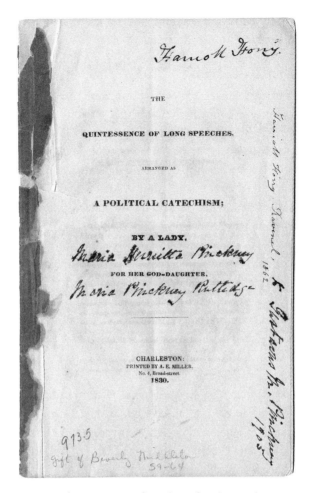

Several generations of Pinckney family members
inscribed their names on the title page of the pamphlet.
Maria Henrietta Pinckney, *The Quintessence of Long
Speeches, Arranged as a Political Catechism,* published
version (1830). (Pamphlet Collection, South Carolina
Historical Society.)

under cover of a classical republican moniker—no "Publius," "Brutus," or
"Caroliniensis" here. This work came from the pen of a lady, a person—female,
presumably white, respectable, of at least the middle class—who had a special
claim to attention and solicitude from the world.

And finally the dedication: "For Her God-Daughter." Maria Henrietta
Pinckney had no children of her own. But the dedication of the essay to an

unnamed female relative, based on a relationship defined by sacred ties and spiritual mentorship, cloaked her political tract in the more socially acceptable guise of domestic religious instruction. The title also suggested a note of private piety shared altruistically with a weary public in need of succor. "I have assembled this catechism to teach my god-daughter," the title page seemed to say. "Perhaps you, too, might benefit from it, neighbor?" In short, the title was masterly, even as it concealed its pretensions to authority.

There really was a goddaughter, however. Her name was Maria Pinckney Rutledge, and she was born in 1803, the daughter of Maria Henrietta Pinckney's first cousin Harriott Pinckney Horry Rutledge. That first cousin (let us call her "Cousin Harriott") was the daughter of Maria Henrietta Pinckney's aunt Harriott Pinckney Horry—sister of Charles Cotesworth Pinckney, and the aunt who had helped to raise Maria Henrietta Pinckney. Cousin Harriott had also been in the party that had accompanied their grandmother Eliza Lucas Pinckney on her final trip to Philadelphia in 1793, when Cousin Harriott was twenty-two years old, and Maria Henrietta was nineteen.

Maria Henrietta Pinckney and Cousin Harriott were of the same generation of Pinckneys. They had spent substantial amounts of time together as children and as young women, including intense periods of travel and family mourning. Cousin Harriott's daughter was Maria Henrietta's namesake and goddaughter. It was to this member of the next generation that Maria Henrietta dedicated her political tract.

Maria Henrietta Pinckney and her sister Harriott were especially close to Cousin Harriott, her husband, Frederick Rutledge, and their eight children. The families spent significant amounts of time together, in the Rutledges' house on Tradd Street or at the Pinckney Mansion on East Bay Street. After Frederick Rutledge died in 1821, Cousin Harriott—like so many Pinckney women before and around her—was left a widow with substantial property to manage. Her children, among them the goddaughter to whom the *Political Catechism* was dedicated, appear to have been regarded by their unmarried Pinckney aunts as treasured nieces and nephews, even though they were in truth the first cousins once removed of Maria Henrietta and Harriott Pinckney. With the passing of the three Revolutionary Pinckney siblings, Maria Henrietta and Harriott stepped into the role of senior members of the family. But as they performed the role, it combined both the traditionally female duty of kin specialists (see *A Notice of the Pinckneys*) and the traditionally male position of patron and financial backer.

A few examples will demonstrate the affection and care that Maria Henrietta and Harriott obviously bore for these young Rutledges. In 1835, a few years after Cousin Harriott's eldest child, Edward Cotesworth Rutledge married, the Pinckney aunts from East Bay bought a plantation called "Belvidere" and gave it to him and his wife.[65] Similarly, in 1849, the surviving aunt (Harriott) gave the family's storied Belmont Plantation, which had been in the family since 1736, to another young Rutledge, the sister of Edward, who was named Harriott Pinckney Rutledge Holbrook.[66]

The presence of Maria Henrietta Pinckney and her sister in the lives of the next generation is clear in the reams of correspondence that the members of the extended family exchanged with one another. Reports in these letters discussed family conversations, and so might appear to belong in the "domestic" category, but for the fact that conversations frequently concerned elections, government, and public affairs in Charleston and the nation. Moreover, Maria Henrietta Pinckney was far from the only political lady in her family.

The election of 1832, which pitted incumbent Andrew Jackson against three opponents (all of whom were essentially running as anti-Jacksonians, and therefore split the vote, helping to ensure Jackson's reelection), was particularly stormy in Charleston because it coincided with the height of the nullification crisis. Edward, one of the young Rutledges, who was at that time a naval lieutenant whose duties included postings in Norfolk, Pensacola, and Havana, received frequent news of the family from his wife, Rebecca Motte Lowndes Rutledge.

One night during election season, when crowds of supporters for the nullifiers paraded through the streets, "the State right ladies of the family replied by a clapping of hands and waving of handkerchiefs," Rebecca reported. Evidently the states'-rights ladies of the family did more than clap and wave; they also provided office space for their partisan allies: "Your Aunts intend to pull down that house next to them, before October, and as they will not refuse lending it, for electioneering purposes, I am very glad indeed of it, for it is not right that they should countenance such doings, besides it gives people a handle by which to pull them to pieces."[67]

In October, with election season coming to a close and the nullification convention approaching, Rebecca wrote again of the Pinckney aunts' political efforts: "The State Righters in Charleston, our Royal cousins included, are quite angry with General Hayne for suppressing bribery in his party; they say he will cause the election to be lost by his scruples."[68] Moreover, Maria Henrietta, noticing that Rebecca was writing to Edward, saw an opportunity to spread her preferred political message: "Your Aunt Maria desired me to tell you when I wrote, that instead of sending you letters, she and cousin H. had sent you two copies of Calhoun and Hamilton's correspondence[,] one to read yourself and one to give to a friend."[69] The Hamilton in question was James Hamilton, Jr., governor of the state. At the time of the Vesey conspiracy ten years earlier, in 1822, Hamilton had been the intendant (mayor) of Charleston who called out the militia and assembled the court of magistrates and freeholders, prompting William Johnson to take up his pen to criticize city leaders' actions.

Other Pinckney women were equally ardent supporters of nullification. "Our Aunts themselves cannot be more anxious to see the Nullifying law passed than I am," wrote Edward's sister Harriott. "[F]or tho' well convinced that it cannot end but in defeat or danger—I am anxious to see the end of it and to see what measures Congress will pursue." She employed a florid historical reference to illustrate her point: "I look forward to seeing Congress send an Embassy to beg our pardon & request our alliance & the Gov. of So. Carolina place his foot on the neck of the Envoy after the manner of Frederick Barbarossa and the Pope some centuries ago."[70]

A few weeks later, when the nullification convention met, Rebecca reported on the activities of other members of the family—the sons of General Thomas Pinckney, who were Maria Henrietta's first cousins, childhood confidants, and co-generationists. "The state convention has met at last[. I]t began its sitting yesterday, and it is said will continue it more than a fortnight," Rebecca wrote. "My two Uncles Cotesworth and Tom are in it." "Tom" was Colonel Thomas Pinckney, who three decades earlier had sent Maria Henrietta word of President Washington's death. Now he and his brother were members of the convention called to decide whether the state would declare the federal tariff laws null and void within its borders.[71]

Rebecca mused about her husband's absence in terms both personal and political. At one point, she contemplated the possibility that he might resign his commission in the U.S. Navy and return home to stand with South Carolina. "I would not have you leave your vessel on any account whatever, while you are an officer. I would have no domestic considerations to interfere with your duty in that calling," she stated. Yet "[i]f the State and General Government should come into actual collision I know that Self Interest would never prevent your coming to defend this State—but in any other case I wish you to remain with your vessel as long as may be necessary."[72] For the first time, the Pinckney family's devotion to the service of the nation was wavering in the face of what they viewed as the conflicting, and superior, claims of South Carolina.

And what of the goddaughter to whom Maria Henrietta Pinckney dedicated her *Political Catechism?* Maria Pinckney Rutledge was another of these young

Rutledges, the younger sister of Edward the naval lieutenant and his sister Harriott the medieval-history enthusiast. She was twenty-seven when her aunt Maria published the *Political Catechism* in 1830. A few years later, in 1838, goddaughter Maria perished in the *Pulaski* steamship disaster, in which more than one hundred people died after a boiler exploded on board the steamer when it was off the coast of North Carolina, en route from Charleston to Baltimore. Maria was traveling with her brother Thomas Pinckney Rutledge and his wife, Frances; all three were lost.[73]

As the inscriptions on the image shown here demonstrate, a copy of Maria Henrietta's treatise was passed through generations of women in the Pinckney family. First, Maria Henrietta's aunt "Harriott Horry," likely the first owner of the book and the source of the inscription at the top of the title page. This was Harriott Pinckney Horry, who died in December 1830. She must, however, have lived long enough to see her beloved niece's political commentary in print. Then, if one reads downward along the side of the page, one encounters another descendant, Harriott Horry Rutledge Ravenel—Maria Henrietta Pinckney's first cousin twice removed, born in 1832—who added her name in 1862. Between these two Harriotts must have been an intervening family member who transmitted the pamphlet, likely Harriott Horry Rutledge. Another descendant, Gustavus Memminger Pinckney, added his name in 1905. The chain of ownership and readership for this pamphlet thus traveled forward in time through five generations of Pinckneys—nearly all of them women—whose lives spanned 164 years, from 1748 to 1912, the reign of George II to the eve of World War I.

The *Political Catechism* and Nullification

The nullification movement initially announced itself on the American political scene in response to the federal tariff of 1828, which protected finished goods (chiefly textiles) and levied taxes on competing European imports. Opponents of the tariff argued that it unfairly burdened certain regions of the country and benefited others—specifically, that it hurt southern agriculture in order to protect northern industry. The chief victims, on the nullifiers' view, were southern planters, who both imported significant quantities of finished goods and exported their raw materials (cotton, indigo, and rice) to Britain. Thus, they argued, southerners paid a disproportionate amount in duties and would be the principal victims of any retaliatory tariffs imposed by Britain. The tariff, which became known to its critics as the "Tariff of Abominations," was signed into law by President John Quincy Adams, in the final year of his presidency, and helped ensure the election of Andrew Jackson in 1828.

When Jackson took office but failed to push for repeal of the tariff, South Carolinians—led by Vice President John C. Calhoun—began calling for their state to cease enforcing the tariff on its substantial import trade. In an anonymous essay of December 1828 known as the "South Carolina Exposition," Calhoun developed the nonenforcement strategy into the doctrine of nullification. Calhoun's theory was that an individual state had the power to call a special convention to determine whether a particular federal law was constitutional. The convention would be empowered to "nullify"—declare null and void within the state—the law. The state convention could also call for a national convention to meet and propose amendments to the Constitution.[74]

In the "Exposition," Calhoun argued that nullification was not extraconstitutional but rather consistent with the structure and text of the Constitution. In addition to laying out the mechanics of nullification and how the conventions would actually work, he focused on the question of sovereignty. For Calhoun, the Union was a compact among the states; therefore, each state retained the power to judge for itself the validity of federal law.[75]

As a young man, Calhoun had attended college at Yale, graduating as valedictorian of the class of 1804, and then studied law at Tapping Reeve's Litchfield Law School. In both places, he had felt alienated from the Federalist ideology that surrounded him. Yet Calhoun had begun his political career in 1810 as a "War Hawk" congressman, supporting the War of 1812 against Britain as well as congressionally funded "internal improvements" such as roads and canals. Calhoun had also drafted the charter of the Second Bank of the United States; served as Monroe's secretary of war; and spent two terms as vice president, under John Quincy Adams and then under Andrew Jackson, before he split with Jackson and resigned in 1832.[76]

The "Exposition" was carefully framed as a theory of constitutional interpretation and enforcement. It was not offered as a mandate for disunion or a blueprint for secession. Calhoun viewed himself as a responsible republican statesman who was offering a theory consistent with the boundaries of the founders' system. He believed himself to be, and at that time was, a moderate and a nationalist compared with some of South Carolina's other political leaders, who were openly skeptical of broad constitutional construction and federal power of the type that Calhoun endorsed while he was in the Cabinet. Between 1828 and 1830, however, Calhoun became increasingly estranged from President Jackson, and more associated with the radical nullifiers of his home state.

This result came about in part because of the machinations of Martin Van Buren, who hoped to win power for his New York wing of the Democratic Party (known as the "Albany Regency"), and to ensure a successful future presidential bid for himself. By stoking Jackson's anger at Calhoun across various fronts, ranging from the politics of Cabinet members' wives' interactions to Calhoun's secret authorship of the "Exposition," Van Buren effectively isolated Calhoun and secured his own position as Jackson's heir apparent.[77]

In an 1831 essay that became known as the "Fort Hill Address," Calhoun elaborated on and amplified his views. He criticized "the error" of those who assumed that "the General Government is a party to the constitutional compact." On the contrary: the "States, as has been shown, formed the compact, acting as sovereign and independent communities." The general government was merely the "creature" of this compact, its agent for certain specified duties, "partaking, in its nature and object, of the character of a joint commission, appointed to superintend and administer the interests in which all are jointly concerned; but having, beyond its proper sphere, no more power than if it did not exist." Therefore, in his view, "the several States, or parties, have a right to judge of its infractions; and in case of a deliberate, palpable, and dangerous exercise of power not delegated, they have the right, in the last resort, to use the language of the Virginia Resolutions, 'to interpose for arresting the progress of the evil, and for maintaining, within their respective limits, the authorities, rights, and liberties appertaining to them.' " Calhoun thus tied his theory directly to Madison's Virginia Resolution of 1798:

> This right of interposition, thus solemnly asserted by the State of Virginia, be it called what it may,—State-right, veto, nullification, or by any other name,—I conceive to be the fundamental principle of our system, resting on facts historically as certain as our revolution itself, and deductions as simple and demonstrative as that of any political or moral truth whatever; and I firmly believe that on its recognition depend the stability and safety of our political institutions.[78]

Calhoun understood the fraught and contested nature of the relationship between federal and local power. He was capable of diagnosing the many competing federalisms that were being articulated in interbellum constitutional debates. His answer to the problem of multiple levels of governmental authority was to turn to structure—the deep structure of the constitutional system. Calhoun believed himself to be part of a continuous and ongoing dialogue with the founders, living in an extended, long founding moment. In this respect, he resembled his Carolina compatriots Maria Henrietta Pinckney and William Johnson. But the solutions these three thinkers offered to the problem of federalism differed, sometimes dramatically.

By 1832, Calhoun was undoubtedly the champion of nullification. His theory of state sovereignty, based on the doctrine that the Constitution guaranteed states the power to "interpose" their own interpretations of federal law over those of Congress, the president, or the federal courts, claimed to be consistent with the republicanism of the founding era. But it also provided a weapon with which to attack the very foundations of the Union. Moreover, Calhoun's constitutional theory also, in his view, justified slavery, which he described as a "positive good" in an 1837 speech on the Senate floor.[79]

Maria Henrietta Pinckney certainly knew Calhoun and discussed politics with him. An 1831 letter from her sister Harriott to their cousin (another Charles Cotesworth Pinckney) remarked, "I wish we could see a little more of the Vice President." This was Calhoun, whose forceful "Fort Hill Address" would first appear two days later. "How shamefully Maria's old favorite hides."[80] Harriott was writing from the Pinckney Mansion in Charleston. Cousin Charles Cotesworth was at his plantation in Pendleton, five miles southeast of Fort Hill, where Calhoun was finishing his address.

One might be tempted to assume that Pinckney's vigorously argued *Political Catechism* was simply an imitation of Calhoun's "Fort Hill Address." But such an assumption would be incorrect. Indeed, it would reverse the timing of the two tracts. Pinckney's pamphlet predated Calhoun's "Fort Hill Address" by nearly eight months. The *Political Catechism* bore a publication date of 1830. As we have seen, a printed copy of it was in the hands of Maria Henrietta's aunt Harriott Horry before the latter's death on December 19, 1830. Moreover, before Pinckney's treatise was sent to the printers, it comprised twenty-eight closely written manuscript pages. And there were at least two manuscript versions, which today survive in the South Carolina Historical Society Archives. They could not have been produced easily or quickly, and would surely have taken Pinckney some time to compose.

Calhoun's "Fort Hill Address," meanwhile, was not published until August 3, 1831. He had been moved to write it after much self-examination and discussion with his political allies in South Carolina; he apparently made his final decision to join the radicals in the wake of that year's Fourth of July celebrations.[81]

In short: Pinckney was not simply parroting the provocative ideas of the controversial vice president. She was, in fact, sketching her own theory of the Constitution and the federal structure that it created.

Maria Henrietta Pinckney, "A Political Catechism by a Lady for Her God-Daughter."
(Pinckney Family Papers [38.00], South Carolina Historical Society.)

In the *Political Catechism*, Pinckney provided a rationale for, and a species of, nullification that differed in important ways from Calhoun's heterodox orthodoxy. To be sure, her *Catechism* had all the markings of the genre, structured as it was in the highly stylized form of questions and answers that would have been familiar to a nineteenth-century audience steeped in the tradition of didactic Christianity:

Question—What do we understand by the Federal Union?

Answer—It is an agreement between Sovereign States, to forbear exerting their sovereign power over certain defined objects, and to exert jointly their sovereign power over other specified objects, through the agency of a General Government. Each State agrees to exert its full sovereign power jointly, for all external purposes; and separately, for all internal purposes, or State concerns.[82]

There was none of Johnson's "tripartite contract" among the people, the states, and the United States to be found here.[83] The United States was not even a party to the agreement; it was, as Calhoun would argue in the "Fort Hill Address" the following year, merely an agent of the contracting parties.

Pinckney went on to canvass the basic tenets of nullification in similar terms to those that were being articulated by Calhoun and others. On the sovereignty question, for example ("Did the States, in forming the Constitution, divest themselves of any part of their Sovereignty?"), Pinckney had this to say: "Of not a particle."

She followed this sharp retort with a longer response that suggested that she, too, might have imbibed some principles of law from her father, General C. C. Pinckney:

> [T]he power exercised by the functionaries of the General Government, is not *inherent* in them, but in the States whose agents they are. The Constitution is their Power of Attorney, to do certain acts; and contains, connected with their authority to act, their letter of instruction, as to the manner in which they shall act. They are the Servants. The power which gives validity to their acts is in their Masters—THE STATES.[84]

The legal analogies would have been right at home in an interbellum southern lawyer's peroration before a court. The states were the principals, and the "functionaries of the General Government" were merely the "agents" of the states. Among these "functionaries," Pinckney presumably would have included Attorney General William Wirt, Justice Johnson, and perhaps even Congress. The Constitution was a "power of attorney" granted to those functionaries for certain limited purposes, not an open-ended grant of discretion. And then, inevitably, the shift to the law of master and servant—the southerner's preferred euphemism for "slave." The federal functionaries were but "the Servants" of the states.

Yet Pinckney's treatise demonstrated that her reading had ranged well beyond reports of common law cases. Concepts drawn from political theory, in particular from the work of Jean-Jacques Rousseau and John Locke, also animated her arguments. Her definition of sovereignty, for example, bears a striking similarity to Rousseau's theory of the general will as described in *The Social Contract*. "What is the meaning of Sovereignty?" Pinckney asked. "It is the will of civil society in the Social Compact, which society is a moral person, whose will, like the will of the human being, cannot be divided without destroying the person; we can conceive the will operating in a thousand various ways, but we cannot conceive its separation into parts; neither can we conceive of the separation of Sovereignty—its unity and life are inseparable."[85]

Compare this to Rousseau's description of the general will: "As long as several men assembled together consider themselves as a single body, they have only *one will* which is directed towards their common preservation and general well-being. Then, all the animating forces of the state are vigorous and simple, and its principles are clear and luminous; it has no incompatible or conflicting interests; the *common good* makes itself so manifestly evident that only common sense is needed to discern it."[86]

Pinckney's grandmother Eliza Lucas Pinckney had been a voracious reader of political philosophy and classical works, as well as novels. In Eliza's letters, she had discussed her reading: Locke, Virgil, and Samuel Richardson's *Pamela*, among others.[87] She and her husband had consciously sought to raise their children, especially Charles Cotesworth Pinckney, along Lockean principles, even writing to friends in London to request that they purchase and send across the ocean a particular type of toy that Locke had recommended.[88]

The most significant component of Pinckney's defense of nullification came in her discussion of the U.S. Supreme Court. Fresh invocations of sovereignty and the Articles of Confederation were the common stuff of virtually every pro-nullification oration and broadside in these years. Pinckney's *Political Catechism* contained a satisfying amount of discussion of the nature of political authority. But her treatment of the Court, both as an institution and in its current incarnation under Chief Justice Marshall, distinguished her analysis from the more conventional nullification tracts. Pinckney had clearly kept up with the reports—not only of the Court's decisions, but also of the arguments and speeches delivered by the lawyers who appeared before it. In order to do so, given that regular reporting of Supreme Court cases was still in its infancy, she would have had to scrutinize the newspapers, which were the only available source of case reporting for much of the nineteenth century. They also typically included the arguments of counsel, at least in high-profile cases involving prominent members of the bar.

Pinckney's critique of the Court singled out Daniel Webster, whom Pinckney derided for having "discovered" a "new version of the Constitution." Pinckney did not cite Webster's argument in *McCulloch v. Maryland*, the 1819 case in which the Court had upheld the constitutionality of the Second Bank of the United States and invalidated Maryland's attempt to tax it.[89] Nor did she refer to Marshall's rhetoric in his *McCulloch* opinion, in which the chief justice conjured a vivid image of a muscular Union built on commercial and military power. "Throughout this vast republic, from St. Croix to the Gulf of Mexico, from the Atlantic to the Pacific, revenue is to be collected and expended, armies are to be marched and supported," Marshall proclaimed.[90] Even without mentioning *McCulloch* by name, however, Pinckney's *Political Catechism* reads as a rebuttal of both Webster's argument and Marshall's opinion in the case.

Pinckney also confuted Webster's recent and vigorous articulation of the nationalist theory of the Union during his widely publicized Senate debate with South Carolina U.S. senator Robert Y. Hayne in January 1830. "I do not admit, that, under the Constitution and in conformity with it, there is any mode in which a State government, as a member of the Union, can interfere and stop the progress of the general government, by force of her own laws, under any circumstances whatever," Webster thundered, as Vice President Calhoun looked on from his seat as president of the Senate. "The people of the United States have declared that the Constitution shall be the supreme law," he continued. "The states are, unquestionably, sovereign, so far as their sovereignty is not affected by this supreme law. But the state legislatures, as political bodies, however sovereign, are yet not sovereign over the people." The agency analogy was also appealing to Webster. But he deployed it to argue that the people of the entire United States, not the states, were the principals: "So far as the people have given power to the general government, so far the grant is unquestionably good, and the government holds of the people, and not of the State governments. We are all agents of the same supreme power, the people."[91]

In the *Political Catechism*, Pinckney skewered "Messrs. Webster & Co." for what she viewed as this groundless theory that the Constitution had been created not by the states, but by the people of the Union:

> They have discovered that the Constitution was not formed by the States in their Sovereign capacity—that it is not a compact between the States— but that it is a Government formed by the people, *en masse*, that is, by the people collected into one nation—that this nation brought the Government into existence. . . . That in forming this National Government, the

people conferred upon the Supreme Court, the power of imposing these certain salutary restraints upon the Sovereignty of the States.[92]

The peril of such heresies was clear. They would lead to "the annihilation of State Rights, and consequently, of the fundamental principles of the Constitutional Liberty, for which our Fathers fought and conquered."[93] The Constitution and the legacy of the Revolutionary generation were at risk. In other words, the theories of "Webster & Co." endangered 1776 as well as 1789.

Pinckney's attack on the Court extended to another Marshall decision that touched on the real-world consequences of abstract notions of state sovereignty. That case was *Martin v. Hunter's Lessee* of 1816, in which the Court had held that state courts were bound to follow the Court's interpretation of federal law.[94] In the course of that lawsuit, as discussed in Chapter 1, the Virginia state judges had insisted that the Constitution had not given the Court the power to act as an "umpire" in any case that happened to involve a federal issue. Justice Story's opinion for the Court had vehemently rejected that claim, insisting that the Supremacy Clause and Article III required that the Court have final authority over all federal issues.[95]

Now Pinckney weighed in, reiterating and amplifying the arguments of the Virginia judges. "The epithet of supreme which gives importance to the Court and imposes on the ignorant, is entirely relative, and imports only that appellative jurisdiction which it may exercise over the subordinate Courts of the *General Government*," she argued. "It is not called supreme, in reference to the other departments of the Government, nor has it any supremacy in reference to the *States*."[96] The Court's power was horizontal and judicial, only. It could reach other federal courts, but it could not act vertically upon the states, nor could it overturn the acts of other branches of the federal government (Congress or the president). In a single dependent clause, Pinckney thus also rejected the holding of *Marbury v. Madison*.[97] In short, the Court's power of review was confined entirely to the decisions of other federal courts.

Pinckney's *Political Catechism* was a formidable, deeply intellectual work of constitutional and political analysis. It is difficult to assess how influential it was, although it is said to have been circulated widely.[98] Notably, the treatise was published by Archibald E. Miller, from whose Broad Street print shop issued many of the most important political publications of the day, as well as almanacs and other items.

Besides her writing, Pinckney was personally involved with the nullification movement in a number of other ways. Family members described Maria Henrietta and her sister Harriott as the family's "Great Politicians" and reported that the sisters talked of transforming the mansion into "Nullification Castle" in the event that the federal government attempted to enforce the tariff.[99]

Moreover, Pinckney and South Carolina governor James Hamilton, Jr., made plans to import a quantity of sugar upon which they would refuse to pay the tariff fees, in an effort to "have a practical test of the working of the tariff law"—and then to bring a judicial challenge to its constitutionality.[100] Speaking to the South Carolina Association, which after its founding during the Vesey crisis in 1822 remained active until the 1850s, Governor Hamilton described his and Pinckney's plan. An account of the event comes from James L. Petigru, the former attorney general who had declined to argue on behalf of the state in *Elkison v. Deliesseline*, and who by 1830 was a leader of the Unionist faction. (In the way of the close-knit Charleston elite, Petigru was also Hamilton's former law partner.) According to Petigru, Hamilton told his audience that he had "shipped a cargo of rice to Havana for a return of sugars," and "he intended to let his sugars go into the custom house stores." If the tariff was not repealed, Hamilton told his audience that "he expected them to go to their deaths with him for his sugars, which was received with great applause."[101]

One year after the publication of the *Political Catechism*, Pinckney made another public affirmation of her nullification principles. The setting was the same State Rights and Free Trade Party celebration of July 4, 1831, at which Senator Hayne proudly invoked *Elkison v. Deliesseline* as a precedent for nullification. A few days before the great assembly, Governor Hamilton had visited the Pinckney sisters at home and asked if Maria Henrietta would publicly deliver a banner to the members of the party, who planned to process throughout the city. Sister Harriott reported Maria Henrietta's response:

> To this my sister immediately objected, saying it would render her too conspicuous for that she had been much more so than she ever intended. . . . He still urged it saying he should take care that there should be nothing of the kind & that she must recollect that she was now identified with the party. His solicitations were expressed with so much eloquence, grace, & enthusiasm that Maria said she would compromise the matter so far that the standard should be presented from this house in the name of the State Rights Ladies & that it must not be mentioned when the account was given as our house, but as the late residence of a distinguished Patriot. To this the Governor agreed when he found her so determined not to deliver it herself.[102]

Maria Henrietta Pinckney had written a tract, but she had couched it in terms of a catechism delivered to a young, female relative. Her pamphlet had publicly demonstrated her association with the State Rights and Free Trade Party. But she refused the governor's request to appear in person before a noisy, rowdy, likely inebriated crowd on the Fourth of July, even in the name of states' rights.

Did this refusal represent an independence of mind, a desire to remain the author of her works, and an unwillingness to be used as a prop in someone else's pageant? Or was it simply obeisance to prevailing norms dictating that upper-class white ladies did not appear in public before large and unruly groups of men? These are difficult, if not impossible, questions to answer.

But if Maria Henrietta Pinckney wanted her words to speak for her, rather than making a spectacle of her person, she succeeded. When the great day of July 4, 1831, arrived, and the procession was making its way along East Bay Street, a "splendid Standard" was presented "in the name of the Ladies, to the Free Trade Party." The standard "was greeted by the multitude with reiterated shouts." "It displayed on one side the Arms of the State; on the other was a Palmetto Tree, at the foot of which were bales of Cotton and barrels of Rice, the whole encircled with the State Rights motto, inscribed in gold, 'millions for defence, not a cent for tribute.' "[103]

These final words, of course, were an echo of C. C. Pinckney's famous retort to the French deputation in 1798, now redeployed by his daughter in a public assertion of the connection between the founding generation and their nullifying children. Maria Henrietta had also used them to end her *Political Catechism*:

> Q. *On whom must Carolina depend in her hour of peril?*
> On the descendants of the patriot band who achieved the Revolution.
> On the descendants of those brave and generous foreigners who united
> with us in that arduous and glorious struggle. On the proprietors of the
> soil—and on those whose motto is "MILLIONS FOR DEFENCE, NOT A CENT
> FOR TRIBUTE."[104]

A decade earlier, when the planter-contrivers of the South Carolina Association were calling for white Charlestonians to join them in assuming the power to enforce the Seamen Act, they had proudly proclaimed themselves "owners of the soil."[105] Pinckney's *Catechism* took this encomium even further. The nullifiers defending South Carolina were not only the owners of the soil; they were also the owners of the Revolutionary past.

In November 1832, when South Carolina's much-anticipated nullification convention finally met in Columbia, two of Maria Henrietta's first cousins were among the delegates. These were Colonel Thomas Pinckney and Charles Cotesworth Pinckney (her godson, "Cotesworth"), the sons of General Thomas Pinckney.[106] Pinckneys were always among the delegates, if not the leaders, at important public meetings. They were like the Johnsons in that respect.

Except that there were no representatives of William Johnson's family at the nullification convention. For the Johnsons, unlike the Pinckneys, there was no lineage that could connect the Revolution and the ratification of the Constitution with the vigilantism of the South Carolina Association in 1822 and 1823 or the nullification convention of 1832.

Two Final Scenes

In March 1835, another Harriet—the English writer and social reformer Harriet Martineau—spent a few days in Charleston as part of her two-year tour of the United States. Martineau was a student of political and social institutions, and an outspoken critic of slavery, which she called "indefensible, economically, socially, and morally."[107]

Martineau's published account of her travels included this scene:

> One lady who had contributed ample amounts of money to the Nullification funds, and a catechism to Nullification lore, amused while she grieved me by the strength of her political feelings. While calling on her, one morning, the conversation turned on prints, and I asked an explanation of a strange-looking one which hung opposite my eye; the portrait of a gentleman, the top of the head and the dress visible, but the face obliterated or covered over. She was only too ready to explain. It was a portrait of President Jackson, which she had hung up in days when he enjoyed her favour. Since Nullification she had covered over the face, to show how she hated him.[108]

The lady, of course, was Maria Henrietta Pinckney. The conversation took place in one of the drawing rooms of the Pinckney Mansion. President Jackson had earned Pinckney's enmity, along with that of every other nullifier, with his "Proclamation to the People of South Carolina" of December 1832, in which he had castigated the nullifiers, rejected their theories of states' rights, and promised full federal enforcement of the tariff laws—by force, if necessary. The proclamation was followed in March 1833 by the Force Bill, which authorized the president to use the military to ensure that federal laws were carried out, protect federal customs officers, prevent unauthorized removal of untaxed goods or ships, and suppress insurrections.[109]

Martineau described herself as "amused" and "grieved" by Pinckney's ideological zeal: "A stranger hardly knows what to think of a cause whose leaders will flatter and cherish the perpetrators of a piece of petty spite like this; yet this lady is treated as if she were a main pillar of the Nullification party."[110]

A few days later, Martineau accompanied Senator Calhoun, Governor Hayne, and their families on a round of city sights. They went "to the public library, to a panorama, and to the arsenal." Again, Martineau was both perplexed and alarmed by the tone with which the two men were received by their fellow citizens, especially the soldiers at the arsenal, which was a U.S. installation.[111] Federal, state, and local authority were always intermixed in interbellum Charleston.

Following a small parade, Calhoun and Hayne removed their hats and delivered remarks to the dozen recruits:

> Mr. Calhoun first, and Governor Hayne afterwards, uncovered and addressed them with as much gravity and effusion of patriotic sentiment, as if we had been standing on the verge of a battle-field. Some of our party were of Union politics; and they looked exceedingly arch during the speechifying. It will be too sad if this child's play should be turned into bloodshed after all, for the gratification of any man's restless ambition, or in the guilty hope of protracting slavery under the reprobation of the whole of society, except a small band of mercenaries.[112]

Just over a year following Martineau's visit to Charleston, on May 13, 1836, Maria Henrietta Pinckney died. She was sixty-two years old. The *Charleston Mercury* (edited by Henry Laurens Pinckney) eulogized her as "[t]he worthy daughter of an illustrious parent" and lauded her "heroic patriotism" during "the darkest hour of our struggle."[113] A notice of her funeral appeared, inviting the "Relatives and Friends of the late Gen. Charles Cotesworth Pinckney" to attend the procession "from her late residence in East Bay, *This Afternoon*, at 4 o'clock."[114] The cortege traveled half a mile south through the streets of the city to St. Michael's churchyard, where Maria Henrietta was buried a few feet from her aunt Harriott and her father.

On May 16, the *Mercury* printed a longer tribute marking "the death of Miss PINCKNEY." Maria Henrietta had never married, and this final memorial read almost as an addendum to her *Notice of the Pinckneys*. "In the recent struggle and triumph of our State, no spirit more pure and enthusiastic than hers gave its aspirations and its energies to the righteous cause of Carolina and liberty,"

the obituary stated. "The resources of an affluent fortune were zealously proffered; and much more, the richer wealth of a mind of great moral and intellectual elevation was most efficiently contributed." She was "[c]onspicuous
among the luminous writers of the time, in expounding the leading Carolina
doctrines, and eloquently enforcing the duties of the citizen." But she remained notable for "the total absence of even the semblance of masculine
obtrusiveness." The encomium ended by situating Maria Henrietta in the line
of her political family:

> However humble and inadequate this tribute to the memory of an ami-
> able and truly noble lady, we offer it in the name of the numerous objects
> of her watchful benevolence, and delicate, considerate and bountiful
> charity . . . in the name of the polished social circle to which she gave
> dignity and refinement; and most of all, in the name of South Carolina,
> to whom she rendered the long cherished name of PINCKNEY yet more
> dear, by a hereditary loyalty, which, illustrating in *the daughter*, the
> blended inspiration of patriotism and filial piety, imparted a fresh ver-
> dure to the chaplet on *the father*'s tomb.[115]

The notice portrayed Maria Henrietta as a republican daughter, moving
through the world in a manner that brought honor to her heredity—in particular, to her storied father. As a recordkeeper, a family chronicler, a beneficent patron, a colorful aunt, and an owner of vast estates and numerous human beings,
she had certainly fulfilled her obligations as a daughter of the house of Pinckney.
But aside from the *Notice of the Pinckneys*, these aspects of her legacy have been
transmitted down the historical record through the letters and reminiscences of
others. Other glimpses reveal her as political actor—through the parade, the
banner, the tariff test case, and the shrouding of Jackson's portrait. In the *Political Catechism*, though, we see her as a "woman of masculine intellect," as her
first cousin twice removed Harriott Horry Rutledge Ravenel, the family chronicler of the next two generations, described her in 1896.[116] "The ladies were as
enthusiastic and as well informed as the men," wrote Ravenel. "One of the best
explanations of the doctrine of State Rights is 'The Quintessence of Long
Speeches or a Catechism of State Rights,' by Miss Maria H. Pinckney, eldest
daughter of General C. C. Pinckney."[117] Of course it took another Pinckney
woman to commit this portrait to paper.

On December 20, 1860, South Carolina became the first state to pass an
ordinance of secession. On April 12, 1861, South Carolinian cannons posted

around the harbor opened fire on federal-held Fort Sumter. Four days earlier, Mary Boykin Chesnut recorded in her diary that she had called at the East Bay mansion to visit Maria Henrietta's sister Harriott, "one of the last of the old-world Pinckneys."[118]

On the night of December 11, 1861, a blaze that came to be known as the "Great Charleston Fire" of 1861 started—from a still-unknown cause—near the corner of East Bay and Hasell streets, two blocks north of the Pinckney Mansion. The fire consumed more than 540 acres of the city, including five churches, many businesses, and nearly six hundred houses.[119] One of those houses was the Pinckney Mansion, still owned by Maria Henrietta's younger sister Harriott Pinckney, who lived until March 1866. Masses of family books, letters, and other documents must have been devoured by the flames. Among these were surely Maria Henrietta's papers.

The *New York Times* carried this account of the fire, which it received from the Richmond *Examiner*:

> The most irreparable of the results of this awful calamity is the whole-sale destruction of the antiquities of our city. Great numbers of those grand old mansions of revolutionary memory, which have given to Charleston the prestige which attaches to every city of the ancient re-gime, now lie blackened and smoldering heaps of ruins. The stately halls in which the rebels of '76 were wont to live and move, are lost to the rebels of '61. The ancestral homesteads of the Heywards, the Laurences, the Pinckneys, the Middletons, the Haynes, and of many other families whose names are entwined with the history of the State, are leveled with the ground.[120]

The fire was believed to have been started by accident. But the symbolism of the massive inferno was impossible not to notice, for Charlestonians and others. The fire destroyed a swath of the city "a quarter of a mile in width and fully a mile in length, through the very heart and oldest quarter of the city." By dawn the next day, "all was a wilderness of smoky ruin," recalled Harriott Horry Rutledge Ravenel in 1906.[121] The newspapers tallied the losses: St. Andrew's Hall, "the scene of solemn separation by the Convention of the State of South Carolina from the United States," and Institute Hall, "in which the act was enthusiastically ratified by the people" and which therefore was "to Charleston, what Faneuil Hall is to Boston." Union gunboats blockading the harbor reportedly "fired a salute during the conflagration."[122]

George N. Barnard, *Ruins of the Pinckney Mansion, Charleston, South Carolina*, 1865.
In this view from the east, the pair of windows on the right-front side of the main
floor mark the location of the library. (National Archives and Records
Administration.)

A Federalism of Legacy and the Local

The story of Maria Henrietta Pinckney, like that of William Johnson, is a
narrative of layers—layers of families and layers of governments, all overlapping each other, all fighting. They fought for control of Charleston and its past.
But the battle was not about nostalgia. It was a struggle over whose vision of
law, politics, and society would command the future.

The case of *Elkison v. Deliesseline*, and the larger controversy over the Negro
Seamen Act, demonstrated the complex interactions at work among associational, city, state, national, and international authorities. Johnson, who was
profoundly embedded in Charleston but pledged his reputation to the United
States, personified the conflicts and struggles among these multiple powers.
Pinckney based her claim to the right to engage in constitutional theorizing on
her own embodiment of the Revolutionary heritage of her family, state, and
nation. Each produced a major written work—for Johnson, the *Elkison* opinion; for Pinckney, the *Political Catechism*—that was a meditation on both their
state's place in the federal republic and their own place in their state. Both

texts were defiant, at times angry, as well as subtle and penetrating. Both were written to instruct. Both were produced by authors who were members of the planter elite, and who viewed themselves as conservators of the city's patriot past, a past that also defined each of their families.

Yet these writings presented wildly divergent views of the nature of the Union. Even in the cradle of what became the nation's greatest conflict between federal and state power, interbellum constitutional debates were fundamentally about the contest for control over far more numerous and variegated layers of authority, meaning, and legacy. Whether on the wharf, in the courthouse, or at the drawing-room writing table, Charleston in the 1820s and early 1830s was pulsating with competing claims to power. By the time the Pinckney Mansion burned in December 1861, however, that multilayered cacophony was rearranging itself into a two-sided argument between state and federal power. That argument was so totalizing and brutal that it blotted out the memory of the previous multivocal struggle.

6 • The Editor and the Faithful Ally

A Federalism of Native Country and People

In July 1831, near the headwaters of the Oostanaula River in what today is northwest Georgia, a newspaper editor and father of three in his late twenties paused from the relentless round of duties that occupied him daily, both at his printing office and at his nearby home, to write to his wife's relatives in Connecticut. After apologizing for not replying sooner to his sister- and brother-in-law's most recent letter, he reported some news from the elder members of that side of the family. "Last mail brought us a letter from our good parents, dated in New Haven," he wrote.

> They say they have so many grand children coming on, some of whom will wish to get an education in Yale, that they aught to be there to take care of them. They express a hope that *some* of our ~~Indian boys~~ papooses may go there. As to that we can say we have but three [yet?] we do [not] know how it will be. William Penn, however, if *we* live and if *he* lives and is not a block head, and above all *if* we have the *means* at our command, will go to New England for *larning*. But you see it depends upon many contingencies.[1]

The father who made these cautiously hopeful plans for his children was Elias Boudinot, a citizen of the Cherokee Nation and the editor of the *Cherokee Phoenix*, the Nation's official newspaper.[2] William Penn, seventeen months old, was the third child of Boudinot and his Connecticut-born, non-Native wife, Harriett Gold Boudinot.[3] William Penn's older sisters, Eleanor Susan and Mary Harriett, were four and three years old, respectively. The girls' education was already underway, by means of spelling books and readers ordered from Boston by their father and sent one thousand miles over land and water to New Echota, the capital of the Cherokee Nation.

The *Phoenix*, like its editor, was thoroughly and proudly bilingual. Its columns carried articles in both English and Cherokee, printed by means of a custom-made set of metal type that reproduced the Cherokee syllabary developed by Sequoyah in 1821.[4] Boudinot himself wrote many of the pieces that appeared in the *Phoenix*; other items were reprinted from the approximately one hundred American and European newspapers with which he had arranged reciprocal subscriptions with the *Phoenix*.

Beginning in 1828, the *Phoenix* was published in a small, log-hewn wooden building on the town square in New Echota. The two-story, frame Boudinot home, with its double-layered white porches, stood a few steps away. The council house, the Nation's seat of government, faced the print shop—a fitting arrangement for two of the Cherokee people's most important political institutions and sites of national self-assertion.

These important developments were background to the moment in July 1831 when Boudinot, writing to his wife's sister and brother-in-law, imagined a future in which his son would attend Yale and his daughters would be educated at New England academies of like stature. Boudinot's letter displayed his customary dry wit, verbal acuity, and skill at conveying multiple subtle meanings. Harriett's parents in New Haven, he wrote, "express a hope that *some* of our"—and then he crossed out the phrase he had initially written, "Indian boys," replacing it with "papooses"—"may go there."

By using the word "papoose," a variant on an Algonquian (not Cherokee) word present in the Anglo-American lexicon since the seventeenth century, Boudinot appears to have been consciously performing an ironic, generic version of Indian-ness to his brother- and sister-in-law.[5] He did this frequently in his letters, sometimes referring to himself as a "son of the forest," a phrase that recurred in non-Native speech in nineteenth-century America to refer to Indigenous men and to signal their exoticness.[6] Similarly, Boudinot's underlining of the word "larning" functioned as the nineteenth-century equivalent of modern "scare quotes," signaling to the reader that he was deliberately using the nonstandard version of the word "learning." Given the New England accent of the period, "larning" might well have been a parodic quotation of a northwestern Connecticut pronunciation—and thus a reminder of the well-traveled Boudinot's familiarity with Yankee mores.

The deliberately chosen words with which Boudinot composed his letters to his New England relations were but one element of his lifelong project to present the Cherokee Nation as a polity that stood equal to—but, crucially, distinct from—the United States. Boudinot's personal experiences in Connecticut during the controversy surrounding his marriage to Harriett, as well as his speaking circuits through churches and lecture halls up and down the East Coast, had made him aware of the surprising picture that he presented to many white Americans. One account of a prayer meeting he had attended in New Haven described him as "a manly, good-looking Cherokee Indian"; other reports noted his fashionable, European-style attire of frock coat, trousers, high collar, and cravat, as well as his facility with the English language.[7]

Indeed, Boudinot made his identity a focal point of his standard lecture. "What is an Indian? Is he not formed of the same materials with yourself?" he asked his largely white audiences. "You here behold an *Indian*, my kindred are *Indians*, and my fathers sleeping in the wilderness grave—they too were *Indians*." He then described his upbringing in terms that began in a pastoral register before shifting to a patriotic mode:

[O]n a little hill, in a lonely cabin, overspread by the forest oak, I first drew my breath; and in a language unknown to learned and polished nations, I learnt to lisp my fond mother's name. In after days, I have had greater advantages than most of my race; and I now stand before you delegated by my native country to seek her interest, to labour for her respectability, and by my public efforts to assist in raising her to an equal standing with other nations of the earth.

Throughout his remarks, Boudinot made clear that his "native country" was not a generic Indian periphery, but a specific political, territorial, and cultural entity: the Cherokee Nation. The speech was published under the title "An Address to the Whites"; the title page denominated the author as "Elias Boudinott, a Cherokee Indian."[8]

For Boudinot, the essence of the Nation was its people. Even more than the ancestral Cherokee lands that he held dear, Boudinot prized the Cherokee people and what he viewed as their rapidly improving culture. He lauded their written language, their adoption of Christianity, and their constitutional form of government. Standing before northern audiences, Boudinot identified himself as "an *Indian*," a representative of "that particular tribe called Cherokees."[9] Despite—or perhaps because of—the fact that he had spent his formative years in New England, Boudinot was committed to his Cherokee identity, which he did not appear to regard as depending on or deriving from a specific physical place. He was always and forever a Cherokee person, whether he was at home in New Echota or campaigning in Philadelphia, Boston, or Washington. Perhaps spending his adolescence far from the Cherokee Nation made

Elias Boudinot, by an unknown artist, n.d. (Courtesy
of Western History Collections, University of Oklahoma
Libraries, Frank Phillips Collection 3487.)

Boudinot all the more conscious of his Cherokee identity. As an expatriate, he
might have been both more aware of his Cherokee-ness and also more dependent on persons, rather than places, as carriers of that identity.

Throughout his highly public life and career, Boudinot devoted himself to
what he clearly regarded as a crusade on behalf of the Cherokee Nation. But as
he matured, he came to distinguish between the Cherokee people, whom he
described as "intelligent and virtuous," and the Cherokee lands that lay within
the chartered limits of four of the United States. In 1832, he described his patriotism as comprising both *"love of the country"* and *"love of the People."* Both,

he said, were the "object[s] of my affection."[10] Yet they were neither equal nor indivisible. By "country," Boudinot referred to the Cherokee Nation in its then-current territorial instantiation. That country could not survive without the people, while the people might be saved even if the country was lost. The people were the indispensable core of Boudinot's conception of Cherokee patriotism. If pressed to choose between the two affections, his mission would be to ensure the "safety" of the people—even if that choice required accepting that the country was lost.[11] If Georgia extended its authority in such a way as to encompass Cherokee lands, then the country was for all purposes lost. Boudinot was a Christian who wore European clothes, but that did not make him an assimilationist. On the contrary: he was a separatist who believed in the preservation of the Cherokee people.[12] If the Cherokees were forced to choose between keeping their land but acknowledging Georgia's power, or losing their land but surviving as a people, he insisted that they must choose the latter. That insistence ultimately cost Boudinot his life.

Boudinot's political activities drew on his formidable skill as a writer and a translator. As the July 1831 letter to his relatives demonstrates, Boudinot was acutely aware of the nuances of language and how they were employed by different speakers and understood by different audiences. After he had filled three sides of a single folded piece of paper, just before he handed the letter to Harriett to add her own message to her sister and brother-in-law, he noted in closing, "I have occupied more of this sheet than I intended to and have left very little space indeed for the S---w. All our wives are known in Georgia by that name."[13]

The word that Boudinot overtly refrained from spelling out in its entirety was "squaw." Like "papoose," the word "squaw" was not a Cherokee term. It was instead a phonetic rendering by European North Americans of an Algonquian term for "woman."[14] By the 1830s, the word was used by white Americans to refer broadly—and often pejoratively—to Native women. Boudinot acknowledged the word's crudeness by using dashes for the middle letters of the term, a common device for writers of the period who sought to avoid repeating profanities (or, in some cases, to conceal the identities of their subjects).[15]

Yet in a letter to the same relatives six months earlier, he had written each letter of the word: "I should like to write a great deal if I had time and room—but Harriett, my Squaw, has been pretty particular."[16] In both letters, Boudinot's use of the term was deliberate and striking. He—a Cherokee man—was employing a pseudo-Indian term that was commonly used by white speakers, and he was using that term to refer to his wife—a white woman—in a letter to her relations in New England. In a single sentence, written in his second language, Boudinot conveyed multiple layers of meaning as well as a commentary on those meanings. Through his linguistic adeptness, he was performing a version of Native identity for an audience of white people who were also members of his extended family, and thereby seizing control.

Perhaps Elias was demonstrating to the Connecticut connection that Harriett had in fact become a Cherokee woman by marrying him and moving to New Echota. He constructed his message through his mastery of layers of language—here, by adopting Euro-American versions of borrowed and bastardized Indian terms. It was a process of translation and re-translation. Typically, when he was referring to his beloved Harriett in letters, Elias used her name or the standard terms of early-nineteenth-century polite epistolary discourse: "my wife," "my companion." Why, then, did he employ a term that would likely have seemed—to him more than to virtually anyone else—both fraught and inaccurate?

One answer may lie in the next sentence of the letter: "All our wives are known in Georgia by that name." *Our* wives—meaning the wives of all Cherokee men, and perhaps of all Indians; *known*—meaning to others, to an audience other than their spouses or themselves; and *in Georgia*—not in the Cherokee Nation, but someplace else, somewhere both linguistically and politically distinct.

That distinct place was the state of Georgia, which was at once alien to and invasive of the Nation. Georgia surrounded New Echota, but in the eyes of the Cherokee Nation, New Echota was not *in* Georgia. The return address Boudinot wrote on the letter conveyed the complex physical and legal location of the Nation: "New Echota C.N. Ga."[17]

For even as Boudinot wrote poignantly in July 1831 of his aspirations for his children's future schooling among the Calvinist elms of New Haven, the Cherokee Nation was under attack by the state of Georgia. The sense of looming catastrophe is palpable in the Boudinots' letter to their Connecticut relatives. Indeed, even the letter that ended on a note of hope started with a veiled reference to violence. Boudinot began his portion of the letter with an allusion to the fact that he had recently been forcibly haled before the state militia and threatened with flogging for his work as editor of the *Phoenix*. With characteristic understatement, he referred to these events only by saying, "[W]e have been in hot water ever since our last to you, that is the masculine portion of us." But his tone grew more serious as he discussed "the Georgia affair," which he described as "a piece of great wickedness": "The last right and in some respects, the most important right of the Cherokees, is to be fought and contended for—their right to the *land*. . . . One thing is certain [:] there is a crisis approaching, both in the history of the Cherokees & the United States. Shall robbery be committed?"[18]

In her portion of the joint letter, Harriett castigated the American public for not doing more to aid the Cherokees, whom she referred to as "our people." The poor health that she was suffering—likely due to the early stages of pregnancy with the couple's fourth child, Sarah—did not impede her from pressing her point to her brother-in-law, the Reverend Herman Vaill: "How are the American people ever to atone for the injuries done the original inhabitants of this Country?"[19]

Fractal Federalism: A Nation within a State within a Nation

From the banks of the Oostanaula to the halls of Congress and the chamber of the Supreme Court, at the lecterns of churches and in the pages of newspapers, the Cherokee Nation was insisting on recognition.[20] But these national assertions were met with other polities' invocations of statehood. Georgia was demanding all the rights that appertained to its position as what it regarded as a sovereign member of the American union. One of these claimed rights was the power to eliminate rival sovereignty claimants within its borders.

The conflict between the Cherokee Nation and Georgia dated from the early eighteenth century, when Georgia was a British colony feeling itself beset by Indian enemies within and French and Spanish competitors without. The struggle continued into the early national period, when the dispute between Georgia and the southeastern (then called southwestern) tribes commanded the attention of a series of presidential administrations and Congresses. But the fight was never only between the Cherokees and Georgia. The question of the legal and political status of the Cherokee Nation always involved at least three parties: the Nation, Georgia, and the United States.

Between 1827 and 1839, the long-seething battles escalated into a multi-sided, constantly shifting war. The parties to that war included on one side the Cherokee Nation, with its own increasingly distinct internal factions; influential and well-funded Christian missionary organizations, notably the American Board of Commissioners for Foreign Missions; and a large coalition of politicians and state-crafters who combined reform-mindedness, Protestant Christian ethics, and opposition to President Andrew Jackson and his program of Indian removal. On the other side were the state of Georgia, the government and people of which were largely unified in their desire to eject the

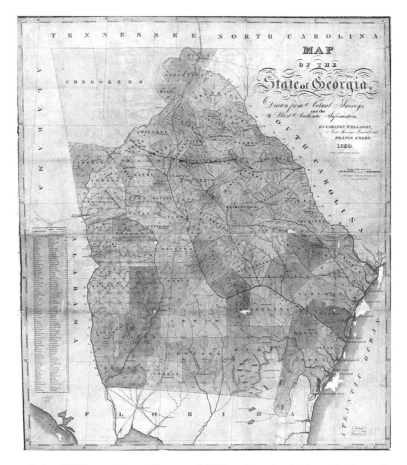

Carlton Wellborn, Orange Green, and William Hoogland, *Map of the State of Georgia, Drawn from Actual Surveys and the Most Authentic Information*, 1830. The Cherokee Nation is the triangular slice at top left. (Geography and Map Division, Library of Congress.)

Cherokees and seize their land; Jackson and his administration; and Jacksonian Democrats in Congress. And one notable set of players held views that overlapped with those of both camps: the justices of the Supreme Court of the United States.

The Cherokee Nation extended across the state lines of Georgia, Alabama, Tennessee, and North Carolina, covering some fifty-three thousand square miles.[21] Its population numbered approximately fifteen thousand people.[22] In 1827, the Cherokee Nation ratified a constitution that provided for a bicameral legislature, an executive branch, a supreme court, elections, and trial by jury, among other elements. In response to the threat the Cherokee constitution represented, the Georgia legislature formally extended the state's jurisdiction to cover the Nation, passing legislation that was designed to take effect in 1830.

In 1828, however, gold was discovered in northwestern Georgia, including within the Nation. Also in 1828, Andrew Jackson won the presidency, after running on a platform that included a promise to compel the southeastern tribes to move west, across the Mississippi River, in a program known as "Indian removal." In 1829, Jackson announced a change in official policy by explicitly stating that the Cherokees had no choice but to submit to the laws of the states in which they resided. After months of fiery debate, in 1830 Congress passed the Indian Removal Act, which authorized Jackson to negotiate with the tribes for their removal to federal lands in the West. Georgia, meanwhile, began enforcing its new laws invalidating all Cherokee laws, both formal and customary, and extending the state's jurisdiction over all white people living within the Cherokee Nation. A newly formed militia, the Georgia Guard, was charged with enforcing these laws.[23]

The Nation fought back. Delegations of Cherokee leaders had been traveling to Washington since the 1820s to meet with the president, the Cabinet, and members of Congress; to negotiate treaties; and to press their case for adherence to existing treaties. In 1828, the first issue of the *Cherokee Phoenix*, edited by Boudinot, appeared. In 1830, the leaders of the Nation confronted the increasingly dire prospects before them by expanding their efforts to a new institution: the Supreme Court.

There, before the Court, the Cherokee Nation waged a constitutional battle that grappled with—and altered—foundational concepts of American law: jurisdiction, sovereignty, and nationhood.[24] A polity that insisted that it was distinct from, but a "faithful ally" of, the United States sought to vindicate its autonomy in the fora of that foreign government.[25] One nation came into the courts of another to obtain recognition, which the plaintiff nation hoped then to deploy against another, hostile, subnational entity.[26] Ironically, in its struggle to remain separate from the United States, the Cherokee Nation shaped American law.[27]

This chapter and the next place the struggle of the Cherokee Nation at the center of the interbellum American constitutional narrative. The story is not simply one of binary conflict between the federal government and the states. It is not a case study in the familiar federalism dynamic brought about by the Civil War and entrenched in the twentieth century. Nor is it a tale of inevitability, in which an Indigenous society was destined to be compelled to give way in the face of American imperialism, Manifest Destiny, racism, or any of the other forces that are correctly associated with, but not entirely constitutive of, the interbellum United States.

Rather, these chapters demonstrate that the controversy over the status of the Cherokee Nation was a renewed and pitched struggle over the status of nonconforming polities that lay within the boundaries of the American federal union. Moreover, some of the most important arguments about this long-controversial question were offered by Cherokee leaders and their lawyers.

The American founders had discarded one canonical version of sovereignty, that offered by William Blackstone, who insisted that a government could contain only a single sovereign, and that any system that attempted to contain multiple sources of governmental authority was definitionally impossible. In the 1770s and 1780s, Americans came to reject this view that a government within a government, or an *imperium in imperio*, was necessarily a "solecism." Instead, they turned to Continental theorists and their own experience under the British Empire to argue that multiple, multilayered sovereignty was not only possible, it was the optimal structure for a republic on the scale of the United States. Many members of the founding generation argued that the specter of the *imperium in imperio* could be banished by building a structure that allocated sovereignty, along with functions, to particular spheres of government. This subject-matter vision of sovereignty, which de-pathologized multiple sovereigns, was the paramount innovation of the American federal republic.[28]

The ideological origins of American federalism lay in answering the following question: What was the status of subpolities—presumed to be the states—within the American federal union? One provisional answer, reached in 1789, was that the division of power based on subject matter (treaties, money, war, post offices) allowed a multiplicity of governments to exist within a single, overarching union. The Constitution not only rejected the solecism view of *imperium in imperio*, it embraced the possibility of multiple overlapping governments, reframing *imperium in imperio* as a virtue and a source of strength. In 1793, Supreme Court justice James Wilson reflected many post-founding Americans' skepticism about sovereignty, writing, "Who, or what, is a sovereignty? What is his or its sovereignty? On this subject, the errors and the mazes are endless and inexplicable."[29]

The urgent question of the interbellum period was a different one, and it was central to the controversy over the Cherokee Nation: How far down—and up—should the rejection of *imperium in imperio* go? By 1789, it was clear that the existence of the states did not necessarily raise *imperium in imperio* problems. But it was not at all clear how sovereign the states were permitted to be with respect to each other or to the general government. Nor was it clear how, or whether, sovereignty could be claimed by other entities that were not states, such as the Cherokee Nation.

In the 1820s and 1830s, the battle over the status of the Cherokee Nation witnessed a resurgence of *imperium in imperio* thinking. But this time, the concern was initially not about the structural integrity of the Union, but rather of the states—indeed, of one state. The state of Georgia feared the Cherokee Nation and hungered for Cherokee lands. Georgia's leaders thus revived the old *imperium in imperio* idea to frame this fear and this hunger in terms of constitutional theory. Georgia claimed that its territorial and political integrity simply did not permit an entity that called itself a nation and insisted on its own constitution and laws to exist within Georgia's boundaries. The argument entailed an inversion of the era's understanding of the law of nations: a state, in the special infranational American sense, seeking to quash a state, in the international sense.[30]

Cherokee leaders understood their polity to be juridically separate from the United States. Nevertheless, they presented their claims as supported by, not antithetical to, U.S. law in all its varied forms—treaties, statutes, executive-branch interpretations, and the Constitution. In their view, the Cherokee Nation was precisely a nation within a nation, a status that had been confirmed over decades of diplomacy, negotiation, and treaty-making.[31] But the relevant nation in which the Cherokee Nation lay was not Georgia, within whose chartered boundaries a portion of the Cherokee lands happened to be situated, but rather the United States. The Cherokee Nation was an allied republic, not an alien body. As Boudinot expressed the relationship, "She will become not a great, but a faithful ally of the United States. In times of peace she will plead the common liberties of America. In times of war her intrepid sons will sacrifice their lives in your defence. And because she will be useful to you in coming time, she asks you to assist her in her present struggles."[32]

Such a view endured long after the Nation was removed from its land by the combined force of Georgia and the United States. In 1937, one Cherokee citizen in Oklahoma described the pre-removal status of the Nation precisely in *imperium in imperio* terms: "The Cherokees had their own government. It was just a little, miniature republic, and each of the five tribes were likewise."[33]

Paradoxically, some of the most creative and closely argued American constitutional reasoning of the early nineteenth century came from individuals dedicated to the principle that their allegiance lay not with the United States but with another nation. Some of those arguments were made in the American press, in Congress, in the White House, and before the Supreme Court. These arguments ultimately did not prevent the Cherokee Nation from being forcibly removed from their eastern lands and marched nearly one thousand miles to territory west of the Mississippi River, along the infamous Trail of Tears.[34]

But the Nation nonetheless seized control of a crucial arena: American constitutional law. Its producers of constitutional discourse included Boudinot; his uncle and his cousin, Major Ridge and John Ridge, both of whom were prominent Cherokee political leaders; and John Ross, principal chief of the Cherokee Nation. Important non-Native supporters of the Cherokees were William Wirt, who represented the Nation before the Supreme Court, and the missionary Samuel Austin Worcester, Boudinot's frequent collaborator and the petitioner in the second case that the Nation managed to bring before the Court. Other participants included Jackson, Georgia governor George R. Gilmer, and—of course— the members of the Court itself, in particular Chief Justice John Marshall.

These arguments were uttered in the highest fora of U.S. law and politics, and they ultimately shaped American constitutional thought and practice. The Cherokees' claims were not precisely about federalism. Nor were they only about sovereignty or jurisdiction, although both of those were vital lodestars of the argument. To cast the Cherokee cases solely as a moment in the origin story of American federalism would be to misinterpret them in light of developments that came later.

Compacts and Intercourse

The Cherokees were part of the larger Mississippian culture, an agriculture-based civilization that emerged in southeastern North America around 800 C.E. In contrast to the languages of their nineteenth-century geographic neighbors—the Muscogee Creeks, Choctaws, Chickasaws, and Seminoles— the Cherokee language developed from the Iroquoian linguistic family, rather than the Muskogean or the Siouan families.

As the British Empire sought to expand its reach across the North American continent in the 1750s and 1760s, the Cherokees played an important role as sometimes allies, sometimes adversaries. During the Seven Years' War (known to the English, and many of their American successors, as the French and Indian War), the Cherokees initially fought alongside the British. But a series of conflicts with both Anglo-American settlers and the British Army sparked a war within the Seven Years' War that became known as the "Cherokee War" or "Anglo-Cherokee War." By 1760, Britain had defeated the Cherokees, seizing land and destroying towns and crops. In 1763, when the Treaty of Paris ended the Seven Years' War, the victorious British Empire consolidated its gains on the continent by issuing the Proclamation of 1763, which prohibited British settlement west of the Appalachian Mountains. The corresponding "Proclamation Line" extended through modern-day North Carolina, touched the edge of South Carolina, and sliced an arc through Georgia. This mapped boundary between settler and Native lands aimed to divide the two populations and appeared to create a "separate and distinct Indian country."[35]

The experience of the war with Britain prompted Cherokee leaders to revise their governmental structure. Prior to the 1760s, Cherokee politics and society were highly decentralized, with identity based more on town or regional affiliation than on any sense of collective political nationhood across the groups that would later come to be denominated the Cherokee Nation.[36] Knowing whether someone belonged to the Lower, Middle, Valley, Out, or Overhill settlement, and knowing which clan claimed them as a member, were the crucial social and political facts, grounded on kinship ties and deeply rooted norms of the common good.[37] After the war, however, Cherokee leaders began to work to knit together these loosely linked settlements. Fighting a war against Britain and its settlers thus spurred the emergence of a Cherokee national identity and what one scholar terms "the dissemination of a broader collective consciousness."[38]

At the same time, the end of the Seven Years' War ensured that among the great powers of Europe, it was Britain—not France, not Spain—that would dominate North America. This sense of imperial hegemony trickled out from the center to the peripheries. Many colonists managed to combine pride in their status as subjects of the triumphant British Empire with the conviction that their own particular colony's government possessed a broad remit that included the powers of lawmaking, taxation, and self-defense. A colonist in Virginia or Pennsylvania could reasonably conceive of himself as simultaneously a wave-ruling Briton and a provincial bearer of the rights of Englishmen.[39] And no colony was more flush with its own heady blend of imperial might and aggressive self-determination than Georgia.

Since its founding in 1732, Georgia had operated as boundary and buffer zone between British and Spanish claims in North America. Georgia was devised by the Crown as a purpose-built frontier, a garrison protecting the rich and profitable colony of South Carolina from Spanish raids or claims— and, not incidentally, serving as a barrier to discourage Carolina's large and growing slave population from attempting to flee south to Florida.[40] Unlike many of Britain's other colonies, Georgia was invested from its beginning with a geopolitical, as well as a mercantile, mission.[41] This sense of purpose instilled in Georgians the belief that they possessed a uniquely powerful position first in the British Empire, and then, after 1776, in the United States.

During the Revolutionary and founding eras, concerns about the presence of Native people and the status of their lands informed debates about trade, war, and property.[42] Georgians were reluctant to relinquish the power to make war on, or treaties with, the Indians, whom they regarded as living on Georgia's land. Throughout the Confederation period, Georgians resisted federal treaty-making on grounds of what Lisa Ford terms "settler sovereignty."[43] But the perceived threat of war with Native nations ultimately convinced Georgians to ratify the Constitution. As Greg Ablavsky notes, Georgians viewed the Union "instrumentally," insofar as "they were willing to offer loyalty and obedience as long as the government fulfilled what they considered its most basic function of protection"—for their property and their broader claims of sovereignty over the land, as against competing Indigenous claims.[44] So deeply engrained was Georgians' understanding of the nature of the Union that it amounted to "an alternate constitutional tradition committed to expansion and dispossessing Indians."[45]

By 1800, white Georgians had grown accustomed to viewing themselves as having earned a kind of demi-nation status, thanks to their service as wardens of the border, holding the South against foreign invasion from without and Indian invasion from within. As a result, they were in a position to bargain with the U.S. government rather than simply acceding to federal demands. In exchange for ceding the so-called Yazoo lands, which comprised most of the area between the Mississippi and Chattahoochee rivers and would later become the states of Alabama and Mississippi, Georgia was able to extract benefits from the United States. In 1802, the state obtained from the federal government a payment of $1.25 million and, more importantly, a guarantee that the federal government would "extinguish, for the use of Georgia, as early as the same can be peaceably obtained, on reasonable terms," the Indian title to all lands within the state's boundaries.[46] Implicit in the agreement was a recognition of the Cherokees' title to their land. But it was recognized only in order to eliminate it.

The Compact of 1802, as it became known, provided a legal foundation for Georgia to argue that its claims to Indigenous land were not only valid exercises of the state's own sovereign power, but also that that exercise had been ratified by the federal government. Because it was styled as a "compact," the agreement sounded in the law of nations: it was a binding commitment between coequal polities, not a command from a superior to an inferior power.[47] The federal government had the authority to "clear"—or, more bluntly, to "extinguish"—Indigenous land title, and a state could demand that the United States exercise that power.[48] The Native nations themselves were not parties to the compact.

Of course, a state could demand, but the general government might not act upon those demands. Despite Georgia's persistent invocation of the compact, and despite the *quid* of the state's cession of its western lands, the *quo* of the federal government's promise to extinguish Native title was not fulfilled for three decades.

Meanwhile, less than a month after commissioners from Georgia and the United States reached agreement on the Compact of 1802, Congress affirmed the supremacy of the federal government over relations with Indigenous nations. Signed into law on March 30, 1802, by President Thomas Jefferson, the Act to Regulate Trade and Intercourse with the Indian Tribes, and to Preserve Peace on the Frontiers was the latest in a series of congressional acts attempting to establish ground rules for Americans' relations with Native tribes and individuals.[49] The Trade and Intercourse Act began in the tradition of Britain's Proclamation Line of 1763, defining in metes-and-bounds detail a "boundary line" between Indian Territory and the United States.

The most important provision of the Trade and Intercourse Act, Section 12, provided that "no purchase, grant, lease, or other conveyance of lands" from "any Indian, or nation, or tribe of Indians, within the bounds of the United States" was valid unless it was made "by treaty or convention, pursuant to the constitution."[50] Congress's message was clear: the only lawful means by which Indian lands could be acquired was through the mechanism of a treaty. Individual purchases of land were not permitted. Nor were the states themselves allowed to negotiate land cessions from Native tribes. The proper mode of transfer was from one nation to another, according to the forms of eighteenth-century international relations. Thus, by implication, the Trade and Intercourse Act recognized some degree of sovereign status in Native governments. The act also entailed a diminished form of sovereignty in states such as Georgia, insofar as it rejected their claimed power to conduct their own foreign affairs with respect to "any Indian, or nation, or tribe of Indians."

Perhaps for this reason, the Trade and Intercourse Act was known by some contemporaries as the "*Non*-Intercourse Act." At both structural and substantive levels, the act operated in permissive as well as restrictive registers. The rules of trade and intercourse with the Indian tribes were under the authority of the United States. The act of 1802 was itself one such rule, an assertion of federal power. Intercourse with the Indian tribes seemed to be a federal matter, notwithstanding Georgia's views on the Compact of 1802.

Politics, 1824: Washington

By the 1820s, conflict between Georgia and the Cherokees seemed both unavoidable and imminent. The federal government had thus far failed to extinguish Cherokee title in the northwest portion of Georgia. Georgia officials in the state capital of Milledgeville and in Washington, where they were vocal members of Congress as well as of the Cabinet, were pressing their claims with increased fervor and occasional violence.

Cherokee leaders, for their part, continued their project of unifying the tribe's disparate towns into a single nation and constructing an overarching government. The National Council that had emerged as the locus of political power in the late-eighteenth-century shift toward greater centralization developed by 1809 into a body with formal executive powers. In 1817, the council launched more fundamental changes aimed at centralizing and bolstering governmental structures in the face of ongoing pressure for land cessions.[51] The reforms, memorialized as the Articles of Government, established a bicameral legislative system, with a thirteen-member National Committee that would draft laws and manage the affairs of the Nation, while town leaders meeting in their annual session of the National Council would act as a legislature, adopting or rejecting the proposed laws.[52] As the preamble to the articles, which some scholars have deemed "the first Cherokee constitution," explained, the principal motivation for the reforms was a fear that a subset of Cherokee citizens might enter into an agreement to surrender some of the Nation's land, which was held in common, to the United States or Georgia: "Whereas fifty-four towns and villages have convened to deliberate and consider on the situation of the Nation, in the disposition of our common property of land without the consent of the members of the Council, in order to obviate the evil consequences resulting in such a course, we have unanimously adopted the following form of the future government of our nation."[53]

As events unfolded in the Cherokee Nation and in Washington in the middle years of the 1820s, the caution of the Cherokee leaders was warranted.

Georgia's belligerence toward Native nations that held land within the state's territory became evident in the 1820s, during the administrations of James Monroe and John Quincy Adams. Like many white Americans of the era, both presidents regarded the presence of Indigenous people within the boundaries of the United States as a problem for national expansion, the security of settler property rights, and—for some commentators—the survival of the tribes themselves.[54]

Beginning with the Washington administration, the federal government had maintained a policy of promoting the "civilization" of "the friendly Indian tribes."[55] Washington, his secretary of war, Henry Knox, and many other statesmen of the early national period believed that Native peoples were capable of being included in the American polity in some capacity—perhaps through assimilation, or perhaps through some other vaguely defined set of policies that maintained a degree of distinction.[56] The key to this planned incorporation was the Indians' "civilization": principally, the shift to a more sedentary, agricultural socioeconomic structure (a shift that for some tribes, including the Cherokee, had in fact already occurred several decades earlier), as well as the spread of literacy and the adoption of Christianity. Knox's vision was that with this transition away from hunting toward husbandry, Native peoples would voluntarily sell their excess land to the federal government.[57] For the first few decades of the United States' existence, then, federal policy aimed at civilizing the Indians in the hope that they would voluntarily cede some significant portion of their lands.

By the 1820s, however, many white Americans had come to regard Indians as a population doomed to disappear. For some commentators, Indian decline was inevitable because Indigenous people constituted a distinct race that was, in the words of Adams's secretary of state, Henry Clay, "essentially inferior to the Anglo-Saxon race."[58] An opinion that might have been slightly more sympathetic to the situation of many Native nations, but that often ended up reaching a similar conclusion, held that as long as Native populations were surrounded by the baneful influences of white settlers—ranging from violence to alcoholism—Indians had little hope of sustaining their culture and autonomy. This view seems to have been shared by Monroe and Adams. Other contemporaries focused on the land itself, viewing Indian claims as illegitimate and as obstacles to the appropriate use of property by the correct proprietors.

However they arrived at their views, by the 1820s many white observers had come to believe that Indigenous nations were fundamentally incompatible with, and had no place in, the American republic. The solution on which many seized was for the government to shift away from a policy of civilization and encouragement and toward an intensified effort to persuade the Native nations to relinquish their lands and "remove" outside the boundaries of the several states, to unorganized federal territory.[59] This persuasion took increasingly stringent forms, but most Americans continued to hew to the belief that removal must be voluntary, not coerced. Georgians, however, were increasingly willing to turn to force. Eager to eject the Cherokee and Creek Nations from their long-held lands, Georgia hounded the federal government to carry out the Compact of 1802 and to begin in earnest a comprehensive program of Indian removal.

The "Indian problem," as it became known in Washington, was the subject of frequent discussions in Congress and within the executive branch. These debates took place in the Cabinet, the site during this period of robust policy-making by a notably accomplished group of statesmen. Federal Indian policy was also made in the War Department, which carried out federal Indian policy first through the Office of Indian Trade and then, beginning in 1824, the Bureau of Indian Affairs.

The Cherokee Nation, for its part, deployed its own cadre of sophisticated diplomats to negotiate with the United States throughout the first two decades of the nineteenth century. In January 1824, a delegation of leading Cherokee officials traveled to Washington, where they spent six months lobbying and negotiating on behalf of their Nation. The Cherokee National Council had recently rejected yet another set of overtures from Georgia seeking tribal lands. At the same time, the Nation was engaged in talks with federal commissioners whom Monroe had appointed to treat with the Nation about potential cessions. In response to all these entreaties, Cherokee officials declared their "fixed and unalterable determination . . . never again to cede *one foot* more of land."[60]

The delegation thus journeyed to Washington in 1824 with several objectives: to reiterate their unwillingness to cede more land; to ask the federal government to remind Georgia that the Compact of 1802 was not a mandate to seize Cherokee lands, but rather specified that land be "peaceably obtained" on "reasonable terms"; to request the one-thousand-dollar annuity owed to the Nation under a prior treaty; and to ask that the unpopular federal agent to the Nation, former Tennessee governor Joseph McMinn, be replaced for alleged corruption and bribery.[61]

As commissioners, the National Council appointed four of the Nation's most prominent statesmen: Major Ridge, John Ross, Elijah Hicks, and George Lowrey. The delegation melded two generations of Cherokee leadership: the senior cohort of Ridge and Lowrey, both of whom had been born in the 1770s; and a younger contingent, Ross and Hicks, who had been born in 1790 and 1797, respectively.

Major Ridge was a famed warrior who had in his youth fought with General Andrew Jackson against the Creeks and the Seminoles. During that campaign, he gained the rank of major in the U.S. Army, which he then made part of his English name.[62] By 1824, Major Ridge had become one of the most important members of the Cherokee government as well as one of the Nation's wealthiest citizens. His holdings included a 280-acre plantation overlooking the Oostanaula River (twenty-six miles southwest of New Echota, near modern-day Rome, Georgia), a ferry, a store, and a work force of thirty slaves.[63]

Lowrey, Ridge's contemporary, was also a member of the national government. Hicks was the son of Charles Renatus Hicks, the assistant principal chief of the Nation.

Ross was one of the Nation's most promising up-and-coming public men: like Ridge, a veteran of the Creek War; president of the National Committee; clerk to the Nation's principal chief, Pathkiller; and a successful businessman. Four years after the mission to Washington, in 1828, Ross was elected principal chief of the Nation, a post he held until his death in 1866.[64]

All four delegates had at least one European parent or grandparent, in many cases a Scottish or Scots-Irish trader or frontiersman who had married a Cherokee woman. Because Cherokee culture followed a matrilineal tradition, the children of these unions were full members of their mothers' clans.[65] Their European heritage had little consequence for their status as citizens of the Nation. Ridge and his family consistently referred to themselves as "full-blooded Cherokees."[66] Some of their white contemporaries persisted in tallying the quantum of Indian "blood" that a particular Cherokee leader was thought to possess, repeatedly pointing out that Ross was "only" one-eighth Cherokee and commenting on what they regarded as his surprisingly light complexion.[67]

Since childhood, Ross (known as "Tsan Usdi," or "Little John") had lived literally at the crossroads of Cherokee and white culture. His father was Daniel Ross, who had emigrated as a boy from Sutherlandshire, Scotland. His mother, Mollie McDonald Ross, was the daughter of a Highlander from Inverness and the granddaughter of a Cherokee woman named Ghigooie.[68] John Ross grew up with his parents and eight siblings as "backwoods aristocrats" in a Cherokee town near present-day Chattanooga, Tennessee, attending Cherokee festivals, and receiving private lessons in English from a tutor before being sent to board at an academy that offered an Anglo-American curriculum.[69]

Ross inherited a trading empire and substantial property, including slaves, from his father. Combined with his rigorous formal education, Ross's business connections made him particularly adept at moving between Euro-American and Cherokee society. The 1824 trip to Washington was not his first mission to the capital. He had traveled there in 1816 to press the Nation's claims, and his fluency in English had made him an important participant in meetings with the Madison administration. With the exception of Major Ridge, who spoke only Cherokee, each of the members of the 1824 delegation had some competence in both Cherokee and English—although, in Ross's case, the Cherokee was only rudimentary. When he later became principal chief, Ross routinely addressed his fellow citizens in English, with an interpreter standing by to convey his words in Cherokee.

When the Cherokee delegation arrived in Washington in early January 1824, they took rooms at Tennison's Hotel at Fourteenth Street and Pennsylvania Avenue, two blocks east of the White House.[70] They then launched their diplomatic efforts, meeting with President Monroe, Secretary of State Adams, and Secretary of War John C. Calhoun, as well as with other Cabinet officials and members of Congress. Along with the official sessions, the members of the delegation attended a whirl of social events, including parties and balls at the White House and at the homes of Adams and Calhoun, among others. At these gatherings, the Cherokee representatives sought to continue arguing their case, to engage in informal suasion, and also to demonstrate, by their very presence, that their Nation had achieved the degree of civilization that the United States seemed bent on demanding from them as a condition of protecting their lands against the increasingly heated demands of Georgia. The Cherokee representatives regarded themselves as diplomats acting on behalf of a distinct nation. Consequently, all affairs with the sister nation of the United States were to be settled through the accepted medium of the law of nations: treaties. Yet their American counterparts required perpetual convincing.

Between January and June 1824, conversations concerning the burgeoning conflict between Georgia and the Cherokees filled the halls of Congress, the chambers of the War Department, and the dining room of the White House. In the evenings, they spilled over into the salons and levees of Washington City's leading hostesses, many of whom were the wives of Cabinet members. The debates unfolded across the capital's variety of elite spaces. Representatives of the Cherokee Nation made certain that they were present—and, crucially, both seen and heard—in each of these theaters of power.

Washingtonians were struck by the delegation's conviviality and social acumen—and by how radically their appearances diverged from the image of the untutored son of the forest that many white Americans had evidently expected. Secretary of State Adams noted the following observations in his diary:

> The manners and deportment of these men have in no respect differed from those of well-bred country gentlemen. They have frequented all the societies, where they have been invited at evening parties, attended several drawing-rooms, and most of Mrs. Adams's Tuesday evenings. They dress like ourselves, except that Hicks, a young and very handsome man, wore habitually a purfled scarf. He and Ross are half-breeds, and Ross is the writer of the delegation. They have sustained a written controversy against the Georgia delegation with great advantage.[71]

Adams's repetition of the word "delegation" to refer to both the Cherokees and the Georgians is notable here. The secretary of state, a scion of one of America's founding families who had spent years mixing with the diplomatic corps of Russia, the Netherlands, and Prussia, was clearly impressed by the seriousness and urbanity of the Cherokee representatives. "They write their own State papers," he observed in his diary, "and reason as logically as most white diplomatists."[72]

The Cherokees were not the only ambassadors from the Southwest who were pressing their case in Washington in early 1824. The capital was a battleground for two delegations that had traveled north to claim the lands northwest of the Chattahoochee River. While Ross, Ridge, Hicks, and Lowrey were chivying along their agenda with Secretary of War Calhoun and others, Georgia's congressional representatives were pressuring the Monroe administration to deny the Cherokees' demands and to inform them that removal was their sole option.

In meetings with the Cherokee delegation, Calhoun urged the envoys to convince their government to cede the Nation's lands to the United States in exchange for a sum of money and unspecified lands west of the Mississippi River. The only alternatives, Calhoun argued, were for the Cherokees to "remain . . . exposed to the discontent of Georgia and the pressure of her citizens" or to convert tribal ownership of land into individual holdings—and, in so doing, to dismantle the Nation from within.[73]

In a series of written responses, the Cherokees—with Ross almost certainly wielding the pen—reiterated their central points: "[T]he Cherokees are not foreigners, but original inhabitants of America." Therefore, "the limits of their territory are defined by the treaties which they have made with the Government of the United States." Moreover, Ross and his fellow delegates cast Georgia's claims as pretensions to power in a domain that was not only outside the state's jurisdiction, but within the jurisdiction of a different polity. The Cherokees, Ross wrote, "cannot recognize the sovereignty of any State within the limits of their territory."[74] The state of Georgia simply could not extend its reach into the Cherokee Nation. To allow it to do so would be to permit a state to interfere with the superior power of a nation. The Cherokees were here seizing the *imperium in imperio* concept for themselves. It was not the Cherokee Nation that was the nonconforming polity; it was Georgia, improperly asserting sovereignty from within the "limits of" Cherokee "territory."

But even these dark exhortations from the secretary of war were not enough to satisfy the Georgians, who were clearly irked at the cordial reception that the Cherokee delegates were receiving in the capital. At one point, Georgia officials objected to the fact that a communiqué from the federal government to the Cherokee representatives began with the salutation "Gentlemen." Adams appeared to give credence to the complaint by characterizing the word choice as "an inadvertency of a clerk, overlooked by Calhoun in signing the paper."[75] Presumably the Georgians, ever punctilious in matters of social and racial hierarchy, would have preferred the communication to begin "Sirs." So inflamed did the Georgians become at what they perceived as a lack of will on the part of the administration that they issued a belligerent letter to the president, the intemperateness of which appears to have stunned President Monroe, who immediately convened the Cabinet to share in his indignation.

Consider the scene: a meeting of the president and his Cabinet, in the second-floor room of the White House known then as the president's office (and today as the Lincoln Bedroom). The sixty-five-year-old president, clad in no-longer-modish knee breeches, visibly aggrieved by the Georgians' stance, declared the letter "an insult." An "insult" was no idle label in this period, given the alacrity with which politicians were prepared to settle affairs of honor on the dueling ground.[76] Adams, who was present at the meeting, noted, "The President said he had never received such a paper." (Note the use of the word "paper"—did the pugnacious item not even qualify as a letter?) Adams's account suggests that Monroe handed the letter around the table so that the members of his (betrousered) Cabinet could view Georgia's enormity with their own eyes. In "terms of the most acrimonious reproach against the Government of the United States," Adams recounted in that day's diary entry, the letter charged the administration "almost in terms with fraud and hypocrisy" and "broadly insinuate[d] that the obstinacy of the Cherokees [was] instigated by the Secretary of War himself."[77]

Peering at the letter as it was passed around, the thus-maligned secretary of war opined as to the identity of the writer based on forensic evaluation. "Calhoun remarked that it was in the handwriting of [Georgia congressman Thomas W.] Cobb, but it was signed by the two Senators, [John] Elliott and [Nicholas] Ware, and by all the members of the House from the State," except one who was evidently not in Washington at the time. Ever a stickler, Calhoun then "dwelt upon its incorrectness with regard to the facts." Adams, for his part, challenged the Georgians' interpretation of the language of the Compact of 1802, which they had invoked as the gravamen of their complaint. The secretary of state "observed that it was a peremptory demand to do by force, and upon most unreasonable terms, that which had been stipulated only to be done peaceably, and upon reasonable terms."[78]

Everyone at the table appears to have agreed that Georgia was in the wrong. Adams referred to "this raging fever for Indian lands," and Calhoun observed that Georgia's "immoral and corrupt" system of granting land by lottery was to blame, insofar as it "instigat[ed] insatiable cupidity for lands."[79] The sense of the room was that Georgia's bellicosity not only toward the Cherokee Nation, but now against the federal government, was a troubling development. "I suspected this bursting forth of Georgia upon the Government of the United States was ominous of other events," Adams brooded to his diary.[80]

The meeting continued for more than five hours while Monroe, Calhoun, Adams, and Secretary of the Navy Samuel Southard batted around potential responses to Georgia. When the assembled company adjourned sometime after three o'clock in the afternoon, they had not agreed on a course of action. Monroe continued to mull his options for more than two weeks.

Finally, after several more discussions in the Cabinet—some with the participation of Attorney General William Wirt and Treasury Secretary William Crawford, a Georgian who in this case took pains to distance himself from his compatriots who had authored the letter—Monroe settled on a plan. He would not forward Georgia's letter to Congress, declining to dignify it with such attention. Instead, the president proposed to send two documents to the Capitol. First, he would transmit a report from Calhoun outlining the actions the federal government had taken in pursuance of the Compact of 1802, which made a brief allusion to the letter from the Georgia delegation. Second, Monroe would send a message reiterating that the Cherokees could not be removed by force, but then stating that since they continued to refuse to cede any additional land despite "all that has been done by the Government of the Union in fulfillment of the compact," there was in fact no further recourse other than using force because of "the absolute necessity that the Indians should remove west of the Mississippi." Finally, Monroe planned to end the message by stating that "nothing further could be done by the Executive." Thanks to this pregnant statement by the president, Adams observed, "there were direct intimations that something should be done by Congress."[81]

Upon hearing Monroe's proposed message, Adams and other members of the Cabinet objected. Far from rebuffing Georgia's insolence, as Monroe had initially intended, they argued that such a message would suggest that there was merit to the state's claims and prompt its leaders to seek redress in Congress. How had a rebuke from the president to Georgia suddenly become an invitation to that recalcitrant state to begin "peremptorily claiming something further, and immediately, from Congress"? Monroe said he would "consider of it further."[82]

The next day, the president sent a reworked version of the carefully worded message to Congress. In it, he stated that "the Indian title was not affected in the slightest circumstance" by the Compact of 1802, and that, despite Georgia's intensifying demands, there was "no obligation on the United States to remove the Indians by force." Indeed, Monroe noted, any effort to remove Native nations by force would be "unjust." Yet the tribes whose lands lay within Georgia ought to be made to understand that removal was in their best interest: "Surrounded as they are, and pressed as they will be, on every side by the white population, it will be difficult if not impossible for them, with their kind of government, to sustain order among them." Still, the goal, at least nominally, was voluntary removal. "[A]ll these evils may be avoided," Monroe wrote, "if these tribes will consent to remove beyond the limits of our present States and Territories." The president concluded by submitting the issue to Congress "under a high sense of its importance and of the propriety of an early decision on it."[83] Monroe sent his message to Congress on March 30, 1824. Congress responded by approving a new round of talks between federal commissioners and Cherokee officials, in the hope of arriving at a final land cession through treaty.

The Cherokee delegates understood the need to direct their campaign at Congress as well as the president. A fortnight after Monroe's message, the Cherokee representatives appeared in person at the Capitol to bring a memorial before Congress. The American people, they hoped, would intercede, and Georgia would be isolated as a rogue state.[84]

Major Ridge, for his part, characterized Georgia's letter to the administration as a gambit aimed at satisfying the Georgia audience. Some months later, he commented through an interpreter, "It is a very hot talk—I suppose it was intended for the people at home."[85] For Ridge, those people at home likely included members of Native nations as well as white Georgians. The former were meant to be intimidated into ceding their lands, while the latter would be bolstered by their state's aggressive insistence on the broadest possible version of sovereignty.

On one level, the Cherokee Nation's Washington campaign of 1824 yielded disappointing results. The detested Agent McMinn remained, and the situation with Georgia remained both tense and unresolved. The delegates had secured one victory, however: payment of the long-overdue annuity of one thousand dollars per year, plus interest, that was owed to the Nation under the Treaty of Tellico of 1804. The delegates' citation of this obligation initially took Calhoun by surprise. But they had prudently brought their own copy of the signed and sealed treaty to Washington. When they laid it before Calhoun, a clerk had to be sent to retrieve the War Department's own "long lost" copy.[86]

In a larger sense, by making this latest official visit to the seat of American government and its spaces of informal politicking, the Cherokee representatives had compelled the elite of the federal government to engage with them as diplomats and see them as emissaries from a society that bore all the requisite markers of nineteenth-century civilization.

What Ross, Ridge, Hicks, and Lowrey could not know, however, was that it was this very civilization that sparked such resentment and covetousness in the citizens of Georgia, solidifying the state's determination to exile the Nation beyond its boundaries. After the same Cabinet meeting that caused Adams to marvel at the skill displayed in the Cherokees' state papers, he recorded a comment from Calhoun that later revealed itself as prescient: "Mr. Calhoun thinks that the great difficulty arises from the progress of the Cherokees in civilization."[87]

Politics, 1826–28: Cherokee Nation

Elias Boudinot, who wrote of his hopes for his children's education in the North, had himself gone to New England for learning. Born around 1804 in the Cherokee village of Oothcaloga in northwestern Georgia, and known during childhood as "Gallegina" ("ᏍᏓᏴ ᎣᎬᏗ" in Cherokee) or "Buck," he was the eldest of nine children of Oo-watie (also known as "David Uwatie" or "David Watie") and Susanna Reese.[88] Oo-watie was the younger brother of Major Ridge; Susannah Reese was the daughter of a Cherokee mother and a white trader.[89] Both Oo-watie and Ridge believed that their children should obtain Anglo-American-style educations. As historian Theda Perdue notes, the fact that the children of these families adopted "Watie" and "Ridge" as surnames (except, of course, for Boudinot) suggests "a move away from matrilineality" and other aspects of traditional Cherokee culture.[90]

At around the age of six, Buck was sent to a Moravian mission school twenty miles north of his parents' home, where he, his cousins John and Nancy Ridge, and several other Cherokee children were taught—in English—reading, writing, arithmetic, history, geography, and Christian doctrine, as well as the "arts of civilization."[91] Buck quickly distinguished himself as one of the most promising students. In 1817, when he was about thirteen years old, he was invited to attend the secondary school run by the American Board of Commissioners for Foreign Missions (ABCFM) in Cornwall, Connecticut.

The aim of the Foreign Mission School, as it became known, was to draw promising young men from non-Christian populations around the world in order to convert and educate them, and then to send them back to their homelands as missionaries. While traveling to New England in the company of the board's officers, Buck was introduced to the prominent New Jersey statesman Elias Stockton Boudinot, who had served in the Continental Congress, become president of the American Bible Society, and was a strong supporter of the education and Christianization of Indian youths. By all accounts, the septuagenarian philanthropist and the young Cherokee scholar struck up an immediate rapport, such that Buck took the elder man's name and was thenceforth known as "Elias Boudinot."[92]

Boudinot remained at the Foreign Mission School in Cornwall for five years. During that time, he excelled at both his academic and his spiritual studies, leading his teachers to praise both the perfection of his mathematical exercises and the cultivation of his soul. In 1820, when he was about sixteen years old, Boudinot converted to Christianity. In 1821, an English visitor to the increasingly famous school noted a highly satisfactory half-hour conversation with "Kub-le-ga-nah Elias Boudinot a Cherokee," who "had gone through a course of history, geography, and surveying, had read some books of Virgil, and was then engaged in studying [William] Enfield's philosophy, over which, indeed, I afterwards found him, when I visited the school. I also saw his trigonometrical copybooks."[93] Another visitor who witnessed the school's annual public exhibition wrote that "the appearance and performance" of Boudinot and his cousin John Ridge "would have done credit to the best white young men of their age." Boudinot, who delivered a declamation, "confuted the idea more completely by his appearance than his arguments, that savages are not capable of being civilized and polished."[94]

Boudinot's success marked him, in the words of the school's principal, as "worthy of a finished education" in theology, so that he could return to the Cherokee Nation as an ordained minister.[95] But instead of matriculating at the Andover Theological Seminary according to plan, Boudinot became ill with a "bilious complaint" and returned to his family in Oothcaloga in 1822, at the age of about eighteen.[96] Boudinot traveled southward by way of Charleston, where he met John Ridge and a few others who were stopping in the city as part of a lecture tour. The mild climate appears to have agreed with Boudinot, who wrote to an ABCFM correspondent that the voyage had had "an astonishing effect on my cough" and had relieved "that pressure on my chest."[97] In December 1822, Boudinot and Ridge arrived in the Cherokee Nation, where the return of "the dear youths from Cornwall" was hailed as they traveled, interpreted, and prayed.[98]

A tumultuous interval followed, for Boudinot, the school, and the ABCFM's entire project of educating future Native missionaries and leaders. During his five years in Cornwall, Boudinot had become acquainted with the family of Benjamin and Eleanor Gold, who were leading citizens of the town and supporters of the Foreign Mission School. Colonel Gold was a deacon of the town's Congregational church, a member of a renowned family of Yale-educated divines, and an agent, or board member, of the school. The Golds' home was frequently the site of school events as well as informal visits from teachers, students, and others associated with the school. Among the eleven Gold children still at home to entertain and converse with the students was the youngest daughter, Harriett Ruggles Gold, who had been born in 1805 and was therefore very close in age to Elias Boudinot. The two became friends. After Boudinot left the school and returned to the Cherokee Nation in 1822, they continued their conversation through a long-distance correspondence. Their letters sparked a courtship, then an engagement, and finally a public controversy that shook the town of Cornwall and reverberated throughout the United States.

The Native scholars at the school had generally received a warm welcome from the people of Cornwall, who appeared proud that their small town in the Litchfield hills had achieved such distinction on the international stage of missionary work. The students of the school had been greeted in church and on the town square, their Christian progress regarded as evidence of their civilization and even brotherhood with upright New England Puritans. But the prospect of young white women from the town "intermarrying" with young Indian men brought out an ugly, racialized resistance.[99]

The first jolt came sometime in 1823, with reports that a local girl, Sarah Bird Northrup, had formed an attachment to Boudinot's cousin John Ridge, son of Major Ridge. Months of scandal ensued. One local newspaper editor excoriated the school on behalf of "the young men of the town, poor white boys" who had been "cast into the shade by their colored and tawny rivals."[100] An even cruder attack lamented "the affliction, mortification, and disgrace, of the young woman [who] . . . throwing herself into the arms of an Indian . . . has thus made herself a *squaw*."[101] As Boudinot's brother-in-law—a white man—later observed, "[T]he papers proclaimed it an outrage, and preachers denounced it in the pulpit—that an *Indian* should go into a civilized community of New England and marry and carry away one of the finest daughters of the land."[102] Shaken but unswayed by the outcry, John Ridge and Sarah Northrup married at her parents' home in Cornwall in 1824.

Sometime within the following year, Harriett Gold announced to her parents her intention of marrying Elias Boudinot. Her parents objected, their general amity toward the civilized young Indian men at the school clearly challenged by the specific prospect of having one of them as a son-in-law. The objection was, as one of Harriett's brothers bluntly put it, "that she was engaged to that Indian E."[103] The Golds had "previously felt that marriages of this kind were not sinful & now they had a severe trial in the case of their beloved daughter," one of Harriett's married sisters wrote to another. "It is a time of great commotion in C[ornwall] still Harriett is meek, though firm as the hills."[104]

Suffering alone while Elias was at his parents' home, Harriett remained firm in the face of what must have been nearly unbearable pressure and criticism from her parents, her siblings, and her brothers-in-law (who saw fit to lodge the most vocal of any objections in lengthy written screeds). The board members of the Foreign Mission School summoned her before them and urged her to quash the rumors and recant her engagement in order to save their institution, which was under attack for fostering such marriages. Harriett also faced the public shame of being asked to remove from her usual place with the choir during Sunday services, while her erstwhile choirmates donned black crepe armbands.[105]

But the most appalling trial for a young woman of twenty must have been to witness herself and her betrothed being burned in effigy on the town green, by her neighbors. Her own brother lit the match. Watching the proceedings from the window of a neighbor's house, it having been determined that she was not safe in her own home, Harriett saw the following spectacle:

> A painting had before been prepared representing a beautiful young Lady & an *Indian*. . . . Evening came on. The church Bell began to toll one would conclude, speaking the departure of a soul. . . . Brother Stephen set fire to the barrel of Tar or rather the funeral pile—the flames rose high, & the smoke ascended—some said it reminded them of the smoke of their torment which they feared would ascend forever. My heart truly sung with anguish at the dreadful scene.[106]

Yet Harriett clearly loved Elias and believed that a life with him in the Cherokee Nation would provide her with a forum for her own missionary zeal, which one historian likens to the vocation of a "Puritan mystic."[107] When she became seriously ill and her life appeared to be in peril, her parents finally gave their blessing to the marriage. One of the brothers-in-law expressed his disgust at the result, blaming "Harrietts [sic] craftiness by making them believe that she should die if she did not have her Indian." Now, he raged, "the whole family are to be sacrificed to gratify if I may so express it the animal feelings of one."[108]

A few lines later, this hostile account revealed the reason for the Golds' reversal of their earlier refusal: "*they could not fight against God—is the reply.*"[109] Harriett's illness and her refusal to abandon Elias convinced her parents that to block the marriage was to attempt to stand in the way of divine will. One friend of the family recorded Harriett's argument: "We have vowed, and our vows are heard in heaven; color is nothing to me; his soul is as white as mine; he is a Christian, and ever since I embraced religion I have been praying that God would open a door for me to be a missionary, and this is the way."[110]

Thereafter, Harriett's parents and sisters became the couple's defenders, remonstrating with the disapproving brothers-in-law. "It is through pride & prejudice—that all this clamour has been raised against Indians," Colonel Gold chided his son-in-law Herman Vaill.[111]

Elias, meanwhile, was in Oothcaloga, anxiously awaiting word from Harriett's parents and reading newspaper reports of the continuing scandal that had erupted in Cornwall. The ABCFM's established strategy of ensuring that favorable accounts of their efforts at the Foreign Mission School were publicized in widely circulated journals now bore the unwelcome fruit of a nationwide audience prepared to gasp at the sensational news of another intermarriage and to castigate the couples, their families, and the school.[112]

The faraway uproar, and the sense that for all his academic and spiritual attainments he would nevertheless be deemed by some an unacceptable husband for a young white woman, appears to have impelled Boudinot into a kind of crisis. Daniel Butrick, a missionary in the Nation who knew Boudinot well, wrote that he was "in great trouble" during this time. Most notably, Boudinot drew criticism from local representatives of the ABCFM for attending a traditional Cherokee ball play on the Sabbath.[113] News of the favorite scholar's apparent lapse reached all the way to ABCFM headquarters in Boston. In a letter to the ABCFM secretary, Jeremiah Evarts, Butrick defended Boudinot as having been distraught by "the shameless conduct of the citizens of Cornwall, & the cruel treatment he has received from those who would claim to be his spiritual fathers." Butrick specifically cited "the smoke of his burning effigy, driven by the fiercest northern blast," as having "occasioned this fall." Reports of the hatred-fueled conflagration on the Cornwall town green had reached the Cherokee Nation.[114]

Many other Cherokee observers were also shocked by the vitriolic response to the marriages. Major Ridge, Boudinot's uncle and the father of John Ridge, put "a plain question" to an ABCFM representative and requested "a plain answer." Ridge's question was whether anything in the Scriptures prohibited Indian men from marrying white women. The official responded that nothing in the Bible disapproved of such marriages and added that he himself favored them.[115] Indeed, as the widely circulated *Niles' Weekly Register* of Baltimore noted in one of its reports on the controversy, no less an authority than former president Monroe had endorsed "an incorporation of the Indian race with the citizens of the United States, by intermarriages."[116]

Harriett and Elias, for their part, would not be shaken from their resolve. A letter from Harriett's father to Elias in which Benjamin Gold refused his and his wife's consent to the marriage was overtaken en route south by a second letter in which the Golds wrote of their change of heart. Fortunately for the couple, the second letter arrived in Oothcaloga before the first.[117]

In the early spring of 1826, Elias Boudinot set off on a speaking and fund-raising tour along the East Coast. Now around twenty-two years of age, he intended to deploy his education, his oratorical skills, and his charisma to make the Cherokees' case before white audiences. He also intended to "visit Cornwall and, I presume, does not intend to leave it without a wife," observed his friend and colleague Samuel Worcester, the Vermont-born Congregationalist missionary who had recently arrived in the Cherokee Nation.[118] In Connecticut, Harriett had been awaiting Elias's arrival since the winter. She wrote to her sister and brother-in-law, "I hope to hear from my *far distant friend* before long

& know how soon I shall go." In the meantime, she was preparing for her marriage and her journey south. "My Box is made & I am trying to fill it with something—have some presents from friends for all which I am very grateful."[119]

Elias's lecture circuit took him to Charleston, New York, Philadelphia, and Boston. Somewhere in his itinerary, he made a trip by stagecoach from Hartford to Litchfield. From Litchfield, he traveled to Cornwall—approaching the town warily and in disguise, as he had received threats to his safety.[120] But no attacks came. On March 28, 1826, at two in the afternoon, he and Harriett were married in the parlor of Harriett's parents' home. The ceremony was performed by a clergyman from the neighboring town, the local Congregational minister having vociferously opposed the match. Brother Stephen, who had ignited the blaze for the effigy burning, was absent from the ceremony, although he did bring himself to greet Elias in a relatively civil manner a few days later, after the couple were married.[121]

The newly married Boudinots then continued on a three-month tour of eastern cities. Elias Boudinot spoke in thronged churches filled with reform-minded, often deeply religious audiences—among them, presumably, his admiring new wife—and raised money for the press and the expensive bespoke type that would permit the Cherokee Nation to begin publishing the *Phoenix*. In Philadelphia, he had his lecture printed as a pamphlet, titled *An Address to the Whites*, in which he enumerated the many ways in which "the Cherokees have improved and are still rapidly improving."[122]

In the summer of 1826, the young couple arrived in the Cherokee Nation, where they set up housekeeping and threw themselves into work that combined missionary zeal, cultural shaping, and nation-building. Their ostensibly personal conflict with the townspeople of Cornwall had become the subject of national attention, connected as it was with the ABCFM's missionary efforts, the fate of the Foreign Mission School (which was shuttered soon after), and the ongoing controversy about the status of Indian lands in Georgia. The venom displayed in the responses to the Boudinot and Ridge marriages stunned the principals. It likely also influenced Elias Boudinot's and John Ridge's understandings of the depth of white animosity toward Indians and tested the cousins' faith that Americans might one day recognize the Cherokees as a nation.[123]

The Founding

In his *Address to the Whites* of 1826, Boudinot enumerated three recent developments that he characterized as together constituting "a powerful

argument in favor of Indian improvement." These were the "invention of letters"; the "translation of the New Testament into Cherokee"; and the "organization of a Government."[124] Within two years of his and Harriett's arrival in
New Echota, the capital of the Cherokee Nation, that list grew to include a new
pair of landmarks: a constitution and a newspaper.

The National Council passed a resolution in November 1826 calling for a
convention or "special council" to draft a constitution for the Nation. Boudinot, in his capacity as clerk to the General Council, recorded the resolution
and rules for debates. Following the election in May 1827, he minuted the
names of the twenty-four delegates. John Ross was chosen as president of the
convention.[125] By the time the special council convened in the summer of
1827, the Nation had undergone a sudden change in leadership owing to the
deaths of two principal chiefs in quick succession. Ross and Major Ridge, as
president of the National Committee and speaker of the General Council, respectively, became acting heads of government.[126]

The Cherokee constitutional convention held its first session on July 4,
1827. The body was "no more representative of the Cherokees than the U.S.
founding fathers were of Americans," with a disproportionate number of
"wealthy, literate, and Christian" members.[127] Three weeks later, on July 26,
the delegates approved the Constitution of the Cherokee Nation.

A dedication to republican principles of representation and separated powers infused the document.[128] The constitution comprised six articles, each of
which was broken into between two and twenty-six sections. Article I began
with a description of the boundaries of the lands "solemnly guarantied and
reserved forever to the Cherokee Nation by the Treaties concluded with the
United States." Then followed a forceful statement of the scope of the authority the constitution was asserting over its territory, as well as a prohibition on
the alienation of those lands by individual Cherokee citizens:

> The sovereignty and Jurisdiction of this Government shall extend over
> the country within the boundaries above described, and the lands therein
> are, and shall remain, the common property of the Nation; but the im-
> provements made thereon, and in the possession of the citizens of the
> Nation, are the exclusive and indefeasible property of the citizens respec-
> tively who made or may rightfully be in possession of them; *Provided*,
> that the citizens of the Nation ... shall possess no right nor power to
> dispose of their improvements in any manner whatever to the United
> States, individual states, nor individual citizens thereof.[129]

CONSTITUTION

OF THE

CHEROKEE NATION,

FORMED BY A CONVENTION OF DELEGATES FROM THE
SEVERAL DISTRICTS, AT

NEW ECHOTA, JULY 1827.

ᏗᎪᏪᎸᎩᎯᎠ ᏣᎳᎩ ᎤᏪᏗᏆᏍᎢ,

ᏗᎳᏫ ᏦᏍᎩ ᎢᎵᏗᏔᏍᎠ ᎤᏔᏇᎢᎠ, ᏣᏍᏫᏂ ᎤᎴᏔ 1827 ᎤᏂᎳᏍᎪᎠ.

We, THE REPRESENTA-
TIVES of the people of the
CHEROKEE NATION in Con-
vention assembled, in order
to establish justice, ensure
tranquility, promote our
common welfare, and se-
cure to ourselves and our
posterity the blessings of liberty; acknowledging with
humility and gratitude the
goodness of the sovereign
Ruler of the Universe, in
offering us an opportunity so
favorable to the design, and
imploring his aid and direction in its accomplishment,
do ordain and establish this

ᎠᏌ ᎡᏂᏫ ᏛᎣᎵᎵᏜ ᎠᏍᎯ᎓ ᏗᎠ-
ᏌᏫ, ᏣᎳᎩ ᎤᎣᎤᎼ ᎠᏯᏗᏇᎠ,
ᏍᏫᎪᎼ ᏛᏯᏗᎯᎵᏛ, ᎠᏕ ᎴᎠ Ꮫ᎓
ᏯᎦᎠᎣᎯᏗᏛ, ᎠᏕ ᏛᎡ ᎢᎯᏕᎣᏫ᎓
ᎸᏗ ᏈᎡ ᏃᎢᎵ ᏣᎳᎩ ᎠᏍᎯ᎓ ᏦᏯᏇ᎓
ᎤᎯᏛᎵᎵᏛ, ᎤᎣᏫ ᏛᏯᏛᎵᏗᎠᏗ᎓
᎓ ᏛᏯᏛ ᏦᏯᎤᎯ ᎲᎢᎡᎤ ᎲᏯ, ᎠᏕ
ᏈᎲᎲ ᎤᎣᏫ ᏔᏫᎯᎵ ᏈᎲᎯᏛᏍᎯᏗ᎓
᎓, ᎡᏯᏫᎤᎵᎠ, ᎠᎠ ᏗᎣᏕᎵᎣᎵ
ᏣᎳᎩ ᎤᏪᏔᎵ ᏛᎩᏇᎣ. ᏍᏇᏫᏗᏗᎣ
ᎡᎠ, ᎲᎡᎣᎼ ᎤᎡᏕᎦᏛ, ᏛᎲᎵᎠᏔᎤᏛ;
ᎠᏕ ᏛᎪᏈᎵᎲᎲ ᎤᎣᏯ ᏔᎤᎠᎲᎤᎼ
ᎲᏯ ᎠᏛ ᎤᎠᏯ ᏔᏫᎯᎵ ᏦᏯᏇᎣᎯᎵ᎓
ᎠᎵ ᎲᎲᏍᎢᎣᎵᎵᏍ, ᎠᏕ ᎤᎣᏯ ᏛᏯ᎓
ᎣᏇᏇᎵᎠ᎓, ᎠᏕ ᏛᎢᎲᎵᎠ᎓, ᏛᎲᏫ᎓
ᎲᎵ.

Constitution of the Cherokee Nation, printed at New Echota in the office of the *Cherokee Phoenix*, 1828. (Courtesy of American Antiquarian Society.)

The purpose of this provision was clear: to bar all Cherokee citizens from acceding to the pressure of the state of Georgia, or of individual Georgians, to sell their lands.

Then came the structural provisions. Article II stated that the power of the government was to be "divided into three distinct departments: the Legislative, the Executive, and Judicial." The legislative power was further divided into two branches, a committee and a council, "each to have a negative on the other, and both to be styled the General Council of the Cherokee Nation." The "Supreme Executive Power" was vested in a principal chief, who was chosen by the General Council to serve a four-year term. In an exception to the stated principle of separated powers, a three-member council was to be appointed by the legislature "to advise the Principal Chief in the Executive part of the Government." Finally, the judicial power of the Nation was to be vested in a supreme court and any inferior courts established by the General Council.[130]

In addition to setting out these institutions, the constitution addressed the issue of who was qualified to claim the "rights and privileges of this Nation." These rights were available to those who had at least one Cherokee parent and another parent who was free and not "of negro or mulatto parentage." If the Cherokee parent was the father, the mother could not be a member of "the African race," and the parents had to have been "living together as man and wife, according to the customs and laws of this Nation." Citizenship was more readily granted in situations where the Cherokee parent was the mother; in such cases, the male parent need only be a "free" man, and there was no requirement that the parents be man and wife. Presumably, this distinction recognized the long history of non-Native traders fathering children with Cherokee women but not residing with their Cherokee families. It also maintained a remnant of matrilineality, insofar as it claimed the offspring of such unions as Cherokee citizens.

The constitution did not specify a precise definition of "Cherokee." Political power was restricted in other ways, however. The right to vote was granted only to "[a]ll free male citizens, (excepting negroes and descendants of white and Indian men by negro women who may have been set free,) who shall have attained to the age of eighteen years." Only "free male Cherokee citizen[s]" were eligible to serve in the General Council. Finally, no person who was "of negro or mulatto parentage, either by the father or mother side," was permitted to "hold any office of profit, honor or trust under this Government."[131]

The Cherokee constitution and the *Cherokee Phoenix* were born of the same impulse: to bolster those elements that made the Nation a nation, in the minds of both its internal and external audiences. These goals were not only those of the white missionaries of the ABCFM. They were widely embraced by Boudinot, his parents and Watie siblings, John Ridge and Major Ridge, John Ross, and many other members of the Cherokee elite. This group included near-aristocrats such as the Ridges and Ross as well as more bourgeois farmers, skilled artisans, and educated professionals such as Boudinot and the Waties. When the first round of elections under the new constitution was held in fall of 1828, these improvement-minded citizens won the highest posts. Three of the top five positions were also filled by individuals who had been members of the 1824 delegation to Washington: Ross as principal chief; George Lowrey as assistant principal chief; and Major Ridge as one of three counselors to the principal chief.

Boudinot, meanwhile, received an appointment from the legislature as editor of the newly created *Phoenix*. His first duty, according to the resolution of the General Council, was "to issue a prospectus throughout the United States & the Cherokee Nation."[132] The specific reference to "the United States" was important. The *Phoenix* was to serve as a vehicle for the political goals of the Nation, flying from New Echota to the far reaches of America and perhaps even to Europe as documentary proof of the Cherokees' accomplishments. Having failed to gain meaningful results in their missions to Washington, the leaders of the Nation determined to wage their campaign on grounds of culture, religion, and morality.

In October 1827, Boudinot released his prospectus, which he then proceeded to disseminate across his wide network of correspondents. It provided a preview of the contents of the *Phoenix*: national laws and documents; accounts of "the manners and customs of the Cherokees, and their progress in Education, Religion, and the Arts of civilized life"; the "principal interesting news of the day"; and "Miscellaneous articles calculated to promote Literature, Civilization, and Religion among the Cherokees."[133] As was the case for most newspapers of the era, many of the interesting and miscellaneous items would be lifted directly from other newspapers (with a line crediting them). The newspaper was to be published weekly, with two hundred copies printed for distribution in the Nation and to the scores of subscribers elsewhere in the United States—including Troy, New York; Mobile, Alabama; and even New England, where Boudinot urged his siblings-in-law to drum up subscribers "if there are any to be had in Connecticut, the land of *intermarriages*."[134]

The first issue of the *Cherokee Phoenix* carried the text of the constitution, printed in both English and Cherokee. It appeared on February 21, 1828, after the much-anticipated press and type had finally arrived after an arduous voyage by steamboat from Boston to Augusta, Georgia, and then two hundred miles overland by wagon from Augusta to New Echota. Boudinot also used the press to produce copies of the constitution in the form of a twenty-eight-page pamphlet that featured the text in both languages, in side-by-side columns.[135]

The purchase of the equipment was handled with great deliberateness. The money came from the Cherokee government and from donations that Boudinot, John Ridge, and others had received during their fundraising travels. The funds were forwarded to the leaders of the ABCFM in Boston, who were authorized to transact the purchase on behalf of the Nation. Nevertheless, the *Phoenix* was persistently dogged by the rumor that the federal government or the ABCFM had paid for the printing equipment, a slight that Boudinot and others resented as casting aspersions on the Cherokee Nation's ability to devise and fund its own projects.

To aid Boudinot's work as editor, the General Council provided for the appointment of a printer. When Boudinot learned that the legislature was offering white printer Isaac Harris a salary that was one hundred dollars per year greater than the three hundred dollars per year that Boudinot had been offered, he first requested a higher salary and an assistant translator, and then refused to take on the editorship.[136] But his contacts at the ABCFM sought to right the inequity by making up the difference, and Boudinot took up the editor's pen.[137]

Harris proved to be a troublesome colleague. He minimized Boudinot's role by "circulating falsehoods, one of which is that the Cherokee Phoenix is under the influence of Mr. Worcester," and another of which was that Harris, not Boudinot, was the author of the paper's original content, Elias reported to Harriett's family. (Harris was a Methodist to boot, a fact that the Presbyterian Boudinot could not help noting.) Within a year, Harris had left, having been fired with a flourish by Boudinot, who had received "full authority from the principal Chiefs to continue or dismiss what printers I pleased." Boudinot delivered the news of the termination first in writing and then, when Harris proved recalcitrant, with an order from the assistant principal chief and a visit from one of the Nation's marshals.[138]

Harris's assistant, John F. Wheeler, a white Kentuckian, proved a more convivial and productive companion in the small printing office. Within a few years, Wheeler and his Cherokee assistant, John Candy, had married Boudinot's sisters Nancy Paschal Watie and Mary Ann Watie, respectively.[139]

The first issue of the *Cherokee Phoenix*, February 21, 1828. (Courtesy of American Antiquarian Society.)

Boudinot designed the *Phoenix* to serve two important purposes. First, the newspaper would benefit the citizens of the Nation by providing them with one of the most important markers of nineteenth-century nationhood. Second, it would present the Cherokees to the American public "not as a tribe struggling toward 'civilization,' but as a society which had already achieved that goal," as historian Theda Perdue puts it.[140] Yet another purpose emerged over the four years of Boudinot's editorship of the newspaper: to articulate a substantive vision of Cherokee nationhood. His work as a writer and editor complemented his lectures and speeches, reaching a far-flung audience and making Boudinot as important a producer of constitutional discourse as the Nation's elected leaders.

For the Nation was engaged in a fight for its existence. The official battle-grounds included the halls of Washington, where deputations of delegates negotiated with the administration of President John Quincy Adams and with Congress, as well as the chamber of the council house at New Echota, where the General Council formulated responses to the increasingly brazen attacks by Georgians on the persons and property of Cherokee citizens.

The third arm of this campaign was the *Phoenix*. It was not simply a pro-Cherokee propaganda machine or a purveyor of assimilationist bromides. It was significant not only because it proved that a Native nation could produce a newspaper, although this achievement was important. The *Phoenix* also offered an argument for what the Cherokee Nation was fighting for. Its columns presented—in both English and, when Boudinot could find the time and space to offer a full translation, in Cherokee—a political and constitutional argument for how a nation could define itself. What was it that made a nation a nation when it was both surrounded by a hostile state that claimed to be sovereign and compelled to maintain diplomatic ties with a sister nation that doubted its very capacity for existence?

Boudinot had fully imbibed the Protestant missionary worldview in which he had been immersed since he was around six years old. He could and did sound priggish and judgmental at times. For example, he contrasted the "intelligent and virtuous portion of the nation" with the "superstitious practices" of what he characterized as a bygone "dark & gloomy" era of Cherokee history, when "the young and middle aged of the males were seen to leave their houses, their faces fantastically painted, and their heads decorated with feathers, and step off with a merry whoop, which indicated they were *real men*, to a ball play, or a meeting of a similar nature."[141] (Given the editor's own scandalous attendance at a ball play not five years earlier, his statement that "we speak from hearsay, for we were born under an era of reformation" must have caused some of his readers, in the Nation and in Boston, to raise a skeptical eyebrow.)

His Anglo-American education, a formative experience that he shared with Ross and John Ridge, as well as his own skill as a writer and theorist gave Boudinot the ability to build his newspaper into a formidable rhetorical and conceptual vehicle for constituting Cherokee nationhood. Yet the *Phoenix*'s power to influence political discourse in the Nation ultimately brought Boudinot into conflict with Ross, such that the principal chief essentially forced Boudinot out of the editorship.

But in the heady early days of the *Phoenix*'s endeavors, that conflict was still in the future. The key to Boudinot's vision of the Nation was his conviction that the existence of the polity depended on maintaining the Cherokees as a distinct "people." As he wrote in 1829 in a letter intended for publication, "As long as we continue as a people in a body, with our internal regulations, we can continue to improve in civilization and respectability."[142]

Even though he firmly believed that the Cherokee people should improve and civilize themselves by abandoning "superstitious practices," becoming literate, and embracing Christianity, Boudinot did not therefore advocate assimilation and integration into white society. On the contrary, he remained more of a separatist than an assimilationist. Perhaps his sense of betrayal by the townspeople of Connecticut, and their burning effigies, shaped his belief that Indians could never flourish if they were in close proximity with whites, who would inevitably regard Native people as inferior.[143] In his editorials, he derided the overtures that came from the federal government encouraging the Cherokees to relocate in the West. "Where have we an example in the whole history of man, of a Nation or tribe, removing in a body, from a land of civil and religious means, to a perfect wilderness, *in order to be civilized*," he queried acerbically in an 1828 editorial.[144]

And yet Boudinot was married to a white woman, a union that, along with John Ridge's marriage to Sarah Northrup, had led to a revision in the Nation's laws to permit the children of white women and Cherokee men—a less common pattern than the decades-old practice of European men marrying Cherokee women—to be counted as Cherokee citizens.[145]

Both Elias and Harriett seem to have regarded their marriage as making Harriett fully a member of the Cherokee Nation. In one of her first letters to her family back in Cornwall after she arrived in the Nation, Harriett wrote of "[m]y Cherokee Father" and "[m]y dear Cherokee Mother." She also noted that she was "pleased with my Cherokee name," which was "Ka-lah-dee"; "it already sounds very natural to me."[146] The Boudinots' busy household in New Echota contained increasing numbers of their own children as well as visiting siblings from Elias's parents' home in Oothcaloga. Elias's younger sister Mary Ann (called "Polly") Watie was a "great favorite" of Harriett's, often acting as interpreter between Elias's parents and Harriett.[147] His younger brother Stand Watie was "much esteemed in the Nation" and occasionally assisted Elias with the *Phoenix*, taking over as editor when Elias traveled north on further fundraising circuits.[148] Visiting missionaries sometimes stayed at the house, including Sophia Sawyer, a teacher from Vermont whom the Boudinots engaged as governess to their children.

Of his work, Boudinot wrote to the Connecticut relatives, "I can assure you I have no time to be idle." He continued: "My duties are complicated. I have no associate in the Management of the paper, so I have to select pieces for publication, & this requires some time in order to be Judicious, & then I have to prepare what little editorial may be seen in the Phoenix, in English & Cherokee, & to write one column a week original in Cherokee with so much other work, is no small matter—one cant [sic] write fast in Cherokee."[149]

As this comment suggests, even a born speaker of Cherokee such as Boudinot found Sequoyah's syllabary sufficiently challenging that English was his preferred language for writing. Boudinot then had to render his English text into written Cherokee. Moreover, Boudinot combined his work on the *Phoenix* with translations of religious tracts, including the Bible and hymns, from English into Cherokee. In this, he was aided by the Presbyterian missionary Samuel Worcester, who was rapidly learning how to speak and write in Cherokee.[150]

Boudinot worked long days, and often into the night, at the printing office. His labors were fueled by tea, coffee, and sugar. One of the annual lists of supplies that the family submitted to the ABCFM included entries for "8 lb. black Tea," "2 lb. green Tea," "1 block-tin Teapot largest size," as well as "50 Reams Super Royal Printing Paper," "2 Canisters Printing ink," and various clothing items, including "1 silk vest," "2 pr. Women's Shoes calf good thick No. 5," and "9 yds. Calico for little girls."[151]

But, as Harriett noted with obvious pride, despite the demands of their daily lives, the Boudinot household did not indulge in spirituous liquors. In response to a letter from her sister, Harriett wrote,

> [Y]ou were about to call your last baby, *temperance*, because you dispensed with rum—what shall we do? We have had 3. without the assistance of a shot of rum—or any kind of ardent spirits. The truth is, we have not bought a drop since we kept house & I hesitate not to say, (without boasting) that my husband is, & *has ever been* a more temperate man—than any of his brothers in law on *my* side.[152]

Harriett's reference to temperance functioned as a further marker of Elias's piety and refinement.

Along with this note to her sister, Harriett also enclosed a letter that their parents wrote during an extended visit they made to New Echota in the autumn and winter of 1829–30. After a forty-seven-day journey in their own carriage, Benjamin and Eleanor Gold arrived in the Cherokee Nation. Harriett's parents were delighted by the reception they received, the people they encountered, and the town square of New Echota, the dwellings of which "would be called respectable in Litchfield county," the Golds reported to Harriett's siblings back in Connecticut. Colonel Gold attended a session of the

National Council and the superior court, noting that both included "a number of learned polished & well Qualified Gentlemen fit to appear in any place in Connecticut."[153] Elias clearly stood in high esteem with his father-in-law: "Mr. Boudinot has much good company and is as much respected as any man of his age. His paper is respected all over the United States, and is known in Europe." The "large and convenient framed house" was also praised.[154]

But the highest encomia were reserved for the grandchildren. Two-year-old Eleanor Susan "appears to know as much as any girl of her age," and one-year-old Mary Harriett "looks out of as hansom pair of black eyes as ever was seen"; new baby William Penn was "s[econd] to no boy of his age."[155] Upon the doting grandparents' arrival, before William Penn had been born, the girls were pronounced "beautiful and interesting children [who] would pass in company for full-blooded Yankees." According to Colonel Gold, Mrs. Gold "says she thinks they are rather handsomer than any she has seen at the north."[156] The Golds' comments suggest a curiosity—and perhaps anxiety—about what they would find in the Cherokee Nation, including just how "Indian" their grandchildren would look. Elias's previous letters to the Golds had noted the children's "real Indian black eyes," a pointed reminder of their Cherokee identity, and of the completeness of his union with Harriett.[157]

By the end of their visit, however, the elderly New Englanders had been thoroughly won over to the cause of the Nation. As Colonel Gold wrote to the family at home, "It seems to me a very great pity that any part of our country should attempt or desire to arrest from this Nation a right which they possess by arts & treaties of the United States—rites I say which they have to the possession & Government of all the lands which they have not ceeded [sic] to the United States."[158]

Colonel Gold's distress at the Cherokees' treatment by "any part of our country"—a reference to the state of Georgia—was well founded. By late 1829, the situation of the Cherokee Nation had become more dire than ever before. In 1828, white settlers had discovered gold in Dahlonega, seventy miles east of New Echota. This development led to incursions by prospectors on Cherokee land and feverish demands on the part of Georgia for the federal government to compel the Nation to remove. The Georgia legislature, meanwhile, had in 1827 passed a set of laws asserting jurisdiction over the Cherokees. The new laws included provisions granting the state courts jurisdiction over crimes committed by or against Georgia citizens in the Cherokee Nation; pronouncing the Cherokees tenants at will on their land; and subjecting all white people residing in the Nation to the laws of Georgia.

But the greatest existential danger to the Nation came from a new act of the state legislature providing that all Cherokee laws and customs would be deemed null and void as of June 1, 1830.[159] In a legislative report that Boudinot reprinted in the *Phoenix*, Georgia claimed "absolute jurisdictional right" over Native lands within the territorial boundaries of the state.[160]

That was Georgia. But there was also the United States to consider. In 1828, the disposition of the federal government toward the Nation underwent a transformation with the election of Andrew Jackson as president.

Long famed as an Indian fighter, Jackson had run on a platform that featured Indian removal as one of its central and most demotically appealing planks.[161] Jackson's disdain for previous administrations' treaty negotiations with Native tribes was well known. In 1817, then-major general Jackson took up his pen in Nashville to write a lengthy letter to President Monroe—on Monroe's first day in office. "The Indians are the subjects of the United States, inhabiting its territory and acknowledging its sovereignty," Jackson stated. Therefore it was "absurd for the sovereign to negotiate by treaty with the subject."[162] Three years later, Jackson again inveighed against treaties, this time in a letter to Secretary of War Calhoun. "It appears to me that it is high time to do away [with] the farce of treating with Indian tribes," Jackson opined. Instead, the tribes should be regulated through legislation. Not foreign but subject, the tribes, in Jackson's view, merited only ordinary statutes, not treaties. "[T]he arm of Government is sufficiently strong to carry into effect any law that Congress may deem necessary and proper to pass for the welfare & happiness of the Indian and for the convenience and benefit of the u. states." Treaties, which implicitly recognized the parties as sovereigns, ought to be replaced by ordinary lawmaking befitting tribes "situate within our declared Territorial limits as a nation."[163] And the executive branch should, Jackson made clear, stand ready to enforce whatever laws Congress chose to enact.

When Jackson took office in March 1829, he instructed his secretary of war and longtime Tennessee confrère, John H. Eaton, to adopt an unyielding policy against the Cherokee delegations. In his annual message to Congress of December 1829, Jackson made clear his administration's position—and reversed his predecessors' policy of keeping distance between the federal executive branch and Georgia's claims against the Native nations. "A portion . . . of the Southern tribes, having mingled much with the whites and made some progress in the arts of civilized life, have lately attempted to erect an independent government within the limits of Georgia and Alabama," Jackson stated. Portraying the tribes as both parvenus and aggressors, he described Georgia

and Alabama as having been "induced to call upon the United States for protection." Jackson then turned the Native claims of nationhood against their
authors:

> The Constitution declares that "no new state shall be formed or erected
> within the jurisdiction of any other state" without the consent of its leg-
> islature. If the general government is not permitted to tolerate the erec-
> tion of a confederate state within the territory of one of the members of
> this Union against her consent, much less could it allow a *foreign and
> independent government* to establish itself there.[164]

Jackson portrayed the Cherokee Nation as a newly arrived pretender to sovereignty. His argument was that the states had existed before the tribes organized themselves into polities; therefore, the tribes could not constitutionally
establish their governments "within the territory" of Georgia. His argument
assumed what appeared to be two incompatible propositions: first, that the
tribes had constituted themselves into "foreign and independent governments"; second, that the rules set forth in the Constitution somehow bound
those foreign and independent governments.

Jackson also swept aside the Monroe administration's careful parsing of the
distinct powers of the president and Congress with respect to removal. Instead, he asserted broad executive might to force the Native nations to choose
between removal and subjecthood. "I informed the Indians inhabiting parts of
Georgia that their attempt to establish an independent government would not
be countenanced by the executive of the United States, and advised them to
emigrate beyond the Mississippi or submit to the laws of those states."[165]

The newly aggressive tone of Jackson's address was matched a few months
later in Congress, into which had swept a Jacksonian majority in 1828. On April
24, 1830, over strident objections and following weeks of debate, the Senate
passed the Indian Removal Act, which authorized the president to grant western
lands to tribes in exchange for their lands within existing state borders, by a
largely party-line vote of twenty-eight to nineteen. The House passed the provision by a narrower margin of one hundred and two to ninety-seven on May 26,
after a lengthy and emotional debate witnessed by members of the Cherokee
delegation. Numerous Jacksonian congressmen declined to support the bill:
twenty-four voted against it, while twelve did not vote.[166] The opponents included many from the West, such as Tennessee congressman David Crockett,
who later called the bill "a wicked, unjust measure."[167] Despite eloquent arguments from allies such as Senator Theodore Frelinghuysen of New Jersey and

Congressman Edward Everett of Massachusetts, Congress had decided to follow the bellicose lead of the president. Two days later, Jackson signed the bill into law.

Seeing that the first two branches of the federal government had joined the state of Georgia and turned decisively against them, Cherokee leaders determined to take their battle to the final remaining branch: the courts of the United States. Perhaps there they might find relief from what Boudinot decried in the *Phoenix* as the "republican tyranny" that was about to eject them from their lands.[168] In February 1829, Boudinot changed the name of the newspaper to the *Cherokee Phoenix, and Indians' Advocate*, suggesting a further widening of its ambitions.

In his editorials, Boudinot expressed impatience and skepticism toward Georgia's claims, now newly amplified by the support of the federal government. "Why were we not told long ago, that we could not be permitted to establish a government within the limits of any state?" he queried in the *Phoenix* in June 1829.[169] As usual, he wrote his pieces in the plurally erudite voice: "we." Later, in response to Georgia's claimed jurisdiction over the entire Cherokee Nation, Boudinot noted mordantly that neighboring states might find their autonomy infringed by Georgia's bold assertions. "We have already noticed the late law of Georgia, making a high misdemeanor, punishable with four years [*sic*] imprisonment at hard labour in the penitentiary, for any white man to reside, after the 1st of March, *within the limits of the Cherokee nation*, (so the copy of the laws we received reads—let the people of Alabama, Tennessee and North Carolina look out—the Georgia legislature is carrying its sovereignty too far)."[170]

Boudinot's observation was a deft maneuver of redirecting Georgia's *imperium in imperio* contentions back against the state itself. In its eagerness to assert jurisdiction over "the limits of the Cherokee nation," Georgia was trammeling on the sovereignty of its neighboring states. But for Boudinot the greater enormity was, of course, Georgia's refusal to recognize the nation within—but not entirely within—its borders. Boudinot was articulating a theory of fractal federalism. The Cherokee Nation was a nation within a state that was within a nation. And he believed this theory to be entirely compatible with—indeed, a natural outgrowth of—distinctly American modes of legal and political thought.

7 • *The Cherokee Nation v. Georgia v. United States*

A Federalism of Fractals

As in their dealings with the executive branch and Congress, the leaders of the Cherokee Nation did not approach the Supreme Court as naïve, unsophisticated, or friendless provincials. On the contrary, the close working relationships that John Ross, Elias Boudinot, and John Ridge maintained with their contacts at the American Board of Commissioners for Foreign Missions's Boston headquarters and in Washington meant that the Nation was able to consult and strategize about how best to bring their dispute with Georgia before the Court.

The Nation in the Court, 1830–33

The passage of the Removal Act by Congress in May 1830 made the issue urgent. That spring, the members of the Cherokee delegation in Washington began interviewing potential lawyers. Through Jeremiah Evarts, secretary of the ABCFM, and Daniel Webster, who was at this time a powerful U.S. senator and political foe of Andrew Jackson, the delegates were introduced to former U.S. attorney general William Wirt.[1]

Wirt was now fifty-seven years old and at the pinnacle of a long and successful legal career. He and Webster were considered the Supreme Court advocates nonpareil of the day. As attorney general in the Monroe and Quincy Adams administrations, Wirt had participated in the Cabinet debates of the 1820s concerning the status of the Cherokee Nation. He had previously met George Lowrey, John Ross, and Major Ridge; he and his family had attended balls and levees with the Cherokee delegates. In his capacity as attorney general, he had rendered an opinion in which he found that the Nation did not

William Wirt, by Henry Inman, 1832. (Boston Athenaeum.)

have the power to impose taxes on U.S. traders operating within the Nation, although he did insist on the primacy of treaties as the basis for Congress's authority over the tribe.[2]

Now, in the spring of 1830, Wirt was approached by the Cherokee delegation about the possibility of devising a case to bring their claims before the Supreme Court. Wirt described the overture to his lifelong friend and confidant, Dabney Carr, now a judge of the Virginia Court of Appeals. "[A]fter the passage of the Indian Bill, some of the most distinguished men in Congress who had opposed it's [sic] passage, Webster, Judge Spencer, Frelinghuysen, & others advised the Cherokee Delegation, then in Washington, to employ counsel to bring the various questions of their rights, under the treaties, before the Supreme court of the U. S.," Wirt wrote. "For this purpose they were introduced to me, when in Washington."[3]

By June, at home in Baltimore, Wirt had fully immersed himself in fact-gathering and strategizing. He initiated an official correspondence with the governor of Georgia, George Rockingham Gilmer. Soon thereafter, Wirt's name appeared in the press as having been professionally consulted by the Cherokee Nation.[4] Wirt harbored apprehensions about taking the case because of its controversial nature. But the canny attorney also understood the value to his clients of putting their case before the general public in order to attract popular sympathy.

Wirt's letter to Gilmer launched one of many tense political episodes surrounding the major drama of the Cherokee Nation's case. In early June, Wirt took up his pen and addressed Gilmer in tones that bore simultaneously the air of an apology, a challenge, and a memo to the file. "A just respect for the state of Georgia, and a desire to avoid a misconstruction which might be attended with evil consequences, seem to me to call for a communication which, under other circumstances, might well be deemed officious and intrusive," Wirt wrote. He then explained his position:

> The Cherokee nation have consulted me, professionally, as to their rights under their various treaties with the United States. . . . I have not sought this consultation. It has been cast upon me in the common and regular practice of my profession. . . . They are civilized and well informed men—they wear our dress, speak our language correctly—and in their manners indicate all the mildness and much of the culture and courtesy of our own best circles.

Following this expository preamble, Wirt set forth his view of the merits of the Cherokees' claim: "It is my misfortune to differ with the constituted authorities of the state of Georgia, on the question of her power to extend her laws into the Cherokee nation."[5]

Having responded to charges that he had instigated the case or encouraged the Cherokees to violence, Wirt turned to procedural details. First, notice: "My object is . . . simply to avoid all appearance of concealment, and all misapprehension or surprise on the part of the state of Georgia." Second, remedies: "[I]n the future measures which may grow out of this controversy, so far as they shall be under my direction, care will be taken to give as little trouble as possible to the constituted authorities of the state of Georgia." Finally, the thorniest issue, sovereign immunity: "The decision may be expedited by making a case, by consent, if that course should suit the views of the state of Georgia."[6]

Wirt was inviting Gilmer to consent to suit on behalf of the state, and thus to waive the defense of sovereign immunity under the Eleventh Amendment.[7] Ratified in 1795, the Eleventh Amendment bars suits "commenced or prosecuted against one of the United States by Citizens of another State, or by Citizens or Subjects of any Foreign State."[8] Given that Wirt was at this point uncertain who his plaintiff might be, Georgia's waiver would in theory allow a non-Georgia individual—for example, a Cherokee citizen—to bring suit against it.

The maneuver of "making a case by consent" was not uncommon at the time. Wirt alluded to this practice in a letter to a Baltimore newspaper regarding his exchange with Gilmer, citing as precedents two of the Court's recent and high-profile cases, *McCulloch v. Maryland* (1819) and *Brown v. Maryland* (1827), both of which Wirt had argued.[9] In both cases, the parties and their lawyers had agreed to stipulate to a given set of facts in order to reach the constitutional issues. In both cases, Wirt observed, "the attorney general of the state . . . co-operated in the measure, and under the instruction of state authorities, gave facility and despatch to the reference of the questions to the decision of the supreme court."[10]

Despite Wirt's typically elegant epistolary style, Gilmer regarded Wirt's overture as a "gross indignity" against Georgia, as the *Georgia Journal* approvingly put it. The governor's reply began with frosty third-person hauteur, then shifted into snide faux literalness:

> The governor of Georgia knows of no reason why he should be notified that professional duty required of you to take fees of all who ask your advice. Georgia claims no jurisdiction over the lawyers of Maryland. . . . Why it should be the *misfortune* of a citizen of Maryland (as you say it is yours) to differ with the constituted authorities of Georgia, is not very clearly understood.

In Gilmer's view, Georgia—slaveholding, Indigenous-land-hungry Georgia—was taking a righteous stand against oligarchs like Ross, Boudinot, and the Ridges, who were "not Indians" but "the children of white men." This "sad state of things" rendered it "obligatory upon the state of Georgia, to vindicate the rights of her sovereignty by abolishing all Cherokee government within its limits," Gilmer argued.[11]

Unsurprisingly, Gilmer rejected Wirt's suggestion that Georgia consent to suit: "No one knows better than yourself, that the governor would grossly violate his duty, and exceed his authority, by complying with such a suggestion."[12] As the *Georgia Journal* jeered: "Has it come to this, that a sovereign and independent state is to be insulted, by being asked to become a party, before the supreme court, with a few savages, residing on her own territory!!!—Unparalleled impudence."[13]

Wirt's attempt informally to structure a case in which the state of Georgia was the defendant had failed. But perhaps he should have anticipated that Gilmer would not consent to the suit. Two notable background points give additional context to the exchange. First, Wirt and Gilmer were distantly related, by marriage, and both were aware of this fact. Wirt's first wife, Mildred Gilmer, who had died in 1799, was the governor's cousin. Moreover, Gilmer's own wife, Eliza Grattan Gilmer, had lived with Wirt and his second wife, Elizabeth, for a few years in Richmond as a girl. Gilmer seemed to regard their connection as adding additional presumption and insult to Wirt's letter.[14]

Perhaps this complex personal history was the reason Wirt had styled his letter to Gilmer as a public document. He sent copies of the letter to his friend Carr, to Principal Chief John Ross, and to President Jackson.[15] To Carr, he wrote, "I am sorry he bears the name of Gilmer—Yet is he a right good fellow in every thing but his Georgia politics." It was precisely those Georgia politics that led Wirt to regard Gilmer as operating under a kind of irrational obsession when confronted with the Cherokee Nation. In this affliction, Wirt believed, Gilmer resembled Jackson and the "set of myrmidons around him":

> [T]he Indian question is the chord of insanity—they are hardly responsible for what they say or do under the influence of the *mania* which has seized them. Heaven knows to what lengths they will carry it supported as they are at Washington. It was with great difficulty they were restrained by the energy of Mr. Monroe and Mr. Adams from moving on the Indians sword in hand but I shall try their metal with the constitution of the U.S. if I can get a question into the supreme court.[16]

The letter to Gilmer became the core of a pamphlet that Wirt composed and had published and circulated. Titled *Opinion on the Right of the State of Georgia to Extend Her Laws over the Cherokee Nation*, the initial run of the twenty-six-page pamphlet was printed in New Echota, on the press of the *Cherokee Phoenix*. This fact was boldly noted on the title page, making the point that the Cherokee Nation was literate, law-abiding, and civilized. The pamphlet was then reprinted by a Baltimore printer, citing the original publisher.[17]

The title of the pamphlet was significant, as Wirt—one of the era's most gifted men of law and letters—was likely well aware. He was presenting his analysis not as an "argument," a "protest," or an "address. It was an "opinion."

Opinions were works of study, scrutiny, and careful reasoning. They were not mere advocacy pieces. Opinions issued from the pens of U.S. government officials—the attorney general, the justices. Opinions were authority.

With this authority, Wirt offered a full-throated rebuttal of Georgia's sovereignty arguments. Georgia officials argued that the Nation could not possess the supreme power of self-government because such a power would constitute an impermissible sovereign-within-a-sovereign, or *imperium in imperio*. Wirt responded: "It is only by begging the question and assuming the right of the neighbouring states to govern the Indians by state laws, within the Indian possessions, that the political solecism of a government within a government is produced." He continued:

> If by a *government within a government*, it be meant that the territory all around the Indians is under the government of several of the States, this is no political paradox, and is not at all the meaning of the axiom in question. It is a thing of every day's consequence, for a small state to be surrounded by the territories of another sovereignty. . . . I see not why the government of Congress, within the D[istrict] of Columbia should not as well be considered *a government within a government* because surrounded by the State authorities of Maryland and Virginia, as that the self-government of the Cherokees within their limits, should be considered *a government within a government* because surrounded by the State authorities of Georgia, Alabama and Tennessee. In both cases, it is a matter of compact: and so long as the compact is respected there is no collision of authorities, but the political relations of the parties are as separate and distinct, and their actions as harmonious, as if they were parted by oceans.

Contrary to Georgia's claims, "the Cherokee Indians are not *people within her territory*. The territory which they occupy is not, *at present*, a part of the *territory of Georgia*."[18]

Wirt's analysis showed the masterly skills of a lawyer who at this point had 144 appearances before the Supreme Court to his name.[19] Wirt developed a line of analysis that provided a theoretical distinction between the Cherokee Nation and the illegitimate *imperium in imperio*, as well as a concrete analogy—Congress and the District of Columbia—that would give his auditors a logical path by which to follow him.

The issue that truly bedeviled Wirt during the summer of 1830 as he analyzed the legal situation of the Cherokees, however, was precisely how he would "get a question into the supreme court" in order to try the Georgians' metal with the Constitution of the United States. The crucial puzzle was how to establish the Court's jurisdiction over the case—and what the specific claim in that case would be.

The most obvious path was to style the case as a suit brought by the Cherokee Nation itself as plaintiff, challenging Georgia's 1830 laws extending jurisdiction over the Cherokee Nation on the ground that they conflicted with federal law. In Wirt's view, the Georgia laws conflicted with a number of different types of federal law: the Indian Commerce Clause and Contract Clause of the Constitution; the Intercourse Acts of 1790 and 1802; and treaties that the United States had signed with the Nation. He shared his views with Ross and with the Nation's local counsel, William H. Underwood of Gainesville, Georgia, with whom he regularly exchanged letters discussing litigation strategy.[20]

According to Wirt's theory of the case, federal power was supreme (perhaps even exclusive) in the domain of jurisdiction over Native nations. Therefore, Georgia's laws were invalid. This approach suffered from one insurmountable problem, though. In order to satisfy the requirements for the Court's appellate jurisdiction under Section 25 of the Judiciary Act of 1789, the fact that the case involved the validity of a federal law had to appear on the face of the record from the state court that had initially heard the case.[21] Wirt had heard from no less an authority than his successor as U.S. attorney general, John Macpherson Berrien (a Georgian), that "the State of Georgia will take care that no case shall ever come to the Supreme court." In order to stymie the appellate process, Wirt vented to Carr, a state judge who heard a case in which a Cherokee citizen challenged state law would "probably refuse to receive and put upon their records any plea which will shew that the construction of treaties was involved, so that the record will contain nothing to found the jurisdiction of the Supreme court under the 25. Section."[22]

Wirt's pessimism proved well founded a few months later, in September 1830, in the case of *Georgia v. Tassel*. George Tassel, a Cherokee man, was tried in the superior court of Hall County, Georgia, on the charge of having "waylaid and killed" another Cherokee man within the Nation, a charge founded on the jurisdiction acts of 1830. Wirt and Ross, who were corresponding regularly at this point, watched the case to determine whether it might provide a vehicle to bring the Cherokees' claims before the Supreme Court. The county court convicted Tassel, and Wirt petitioned the Court for a writ of error under Section 25. Chief Justice John Marshall granted the writ and ordered Georgia to appear before the Court the following January. Ten days later, however, despite the pending order from the Court, the state of Georgia executed Tassel.[23]

In a further example of the small world of the early-nineteenth-century bar, or perhaps of the many connections of William Wirt, the trial court judge in the *Tassel* case, Augustin Smith Clayton, was also a distant relation of Wirt's: he was the stepson of Wirt's elder sister Elizabeth Wirt Carnes Clayton.[24]

From New Echota, Boudinot fired off an outraged volley in the pages of the *Phoenix*. He likened Georgia's conduct in executing Tassel, thereby defying federal authority, to the increasingly vocal claims being made by the nullifiers in South Carolina. As we saw in the previous chapter, John C. Calhoun's *Exposition* had appeared in 1828. Sometime before December 1830, Maria Henrietta Pinckney's *Political Catechism* was published. Meanwhile, from Boudinot's pen in the Cherokee Nation, came this:

> The conduct of the Georgia legislature is indeed surprising—one day they discountenance the proceedings of the nullifiers of South Carolina—at another, they even out-do the people of South Carolina, and authorize their governor to hoist the flag of rebellion against the United States! If such proceedings are sanctioned by the majority of the people of the U. States, the Union is but a tottering fabric, which will soon fall and crumble into atoms.[25]

Wirt, too, was keenly aware of the growing convergence between Georgia's and South Carolina's rejections of federal supremacy. Perhaps he recalled his argument in the Fairfax lands case sixteen years earlier, during the great standoff between the Virginia Court of Appeals and the U.S. Supreme Court that had culminated in *Martin v. Hunter's Lessee*.[26] Significantly, *Martin* was also a case involving federal treaties. Arguing before the Virginia court in 1814, Wirt had portrayed the Supreme Court as the "one revisionary, superintending power" capable of binding the Union together and enforcing the Constitution. The alternative, he had contended, was a "disorganized, disjointed, jarring and clashing chaos of jurisprudence."[27] Judge William H. Cabell, Wirt's brother-in-law, had rejected this "umpire" vision of the federal judicial power. But how else, Wirt asked in 1814, could "the judicial power of the United States extend to *all* cases arising under treaties, if the state courts decide *finally* all cases brought before them?"[28]

Now, in 1830, with Georgia's governor, courts, and legislature challenging the supremacy of another set of federal treaties, Wirt turned to the Supreme Court. This time, however, he was no longer a green attorney scrabbling to gather his notes in the late-night coach and facing a mortifying set-down at the doeskin-gloved hands of a famed orator and onetime attorney general. Now he was the illustrious orator and renowned attorney general.

Representing the Cherokee Nation appealed to Wirt as something more than simply an opportunity for a fee or a chance to have his name in the public prints of Washington City. Wirt's practice was thriving—perhaps too much, as his increasingly frequent bouts of ill health suggested—and he knew that the Nation's funds were limited. Yet he took the case because he believed that the Cherokees had valid legal claims, and he condemned the actions of Georgia and the Jackson administration. As early as 1828, when he was still attorney general, Wirt had expressed his views to President John Quincy Adams—to the latter's evident puzzlement. "Mr. Wirt came," Adams noted in his diary. "I had a very long conversation with him about the Cherokee Constitution and the Indian titles to lands. He seems not to have considered thoroughly the nature of the Indian title, and to suppose that it is a permanent possession of the soil, like that of the white people."[29] The views that Adams dismissed in 1828 as at best hasty, and at worst mistaken, became the core of the arguments that Wirt made before the Court in 1831 and 1832.

But first Wirt and the Cherokees had to overcome the jurisdictional obstacles. In Wirt's view, the execution of Tassel foreclosed the possibility of getting a case before the Court via its appellate jurisdiction. Wirt therefore turned to the only other avenue: the Court's original jurisdiction.[30] Such a suit required delicate structuring. It would have to be brought in the name of the Cherokee Nation itself against the state of Georgia so that it came within both the federal courts' jurisdiction ("Controversies . . . between a State . . . and foreign States, Citizens, or Subjects") and the Supreme Court's original jurisdiction ("Cases . . . in which a State shall be a party").[31] Establishing that the Nation itself was the plaintiff was also necessary in order to avoid Eleventh Amendment problems. As long as the suit was brought against a U.S. state (Georgia) by a foreign state itself (the Cherokee Nation), and not by the citizens or subjects of that state, it could plausibly be argued that the suit was not barred by the Eleventh Amendment.

The trickiest point for the suit was also the most crucial: establishing that the Cherokee Nation was a foreign state for purposes of jurisdiction. Wirt was not confident that this argument would convince the Court. In a lengthy letter to Carr in which he unburdened himself of all his worries about the case (was he "playing the part of a traitor to my own country and of a false and most pernicious advisor to the Cherokees whom I was about to involve in ruin under the pretence of aiding them"?), Wirt implored Carr to send his views on the question whether the Nation should be classified as a foreign, or "alien," state.[32]

Embedded within this question about the Nation's status was a question that touched on the separation of powers under the U.S. Constitution: Which branch of the federal government had the power to make such a decision? Was such a question open to judicial analysis, or was the president's determination of the Nation's status dispositive?

The separation-of-powers question so troubled Wirt that he sought counsel from New York chancellor James Kent, and from Chief Justice Marshall himself.[33] To his cherished Carr, Wirt sent this request: "Would there be any impropriety in your conversing with the Chief Justice on this subject, as a brother Judge, and giving me his impressions of the political character of this people, in the respect I have mentioned?" The precise question on which Wirt wanted guidance was whether Marshall considered "the courts of the nation constitutionally bound by the declaration of the Executive Branch" that the Nation was "not a Sovereign State, so that the prior implications, by treaty, of their sovereignty will be judicially considered as superseded by such Presidential declaration?"[34] Wirt hastened to add that he would ask Marshall the same question if he himself were in Richmond rather than Baltimore. He hoped that Marshall would understand the question in the manner it was intended: as an effort to "prevent embarrassment & mischief" by obtaining "a correct understanding of the full scope of the decisions heretofore pronounced."[35]

Carr duly sent Wirt's letter to the chief justice and invited his comment. Marshall returned Wirt's letter to Carr, writing to Carr that although his "own sense of duty" prevented him from opining on Wirt's "delicate" and "very interesting" inquiries, he was not offended by "the frank and open application." In closing, Marshall offered a clue to his views, stating that he wished that "both the Executive and legislative departments had thought differently" on the question of Indian removal.[36]

By the end of 1830, the case was ready to proceed. Ross and Wirt exchanged a series of letters in which they discussed details of notice, service of process, the form of affidavits, and signatures. Ross himself took to the roads, riding to Milledgeville and Augusta over six days in December 1830 personally to serve the documents on Governor Gilmer and the attorney general.[37]

Ross sent the completed affidavits to Wirt on January 1, 1831. The covering letter briefly discussed Wirt's fees, for the payment of which the Nation was perpetually in arrears because the federal government had halted its treaty-mandated annuity payments to the Nation. Ross then closed with a postscript that reads as a small assertion of power from a client to his lawyer: "You will please to stick the documents together. I have no time to do it."[38] In the era

John Ross, by Alfred M. Hoffy, copy after Charles Bird King, ca.
1843. (National Portrait Gallery, Smithsonian Institution; gift of
Betty A. and Lloyd G. Schermer.)

before staplers, such papers were typically fastened together by wax, either
melted or in wafer form.[39]

Two months later, on Saturday, March 5, 1831, the case of *Cherokee Nation v.
Georgia* commenced in the Supreme Court of the United States.

When the arguments began, Wirt was battling illness as well as suffering
under a new sorrow that nearly broke him. His sixteen-year-old daughter, Agnes, had died suddenly on December 30, little more than two months previously, from what doctors identified as dysentery.[40] "O I am so so weary—altho'

I have now only a few more days of court, I dread them," he wrote to his wife, Elizabeth, a week after the case began, from his rooms at Gadsby's Hotel on Pennsylvania Avenue at Sixth Street.[41]

Wirt's former Cabinet colleague John Quincy Adams paid him a visit at his lodgings. The pair spent nearly two hours venting their opposition to Jackson and sharing their fears for the country's political future. Wirt's "anticipations are as gloomy and more desponding than my own," Adams observed. "He sees, as I do, all the dangers impending over the Union, but has not the same hope that I indulge of the preservation of the Constitution by the effect of new interests and passions and parties, to spring from the revolutions in Europe and their influence upon our affairs." Of Adams's recent election to the House of Representatives, Wirt stated that "he had no doubt that I should be personally ill treated and insulted." When Adams asked if this was a legitimate reason for him to decline to serve, however, Wirt replied, "[C]ertainly not."[42]

In addition to his emotional strain and the labors of the case, Wirt was also troubled by recurring nightmares—"the *incubus*," as Elizabeth termed the affliction in her worried letters from their Baltimore home. "I think my mind would be somewhat relieved, if one of your children were with you, for the few days of hard labor that is before you," Elizabeth wrote to her husband. She hoped that "one of the girls" might be able to aid their overworked father. She contemplated dispatching two of their children, twenty-year-old Catharine and fifteen-year-old William, Jr. (called "Will" by the family), to "keep all quiet while you take your *siesta*—and to help you to examine for authorities at night." Elizabeth briefly feared that Catharine might not be able to make the journey—"next week is the time for dear C to be *indisposed*," Elizabeth wrote delicately to William, who presumably would have understood the reference to Catharine's menstrual cycle.[43]

Soon, however, the plans were settled. At noon on Monday, March 14, Elizabeth saw her daughter and son, along with their escort, Navy lieutenant Louis Goldsborough—the fiancé of another daughter, Liz—into one of Beltzhoover & Company's vaunted "safety coaches" for the five-hour trip to Washington. An enslaved maid named Polly also accompanied the younger Wirts to Washington. Catharine "will feel more protected by having her own maid in the room with her," Elizabeth wrote to William.[44] Shortly after Catharine, Will, Goldsborough, and Polly boarded the coach, it stopped at the home of Roger Brooke Taney to collect more passengers. Catharine, who was acquainted with the Maryland attorney general and his daughter Anne, introduced them to Will and Goldsborough, and they spent several miles in pleasant conversation.[45]

Upon the party's arrival in Washington, Catharine immediately wrote to her mother to report on the trip and their accommodations, noting, "Polly is airing our night-clothes by Father's fire in the other room. William is going to sleep in Mr. Farleys [*sic*] cot-bed." (Mr. Farley was Catharine's fiancé, although she later ended the engagement upon learning that her intended was "*a confirmed deist.*")[46] Catharine wrote that she and Polly would sleep in the parlor, "w[hic]h is not dear Mother fronting the avenue, but the back street with a corner-glimpse of the avenue." "It is however a very neat and pleasant room."[47]

In a different chamber down Pennsylvania Avenue, Wirt and John Sergeant continued to argue the Nation's case before the Court. No opposing counsel occupied the other table, the state of Georgia having declined to appear. In his peroration, Wirt appealed to the sentiments of the justices and his broader audience, describing the "cause" of this "unfortunate people" as "one that must come home to every honest and feeling heart."[48]

Despite Wirt's fatigue, his final argument on March 14 was described by one observer as "one of the most splendid discourses ever pronounced in that Court, and as powerful in argument as it was beautiful in diction."[49] John Quincy Adams, now representing Massachusetts's Eleventh Congressional District in the House of Representatives, walked from his home to the Capitol to hear Wirt's closing argument. Over the course of their long service together as Cabinet secretaries, and then during Adams's presidency, Adams came to hold Wirt in high esteem. "His health is much broken down, but his voice is strong, and his manner animated beyond the condition of his strength," Adams recorded in his diary. "After finishing the argument upon the constitutional points, and chiefly upon the jurisdiction of the Court, he concluded by a short appeal to the sympathies of the case, in a low tone of voice and that accent of sensibility which becomes doubly impressive by being half subdued. The deep attention of the auditory was the indelible proof of its power. His argument was little more than a repetition of what had been said by Sergeant. His pathos was his own."[50]

On the evening of Monday, March 14, after the final day of argument in the case, Catharine reported to her mother that she had overseen professional and social business in the Wirts' suite of rooms, managing a steady and varied stream of callers while her father was out:

His two Indian clients have just come to the door, but seeing he is gone out, said they wd. call again presently. . . . Mr. Taney came in a few moments—Mr. Marshall & Judge Story wrote answers to Father's notes begging him to take care of himself & not overwork himself. [Younger brother] Henry, Mr. Taney praised for graceful horsemanship so much![51]

On March 18, Marshall issued an oral decision from the bench, as was the custom of the Court. John Ridge, a member of the Nation's delegation, was present in the chamber.[52] Marshall began with words that must have struck careful listeners as ominous: "If courts were permitted to indulge their sympathies, a case better calculated to excite them can scarcely be imagined." That "if," pregnant with counterfactuals.[53]

But then Marshall turned to the jurisdictional question, which he phrased as "Do the Cherokees constitute a foreign state in the sense of the Constitution?" In order for the case to proceed to the merits, the answer to this question had to be affirmative.

Marshall acknowledged Wirt's and Sergeant's claims that the Nation was "not a state of the Union." But that did not mean that it was a foreign state within the meaning of Article III. The relationship between "the Indians"—Marshall did not in this sentence specify whether he was referring to the Cherokee Nation or to Native peoples in general—and the United States was "marked by peculiar and cardinal distinctions which exist no where else." A key point for Marshall was the language of treaties, which stated that the tribes were "under the protection of the United States." To be sure, the Indians' "unquestionable right to the lands they occupy" could be extinguished only by "a voluntary cession to our Government"—not by coercion, and not to the government of a state.

But then the chief justice delivered the blow to the Nation's jurisdictional claims. "It may well be doubted whether those tribes which reside within the acknowledged boundaries of the United States can with strict accuracy be denominated foreign nations," Marshall stated. "They may more correctly perhaps be denominated domestic dependent nations."[54]

The Cherokees were a nation, then. But it was a qualified nationhood: domestic and dependent, and therefore insufficient to achieve the status of a foreign state.

On the overarching issue captured in the heading of the case—the sovereignty of the Cherokee Nation versus that of the state of Georgia—Marshall declined to speak directly. The fact that the Nation sought to enjoin the state legislature from "the execution of certain laws" appears to have troubled him.[55] "[T]he Court is asked to do more than decide on the title. The bill requires us to control the Legislature of Georgia, and to restrain the exertion of its physical force. The propriety of such an interposition by the Court may be well questioned. It savours too much of the exercise of political power to be within the proper province of the judicial department," he stated.[56] But then Marshall offered a small but hopeful sign to the Nation. "The mere question of right might perhaps be decided by this court in a proper case with proper parties," he observed. Here, the jurisdictional issue rendered answering this question "unnecessary."[57] But the comment was a beacon pointing toward a potential future litigation strategy.

In the immediate aftermath of the decision in *Cherokee Nation*, Marshall made additional efforts to highlight the "nation" element of the "domestic dependent nations" concept that he had devised. During the course of the justices' deliberations, Joseph Story and Smith Thompson stated that they intended to dissent.[58] In their view, the Nation constituted a foreign state for purposes of Article III, and the Nation was entitled to the injunction it sought. Marshall urged Story and Thompson to pen a dissenting opinion for publication.[59]

Boudinot reprinted a summary of the decision in the *Phoenix*, along with his own commentary. He challenged the view of those who regarded the case as sustaining "the pretensions of Georgia & the views of the Executive," pointing out that the Court had not reached the substantive issues that the case presented, only the jurisdictional question. Boudinot also found a hopeful note in Marshall's statements that the Cherokees were owed protection from the general government.[60] As in his *Address to the Whites* of 1826, Boudinot described the Cherokees as the "faithful allies" of the United States. The Nation must, he urged, cling to this separate status.

Just below this report of the case, Boudinot printed three items that highlighted the urgency of the Nation's situation. One reported on yet another arrest of a Cherokee citizen by state authorities: "We understand on Wednesday morning Mr. John A. Bell of Coosewaytee was arrested by a detachment of the Georgia Guard. Mr. B. is a native and what the charge was we are unable to say; and in fact it is impossible to know, for these law officers go to work without a written precept." Another was a reminder of both the labor involved in producing the newspaper and the tangibility of the finished article: "Our printers being unable to issue a sheet of a usual size, we present our readers with a smaller sheet." A small but telling notice occupied the bottom right-hand corner of the page: "MR. WIRT'S OPINIONS Printed in pamphlet form for sale at this office."[61]

Georgia was aggressively extending its reach into the Nation and upon its people. The Supreme Court had held that it was unable to hear the Nation's petition for relief. The messages that Boudinot sent out from the printing office in New Echota should be understood as supplements to those petitions.

The columns of the *Phoenix* presented legal claims, asserted cognizable injuries, articulated chains of causation, and prayed for relief. They spoke in terms of Christian morals as well as constitutional law, presenting a brief for the Cherokee Nation to the tribunal of the broader American audience. As Wirt was the Nation's advocate before the Court, so was Boudinot its orator in the printed arena of public discourse.

Enforcing

In the final paragraphs of his opinion in *Cherokee Nation v. Georgia*, Marshall acknowledged that the Court lacked the power to "control the legislature of Georgia" or to "restrain the exertion of its physical force."[62] Even the Court's gains in institutional might since the days of *Martin v. Hunter's Lessee* did not allow it to exert direct influence on state lawmaking or enforcement of those laws. But the Court's authority did extend to declaring state laws "unconstitutional and void," and it also had the power to hear appeals brought by defendants who had been convicted in state court of violating state criminal law.[63]

While the Court was hearing arguments in *Cherokee Nation v. Georgia*, another case that satisfied these jurisdictional criteria was already in train. In March 1831, missionary Samuel Worcester, Boudinot's close friend and translation colleague, was arrested by Georgia authorities. His crime was failing to obtain the state license and swear the oath of allegiance that a newly enacted Georgia law required of white persons living in the Nation.

Worcester and several of his fellow missionaries had deliberately courted prosecution under the state law in the hope of gaining an entrée to the Supreme Court for the Cherokees' claims. In these resistance efforts, Worcester and his colleagues had the full support of their ABCFM associates. "We consider it certain, that not one of you will accept any license from Georgia,—that you will do nothing indeed, which admits or implies, that Georgia has any jurisdiction over the Cherokee territory," Jeremiah Evarts and David Greene exhorted Worcester from Boston.[64] In a letter that was at that point already on its way to ABCFM headquarters, Worcester assured Evarts of his solidarity with the Cherokees, writing that he would "rather suffer with and for the Cherokees, than to discourage them by having it said that the Board and its missionaries could not trust the Supreme Court of the United States."[65]

The missionaries' plan to use their arrests and convictions to bring a test case before the Court foundered on Georgia officials' determination to thwart those efforts, however. When Worcester and his colleagues were haled before the Gwinnett County Superior Court, their defense lawyers ready to argue that the state law was unconstitutional, Judge Augustin Smith Clayton ordered the missionaries released. Clayton, who one year previously had served as the judge in the murder trial of George Tassel, now held that the missionaries were exempt from the law because they were federal agents—Worcester because he was postmaster of New Echota, and others because their sponsoring organizations received federal funding.[66]

As postmaster, Worcester was undoubtedly a vector by which federal power reached into the Cherokee Nation. Ironically, in this instance federal power had worked to support Cherokee autonomy. The post office was indispensable to Boudinot's efforts to fight the Nation's battle through the pages of the *Phoenix*. It carried those sheaves of letters addressed and return-addressed "New Echota C.N. Ga" between the Boudinots and their far-flung correspondents. Official Cherokee governmental communiqués, missionaries' petitions, even orders for textiles, coffee, and paper routinely passed through the hands of the New Echota postmaster.

Now, however, the shield of federal immunity hampered Worcester's efforts to win the Nation a hearing before the Supreme Court. Indeed, Clayton likely issued his ruling in order to stifle the challenge to the law.[67] Georgia governor Gilmer, however, appears to have relished the opportunity to vanquish the missionaries' efforts at "exciting the Indians to oppose the jurisdiction of the state," as he wrote to Worcester and his associates.[68] At Gilmer's request, Postmaster General William Taylor Barry removed Worcester from the New Echota postmastership, and Secretary of War Eaton opined that the missionaries should not be deemed federal agents.[69] The path was now clear for Georgia to renew its prosecution of Worcester and his associates. "You are therefore advised to remove from the territory of Georgia, occupied by the Cherokees" within ten days, or else face "punishment," Gilmer wrote to Worcester.[70]

To make his meaning unmistakably clear, the governor sent his message to Worcester by the hand of a colonel of the Georgia Guard. The letter soon made its way from Worcester to his friend Boudinot, who printed it in the pages of the *Phoenix*, under the headline "Progress of Oppression." In a companion piece, titled—with heavy irony—"Post Office Reform," Boudinot unleashed a mocking critique of Georgia's and Jackson's maneuverings:

> Who would have thought it?—but so it is—The *searching operation* of the government has penetrated into the wilderness! New Echota has fallen under the proscription of major Barry, the post master general. On last

Monday our worthy post master, rev. S. A. Worcester, who has given general satisfaction for the faithful and able manner in which he has discharged the duties of his office, was turned out. . . . The present administration must be lynx-eyed if they can see from Washington "public interest" suffering in these woods, and if they can "promote" it in this manner.[71]

With the obstacles of federal immunity removed from their path, Georgia officials arrested the defiant Worcester and ten other missionaries on July 7, 1831, and marched them, in chains, more than eighty miles overland to the county seat.

During this time, Worcester was busily corresponding with the ABCFM in Boston and with Wirt, who had agreed to represent him. Wirt hoped that Worcester's case would give him another opportunity to argue the Cherokees' cause before Supreme Court. In order to do so, however, Worcester had to maintain his resolve. To prevent the case from becoming moot and to preserve his standing as a potential plaintiff-in-error, Worcester would have to remain within Georgia's jurisdiction. Wirt warned Worcester of the risks, counseling, "It is for yourself alone to consider whether you choose to become the victim by whose suffering this question is to be raised."[72]

Worcester was determined, however. He applied to the governing committee of the ABCFM for financial support, which they granted.[73] As Worcester, Wirt, the ABCFM, and Cherokee leaders had anticipated, Worcester and his fellow missionaries needed all the resolve they could muster. In September 1831, Worcester, his colleague Elizur Butler, and nine others were found guilty of violating the state licensing and oath law. The Gwinnett County judge—Augustin S. Clayton again—sentenced them to four years' hard labor in the state penitentiary at Milledgeville.[74]

From their offices, known as the "Missionary Rooms," in Boston's Cornhill, ABCFM officials viewed themselves as fighting a multifront war not only on behalf of their own ministers, but on behalf of the Cherokee Nation. One field of battle was Worcester's challenge to his conviction under Georgia law, which implicated the larger question of Georgia's power to regulate the Nation. Consequently, ABCFM leaders followed the litigation closely. They asked Wirt to send them copies of all advice he sent to Worcester, and they paid Wirt's fees for his representation of the missionaries.[75]

Another crucial theater was that of politics and public opinion. These were Boudinot's arenas. In December 1831, while the records from the Gwinnett County trial were making their way to the Supreme Court for its January session, Boudinot was already in Washington. There, he was lecturing, meeting with the Nation's political supporters, and raising money. He was also in regular contact with the ABCFM in Boston, with the secretary, David Greene, minuting their correspondence in the board's records.[76]

On February 20, 1832, arguments in *Worcester v. Georgia* commenced in the Supreme Court. Again, the Nation was represented by Wirt and Sergeant. Both lawyers were now also candidates in the coming presidential election. Sergeant was the vice-presidential candidate of the National Republican Party, joining Henry Clay on the ticket. Wirt had received the nomination of the Anti-Masonic Party at its convention in Baltimore in September 1831.[77] He was surprised by the nomination but regarded it as both an honor and an opportunity to aid in galvanizing the opposition to Jackson's reelection—"the immediate ejection of the hero, by a union of the whole opposition," as Wirt put it.[78]

Wirt was now combating Jackson on two highly public and visible fronts: as the lawyer for the Cherokee Nation and as a presidential candidate. Wirt's letters suggest both deep fatigue as well as a profound anxiety for the future of the republic. To Carr, he wrote, "[I]n my heart, my dear friend, I am very weary and sick of public life and it's affairs." He continued:

> [W]e have become a nation of fools and blackguards—such a President & such a set of myrmidons around him—such scenes as are passing under his very nose & by his management—and the people so enamored of the poor & desp[i]cable image which they have set up—so much faction, corruption, intrigue, and impenetrable & imperturbable stupidity and infatuation pervading the whole community—with such a prospect of things becoming worse & worse, 'till the scene winds up with a *protectorate* or a dissolution of the union.[79]

Again, the state declined to appear. Wirt did not lack for an audience, however. "House very thin," Adams noted in his diary for February 21, the first day that Wirt argued. "Mr. Wirt was arguing a cause before the U.S. Supreme Court for certain missionaries to the Indians imprisoned by the State of Georgia. This is a cause of deep interest, and there were fifty or sixty members of the House who left their seats to hear him."[80]

Again, the core of Wirt's and Sergeant's three-day arguments was that the Georgia laws under which the missionaries had been prosecuted, and "the entire system of laws by which the state had assumed jurisdiction over the Cherokee territory," were unconstitutional interferences with U.S.-Cherokee treaties and with the federal government's exclusive power over Indian affairs.[81]

A dozen years later, Story told his Harvard law students that "Judge Marshall was affected to tears by the eloquent peroration of Wirt."[82] Story described his own reactions in a contemporaneous letter to his wife, Sarah Wetmore Story. "We have had from Mr. Wirt and Mr. Sergeant, in the past week, some fine arguments in the Cherokee case, brought before us in a new form," he wrote. "Both of the speeches were very able, and Mr. Wirt's, in particular, was uncommonly eloquent, forcible, and finished."[83] Story noted pointedly that "no person appeared for the State of Georgia." But Story laid blame on Jackson and Congress as well. "I confess that I blush for my country, when I perceive that such legislation, destructive of all faith and honor towards the Indians, is suffered to pass with the silent approbation of the present Government of the United States."[84]

Marshall issued his opinion for the Court nine days later, on March 3, 1832. It was a victory for Worcester, Butler, and the Cherokee Nation. The Court invalidated the Georgia law under which the missionaries had been convicted as well as the act extending Georgia's jurisdiction over all Cherokees within the state's borders.

The seventy-six-year-old chief justice read his opinion from the bench, for an hour and fifteen minutes, in a "feeble" voice. As one newspaper reported, "[S]o anxious were the audience to hear him, that the space in rear of the Justices, and in front of the bench, was crowded with members of Congress, Gentlemen of the bar, and visitors."[85] Marshall's beloved wife, Polly, had died the previous December, a blow that had left him deeply shaken.[86] Marshall was also still recovering from a brutal surgical operation five months earlier. The chief justice had traveled to Philadelphia by steamboat to seek treatment from famed physician Philip Syng Physick for the bladder stones that caused him excruciating pain when walking and required him to use a special cushioned seat in his carriage.[87] The procedure, conducted without anesthesia, resulted in the removal of more than a thousand stone fragments from Marshall's bladder. Thirty-seven days after the operation, in November 1831, Marshall had recovered sufficiently to begin the journey home aboard the steamboat *William Penn*.[88] After three days of travel, he was back in Richmond, in time to preside over his circuit court the following day.[89]

Now, in March 1832, Marshall delivered a decision that vindicated the rights of the missionaries and the Nation. On behalf of a five-justice majority that included, in addition to himself, Joseph Story, Gabriel Duvall, Smith Thompson, and John McLean (who filed a separate concurrence), Marshall stated, "The treaties and laws of the United States contemplate the Indian territory as completely separated from that of the States, and provide that all intercourse with them shall be carried on exclusively by the Government of the Union." The "Indian nations," he continued, "had always been considered as distinct, independent political communities retaining their original natural rights as undisputed possessors of the soil, from time immemorial, with the single exception of that imposed by irresistible power, which excluded them from intercourse with any other European potentate." Since that time, American law had consistently regarded the Native nations as independent polities: "The Constitution . . . admits their rank among the powers who are capable of making treaties. The words 'treaty' and 'nation' are words . . . having each a definite and well understood meaning. We have applied them to Indians as we have applied them to the other nations of the earth. They are applied to all in the same sense."[90]

Therefore, Marshall held, the Georgia court's conviction of Worcester and Butler "was pronounced by that court under colour of a law which is void, as being repugnant to the Constitution, treaties, and laws of the United States, and ought therefore to be reversed and annulled." Marshall also announced that the judgment of the Supreme Court would be accompanied with a "special mandate" that would "go from this Court to the said Superior Court to carry this judgment into execution."[91]

Precisely what would happen next was the subject of intense debate and speculation. The structure of the judgment and mandate acknowledged that the Court lacked the power itself to reverse Worcester's and Butler's convictions and enter judgment on their behalf. Those steps could be accomplished only by the state court. As in *Martin v. Hunter's Lessee*, the case raised profound questions about how the Supreme Court ought to deal with a defiant state court. Now, however, the defiance was emanating from the governor and legislature of the state as well. Moreover, the "revisionary, superintending power" that Wirt had argued for in 1815 now aimed not only at safeguarding federal supremacy, but also at protecting Cherokee sovereignty. In this symmetrical spectrum of fractal federalism, there were nations at each end, with a state in the middle. But the state was fully, violently committed to denying the possibility that such a spectrum could even exist.

A fortnight after Marshall handed down his decision, Worcester and Butler's attorneys in Georgia presented the special mandate to the Georgia court and moved for reversal of judgment and for a writ of habeas corpus. Judge Clayton had been elected to Congress, but his successor, Charles Dougherty, proved determined to follow his lead. Dougherty denied the motions, "*disregarding* altogether the Mandate of the Supreme Court," and rejected the attorneys' request for a record of the proceedings. In so doing, Dougherty frustrated the lawyers' efforts to preserve the possibility of carrying the missionaries' suit back to the Supreme Court.[92]

Events now reached both a standstill and a crisis. The Supreme Court had spoken, but it was not at all clear that anyone who was disposed to listen had the power to execute the Court's judgment. Section 25 of the Judiciary Act of 1789, as we have seen, authorized the Supreme Court to review the decisions of state courts. According to Section 25, a final judgment or decree from "the highest court of law or equity of a State in which a decision in the suit could be had" could be "re-examined and reversed or affirmed in the Supreme Court of the United States."[93] The procedure by which the Court was to carry out this reversal or affirmance was to remand the case to the state court. The state court, in turn, was to enter judgment according to the terms of the Supreme Court's judgment. These procedures were not simply courteous niceties. They were widely viewed as both necessary recognitions of state autonomy as well as requirements established by an act of Congress.[94]

Marshall and his fellow justices hoped that the Georgia courts would choose to comply with this delicate process. But, as Judge Dougherty of the county court demonstrated when he chose to disregard the special mandate, it was only a hope, not a requirement. For a subsequent clause of Section 25 read as follows: "except that the Supreme Court, instead of remanding the cause for a final decision as before provided, may at their discretion, if the cause shall have been once remanded before, proceed to a final decision of the same, and award execution."[95] In other words, the Supreme Court could remand a case to the state court and hope that the state court would, as a matter of comity, enter judgment accordingly. If the state court refused to enter judgment, however, the Court could not order it to do so. According to the statute, the only scenario in which the Court could *itself* "proceed to a final decision" and "award execution" was if the case had been once remanded to the state court, and the state court had declined to act. In that situation, the judgment could be executed by a federal marshal, acting under the authority of the president.[96]

Until the case had reached that procedural posture via a return trip to the Supreme Court, however, the Court was without the means of enforcing its judgment. Upon Dougherty's refusal to enter the Court's mandate in the county court, the missionaries' lawyers had immediately sent a messenger to Washington to seek a second order and execution from the Court pursuant to the Section 25 procedure. But by the time the messenger reached the Capitol, the Court had already adjourned.[97] Thus, when a county-court judge denied motions supported by the weight of a Supreme Court judgment, federal law offered no immediate recourse. The parties' only option was to return to the Supreme Court at its next term—in January 1833, ten months away.

Wirt, who was actively monitoring the proceedings from his home in Baltimore, worried that the lack of a record from the county court might prove an insurmountable procedural obstacle to further review by the Supreme Court. He exhorted his congressional contacts to take up a set of judicial reform bills. In addition to eliminating the second-mandate requirement of Section 25, Wirt proposed granting the federal courts the novel power to issue writs of habeas corpus to persons held in state custody.[98] Had Justice Johnson had this habeas power in 1823, he would have been able to order Henry Elkison, charged with violating South Carolina's Negro Seamen Act, released from the Charleston jail.[99]

In his *Cherokee Nation* argument in 1831, Wirt had presciently insisted that the president was constitutionally obligated under the Take Care Clause of Article II, as well as the Militia Act of 1795, to "call out the military power of the country to enforce the execution of the laws." Those laws, Wirt argued, necessarily included the decisions of the Supreme Court. "It is not for [the president], nor for the party defendant, to sit in appeal on your decision," he told the Court. "It is your function to say what the law is. It is his to cause it to be executed."[100] Nevertheless, the law as it stood—in the form of Section 25— clearly required that the case have been "once remanded before" in order for the Supreme Court itself to order execution of its judgment.

Now, one year later, as he watched Georgia defy the Court's decision in *Worcester*, Wirt believed that the constitutional system had reached a crisis. The crisis had both federalism and separation-of-powers components: Georgia versus the United States, and the president versus the Court. But Wirt was also canny enough to realize that these seemingly distinct conflicts were in fact united by Jackson himself. Since his first days in office, Jackson had made clear that he would not interfere with Georgia's policy of harassing the Cherokees and attacking the jurisdiction of the Nation.[101] Jackson's supposed statement upon hearing of the *Worcester* decision, "John Marshall has made his decision, now let him enforce it," was almost certainly apocryphal.[102] Enforcement of the Court's judgment was not required of Jackson until the case had satisfied the statutory requirements and made a return trip to the Court.

Nevertheless, Wirt and many others held Jackson at least partially responsible for Georgia's defiance. "Gen. Jackson could by a nod of the head or a crook of the finger induce Georgia to submit to the law," wrote Congressman Lewis Williams. "It is by the promise or belief of his countenance and support that Georgia is stimulated to her disorderly and rebellious conduct."[103] To Wirt, bolstering the Court's power over the states was necessary to counterbalance presidential aggrandizement. "[T]his resistance on the part of Georgia is creating a strong interest for the authority of the Supreme Court," Wirt wrote to Williams.[104]

Story struck a more fatalistic note in a letter to George Ticknor five days after the Court had decided *Worcester*:

> Georgia is full of anger and violence. What she will do, is difficult to say. Probably she will resist the execution of our judgment, and if she does, I do not believe the President will interfere, unless public opinion among the religious of the Eastern and Western and Middle States, should be brought to bear strong upon him. The rumor is, that he has told the Georgians he will do nothing. I, for one, feel quite easy on this subject, be the event what it may. The Court has done its duty. Let the nation now do theirs. If we have a Government, let its command be obeyed; if we have not, it is as well to know it at once, and to look to consequences.[105]

Both Wirt and Story had been at the center of the earlier confrontation between the Supreme Court and a state in *Martin v. Hunter's Lessee*. Story's expansive reading of federal judicial authority, built on Wirt's concept of a single "revisionary, superintending power," had managed to stave off the Virginia judges' theory of state judicial supremacy. But the Virginia judges had themselves been cognizant of other fissures in the federal fabric, holding back their opinion until after the end of the War of 1812 and the Hartford Convention's threatened New England separation. The Virginians regarded themselves as defenders of the Union.[106] Their judges claimed interpretive power over issues of property, contract, and vested rights that only tangentially—*pace* Story—touched on the federal government's treaty power.

Georgia, however, was making a different kind of claim. The state asserted the power to act like a nation, and to deal with the Cherokee Nation as though the Nation were something less than a state. Georgia rejected the Court's superintending power, as well as any systemwide umpire. It insisted that it had the power to engage in treaty-making—or, more accurately, to ignore federal treaties—with Native nations. Little about the bellicose arguments emanating from the state's courts, legislature, or governor sounded in terms of union, at least as that term had been understood since 1815. Georgia, like South Carolina, now demanded complete control over all persons and lands within its borders. Moreover, Georgia was willing to defend this power even if that meant flouting a judgment of the Supreme Court that was directly binding on the state. The difference was evident to Wirt and Story. In the spring of 1832, both increasingly believed that something was deeply wrong, perhaps fundamentally and irreparably so, in the American constitutional system.

Brief Victory

Elias Boudinot, like many other Cherokee leaders, experienced a surge of optimism when he learned of the Court's decision in *Worcester v. Georgia* in early March 1832. That spring, Boudinot was traveling through the North on another speaking and fundraising tour with John Ridge. The need for such efforts had become more acute since the passage of the Indian Removal Act in 1830, and the Jackson administration's subsequent decision to cease its treaty-required payment of an annual annuity to the Nation for prior land cessions. The loss of the annuity revenue meant that the Cherokee government had fewer funds to direct toward the *Phoenix*. Boudinot, therefore, returned to his northern circuit of public addresses and appeals for contributions to the newspaper.[107]

Fittingly, the cousins were at the offices of the ABCFM in Boston when the news reached them on March 7, four days after Marshall announced the ruling. Boudinot recounted the moment in a letter that day to his brother Stand Watie, who was in New Echota overseeing the *Phoenix* in his absence:

> Expectation has for the last few days been upon tiptoe—fears and hopes alternately took possession of our minds until two or three hours ago Mr. John Tappan came in to see us, and asked us whether we could not dine with him to-morrow. He said his brother had just arrived in the city from Washington, and he supposed we were prepared to hear bad news—(a chill went through my heart). Mr. Ridge observed, "No, we are not prepared." He then told us of the true state of the case, and produced a paper which contained an account, and tried to read to us, but he was so agitated with joy he could hardly proceed. . . . These little incidents manifest the feeling, the intense feeling, on that question.[108]

Boudinot, Ridge, and their associates at the board were jubilant. "I will take upon myself to say that this decision of the Court will now have a most powerful effect on public opinion. It creates a new era on the Indian question,"

Boudinot wrote to his brother. "The laws of the State are declared by the highest judicial tribunal in the Country null and void. It is a great triumph on the part of the Cherokees so far as the question of their rights were concerned. The question is for ever settled as to who is right and who is wrong."[109]

Moreover, Boudinot observed, the decision of the Court fundamentally changed the nature of the conflict: "It is not now before the great state of Georgia and the poor Cherokees, but between the U.S. and the State of Georgia, or between the friends of the judiciary and the enemies of the judiciary." Instead of the Cherokee Nation having to fend off Georgia and the federal government on its own, the Court had asserted itself as the constitutional arbiter of the federal government. As a result, Boudinot hoped, the Nation would have the U.S. government behind it, facing down Georgia.[110]

Still, Boudinot remained cautious. He took pains to specify what portions of his report could be shared, and which should be withheld from public consumption in New Echota, and in particular from the columns of the *Phoenix*. He also understood the delicate and contentious political landscape in which the Court was operating. "Publish nothing in regard to the Presidential election—about Clay or Jackson, and copy little of what is said about the S[upreme] C[ourt]," he instructed Watie. "A great deal will be said but let us only look on and see—I shall write again soon." He ended the letter with a message to be conveyed to his wife, Harriett: "Tell H. I *do* behave myself."[111]

With elation came renewed zeal. The *Worcester* result was a "glorious decision" and a "momentous event," Ridge wrote to Watie. But "the contest is not over." On the contrary: this was the crucial moment to seize victory—not only for the Cherokee Nation but also for the Court. It was time "to settle the matter either for us and all the friends of the Judiciary or against us all!" Ridge thus explicitly aligned the Cherokees' campaign for sovereignty with the Court's battle against the executive—and Marshall's conflict with Jackson. "[T]he Chicken Snake General Jackson has time to crawl and hide in the luxuriant grass of his nefarious hypocracy [*sic*] until his responsibility is fastened upon by an execution of the Supreme Court at their next session," Ridge wrote. "Then we shall see how strong the links are to the chain that connect the states to the Federal Union. Upon this subject the Union pauses and stands still to look upon the crisis our intellectual warfare has brought them and the Cherokee question as it now stands is the greatest that has ever presented itself to the consideration of the American People."[112]

Ridge was watching the aftermath of the Court's decision with the eyes of both a sophisticated user of American law as well as an observer witnessing the growing struggle to define the "chain" connecting "the states to the Federal Union." He was clearly proud of the impact the Cherokees' arguments had had on American law and politics. The Nation's "intellectual warfare" had wrought a "crisis" to the American people. The question now was whether that body politic had a "proper head"—a suitable executive who would neither give in to the "menacing attitude" of the "foolish Georgians," nor gamble with the "permanency of the general government."[113]

In the spring of 1832, however, the relief and elation began to wear off for both Boudinot and Ridge, leaving in its place a newfound skepticism. Increasingly, they came to view "the people" as the core of the Nation. Still, the Cherokee delegates continued to prosecute their diplomacy at the highest levels of the U.S. government. In April, Ridge met with Jackson at the White House. Jackson advised Ridge to "go home and advise his people that their only hope of relief was in abandoning their country and removing to the West." After the meeting, Jackson wrote to his longtime confidant John Coffee, "I believe Ridge has expressed despair, and that it is better for them to treat & move—in this he is right. . . . [I]f a colision [sic] was to take place between them & the Georgians, the arm of the Government is not sufficiently strong to preserve them from destruction."[114]

The possibility of a treaty followed by voluntary removal also occupied the minds of the ABCFM officials in Boston, who were in regular communication with Ridge and Boudinot. Greene urged Ridge to wait a year before beginning treaty negotiations. "By that time the Court, the president, and Congress will all have had ample opportunity to take all the requisite measures for enforcing the decision, and the question will probably have been brought to an issue, whether that decision is to be regarded or not," Greene maintained.[115] Again, the enforcement issue was central.

The ABCFM sent a similar message of fortitude to missionaries Worcester and Butler, who remained in the Georgia penitentiary. They spent their days working as cabinetmakers and their evenings and Sundays leading prayer services for their fellow inmates.[116] They also remained steadfast in their refusal to accept pardons from the governor. On the same day as his just-quoted letter to Ridge, Greene wrote to Worcester, urging him to resist the proffered pardon. To do otherwise was "to cause the authority of the court to be contemned before the whole country," Greene wrote.[117] Again, the message was clear: wait and see; do not give in to Georgia; do not endanger the standing and authority of the Court.

The justices were also continuing to ponder the situation of the Cherokee Nation. Two months after the decision, in May 1832, Justice John McLean invited Boudinot, Ridge, James Martin, and William Shorey Coodey (Ross's nephew) to a private meeting. McLean had concurred in *Worcester*, writing that although the Nation possessed the power of "self-government," its status as an "interior independent power" within the state of Georgia meant that this self-government was "undoubtedly contemplated to be temporary." A Native nation's presence within the territory of a state might "seriously embarrass or obstruct the operation of the state laws," McLean observed. Therefore, "[a] sound national policy does require that the Indian tribes within our states should exchange their territories, upon equitable principles, or, eventually, consent to become amalgamated in our political communities."[118] In the meeting, the justice urged the delegation to consider voluntary removal. Continuing to fight in the courts would be ruinously expensive and likely fruitless; far better to move west and "become a Territory with a patent in fee simple to the nation for all its lands."[119]

In letters to Ross, McLean offered the same advice. "I have come to the conclusion, that every consideration which should influence you as a people, is in favor of your removal West of the Mississippi," McLean wrote to the principal chief.[120] "Where has an Indian Community flourished long, which has been surrounded by a White population[?]" In Georgia, such a scenario had led to increased "excitement in the people" and "a corrupting and licentious intercourse," McLean warned.[121]

That word again: "intercourse." It had been the organizing rubric for numerous acts of Congress regulating relations between the United States and Native nations since 1790. It was bound up with notions of commerce—commerce "with the Indian tribes," as well as "among the states," thanks in large part to Wirt's framing of the domestic commerce power in *Gibbons v. Ogden*.[122] But McLean was invoking a more dangerous, pestilential version of intercourse, one that was "corrupting and licentious." In his view, the Cherokees would be unable to fend off such infection. Despite the degree of "civilization" they had achieved, they were doomed. And, he observed pessimistically, law was powerless to stop this process: "The laws restrain the good, but the profligate part of society, in defiance of all injunctions and penalties, will intrude into the Indian Country and disseminate their vices among its inhabitants."[123]

Reversals

By the summer of 1832, Ridge, Boudinot, and the rest of the delegation had returned to New Echota. The situation in Georgia was increasingly grim. On

August 1, 1832, Boudinot resigned as editor of the *Phoenix*. His willingness to contemplate a treaty and removal had become known, and he had faced pressure from Ross and many members of the General Council to temper those views. Instead, he ceded his post.

In his final edition of the *Phoenix*, Boudinot announced that he was stepping down and published the letter of resignation he had sent to Ross. Boudinot believed that he, as editor, had a moral and political obligation to present the Cherokee people with a candid view of the choices before them, and the consequences of those choices. Having himself reached the bitter conclusion that removal was the least destructive option for the Nation, he could not stomach serving as editor if he was barred from even discussing removal. It was "the duty of every citizen to reflect upon the dangers with which we are surrounded—to view the darkness which seems to lie before our people—our prospects, and the evils with which we are threatened—to talk over all these matters, and, if possible, come to some definite and satisfactory conclusion, while there is time, as to what ought to be done in the last alternative," he wrote to Ross, and to his fellow Cherokees. If the government was unwilling to permit the *Phoenix* to air dissenting views in weighing the Cherokees' prospects, Boudinot was equally unwilling to continue serving as editor.

> I could not consent to be the conductor of the paper without having the right and privilege of discussing these important matters—and from what I have seen and heard, were I to assume that privilege, my usefulness would be paralyzed by being considered, as I have already been, an enemy to the interests of my country and people. *I love my country and I love my people, as my own heart bears me witness, and for that very reason I should deem it my duty to tell them the whole truth, or what I believe to be the truth.* I cannot tell them that we will be reinstated in our rights, when I have no such hope, and after our leading, active, and true friends in Congress, and elsewhere, have signified to us that they can do us no good.[124]

Ross presented Boudinot's letter of resignation to the General Council, accompanied by a strongly worded rebuttal of his own. "The *views* of the *public authorities* should continue and ever be in accordance with the *will of the people*; and the *views of the Editor of the National paper* be the same," Ross insisted.[125] The principal chief thus rejected Boudinot's claim that the "conductor" of the *Phoenix* had a "right and privilege" to use the paper to tell the Nation "the whole truth" as the editor saw it. Rather, the editor's job was to represent the views of the "public authorities," which were necessarily in accordance with the will of the people. The *Phoenix* was the "*National paper.*" As the national paper, it had a duty to reflect the views of the government. Any other approach would harm the Nation. "The love of our country and people, demands *unity of sentiment and action* for the good of *all.*"[126] Shortly thereafter, Ross's brother-in-law Elijah Hicks was appointed by the council to take over the editorship.

In October 1832, the Georgia legislature authorized a lottery for Cherokee lands, despite the fact that those lands remained in the possession of their Native owners. The homes and fields of high officials were not exempt from the proceedings. After one trip, Ross returned to his plantation at Head of Coosa, roughly twenty-five miles southwest of New Echota, to find that a "fortunate drawer," in the words of the lottery statute, and his family were occupying the house. Critics of the lottery frequently used the phrase "fortunate drawer" ironically.[127]

Just a few month earlier, in April 1832, John Ridge's elderly father, Major Ridge, had joined some eighty other citizens of the Nation in signing a circular letter from the Cherokee government rejecting "any artifices" that might be used by the Jackson administration "to divide & distract our people" into splitting into factions. The letter was sent to the various districts of the Nation and warned them against entering into separate treaty negotiations with the administration. "[N]o individuals have a right to make a Treaty, that right being vested in the lawful council of the nation," the letter declared.[128] No subset of Cherokee individuals could lawfully enter into a treaty with the U.S. government.

By the fall of 1832, however, the Ridges, Boudinot, and others were increasingly convinced that a treaty and removal were the only viable means of preserving the Nation and its people. But, as demonstrated by Boudinot's removal from the editorship of the *Phoenix* for entertaining the possibility of a treaty, Ross and his supporters were determined to continue fighting for the land.

Events outside the Nation in late 1832 further altered the landscape of the Cherokees' resistance to Georgia. As Jackson's reelection was becoming a fait accompli, South Carolina's nullification convention was assembling and, on November 24, adopted an ordinance nullifying the federal tariffs of 1828 and 1832. On December 10, Jackson issued his Nullification Proclamation, in which he suggested that he might forcibly put down the defiant South Carolinians if they persisted in defying federal law. The administration and its allies sought to portray the nullifiers as pariahs making claims far more radical than

Andrew Jackson, by Ralph Eleaser Whiteside Earl, 1836–37. (Smithsonian American Art Museum.)

the standard state-sovereignty arguments that had circulated for decades. In order to ameliorate the crisis in South Carolina and to prevent it from spreading, Georgia had to be mollified. In order to enable Jackson to hold firm to his threats against the nullifiers, the fact of his inaction in the wake of *Worcester* had to be minimized and distinguished. As a result, the impetus to continue fighting against Georgia began to dwindle on the part of many of the Cherokees' supporters outside the Nation.[129]

With Worcester and Butler preparing to return to the Supreme Court for its 1833 term, a host of disparate political actors mounted a campaign to squelch the case. The governor of Georgia, seeking a middle ground between uniting with the South Carolina radicals and alienating his own fellow state-sovereigntists, oversaw the repeal of the law under which they had been convicted. Vice-president-elect Martin Van Buren, Secretary of War Lewis Cass, and Georgia U.S. senator John Forsyth urged Wirt to intercede with the ABCFM. On Christmas Day 1832, the board's governing committee adopted a resolution stating that "in view of the changed circumstances," it was "inexpedient for Messrs. Worcester & Butler to prosecute their case further before the Supreme Court of the United States." An accompanying resolution stated the committee's belief that the "best good" of the Cherokee Nation would be served by signing a removal treaty.[130] The news of the resolutions was conveyed to Ross shortly thereafter.

On January 8, Worcester and Butler informed Wirt and Sergeant that they did not wish to seek a second writ of error from the Court, citing "considerations of a public nature." The missionaries refused to admit guilt, but the governor bristled at any slight to Georgia's authority. A highly stage-managed compromise was reached. Rather than issue a pardon directly to Worcester and Butler, the governor would direct his order to the keeper of the penitentiary, who would then release them.[131] The release finally took place on January 14, 1833.

Two days later, Jackson requested authorization from Congress to use armed force to compel South Carolina to comply with the federal tariff laws. Georgia, meanwhile, earned scorn from its neighboring state. On March 2, Congress passed the Force Act, granting Jackson the authorization he sought, and a new compromise tariff bill.[132] Two days after that, Jackson was inaugurated for a second term. On March 15, South Carolina's nullification convention repealed the ordinance of nullification. At the same time, in a final show of defiance, the convention declared the Force Act null and void.[133]

The might of the federal government had finally been brought to bear against a rebellious state. But that state was South Carolina, not Georgia. Georgia remained free to claim that its defiance had been vindicated, and that it had bested Marshall and the Court. Paradoxically, the victory for federal supremacy in South Carolina permitted Georgia's vision of complete territorial sovereignty—"absolute jurisdictional right"—to prevail. Fractal federalism, in which a nation contained a state that contained (partially) a Nation, was cast to the solecism pile. The *imperium* of Georgia was total, and it grudged only the thinnest of *imperia* to the Union above it. The price of that slender victory for the United States was to be charged to the immeasurable suffering of the Cherokee Nation.

As Boudinot, the Ridges, and their fellow members of the emerging Treaty Party continued to warn of what Boudinot had called "the darkness which seems to lie before our people," the Nation lost one of its most dedicated allies on the stage of U.S. law and politics.

William Wirt died in Washington on February 18, 1834, at the age of sixty-one, after a sudden illness. He had just begun his usual grueling season of arguing cases before the Supreme Court. He and his wife, Elizabeth, had hoped that it would be his final session before the Court, and that their increasingly precarious finances would allow them to move to a plantation in Florida that they, along with a few of their daughters and sons-in-law, had been developing, and that had become the focus of the couple's hopes for their future.[134]

Instead, Wirt took ill after walking with his daughters Catharine and Ellen, and Alexander Randall (whose brother Thomas was married to another Wirt daughter, and who would himself marry Catharine in 1841), from the Wirts' boardinghouse to church services at the Capitol and back on Sunday, February 9. His condition rapidly grew more serious, from a cold to a high fever to what doctors diagnosed as erysipelas. After several days of treatments, including hot bricks, poultices, blistering (on the head, arms, and legs), and the application of "[f]orty leeches . . . two or three different times, to the left temple and behind the right ear," with his wife and three of his daughters at his bedside, Wirt died on the morning of February 18.[135]

The most detailed account of Wirt's final days comes from a letter written four days after his death by Catharine to her aunt Eliza Wirt Carnes Clayton of Augusta, Georgia. Eliza Clayton was William's older sister, who had married Judge Peter Carnes. Carnes was the onetime balloonist of Bladensburg; the former husband of William and Eliza's mother, Henrietta Wirt; and, as persistent rumors suggested, the father of William. In 1789, the teenage William had traveled from Maryland to Georgia to visit Eliza and Peter Carnes, a sojourn that he later claimed had moved him to shift his career ambitions from the church to the law.

Adding to the many layers of renown attached to Aunt Eliza was the fact that she was also, thanks to her second marriage after Carnes's death, the stepmother of Augustin Smith Clayton—the Georgia county-court judge who had presided over the *Tassel* case as well as the first trial of Worcester, Butler, and the other missionaries. That connection made William Wirt the stepuncle of the trial-court judge whose rulings had sparked the legal conflagration that became *Cherokee Nation v. Georgia* and *Worcester v. Georgia*. In a further remarkable instance of the web of family and law, that same Clayton—"your dear son, Judge C.," as Catharine referred to him—had called at the Wirts' home in Washington during William's last illness.[136]

Catharine's narrative of her father's last days was suffused with the rhetoric and imagery of the era's Protestant culture.[137] Many of Wirt's friends noted that he had become more outwardly devout since the death of his daughter Agnes in 1830. Catharine's letter emphasized those elements of the deathbed scene. Catharine described her suffering, bedridden father as initially preoccupied by "his law cases." Wirt "would call us to him by name, and then begin, as if he was addressing the judges of the supreme court, carrying on a continuous argument for several sentences together." Toward the end, however, the professional cares were replaced by thoughts of salvation, hopes of reuniting with the children lost, and concern for the family left behind.

> [My mother] approached the bed-side—he looked at her, and said, "*Wife, I am going before you!*" I feared this would overpower her; but God upheld her, and she answered meekly . . . "There are five of our children in heaven now, waiting to receive you, and you leave five more on earth under my care—it will only be for a little while, and we, too, shall come and join you."[138]

The Philadelphia-based *Christian Advocate* published Catharine's letter under the title "The Last Days of William Wirt, Esq.," noting that it was reprinting the letter, along with an editor's introduction, courtesy—ironically—of the *States' Rights Sentinel* of Augusta, Georgia.[139] Augusta was, of course, the residence of Aunt Eliza, the recipient of Catharine's letter.

Catharine was the daughter who had been sent to Washington to aid her father when he was arguing the Cherokee cases. Now she was penning a literary tribute to him—a tribute that began in chats with a Georgia judge, developed in a letter to a Georgia aunt, and was first presented to the world in a Georgia newspaper devoted to the principles her father had spent his final energies in combatting. It was a strangely fitting postscript.

When news of Wirt's death reached the Supreme Court chamber, the Court immediately adjourned.

John Quincy Adams found himself deeply distressed by Wirt's death. The sight of black crape tied to the knocker of the door of Wirt's lodgings on the morning of his death launched the sixty-six-year-old congressman and former president into a melancholy train of reminiscences. "And thus pass away in succession the glories of the world. He has not left a wiser or a better behind," Adams mused. Adams proceeded to the House for an ordinary day's business. On February 20, he attended Wirt's funeral, joining in the procession from Wirt's lodgings to the "Eastern Branch burying-ground"—known today as Congressional Cemetery. The House of Representatives adjourned (over the objection of a member from South Carolina) because so many members wished to attend the funeral. Also in attendance were President Jackson, Vice President Van Buren, Attorney General Benjamin F. Butler, and four other Cabinet secretaries, as well as "many members of both Houses of Congress, and a large concourse of citizens."[140]

The official rites were observed. Nevertheless, Adams felt unsettled. More ought to be done, he believed. "There was no religious service at the house, and only a short prayer at the grave, by Dr. Post, in which the only qualities of the deceased which he noticed were his piety and religious faith," Adams brooded. Post was the Wirt family's longtime Presbyterian minister; he had prayed with Wirt in his final hours. But Adams clearly felt that the clergyman's graveside devotionals did not do justice to the full scope of Wirt's personality or intellect. "[F]or the rest of the day I was unable to attend to anything of the multiplicity of business in which I was involved," Adams wrote in his diary.

> I could think of nothing but William Wirt—of his fine talents, his amiable and admirable character, the twelve years during which we had been in close official relation together, the scene when he went with me to the Capitol, his warm and honest sympathy with me in my trials when President of the United States, my interviews with him in January, 1831, and his faithful devotion to the memory of Mr. Monroe. These recollections were oppressive to my feelings.[141]

It was a striking tribute from a patrician colleague who had once sniffed at Wirt's "County Court" tendencies. Over a long course of years spent working side by side, however—whether debating the nuances of Vattel, jousting over the scope of presidential power, or uniting against South Carolina's Negro Seamen Act—Adams and Wirt had developed a bond of mutual respect and warm collegiality that seems to have taken even Adams by surprise. Reminiscences of their long association now washed over Adams's memory. The "scene when he went with me to the Capitol" was the day of Adams's inauguration as president, March 4, 1825, when the anxious president-elect traveled from his home to the Capitol accompanied in his carriage by Wirt and Secretary of the Navy Samuel L. Southard, the two holdover officers from the close-knit Monroe Cabinet, in which Adams had also served.[142]

The oppressive recollections continued to haunt Adams throughout the night of the burial. To exorcise them, he prepared an address sketching "the remarkable excellencies in the character of Mr. Wirt," which he "endeavored to concentrate . . . in words as few as possible." But he feared "insuperable obstruction" from the Democrats in the House, whom he anticipated would block any effort to honor the memory of one who had been a "formal and dreaded candidate in opposition to the re-election of Andrew Jackson." As he walked to the Capitol the morning after Wirt's funeral, Adams became determined to find a means of memorializing what he regarded as Wirt's brilliant and intrepid service to the nation. When House Speaker Andrew Stevenson of Virginia rejected Adams's request to cause the House journal to "notice the decease of Mr. Wirt as being the occasion of the adjournment yesterday," Adams resolved to achieve his purpose through a creative parliamentary maneuver.[143] He would ensure that Wirt's death, and the mark of respect that the adjournment of the House on the day of his funeral represented, would be recorded in the official journal of the House.

Adams asked the speaker "if he would object to my asking the unanimous consent of the House that the entry [noting Wirt's death] should be so made. He said, certainly not. Accordingly, when the House met, I made my proposal, and delivered my short address of five minutes." Adams then stated that if there was any objection to his proposal, he would withdraw it.

> The Speaker said he could not have the entry made without the authority of the House, and he should consider it as granted if he should hear no objection made to it. [Pennsylvania congressman] Joel K. Mann, precisely the rankest Jackson man in the House, said no. There was a general call upon him from all quarters of the House to withdraw his objection, but

he refused. Blair, of South Carolina, rose, and asked if the manifest sense of the House could be defeated by one objection. The Speaker said . . . that the House was competent to give the instruction upon motion made. I was then called upon by perhaps two-thirds of the voices in the House, "Move move—move"—and said . . . as only one objection had been heard, which did not appear to be sustained by the general sense of the House, I would make the motion that the addition should be made which I had proposed in the journal. The Speaker took the question, and nine-tenths at least of the members present answered aye.

Adams had succeeded. The House journal noted that the adjournment was "for the purpose of affording the Speaker and the members of this House an opportunity of attending the funeral obsequies of William Wirt, deceased." At last, Adams seemed satisfied that he had fulfilled his duties as a colleague and friend of Wirt. "My anxious feeling was relieved."[144]

Wirt, the striver turned litterateur turned statesman, would doubtless have been deeply moved by Adams's efforts and the nation's encomia. More than two decades previously, when he was just embarking on his *Life of Patrick Henry* and the attorney generalship lay in the unknown future, William had mused in a letter to Elizabeth on words, deeds, mortality, and the elements of a worthwhile life:

> The idea has always been very dismal to me, of dropping into the grave like a stone into the water, and letting the waves of Time close over me, so as to leave no trace of the spot on which I fall. For this reason, at a very early period of my youth, I resolved to profit by the words of Sallust, who advises, that if a man wishes his memory to live forever on the earth, he must either *write* something worthy of being always read, or *do* something worthy of being written and immortalized by history.[145]

Between *Worcester v. Georgia* in February 1832 and his death in February 1834, Wirt argued at least another ten cases before the Supreme Court. These appearances included the first round of *Charles River Bridge v. Warren Bridge*, the landmark case concerning state power and economic development that would eventually be decided by the Taney Court in 1837.[146] But it was through his representation of the Cherokee Nation—his printed *Opinion* and his oral arguments—that Wirt sought to satisfy his deepest drives as a writer, a lawyer, and a man. Into this work he poured his ambitions to write something worthy of being always read and to do something worthy of being written about and immortalized.

"Our Prospects, and the Evils with Which We Are Threatened," 1835–38

Wirt's death, the denouement of the nullification crisis, the release of Worcester and Butler, and the ABCFM's withdrawal of support for further proceedings before the Supreme Court effectively ended the Cherokee Nation's hopes of using the American courts to defend its sovereignty. The strategic issue to be debated then became whether to continue to hold firm against the administration, while calling upon the aid of the Nation's supporters in Congress and in the broader public, or to open negotiations for a removal treaty.

A series of special councils of the Nation convened in Red Clay, across the border in Tennessee to avoid the reach of the Georgia Guard. There, Cherokee citizens debated whether to accept the federal government's offer of western lands in exchange for removing from within the state of Georgia. In a message to the General Council, Ross noted "the abuses and aggressions which have been committed, and are now committing, upon them under state authority," but urged his fellow citizens to hold firm. "Owing to the peculiar situation in which our public affairs are placed by the position taken by the President of the United States, there is no alternative left the nation at present, but to persevere in the peaceable course of asserting & maintaining our clearly acknowledged rights where we are," Ross argued. It was a rebuttal to the arguments of Boudinot, the Ridges, and others who were urging the Nation at least to consider the possibility of a treaty. "[I]t would be folly in the extreme for the nation ever to think of conceding any of those rights, under existing circumstances," Ross stated.[147]

Early in 1835, Boudinot and Ridge again traveled to Washington, where they discussed the details of a treaty with Secretary of War Lewis Cass. At the same time, Ross and another delegation also met with Cass. Cass conveyed a blunt message from Jackson to Ross. The president, Cass stated, was willing to aid the Cherokees. But "any arrangement short of a general removal of your people, would neither relieve the difficulties of the present, nor prevent those of the future." On the contrary: "The laws of the State where you might reside, would immediately interpose with all those consequences which are known to you."[148]

It is notable that Jackson's message, as channeled through Cass, used the term "interpose," given the use of that term—and its cognate, "interposition"—by the South Carolinian nullifiers. If the Cherokees persisted in demanding a "permanent establishment" in their "present situation," the laws of the state "would immediately interpose," with violent consequences. Jackson's statement was further proof that he regarded Georgia's assertions of sovereignty as valid, worthy of federal protection, and altogether different from those made by South Carolina.

Boudinot, John Ridge, Major Ridge, Stand Watie, and a number of others saw themselves as realists who reluctantly accepted that Georgia would not allow the Nation to survive within its limits. In 1832, upon his resignation as editor of the *Phoenix*, Boudinot expressed his view of Cherokee nationhood in an impassioned letter to the new editor:

> In one word, I may say that my patriotism consists in the *love of the country*, and *the love of the People*. These are intimately connected, yet they are not altogether inseparable. They are inseparable if the people are made the first victim, for in that case the country must go also, and there must be an end of the objects of our patriotism. But if the country is lost, or is likely to be lost to all human appearance, and the people still exist, may I not, with a patriotism true and commendable, make a *question* for the safety of the remaining object of my affection?[149]

In 1837, Boudinot published this and others of his letters, as well as a new essay, in a pamphlet titled *Letters and Other Papers Relating to Cherokee Affairs; Being a Reply to Sundry Publications Authorized by John Ross*. Because Boudinot no longer had access to the *Phoenix* printing office, the sixty-six-page pamphlet was printed in Athens, Georgia, some 120 miles southeast of New Echota.

As the title of the pamphlet made clear, Boudinot and his associates in the Treaty Party had come to believe that they were fighting the principal chief for the survival of the Nation. In their view, the Nation was constituted more by its people than by its homeland in northern Georgia. Indeed, Boudinot's writings increasingly focused on "the moral condition of this people." Boudinot implored Ross,

> Look, my dear sir, around you, and see the progress that vice and immorality have already made! See the spread of intemperance and the wretchedness and misery it has occasioned. . . . [A]s a people, we are making a rapid tendency to a general immorality and debasement.[150]

Boudinot was again making a separatist argument for the treaty. Removal with the protection of a treaty would allow the Cherokees to realize the hope that Justice McLean had offered when he met with the delegation in the spring of 1832: to hold territory in fee simple, guaranteed by a federal patent, perhaps with a congressional delegate.[151] Otherwise, Boudinot insisted, the Cherokees would inevitably become "[s]ubject . . . to the laws of the States." The ensuing "moral pestilence" would "finally destroy our nation."[152] Independent existence—sovereignty—within the boundaries of a U.S. state was no longer a possibility.

In December 1835, U.S. commissioner John F. Schermerhorn called for another special council, this time to be held at New Echota. Some three or four hundred residents of the Nation traveled to the town—which had been replaced as the Cherokee capital by Red Clay, Tennessee, in 1832—for the session, which began in the old council house on December 22.[153] The purpose of the assembly was clear to all: to debate, and likely vote on, a treaty. It was not an official meeting of the Cherokee government, however, for Ross and a small number of delegates had departed for Washington earlier that month.

Boudinot and Major Ridge were among the most impassioned advocates of the proposed treaty. (John Ridge and Boudinot's brother Stand Watie, who also supported the treaty, were reluctantly traveling with Ross, at his urging.) One of the onlookers at the treaty council was a young white man named John W. H. Underwood, the son of the Nation's local lawyer, William Underwood, who had assisted Wirt in preparing the cases for the Supreme Court. Several decades later, John Underwood recorded his recollections of the meeting. With Boudinot interpreting, Major Ridge addressed the gathering. He spoke as an elder and a warrior. "I am one of the native sons of these wild woods. I have hunted the deer and turkey here, more than fifty years. I have fought your battles, have defended your truth and honesty, and fair trading," Ridge reminded his audience. "There is but one path of safety, one road to future existence as a Nation. That path is open before you. Make a treaty of cession. Give up these lands and go over beyond the great Father of Waters."[154]

Soon after Major Ridge delivered his emotional remarks, which Underwood reported moved many of "the fathers and mothers of the tribe" to tears, Boudinot spoke. He was now around thirty-one years old. He had spent most of his life studying and producing words, in both Cherokee and English, and deploying them in elegant, compelling arguments. It was his great skill and gift. He had courted Harriett in letters sent from New Echota to Cornwall; he had helped to build the Nation in the columns of the *Phoenix*; and he had spun images and biblical text into speeches capable of drawing money from easterners' purses and political support from their representatives. But now came one of his most momentous tests.

"Elias Boudinot then arose and poured forth the inspiration of genius," Underwood wrote. He quoted Boudinot's remarks, which were presumably in English, assuming that Underwood comprehended their meaning at the time and was able to give at least some account of them fifty years later:

> I know I take my life in my hand, as our fathers have also done. We will make and sign this treaty. Our friends can then cross the great river, but [Ross's allies] will put us across the dread river of death! We can die, but the great Cherokee Nation will be saved. They will not be annihilated; they can live. Oh, what is a man worth who will not dare to die for his people? Who is there here that will not perish, if this great Nation may be saved? When we fall in this heroic attempt, our souls will pass to the happy hunting grounds of the Great Spirit, where no foes dare molest us in our rights. The Captain of our Salvation will command us and we will sing His praise forever and evermore.[155]

Even in this moment of crisis, for Boudinot, the people were the Nation, and the Nation was the people. As Harriett had once remarked, Ross and his party were "lovers of the land," while her husband and his associates were "lovers of the people."[156]

The council appointed a committee of twenty men to negotiate specific treaty terms. At six o'clock on the evening of December 29, 1835, the committee convened in the Boudinots' parlor. Also present were Commissioner Schermerhorn and a few witnesses. Before them lay the draft treaty that the Nation had been debating for months. The treaty ceded the Nation's land within the boundaries of Georgia in exchange for a grant of lands west of the Mississippi River, to which the Nation was to hold title in perpetuity, as well as a five-million-dollar payment from the federal government; five hundred thousand dollars in funds for education; full compensation for all property remaining in the East; and a delegate in Congress.[157] The treaty was read aloud slowly and with ceremony. For several hours, there was muted discussion, pipe smoking, but no actual signing. Finally, sometime after eleven o'clock, the committee members took up the pen. All twenty signed, nine by name and eleven by making their marks. Boudinot was the fifth to sign, according to Underwood. By ten minutes before midnight, the treaty was signed, and the signatures witnessed.[158]

The signers of the Treaty of New Echota understood that by putting their names to the agreement, they were violating both customary and formal Cherokee law that prohibited individual members from selling or conveying land.

They also understood themselves to be risking their lives. A statute known as the "Blood Law," which the Cherokee legislature had passed in 1829, prohibited such sales absent authorization from the National Council. Major Ridge had been a vocal proponent of the law, which was passed out of concern that mounting pressure and harassment from Georgia would impel some Cherokees to engage in unauthorized land sales. The penalty for violating the law was death.[159] Traditional law, which continued to inform how controversies were handled, emphasized community norms and maintaining social harmony, public consensus, and a clan-based system of justice.[160] This context explains the statement that Major Ridge is reported to have uttered as he placed his mark on the treaty: "I have signed my death warrant."[161]

On the day after the signing, the treaty received the unanimous approval of the council that was assembled at New Echota.[162] The council also dispatched the members of the committee of twenty to Washington, led by Major Ridge. It was hoped that they would be able to prevail upon Ross and the rest of the official contingent to agree to the treaty. At that point, the unified Cherokee leadership would forward the treaty to the Senate for ratification.

By early February 1836, the members of the treaty committee had arrived in Washington. John Ridge and Stand Watie, who had at that point been in the city with Ross's group for several weeks, moved their lodgings to the hotel where Major Ridge, Boudinot, and the other signers had taken rooms. They also added their signatures to the treaty. "The Ross party here already count my death as certain," John Ridge observed, echoing his father's dark prophecy. "What will that be to the joy which the treaty will ultimately give to the Indians?"[163] Ross, meanwhile, did not reply to the treaty group's communications or its request for his delegation to join them in signing.

The Treaty of New Echota, as it became known, was ratified in the U.S. Senate with a one-vote margin, despite acrimonious debate in both houses and a petition delivered by Ross and signed by sixteen thousand Cherokee citizens calling for the treaty to be declared void. Jackson signed the treaty into law on March 1, 1836. Nevertheless, Ross continued battling to overturn the treaty, attacking both its substance and the unlawful procedure by which it was adopted. The Cherokee General Council passed a resolution declaring the treaty null and void.[164] When Martin Van Buren took office as president in March 1837, he denied Ross's requests to renegotiate the treaty.

Prophecies, 1836–39

Elias Boudinot, his uncle Major Ridge, and his cousin John Ridge were correct in their predictions that by signing the treaty, they had ensured their own deaths. But first, other deaths intervened.

One great loss came as the Boudinots were preparing to leave their home in New Echota and remove to the West. On August 15, 1836, Harriett Boudinot died, perhaps from an illness related to the pregnancy and childbirth she had undergone three months before. Elias Boudinot was distraught. He was left without his "dear companion" and was now the sole parent of six small Boudinots under the age of nine: Eleanor Susan, Mary Harriett, William Penn, Sarah Parkhill, Elias Cornelius, and Frank Brinsmade.[165]

The day after Harriett died, Elias took up his pen to perform the sad duty of conveying the news to her parents in Connecticut. "Harriet is no more—she died yesterday morning, 19 minutes after 1 o'clock, and about 3 o'clock in the afternoon, we consigned her mortal remains to our mother earth, there to lie until God shall raise the dead," he wrote. He then chronicled Harriett's final hours, emphasizing her Christian fortitude in the face of suffering, the words of pious exhortation she had offered their assembled children, and her hope of salvation.

> Upon my inquiring how she did, she said, "I am in great distress, (meaning her bodily distress,) I hope this is the last night I shall spend in the world—then, how sweet will be the conqueror's song!" I inquired whether her darkness was removed. "Yes." You can look to the Redeemer and consider him yours? "Yes." . . . "Tell father Watie [Elias's father]," she said, "to pray that my death may be easy, and that it may be to the glory of God." Her paroxysm returned, and here the conversation ended.[166]

As with Catharine Wirt's account of her father's last days, Elias Boudinot's account was doubtless shaped by the era's specific religious and cultural frames. Still, the narrative is striking in its echoes of the couple's earlier letters. The combination of missionary and political zeal that they shared is evident in the catechistic nature of the exchange. Their optimism about the potential for Cherokees and Euro-Americans to coexist, and indeed to intermarry and connect their families up and down across the generations, is demonstrated by Harriett's reference to her husband's father and, elsewhere in the letter, to the Boudinots' children.

And yet Elias's letter also displays his realist side and his terrible frustration with the state of the Cherokee Nation. The claims of Ross and the anti–Treaty Party to be preserving the Nation's land rang hollow at the very moment when they were most needed. For Elias had had to seek permission to bury Harriett "on a hill near the little spring occupied, I think, by Mr. Tarvin, when you were here, as you go out to Oogillogy," he wrote to Harriett's parents. The Golds' memories of their happy trip to New Echota in 1829 might allow them to envision the exact place. But "[a]s I have not a foot of ground that I can call my own, I had to ask of the proprietor the privilege of depositing her beloved remains on his land, and I have consigned her ashes to his protection." He would always be attached to that piece of land near the spring. The tie came through Harriett, and through the "links, dear to you"—the children, on whose behalf he hoped the Golds "will still consider me as being near to you." He signed the letter "I am, as ever, your dutiful son. Elias Boudinott."[167]

A few months later, the letter was printed in a New York newspaper, under the title "Last Hours of Mrs. Boudinott.[168] One cannot help wondering whether Elias Boudinot used his formidable network of newspaper connections to ensure that Harriet received an appropriate memorial in print, and in the East.

The missionary Sophia Sawyer, who had been the Boudinot children's teacher, described the situation of the household in a letter to David Greene of the ABCFM:

> Mr. Boudinott is a man, as you know, of the finest sensibilities—very domestic in his feelings and habits—has lost one of the most lovely women in the world—at a time too, the most trying in the history of nations or individuals six children hanging now solely on a father's care—the eldest has entered her tenth year—the youngest only a few months old. I fear for him amidst the wreck of his nation.[169]

In subsequent months, Boudinot was at times "sick in bed" and in "very low spirits."[170] The following year, in May 1837, he married again. His second wife was a white missionary from Vermont named Delight Sargent. In a letter to the Golds informing them of his marriage, he emphasized her kindness and her similarity to Harriett: "I can assure you, and all your friends in this Nation will assure you, your dear grand children could never expect a better friend, a better mother."[171]

As the Boudinot household collapsed, the wreck of the Eastern Cherokee Nation was approaching completion. In the fall of 1837, the Boudinots, along with John and Sarah Ridge and their children; several members of Boudinot's family; and a few other families, began the journey to the Cherokee Nation West—lands west of Arkansas that today constitute a portion of the state of Oklahoma.

The Boudinot-Ridge party's trip was comparatively easy: they traveled in carriages and brought along their livestock. Their route took them through western Tennessee. Notably, during a stop at Nashville, Ridge and Boudinot paid a visit to former president Jackson at his plantation, the Hermitage.[172] The Ridges also brought a number of enslaved people with them.[173] Upon reaching Indian Territory, the families dispersed to different places they had selected for their homes. The Ridges settled at Honey Creek, where Major Ridge and another group who had arrived a few months earlier had begun farming. Oo-watie and his family, including Boudinot's brother Stand Watie, also made the journey in 1837. The Boudinots ended their travels at Park Hill, near present-day Tahlequah, Oklahoma, where they joined Samuel and Ann Worcester, who had settled there one year earlier. As in New Echota, the families would be neighbors. Boudinot and Worcester planned to continue their work of translating books, in particular the Bible, from English into Cherokee.[174]

The Boudinot-Ridge party had set out nearly a year before the main body of the Cherokees were forced to leave their homes in the Nation. In the summer of 1838, according to the deadline set forth in the Treaty of New Echota, some sixteen thousand Cherokee men, women, and children began the forced journey westward that became known as the "Trail of Tears."[175] Many of them had spent the previous months in squalid camps and stockades, overseen by American troops under the command of General Winfield Scott. In one of few concessions by Secretary of War Joel Poinsett, the removal process was organized by Ross, who was named superintendent, rather than by Scott and the Army.

The groups traveled in thirteen detachments, each of which comprised around one thousand people. Each detachment was led by a "conductor," a trusted Cherokee man appointed by Ross. The detachments traveled west along one of several routes; the most widely used of these ran northwesterly across Tennessee and then through southwestern Kentucky before turning west to cross the southern tip of Illinois, much of the width of Missouri, and finally turning south at Springfield, Missouri, to cross into Arkansas and Indian Territory. This route covered 826 miles by land and water. At least four thousand people, one-fourth of the Cherokees who walked the trail, died along the route, among them Ross's wife, Quatie, who died near Little Rock, Arkansas, and was buried near the trail.

In June 1838, Georgia militia general Charles Floyd sent a report to Governor George Gilmer, who had recently been returned to office. From New Echota, Floyd wrote:

> I have the pleasure to inform your excellency that I am now fully convinced there is not an Indian within the limits of my command, except a few in my possession, who will be sent to Ross' Landing to-morrow. My scouting parties have scoured the whole country without seeing an Indian, or late Indian signs. . . . [N]one can escape the vigilance of our troops. Georgia is ultimately in possession of her rights in the Cherokee country.[176]

Floyd's bombast was premature. Detachments of Cherokees continued leaving the Nation through November 1838. The trip took between three and six months, meaning that the groups that left in late fall had to struggle to keep moving through the depths of winter.[177]

When the surviving detachments arrived in the Cherokee Nation West in the spring of 1839, they found the members of the Boudinot and Ridge families already established there, along with the "Old Settlers," Cherokees who had moved from Arkansas and other areas in previous years. The experience of the terrible hardships suffered on the Trail of Tears stoked further resentment toward the signers of the Treaty of New Echota. As missionary Elizur Butler observed, "*All* the suffering and *all* the difficulties of the Cherokee people [were] charge[d] to the account of Messrs. Ridge and Boudinot."[178]

Daniel Butrick, another ABCFM missionary who had known Ridge and Boudinot since they were children at the mission school in the Cherokee Nation, accompanied the Cherokees on the journey west. He watched with trepidation the building anger toward the Treaty Party, and he went so far as to urge Boudinot and Ridge to "address a communication to the general council, acknowledging the importance of the law they had violated"—the Blood Law of 1829.[179] In early June 1839, Butrick addressed a more explicit plea to Boudinot. Butrick began by noting his close friendship with Boudinot and his family. Then he proceeded to admonish Boudinot for signing the treaty:

> [Y]ou . . . plunged yourself into such a thorn hedge, that I would not, and cannot get to you, without tearing myself to pieces, and getting out of sight and hearing almost of the entire Cherokee nation. You will readily perceive what I want you to do, that is, to come out of that hedge to your people, and tell them you are sorry you ever went into it. It appears to me

that justice to yourself,—to your friends,—to the church of Christ, and especially to the mission, requires this.[180]

Butrick's message was clear: by signing the treaty, Boudinot had broken the law, plunging himself into "a thorn hedge" so dense that Butrick could not aid him without destroying the credibility of the missionaries and their project in the Nation.

In the summer of 1839, the first one following the arrival of the "Late Immigrants" from the East, the reckoning came. Several of the Nation's leaders, acting without Ross's knowledge, met secretly to deliberate on the crimes committed by Boudinot, the Ridges, and the others who had signed the treaty. Finding them guilty of violating the Blood Law, the group then asked three men from the clan of each of the accused to set the penalty. Clan members deliberated on the punishment only for those who were of their same clan. The proceedings combined customary clan-based justice with more recent national law such as the Blood Law.[181]

Each of the signers was sentenced to death. The members of the secret meeting then drew lots to decide who would carry out the punishment. Allen Ross, a son of John Ross, was present at the meeting. He recalled that "numbers were placed in a hat for each person present; twelve of these numbers had an X mark after the number which indicated the Executioners." The younger Ross was not allowed to draw a lot, however. Instead, he was told "to go to my father's home on the evening before this execution" and "to stay with my father that night and the next day and if possible to keep him from finding out what was being done."[182]

On the morning of Saturday, June 22, several groups of men fanned out across the new Cherokee Nation to carry out the agreed-upon sentences.

John Ridge was dragged from his bed, pulled into the yard of his house, and—while his wife and children were physically restrained from intervening—stabbed twenty-five times until his jugular vein was severed. His body was then trampled underfoot. Still, he attempted to get up; as his then-teenage son John Rollin Ridge later recalled, "Then succeeded a scene of agony . . . which might make one regret that the human race had ever been created. It has darkened my mind with an eternal shadow."[183]

Meanwhile, a separate group of killers arrived at Park Hill, where Boudinot was in the process of building a new house next door to that of the Worcesters. When Boudinot came out of Worcester's house, the men approached him and asked him for medicine, a service he frequently provided to members of the community. As Boudinot turned to walk toward Worcester's mission, one of the men fell behind and stabbed Boudinot in the back with a large knife. Boudinot then shrieked and fell, at which point another of the men struck him in the head several times with a tomahawk. Some accounts stated that he was also shot.

Boudinot's sister Nancy Wheeler, who had married his old colleague John Wheeler, printer of the *Phoenix*, was apparently present at the scene. John Wheeler later described what his wife had witnessed on the day her brother was killed: "When the group of men were nearing the house Boudinot was attacked. He ran from the woods, after being hacked in the forehead and face with a tomahawk, and with blood streaming down his face, he fell on the doorsteps of his house and died with his head in his sister's (Nancy Wheeler's) lap. He had also been shot and stabbed in the back."[184]

Boudinot's wife, Delight, and Samuel Worcester were also present, looking on in helpless horror. Worcester described the scene: "He lived until we received word, and arrived at the spot to see him breathe his last, but he was insensible to surrounding objects, groaning only, but without motion or speech."[185] Worcester reportedly cried, "They have cut off my right hand!" The killers were "pursued a few rods into the woods, where they joined a party of armed men on horseback, and made their escape."[186]

The third victim was Major Ridge, shot while riding his horse down a road just over the border in Arkansas. Sarah Ridge had sent a messenger to tell him of John Ridge's killing and to alert him of his own certain attack, but the warning arrived too late. Compared to the punishments that were meted out to his son and nephew, his end was relatively quick and merciful: five shots to his head and body.[187] Perhaps the difference was meaningful, a recognition of his status as an elder and his long years of service to the Nation as both a leader and a warrior.

Another group had been dispatched to carry out the sentence against Boudinot's brother Stand Watie, but he received warning from Delight Boudinot and Samuel Worcester at Park Hill in time to escape. According to some accounts, he appeared at Worcester's home in Park Hill that evening, where his older brother's body was lying. Watie was said to have looked at Boudinot's mangled remains and then informed the assembled family members and friends that he would give ten thousand dollars to anyone who informed him of the names of the perpetrators.

Boudinot and John Ridge were buried on the same day, some sixty miles apart, near each of their respective homes. Worcester, presiding over Boudinot's funeral, eulogized his friend's "loveliness, integrity, and Christian worth." In deciding to sign the treaty, Boudinot had been moved by "his desire for the good of his people." The decision, Worcester said, was the only questionable action he had ever known Boudinot to take.[188] After these brief remarks, an "unmarked slab of stone, rough and hastily hewed" was laid atop the grave.[189] Worcester's daughter later remarked that "she never knew her father to speak so strongly of the Christian character" of anyone else as he did of Boudinot, "though he did not follow his advice against signing the treaty."[190]

Shortly after the funeral, Worcester took up his pen to write, as Boudinot had done so many times before, to Harriett's family in Connecticut. Now Worcester sent "afflictive intelligence" of "a dear friend, a most intimate companion, and a most valued helper," who was also "your brother-in-law." Boudinot, he wrote, "has fallen by the hands of assassins!" After describing all three of the killings that had taken place four days earlier, Worcester attempted to set the events in context. "Undoubtedly the part which they took in relation to the treaty has been the cause of these inhuman assassinations. I would that my beloved friend Mr. Boudinot had had no part in that transaction; yet I have no doubt of the sincerity of his own conviction that he was doing right, and hazarding his life for the good of his people. He was a great and good man."[191]

Then, showing himself to be Boudinot's true and sympathetic friend, Worcester shifted his focus to the children: "Mr. Boudinot had requested his wife, if he should be taken away, to go with the children to their friends and hers in New England, which she intends to do as soon as circumstances allow." Knowing as he did that he had put his life at risk by signing the treaty, Boudinot had made plans for his children. In the event that he was killed, Delight was to take them far away from the Nation that he had fought to save.[192]

With the letter to the Boudinots' Connecticut relatives, Worcester had memorialized not only the events of June 22, but also Boudinot's actions and the beliefs that had motivated them. Again, a letter writer sought to frame a life just passed. Unlike Catharine Wirt's missive to her aunt or Elias's epistle to Harriett's parents, however, this letter was to remain private, unpublished, outside the public world of the press. "You will communicate this melancholy intelligence to Col. Gold and to the different branches of the family," Worcester wrote to Boudinot's brother-in-law. "But be so kind as not to suffer this letter or any part of it, to be put in print."[193]

Coda

Immediately following the killings, Stand Watie assembled a group of fifteen men to aid him in searching for his brother's and the Ridges' killers.

For a time, he and other treaty signers also took refuge at the U.S. military installation at Fort Gibson. Ross's supporters, meanwhile, gathered around him, numbering in the hundreds and insisting that the principal chief travel with a bodyguard.[194]

Several individuals were rumored to have been among the killers, but given that many Cherokees viewed them as having acted lawfully, they never faced criminal sanctions. U.S. military authorities launched a search at the behest of the Commissioner of Indian Affairs, and some Arkansawyers demanded that Major Ridge's killers be found and tried, but the efforts proved futile. Perhaps it was deemed better not to know for certain.

Supporters of Watie, the Ridges, and Boudinot maintained a years-long feud against Ross and his supporters. In 1842, Watie faced trial in Arkansas for the killing of James Foreman, who was widely believed to have been one Major Ridge's attackers. The jury acquitted him on the ground of self-defense.[195]

But the internal division within the Cherokee Nation endured for several more decades. In the Civil War, the Nation split into northern and southern wings. Ross, who began the war by supporting the Confederacy but ultimately sided with the Union, continued as principal chief of the Cherokee Nation until his death in 1866. Stand Watie fought for the South, becoming a brigadier general in the Confederate Army and leading a famed unit, the First Cherokee Mounted Rifles. He was the only Native soldier to achieve the rank of general on either side in the Civil War. He was also the last Confederate general to lay down his arms, in June 1865, more than two months after Robert E. Lee's surrender to Ulysses S. Grant at Appomattox.

One of Stand Watie's most trusted officers was his nephew, Lieutenant Colonel Elias Cornelius Boudinot, the fifth of Elias and Harriett Boudinot's six children.[196] Born in New Echota in August 1835, four months before his father signed the treaty, Cornelius (as he was known) was sent east after the 1839 killings to be raised by his mother's relatives. As their father had hoped, the Boudinot siblings obtained "larning" in New England. After attending preparatory schools in Vermont and Connecticut, Cornelius moved west to Arkansas, where he read law and was admitted to the bar, as well as becoming a newspaper editor.

The younger Boudinot's activities also came to include politics. In addition to his service in the Confederate Army, Cornelius was elected the Cherokee Nation's delegate to the Confederate Congress. In 1870, he became the first Native lawyer to argue before the U.S. Supreme Court.[197]

A Federalism of Fractals

The struggle of the Cherokee Nation to win recognition of its sovereignty from the United States demonstrates the necessity for broadening our conception of nineteenth-century American constitutional law, and in particular for reframing the concept of federalism. The arguments that Elias Boudinot, John Ross, and John Ridge made, along with those of their allies William Wirt, John Sergeant, and the officers of the ABCFM, changed what "federalism" meant to interbellum Americans. They articulated a theory of fractal federalism—a telescoping series of federalisms, plural. The Cherokee Nation was a nation within a state that was itself within a different nation. They believed this conception to be congruent with American legal and political modes of thought and practice.

Clearly, in an important sense, the Nation lost its battle against Georgia. But that fact does not mean that Boudinot and his compatriots were wrong, or that their arguments were ungrounded or wildly improbable. Events in South Carolina in the 1830s suggested a federalism of the local, with local power controlled by elites who, when they crossed a certain line, met with the full force of the federal executive branch. After the 1830s, that dynamic became the modal type of interaction among the many layers of governments that constituted the Union.

The situation of the Cherokees was different. The federalism of *Cherokee Nation v. Georgia v. United States*—a case that was never brought, and could never have been brought, before the Supreme Court, no matter how many machinations Wirt might have conjured—was a complex set of relationships. It was not a binary between federal power and state power. The local was the national was the international. The relationships were so tangled, crossing vertical levels of government as well as horizontal branches within a single layer, that the straightforward solution—enforcing the Supreme Court's mandate—became impossible. The result was that Georgia was able to nullify federal law. The price of rebutting South Carolina's claimed power of nullification was permitting Georgia to do the same, albeit to a different branch of the federal government.

It was left to their children—Catharine Wirt, Elias Cornelius Boudinot, and their siblings and co-generationists—to sift through the wreckage and determine which, if any, elements of these federalisms were worth saving.

8 • The Customs of Commerce

A Federalism of Jealous States

The Constitution is much better understood at this day than it was at
the time of its adoption.

—Abel Upshur, *A Brief Enquiry into the Nature and Character of Our
Federal Government*, 1840

Robust arguments for each state's dominion over its own territory did not
issue only from the South in the mid-interbellum period of the late 1830s and
the 1840s. By 1837, states throughout the Union were articulating increasingly
forceful arguments insisting on their authority to regulate any items or persons
that crossed over the border and entered the state.

The debates surrounding the steamboat monopoly in *Gibbons v. Ogden* had
offered a hopeful vision in which the Commerce of the Union staved off destruction
and decline. Avoiding the specter of internecine war had been the
message of both Thomas Addis Emmet's and William Wirt's *Aeneid*-laden rhetorical
arabesques in their opposing arguments before the Court in 1824.[1] In
the late 1830s, however, the idea of the Commerce of the Union appeared to
have lost its luster. This shift occurred because contemporaries no longer
wished to search for a shared substantive vision of national commerce. Perhaps
they had ceased to believe that such a vision was even possible. Instead
of asking whether a given activity extended out from the local realm to meld
with commerce among the states, with foreign nations, or with the Indian
tribes, they began asking a different question: Did the activity come into the
state, and in so doing become part of the state's autonomous ambit?

Contemporaries thus turned to concurrent power. They embraced the idea
that the states claimed coequal spheres of governmental authority with those

covered by the general government. Chief Justice John Marshall had suggested in his *Gibbons* opinion that the commerce power might lie exclusively in the hands of Congress.[2] As prior chapters have illustrated, the possibility of federal exclusivity over commerce carried important consequences for debates over migration by Black people, the importation of slaves, taxation of foreign goods, and jurisdiction over Native lands and people. This crucial but unsettled doctrinal point increased the salience of other species of governmental authority—especially the police power.

This growing formalism regarding state lines owed much to the ideological paths laid down by South Carolina and Georgia in the previous decade. But it was not only a strategy for protecting slavery, expropriating Indigenous land, or asserting southern sectional identity. New England states such as Massachusetts, New Hampshire, and Rhode Island demanded recognition of what they regarded as their sovereign power to order their internal affairs, as did the Mid-Atlantic dynamo, New York.

The mid-interbellum turn to concurrent power represented more than a reactionary flight to marshal local power or a cloak for attacking whoever was in charge at the center of government. These are tempting, but partial, explanations. They overlook the growing sense of dissatisfaction among producers of constitutional discourse with focusing the debate entirely on the project of defining national power.

By the late 1830s, it was clear that all sides in the political and legal battles of the day had something to fear from a strong national government. Southern slaveholders worried about the prospect of a federal ban on the interstate slave trade. Antislavery activists and abolitionists feared the opposite: increased federal support for slavery, in the form of a stronger fugitive slave law. All sides were anxious about the status of federal territories, which would eventually become states, and which would therefore affect the degree of control each region exercised in Congress. Representatives of northern and Mid-Atlantic port cities, for their part, fretted about an influx of undesirable migrants from Europe. Concurrent power offered both a theory and practice that seemed to avoid the hollowness and malleability of competing claims to national power.

Moreover, the turn to the states also meant attending to sub-state levels of government, such as cities, in ways that the federal-state binary largely overlooked. The relentless focus on concurrent power in the mid-interbellum period brought with it a renewed interest in jurisdictional multiplicity at the state and local levels. It was not fractal federalism; these infra-state entities did not claim the status of nations, unlike the Cherokee Nation. But they were claimants to regulatory power, and they mattered for purposes of apportioning control over activities, goods, and people who crossed into the territory of their particular state.

"The Constitution is much better understood at this day than it was at the time of its adoption," wrote Virginia judge Abel Upshur in his 1840 rejoinder to Justice Joseph Story's *Commentaries on the Constitution of the United States,* published seven years earlier.[3] Perhaps the Constitution was much better understood in 1840 than it had been during the founding period. Or perhaps Upshur and his contemporaries simply believed, or wanted to believe, that it was. A few years after making this statement, Upshur became secretary of the navy, then secretary of state, in John Tyler's Cabinet. Upshur's former law teacher Wirt would doubtless have cautioned him and his generation against becoming overly confident in the superiority of their powers of constitutional interpretation.

The Voyage of the *Emily*: Migration and Commerce

The ship that triggered the mid-interbellum explosion of jurisdictional multiplicity was, like so many others of its day, a modest packet carrying passengers from the British Isles to the United States. The *Emily* arrived in the port of Perth Amboy, New Jersey, in August 1829 after a roughly forty-day voyage from Liverpool. The ship carried 129 passengers, of whom seventy-two were English, fifty-five were Irish, and two were American.[4] According to the manifest that the ship's master, William Thompson, submitted upon reaching Perth Amboy on August 21, the oldest passenger aboard the *Emily* was Thomas Chadwell, age sixty-two, an English weaver. The youngest was two-month-old Emily Maria McDonald, the daughter of Thomas and Catherine McDonald, lately of Ireland.[5]

The swell of westward transatlantic migration in the early nineteenth century was such that the *Emily* was hardly notable for having borne 129 souls across 3,140 miles of ocean.[6] Instead, the ship's fame came from what happened at the end of its journey, at the Manhattan docks. Six days after making landfall in New Jersey, the *Emily* and its master unleashed a conflict of constitutional law that roiled the city of New York, the federal bench, and the Supreme Court over the course of eight years of litigation. In so doing, it marked the arrival of a new phase of interbellum federalism.

For the *Emily*'s voyage from Liverpool did not end in Perth Amboy, although some number of passengers likely debarked there. The following week,

Thompson sailed the ship thirty miles north into New York Harbor, arriving in New York City on August 27. The ship and its crew were surely busy that Thursday, unloading cargo and disgorging passengers into the hubbub of oyster-mongers, errand boys, and tradesmen's drays that crowded the quays of Lower Manhattan. Captain Thompson had duly filed the required portside paperwork across the river in New Jersey. But, for some reason, he failed to be equally punctilious in New York.

Thompson's failure to file a New York version of the manifest that he had just filed six days earlier in New Jersey proved to have serious consequences. As an initial matter, it subjected him, as master of the *Emily*, to enormous monetary penalties. An 1824 New York law titled "An Act Concerning Passengers in Vessels Coming to the Port of New-York" obliged "the master of any ship arriving at the port of New-York from any country out of the United States or from any other of the United States than this state," within twenty-four hours of the ship's arrival, to

> make a report in writing, on oath or affirmation, to the mayor of the city of New-York, or in case of his sickness or absence, to the recorder of the said city, of the name, place of birth, and last legal settlement, age and occupation of every person who shall have been brought as a passenger in such ship or vessel on her last voyage from any country out of the United States, into the port of New-York, or any of the United States, and from any of the United States, other than this state, to the city of New-York ... under the penalty, on such master or commander, and the owner or owners, consignee or consignees of such ship or vessel, severally and respectively, of seventy-five dollars for every passenger neglected to be reported as aforesaid.[7]

Seventy-five dollars in 1829 is worth approximately $2,500 today. At the time the *Emily* had arrived in New Jersey, it had carried 129 passengers. Thompson's failure to file a report upon reaching New York City thus subjected him to a penalty of $9,675—or $319,400 in 2023 dollars.[8]

Mayor Walter Bowne, apparently intent on recovering the prodigious fee due to the city as a result of the *Emily*'s insufficiently documented entry to the port, initiated an action in the superior court of New York City. The suit named as defendant not Thompson, but George Miln, the consignee of the ship.

The *Emily* arrived in New York City in August 1829, the fifth month of Andrew Jackson's first presidential term. The case was not decided until February 1837, three weeks before Jackson left office and his protégé Martin Van Buren took the oath of office. In the intervening eight years, the case increasingly became an exemplar of its complex constitutional and political moment. The case that arose as a result of Captain Thompson's failure to file papers with municipal officials churned its way through the dockets of numerous courts, from state court to federal circuit court to the Supreme Court of the United States. Indeed, one might fairly say that the case was heard by not one but two Supreme Courts of the United States, as it was argued twice before Chief Justice Marshall, in 1834 and 1835, and then again before Marshall's successor, Chief Justice Roger Brooke Taney, in 1837.

The case, captioned *Mayor, Aldermen, and Commonalty of the City of New York v. George Miln*, both created and reflected the constitutional reality of the 1830s. In this tumultuous core of the interbellum era, *Mayor of New York v. Miln* demonstrated the fallacy of efforts by both contemporaries and historians to cabin American federalism into a matched pair of compartments labeled "federal" and "state." *Miln* both described and gave normative weight to a different version of federalism. The world of *Miln*—in its facts, the arguments of the lawyers, and the Court's eventual, tortured holding—was inescapably a world of jurisdictional multiplicity. The "Mayor, Aldermen, and Commonalty of the City of New York" were the plaintiffs and the primary drivers of the action against the *Emily*. On the other side, meanwhile, was a merchant who was better connected than he initially appeared. In the background were a host of other governmental actors, all with good claims of authority over the port of New York City: other municipal officials; federal customs officers in the port with a long history of extending loans to local merchants at the United States' expense; a Treasury Department newly intent on reforming the nation's customshouses; and a president, Jackson, who used rotation of federal office (also known as patronage or the spoils system) as a tool of both reform and control.[9]

The central conflict in *Miln* might at first appear as simply another in a long train of clashes between a state and the federal government. On this view, even the combatants seem familiar: the state of New York versus the federal government. Indeed, the same year that the New York legislature passed the Passenger Act had also witnessed the Marshall Court's monumental decision in another case involving waterborne transportation around New York City, the "great steamboat case" of *Gibbons v. Ogden*.[10] In *Gibbons*, the Court held that a different New York statute—one granting a monopoly over steamboat travel on the Hudson River—conflicted with Congress's exercise of its commerce power in the federal coasting statute of 1793.[11]

Yet as Chapter 3 argued, *Gibbons* must be understood not only as a contest between state and federal power, but as a well-funded, hard-fought, high-pro-file installment in a longer debate about the meaning of the federal Union it-self. The central question for nearly everyone involved in *Gibbons* concerned the nature of the Union: For what purpose did the Union exist, if not to har-monize and oversee the Commerce of the Union? Lawyers and commentators frequently cited the example of the British Empire and its series of Navigation Acts. The meaning of federal union was underspecified and contested, and the scope of the federal government's powers were therefore also subject to de-bate. But if a union served any useful purpose, surely a central aim was to make commerce—"intercourse," to use the term Attorney General Wirt sup-plied during oral arguments before the Marshall Court—function smoothly. Commerce "always implies intercommunication and intercourse," Wirt main-tained. "This is the sense in which the constitution uses it; and the great na-tional object was, to regulate the terms on which intercourse between foreigners and this country, and between the different States of the Union, should be carried on."[12] The Union was *for* commerce; therefore, the Union in some sense *was* commerce.

Of course, not all commercial activity occurred at the level of the union, a point that occupied many hours of the *Gibbons* advocates' declamatory rock-etry. As Emmet, one of the lawyers for the claimant under the New York mo-nopoly, put it, an "immense mass" of state laws regulated all sorts of activities, from local manufactures to the treatment of indentured servants to the do-mestic slave trade.[13] Local governments had long regulated economic and commercial activities. Such activities might be *commercial*. But were they *Com-merce*? Were they subject to the special regulatory power of Congress acting under Article I, section 8, clause 3—the Commerce Clause?[14]

The connections between *Gibbons* and *Miln* were not accidental. *Gibbons* was understood to be an epochal case at the time it was decided, and it has remained so ever since.[15] Its holding was both monumental and obscure. Had Chief Justice Marshall really pronounced the commerce power to be exclusive in the federal government? Or had he only feinted at that possibility, planting a bit of flickering dicta in a tribute to the oratory of Daniel Webster as well as a signpost marking a genuinely unsettled question?

The *Gibbons* decision answered the question presented: Gibbons could run his steamboats on the Hudson River, despite Ogden's Albany-bestowed mo-nopoly grant. But *Gibbons* said so much more. The opinions of Marshall and his irascible brother justice, William Johnson, along with the arguments of counsel reprinted in the nation's newspapers as well as in the ninth volume of Henry Wheaton's reports, set forth a theory of the Union. The Union and the Commerce of the Union were inextricable and mutually constitutive.

In contrast to the political theory sketched by *Gibbons*, *Miln* was a puzzle requiring canny lawyering and the willingness—or, really, the brazenness—to draw doctrinal lines across broad swaths of submerged murk. The Commerce of the Union was still integral to defining the Union. There was regular commerce going on everywhere in the market-revolutionized republic, and then there was the special "Commerce with Foreign Nations and Tribes and among the States." But by 1837, when the Taney Court finally issued a decision in the case, "commerce" had taken on a more structural, institutionally grounded meaning. Commerce was a type of power that Congress held. It was a tool, a head of lawmaking authority. It was, in short, more instrumental and less existential.

The combination of jurisdictional multiplicity with the commitment to commerce as both a power and an objective of American governments, plural, meant that interbellum constitutional debates were nearly always about commerce and the Union. Moreover, as the Union expanded to include more states and vaster land claims, determining what kind of union the Union was required answering questions about what interstate borders meant and whether they mattered. In particular, the question was: Who had the authority to decide who might enter, who might exit, and what conditions applied for vessels, goods, and—most significantly—persons crossing those borders? By the 1840s, the scale of migration—the sheer number of ships arriving in ports such as New York—compelled jurists, commentators, and politicians to grapple with the many tangled lines of power that met at the nation's docks.

In 1824, the decisive analytical point for the *Gibbons* Court was that the steamboats in question, Thomas Gibbons's *Bellona* and *Stoudinger*, were passenger ships and thus covered by the federal coasting statute.[16] The focus of Marshall's opinion was the ships themselves, rather than the passengers they were carrying back and forth across the New York–New Jersey border. It was a steamboat-level analysis. The several states were but portage points, insular nodes in the continental stream of the Commerce of the Union: "The commerce of the United States with foreign nations is that of the whole United States. Every district has a right to participate in it. The deep streams which penetrate our country in every direction pass through the interior of almost every State in the Union, and furnish the means of exercising this right."[17]

A few years later, the Court took up related questions about the crossing of interstate borders. In *Brown v. Maryland* (1827), the issue was whether Maryland could require a merchant to pay a state license fee in order to sell a package of imported textiles; the Court said that it could not.[18] In *Willson v. Black Bird Creek Marsh Co.*, decided in March 1829—five months before the *Emily* made its manifestless arrival in New York City—the Court held that Delaware could authorize a dam to be built across a "sluggish, reptile stream" even if the dam impinged upon navigation and therefore, arguably, upon the federal commerce power.[19] *Gibbons, Brown,* and *Willson* were foundational decisions about what constituted the Commerce of the Union. Each involved assertions by multiple levels of government of the power to regulate commerce. They also all focused on border crossings by vessels and goods.

A parallel line of cases in the 1820s and 1830s took on the issue of persons crossing borders. As previous chapters have explored, many of these cases came before the justices when they were riding circuit. The justices were thus hearing the cases while physically in the vicinage in which the cases arose, immersed in the many layers of government that clamored for their own rules and powers to apply. In the summer of 1823, Justice William Johnson informed a thronged and stifling courtroom in his hometown of Charleston that South Carolina's Negro Seamen Act was repugnant to not one but two heads of the federal commerce power—the foreign and the interstate commerce clauses.[20] Ranks of governmental actors from the British Foreign Office down to the Charleston harbormaster were involved in the case, as was the South Carolina Association, operating as the litigation arm of the plantocracy. Johnson, himself a slaveowner, nonetheless understood that South Carolina was attempting to wield power far beyond the confines of its supposedly internal affairs.

As the South Carolina case suggests, disputes about persons and goods crossing borders implicated national as well as state boundaries. In 1832, in *Worcester v. Georgia*, the Marshall Court employed another part of the Commerce Clause—the "With the Indian Tribes" head of Congress's power—to hold that Georgia did not have the authority to control who entered the Cherokee Nation or the conduct of persons—even white persons—while there.[21] As we saw in Chapters 6 and 7, Georgia insisted that the fact that the Cherokee Nation was located within the state's territorial boundaries gave the state the authority to regulate persons and activities within the Nation. To permit otherwise would be to allow a nation to exist within a state, which Georgian officials argued would amount to an *imperium in imperio*, or a government within a government.[22]

Worcester is often viewed as a case about the sovereignty of nations. But it was also a case about which level of government possessed the power to regulate the crossing of persons and goods over a particular set of borders. Indeed, it was precisely the radical jurisdictional multiplicity at issue in *Worcester* that raised the fury of Georgia and in turn made it such a controversial case. The Supreme Court of the United States was prepared to uphold the power of the Cherokee Nation to govern who entered its territory, even when the Nation was physically situated largely within the boundaries of Georgia, because the Constitution placed all matters involving commerce with the Indian tribes exclusively within the purview of the federal government. *Worcester*, like *Cherokee Nation v. Georgia* before it, required the Court to articulate the relationship between the Union and its commerce powers. And like the Cherokee cases, *Miln* put the regulation of persons crossing borders at the center of the inquiry.

By the time the Court decided *Miln* in 1837, debates about commerce were increasingly about apportioning control among multiple overlapping jurisdictions. In addition to the existential question—"What is a commercial union?"—lawyers and jurists struggled with a jurisdictional one—"Which governments will regulate in this particular domain?" The controversy centered on which among many contesting levels of government would do the regulating. Interbellum federalism assumed many more levels of government than just the states and the federal government. To overlook this acceptance of jurisdictional multiplicity is to misunderstand the true nature of the debates over commerce in this period.

In keeping with the shift from defining the nature of the Union to apportioning control, the emphasis of the commerce-power inquiry also changed in the 1830s. In *Gibbons*, the lawyers and the justices had sought to define what the Commerce of the Union was. Webster's suggestion that the federal commerce power was exclusive, and Marshall's delphic endorsement of that suggestion, placed "the thing to be regulated"—navigation—in the context of the "uniform whole"—the Commerce of the Union.[23] By the late 1830s, lawyers and judges were less focused on theorizing the nature of the whole Commerce and more on the movement of specific things to be regulated. Ships, passengers, imported goods—all were unquestionably subjects of regulation. But not all of them were "Commerce" in the Article I sense.[24] The immense mass of commercial regulation that had existed in the states, and before that in the colonies, required a more precise definition of which types of commerce belonged to which levels of government. As *Gibbons* had demonstrated, defining the Commerce of the Union was a difficult endeavor. Thus, in the 1830s, the lodestar of judicial federalism shifted from "Commerce" to "articles of commerce."[25] Instead of trying to compass the sun directly, the task became to hunt for evidence of its reflected light.

The Taney Court and Federalism

Contrary to many assumptions, both then and now, the contenders were far more numerous than the simplistic federal-versus-state binary would suggest. Interbellum federalism of the late 1830s was thus fundamentally different from the archetypal federalism of later periods. Yet that latter binary has been retrospectively grafted onto our understandings of the period.

Existing scholarship on *Miln* and the Taney Court's subsequent cases involving the commerce power tends to sound a few repeated themes. One theme, dating back to Taney's appointment as chief justice in 1836, emphasizes the differences between the Marshall Court and the Taney Court to varying degrees. In place of the Marshall Court's nationalism, behold the Taney Court's insistence on states' rights. If Marshall was the Great Chief Justice, the indispensable founding-era jurist, Taney was the crabbed lackey of President Jackson, placed on the Court as a reward for his political loyalty as the Treasury secretary who carried out the president's order to drain the coffers of the Second Bank of the United States. If Marshall embodied the boardinghouse-living, unanimous-opinion-writing, madeira-sipping Court between 1801 and 1835, Taney stood for the fractious, political-wind-minding mediocrity of the Court from 1836 to 1864. The Taney era, in sum, is a study in decline.[26] Even those scholars who question the conventional heroic account of the Marshall Court and its nationalism nonetheless tend to accept the declension narrative of the Taney era.[27]

The other theme in many studies of the Taney Court is, of course, slavery. Chief Justice Taney himself was responsible for the execrable majority opinion in *Dred Scott v. Sandford* (1857), which generations of constitutional scholars have rightly condemned as wrong even on its own terms: wrong on the history, wrong on the law, and wrong in its conception of the judicial role.[28]

Issues concerning slavery, and more broadly race, suffused the Taney Court's jurisprudence—as they had done for the Marshall Court as well. Previous chapters have examined the degree to which controversies concerning race, and specifically the status of Black persons, were at the center of much of the interbellum courts' federalism doctrine. Again, some of the most provocative statements came from the lower federal courts, including the justices sitting on circuit.

Race and slavery were constantly present in the early-nineteenth-century Supreme Court, even when they were not squarely at issue in a given case. The issue of slavery's expansion into new states gained particular salience in the

Roger Brooke Taney, by Jesse H. Whitehurst, ca. 1857. (National
Portrait Gallery, Smithsonian Institution.)

debates surrounding the Missouri Compromise of 1820. Southern sectionalist
ideology gained new converts by raising the specter of a federal government
flush with expanded national power and moving to outlaw slavery in the territories, the District of Columbia, or even the slaveholding states.

In fact the federal government had a decided structural tilt toward the slaveholding South.[29] But the slaveholders were effective conspiracy theorists,
managing to convince many of their contemporaries that any increase in federal power could be hostile toward slavery, even though the slaveholding South
controlled at least two branches of the federal government throughout the

interbellum period. A crucial component of the federal-versus-state binary was thus born in this era.

Many scholars, searching for coherence in the messy federalism jurisprudence of the Taney Court, settle on an explanation that combines two elements: slavery and states' rights.[30] According to one widely held version of this interpretation, the protection of slavery was the objective, and states' rights was the doctrinal pathway to achieve it. As one account puts it, concurrent sovereignty was a "useful strategy" that allowed legal and political actors to "manage the slavery question" while avoiding the vexed issue of federal exclusivity.[31]

At least two problems afflict the argument that the combination of slavery with states' rights provides the sole explanation for the Taney Court's federalism decisions, however. First, states' rights arguments did not necessarily tend in a proslavery direction. On the contrary: the content of states' rights depended on the particular state—and on the wishes of its legislature, courts, and voters. As the next chapter explores, a number of states passed anti-kidnapping statutes that were specifically aimed at protecting Black persons, whether fugitive or free, from being seized and forcibly carried out of the state. Other states went so far as to adopt the language of nullification, arguing that federal officials and even the Supreme Court lacked the power to overturn state-court decisions or to compel state officials to enforce the federal fugitive slave laws. To assume that the argument in *Miln* about whether persons were articles of commerce was really, and only, about whether the federal government would be able to regulate slavery, and further that federal regulation would necessarily involve restriction and limitation, is to insist that the interbellum period was governed by a federal-state federalism binary that did not became dominant until the Civil War.

Second, the numerosity of the justices' opinions, their quarrelsomeness, and their general disagreement even about the relevant terms of the debate in *Miln* and the subsequent cases casts serious doubt on the strong form of the "because of slavery" explanation. The justices and the members of the Supreme Court bar held widely divergent views about crucial issues including whether the commerce power was exclusively federal; the possibility that the states held concurrent power over commerce; the scope of the states' reserved police powers; whether migrants, passengers, indentured servants, and slaves were all similarly situated as subjects of regulation; and even what the ground rules were for lodging a dissenting opinion or communicating directly with the Supreme Court reporter. Some justices owned slaves, while others did not; some justices were from the South, while others were from the Mid-Atlantic,

the Northeast, or the West; and the particular views they held on a given federalism question often did not align with their regional identity or their personal
comfort with purporting to own other human beings.

It is undeniable that issues of race and slavery were inextricably connected
with questions of federalism in the interbellum era. But those connections
were complex and ran in multiple directions. Clearly, it was a horrifically ugly
period of U.S. history in which the majority of white Americans were
apparently able to accommodate themselves to the knowledge that their nation protected and profited from chattel slavery. To recognize this historical
fact does not tell us about the motivations or thought processes of lawyers or
judges. Few people are able to formulate a goal and then structure all their actions in such a way as to bring about that goal.[32] Fewer still are able to carry out
such a project and then leave a reliable trace of it in the records that survive
them. The blunt "because of slavery" argument both proves too much and too
little. Too much because it does not acknowledge the virulent conflict on display among the justices' opinions. Too little because it provides only a static
interpretation, without accounting for the change and common-law development evident in the full sweep of interbellum commerce-power cases.

The three Commerce Clause cases following *Miln*—*Groves v. Slaughter*
(1841), the *License Cases* (1847), and the *Passenger Cases* (1849)—generated a
total of twenty-one opinions. They are, to be sure, nightmarishly baroque in
their doctrinal chopping and parsing, such that they do not lend themselves to
excerpting in constitutional law casebooks. Only *Cooley v. Board of Wardens*
(1852), in which the Court essentially threw up its hands and announced what
commentators too generously term a "pragmatic" standard of "selective exclu-
siveness," tends to deserve a place—albeit in the notes following *Gibbons*.[33]

Miln: A List Not Made and a Case's Circuitous Journey

When Captain Thompson failed to file a report of the *Emily*'s passengers
with New York City officials within twenty-four hours of the ship's arrival on
August 27, 1829, he triggered the penalty provisions of New York State's 1824
Passenger Act. Within a few weeks, the city responded according to the procedures set forth in the statute, by initiating an action of debt in the superior
court for New York City.

The suit was brought in the name of the "Mayor, Aldermen, and Commonalty of the City of New York" and named as defendant George Miln, the consignee of the vessel. The statute permitted the city to choose any or all of a

number of potential defendants: the master or commander of the ship, the owner of the ship, or the consignee. The consignee, sometimes also called the "receiver," was the person or entity who was financially responsible for the cargo—in other words, the buyer. Consignees did not necessarily own the ship, but they were responsible for paying duties on the cargo.

As we saw in the context of Charleston, the consignee played a central role in the world of early-nineteenth-century commerce. Ships such as the *Emily* carried cargo as well as passengers. When the ship arrived in port, U.S. customs officials—the collector of the port and other officers of the federal revenue—inspected the ship, received the required manifest from the captain, and assessed import duties. In an era without a federal income tax, customs duties supplied the bulk of the federal government's revenues. In the period from the nation's founding to the end of the War of 1812, customs proceeds amounted to 86 percent of the federal government's total revenue.[34] The war ended in 1815, but its expenses lingered in the form of a substantial national debt. Under the Monroe and Quincy Adams administrations, the federal government launched new efforts to collect duties at the nation's ports. In 1816, total customs revenues amounted to $36.3 million; in 1825, the total was $20.1 million.[35]

Federal customs officers were among the most visible agents of the federal government in America's port cities. Like the post office and, in some cities, the federal courthouse, the stolid customshouse embodied the authority of the United States. The chief official, the collector of the port, was appointed by the president and charged with enforcing the revenue laws passed by Congress.

Yet customs officers were also deeply enmeshed in local political and economic networks. One of the chief vectors connecting the customs officials of a given port with the merchant population that they were meant to be regulating was the customs duty bond. These bonds allowed importers of goods to collect their merchandise while postponing the payment of duties for a period of time, typically three or six months. They also permitted the collectors to issue loans on behalf of the federal government based on their own authority. The system was an important source of credit for merchants, who relied on the ability to postpone payment on goods they imported and then sold. Markets in the bonds soon developed.

As for the collectors, the bonds were "an important tool with which to negotiate authority among the merchants in their community."[36] The collectors enjoyed a broad ambit of discretion, which they used to extend credit to their merchant associates, a boon from which the collectors could and did profit.[37] The ensuing commercial networks also helped the collectors advance their own economic, political, and social standing in their cities. Early-nineteenth-century American merchants and shipowners were thus accustomed to dealing with the federal government and its officers as a part of their regular cycle of buying, selling, and borrowing against goods and merchandise.

In 1819, the federal government extended its portside reach to cover a new category: passengers.[38] Congress had previously regulated the entry of a range of persons: indentured servants, redemptioners, and, after 1808, enslaved people.[39] The transportation of these individuals was generally regarded as a type of trade, although the terms "migration" and "importation" were sometimes used.[40] But the 1819 act was different. Motivated by concerns about overcrowded ships, Congress created a distinct domain of immigration law— a domain that comprised only voluntary, white migrants.[41] The resulting Act Regulating Passenger Ships and Vessels, known as the "Steerage Act," required the master or captain of any passenger ship arriving in an American port to record, and report to the U.S. secretary of state, the age, sex, occupation, home country, and intended new country of each passenger.[42]

When Captain Thompson submitted a manifest for the *Emily* in New Jersey on August 21, 1829, he was complying with the Steerage Act. The list bore Thompson's attestation that it was "a just and true account of all the passengers received on board the Ship Emily whereof I am Master from Liverpool." It was certified by James Parker, the federally appointed collector of the port of Perth Amboy.[43]

Thompson may have also submitted a similar list to New Jersey, pursuant to state law. State officials did not view the federal passenger act as automatically displacing long-standing state laws regulating the entry and behavior of persons.[44] Many states had passed such laws in the late eighteenth century, and before that time many colonial legislatures had regulated the movements of certain categories of persons, most notably poor people ("paupers," in the terminology of the day), vagrants, and free people of color. Such regulations were understood to be integral to the state's power to regulate the health, safety, and welfare of its people—in other words, its police power.[45]

The police power had long been linked with republican notions of the commonwealth and the public good. But it had also traditionally scrutinized the movement of some persons more than others.[46] It was also notoriously difficult to define. Of the police power, Ernst Freund wrote in his 1904 treatise of that name, "The term police has never been clearly circumscribed." He continued:

"In the decision of the courts we find the term police coupled with internal commerce and domestic trade; health and safety measures are commonly ascribed to it . . . and the general tendency is to identify it with the whole of internal government and sovereignty, and to regard it as an undefined mass of legislation."[47]

Freund's "undefined mass of legislation" echoes the recurring phrase from *Gibbons*, which gained new life in *Miln*: the "immense mass" of state legislation governing commercial activities. Indeed, for the first use of the term "police" as "a division of legislation," Freund cited New York's Revised Statutes of 1829.[48] Thus, in the same year in which the captain of the *Emily* failed to supply the passenger list to New York City officials, the state of New York was growing ever more assertive in claiming the very powers that Captain Thompson seemed to be flouting.[49]

From Castine, Maine, to New Orleans, the port was a site in which many levels of governmental authority came together, made demands of individuals, and sometimes collided. At the port of New York in August 1829, George Miln found himself the defendant in a lawsuit brought by the city and seeking penalties in the amount of fifteen thousand dollars.[50]

But who was George Miln?

Longworth's American Almanac, New-York Register, and City Directory for 1829 contained a listing for "Geo. Miln & Co.," commission merchants. The business was located at 64 Pine Street, between Pearl and William streets—equidistant between the U.S. customshouse to the west and the Tontine Coffee House to the east. If Miln walked past the coffee house and continued two more blocks east, he would arrive at Coffee House Slip on the East River. The directory listed Miln's primary address—presumably his home—as 4 Hamersley Street. (Hamersley Street later became the diagonal western line of Houston Street.) By 1832, Miln had moved his business a few blocks east, to 62 Front Street.[51]

Miln himself was a migrant, and a relatively recent one. Immigration rolls record the arrival in New York City in May 1822 of one George Miln, age twenty-eight, aboard the brig *Resign*. His occupation was listed as "merchant," and he had sailed for America from Greenock in Scotland.[52] Greenock was a port with connections to several cities in the United States, including Charleston, as Chapter 4 discussed. Miln was therefore around thirty-five years old in 1829, when the *Emily* arrived in New York City carrying its hundred-odd passengers and Miln's shipment of goods.[53]

It is difficult, if not impossible, to explain why Captain Thompson did not file the passenger list that New York law required. But when the city looked to extract the statutory penalties, it targeted Miln. This fact suggests that Geo.

Miln & Co. was prospering enough to be worth pursuing for fifteen thousand dollars ($495,200 in today's dollars).

But Miln—or his attorney, Andrew S. Garr, who kept offices at 7 Nassau Street, conveniently located across the street from the federal customshouse—then made a procedural move that had far-reaching consequences for both Miln's case and federalism doctrine. Miln was the defendant, and Miln was apparently still a British subject, which permitted him to remove the case from state court to federal court.[54] Miln's status as an alien permitted him access to the federal circuit court, even though the basis of the case was a state-law cause of action. Indeed, this so-called alienage jurisdiction was one of a very few bases of original jurisdiction in the lower federal courts during this period.[55] If Miln had not been a foreign national but instead a citizen of New York, he would have had no choice but to defend his suit in New York state court. Instead, his trial began in federal court.

The Case

In October 1829, the case of *Mayor of New York v. Miln* came before the U.S. Circuit Court for the Southern District of New York, which was part of the Second Circuit. Hearing *Miln* were U.S. district judge Samuel Rossiter Betts and Associate Justice Smith Thompson. Betts was a Democratic-Republican who had been nominated to the federal bench by President John Quincy Adams in 1826. Thompson was also a Democratic-Republican as well as a close associate of Martin Van Buren, one of the two New York political kingmakers who divided the state between them.[56] (The other was Governor George Clinton, famed as the political force behind the Erie Canal—completed in 1825 and known as "Clinton's Ditch.")

Miln's progress through the courts then seems to have stalled. Having successfully gotten himself into federal court, Miln then demurred to the city's claims—repeatedly. To each of the two counts in the city's declaration, Miln responded that the counts "are not sufficient in law for the said plaintiffs to have or maintain their aforesaid action thereof against him, the said defendant, and that he . . . is not bound by the law of the land to answer the same, and this he is ready to verify; wherefore . . . the said George Miln prays judgment, and that the said plaintiffs may be barred from having or maintaining their aforesaid action thereof against him."[57]

In essence, Miln answered the city's claims by saying that the city had failed to state a claim against him. The city's rejoinder was equally blunt: the mayor, aldermen, and commonalty "say . . . that the said declaration, and the matters therein contained . . . are sufficient in law for them . . . to maintain their afore-said action thereof against him, the said George Miln defendant."[58]

Demurrers were not uncommon in early-nineteenth-century litigation. What followed was less typical, however, and more surprising. The federal circuit court declined to rule on the demurrer. The city had asserted its claims. Miln had said: you have no claim. The city had said: yes, we do. Yet Justice Thompson and Judge Betts seemed unable or unwilling to reach a conclusion. They refused to dispose of the case in October 1829, and they persisted in continuing it on five successive hearings between May 1830 and October 1832.[59] Six times the record reflects a hearing of the case followed by this re-sponse from the judges: "[T]he said court now here are not yet advised what judgment to give of and upon the premises," and a future date was named on which the parties would "hear judgment thereon."[60]

For some reason, the circuit court continued this relatively straightforward case six times between 1829 and 1832. Explaining why judges Thompson and Betts kept *Mayor of New York v. Miln* lingering on the docket for three years is difficult. With such a sparse record, deciding whether Miln was obliged to pay the statutory penalty did not involve gathering additional facts or weighing evidence. Really, it was simply a matter of determining whether the city had stated a claim, since Miln did not dispute that Captain Thompson had failed to submit the passenger list or that he himself had refused to pay the fine.

Suddenly, in October 1832, after three years of delay, there was a develop-ment in the case. After six paragraphs of repetitive demurring, the record of the circuit-court proceedings offered the following startling announcement:

> *The following point was presented on the part of the defendant, viz.*
>
> That the act of the Legislature of the State of New York, mentioned in the plaintiffs' declaration, assumes to regulate trade and commerce be-tween the port of New York and foreign ports, and is unconstitutional and void.[61]

Three years into the litigation, Miln had for the first time raised the consti-tutional issue. New York's Passenger Act was "unconstitutional and void" be-cause it "assume[d] to regulate trade and commerce" among the states and with foreign nations. In terms of constitutional law, Miln had just uttered cru-cial magic words.

No response from the city was recorded. But Miln's invocation of the talis-manic phrase "unconstitutional and void" triggered immediate action from the jurists. Faced with Miln's constitutional argument, Justice Thompson and Judge Betts found that they could not agree on a judgment. They, too, had magic words—procedural words that would pass the case on to be decided by the Supreme Court of the United States. All at once, Thompson and Betts seemed to bestir themselves from their three years of torpor toward *Miln*, to disagree on the constitutional question, and to issue a certificate of division.[62]

Facing the prospect of crushing fines and paying lawyer's fees for the ongoing defense of his suit, Miln nonetheless had demurred repeatedly for three years before raising the constitutional issue and challenging the New York law as an infringement on Congress's commerce power. Marshall had hinted in *Gibbons* that the federal commerce power might be exclusive, but even if it was not, the existence of the federal passenger act of 1819 might have been sufficient for a court to find a collision between state and federal law, and therefore to invalidate the state law. A defendant who wanted the case to disappear would surely have thought it worthwhile to raise the constitutional issue. A defendant who wanted to make a point by taking a test case to the Court would have done so as well. Yet George Miln remained taciturn, issuing demurrer after demurrer until October 1832. Combined with the circuit court's willingness to continue the case, Miln's delay in raising the commerce-power claim is, quite simply, baffling. But the case's slow start—state court, then federal circuit court for three years—suggests that the parties did not initially regard it as an obvious constitutional watershed. In this respect, *Miln* was singularly unlike its in-state predecessor, *Gibbons*. *Miln* became an epochal case after starting its career in decidedly un-epochal trappings.

Miln before the Supreme Court: The Marshall Variations

The federal circuit court's certificate of division had directed that *Miln* be placed on the Supreme Court's docket for the January 1833 term. But in keeping with the case's history of slow movement, it did not come before Marshall and the rest of the Court until the subsequent year. In January 1834, the Court heard arguments in *Miln*. But here again, the progress of the case was blocked by a series of procedural obstacles and staffing problems. At the same time, the constitutional import of the case was becoming clearer, which had the somewhat paradoxical effect of causing Marshall and his fellow justices to slow its process. They could not have anticipated what the result of this strategy would be.

The long-smoldering drama of *Miln* took the stage before the Court on January 23 and 24, 1834. The basement courtroom in the Capitol looked much as it had for the past fifteen years. But the Court's membership had begun to change, between the expected illnesses and deaths as well as the continuation of Andrew Jackson's presidency into a second term. When the arguments in *Miln* began, the Court comprised seven members: Marshall, William Johnson, Gabriel Duvall, Joseph Story, Smith Thompson, John McLean, and Henry Baldwin. McLean and Baldwin had both been appointed by Jackson, in 1829 and 1830, respectively. Only five justices were actually present in the chamber in January 1834, however, for both Johnson and Duvall were absent owing to illness.

As the constitutional stakes of *Miln* had increased, so too had the need for advocates of stature to represent the parties. Two veteran members of the Supreme Court bar appeared: for the city, David B. Ogden; for Miln, Walter Jones. The case was argued over two days, but the account in Peters's reports was thin: a summary of the New York statute; a restatement of Miln's demurrer; and the disputed point on which the circuit court had issued the certificate of division: "That the act of the legislature of the state of New York . . . assumes to regulate trade and commerce between the port of New York and foreign ports, and is unconstitutional and void."[63]

What followed was described as "the opinion of the Court," which Marshall had issued on January 30, six days after the lawyers finished their arguments. But it was less an opinion than a statement by Marshall that he would not be offering an opinion. With respect to *Miln* and the preceding case, *Briscoe v. Bank of Kentucky*, which raised a different constitutional point, Marshall announced:

> The practice of this court is, not (except in cases of absolute necessity) to deliver any judgment in cases where constitutional questions are involved, unless four judges concur in opinion, thus making the decision that of a majority of the whole court. In the present case four judges do not concur in opinion as to the constitutional questions which have been argued. The court therefore directs these cases to be reargued at the next term, under the expectation that a larger number of the judges may then be present.[64]

With these words, Marshall signaled that the Court was divided on the constitutional issues presented by the case. Marshall was citing something more than a simple quorum rule here. Nor was this a predecessor of the modern "rule of four," according to which four justices must agree in order for the Court to grant *certiorari* in a given case. On the contrary: the rule Marshall invoked applied only to constitutional cases, suggesting that fewer justices could capably handle admiralty cases, cases involving ambassadors, and all the other varieties of matters on the docket.

Instead, Marshall was revealing something substantive about the views of the justices. They disagreed. And even he was unable to wield his storied charisma and herd them into unanimity. The seventy-eight-year-old chief justice still appeared remarkably youthful in portraits, but he suffered from kidney stones, despite the excruciating surgery he had undergone two years before at the hands of Dr. Physick.

Marshall likely canvassed his fellow justices for their views on *Miln*. Story agreed with him that the New York law interfered with the federal commerce power, based either on federal exclusivity or on actual collision with Congress's Steerage Act. That made two justices. But the norm as Marshall had stated it required that four justices "concur in opinion . . . as to the constitutional questions which have been argued." The chief justice was apparently unable to marshal the two additional votes he needed. Reading their later opinions retrospectively, one can hypothesize that Thompson (who had already heard the case—repeatedly—on circuit), McLean, and Baldwin were either unsure but inconvincible, or else inclined to uphold the New York law. Faced with this array of opinions with which he disagreed, Marshall joined the pattern of judicial behavior that *Miln* seemed to have elicited for the past five years. He delayed.

The following year, when *Miln* came before the Court again, Marshall's expectation that a larger number of justices would be present proved mistaken. By February 1835, Johnson had died, his seat filled by James Moore Wayne of Georgia. Duvall had resigned and had not yet been replaced. The lawyers in the chamber appeared to understand that something unusual was happening, that the façade of the Marshall Court was cracking, and that questions that would once have been slightly out of order could now be put to the justices. Richard Peters gives the following report:

> Mr Ogden, for The Mayor, &c. of New York; and Mr Wilde, for George Briscoe and others, inquired, if the court had come to a final decision as to the argument of the cases involving constitutional questions at the present term.
>
> Mr. Chief Justice MARSHALL. The court cannot know whether there will be a full court during the term, but as the court is now composed, the constitutional cases will not be taken up.[65]

That was all. Five months later, in July 1835, Marshall was dead. When the Court reconvened in March 1836, Roger Brooke Taney was chief justice. Duvall's seat had been filled by Philip Pendleton Barbour of Virginia. The appointments of both Taney and Barbour were made by President Jackson.

When *Miln* came before the Court yet again, in January 1837, its strange history of interruption and delay was compounded by its uncanny, almost undead quality. *Miln* was one of a trio of cases, along with *Briscoe v. Bank of Kentucky* and *Charles River Bridge v. Warren Bridge*, that had remained in procedural limbo. Marshall's intention had been to postpone the cases to a later term, likely in the hope of bringing his colleagues around to his views. But the result had been that the cases had been argued, debated by the Marshall Court, then reargued (often by an entirely different cast of lawyers), and debated anew by the Taney Court.

Clearly, those earlier arguments had no preclusive effect, and the opinions of the justices of the *ancien régime* of Marshall's era mattered little. And yet the echoes were there, in the chamber and, as became clear, in the official reports of the cases. They haunted the doctrine for more than a decade after *Miln* was decided.

Miln, Decided

When the clerk called the case of *Mayor of New York v. Miln* on January 27, 1837, did anyone flinch or perhaps suppress a sigh? More lawyers were in the Court's chamber this time. For the city, David B. Ogden was joined by a Mr. Blount, whose first name resists strenuous efforts at discovery. Merchant George Miln was represented again by Walter Jones as well as Joseph M. White. Peters prefaced his summary of the lawyers' arguments with the following deceptively anodyne statement: "The case was argued at a former term of this Court, and the justices of the Court being divided in opinion, a re-argument was directed."[66]

The attorneys for the city emphasized three main points in support of the validity of New York's Passenger Act. First, they noted, the states had traditionally and uncontroversially held such powers. Blount cited a lengthy list of regulations that states had routinely passed since the 1780s, with categories including "quarantine laws," "passenger laws," "pilot laws," "wreck laws," "laws relating to coloured passengers and seamen," and "harbour regulations."[67] It was the "immense mass of legislation" argument from *Gibbons* all over again.

Second, the city's lawyers made a categorical claim: the New York law, like the other laws in Blount's list, was "not a commercial regulation in the sense contemplated in the constitution; but a police regulation." Correctly understood, the New York law was "part of the system of poor laws." Blount made the connection to public safety explicit, invoking an array of what his audience would recognize as threats to municipal order: "[T]he law in question is altogether a police regulation: as much so as laws prohibiting entrance into a walled city after dark; laws prohibiting masters from bringing convicts into the state; or the laws prohibiting free negroes from being introduced among slaves."[68]

Each of Blount's examples in this passage concerned persons moving into areas where they were not supposed to be. They also alluded to perils that the police power was intended to address in the specific context of cities and densely populated areas.[69] Entrance into a walled city after dark was clearly such an example, albeit a medieval one. But the reference to "free negroes . . . being introduced among slaves" was also a particular concern for white urbanites. As we have seen, urban slaveholders constantly feared that the proximity between free and enslaved Black people would lead to the fomenting of revolts. In Charleston, for example, where the Vesey conspiracy had unfolded in 1822, slave quarters and work yards were squeezed into city-scaled lots. Kitchens, stables, laundries, and magnolia-planted allées tended by enslaved workers abutted alleyways traversed by free people of color. Port cities, too, were notorious nests of radicalism.[70] The police power was a necessary tool to be wielded by municipal authorities, who understood the special dangers posed by certain groups of mobile individuals.

Finally, the city's lawyers insisted that the power to regulate commerce was not exclusively vested in the federal government but rather was shared by the states. This was again a theory of concurrent commerce power, akin to that offered by the lawyers arguing on behalf of the state grant in *Gibbons* and other previous cases. The key to this argument was that the domain of commerce was shared, or concurrent, between the regulatory authorities of the federal government and those of the state, subject to the limitation that followed from the Supremacy Clause of the Constitution: the state regulation could not interfere with federal power already exercised over the subject in question. With this conceptual ground laid, the city then had to demonstrate that the New York law did not actually conflict with federal law, in particular Congress's passenger act of 1819.

Ogden labored especially hard to show that no such collision existed. Taking "conflict" to mean "incompatibility," Ogden insisted that the laws were compatible and could coexist. "All the provisions of the laws of the United

States are left in full force," Ogden maintained. The New York law merely "superadds other regulations, deemed necessary for the prevention of the introduction of paupers, and to prevent the city being charged with the support of the outcast population of foreign nations."[71] Again, the threat was especially acute for cities.

Ogden also indulged in a bit of overt *ad hominem* nativism against the Scottish-born Miln. "The defendant states himself to be an alien," he observed. "[B]ut it is a fact worthy of notice, that, although a stranger among us, he has undertaken to teach us constitutional law."[72] New York had not been so finicky in its aversion to foreign-born lawyers just thirteen years before. In *Gibbons*, the claimant under the New York monopoly had been represented by Thomas Addis Emmet, a native of Cork, Ireland; a known associate of Irish revolutionaries; a onetime New York attorney general; and later a state judge. In an earlier round of *Miln*, Emmet's son Robert had represented the city before the federal circuit court.

Miln's lawyers, Jones and White, attacked the city's arguments along two main fronts. First, they portrayed the New York Passenger Act as in direct conflict with the federal Steerage Act. Second, they fought back against the city's portrayal of the state law as fundamentally local, aimed at addressing the special problems of cities, and thus following in a long line of police power regulations.[73]

Fundamentally, Miln's lawyers were challenging the city's vision of how jurisdictional multiplicity ought to be applied in this arena. The city insisted that the Passenger Act fit comfortably within the ambit of the municipal level of government. It was a state law designed to give local authorities control over their port—as the refrain of "the mayor, aldermen, and commonalty" suggested. It was about regulating articles of commerce and people in commerce. Miln's attorneys, in contrast, invoked a vision more akin to *Gibbons*'s Commerce of the Union. Jones focused on the impact of the New York law on both interstate and foreign commerce, arguing that it

> interferes with a very important part of the commercial operations of the country; it affects the employment of the ships and vessels of other states, besides those of New York; it goes across the ocean, and interferes there with the operations of packet ships, prescribing the description of persons who may be brought on board of them; and subjecting the masters and owners of the vessels to duties and liabilities, which do not exist under the laws of the United States, and cannot therefore be imposed by a state law.[74]

The state law "affects the navigation of all countries, as connected by their commerce with this country." New York City was not just another port or another town, Miln's lawyers insisted. It was "the great throat of emigration."[75]

Less than three weeks after the *Miln* arguments concluded, on February 16, 1837, the Court handed down its decision. Justice Barbour wrote for the Court, upholding the New York Passenger Act. A state could constitutionally regulate passengers arriving in its ports from out of state or from outside the United States. Justice Story filed a dissenting opinion.

Barbour's opinion avoided the question whether the commerce power was exclusively held by the federal government. Webster's gambit in the *Gibbons* arguments, and Marshall's open-ended musing in his opinion in that case, remained unsettled to dog the doctrine for another fifteen years. Citing the "internal mass of legislation" language that had come from Webster and Wirt's opponents Emmet and Oakley in *Gibbons*, Barbour likened the state law to "[i]nspection laws, quarantine laws, health laws of every description, as well as laws for regulating the internal commerce of a state."[76]

The potential for collision with federal law still might be a concern, but the principal analysis was now to categorize the nature of the power at work. The New York Passenger Act, Barbour wrote, "is not a regulation of commerce, but of police; and . . . being thus considered, it was passed in the exercise of a power which rightfully belonged to the states."[77] The regulation of passengers who had entered New York was a fundamentally internal affair, Barbour insisted. It was not navigation; it was not intercourse; it was not the Commerce of the Union. It was simply the state exercising its long-established customary powers.

The most controversial point of Barbour's opinion was the one that addressed an issue that no one else appeared to have contemplated raising. Barbour argued that the subjects of the New York law were the passengers themselves. Since persons could not be considered articles of commerce, he contended, they could not be reached by the federal commerce power. After comparing *Miln* with *Brown v. Maryland*, in which the Court invalidated a state licensing requirement on the sale of imported cloth because the license interfered with the federal commerce power, Barbour rejected the analogy. In *Brown*, the goods "were the subjects of commerce." That was all well enough for goods, Barbour opined. "But how can this apply to *persons*? They are not the subject of commerce; and, not being *imported goods*, cannot fall within a train of reasoning founded upon the construction of a power given to congress to regulate commerce, and the prohibition to the states from imposing a duty on imported goods."[78]

Barbour's statement appears bizarre to modern eyes. Was it really possible for a justice of the Supreme Court in 1837—one who came from a family of wealthy Virginia slaveowners, no less—to be so amazed that anyone might think that persons were the subjects of trade and commerce?[79] Or was Barbour referring to commerce in its specific constitutional sense, as the commerce that could be regulated by Congress?

Here again, *Miln* stood at the confused nexus among the legal regimes governing slavery, indentured servitude, and immigration.[80] Some scholars regard Barbour's opinion as evidence of the blunt version of the "because of slavery and states' rights" argument. On this understanding, Barbour was perfectly comfortable categorizing enslaved people as subjects to be bought and sold. His view, which he presented as both descriptive and normative, allowed for commerce in persons. But he could not, or would not, make the conceptual move of linking the buying and selling of persons with a constitutionally significant commerce in persons because to do so would be to open the path for federal regulation of slavery and the interstate slave trade. Therefore, he adopted the disorienting and cynical view expressed in *Miln*. Persons were not subjects of commerce, in the constitutional sense. Therefore, federal power did not reach them, and states were free to regulate—and, crucially, exclude—such persons as they saw fit.

Barbour's fellow justices seemed perplexed by his assertion that persons were not subjects of commerce. Thompson, who had heard *Miln* in its many iterations while on circuit, wrote a concurring opinion upholding the New York law as an exercise of concurrent state power over commerce.[81] Thompson also expatiated on the timing, form, and scope of the certificate of division that had brought the case before the Court, a set of topics that he was, of course, uniquely qualified to address.[82]

Story dissented, offering a robust defense of federal power over the Commerce of the Union. He dismissed as "impossible" Thompson's theory of concurrent state and federal power over commerce. Such a view would, Story said, amount to a recognition of "the double operations of distinct and independent sovereignties."[83] Jurisdictional multiplicity was of course a fact of the Union. But "supremacy" and "uniformity" remained Story's watchwords. In case anyone doubted the conviction with which Story held to these principles, he pronounced a closing benediction upon himself: "In this opinion I have the consolation to know that I had the entire concurrence, upon the same grounds, of that great constitutional jurist, the late Mr. Chief Justice Marshall."[84] Not only did Story cite Marshall's support for his own views; Story made so bold as to serve as medium for the late chief justice himself.[85]

Miln was a case about legacies. It was haunted by the arguments, decisions, and possibilities left open by *Gibbons*. It had once been touched by the hand of Marshall, and that hand reached forward, via Story's pen, to visit praise on Story and condemnation on Barbour, Thompson, and the rest of the Court.

Commerce and People, Commerce in People: The Argument Deepens

A dozen years after *Miln* was decided, its legacy remained unsettled. In the *Passenger Cases* of 1849, in which the justices faced an analogous set of state laws known as "alien taxes," the meaning of *Miln*—in particular, how it had or had not changed *Gibbons*—continued to be so unstable that it required a gloss from the Court. In a bravura display of using whatever means were available to criticize colleagues past and present, to cast doubt on the reporting process, and to skewer the Court's internal norms, Justice Wayne unleashed a fusillade of revelations that signaled how deeply divided the Court remained over *Miln*.

In his concurring opinion in the *Passenger Cases*, Wayne announced that at the time of *Miln*, a four-justice majority of what was then a seven-member Court had in fact disagreed with Barbour's view that commerce did not comprehend "the intercourse of persons or passengers." In other words, four justices believed that commerce *did* include persons. Barbour had added that language at the last minute and without adequate consultation, according to Wayne. Four justices had also concluded that the commerce power was exclusive in the federal government. But Peters's report had inadvertently omitted Baldwin's opinion, and Taney had called Wayne's recollections into question. Taking all these circumstances into account, Wayne stated, the putative opinion of the Court in *Miln* was in fact supported by only two votes: Barbour's and Taney's.[86]

Wayne clearly felt that *Miln* had left the doctrine in such disorder that a public clarification was required. "I have made this narrative and explanation, under a solemn conviction of judicial duty, to disabuse the public mind from wrong impressions of what this court did decide in that case," he wrote.[87] It was an astonishing and stark view of the thorny inner workings of the Court. Much had changed since the collegial days of the Marshall Court.

As the lingering aftershocks of *Miln* suggest, the eight-year travails of the case marked a transition between the Marshall and the Taney courts. It was understood to be so by the justices and by the wider public. The next set of cases in which the Court confronted jurisdictional multiplicity through the lens of the commerce power took place against a dramatically different back-drop of politics, war, and foreign affairs.

The Angry Forties

The 1840s were a tortured and tumultuous decade worldwide. Revolutions shook Europe; Karl Marx and Friedrich Engels's *Communist Manifesto* announced a new vision of economics and society; and the crop failures and famine of the "Hungry Forties" ravaged many countries, with the most brutal effects in Ireland. Between 1845 and 1849, the Great Famine and its accompanying diseases killed one million people and drove one million more to emigrate, reducing Ireland's population by between 20 and 25 percent. Large numbers of those migrants took passage to America, especially to New York City and Boston.[88]

Additional upheavals roiled the United States, even as the nation expanded and claimed lands from a variety of other nations, both settler and Indigenous. The annexation of Texas in 1845 placed the issue of slavery's expansion squarely at the center of political debate. President James K. Polk, the hand-picked heir to Andrew Jackson derided as the "dark horse" because of his sudden rise to Democratic Party leadership in 1844, followed his Texas triumph with a war against Mexico that lasted from 1846 to 1848.[89] At the end of these explicitly expansionist efforts, the United States gained control of territory that became the states of Texas, California, Nevada, New Mexico, Arizona, Utah, Washington, and Oregon, in addition to areas later within the states of Oklahoma, Colorado, Kansas, Wyoming, and Montana.

At the outset of the Mexican-American War, Congressman David Wilmot of Pennsylvania had offered on the floor of the House a controversial proposal to ban slavery in lands acquired from Mexico. The Wilmot Proviso, as it became known, was ultimately voted down. But its effects endured for decades. It emboldened antislavery and abolitionist activists, inflamed proslavery forces, split the Democratic Party, and deepened sectional rifts that had just barely been contained by the party system for the past decade. In America, the appetite driving the Hungry Forties was not only that of the working classes for bread but also the keener gnaw of the southern plantocracy for control beyond the boundaries of their own states. They were not unopposed, however. In Rochester, New York, in 1847, Frederick Douglass—recently returned from two years in Britain and Ireland—launched his first abolitionist newspaper, the *North Star*.

The Supreme Court was also in a period of transition in the 1840s. In 1837, at the behest of outgoing president Jackson, Congress added two new circuits to the federal courts and expanded the Court by two seats, for a total of nine justices. Death claimed four of the justices who had decided *Miln*: Barbour in 1841, Thompson in 1843, Baldwin in 1844, and Story in 1845. They were replaced by Peter V. Daniel, Samuel Nelson, Robert C. Grier, and Levi Woodbury, respectively. The two new seats were occupied by a brace of Van Buren appointees: John Catron and John McKinley. Of the bench that had decided *Miln*, only three remained: Taney, McLean, and Wayne.

The *Passenger Cases* were first argued before the Court in 1845, although they had been on the docket since 1843. By the time the Court handed down its decision in 1849, comprising eight separate opinions and no opinion of the Court, much had changed—both in the basement courtroom at the Capitol and in the wider world. The long era of Marshall had receded into the past, and the age of Jackson had been supplanted by a fractured political landscape dotted with Whigs, Free Soilers, and such exotic species as Barnburners, Young Americans, and Know-Nothings. Arguments about commerce were still central to these reframed controversies. Over the course of the decade, however, most of the participants came to abandon any notion of defining and protecting the "Commerce of the Union" as a holistic, normative goal.

Yet several links connected the constitutional and political strife of these "Angry Forties" with the commerce conflicts of the twenties. One such link came in the person of one who exerted a profound influence in both the political and legal spheres, as well as in the executive and legislative branches of the federal government, until his death in 1852: Daniel Webster of Massachusetts.

Webster's career as a lawyer and statesman attracted encomia from many of his contemporaries. He was "the completest man," according to Ralph Waldo Emerson. Other awestruck observers called him "Black Dan," inspired by one of his brooding, tousle-haired portraits, and "Godlike Webster."[90] His 1830 speech in reply to Senator Robert Y. Hayne of South Carolina, in which Webster denounced the doctrine of nullification, has been deemed the most famous speech in the history of the Senate, memorialized in an epic painting, and quoted in generations of schoolhouse recitations: "Liberty *and* Union, now and forever, one and inseparable!"[91]

However robust Webster's defense of the Union, though, its substantive content was elusive. He was a nationalist, but a conservative one.[92] Webster subscribed to a "political religion," as the young lawyer Abraham Lincoln extolled before the Young Men's Lyceum of Springfield, Illinois, in 1838.[93] Unlike Lincoln's faith, however, which centered on "reverence" for "the Constitution and Laws," the focus of Webster's veneration was the Union it-self. The foundation of Webster's political creed was associational, structural, and juridical.[94]

In 1850, twenty years after his 1830 incantation of "Liberty *and* Union," Webster's embrace of the Union reached its apotheosis in his speech before the Senate advocating what became known as the "Compromise of 1850." Ap-pearing before his colleagues "not as a Massachusetts man, nor as a northern man, but as an American, and a member of the Senate of the United States," Webster urged them to support Henry Clay's package of proposed bills, in-cluding a strengthened federal Fugitive Slave Act. Such was the price, Webster argued, of maintaining "that quiet and that harmony which make the bless-ings of this Union so rich and dear to us all."[95] He thus rejected the claims of both the nullifiers and the "abolitionists and fanatics of Massachusetts."[96] In Webster's view, the Union was its own *raison d'être*. It neither had nor wanted any other substantive purpose.

In the two decades between Webster's 1830 and 1850 speeches on the na-ture of the Union, he represented Massachusetts in the Senate, served as sec-retary of state in the Harrison and Tyler administrations, and was a candidate for the presidency. He was also a busy lawyer, especially in the 1840s, when he frequently appeared before the Supreme Court.

Webster never stinted on noting the magnitude of his own activities. In an 1849 letter to a longtime friend, Webster bemoaned the hectic whirl of his days spent thundering before the bar of the Supreme Court and then racing upstairs to the Senate chamber directly above: "I am overwhelmed with labor; obliged to study from five to eleven A.M.; be in court from eleven to three; and all the rest of the day in the Senate till ten o'clock."[97]

In his capacity as a lawyer, Webster was at the center of the Court's Com-merce Clause cases in the 1840s. His contributions to the doctrine were foun-dational, for he had been, in a sense, present at the creation. In *Gibbons* in 1824, Webster had made the far-reaching argument that Congress's power over commerce among the states was exclusive, and therefore that the state could not regulate commerce, even if Congress had not yet acted. The Court, in particular Marshall and—even more—Johnson, were drawn to Webster's argument. But in the end, the Court in *Gibbons* rested its decision on Wirt's more nuanced view of a shared federal-state zone of commerce powers and the presence, however tenuous, of an actual conflict with the federal coasting statute.

Webster, occupied with his work in Congress, did not participate in the commerce cases of the late 1820s. In the decade following *Gibbons*, Wirt was clearly the leading member of the Supreme Court bar on issues pertaining to the federal-state relationship, in particular the three strands of the Commerce Clause: commerce with foreign nations, among the states, and with the Indian tribes. But, as we have seen, Wirt died suddenly in 1834. By 1841, Webster was back before the Court.[98]

Webster's career as a producer of constitutional discourse spanned the interbellum period. He managed to cross the cultural and technological boundary between etched profile portraits and stern daguerreotypes, arguing about and shaping the constitutional law of commerce at several of its most critical moments. Webster's return to dominance as a constitutional lawyer in the 1840s paralleled the return of the interstate commerce power to the forefront of the Court's docket at that time. In *Gibbons*, Webster and Wirt had presented both a sweeping narrative of the commercial Union as well as a set of common-law rules for deciding cases involving jurisdictional multiplicity. *Miln* tested those rules against a robust vision of the police power of the states and municipalities. The *Passenger Cases* applied the stresses of slavery, sectionalism, and foreign immigration to the mix. The 1820s, it turned out, were never dead. They were not even past.[99]

Northern States, Police Powers, and Migrants

The "*Passenger Cases*" was the combined name for a pair of cases from Massachusetts and New York that arrived at the Supreme Court by way of a writ of error to each state's highest court, pursuant to Section 25 of the Judiciary Act of 1789. Throughout the early nineteenth century, Section 25 was buffeted by attacks and repeal efforts led by critics of the Court's power to reverse state court decisions.[100] The cases that constituted the *Passenger Cases* came to the Court from the states: *Norris v. City of Boston* from Massachusetts, and *Smith v. Turner* from New York. They therefore raised both procedural and substantive questions about how interbellum jurisdictional multiplicity would function.

Both the Massachusetts and New York cases involved state laws imposing taxes on passengers arriving by ship, whether from another U.S. state or from a foreign port. Known as "alien taxes," the regulations required the master, owner, or consignee of the ship to pay a set amount per passenger. The New York law specified a tax of $1.25 per steerage passenger arriving from a foreign port, and twenty-five cents per passenger if the ship was a U.S. vessel arriving from a domestic port. The tax was reduced for ships arriving from New Jersey, Connecticut, and Rhode Island. The Massachusetts statute imposed a tax of two dollars per passenger without differentiating between ships arriving from U.S. versus non-U.S. ports.

In both states, the revenues collected from the taxes were to be turned over to the city or town to be used for municipal purposes. In New York, the funds were designated "hospital moneys" to be used by the marine hospital. In Massachusetts, the funds were to be paid into the municipal treasury "to be appropriated as the city or town may direct for the support of foreign paupers."[101] Versions of each state's law had been in effect since the immediate post-Revolutionary period—1788 in New York, and 1789 in Massachusetts.[102]

In subsequent decades, both states added additional requirements for passenger ships. In 1824, the year *Gibbons* was decided, New York enacted the Passenger Act at issue in *Miln*, followed in 1847 by a new bonding requirement. Massachusetts passed its Act Relating to Alien Passengers in 1837, the year *Miln* was decided.[103] State passenger regulations thus arrived in the same years in which the Court decided major Commerce Clause cases touching on immigration.

Some contemporary observers drew parallels between state laws regulating alien passengers and those that policed free Black sailors who arrived in ports such as Charleston, Norfolk, and Savannah. As we have seen, Marshall, writing to Story in 1823, shortly after Johnson's decision in *Elkison v. Deliesseline*, explicitly likened South Carolina's Seamen Act to the Massachusetts passenger acts:

> You have, it is said, some law in Massachusetts not very unlike in principle to that which our brother has declared unconstit[utional]. We have its twin brother in Virginia, and a ca[se was] brought before me in which I might have considered its constitutionality had I chosen to do so; but it was not absolutely necessary, &, as I am not fond of butting against a wall in sport, I escaped on the construction of the act.[104]

The Massachusetts act to which Marshall referred was likely the statute of 1820 titled "An Act to Prevent the Introduction of Paupers, from Foreign Parts or Places." It required shipmasters who arrived at any port or harbor within the Commonwealth to pay a bond to the town for any passengers "landed" who, in the opinion of the selectmen or overseers of the poor, were "liable to become chargeable for their support to the Commonwealth."[105]

As Marshall's comments suggest, he viewed Massachusetts' passenger laws as analogous to South Carolina's and Virginia's Seamen Acts. Each drew on the states' traditional police powers over public health and safety, and each asserted the state's power to regulate its internal affairs, even when such regulation affected individuals who had arrived through the channels of foreign or interstate navigation. Yet Marshall also implied that there was some distinction to be made between the South Carolina law and its "twin brother" in Virginia on one hand, and the "in principle" "not very unlike" law from Massachusetts.

Despite Johnson's and Wirt's judgments that the South Carolina Seamen Act was unconstitutional, officials in Charleston continued to enforce it through the 1830s and 1840s. In 1831 and 1832, Jackson's first and second attorneys general—John M. Berrien and Roger B. Taney, respectively—supplied new opinions in which they reached the opposite decision from Wirt's. A succession of British officials harangued a series of American presidents, secretaries of state, and legislators, exhorting them to intervene to stop South Carolina from seizing Black British sailors.[106] But the Jackson, Van Buren, Tyler, and Polk administrations were unwilling to compel South Carolina to halt enforcement of its laws, despite their obvious interference not only with foreign commerce but also with the executive branch's power over foreign affairs.

In 1844, Massachusetts took direct state-to-state action. The Massachusetts legislature appointed Samuel Hoar, an eminent lawyer known as the "Squire of Concord," as a commissioner to travel to Charleston and bring a case there challenging the seamen laws. If, as was expected, the plaintiff seaman lost, the case could then be appealed (if it originated in federal court) or brought via writ of error (if a state court) to the Supreme Court.[107] Hoar, however, was driven out of Charleston by an angry mob in December 1844. In his subsequent report to the Massachusetts legislature, Hoar inveighed against South Carolina's aggrandizement of its police powers. Now the issue was personal: not only did the state refuse entry to free Black sailors under the guise of maintaining public order, it blocked a white visitor from Massachusetts on the ground that he was a "foreign agent." Did the Constitution have "the least practical validity or binding force in South Carolina?" Hoar demanded. "Are the other States of the Union to be regarded as the conquered provinces of South Carolina?"[108]

Hoar would likely have rejected Marshall's 1823 analogy between the South Carolina Seamen Act and the Massachusetts passenger laws. But as the two states lobbed commissioners, memorials, and rhetoric at each other in the 1840s, certain similarities echoed. Both acts presumed that under certain circumstances, a state could cite its police powers to block entry of a person who had traveled in interstate or foreign commerce.

Webster was skeptical of the validity of the both species of state law. Writing to his junior associate John Plummer Healy in 1845, Webster characterized the Massachusetts license laws as repugnant to acts of Congress and akin to the South Carolina Seamen Act: "Every thing may be said agt. them, which Massachusetts says agt. So. Carolina."[109] The controversies of the 1820s were reverberating, with increasing volume, in the 1840s.

The pair of cases that became the *Passenger Cases* involved ships that had arrived in the ports of Boston and New York City from outside the United States. The question before the Court was the lawfulness of state passenger acts "imposing a tax upon foreigners arriving in a foreign ship from a foreign port."[110] The cases were therefore similar to *Miln*, which had involved a ship from Liverpool arriving in New York City.

Indeed, the Massachusetts case, *Norris v. City of Boston*, arose out of facts that took place four months after *Miln* was decided. The schooner *Union Jack*, out of St. John's, Newfoundland, arrived in Boston in June 1837 with nineteen passengers aboard. The master, James Norris, also hailed from Her Majesty's Province of Lower Canada, for he was a resident of New Brunswick. Norris paid the required thirty-eight dollars in tax to the Boston boarding officer, "under a protest that the exacting [of] the same was illegal" and filed suit in the state court of common pleas to recover the money.[111] After losing in the trial court, Norris appealed to the Massachusetts Supreme Judicial Court, where in November 1842, following a special verdict from the jury, the court upheld the statute and awarded judgment in favor of the city.[112]

The New York case, *Smith v. Turner*, arose four years later and followed similar outlines. George Smith was the master of the British ship *Henry Bliss*, which arrived in New York City from Liverpool in June 1841 with 295 steerage passengers. William Turner, the state-appointed health commissioner of the port of New York, demanded the statutory $295 tax, but Smith refused to pay. Turner brought suit on behalf of the city; Smith demurred; and the Supreme Court of Judicature gave judgment for the city. Smith appealed to the Court for the Trial of Impeachments and Correction of Errors, which affirmed the trial court's judgment in favor of the city, and upholding the statute, in October 1843. The highest courts of both Massachusetts and New York thus upheld their respective states' passenger acts against challenges by the masters of two British vessels.

Both courts cited *Miln* as precedent for their holdings.[113] Yet much had changed in just the six years since *Miln* was decided. The context in which the states' power over passengers operated was undergoing both internal and external transformations. The depths of the Irish Famine were still roughly two years in the future. But another Irish development was spurring migration from Europe to the port cities of America's eastern seaboard. In April 1838, the wooden-hulled sidewheeler *Sirius* arrived in New York after an eighteen-day voyage from Cork City, the world's first westbound Atlantic crossing powered entirely by steam.[114] Sailing ships continued to transport passengers and freight across the ocean, but the advent of steam travel dramatically changed the nature of migration, shortening the trip from Europe to the United States from a minimum of five to six weeks under sail to less than two weeks by steam. Return trips became more feasible, which in turn altered the demography of migration, for example, permitting more single men to migrate temporarily, rather than entire families migrating permanently.[115]

The ongoing battle over the Seamen Acts confirmed that ports were crucial sites at which local, state, federal, and international authority converged and collided. In these arenas, the police powers of states such as Massachusetts and New York were not operating only internally. New York lawmakers, for example, had put into place an array of regulations, including the passenger list requirement in *Miln* and quarantine laws, and established the post of health officer. In contrast to the poor laws, the era's paradigmatic example of police-power regulation, the New York and Massachusetts passenger acts regulated not paupers who were within the polity, but rather passengers who were in the process of arriving in the state by means of navigation. The statutes levied a tax on passengers. That tax was to be paid by the ship masters or their companies. The acts then permitted the shippers to "demand and recover from each person the sum paid on his amount."[116] The effects of this putatively internal regulation would clearly extend outward, to foreign ship captains, the shipping companies, and governments.

Webster's Lawyering

As the controversy over the alien tax laws mounted, Senator Webster appears to have grown increasingly skeptical of the policies of his home state. In January 1839, as the events in the *Passenger Cases* were unfolding in Boston and on the horizon in New York, Webster recorded receipt of a fee for his services as lawyer for the commonwealth of Massachusetts.[117] Six years later, he was at the forefront of constitutional litigation challenging the state's regulations under color of the police power: the passenger taxes, as well as a scheme that licensed and regulated the sale of imported liquor.

His work at the bar of the Supreme Court in the 1840s placed Webster in forceful opposition to the Massachusetts State House on Beacon Hill, which Oliver Wendell Holmes, Sr., soon thereafter deemed "the Hub of the Solar System."[118] Webster was a central figure among Boston's professional and social elite, as well as the confidant of such legal and intellectual luminaries as Story and George Ticknor, the humanist and Harvard professor. Webster was also connected by marriage (his second) to the wealthy LeRoy family of New York merchants and (via his daughter) to the Boston merchant family of Appleton.[119] When he was not in Boston or in Washington, Webster's domain was his 150-acre estate at Marshfield, thirty miles southeast of Boston. In short, Webster was the political and legal leader of the Whig commercial elect of New England. He was also in perpetual need of funds.[120]

The *Passenger Cases* appeared on the Court's docket in 1843 and 1844. But arguments did not begin until December 1845, when the Court finally heard the New York case, *Smith v. Turner*.[121] Webster appeared on behalf of the ship's master, George Smith, who was challenging the state passenger law. The following year, the Court heard arguments in the Massachusetts case, *Norris v. City of Boston*, with Webster and Rufus Choate (who had studied law under Wirt) for that ship's master, James Norris.[122] In 1847 and 1848, both cases were argued before the Court. In total, the *Passenger Cases* were argued on at least four separate occasions across as many Court terms. Four lawyers appeared on behalf of the shippers: Webster, Choate, David B. Ogden, and Jonathan Prescott Hall. Four different lawyers appeared for the states: John Van Buren (son of former president Martin Van Buren) and Willis Hall for New York, and John Davis and George Ashmun for Massachusetts.

The cases mattered to a variety of parties beyond the ship's masters and the municipal and state authorities. The alien taxes potentially affected anyone with an interest in the transatlantic passenger trade. The shipping companies were liable for the taxes and then extracted those amounts from their (often destitute) steerage passengers, many of whom might not be able to afford a higher ticket price. And since most of the affected shipping interests were not American but British companies, the international business community had a stake in the outcome of the cases.

Indeed, British government officials appear to have felt that the passenger taxes endangered their nation's commercial interests. Having failed to stop the legislation, they turned to the courts, occasionally engineering legal challenges to the laws. A short item appeared in newspapers in New York and Washington, D.C., in March 1849, chronicling the involvement of Robert C. Manners,

British vice consul at Boston, in organizing and financing the cases. In 1837, when the Massachusetts legislature began considering the passenger tax, Manners "addressed a protest" to the chairman of the relevant committee, arguing that the act would be "contrary to the Convention existing between the United States and Great Britain."[123]

The legislation was, of course, passed. But Manners continued his fight. He "caused protest to be made, on payment of the tax, denying its constitutionality, and declaring it contrary to existing treaties." The diplomat also took to the courts, working through lawyer Theodore Otis to find plaintiff Captain Norris of the Newfoundland schooner *Union Jack*, "with a stipulation that he (Norris) should be protected against all cost and charges to which the suit might give rise."[124] Norris lost in the trial court and the Supreme Judicial Court of Massachusetts. When the case went up to the U.S. Supreme Court on writ of error, "Daniel Webster was engaged," and he and Choate argued and re-argued the case. Thus, the author of the piece concluded, "for nearly 12 years, Mr. Manners has opposed the tax as unconstitutional, and for nearly ten years has caused it to be litigated." The echoes of South Carolina's Seamen Act are striking. Yet again, an ostensibly local regulation passed pursuant to the state's police power had far-reaching, even transatlantic, consequences.

As the March 1849 newspaper piece noted, while the *Passenger Cases* were pending, "most owners and consignees of emigrant vessels paid the tax under protest."[125] As a result, the shipping interests behind the vessels stood to recover significant sums in damages if they prevailed in their suits. It was an impetus to keep fighting, to employ the best counsel, and to give the lawyers a stake in the recovery.

Here was another key piece of the structure surrounding the *Passenger Cases*. Webster entered into a contingency fee agreement in 1847, and again in 1849, with a group of merchants who combined to retain Webster, pay his and Choate's costs, and tender to Webster a quarter of any amounts recovered. The original subscribers included Harnden & Co., a messenger service operating in the Northeast that had recently begun "importing European laborers for placement in the West," as well as Enoch Train and Samuel S. Lewis, both of whom were also merchants who imported workers from abroad.[126]

The official report of the *Passenger Cases* reveals surprisingly little about what Webster actually said in his arguments before the justices. Reporter Benjamin Chew Howard, faced with eight lawyers arguing over the course of four years, appears to have tossed away his steel pen and abandoned the effort to give anything like a transcript of the case in the order that it unfolded. Instead,

Howard cobbled together an explicitly artificial pastiche, beginning with a summary of each of the two cases and then including selected portions of some but not all of the attorneys' arguments. "It is impossible to report all these arguments," Howard pleaded. "If it were done, these case alone would require a volume." Howard then explained his editorial method with a startling degree of candor: "The Reporter selects such sketches of the arguments as have been kindly furnished to him by the counsel themselves, and omits those for which he would have to rely upon his own notes." Previous reporters had similarly relied on notes provided to them by lawyers after the fact, occasionally giving rise to situations in which one attorney's deadly on-the-spot riposte appeared much less damaging in print because his opponent had doctored the notes he provided to the reporter, such that the printed report showed him anticipating what in the courtroom had taken him by surprise.[127]

Howard printed virtually nothing of Webster's or Choate's arguments, other than a telegraphic three-point list of their principal arguments in the Massachusetts case. Perhaps they had not given him their notes. A few records of Webster's arguments in the *Passenger Case* have survived in newspaper accounts, however.

Webster was extremely voluble in discussing the *Passenger Case* in his private correspondence. In a February 1847 letter to his son Daniel Fletcher Webster (known as Fletcher), Webster was highly critical of the alien tax, the Massachusetts legislature, and the justices of the Court:

> It is strange to me how any Legislature of Massachusetts could pass such a law. In the days of Marshall & Story it could not have stood one moment. The present Judges, I fear, are quite too much inclined to find apologies for irregular & dangerous acts of State Legislation; but whether the law of Massachusetts can stand, even with the advantage of all these predispositions, is doubtful. There is just about an even chance, I think, that it will be pronounced unconstitutional.[128]

Webster was opining that the *Miln* majority—which, as we have seen, was both thin and unstable—was an outlier. Was Webster correct that such a law as the alien tax "could not have stood one moment" in the days of Marshall and Story? Almost certainly, Story (who had died in September 1845) would have found it unconstitutional. Story had, after all, dissented in *Miln*, insisting in that case—which had involved a similar statute—that the recently deceased Marshall had shared his view. Johnson, given his opinion in *Elkison*, would likely have agreed with Story. Indeed, it was Johnson's sweeping decision on the South Carolina law that had prompted Marshall's September 1823 letter to Story. As for Marshall, he himself had noted that he had escaped having to rule on the constitutionality of Virginia's version of the Seamen Act through statutory construction.[129]

Webster continued to air his concerns about the reconstituted Court in his private letters. Writing in December 1847 to Robert Bowne Minturn, a New York merchant and the city's commissioner of immigration, Webster was again certain that the state law—this time, the New York act—ought to be invalidated. He was less certain that the Court would reach what he regarded as the right decision:

> Looking to the case itself, I should say there was little doubt that the New York law would be pronounced to be repugnant to the Constitution of the United States, & therefore void. But when I consider the state of things on the Bench, & the known differences of opinion among the Judges, on all Constitutional questions, I am constrained to regard the result as doubtful.

The actual provisions of the law left little doubt in Webster's mind that the police power justification for the New York law was insufficient. He was convinced that the law was a tax on foreign and interstate commerce, not a regulation in the name of the *salus populi*. Yet he was also a realist. The "state of things on the Bench" and the justices' "known differences of opinion" on "all Constitutional questions" were, to Webster, entirely distinct from the merits of "the case itself."[130]

Throughout the *Passenger Cases*, Webster frequently communicated with the clerk of the Supreme Court, William Thomas Carroll, about the Court's schedule. He also occasionally wrote to friendly justices—McLean, Wayne, and Woodbury—to inquire whether a decision in the case might be forthcoming. At least one such communication took advantage of modern technology. On December 17, 1847, Webster, who had returned north to handle his practice and to tend to his rheumatism, sent a telegram from New York City to Carroll in Washington: "Will the Constitutional case be taken up on Monday answer by telegraph D. Webster."[131] Later that month, the Court again heard arguments in the *Passenger Cases*, for which Webster returned to Washington. But the case was wearing on him. As he wrote to his son Fletcher, "At present, I am quite engaged in these old causes, now on second argument. I am tired of these Constitutional questions. There is no Court for them."[132]

By "[t]here is no Court for them," Webster seems to have been comparing the Court of the late 1840s with that he had argued before in his previous constitutional outings of the 1820s. Sounding a theme that he and Wirt had emphasized in their *Gibbons* arguments twenty-three years previously, Webster criticized New York for forgetting that it owed much of its prosperity to its membership in the Union. Before the Court, Webster argued that New York was "the mere distributing point of the imports of the Union." The ships that arrived in New York Harbor, and from which the state was now collecting significant tax revenue, were there only because the harbor was the mouth of the Commerce of the Union. New York should not be permitted to benefit from accidents of geography to fill its own coffers with the fruits of foreign and interstate commerce. "Unaided by the rest of the Union, New York would be as nothing, a huge deformity, a *caput mortuum* [death's head], and nothing more," Webster insisted before the Court.[133]

Massachusetts also received a lambasting from Webster for its arrogance and selfishness in adopting a passenger tax. In his argument before the Court in the Massachusetts section of the *Passenger Cases*, Webster drew directly from his arguments in *Gibbons*: "Massachusetts has no more right to assess a burden upon commerce in the waters of Massachusetts, geographically speaking, than New Hampshire has; for *Massachusetts has no navigable waters, has no commerce. They are all United States waters, United States commerce.*"[134] Massachusetts had no commerce because the only activity that merited the title of "commerce" was that of the nation as a whole. Webster's "United States commerce" was an invocation of the Commerce of the Union.

The next step in Webster's logic was the principle that commerce—whether interstate, foreign, or with the Indian tribes—was subject to the exclusive power of Congress, not the states. Here Webster returned to his most far-reaching argument in *Gibbons*, without Wirt to temper it and make it palatable to a cautious bench. "This court has decided that Congress possesses the exclusive power to regulate commerce," Webster stated.[135] Marshall had in fact explicitly left this point undecided in *Gibbons*.[136] This post-*Gibbons* uncertainty was evidenced by precisely the train of Commerce Clause litigation that included the *Passenger Cases* themselves. But Webster simply treated Marshall's observation as though it settled the question. For proof of the settlement, Webster cited McLean's concurring opinion six years before, in the 1841 case of *Groves v. Slaughter.*[137]

Commerce-Power Paradoxes

Groves was the case in which Webster had resumed his constitutional practice before the Court. The suit arose out of a Mississippi transaction for the purchase of enslaved people. An 1832 amendment to the state constitution outlawed the introduction of enslaved persons into the state for sale. Webster and his co-counsel, Henry Clay and Walter Jones, represented slave trader Robert Slaughter, who was seeking to recover on notes given in payment by John W. Brown for "a number of slaves" purchased by Brown at Natchez in December 1836. (Moses Groves was one of the endorsers of the notes.)

Webster and his colleagues argued that the Mississippi provision, which had been passed not on the basis of moral qualms but at least in part in order to protect the in-state market in slaves, was void because it conflicted with the exclusive federal power over interstate commerce.[138] The interstate commerce in question was the interstate trade in enslaved people. That trade was undergoing a period of immense profitability in these decades.[139] The fundamental issue at the heart of the case was whether the interstate slave trade was in fact commerce, and therefore subject to congressional regulation, perhaps even exclusive congressional regulation.

Miln had held that persons were not articles of commerce, although as we have seen, that piece of Barbour's *Miln* opinion had been criticized from the moment it was issued. In *Groves*, which was decided four years after *Miln*, the Court dodged the fundamental and difficult issue of whether the commerce power extended to the regulation of the interstate slave trade. In a five-to-two decision, with Thompson writing for the majority, the Court held that the Mississippi constitutional provision was not self-executing. Absent enacting legislation, the provision did not bar the sale of enslaved individuals that gave rise to the dispute.[140] Slave-trader Slaughter could collect payment on the notes, and the Court escaped having to decide whether the Mississippi provision was "repugnant" to the U.S. Constitution—and therefore whether the federal commerce power reached the interstate slave trade.

Unwilling to avoid the deeper issue of the relationship between the commerce power and slavery, however, McLean wrote separately. McLean was a lifelong abolitionist, although his perpetual quest for political office caused some contemporaries as well as later commentators to doubt the sincerity of his convictions. Yet the combination of McLean's western identity, his political calculations, and his staunch Methodism suggests that the Ohio justice did indeed hold strong antislavery views.[141]

In *Groves*, those beliefs led McLean to concur with the majority. In what might appear a paradoxical array of results, the antislavery justice affirmed the circuit court's judgment in favor of Slaughter. McLean's analysis relied on three premises. First, McLean upheld the exclusive nature of the federal commerce power. "In the case of *Gibbons v. Ogden*, this Court decided that the power to regulate commerce is exclusively vested in Congress and that no part of it can be exercised by a state," he wrote.[142] Second, he denied that the federal commerce power applied to the prohibition of the interstate slave trade. Third, he insisted on the "local" nature of slavery regulations, writing, "The power over slavery belongs to the states respectively."[143]

The seeming puzzle is resolved, however, when one attends to McLean's extended discussion of his home state. The Ohio Constitution, McLean noted, "declares that there shall be neither slavery nor involuntary servitude in the state, except for the punishment of crimes." He continued:

> The power vested in Congress to regulate commerce among the several states, was designed to prevent commercial conflicts among them. But, whilst Ohio could not proscribe the productions of the south, nor the fabrics of the north, no one doubts its power to prohibit slavery. And what can more unanswerably establish the doctrine that a state may prohibit slavery, or, in its discretion, regulate it, without trenching upon the commercial power of Congress? . . . Each state has a right to protect itself against the avarice and intrusion of the slave dealer; to guard its citizens against the inconveniences and dangers of a slave population. . . . The right to exercise this power, by a state, is higher and deeper than the Constitution.[144]

McLean's discussion of Ohio laid bare the stakes of the controversy. Marshall's opinion in *Gibbons* had established that the commerce power was exclusive in the federal government. McLean agreed with this, citing "the necessity of a uniform commercial regulation."[145] But he feared the potential result of extending such regulatory power to cover the interstate traffic in enslaved people. Faced with a choice between allowing one slave trader to profit from what McLean regarded as his immoral activities, versus creating a doctrinal pathway for Congress to enact legislation protecting the interstate slave trade, and with it spawning a host of future Slaughters, McLean decided to write an opinion that looked to the future, even if doing so meant handing a victory to the slave trader currently before him.

For McLean and his fellow critics of slavery, the future was marked by fear of the policies that might be enacted by an emboldened general government. Congress, whether with an affirmatively proslavery majority or simply agnostic but compromise-minded, might well decide to pass legislation under the rubric of commerce that would effectively bar states such as Ohio from banning slavery. Federal power was neither necessarily supportive of nor hostile to slavery.

Indeed, many defenders of slavery in this period openly advocated a world of exclusive federal power over commerce. Slaughter's lawyer (and Webster's co-counsel) Henry Clay had offered just such an argument before the Court. The "power, given by the Constitution of the United States, to regulate commerce," was not "one in which the states may participate," Clay insisted. He did not conceal the fact that slaveholding interests believed that they would benefit from exclusive federal control of commerce. On the contrary, Clay presented this allocation of power as both constitutionally required and sectionally preferred, with what he implied was binding effect: "It is exclusive. It is essentially so; *and its existence in this form is most important to the slave-holding states.*"[146]

In contrast, Clay argued, permitting concurrent power over commerce—by allowing the state constitutional provision to invalidate the promissory notes—would amount to endorsing the goals of an increasingly vocal element in American politics, "the abolitionists." The "argument for the plaintiffs in error" that the Mississippi constitutional provision barred repayment of the note, Clay observed, was "on the abolition side of the question."[147] Clay thus aligned arguments for concurrent commerce power—which, ironically, would here have reinforced the authority of a deep southern slave state—with abolitionist sentiment.

Moreover, abolitionists and concurrent-power advocates both misunderstood the nature of the commerce power, Clay suggested. The fundamental purpose of the commerce power was "to regulate commerce; to sustain it, not to annihilate it. It is conservative. Regulation implies continued existence—life, not death; preservation, not annihilation; the unobstructed flow of the stream, not to check or dry up its waters."[148] Clay thus portrayed the slaveholding interests as not only the beneficiaries but the defenders of the Constitution's proper distribution of authority.

The claim that upholding state law amounted to endorsement of abolition is surprising when viewed from the perspective of modern historiographical assumptions about the state-federal binary and the valence of federal power. But opponents of slavery found refuge in state sovereignty. The substantive orientation of federal power depended largely on the preferences of those in control of Congress—preferences which were themselves shaped by structural aspects of the Constitution.

Webster's Strategy

What did Webster hope to accomplish by citing McLean's *Groves v. Slaughter* concurrence in his *Passenger Cases* arguments before the Court in 1847 and 1848?

Webster was attempting several acts of transformation. First, he was recasting *Gibbons* as having held that the commerce power was exclusive in the hands of Congress. Citing *Miln*'s citation of *Gibbons* worked a subtle reinterpretation of the older case while submerging in precedent the fact that any change was taking place. Second, Webster was not only distinguishing *Miln* but sidelining it.

Webster argued that Massachusetts and New York had erroneously read *Miln*. *Miln* "gave rise to the idea that a door had been opened thereby to the States, to enable them to raise revenue out of the exercise of the commercial power." But Webster maintained that this was a misunderstanding of *Miln*. The passenger law upheld in *Miln* "was no regulation of commerce," unlike the Massachusetts and New York alien taxes at issue in the *Passenger Cases*.[149] Rejecting *Miln*'s commerce-person distinction, Webster argued that "it is yet to be proved that a tax on the importation of persons is not a tax on imports."[150] This point was salient because Article I, section 10, of the Constitution prohibited states from "lay[ing] any Imposts or Duties on Imports or Exports, except what may be absolutely necessary for executing [their] inspection Laws."[151] As a category, taxes on imports or exports, aside from those attached to inspection laws, were thus the exclusive purview of Congress. The alien taxes thus ran afoul of two strands of exclusive federal power: the commerce power and the power to regulate imports and exports.

The "Commerce of the Union" vision was back, according to Webster. Shared power over commerce was impossible. "Here are two laws, or systems of laws, over the same subject," Webster maintained. "Are not the objects and ends of the Massachusetts law repugnant to the objects and ends of the laws and Constitution of the United States?"[152]

One year later, in December 1848, Webster made his final argument in the *Passenger Cases*. He wrote to Fletcher that based on his reading of the justices' demeanor, "tho' we shall get 4 Judges, I fear we may not a 5th."[153] The case had finally concluded.

But after such enormous efforts, anxiety for a decision only increased. Webster wrote to McLean with an unsubtle inquiry as to whether a decision might be imminent. "I would stay for the *decision*, if it be likely to come soon, & *to be worth waiting for*," Webster hinted.[154] Six days later, the normally loquacious McLean sent a pithy note that read, in its entirety: "We had no consultation last night. But rest easy. I think there will be a right decision. J McLean."[155]

McLean's reply was cryptic, but Webster appears to have taken it as a statement that the Court had decided the case in favor of his merchant clients and against the states. Upon receiving McLean's letter (on the day it was written), Webster immediately wrote to his friend Edward Curtis, a fellow Whig and the former collector of the port of New York, asking Curtis to help him negotiate a larger retainer from the New York merchants who had engaged him to argue that half of the *Passenger Case*. Webster conveyed McLean's message, without attributing it to him by name: "*We shall succeed in the cause*, as I now believe. If no Judge dies, or is obliged to leave the Bench, within 15 days, the New York judgment will be reversed." Quoting McLean without attribution, Webster wrote, "Today, I am told to 'rest easy.' "[156]

Far from resting easy, however, Webster moved to avail himself of the next wave of legal action: suits to recover damages from the state treasury. As soon as the Court declared the state laws invalid, merchants and others who had paid the statutorily required taxes would be able to take advantage of the preclusive effect of the Court's judgment by bringing suit to recoup those amounts. With large amounts to be paid to the claimants, Webster predicted that "Further professional advice may perhaps be needed, &c. &c." The always-cash-strapped Webster became practical: this was the time to seek "an *enlarged contingency*," he wrote to Curtis.[157]

A few days later, the renewed fee agreement with Webster for the Massachusetts case was signed by nineteen additional subscribers—an enlarged contingency indeed. The new names read as a parade of Bostonian worthies: Wm. Appleton & Co., A. Hemenway, Samuel Fay, and John E. Lodge. All were merchants engaged in the business of importing laborers from Europe.

The triumphant Webster exhorted his Boston associate to visit the subscribers "& bring suits on the *oldest* claims at once, to prevent the running of the Statute."[158] With a favorable decision from the Court imminent, the next step was to file each claimant's suit against the state to recover amounts paid in passenger taxes over the past dozen years. The more the claimants recovered, of course, the more Webster would earn in fees.

McLean's message of January 3, 1849, convinced Webster that he had prevailed, and that the state passenger laws would be invalidated. The Court did not issue its official decision for another month, on February 7. In the intervening weeks, however, the decision in the *Passenger Cases* was an open secret among Court-watchers and in Washington society.[159]

The decision, when it came, was messy. A five-justice majority held that the state alien taxes were unconstitutional. The majority comprised John McLean, James M. Wayne, John Catron, Robert C. Grier, and John McKinley. The four dissenters were Roger Taney, Peter V. Daniel, Levi Woodbury (giving the lie to Webster's earlier hopes), and Samuel Nelson. But there was no opinion for the Court. Instead, there were eight separate opinions. One can imagine Reporter Howard's dismay.

The chaotic nature of the opinions, following on the years of arguments and reshuffling of lawyers, have led many commentators to dismiss the *Passenger Cases* as at best unhelpful, and at worst as evidence of doctrinal confusion and the brute triumph of politics over law.[160] The 290-page case in the seventh volume of Howard's reports resists interpretation. Awash in political and personal squabbling, dishonesty about slavery, doctrinal legerdemain, and pathetic judicial imitation of the glory days of the Marshall Court, the case seems to encapsulate everything that is wrong with antebellum constitutional law. There is no clear rule; that would come—albeit only illusorily—in the 1852 case of *Cooley v. Board of Wardens*.[161]

But this interpretation is wrong. The *Passenger Cases* are complex, frustrating, and at times tedious. But they are an untidily perfect, in the sense of accurate, window into interbellum constitutional debates. There was no bright-line rule because no bright-line rule was possible.

McLean, true to his predictions to Webster and his own concurring opinion in *Groves v. Slaughter*, held that the commerce power was exclusively federal; that the state alien tax laws were regulations of commerce; and that they were therefore invalid. The contested meaning of *Gibbons* received more support as it was recast in doctrine. Wayne's opinion struck many of the same notes. Others in the majority (Catron) emphasized the treaties with Great Britain governing shipping and immigration, as well as Congress's power over naturalization of citizens. Grier seemed particularly aggrieved by the revenue-raising aspect of the passenger taxes.

The dissenters presented a similarly broad array of justifications for the passenger laws. Taney, who wrote to his son-in-law that "this opinion is supposed to be the best I have delivered from the Bench," insisted that the laws were valid exercises of the states' police powers.[162] The states had full authority to exclude any persons that they thought proper, and the Constitution could not compel them otherwise. Taney was clearly mindful of the analogy to the Seamen Acts and the increasingly urgent issue of fugitive slaves. Both points had been raised by the lawyers for the states in the oral arguments.

Massachusetts and New York might have been "northern" states, but the North-South dichotomy did not capture the full complexity of the states' views on their own claims to sovereignty. This complexity was not evidence of confusion, but rather a reflection of the tangled lines of nationalism, states' rights, and slavery in the interbellum era of jurisdictional multiplicity. As Webster's own career demonstrated, neither "northern" nor "nationalist" necessarily equaled "antislavery."

Union and Its Discontents

The year after the *Passenger Cases* were decided, Webster delivered his "Seventh of March" speech in defense of the Compromise of 1850. It was hailed by some observers as yet another magisterial performance by Godlike Webster, holding the Union together against the forces of section. Others, however, castigated Webster for putting the Union above morality, and for clinging to a Constitution that many critics as well as defenders of slavery viewed as enabling the system of human bondage.

Shocked by Webster's full-throated support of the compromise, the poet John Greenleaf Whittier, a Massachusetts Quaker, penned a poem called "Ichabod" (from the Hebrew for "inglorious"). The poem, published in the same year as the compromise, mourned what Whittier regarded as Webster's perfidy. Its final stanzas read:

> Of all we loved and honored, naught
> Save power remains;
> A fallen angel's pride of thought,
> Still strong in chains.
>
> All else is gone; from those great eyes
> The soul has fled:
> When faith is lost, when honor dies,
> The man is dead!
>
> Then, pay the reverence of old days
> To his dead fame;
> Walk backward, with averted gaze,
> And hide the shame![163]

In 1852, Webster sought the Whig Party's nomination for president, but the party selected General Winfield Scott—the hero of the Mexican-American War and the Army official who had overseen the removal of the Cherokees—instead. Webster served as secretary of state in the Fillmore administration until October 1852, when, from a combination of injuries received in a fall from his horse and cirrhosis of the liver, the man was dead.

A Federalism of Jealous States

Despite the efforts of Webster and his fellow compromisers, by 1850 the Union rested on an increasingly thin and fragile foundation. The American union was, in the eyes of contemporaries, decidedly not a nation. It depended for its existence on being something less unified and uniform than a nation. It was an altogether more diffuse and perpetually unbalanced structure.

In contrast to twentieth- and twenty-first-century debates about federalism, for the most part the participants in the interbellum contest over jurisdictional multiplicity were not playing to win control of the center of government. Arguments for states' rights emerged not because the group making them was out of power in Washington. Rather, the ubiquitous invocations of state autonomy, police power, and state boundaries bespoke a general retreat, by all sides, to local redoubts of governmental power. Unlike the modern federal-state dyad, in which a victory for the state peripheries is generally viewed as coming at a cost to the federal center, the mid-interbellum period witnessed a widespread embrace of state power across the entire American landscape. At the same time, fear of one's political and ideological opponents gaining control of the federal government was pervasive, regardless of who was actually in control in Washington.

The result was increased and polyvocal conflict, as different states with distinct ideas and interests clashed with each other over regulatory subjects ranging from immigration to quarantines to liquor to slavery. Massachusetts and New York claimed the power to tax alien migrants; New Hampshire, Rhode Island, and Massachusetts imposed temperance-based liquor restrictions; South Carolina asserted its right to jail free Black seamen; and Virginia prohibited free Black people from taking up residence in the state. All claimed concurrent power to regulate these subjects of commerce and migration. All insisted on a domain of state authority.

The dynamic was reminiscent of the baneful scenes that William Wirt and Thomas Addis Emmet had each sought to conjure in their closing arguments in *Gibbons v. Ogden* in 1824. The acts of retortion and retaliation against New York's steamboat monopoly by neighboring states; the loss of the state's status as the seat of a republican empire of commerce—in *Gibbons*, these were fearsome specters. Two decades later, they appeared to many contemporaries to have come to pass. The hopeful vision of the Commerce of the Union might always have been a naïve illusion. By 1850, however, the Commerce of the Union had been replaced by the many Compromises of the Union—and, to many observers, by a compromised Union.

9 • The Fugitive Slave Laws, States' Rights, and Northern Nullification

A Federalism of Federalisms

If the Sup[reme] C[our]t has the power which it claims, then are
all the rights of the States subordinated to this central Power. I am
disposed to believe that the authors of the Constitution did not
foresee the dilemma presented. . . . God grant that Wisconsin may not
fail to protect her own rights and the rights of her citizens in the
exigency now before her!

—Charles Sumner, 1856

I am for a dissolution of the Union—decidedly for a dissolution of the
Union! Under an abolition President, who would wield the army and
the navy of the Government for the abolition of slavery, I should be for
the union of these States.

—Frederick Douglass, 1860

In a courtroom in the center of a medium-sized American city in the middle of the nineteenth century, an ambitious young lawyer stood up and delivered a paean to the states. "We plant ourselves upon the doctrine of the
sovereignty of the States," he informed his audience. "I do not belong to that
school, of late increasing among us, which seems to teach that the States are
to look up to the Departments of the Federal Government, with all the submis-
sive deference with which a serf is to listen to the commands of his master."[1]

The lawyer's argument was warmly received by the presiding judge. "Without the States there can be no Union," the judge observed in his decision the
following week. "The abrogation of State sovereignty is not a dissolution of the

Union, but an absorption of its elements." Conjuring the specter of a "consolidation," in which the states—"the last hope of free representative federative government"—would be "swallowed up by the Federal Government," the judge satisfied himself that he, at least, had done his part to preserve the "solemn compact" of the Constitution. "I want my skirts to be clear," he noted, so that "posterity may not lay the catastrophe to my charge."[2]

These champions of state sovereignty were not declaiming before a gallery in Charleston or Milledgeville. They did not count the recently deceased John C. Calhoun among their political idols. Nor did they fancy themselves defenders of the planter aristocracy. They were not southerners, and they were not defending slavery. These encomia to states' rights were uttered in a courtroom in Milwaukee, Wisconsin, by attorney Byron Paine and Wisconsin supreme court justice Abram D. Smith.

Between 1854 and 1861, Wisconsin was the site of one of the most remarkable confrontations among federal, state, and local levels of government in the entire interbellum period. The series of events—known variously as the "Glover Rescue," the "Booth War," or by the name of the Supreme Court case that they generated, *Ableman v. Booth*—featured a challenge to the federal Fugitive Slave Law of 1850, a formerly enslaved man's flight to freedom across state and eventually national borders, violent clashes between law-enforcement officials and crowds, round after round of litigation in state and federal court, and the advent of the Republican Party.[3] At each stage, newspapers not only chronicled events but participated in them, helmed as the papers were by editors who were also lawyers, agitators, and parties to the litigation. The political and legal storm that swept Wisconsin did not abate until the eve of the Civil War—and even then one might more accurately say that the swell was only absorbed into an even more toweringly large hurricane.

But here we must be careful not to be carried away by rhetoric or teleology. Histories of American law and politics in the 1850s tend to slide into apocalyptic language and easy presumptions about causation. One begins, in short, to hunt for origins of later-occurring events, and in so doing risks misrecognizing earlier things—actions, words, statements—for their later versions.

The crisis of the 1850s was clearly among the causes of the Civil War. But causation does not run backward. Observers in the 1850s were speaking in and to their own moment. They were not speaking as they did because they knew that a civil war was coming. Therefore, we should not use the Civil War to explain them or their statements.

Commentators living in the 1860s had lived through the 1850s, and the experience of the 1850s shaped their understanding of what followed: secession, war, and, eventually, emancipation. But the experience of the war did not—of course, could not—have shaped understandings of people living in the prior decade. The fact of the war should not be transmuted into an explanation for Senator William H. Seward's warning in 1858 of an "irrepressible conflict" between "antagonistic systems" of free and enslaved labor.[4] Although Seward's admonition reveals the state of mind of some observers in 1858, it should not necessarily guide a later historian's analysis of that moment. The importance of Seward's statement does not depend on the fact of events that took place at Fort Sumter in April 1861. The fact that the conflict came at all, or came when it did, adds a degree of prophecy to his words. But a historian understands that the significance of the words lies in what they say about their own moment.

Similarly, what we take the Civil War to mean now, looking back across a chronology that includes not only the war but Reconstruction, the twentieth-century civil rights movement, and modern reckonings over racial justice, does not necessarily tell us what the war meant at the time.

The crisis that shook Wisconsin and the nation in the 1850s was important because it involved more forceful claims of states' rights and a more effective and consequential demonstration of state nullification of federal law than any previous events in the nation's history. Virtually the entire state government— from the legislature to multiple county sheriffs—resisted federal law. Mass public meetings, newspaper editorials, and broadsides attacked the Fugitive Slave Act, passed by Congress in 1850 as part of the package of legislation known as the "Compromise of 1850."[5] A host of officers of the United States, including marshals, commissioners, and a federal district judge, sought to enforce the law, only to be met with mobs, violence, and breakneck wagon chases through city streets and along rural plank roads. The third paragraph of Wisconsin's constitution, ratified in 1848, prohibited slavery.[6] In the name of this constitution, and of what Byron Paine termed "the doctrine of the sovereignty of the States," not only the state government but the people of Wisconsin themselves denied the authority of the federal government, even defying a unanimous Supreme Court's 1859 decision in *Ableman v. Booth*.

The events surrounding Joshua Glover's escape from bondage, Sherman Booth's prosecution, and Stephen Van Rensselaer Ableman's efforts to enforce his duties as a federal marshal challenge modern notions of federalism and the federal-state relationship. In Wisconsin, the language of interposition and states' rights was invoked not by southerners seeking to insulate their regional political and economic system against a liberty-propagating central government, but rather by the residents of a state that was at the time of its admission the furthest northwest in the Union.[7]

In this way, the controversy in Wisconsin upends many assumptions about how federalism operated in the early-nineteenth-century United States. The seeming inversion of federalism that the *Ableman* events appear to present was in fact yet another illustration of interbellum views of jurisdictional multiplicity. The Wisconsin crisis of the late 1850s illustrates the many varieties of interbellum federalisms, plural. These interbellum federalisms were distinct from the more familiar dualistic opposition between federal and state power that emerged during Reconstruction, and that tends to dominate modern discussions of the concept.[8]

Wisconsinites bridled at the invasion of the territory of their state by what they regarded as an illegitimate exercise of extraterritorial power by other states. Those other states—southern, slaveholding states—had captured the machinery of the federal government and deployed it with increasing vigor over the nineteenth century to ensure that their putatively local, "domestic" institution was protected and projected nationwide. Deemed by contemporaries the "Slave Power" but more aptly termed the "Slavers' Power," this political and economic minority benefited from structural provisions of the U.S. Constitution—in particular, the Three-Fifths Clause; the Fugitive Slave Clause; and the temporary bar on congressional regulation of the interstate slave trade—to consolidate an outsized power over the national government.[9] For many observers in Wisconsin, the problem was that mere sister states—equals in the jurisdictional hierarchy—were arrogating to themselves the power to dictate their own state's internal affairs. The slaveholding interests that had long dominated their own numerous states, with the apparent acquiescence of a large portion of the rest of the American electorate, now seemed to be extending their grasp beyond the boundaries of their own localities and inserting their will into the domain of other states. To the outrage of Wisconsinites, the weapon of this attack was a federal statute. To this invasion they objected.

The allies of Glover and Booth objected not only to the dignitary assault on their state's sovereignty, but to the practical effect of what they regarded as the Slave Power's control of Congress, the presidency, and the Supreme Court. The core of their resistance to federal authority was resistance to "being made SLAVES or SLAVE-CATCHERS, and to having the Free Soil of Wisconsin made the hunting-ground for Human Kidnappers," in the words of a broadside that was widely circulated in Milwaukee in April 1854.[10] The broadside called on residents to attend an "Anti-Slave-Catchers' Mass Convention" at which a "State League" would be formed.

The language was not unlike that we have seen in previous chapters being used by mass gatherings and planters' associations in South Carolina decrying Congress's tariff, or in Georgia denying the Supreme Court's power to recognize Native nations. If anything, Wisconsin's claims were more sweeping, its defiance more absolute. To be sure, Wisconsin's assertions of state sovereignty ultimately put it on the right side of history. But in historical terms, the *Ableman* events demonstrate the capaciousness of interbellum federalisms and the profound appeal of arguments based on the special role of the states—even on the western shores of Lake Michigan, and even on what became the eve of war.

The Ordeal of Joshua Glover, Part I

The individual whose actions launched the crisis in Wisconsin was not a party to any of the ensuing lawsuits. Nor was he present in the jurisdiction when the legal battles over the scope of federal enforcement and the availability of habeas corpus began. His name was Joshua Glover; he was enslaved; and it was his decision to escape bondage that propelled the following events into motion.

In the spring of 1852, Glover, who was in his late thirties to early forties, escaped the three-hundred-acre Missouri plantation of Bennami Stone Garland and traveled north for six or seven weeks, eventually stopping in Racine, Wisconsin.[11] Located at the mouth of the Root River, Racine was a growing harbor town with a population of more than five thousand people, of whom some sixty were defined by the 1850 federal census as "black" or "mulatto."[12] Racine was also famous as a stronghold of antislavery sentiment, much of it carried to the area by settlers from New York and New England whose Congregationalist religion, Whig politics, and reformist embrace of temperance and other social movements inclined them to be hostile to slavery.[13] Glover found work at Rice and Sinclair's lumber mill outside of town, and he rented a cabin near the river from his employers. In addition to his work at the sawmill, Glover became known in the community, in part because he used his carpentry skills to make items that he sold to other residents of Racine.[14]

The new life that Glover had created for himself lasted for only two years, however. On the night of Friday, March 10, 1854, Glover and two friends—

Joshua Glover, the Fugitive Slave.

"Joshua Glover, the Fugitive Slave." From Chauncey C.
Olin, *Reminiscences of the Busy Life of Chauncey C. Olin*, in
A Complete Record of the John Olin Family . . .
(Indianapolis: Baker-Randolph, 1893). (Wisconsin
Historical Society, WHI-6270.)

both of whom were also African American men—were playing cards in Glover's cabin when a group of five white men knocked loudly on the door and were admitted by one of Glover's companions.[15]

The five men were Garland, who had traveled from Missouri to exercise what was known as his "right of recaption"; an officer of the St. Louis police by the surname of "Melvin"; deputy U.S. marshal Charles C. Cotton of Milwaukee; deputy U.S. marshal John Kearney of St. Louis; and a farmer named Daniel F. Houghton who appears to have been a willing participant in many such raids. Garland was armed with a pistol; Cotton wielded handcuffs; and Kearney carried a whip. After a struggle in which Glover was struck in the head

with the handcuffs and the butt of the whip, he was dragged to one of two waiting wagons. His head was bleeding, and he was wearing only thin clothes
against the wet, snowy, late-winter weather.[16]

The Fugitive Slave Legal Complex

As brutal as Garland's capture of Glover was, the proceedings were lawful
under the Fugitive Slave Act of 1850. The act established a federally enforced
process by which slaveowners could recover fugitive slaves, even if those rendition efforts involved following the enslaved person across state lines and
into free states. Fugitives were not permitted to testify or demand a jury trial.
Slaveowners were permitted to bring damages suits against anyone who interfered with rendition, and such persons might also be subject to fines. The act
provided for summary process according to which a "claimant" (the slaveowner) who offered "satisfactory proof" that the person in question was his or
her slave, often after having "seiz[ed] and arrest[ed] such fugitive," would receive a certificate from a federal commissioner that would authorize the slaveowner to remove the fugitive "to the State or Territory from which such
persons may have escaped or fled."[17] The commissioner received a fee for his
services: five dollars for proceedings in which the commissioner determined
that the person in question was not a fugitive, and ten dollars if he ruled in
favor of the claimant.

A previous federal statute, the Fugitive Slave Act of 1793, had contained
similar provisions. But in the 1850 act, Congress added a key element to enable the smooth functioning of the federally supervised rendition process: the
involvement of federal commissioners. Between 1793 and 1850, a number of
states—including Massachusetts and Pennsylvania—passed anti-kidnapping
statutes that were specifically aimed at protecting Black persons, whether fugitive or free, from being seized and forcibly carried out of the state. Some states,
citing their police powers over individuals located within their borders, also
prohibited state officials from carrying out the mandates of the act.

In *Prigg v. Pennsylvania*, decided in 1842, the Supreme Court upheld the
1793 law.[18] Justice Joseph Story wrote that the law was required by the terms of
the Fugitive Slave Clause of Article IV of the Constitution, willfully miscon-
struing the history of the drafting of the Constitution in order to bolster the
claim that adoption of the clause was necessary in order to obtain South Carolina's and Georgia's agreement, and thus enshrining extraterritorial protection of slavery as a fundament of the American constitutional order.[19] Story

held that state personal-liberty laws that thwarted enforcement of the 1793 act were invalid, but he also ruled that state officials could not be forced to aid in the rendition process. Some states interpreted *Prigg* as an invitation to pass laws barring their officials from carrying out the act.[20]

Consequently, in 1850, Congress passed a newly strengthened fugitive slave law. It was one component of the Compromise of 1850, a suite of bills engineered by Senators Henry Clay of Kentucky and Stephen A. Douglas of Illinois. The compromise aimed at tamping down sectional discord primarily by settling the question whether territories acquired in the Mexican-American War would be admitted as free states or slave states, and secondarily by addressing the issues of fugitives and the slave trade in Washington, D.C.[21]

As contemporaries and later observers noted, the "compromise" in fact yielded much to the slaveholding sections of the nation. Its defenders, including Senator Daniel Webster of Massachusetts, portrayed the compromise as the price of preserving the Union.[22] The compromise legislation was opposed by President Zachary Taylor, the "Hero of Buena Vista" whose fame for his victories as a major-general in the Mexican-American War carried him into the White House in the election of 1848. But the term of Taylor, the last representative of the Whig Party to be elected president, proved fleeting when he died suddenly in July 1850. Taylor's successor, Millard Fillmore, supported the compromise, lauding it as "a final settlement" of the sectional disputes surrounding slavery.[23]

When it was enacted in September 1850, the compromise was greeted by a variety of reactions. Reports of crowds huzzahing the salvation of the Union were matched by worries from both northern and southern observers that their respective regions had capitulated.[24] The next two presidents, Democrats Franklin Pierce of New Hampshire (1853–57) and James Buchanan of Pennsylvania (1857–61), made enforcement of the compromise—and in particular, the Fugitive Slave Act—a central policy imperative of both of their administrations.[25]

Unlike the Fugitive Slave Act of 1793, the act of 1850 did not rely on state officials for its enforcement. Its chief innovation was the deployment of federal commissioners as the executive-branch complement to Congress's regulation of fugitives. The post of the federal commissioner predated the Fugitive Slave Act; their duties were "analogous to those performed by local magistrates or justices of the peace for the states."[26] But the 1850 act empowered federal judges, including those operating in the territories, to "enlarge the number of commissioners"—who would have concurrent jurisdiction with district and circuit judges—specifically in order to augment the rendition process.[27] The act's reliance on federal commissioners avoided the problems that Story had identified in his *Prigg* opinion, with state officials refusing to execute, or interfering outright with, the federal fugitive slave laws. Instead, the act established a smooth channel of federal power, from Congress's act to the locally embedded, but—crucially—federally appointed and remunerated, officials on the ground who would enforce it.

To live as a self-emancipated person under the regime of the Fugitive Slave Act was to dwell in constant fear of a knock on the door, even for those who managed to make their way to comparatively friendly locales such as Racine. The extraterritorial reach of the act invited slaveholders and their agents, the notorious slave-catchers, to pursue their human property across state lines and to enlist the support of the federal government to aid them in their claimed "right of recaption." This support came in the form of the commissioners who stood ready to issue certificates of removal, as well as in more immediate assistance from federal marshals from both the slaveholder's home jurisdiction and the locale of their search.

The first case in which a fugitive slave was seized in New England under the act of 1850 was that of Shadrach Minkins. Minkins escaped enslavement in Norfolk, Virginia, and made his way to Boston, where he found a job as a waiter at the Cornhill Coffee House and Tavern on Court Street, in the heart of what was then and still remains the city's financial district. In February 1851, less than a year after Minkins's arrival in Boston, he was arrested at the coffee house by a group of men, led by deputy U.S. marshal Patrick Riley, to whom Minkins had just served coffee.[28] Minkins's captors then forced him to accompany them to the courthouse one block away, where a large crowd had gathered, some of them abolitionists and members of Boston's newly reconstituted Vigilance Committee, and some doubtless simply hoping for a spectacle.[29]

A few days later, when Minkins was present in the courtroom following a hearing, a group of about twenty Black men, led by antislavery activist Lewis Hayden, "raced to where he stood, seized him 'by the collar and feet,' and fled toward the courtroom door."[30] The rescuers overcame two constables and rushed through the doors and out onto Court Square, still dragging Minkins.[31] Witnesses reported that Minkins was battered but defiant during the rescue, declaring, "If I die, I die like a man" and "I will never be a slave."[32] One of Minkins's lawyers, Richard Henry Dana, Jr., characterized the commotion in his journal: "Such Cheers, & shoutings!"[33] Through the efforts of a network of

Black activists, including Hayden and Minkins's lawyer Robert Morris, Minkins was hidden in a series of homes, moving from Boston to Watertown to Cambridge to Concord, then to Leominster in western Massachusetts, and from there north through Quebec.[34] Minkins spent the rest of his life in Montreal, where he owned a number of barbershops and restaurants—one of which he named "Uncle Tom's Cabin"—until his death in 1875.[35]

News of Minkins's sensational "rescue," as it was termed, immediately traveled out over the telegraph wires and gripped the public imagination through extensive reports in newspapers and periodicals. The rescue galvanized both foes and defenders of slavery. Antislavery activists and abolitionists regarded the rescue as an instance in which what Senator William H. Seward of New York praised as "a higher law than the Constitution" prevailed over the terrestrial requirements of the fugitive-slave complex.[36]

Supporters of slavery, however, viewed the rescue as the action of a lawless mob. The rescue of Minkins, as well as other widely reported rescue attempts—not all of them successful—spurred federal officials to greater measures, including mustering larger groups of armed men to surround courtrooms in which rendition proceedings were taking place. In April 1851, also in Boston, another fugitive named Thomas Sims was arrested and brought before Commissioner George T. Curtis—brother of attorney Benjamin Robbins Curtis, who was appointed to the U.S. Supreme Court by President Fillmore five months later. Despite the efforts of his lawyers, Sims was forced to return to Georgia and re-enslaved.[37]

The Ordeal of Joshua Glover, Part II

Despite Boston's distance from both Bennami Garland's farm outside St. Louis and Joshua Glover's shanty near Racine, all the parties to the events that unfolded in Wisconsin in the spring of 1854 were likely aware of the violence, and the potential for freedom or enslavement, surrounding the Minkins and Sims proceedings.

When Garland gathered his group to capture Glover, he had made sure to cloak the raid in all the trappings of legality under federal law. Before setting out for Wisconsin, Garland had appeared before the Court of Common Pleas in St. Louis to obtain a proof of his property in Glover.[38] He then proceeded to Wisconsin, where he conducted some business in Milwaukee. He retained the firm of Arnold and Hamilton as his lawyers, and at their offices at the corner of Water and Wisconsin streets—then, as now, the heart of downtown

Milwaukee—he signed an affidavit stating that he was the owner of Glover.[39] The next stop was the most important: a visit to U.S. district judge Andrew G. Miller, who issued a warrant for Glover's arrest.[40] Having completed the required federal procedures, Garland—along with deputy federal marshal Cotton and St. Louis police officer Melvin, who had traveled north to aid in Glover's capture—proceeded twenty-five miles south to Racine to transform that mundane paperwork into cold bondage.

On the night of Friday, March 10, after Garland and his four-man posse—now including marshal Kearney and citizen Houghton—wrestled the bleeding Glover into a hired wagon, the captors split into two groups. Kearney and Houghton took one wagon and returned to Racine. By that time, word of Glover's capture had reached town—possibly through the efforts of William Alby, one of Glover's card-playing companions, who had fled during the struggle. When they reached the livery stable, Kearney and Houghton were met by a group of citizens that included the sheriff of Racine County, Timothy D. Morris. Morris questioned Kearney and Houghton and, apparently unsatisfied with their responses, arrested them on suspicion of kidnapping, assault, and battery.[41] A Wisconsin state official thus arrested a federal marshal and a citizen (who might have been acting as his assistant) on state-law charges, despite the fact that the marshal claimed that his actions were authorized by a warrant issued by a federal judge.

The other wagon, driven by Garland or Marshal Cotton, carried the injured Glover (concealed by a buffalo robe) and, according to some reports, Glover's other companion, Nelson Turner, who at some point exited the wagon.[42] Garland and Cotton then headed north. They apparently preferred to drive twenty-five miles through the night to Milwaukee, through March winds blowing off nearby Lake Michigan, rather than lodge Glover in the Racine jail, where the town's prevailing hostility to the Fugitive Slave Act might lead to a rescue attempt.[43] They reached Milwaukee (population twenty thousand in 1850, climbing to forty-five thousand by 1860) at around three in the morning.[44]

News of Glover's arrest had preceded them to Milwaukee, however. Reports of the struggle at Glover's cabin had traveled throughout Racine the night before—from the livery stable to the mill owner to the abolitionist editor of the *Racine Advocate*. The editor, Charles Clement, made sure that an item describing the events appeared in the newspaper's Saturday edition.[45] Even more important, he availed himself of technology to spread the news where it was most needed. The telegraph had reached Wisconsin only seven years before, in 1847.[46] Now Clement used it to send word of Glover's capture up twenty-five

Sherman Booth, n.d. (Wisconsin Historical Society, WHI-9485.)

miles of wire to his colleague and fellow abolitionist Sherman Booth, editor of the *Milwaukee Free Democrat*.

Here enters into the narrative the individual whose name became largely synonymous with the crisis of Wisconsin law and politics in the latter half of the 1850s. Joshua Glover's decision to flee north set events in motion, and Sherman Booth's reaction to those events earned him notoriety, praise, condemnation, and a place in the captions of numerous cases in state and federal court.

Glover's and Booth's paths crossed only briefly, on Saturday, March 11, 1854, in the hours leading up to the melee that engulfed Milwaukee's Courthouse Square that day. They might not have spoken more than a few sentences to each other. But the combined effect of their actions carried ramifications that extended far beyond themselves, throughout Wisconsin and the nation.

Like many of his fellow Wisconsin "old settlers," Booth was originally from New York.[47] Born in 1812 in the town of Davenport in the central part of that state, Booth was drawn to social reform as a young man, becoming an agent of the New York State Temperance Society in 1837, when he was a twenty-five-year-old teacher. A gifted orator, he matriculated at Yale University in 1838, where he supported himself by continuing to work as a teacher.[48] In 1839, during his senior year, Booth was one of a handful of Yale students hired by abolitionists to teach English to the enslaved Africans who had been captured aboard the Spanish ship *Amistad* and then jailed in New Haven.

Booth's family had long held antislavery sentiments, and his experience with the *Amistad* captives appears to have propelled him to become an even stronger critic of slavery. He became a member of the new Liberty Party, which endorsed abolition but distinguished itself from the radical abolitionism of William Lloyd Garrison. The Garrisonians eschewed any participation in the American political process, viewing it as irredeemably tainted by the "pro-slavery, war-sanctioning Constitution of the United States," which they deemed "a covenant with death."[49] In contrast to the Garrisonians' cry of "No Union with Slaveholders," the Liberty Party engaged in the political fray. Booth became the state agent and organizer for the party in Connecticut. In 1848, Booth served as chief secretary for the Liberty Party's convention in Buffalo, which brought the party together with three others (the Conscience Whigs, the New York Barnburners, and the Free Soil Democrats) on a "Free Soil" platform. The Free Soil coalition nominated former president Martin Van Buren and Charles Francis Adams as its candidates for that year's presidential election. The Free Soilers were defeated at the polls, bested by the Whigs' Taylor/Fillmore ticket. But the "free soil, free labor" ideology had deep roots, ultimately becoming the core principle of the Republican Party, which was founded a few years later, in March 1854, in Ripon, Wisconsin—just as the Glover events were unfolding.[50]

Also in 1848, as the Liberty Party was preparing its platform, Sherman Booth left Connecticut and moved to Prairieville (later renamed Waukesha), Wisconsin. There he became the owner and editor of a newspaper called the *American Freeman*. Shortly thereafter, Booth moved himself and the paper to Milwaukee, renaming it first the *Wisconsin Freeman*, and then the *Wisconsin Free Democrat*.

From the standpoint of an individual in Glover's situation, there could have been no better person in the city of Milwaukee than Booth to have received the first word of Glover's capture. By nine o'clock on the morning of Saturday, March 11, Booth was in possession of the telegraphed news from Racine. A commanding man who seemed always to be certain of his mission, Booth then proceeded to the Milwaukee courthouse to demand information from federal officials. Had a fugitive slave indeed been captured in Racine and brought to Milwaukee by wagon, in the dead of night?

At that same moment in Racine, the "largest meeting of citizens ever assembled" there was underway in the town's courthouse square.[51] In keeping with the established custom of interbellum reformers, a committee was formed, and resolutions were drafted. The first two resolutions decried the attack on Glover as "an outrage upon the peaceful rights of this assembly" carried out "without the exhibition of any papers." Glover, they insisted, was entitled to a jury trial. A third resolution, in the name of the citizens of Wisconsin, declared "the Slave-catching law of 1850, disgraceful, and *also repealed.*"[52] A delegation of one hundred men was assembled to travel by steamboat up Lake Michigan to Milwaukee, in the company of Racine sheriff Morris. There, they planned to serve arrest warrants on Garland and Cotton for the assault and battery of Glover.[53]

While the Raciners were steaming northward up the lake, Glover was in a cell in the Milwaukee jail. The jail occupied a wing of the courthouse that dominated the city's main public square. Facing south across Oneida (now Wells) Street and bounded by Jefferson Street on the west and Jackson Street on the east, the courthouse was a low-slung white structure whose squat cupola and pillars suggested Greek Revival pretensions. It housed the U.S. District Court for the District of Wisconsin, the Milwaukee county courts, and the county jail. There was no separate federal jail, a fact that became salient later that day. Multiple layers of government—federal, state, and county—occupied the same physical space. This was the case despite the ostensibly clear channels of federal and state authority that the Fugitive Slave Act had created. The legal structure aimed for separation, but the reality was messiness and overlap.

Booth's efforts to glean information from two federal officials—Deputy Marshal Cotton, who had arrested Booth in Racine the night before, and Judge Miller, who had signed the warrant at slaveholder Garland's request a few days earlier—yielded little. Cotton denied that he had "kidnapped" anyone, and Miller acknowledged only that the warrant had issued.[54]

In the environs of Courthouse Square, Booth encountered General James H. Paine, a leading attorney who, like Garland's lawyers, kept offices near the busy intersection of Water and Wisconsin streets.[55] Paine was also an abolitionist and had been a member of the Ohio Liberty Party. In Ohio, Paine had worked alongside the famed Salmon P. Chase, whose work on behalf of freedom seekers had won him the sobriquet "attorney general for fugitive slaves."[56] Paine had learned that a fugitive slave was being held in the city jail, thus confirming what Booth had read in the Racine telegram.

The lawyer and the editor then joined forces, each according to his profession. Together, Paine and Booth managed to visit Glover in his jail cell. During their interview, Paine took an affidavit from Glover describing the facts of his abduction. Paine then carried the affidavit along with a copy of the federal warrant for Glover's arrest, signed by Judge Miller, to the home of Milwaukee

COUNTY BUILDINGS FROM 1836 TO 1870.
Court House erected in 1836 and donated to the County of Milwaukee by Solomon Juneau

Courthouse Square in Milwaukee. The courthouse is at center, and the jail is visible at right. Henry Seifert and James Lawton, "County Buildings From 1836 to 1870," ca. 1870. (Wisconsin Historical Society, WHI-40833.)

county judge Charles E. Jenkins. There, Paine asked Jenkins for a writ of habeas corpus on behalf of Glover, which Jenkins granted.[57] Jenkins's accompanying order tacitly recognized the many strands of jurisdiction that controlled Glover's situation. The order was directed to the federal marshals who had arrested Glover, and to the county sheriff in whose custody Glover actually was, in the county jail. To add another layer of governmental authority, the city marshal was to serve the order on the federal marshals and the county sheriff.[58]

Booth, meanwhile, called upon his talents as a writer, polemicist, and agitator to spread the news that a fugitive slave was being held in the jail in Courthouse Square. The precise actions he took were disputed by contemporary observers. One fact was certain: Booth returned to the offices of the *Free Democrat* at the corner of Spring Street and West Water Street (now Wisconsin and Plankinton avenues). There, Booth printed sheaves of handbills describing Glover as having been "kidnapped" and local officials as having been "pressed" into doing the federal government's bidding, and calling on his fellow Milwaukeeans to mobilize and to demand a fair trial for Glover.[59]

What happened next was less clear. According to most reports, Booth, Paine, and other leading citizens met in Booth's office. At that meeting, someone reported that the federal proceeding against Glover was scheduled to go forward, despite the state judge's grant of the writ of habeas corpus. Booth and Paine decided to call a public meeting at Courthouse Square. Church bells were rung and handbills were passed out to spread word of the gathering. As part of the mobilization effort, Booth mounted his horse and rode through the streets of the city, shouting. But what did he shout? In his own narrative, published in the *Free Democrat*, Booth said that he cried, "A man's liberty is at stake!" Other accounts had him uttering far more incendiary words, however: "Freemen to the rescue!" or "Ho, to the rescue! Ho, to the rescue!"[60]

In the context of the Fugitive Slave Act, the exhortation "to the rescue" had gained a specific meaning, especially given the rescues and attempted rescues of Minkins, Sims, and others. If Booth had ridden through the streets urging his fellow residents to "rescue" Glover, he risked prosecution under Section 7 of the act, which provided that "any person" who

> shall rescue, or attempt to rescue, such fugitive from service or labor, from the custody of such claimant, his or her agent or attorney, or other person or persons lawfully assisting as aforesaid ... shall, for either of said offences, be subject to a fine not exceeding one thousand dollars, and imprisonment not exceeding six months, ... and shall moreover forfeit and pay, by way of civil damages to the party injured by such illegal conduct, the sum of one thousand dollars for each fugitive so lost as aforesaid.[61]

From this point, events moved increasingly rapidly, filling an already-long Saturday with still more scenes of drama. The tolling of the bells and the distribution of the handbills did their work. By two thirty p.m., the crowd in Courthouse Square numbered between three thousand and five thousand people, according to several estimates.[62] The assembly was a diverse one, including the acting mayor, other city officials, and wealthy merchants, as well as a sizable contingent from Milwaukee's German immigrant population.[63] Speaker after speaker mounted the makeshift rostrum, many of them delivering impromptu lectures on the constitutionality of the Fugitive Slave Act, the writ of habeas corpus, and the right to a jury trial. Votes were taken on a series of resolutions demanding a jury trial and habeas corpus proceedings for Glover and other fugitives.

The committee directing the meeting included Booth; James Paine; Paine's son Byron Paine, a promising young attorney; John Rycraft, a mason and contractor; Dr. Erastus Wolcott, a prominent physician and civic leader; and Abram Henry Bielfeld, a real-estate conveyancer and a leading member of the German community. As in Boston, a "vigilance committee" was formed and charged with ensuring that the mass meeting's resolutions were adhered to by federal and state officials in the city.

And yet the federal officials remained unmoved. Faced with the writ of habeas corpus that had issued from Judge Jenkins of the county court, deputy U.S. marshal Cotton consulted federal judge Miller. Was the federal marshal compelled to take a prisoner held under federal authority before a county judge to justify his detention? The county sheriff, Herman Page, to whom the county judge's writ was also directed, faced a different question. What authority did he have to take a federal prisoner who was physically in the county jail but not technically in county custody before a county judge? Judge Miller advised Cotton to ignore the writ.[64] Cotton did so, but he clearly became concerned about the growing, and increasingly agitated, crowd outside the courthouse. Because Cotton's superior, U.S. marshal Stephen Ableman, was apparently out of the city at the time, another federal official stepped in. John Randolph Sharpstein, the U.S. attorney (or, as the position was then called, district attorney) for Wisconsin, summoned assistance in the form of a federal military battalion. In addition to his duties as U.S. attorney, Sharpstein was, like Booth, a newspaper editor; his paper was the *Milwaukee Daily News*. Someone else—perhaps Sheriff Page—requested the presence of local militia and fire companies. But no military support arrived.

At five o'clock, the tension reached its crest. Word reached the crowd that Judge Miller refused to acknowledge the county-court writs, and that Glover would remain in custody for two more nights before finally receiving a hearing on Monday. A report circulated through the crowd that Miller had said "that the writ of habeas corpus should not be obeyed and that no earthly power should take Glover from the jail before Monday."[65] Some among the throng suspected this was a feint to give the federal authorities an opening to spirit Glover away in the night, sending him back to bondage in Missouri. As the angry murmurs swelled, there was another development. The hundred-person delegation from Racine arrived by steamboat and marched through the streets to the jail while the bells pealed, bearing warrants from the Racine sheriff for the arrest of Garland and Deputy Marshal Cotton.

The infusion of the Racine contingent appears to have reenergized the assembly in the square. Perhaps it provided an excuse to act. Booth addressed the crowd, followed by an abolitionist lawyer named Charles Watkins. Booth "explained to the Racine delegation what had been done and denounced the Fugitive Slave Act. But he cautioned the people against violence." Then Watkins spoke: "Mr. Watkins said it was an outrage to keep Glover in jail over the Sabbath without medical aid, as he had been badly assaulted, maimed, and covered with blood by the cruel treatment of Garland and United States Marshal Cotton; that there were times when the people must take the law into their own hands, but whether the present was such a time the people must judge. He would give no advice on that point."[66]

The vigilance committee then met briefly with the Racine group, at which point "it was decided to report at the American House, take tea and consult as to the best course to be pursued."[67] The American House was a popular hotel on the other (west) side of the Milwaukee River, just over half a mile from Courthouse Square, nearly adjacent to Booth's newspaper office at Spring and West Water streets. It was also, according to the city directory, U.S. marshal Ableman's preferred hostelry when he was visiting Milwaukee from his home near Baraboo, in the town of Ableman, which he had founded.[68]

Some scholars express skepticism toward Booth's and Watkins's intentions here, suggesting that their comments were "self-serving," insofar as they alluded to direct crowd action (namely, breaking Glover out of the jail) but then gave themselves deniability with their disingenuous cautions against violence.[69] Whatever meaning the speakers intended for their words, the crowd evidently heard in them permission to act, in the revolutionary tradition of the "people out of doors."[70] Chauncey Olin, who aided Glover's escape beyond the city limits, later recalled the events:

> [T]he crowd made a rush for the jail. On arriving there, a demand was made for the keys of the jail of the under-sheriff of the jail, S. S. Conover. But the request was denied, whereupon, about twenty strong and resolute men seized a large timber some eight or ten inches square and twenty feet long and went for the jail door; bumb, bumb, bumb, and down came the jail door and out came Glover. About this time the United States Marshal made his appearance on the scene, and a rescue was attempted from those who had Glover in their possession, and for about twenty minutes or half an hour the devil was to pay.[71]

One of the leaders of the group that breached the door of the jail was James Angove, a young carpenter who had recently arrived in Milwaukee from Cornwall, England. Recalling the events several decades later, Angove explained the sudden appearance of the twenty-foot-long timber:

The leaders demanded the keys of the jail, but the jailer refused. The crowd stood still. The lumber for St. John's cathedral, then in process of erection, was all over the street. When the jailer refused the keys, I picked up a six-inch beam and said to the crowd: "Here's a good enough key." In a minute taller men than I had the timber, and made a battering-ram of it, breaking in the door.[72]

The cornerstone of St. John's Cathedral, the seat of the Catholic Diocese of Milwaukee, had been laid in 1847. The cathedral was completed and consecrated in 1853, but as Angove's recollections suggest, building materials were still present on the site. The cathedral still stands on Jackson Street, facing the site of the courthouse where the Glover rescue took place. Courthouse Square is now known as "Cathedral Square."[73]

As they raced away from the courthouse, Glover and his rescuers managed to evade the pursuing federal officials. The rescue party headed west toward the river, "about one thousand people following in the wake," according to one report.[74] Upon reaching East Water Street, the city's main north–south artery, Glover and his companions turned south, presumably aiming for the main roads running out of the city and toward more hospitable precincts. Some accounts report that Glover "doffed his cap" to the crowds and cried, "Glory, Hallelujah!" during the chase, while Booth accompanied the group on horseback as far as the bridge over the Milwaukee River.[75]

As Olin recalled:

Sometimes it seemed as though the marshal and sheriffs' posse would rescue [Glover] from the angry populace, but on they went from Wisconsin street to East Water street, and down East Water street to what was then called Walkers Point bridge, while the crowd was constantly increasing. But the victory was for the rescuers. On arriving at the bridge, John A. Messenger, a Democrat, came along and wanted to know what was up. What was this large crowd in search of, was his inquiry. After being told, he said, Put that man into my buggy, and no quicker said than done, and away he went with the whole posse of the United States Government in his wake.[76]

The "whole posse of the United States Government" was pursuing one fugitive slave, and the people of Wisconsin—including such unlikely accomplices as recent immigrants, members of the bar, and Democrats—were clearly determined to help him escape.

And they succeeded. With the help of the network of abolitionists who ran the Underground Railroad in Wisconsin, Glover traveled from Milwaukee west to Waukesha, then back south to Racine to await safe passage to Canada. By April 19, 1854—forty days after he was arrested—Glover had arrived in Etobicoke, Ontario, a rural town on the outskirts of Toronto that counted some thirty-six Black émigrés from the United States among its population.[77] He found work as an agricultural laborer and rented a house from Thomas Montgomery, an Irishman from County Fermanagh who owned a busy inn that bore his name. Over the next decades, Glover married twice; both of his wives, Ann (who died in 1872) and Mary Ann (who died in 1881), were white Irishwomen.[78] After a conviction for a misdemeanor stabbing of a white man in 1884, Glover served three months in prison, escaping what would likely have been a much harsher penalty without the Montgomery family's assistance in retaining a lawyer and locating witnesses.[79] In June 1888, Glover died in the York County House for the Aged; the death certificate listed his age as eighty-one.[80]

A States' Rights Convention

Through the ructions of March 10 and 11, 1854, a sizable portion of the people of Wisconsin denied the lawfulness of the Fugitive Slave Act through both words and acts: the words of the resolutions adopted by the thousands of people who attended the public meetings in Racine and Wisconsin, and the acts of the individuals who had broken the jail, fought off the federal marshals, and helped Glover escape the city and travel to Canada. More than anyone, Glover had personally thrown off the Fugitive Slave Act's entire regime, denying by his every deed that he was subject to its dictates, ineligible for due process of law, or subject to enslavement.

After the buggy carrying Glover had rattled over the Walker's Point Bridge and out of town, the antislavery people of Milwaukee escalated their campaign against the Fugitive Slave Act. They worked through two channels: the people themselves, in crowds and mass meetings; and the courts, in particular the Wisconsin state courts.

Events occurring beyond Wisconsin in the spring of 1854 added new urgency to the fight. In January of that year, Senator Stephen A. Douglas of Illinois had introduced a bill in Congress proposing to settle the slavery issue once and for all. The Kansas-Nebraska Act, as it became known, overrode the Missouri Compromise of 1820, the previous congressional regulation of slavery in federal territory, which had drawn an east–west line and prohibited slavery to the north of that line. Instead, Douglas extolled the virtues of "popular sovereignty": leaving the slavery issue to the voters of each new state—who were uniformly male and white—as it sought admission to the Union.[81] After weeks of impassioned, vituperative debate in Congress and throughout the nation, and despite a fusillade of attacks from antislavery leaders such as Charles Sumner and Salmon P. Chase, the bill was passed by Congress and scheduled to take effect on May 30, 1854.

With Glover on his way to Canada but the Kansas-Nebraska Act looming, the people of Wisconsin mobilized. As their Revolutionary forbears had done, they adopted the mechanism of the convention. Conventions had long been understood as a political mode through which the people themselves could act outside the established institutions of government. The concept had a long history in American and Anglo-American law and politics, dating at least from the time of the English Civil War, when resistance to the Stuart monarchy had taken the form of conventions of the people, which sometimes produced written resolutions or agreements.[82]

The paragon of conventions for interbellum Americans was, of course, the Constitutional Convention, which had broken outside the dictates of the Articles of Confederation to produce the Constitution. In the early nineteenth century, the rhetorical and ideological weight of the convention made it the favored mode for organizing dissident political views, especially those that sought to resist some particular exercise of authority by the central government. An especially notable recent convention for Americans of the 1850s was the South Carolina nullification convention of November 1832, discussed in Chapter 6, which had declared the federal tariffs of 1828 and 1832 void within the state.

Four weeks after Glover's rescue, in early April 1854, a new wave of handbills and newspaper notices began appearing in Milwaukee. The circulars invited the public to attend an "Anti-Slave-Catchers' Mass Convention" to be held at Young's Hall, one of the city's largest assembly spaces, at the northeast corner of Main Street (now Broadway) and Wisconsin Street. The date of the convention was significant: April 13, the birthday of Thomas Jefferson, which was traditionally celebrated throughout the nation—especially by Democrats—with political gatherings, toasts, and acts of partisan theater that were sometimes scripted, sometimes impromptu.[83] The convention was organized by Booth as well as two other leaders of the public meeting in Courthouse Square: Rufus King, editor of the *Milwaukee Sentinel*, and Erastus Wolcott, the physician who had been elected president of that earlier assembly.

The broadside announcing the convention spoke in explicit terms of state sovereignty and resistance to federal power. Calling on the people of the state who were "opposed to being made SLAVES or SLAVE-CATCHERS, and to having the Free Soil of Wisconsin made the hunting-ground for Human Kidnappers," the notice called for the formation of a "STATE LEAGUE." The purposes of the state league were

> to defend our State Sovereignty, our State Courts, and our State and Na-
> tional Constitutions, against the flagrant usurpations of U.S. Judges,
> Commissioners, and Marshals, and their Attorneys; and to maintain in-
> violate those great Constitutional Safeguards of Freedom—the WRIT OF
> HABEAS CORPUS, and the RIGHT OF TRIAL BY JURY—as old and sacred as
> Constitutional Liberty itself.

The mission of the convention could not have been framed in starker terms. The state league aimed to defend the integrity of the state itself, and of its institutions, by wielding the guarantees of the U.S. Constitution—the frame of the entire federal republic—against the illegitimate exercise of power by the agents of the center. In other words, the antislavery people of Wisconsin were claiming the Constitution on behalf of themselves, their state, and fugitives such as Glover. In so doing, they charged federal officials—the "U.S. Judges, Commissioners, and Marshals"—with abandoning the "great Constitutional Safeguards of Freedom" embodied in the writ of habeas corpus and the jury trial. The convention's organizers also objected to federal authorities' use of Wisconsin as their forum for operating. The rights of those "who are prosecuted, and to be prosecuted in Wisconsin" by the "agents and executors of the Kidnapping Act of 1850" must be protected by the "freemen of Wisconsin," acting in "the spirit of our Revolutionary Fathers."[84]

When the convention met on April 13, its audience included several hundred people, including many from Racine, and many who had traveled as far as one hundred miles to attend the gathering.[85] The attendees began the meeting by appointing officers. Byron Paine, the young lawyer who was the son of General J. H. Paine and who had galvanized the crowd in Courthouse Square on the day of Glover's rescue, was elected secretary of the convention.

The assembly adopted an official statement that charged "the officers of the United States" with attempting "to deprive an inhabitant of this State of his liberty, without a trial by jury," which required "the people to take measures for the protection of their constitutional rights, and to express their opinions concerning the respective powers and duties of the State and National Government."

"Anti-Slave-Catchers' Mass Convention!" handbill, 1854.
(Wisconsin Historical Society, WHI-1928.)

Then, in language that borrowed directly from Madison's and Jefferson's Virginia and Kentucky Resolutions of 1798, the statement laid out its view of the U.S. constitutional structure:

> That we do explicitly and peremptorily declare that we view the powers of the Federal Government as resulting from the compact to which the States are parties; as limited by the plain sense and intention of the instrument constituting that compact; as no further valid than they are authorized by the grants enumerated in that compact; and that in case of a deliberate, palpable, and dangerous exercise of other powers, not granted by the said compact, the States who are the parties thereto have the right, and are in duty bound to interpose for arresting the progress of the evil, and for maintaining, within their respective limits and authorities, rights and liberties appertaining to them.[86]

The Union was a "compact"; the states were the "parties" to that compact; and they were "duty bound to interpose" when their agent—the general government or its officers—threatened the "dangerous exercise" of powers that did not rightfully belong to it. This paragraph was a nearly verbatim quotation from Madison's Virginia Resolution.[87] Booth, Paine, and the other antislavery Wisconsinites were invoking a specific version of the "spirit of our Revolutionary Fathers," one that insisted on a constitutionally required duty of the states to check the federal government. In this respect, they also echoed the arguments of Maria Henrietta Pinckney, who had reminded her audience of her personal connection to the founding generation in order to support her arguments for South Carolinian nullification.

Indeed, the drafters of the convention statement surely understood that the words "compact" and "interpose" had acquired additional layers of meaning in the decades since 1798. In his "Fort Hill Address" of July 1831, Vice President John C. Calhoun—at that point increasingly estranged from President Andrew Jackson over South Carolina's claimed power to nullify federal tariffs—had also cited the Virginia Resolution to support his view of state power. "The great and leading principle," Calhoun wrote, was "that the Constitution of the United States is, in fact, a compact, to which each State is a party . . . and that the several States, or parties, have a right to judge of its infractions." In the event of a "deliberate, palpable, and dangerous exercise of power not delegated," the states had the right "in the last resort, to use the language of the Virginia Resolutions, 'to interpose for arresting the progress of the evil, and for maintaining, within their respective limits, the authorities, rights, and liberties appertaining to them.' "

This right of interposition, thus solemnly asserted by the State of Virginia, be it called what it may—State-right, veto, nullification, or by any other name—I conceive to be the fundamental principle of our system, resting on facts historically as certain as our revolution itself, and deductions as simple and demonstrative as that of any political, or moral truth whatever; and I firmly believe that on its recognition depend the stability and safety of our political institutions.[88]

When the members of the Anti-Slave-Catchers' Mass Convention used the phrase "deliberate, palpable, and dangerous" to describe the powers that the federal government was claiming in the Fugitive Slave Act, they were explicitly borrowing the words of Madison, which they and their audience also recognized as having acquired a more recent gloss from Calhoun.

Yet the members of the Milwaukee convention surely also knew that they were using this language in the service of a project that was anathema to Calhoun: an attack on the constitutionality of the Fugitive Slave Act. Calhoun had died on March 31, 1850; his final speech in the Senate, on March 4, was an attack on the proposed Compromise of 1850. The ailing Calhoun was so weak that his forty-two-page address had to be read aloud by a colleague. In the speech, Calhoun called on "the North" to "do her duty by causing the stipulations relative to fugitive slaves to be faithfully fulfilled—to cease the agitation of the slave question, and to provide for the insertion of a provision in the Constitution, by an amendment, which will restore to the South, in substance, the power she possessed of protecting herself before the equilibrium between the sections was destroyed by the action of this government."[89] Five months later, in September 1850, Congress passed the Compromise of 1850.

The core of the Milwaukee convention's official statement was this provision:

> That the Constitution of the United States contains no express grant of power to Congress to legislate on the subject of reclaiming fugitives from labor, neither is such legislation necessary or proper to carry into execution any express grant, and therefore the act of Congress of 1850, commonly called the Fugitive Slave Law, is unconstitutional and void, and all power to legislate upon that subject rightfully belongs to the states.

The act was "a glaring usurpation of power by the Federal Government," "odious and unjust in its provisions, dangerous to the liberties of the people, and destructive to the sovereignty of the States." Therefore, the statement insisted, "[I]t is the duty of the State Government by all its departments to protect by every legal means, the liberties of its citizens from all encroachments by virtue of said act."[90] This was a call to action, to be sure, but it stopped just short of calling for outright resistance to federal law.

Bolder language characterized the "Declaration of Sentiments" adopted by the convention.[91] The eight provisions of the declaration included a statement that "All persons in the State of Wisconsin, irrespective of birth, condition, or color, are presumed to be free." Another stated, "The Fugitive Slave Act of 1850 is unconstitutional and void," listing three reasons: it exceeded Congress's power; it annulled the writ of habeas corpus; and it abrogated the right of trial by jury.

U.S. district judge Andrew Miller was specifically named and condemned for his actions in Glover's case:

> The refusal of Judge Miller to allow the writ of habeas corpus in favor of Glover to be obeyed by the officers under his control, and his abuse of that writ in discharging Garland from arrest under process from a State court for assault and battery, on the ground that Garland, by virtue of an affidavit that any person was his slave, had a right, with or without process, to seize such person, and use any amount of evidence necessary to subdue him, and make him his slave, furnishes just cause of alarm to the people of this State and deserves their severest condemnation.[92]

Having censured Miller, the Declaration of Sentiments finished by calling upon Wisconsinites to oppose "by all peaceful, legal and constitutional means" the Fugitive Slave Act's "encroachments upon the sovereignty of the State, and the rights and liberties of the people."[93] True to long-standing norms about how conventions operated, the members then charged the people of the state to "meet in their respective localities" and adopt the Declaration of Sentiments. The energy of opposing the Fugitive Slave Act was thus flung outward from Young's Hall, to the people in their localities across the state. Through this centrifugal dynamic, the rights of the state and its people—including individuals such as Glover—would be amassed and defended, and the people would resist being pressed into service as either "slaves" or "slave-catchers."

The Battles of Sherman Booth

Immediately upon Glover's escape from Milwaukee, Sherman Booth took center stage in the controversy, and thus he now does in this narrative. Booth's reformist zeal was accompanied by a self-dramatizing streak that was useful for rallying crowds and turning out polemical copy. He was at times bombastic and self-righteous, and he clearly alienated many of his contemporaries, even some who shared his political opinions.

As Booth was printing and distributing handbills in the streets and address-ing mass gatherings, he was also in court, facing judicial process or bringing his own actions. Over the course of twelve years, from March 11, 1854—the day of Glover's escape—to 1866, Booth was constantly suing, being sued, or both in connection with the events that took place in Courthouse Square.

Booth's legal travails began within days of Glover's rescue. On March 15, 1854, U.S. marshal Stephen Ableman arrested Booth and charged him with "unlawfully aid[ing] and abet[ting] a person named Joshua Glover . . . to es-cape from the lawful custody of Charles C. Cotton, a deputy of the Marshal of the United States for the District of Wisconsin."[94] The U.S. commissioner in Milwaukee, Winfield Smith, also issued warrants for the arrest of others who had been involved in the events at Courthouse Square, including lawyers Charles Watkins and James Paine. Correspondence among U.S. attorney gen-eral Caleb Cushing; Solicitor of the Treasury Farris B. Streeter, who oversaw federal district attorneys throughout the nation; and John Sharpstein, the dis-trict (U.S.) attorney for Wisconsin indicates that the events in Milwaukee had drawn the concern of the Pierce administration.[95] The message was clear: the Fugitive Slave Act would be enforced, and the leaders of the mob would be punished. The federal government was fighting back.

On March 21, 1854, Booth appeared before Winfield Smith, the federal commissioner in Milwaukee. Smith had been appointed to the post of com-missioner by U.S. district judge Miller shortly after Smith had been admitted to the Wisconsin bar in 1850.[96] What might in other circumstances have been a routine preliminary hearing in the commissioner's court quickly escalated to a public spectacle. Booth himself spoke at length, as did his lawyer, James Paine. Sharpstein, representing the federal government, charged Booth with participating in the rescue as part of a riot that had committed acts of vio-lence.[97] Commissioner Smith found probable cause to hold Booth on bail in the amount of two hundred dollars.[98]

This proceeding before the commissioner launched a lengthy series of cases that can be grouped under the heading "the Booth litigation." Although the procedural details were intricate, the overarching themes were relatively straightforward. The federal government, acting through Judge Miller, Com-missioner Smith, Marshal Ableman, and Deputy Marshal Cotton, among oth-ers, charged Booth (among others) with aiding and abetting in the escape of

Glover. Booth sought redress from the Wisconsin state courts, arguing both the process by which he had been haled into federal court was defective, and that the statute under which he was being prosecuted—the Fugitive Slave Act—was unconstitutional. Booth thus sought protection from the state against what he argued was an invalid federal law. In this way, Booth's case was an inversion of prior suits in which an individual sought redress from one government against prosecution by another. In Charleston in 1823, Henry Elkison had turned to the federal courts to challenge his imprisonment under South Carolina's Seamen Act. Now, in 1854, Booth—like Joshua Glover prior to his rescue from jail—attempted the opposite maneuver, calling on the state courts to shield him from federal law.

The river of the Booth litigation also involved a few tributaries: the Wisconsin state-court proceedings against slaveholder Bennami Garland, charging him with assault and battery on Glover; a federal damages suit brought by Garland against Booth, seeking the claimed value of Glover (eighteen hundred dollars) plus expenses, for a total of four thousand dollars; and federal prosecutions of a few other prominent participants in Glover's rescue, including John Rycraft, who was alleged to have helped break down the door of the jail, and John Messenger, who drove Glover across the bridge and out of town in his fleet buggy.[99]

Booth's confrontations with federal authority began with his hearing before Commissioner Smith in March 1854. Two months later, Marshal Ableman detained Booth. Through his lawyer Byron Paine, Booth applied for a writ of habeas corpus to Justice Abram D. Smith of the Wisconsin Supreme Court. Because the court was in its vacation, and Smith was at home in Milwaukee, the arguments were held before Smith alone. This was the proceeding with which this chapter began. "We plant ourselves upon the doctrine of the sovereignty of the States," Paine announced. He then invoked the foundational texts of states' rights doctrine: the Virginia and Kentucky Resolutions and Hayne's portion of the debate with Webster. Paine also reframed several of the U.S. Supreme Court's most pro-Union decisions—*Martin v. Hunter's Lessee, McCulloch v. Maryland, Gibbons v. Ogden*—to support his arguments.[100] Federal district attorney Sharpstein appeared on behalf of the government, citing *Prigg v. Pennsylvania* and the decision of the federal commissioner in the case of the fugitive Thomas Sims to support his argument for the validity of the Fugitive Slave Act.[101]

Just over a week after the hearing, Justice Smith issued his decision in *In re Booth*. Smith held that the warrant under which Booth was held was insufficient, and that the Fugitive Slave Act was unconstitutional.[102] "I solemnly believe that the last hope of free representative federative government rests with the States," Smith wrote. The Constitution "not only confers *powers* upon the Federal Government, but it guaranties *rights* to the States and to the citizens. . . . It is an instrument of grants and covenants." The defect of the Fugitive Slave Act lay in its deprivations of the due process of the alleged fugitive, in violation of the Fifth Amendment to the Constitution: "The law of 1850, by providing for a trial of the constitutional issue, between the *parties* designated thereby, by officers not recognized by any constitution, State or national, is unconstitutional and void." Smith therefore ordered Booth's discharge.[103] One month later, in July 1854, the full Wisconsin Supreme Court heard the case—evidently on Marshal Ableman's motion—and upheld Justice Smith's grant of habeas relief to Booth.[104]

Apparently undaunted, within days of the Supreme Court's decision, Ableman again arrested Booth, this time on a warrant from U.S. district judge Miller, rather than on a warrant from the federal commissioner. Again Booth sought habeas relief from the Wisconsin Supreme Court, this time represented by the elder Paine. But in this case, captioned *Ex parte Booth*, the court declined to grant Booth's petition. The court held that it could not issue a habeas writ on Booth's behalf to the marshal and sheriff. To do so, wrote Chief Justice Edward V. Whiton, would be to interfere with the jurisdiction of the federal court in a pending case. Unlike Booth's previous habeas petition, in which he had challenged the commissioner's warrant, here the jurisdiction of the federal court had already attached, and the state court was barred from issuing its writ. To act otherwise would be to "do an act which would prevent the court of the United States from proceeding to try and determine a case now pending before it, and of which it has exclusive jurisdiction," the chief justice wrote.[105] By issuing the warrant for Booth's arrest, U.S. district judge Miller had effectively blocked the state court from acting. The state courts could only wait for the federal proceedings to run their course.

The friction between the two systems resembled the tense overlap that we have seen in cases such as *Elkison v. Deliesseline* and *Worcester v. Georgia*. Unlike the examples of South Carolina and Georgia, however, the hierarchy here was reversed. The state court was forced to halt and defer to the ongoing federal proceedings.

The weight of the judicial power of the United States continued to press down on Booth. In a pair of federal cases in early 1855, he and Rycraft—who had allegedly battered down the door of the Milwaukee jail—were convicted on charges that they "knowingly and wilfully did aid, abet, and assist one

Joshua Glover to escape from the custody of Charles C. Cotton, then and there being a deputy of the Marshal of the United States for the District of Wisconsin."[106] The cross-system litigation continued when Booth and Rycraft each brought a new habeas petition to the Wisconsin Supreme Court. The federal proceedings having terminated, the state high court this time granted the petitions. The Wisconsin justices held that the federal courts lacked jurisdiction to convict Booth and Rycraft for the common law crimes of aiding, abetting, and assisting the escape of a prisoner.[107]

The dogged interventions of the Wisconsin Supreme Court had not escaped the notice of higher federal authorities. U.S. attorney general Caleb Cushing, acting in accordance with instructions from President Franklin Pierce, undertook to bring the case before the Supreme Court of the United States.[108] In April 1855, the Court issued a writ of error to the Wisconsin Supreme Court for *In re Booth* (the original habeas case) and *In re Booth and Rycraft* (the later habeas case). The Wisconsin Supreme Court, however, returned the writ—and with it the record—in only one of the two cases.[109] To the other case, the state court made no reply. Attorney General Cushing nevertheless "filed a copy of the record" that he had managed to obtain and moved the Supreme Court to docket the case and schedule it for argument.[110]

Writing for the Court, Chief Justice Roger Taney held that the "refusal of the clerk" of the Wisconsin Supreme Court "cannot prevent the exercise of the appellate powers of this court; and the court will take such order in the case, as will enable it to fulfil [sic] the duties imposed upon it." But Taney expressed a desire to proceed cautiously "in a matter of so much gravity and importance." The Court would therefore "lay a rule upon the clerk to make the return required by the writ of error." It was a direct order from the U.S. Supreme Court to the Wisconsin Supreme Court. Taney was essentially giving the state court a final warning, and with it an opportunity to adhere to the usual courtesy of giving the case to the Supreme Court rather than the Court simply taking jurisdiction. "It is therefore ordered, that the clerk of said supreme court of the State of Wisconsin do make due return of the said writ of error, pursuant to the mandate therein contained, and according to the laws of the United States," on or before the first day of the Court's next term, in December 1856.[111]

The Wisconsin court, however, refused to comply with the Supreme Court's order. When the Court ended its next term in March 1857, the new Buchanan administration was unwilling to brook further intransigence from the state. The two Booth cases, with only a copy of the record for one of them, were calendared for the following term.

After additional delay, in part owing to the federal government's efforts to deal with ongoing resistance in Wisconsin, the cases came before the Supreme Court on January 19, 1859. Arguing on behalf of the government was U.S. attorney general Jeremiah Sullivan Black. No counsel appeared for Booth.[112]

On March 7, Taney issued a unanimous opinion for the Court. Unsurprisingly, the decision completely rejected the claims of both Booth and the Wisconsin Supreme Court. A state court had no power to invalidate a federal law as unconstitutional. Moreover, a state court lacked authority to issue a writ of habeas corpus for prisoners held in federal custody. Taney's opinion did not cite a single authority—not even *Martin v. Hunter's Lessee*, which as we have seen, would have provided some of the most forceful language the Court's decisions offered against claims of state power. The position advanced by the Wisconsin Supreme Court, Taney stated, would "subvert the very foundations of this Government."[113] The Fugitive Slave Act, meanwhile, was "in all of its provisions, fully authorized by the Constitution of the United States."[114]

Unacknowledged echoes of *Martin* recurred throughout Taney's opinion. "[T]he supremacy of the State courts over the courts of the United States, in cases arising under the Constitution and laws of the United States, is now for the first time asserted and acted upon in the Supreme Court of a State," the chief justice wrote.[115] But state courts had asserted, or at least tested the possibility of asserting, supremacy over the courts of the United States in a number of cases over the previous half-century. This was the dynamic not only in *Martin*'s confrontation between the Virginia Court of Appeals and the U.S. Supreme Court, but also in the Georgia court's response to Marshall's writ of error in *State v. Tassel* or the Court's decision in *Worcester*, as well as in the South Carolina courts' refusal to be bound by Johnson's circuit-court opinion in *Elkison v. Deliesseline*.

Yet portraying Wisconsin's claims of state sovereignty as novel was essential to the Court's forcefully worded opinion, along with the citation-free flow of language that suggested political theory derived from first principles rather than the chopping of doctrine. Taney and his fellow justices insisted that the "propositions" on which Wisconsin relied were "new in the jurisprudence of the United States, as well as of the States." On this the justices could, apparently, all agree—even across the gulf that separated Taney from Justice John McLean, who had penned a fierce dissent in *Dred Scott v. Sandford* two years earlier.[116] In response to its efforts to adopt the strategy in which South Carolina and Georgia had successfully wrapped themselves, Wisconsin met a unified, univocal wall of judicial supremacy.[117]

The Constitution "contemplates the independence of both governments," wrote Judge William H. Cabell of the Virginia Court of Appeals in 1815. "It must have been foreseen that controversies would sometimes arise as to the boundaries of the two jurisdictions. Yet the constitution has provided no umpire, has erected no tribunal by which they shall be settled."[118]

Lawyer William Wirt and Justice William Johnson had responded by insisting on the need for a "revisionary, superintending power," in Wirt's words.[119]

Now, in 1859, the Court reframed the issue. The question was not whether there was *any* umpire or revising power in the constitutional system. Rather, the question was whether a state could claim that power, and thereby defy the force of the Union—the brittle, compromise-built, eggshell Union. The Court's answer was that a state that did not agree with the Union—a part that dissented from the whole—had no remedy. "[A]lthough the State of Wisconsin is sovereign within its territorial limits to a certain extent, yet that sovereignty is limited and restricted by the Constitution of the United States," Taney maintained. "[T]he sphere of action appropriated to the United States is as far beyond the reach of the judicial process issued by a State judge or a State court, as if the line of division was traced by landmarks and monuments visible to the eye."[120] The judicial power of the United States was strong, but it sat atop an unstable federal structure:

> [I]f the Supreme Court of Wisconsin possessed the power it has exercised in relation to offences against the act of Congress in question, it necessarily follows that they must have the same judicial authority in relation to any other law of the United States, and, consequently, their supervising and controlling power would embrace the whole criminal code of the United States, and extend to offences against our revenue laws, or any other law intended to guard the different departments of the General Government from fraud or violence.[121]

A single state exercising "supervising and controlling power" by deciding what effect federal law would have within its territory was the new solecism, in the eyes of the Court. The content of the specific federal law at issue—the Fugitive Slave Act—was at best irrelevant, at worst essential, to the justices' decision. Moreover, the fact that the state might be claiming not a full-blown right of nullification but only a relatively modest power to allow its judges to issue writs of habeas corpus to persons in federal custody appears not to have mattered to the Court.

The final sentence of the Court's opinion left little room for doubt or discretion: "The judgment of the Supreme Court of Wisconsin must therefore be reversed in each of the cases now before the court."[122] If Booth had hoped for a *Passenger Cases*–style mass of fractured opinions, he would have been sorely disappointed. But Booth, being a provocative sort, nevertheless found ways to use the Court's opinion.

In August 1859, the new federal district attorney for Wisconsin, Don Alonzo Joshua (D. A. J.) Upham, received the Supreme Court's mandates in the Booth cases from U.S. attorney general Black, with orders to present them to the Wisconsin Supreme Court. Upham did so a month later. But the justices of the state high court declined to file the mandates. Booth himself was reindicted and arrested on new federal charges in March 1860.[123] Undeterred, he sought yet another habeas writ from the Wisconsin Supreme Court. The Wisconsin justices split evenly on the question whether Booth was entitled to habeas relief, despite the Supreme Court's ruling. But the result was that no relief was granted to Booth.[124] Five months into his prison term, which he was serving in the newly built federal customshouse in Milwaukee, Booth was forcibly broken out by a group of supporters. He remained at large for several months, residing in the state prison at Waupun, where prison commissioner Hans Heg granted him sanctuary, and occasionally speaking at meetings of political sympathizers. In October 1860, he was captured at one such event, and sent back to federal confinement in the Milwaukee customshouse.

Wisconsin v. The United States

The stakes of the Fugitive Slave Act and the federal regime devoted to its enforcement could not have been more clear for Joshua Glover, Thomas Sims, or for any other fugitive or enslaved person who contemplated the possibility of escape. But what, in the end, were the stakes of the battle over the Fugitive Slave Law for Booth, the Paines, the jail-door-batterer James Angove, the escape-carriage driver John Messenger, or the thousands of other Wisconsinites who attended the meeting in Courthouse Square or the convention at Young's Hall? If a wild-eyed Sherman Booth pressed a still-damp broadside into your hand outside Marshall and Ilsley's bank at the corner of East Water and Huron, what made you decide to turn north and walk a few blocks to join the noisy, volatile, possibly inebriated crowd? And what did you think when you heard Booth and Paine talking of compacts and interposition, citing Mr. Madison and that angry South Carolinian, Calhoun?

Another way of framing the question is to ask why so many Wisconsinites found states' rights a compelling ideology in the 1850s. Did they believe in what they were arguing? Or was it simply an easy and available argument, a species of what moderns would call "cheap talk"?

A few facts to consider:

In February 1857, while the Booth litigation was making its way through state and federal court, and while the case of *Dred Scott v. Sandford* was pending before the U.S. Supreme Court, the Wisconsin legislature passed a personal liberty law.[125] The law set out protections for "any inhabitant of State" who was "about to be arrested or claimed as a fugitive slave," including making available the writ of habeas corpus, requiring that the county district attorney be informed when any inhabitant was so threatened, setting fines for representing that a free person was a slave, and requiring testimony by two witnesses to prove that an individual was in fact a slave.[126] The statute also provided that the state would cover the costs of the habeas proceeding "whenever the same would be otherwise chargeable to the person arrested or claimed as a fugitive slave."[127]

On March 19, 1859, twelve days after the U.S. Supreme Court handed down its decision in *Ableman v. Booth*, the two houses of the Wisconsin legislature passed a joint resolution "relative to the decision of the United States supreme court, reversing decision of the supreme court of Wisconsin." Referring by name to Booth and his petition for a writ of habeas corpus, the resolution excoriated the U.S. Supreme Court for "assuming jurisdiction in the case before mentioned, as an arbitrary act of power, unauthorized by the constitution, and virtually superseding the benefit of the writ of habeas corpus, and prostrating the rights and liberties of the people at the foot of unlimited power." The Court's "assumption of jurisdiction" was "an act of undelegated power, and therefore without authority, void, and of no force."

In addition to this attack on the supremacy of the Court's decision, the legislature addressed the fundamental question of the nature of the Union. Their statements sounded more in the tradition of the Virginia judges in *Martin v. Hunter's Lessee* four decades earlier than in the language of Story, Marshall, or Webster. The Constitution, the legislators maintained, was the fruit of a "compact among parties" having "no common judge" but rather leaving each party with "an equal right to judge for itself."[128] Not "the party which now rules in the councils of the nation" but rather the Constitution itself was the proper judge of the scope of the general government's powers. The "several states which formed that instrument, being sovereign and independent, have the unquestionable right to judge of its infraction." The "rightful remedy" for "all unauthorized acts done or attempted to be done under color of" the Constitution was "a *positive defiance*" by the sovereign states.[129]

On April 28, 1859, the clerk of the U.S. Supreme Court, William T. Carroll, carried a copy of Chief Justice Taney's opinion in *Ableman v. Booth* to the White House, where he delivered it to President James Buchanan. According to Carroll, Buchanan told him, "[T]he Supreme Court and the Executive should stand shoulder to shoulder in such a crisis, that they might be able to resist the fanaticism of both the North and the South."[130]

Seven months later, in November 1860, Abraham Lincoln was elected to the presidency. Immediately, South Carolinians began planning a secession convention. Buchanan had been unable to make good on his statement to Carroll that he would execute the order of the U.S. Supreme Court in the Booth case. Booth had been re-arrested, but the Wisconsin Supreme Court remained intransigent, refusing to recognize the U.S. Supreme Court's mandate, to the chagrin of ill-tempered U.S. attorney general Jeremiah Black. Republicans had swept into power in Wisconsin and other states, and they had just elected their first president of the nation.

And so, when President Buchanan delivered his fourth and final annual message to Congress on December 3, knowing that Lincoln would succeed him, he began with some harsh words:

> The long-continued and intemperate interference of the northern people with the question of slavery in the southern States has at length produced its natural effects. The different sections of the Union are now arrayed against each other, and the time has arrived, so much dreaded by the Father of his Country, when hostile geographical parties have been formed.[131]

Then followed blame:

> All the courts, both State and national, before whom the question has arisen have from the beginning declared the fugitive-slave law to be constitutional. The single exception is that of a State court in Wisconsin, and this has not only been reversed by the proper appellate tribunal, but has met with such universal reprobation that there can be no danger from it as a precedent.

After these statements, the last two clauses of which were more aspirational than factual, Buchanan offered the faintest of hope, phrased in the subjunctive mood: "Let us trust that the State legislatures will repeal their unconstitutional and obnoxious enactments. Unless this shall be done without unnecessary delay, it is impossible for any human power to save the Union."[132]

Even as he inveighed against Wisconsin's pertinacity, Buchanan tacitly acknowledged the force of the state's position. In the face of the state's refusal to adhere to the mandate of the U.S. Supreme Court, the president could do little. Nearly three decades earlier, President Andrew Jackson had been able to threaten South Carolina's nullifying legislature and governor with the Force Bill, which authorized him to deploy the military to collect import duties if the state refused to allow the federal revenue officials to do so.[133] The state had ultimately backed down.

But the nullification crisis was a standoff between Congress and the president on one hand, and the state legislature and governor on the other. Courts were different. As Byron Paine had argued before the Wisconsin Supreme Court in May 1854, "[W]hatever objections might be urged against the actual exercise of the right of resistance by the legislative or executive departments of the State, cannot be urged with equal force against the action of its Judiciary. . . . [I]t follows as a necessary consequence of State sovereignty that upon all questions touching that sovereignty, the Judiciary, as one of the great departments of the State, is to decide independently of all other tribunals upon earth."[134] As Justice William Johnson had learned when sitting on circuit in his hometown of Charleston in 1823, even if a federal court held that a state law violated the U.S. Constitution's foreign and interstate commerce clauses, the state could prevail by simply ignoring the judicial decision.

Buchanan's plaint in December 1860 was apt insofar as it identified the actors who held all the power at that moment. "Let us trust that the State legislatures will repeal their unconstitutional and obnoxious enactments," the president told his audience. But what if they did not? He was speaking of Wisconsin, but his words were equally appropriate for South Carolina in the 1820s and 1830s. State sovereignty, taken to its extreme, clearly would destroy the Union. As would decades of protection and special favors for an institution that claimed to be local but in fact demanded absolute extraterritorial fealty to its regime. And there was the difference between the Wisconsin and the South Carolina species of state sovereignty. Wisconsin was objecting to the terms of union that the southern slaveholding states demanded, while South Carolina was rejecting the concept of union itself.

Dissolution and Reconstitution of the Union

Also on December 3, 1860, the day of Buchanan's annual address in Washington, the famed abolitionist orator, author, and editor Frederick Douglass addressed a rowdy, violent gathering at Tremont Temple in Boston. The occasion for the meeting was to mark the one-year anniversary of the execution of John Brown, who had led the assault on the federal arsenal at Harpers Ferry, Virginia, in October 1859.[135] The Tremont Temple assembly dissolved into a full-blown brawl, ending when the city police cleared the hall. The abolitionists removed to a Black church on Joy Street, where the forty-two-year-old Douglass, fresh from having fought the attacking mob "like a trained pugilist," again took the lectern.[136]

The purpose of the meeting, Douglass noted, was to "discuss the best method of abolishing slavery." Douglass declared himself in favor of "the John Brown way." The "moral and social means of opposing slavery" had had "a greater prominence, during the last twenty-five years, than the way indicated by the celebration of this day." The "John Brown way" of attacking slavery, Douglass explained, was "not only to appeal to the moral sense of these slaveholders." Rather, abolitionists had a "need, and a right, to appeal to their fears." One means to make the slaveholders "uncomfortable," Douglass argued, was to aid slaves in escaping. Another was to make the individual slaveholder "feel that there is death in the air around him." The "Negroes of the South must do this," Douglass urged, by making the slaveholder "feel that it is not so pleasant, after all, to go to bed with bowie-knives, and revolvers, and pistols, as they must."[137] The Fugitive Slave Act received specific mention. "The only way to make the Fugitive Slave Law a dead letter is to make a few dead slave-catchers," Douglass exhorted his audience. The response, according to the account published a few weeks later in *Douglass' Monthly*, was "[l]aughter and applause."[138]

In his remarks that December evening, Douglass made clear the connection between the arguments for the Union and the past decades' compromise measures, chief among them the Fugitive Slave Act. Douglass flipped the pro-Union slavery apologists' assertions on their head. Not only was the Union not worth preserving at the cost of alleged fugitives' freedom, but that freedom could be better protected if the Union were broken apart. "Something is said about the dissolution of the Union under Mr. Lincoln or under Mr. Buchanan. I am for a dissolution of the Union—decidedly for a dissolution of the Union! Under an abolition President, who would wield the army and the navy of the

Frederick Douglass, 1856. (National Portrait Gallery, Smithsonian Institution.)

Government for the abolition of slavery, I should be for the union of these States," Douglass proclaimed. "If this Union is dissolved, I see many ways in which slavery may be attacked by force, but very few in which it could be attacked by moral means."[139]

In contrast to the argument that the Republican Lincoln would provoke a rupture of the Union, Douglass challenged the notion that the Union was worth preserving for its own sake. If saving the Union meant adhering to a Buchanan, then what, Douglass asked, was the point of the Union?

My opinion is that if we only had an anti-slavery President, if we only had an abolition President to hold these men in the Union, and execute ... that part of the Constitution which is in favor of liberty, as well as put upon those passages which have been construed in favor of slavery, a construction different from that and more in harmony with the principles of eternal justice that lie at the foundation of the government—if we could have such a government, a government that would force the South to behave herself, under those circumstances I should be for the continuance of the Union. If, on the contrary—no *if* about it—we have what we have, I shall be glad of the news, come when it will, that the slave States are an independent government, and that you are no longer called upon to deliver fugitive slaves to their masters, and that you are no longer called upon to shoulder your arms and guard with your swords those States—no longer called to go into them to put down John Brown, or anybody else who may strike for liberty there.[140]

Even as South Carolina was in the process of selecting delegates for its secession convention, Douglass was inviting the slaveholding states to form "an independent government." Only then, he contended, would an antislavery president, leading a Union that no longer compromised with slaveowners, be possible. Only then would "you"—the white, northern members of his Boston audience— no longer be "called upon to deliver fugitive slaves to their masters" or "to shoulder your arms and guard with your swords" states such as South Carolina.[141]

A few weeks later, on December 20, Douglass's qualified hopes were partially vindicated when the South Carolina convention voted unanimously in favor of secession. In January 1861, with Buchanan still in office and Lincoln's inauguration two months away, Douglass speculated on what secession meant, and whether the federal government would continue its appeasing ways. In an essay titled "Dissolution of the American Union," Douglass began with a declaration: "The event so long and so loudly threatened by the State of South Carolina, and dreaded by the other States, has at last happened, and is a matter of history." But then his tone turned acerbic, jibing at the many rhetorical flourishes that had been used by secessionists in recent weeks to characterize their actions:

She has seceded, separated, repealed, quitted, dissolved the Union, declared her independence, set up for herself, assumed a place among the sisterhood of nations, pulled down the star spangled banner of the great American Confederacy, and upon innumerable pine poles has unfurled the Palmetto flag, preferring to be a large piece of nothing, to being any longer a small piece of something.[142]

It was a masterly melding of satirical boilerplate and a plain but damning coda.

Douglass's language also conveyed a sense of inconclusiveness. Secession "seems a newly invented game, and the people are much delighted with it," he wrote. "And yet . . . there is an undercurrent of doubt, uncertainty, distrust, and foreboding." The "ship"—South Carolina—"is still anchored in the safe harbor of the Union, and those having her in charge seem, after all, rather reluctant about venturing out upon the untried billows of the dissolution sea."[143] For Douglass, who had declared himself "for a dissolution of the Union," the question was urgent: Had the Union in fact been dissolved?

This inquiry, as Douglass framed it, had two parts. First, what did South Carolina need to do in order to perfect its status as "the new Republic"? Second, what did the U.S. government need to do in order to allow itself to treat the seceded states as something apart from the Union, and thus as no longer entitled to claim the benisons of compromise?

Based on South Carolina's utterances, the state had begun to break free from the Union. "She is out of the Union, on paper, in speeches, letter, resolutions, and telegrams," Douglass catalogued. But he expressed skepticism that South Carolina could accomplish true secession, secession in fact, through mere words. "The head and front of her independence hath this extent, no more," he observed. Yet

[t]he postal arrangements of the United States are still extended over her; the revenue laws of the United States are still enforced in her ports, and no hand, thus far, has been lifted against the one or the other. The United States flag yet waves over Fort Moultrie, and a United States revenue cutter is lying in Charleston harbor. The South Carolinians have accomplished what they call peaceful secession—a thing quite as easily done as the leaving of a society of Odd Fellows, or bidding goodnight to a spiritual circle. But, unfortunately, human governments are neither held together, nor broken up by such mild and gentle persuasives as are implied in the soft phrase—peaceful secession. Theirs is a voice of command, not of persuasion. They rest not upon paper, but upon power. . . . The work is not done yet.

The "work" was "not done yet"—by this Douglass meant the work of splitting apart from the Union and creating a new republic. Notably, his focus was on what was required of South Carolina to perfect its secession. How could secession break the "moorings that bind these States together"? Only "by opinion, backed up by force." Fiery proclamations were useful as "opinion" but incomplete insofar as they lacked "force."[144]

In order to make the separation real, South Carolina had to cut the cords of law, politics, and institutions that tied it to the Union. This work was more difficult than it might have initially appeared, Douglass noted. It involved more than the mere declaration that the state was revoking its consent to join the Union. The connections ran deeper, the tendrils of federal power longer, the lattice of interlocking general and local power denser. South Carolina "must exclude the mail service, put an end to United States Post Offices, drive United States Custom House officers from her ports, capture public property, take the forts and arsenals, and drive out every officer from her borders who holds and exercises any authority whatsoever under the Government of the U.S."[145]

It was as though Douglass were reciting a list of the actors in the constitutional dramas of the past five decades, from *The Brig Wilson* to *Ableman*, each of which had involved numerous layers of governmental power. For South Carolina to secede, he suggested, the entire structure of jurisdictional multiplicity that constituted American federalism would have to be dismantled.

And even then, South Carolina was "still in the Union." The "right of South Carolina to secede . . . depends upon her ability to do so, and to stay so," he argued. Again, the standard was not words alone but actions and recognition on the part of other powers. The state would have to "whip the Federal Government and scourge and keep it beyond her borders, and compel the United States to regard her as other than a revolt province." Only then could it "get out of the Union."[146] The same requirement applied to other states that might follow South Carolina into secession. Those states—Douglas specifically mentioned "the cotton States" of the Deep South—would "have to extinguish the life of the Federal Government within their limits, and keep that extinguished." But such total annihilation of federal power was unlikely to succeed, in Douglass's view. It could be achieved only "*by force, by treachery, or by negotiation; and to neither will Abraham Lincoln succumb.*"[147]

Douglass recognized that the federal government had always been present and operating within the states. Federal power had always been emanating across and through state borders. Even at the very zenith of state sovereignty in December 1860, there was no clear separation between state and federal power in practice. Extricating South Carolina from the Union was more than a matter of conventions and ordinances. The post office, the revenue cutter, the customshouse—all these would have to be dismantled.

In a February 1861 essay titled "The Union and How to Save It," Douglass noted the pattern of activities carried out by the seven states that had seceded at that point: "They fall to seizing forts, arsenals, arms and ammunition, capturing Custom Houses, Post Offices, tearing down the national flag, and firing upon an unarmed Government vessel, with the national flag flying at her masthead."[148] Absent this attack on the federal institutions within, a state could not transform itself from a mere one of the "several States" to a member of the sisterhood of nations. The seceded states' actions themselves confessed the interlocking, overlapping facts of federal and state power. The Union was not a binary arrangement between the general government and the states, or even a compact among the states. Instead, it was a dense and many-threaded fabric. Despite the "how-to" title of Douglass's February 1861 piece, the final sentence suggested that the Union might not in fact be worth saving, precisely because it comprised such interwoven governments, morals, and compromises. "If there is not wisdom and virtue enough in the land to rid the country of slavery, then the next best thing is to let the South go to her own place," Douglass wrote, "and be made to drink the wine cup of wrath and fire, which her long career of cruelty, barbarism and blood shall call down upon her guilty head."[149]

On March 2, 1861, his second-to-last day in office, President Buchanan remitted the fines that Sherman Booth owed and ordered him released from custody. Booth had been held for five months in the federal customshouse in Milwaukee.[150] Two days later, Abraham Lincoln was sworn as president, with the oath administered by Chief Justice Roger Taney.

A Federalism of Federalisms

One can tell at least four possible stories about the Wisconsin crisis of the late 1850s, as it developed into—but was not resolved by—the case of *Ableman v. Booth.*

The first story downplays the meaning of the states' rights claims that Wisconsinites made during the rescue of Glover and the struggle over the Fugitive Slave Act. This account portrays *Ableman,* using the case name as a shorthand for the entire conflict, as a blip. According to this view, the invocations of states' rights by northern antislavery and abolitionist actors were less heartfelt, more strategic, and therefore less real than those trumpeted by their compatriots to the south.

This interpretation can be found in David M. Potter's book *The Impending Crisis, 1848–1861*, which won the Pulitzer Prize for History in 1977. Potter described Wisconsin's first burst of defiance as "involv[ing] nullification in a form that John C. Calhoun had not advocated." With Taney's opinion, however, the U.S. Supreme Court "ended this case," and, Potter suggests, the ostensibly normal alignments were resumed. "[T]he Wisconsin court, perceiving that it was a tactical error for antislavery men to support doctrines of state sovereignty, acquiesced in the decision."[151] As we have seen, however, the Wisconsin court did not acquiesce; on the contrary, joined by the state legislature, it continued to defy the mandate of the Court. But the identifications with states' rights are treated as fixed and incapable of change. Within five years, according to Potter, "the South resumed its traditional role as the chief defender of states' rights and the North was again identified with the acceptance of federal authority." In the end, however, Potter treats all these beliefs as simply epiphenomenal of the parties' substantive views: "The events of the fifties offered a telling demonstration that the attitudes of various groups in a society toward upholding the law [are] in direct proportion to their approval or disapproval of the law which is to be upheld."[152] Arguments based on ideas about constitutional law and politics, on this view, are mere manifestations of some preexisting core set of policy preferences.

The second story of *Ableman* portrays the case as the culmination, ironic in some ways, of the Marshall Court's nationalism. On this view, when Chief Justice Taney, writing for a unanimous Court, castigated Wisconsin's claims as tending to "subvert the very foundations of this Government," he was following in the doctrine line laid down by his predecessor in cases such as *Martin v. Hunter's Lessee* and *McCulloch v. Maryland*. Judicially enforced federal supremacy was the lodestar of this analysis. In *Ableman*, Taney thus "completed the work of the Federalists," producing both a "blunt statement of governmental hierarchy within the American nation" and an "eloquent rationale for the subordination of state governments to a centralized authority."[153] This second story of *Ableman* is therefore a tale of continuity. The trajectory might appear controversial, given both conventional assumptions about the valence of nationalism and states' rights, and the conventional view that the Marshall Court stood for nationalism while the Taney Court enacted a largely centrifugal agenda. Indeed, the account is aimed to provoke, both by challenging the heroic mythology of Marshall and by raising Taney from a proto-Confederate to a defender of the Union.

The final two stories of *Ableman* are about limits.

One of these accounts views *Ableman*, and the crisis that gave rise to it, as demonstrating the limits of appeals to the Union after 1850. As we have seen, Daniel Webster, Joseph Story, and many others—including numerous federal commissioners charged with carrying out the Fugitive Slave Act—valorized the Union on its own terms, as a good in and of itself.[154] The ideology of union underpinned Webster's support for the Compromise of 1850, Story's opinion in *Prigg*, and the actions of many officials in Wisconsin and elsewhere who sought to carry out federal law in the face of states' rights resistance. Invocations of the Union in the interbellum period are attractive to current-day observers, insofar as they seem familiarly, comfortably congruent with the moral and military victors of the war that followed. As the critiques articulated by Paine, Booth, and Douglass throughout the 1850s showed, however, some contemporaries were frustrated by the thinness of these cries of "Union." Even worse, for some, was the fact that adhering to the Union often brought with it a quietism that shied away from forceful critiques of what they regarded as the slavocracy that ruled the nation. By the "secession winter" of 1860–61, many of these critics were increasingly questioning the necessity of the Union.

The final story of *Ableman* focuses on the opinion of the Supreme Court. It was, as we have seen, a unanimous opinion. Taney wrote for himself and for eight associate justices: John McLean, James M. Wayne, John Catron, Peter V. Daniel, Samuel Nelson, Robert C. Grier, John A. Campbell, and Nathan Clifford. Of these silent concurrences, the most notable is that of McLean. As we have seen, McLean was an avowed antislavery man who had written a powerful dissent in *Dred Scott* in 1857. Two years later, in *Ableman*, however, he signed on without comment to Taney's complete rejection of Wisconsin's claimed power to invalidate a federal statute and to issue habeas relief to a federal prisoner. Even for an Ohio abolitionist, such claims were evidently beyond the boundary of permissible constitutional discourse—at least when they challenged the authority of the Supreme Court of the United States.

Perhaps the most compelling story of the Wisconsin crisis of the 1850s is the one that highlights the many varieties of interbellum federalism. In December 1860, South Carolina seceded in the name of states' rights. One year earlier, in 1859, Wisconsin had resisted federal authority in the name of states' rights. One year later, in 1861, Wisconsin would take up arms for the Union in the name of states' rights.

Epilogue

In late July 1885, Ulysses S. Grant, former president of the United States and commanding general of the Union Army, was racing to finish writing his *Personal Memoirs* while suffering from what he knew to be fatal throat cancer. Within days of completing the *Memoirs*, the sixty-three-year-old Grant was dead.

The bulk of the *Memoirs* focused on Grant's military career, first as an infantry lieutenant in the Mexican-American War and then his rise from colonel to lieutenant general in the Civil War. The tone throughout was decidedly retrospective but relatively brisk and unadorned. In the conclusion, Grant allowed himself more license to reflect and to place the great events he had lived through in a broader historical context. The most monumental of these events, the Civil War, formed the architecture of the conclusion, just as it had Grant's own life.

Grant began the conclusion with a stark statement of fact: "The cause of the great War of the Rebellion against the United States will have to be attributed to slavery."[1] He then devoted several paragraphs to a sophisticated legal and political analysis of the coming of the conflict. Grant seemed to be attempting to answer the question of why the war burst forth when it did. How did the fragile, compromising, compromised interbellum Union take the steps to become the Union that fought the Confederacy? To address this question, Grant looked to the connection between slavery and federalism.

> Slavery was an institution that required unusual guarantees for its security wherever it existed; and in a country like ours where the larger portion of it was free territory inhabited by an intelligent and well-to-do population, the people would naturally have but little sympathy with

demands upon them for its protection. Hence the people of the South were dependent upon keeping control of the general government to se-cure the perpetuation of their favorite institution.[2]

In Grant's view, slavery was an "institution" that was not typical of the en-tire United States, and that therefore "required unusual guarantees for its se-curity" in the places where it did exist. The people of the free territory that constituted the rest of the country were not disposed to be burdened with these unusual guarantees. They had "little sympathy" with "demands" made by upon them by the slaveholding regions of the country. (Notably, Grant used the more colloquial term "country" rather than the word "nation," with its con-notations of a centralized nation-state.) Therefore, the "people of the South" were "dependent upon keeping control of the general government to secure the perpetuation of their favorite institution."

Consider Grant's phrasing here: "keeping control" and "perpetuation of" slavery. The white southern slaveholders as a group already had control of the general government, and they wanted to maintain that control in order to con-tinue the already-existing institution of slavery. Grant implied that keeping this control required effort, because it was not the natural state of political af-fairs, given that the "larger portion" of the country was "free territory."

And, Grant suggested, there was something defective in this political struc-ture. A group that was bent on entrenching its favorite institution was doing so by cementing its grasp on the general government. A set of local, or per-haps regional, interests was controlling the center.

A region was improperly driving the policy of the Union as a whole, in Grant's view. And they were apparently able to exert their will in this way—to capture the general government—not because they executed a sudden power grab, but be-cause they had been allowed to do so over the course of decades. "They were enabled to maintain this control long after the States where slavery existed had ceased to have the controlling power, through the assistance they received from odd men here and there throughout the Northern States," Grant argued.[3]

The greatest impetus toward conflict, according to Grant's narrative, was the Fugitive Slave Act of 1850 and its effects on northern sentiment. The "peo-ple of the South"

saw their power waning, and this led them to encroach upon the pre-rogatives and independence of the Northern States by enacting such laws as the Fugitive Slave Law. By this law every Northern man was obliged, when properly summoned, to turn out and help apprehend the runaway slave of a Southern man. Northern marshals became slave-catchers, and Northern courts had to contribute to the support and protection of the institution.[4]

This was Grant's account of why the Civil War came: the sense in the North that the "people of the South"—by which he meant the white people—had illegitimately seized control of the federal government. In so doing, they had arrogated to themselves the power to direct policy in the North. The southern slaveocracy was essentially using the general government to launder its naked power, cloaking it in the authority of the center in order to command other states to carry out its will. Southern states were reaching into the internal affairs of other states—piercing through the northern states' sovereign borders—in a manner that Grant viewed as subversive of the foundations of the American federal system.

Moreover, this invasion of northern states' spheres was not only an offense to abstract structures of federalism. It touched the dignity of the free states as states, as well as that of their citizens. The Fugitive Slave Act of 1850 made slave-catchers of northern marshals and compelled northern courts to enforce the institution of slavery. In doing so, it insulted them. In insulting them, it spurred them into action:

> This was a degradation which the North would not permit any longer than until they could get the power to expunge such laws from the statute books. Prior to the time of these encroachments the great majority of the people of the North had no particular quarrel with slavery, so long as they were not forced to have it themselves. *But they were not willing to play the rôle of police for the South in the protection of this particular institution.*[5]

Grant's account of reactions to the Fugitive Slave Act explains how and why states' rights claims became increasingly important to northerners after 1850. It also illustrates several crucial aspects of the interbellum Union. In highlighting what many northerners viewed as an unacceptable invasion of the prerogatives and independence of their states, Grant's explanation illuminates the constitutional climate of the 1850s. Ironically, states' rights ideas were largely responsible for transforming the Union of compromise into the Union of liberty.

The Fugitive Slave Act made the harms of slavery feel immediate to people who increasingly identified themselves by the amorphous terms "northerners," and also many of those who described themselves as "westerners" and "easterners." The "North" was a notional region, defined largely in contrast to the "South." But these were highly permeable definitions. Grant's native state of Ohio, for example, was both "northern" and "southern" as well as "western." The same was true of Abraham Lincoln's home state of Illinois, as well as Missouri, the admission of which in 1821 had formed a flashpoint in the era's political and legal debates.[6]

The galvanizing effect of the Fugitive Slave Act came from the shock it administered to many Americans living in states that did not formally recognize slavery. By requiring them to "play the rôle of police for the South," to "turn out and help apprehend the runaway slave of a Southern man," the act not only made them morally complicit in the institution of slavery; it commandeered their labor on behalf of someone else. For many people, especially white men steeped in the powerful free labor ideology of the era, this compelled service was tantamount to impressment, even theft.[7] It was the corvée. It was a form of slavery, a "degradation" to both northern people and states: coerced labor from the people, and invasion of the states. It was not remote harm to an abstract Union, but rather concrete injury to the people and the states—the other parties to William Johnson's tripartite contract. In response, the people of Wisconsin, Pennsylvania, and Massachusetts, among others, defended themselves in the language of states' rights. Because of states' rights, they joined what became the cause of the Union of liberty.

Even the expansion of commerce and transportation networks served this incursion of southern power into northern states, according to Grant. "In the early days of the country, before we had railroads, telegraphs, and steamboats—in a word, rapid transit of any sort—the States were each almost a separate nationality," Grant observed. So far, the story was a familiar one: in the beginning, there was fragmentation and localism. But then Grant's narrative took a different turn: "At that time the subject of slavery caused but little or no disturbance to the public mind. But the country grew, rapid transit was established, and trade and commerce between the States got to be so much greater than before, that the power of the National government became more felt and recognized and, therefore, *had to be enlisted in the cause of this institution.*"[8]

The claim that the growth of trade and travel led to an increased sense of the country as a nation was a familiar one to contemporaries, and it recurs in historians' accounts.[9] As Grant suggested, however, this nationalism could be employed by whoever controlled the federal machinery. Commerce, transportation, communications—as these grew, so too did the power of the general government. As that power "became more felt and recognized," it too "had to be enlisted in the cause of this institution"—slavery.

This story was not a Whiggish one of inevitable progress, in which national commerce and national governmental power expanded in a healthy tandem relationship that eroded parochial local interests. Rather, it was a pessimistic tale of capture and hegemony. Commerce grew; the sense of the country as a nation grew; and so too did their value to the slaveholding power. Grant charted a trajectory from localism—each state "almost a separate nationality"—to interconnection and intercourse. This transition was not necessarily salutary, nor was it necessarily harmful. In the specific context of the 1850s, however, the shift became a catalyst for many in the North to move from toleration of or indifference to the institution of slavery, to viewing the institution as an attack on themselves and their states. Many of those who came to support the cause of Union did so because they believed that a mere part of the country was exercising control over the whole.[10] Such an arrangement, they believed, was a perversion of the structure of the federal republic.

As this book has demonstrated, the interbellum period was defined by jurisdictional multiplicity and overlap. During these four and a half decades, federal power permeated the states. Federal authority was exercised in the ports, as we have seen; it was diffused through the post offices; it emanated from the courtrooms (some of which shared quarters with state and local judiciaries); its officers interviewed ship captains, inspected cargoes, and drew up schedules of import duties. Federal officers also captured and processed alleged fugitives, confining them in jails and trying them in courtrooms even when doing so required borrowing those spaces from states or counties. This interconnectedness was the reason for Frederick Douglass's observation in January 1861 that the only way for South Carolina to "get out of the Union" was to "exclude the mail service, put an end to United States Post Offices, drive United States Custom House officers from her ports, capture public property, take the forts and arsenals, and drive out every officer from her borders who holds and exercises any authority whatsoever under the Government of the U.S."[11] In order to "get out of the Union," the state would have to get the Union out of it.

Even at the individual level, federal power diffused into local spaces. Federal allegiances and outlooks, once established in even the most proud provincial bosom, proved surprisingly tenacious. "My reputation is the property of the United States," wrote William Johnson, devoted son of Charleston, in 1822, as he prepared to confront the self-designated proprietors of his state's soil. Onetime Jefferson protégé William Wirt, whose "Virginian Constitutional scruples" had initially so irritated his Cabinet colleague John Quincy Adams, spent the final years of his career battling Georgia's claim of a state sovereignty so potent that it could summarily extinguish the Cherokee Nation.[12] Joseph Story, scion of an old Massachusetts family, found the appeal of a Union based on legal uniformity so powerful that he interpreted the Fugitive Slave Clause of the Constitution as an inexorable command to Congress and the states.

Interbellum federalism was a congeries of multiple powers overlapping and acting upon the same people, places, and activities. Line-drawing and formalism were thus, paradoxically, widely engaged in by contemporaries. To see this point, one need only consider the disputes over enforcement of the U.S. Supreme Court's orders in *Martin v. Hunter's Lessee*, *Worcester v. Georgia*, and *Ableman v. Booth*. State authorities insisted that every punctilio of respect and dignity be afforded them. Otherwise, they withheld trial-court records, declined to send counsel to argue on their behalf, and refused to comply with mandates. Federal officials, too, demanded that borders be observed and jurisdictions respected. Consider Chief Justice John Marshall's delicate treatment of the interlocking Virginia and congressional acts in the case of *The Brig Wilson*, Johnson's strenuous efforts to shape and guide a case challenging South Carolina's Seamen Act into his court, and Wirt's and Principal Chief John Ross's fastidious attention to the pleadings and the parties in the Cherokee cases.

Throughout the early nineteenth century, federal power routinely reached into local domains. The whole—the Union—could and did influence events, even down to the level of the dock, the market, and the mayor's court. But the parts—the states—did not generally assume the power to reach across and into each other's realm. In 1850, however, this norm appeared to many contemporaries to have changed.

"Even though the southern people will not so much as listen to us, let us calmly consider their demands," Abraham Lincoln urged his audience at New York City's Cooper Union in February 1860. Lincoln, who two years earlier had lost his campaign for one of Illinois's U.S. Senate seats to Stephen A. Douglas, was now positioning himself as a potential candidate for the upcoming presidential election. "The question recurs, what will satisfy them?" Lincoln asked.

> This, and this only: cease to call slavery *wrong*, and join them in calling it *right*. And this must be done thoroughly . . . we must place ourselves avowedly with them. Senator Douglas's new sedition law must be enacted and enforced, suppressing all declarations that slavery is wrong, whether made in politics, in presses, in pulpits, or in private. We must arrest and return their fugitive slaves with greedy pleasure. We must pull down our

Free State constitutions. The whole atmosphere must be disinfected from all taint of opposition to slavery, before they will cease to believe that all their troubles proceed from us. . . . Holding, as they do, that slavery is morally right, and socially elevating, they cannot cease to demand a full national legal recognition of it, as a legal right, and a social blessing.[13]

Lincoln's argument was clear: the "southern people" would not be content with acquiescence from the rest of the nation. Lincoln was willing to agree to nonintervention. "Wrong as we think slavery is, we can yet afford to let it alone where it is, because that much is due to the necessity arising from its actual presence in the nation," he told his audience. But, he noted, passivity would not satisfy the southerners. They would inevitably demand "a full national legal recognition" of slavery. At that point, Lincoln argued, the northern states must resist. "[C]an we, while our votes will prevent it, allow it to spread into the National Territories, and to overrun us here in these Free States?" His answer was unequivocal: "If our sense of duty forbids this, then let us stand by our duty, fearlessly and effectively."[14]

In Lincoln's view, the preferences of a part of the whole—the "southern people"—ought not be permitted to dictate how the federal territories and the free states would be governed. The territories were, pursuant to the Constitution, under the exclusive authority of Congress. The free states were coequal in power to the slaveholding states. There was simply no basis in American federalism for a handful of states, acting as states, to arrogate to themselves the status of umpire—not only over other states, but over Congress itself. Not even the most forceful states' rights arguments made by the Virginia judges in *Martin v. Hunter's Lessee* had contemplated such an arrangement.

In interbellum constitutional discourse, the opposite of "federal" was not "state." It was "local." Lincoln's phrasing of his central question illustrated this crucial point: "Does the proper division of local from federal authority, or anything in the Constitution, forbid *our Federal Government* to control as to slavery in *our Federal Territories*?"[15] A binary state-federal model does not accurately describe American federalism between 1815 and 1861. In both theory and fact, the constitutional structure of the period was characterized by jurisdictional multiplicity, concurrent power, an almost-obsessive focus on commerce, and surprising valences of both federal and local authority.

The federalisms of the interbellum United States were many and varied. Those today who would seek a strict demarcation between state and federal spheres must look elsewhere than early-nineteenth-century history, text, structure, or practice to find such a separation.

Notes

Introduction

1. See Bruce Ackerman, *We the People: Foundations* (Cambridge, Mass.: Harvard University Press, 1991), 31–32, setting forth a "dualist" model of constitutional democracy characterized by a "recurring cycle of normal, then constitutional, then normal politics" that operates in a "cyclical pattern."

2. Akhil Reed Amar, *The Words That Made Us: America's Constitutional Conversation, 1760–1840* (New York: Basic Books, 2021), x–xiii.

3. William H. S. Demarest, *A History of Rutgers College, 1766–1924* (New Brunswick, N.J.: Rutgers College, 1924), 291.

4. William Wirt, *An Address, Delivered before the Peithessophian and Philoclean Societies of Rutgers College*, 2nd ed. (New Brunswick, N.J.: Terhune and Letson, 1830), 10.

5. For a foundational account along these lines, see Edward S. Corwin, *The Commerce Power versus States' Rights* (Princeton: Princeton University Press, 1936).

6. William Henry Seward, *The Irrepressible Conflict: A Speech by William H. Seward, Delivered at Rochester, Monday, Oct 25, 1858* (New York: New York Tribune, 1860), 2.

7. See, e.g., Neil Binderglass, Stephanie Dyson, and Jane McGuinness, "Administrative History of the Peithessophian Society of Rutgers College" (1994), Special Collections and University Archives, Rutgers University Libraries, New Brunswick, N.J.; Wirt's address "remained popular for much of the nineteenth century since it appeared to foreshadow the coming Civil War."

8. Wirt, *Address*, 10.

9. Id., 11.

10. Id., 14.

11. Id.

12. See Eric Foner, *The Second Founding: How the Civil War and Reconstruction Remade the Constitution* (New York: W.W. Norton, 2019).

13. See Daniel J. Hulsebosch, *Constituting Empire: New York and the Transformation of Constitutionalism in the Atlantic World, 1664–1830* (Chapel Hill: University of North Carolina Press, 2005), 88.

14. See Alison L. LaCroix, *The Ideological Origins of American Federalism* (Cambridge, Mass.: Harvard University Press, 2010).

15. See Alison L. LaCroix, "Rhetoric and Reality in Early American Legal History: A Reply to Gordon Wood," 78 *University of Chicago Law Review* 733, 757–78 (2011).

16. Charles Sellers, *The Market Revolution: Jacksonian America, 1815–1846* (New York: Oxford University Press, 1991); Sven A. Beckert, *Empire of Cotton: A Global History* (New York: Alfred A. Knopf, 2013); Daniel Walker Howe, *What Hath God Wrought: The Transformation of America, 1815–1848* (New York: Oxford University Press, 2007).

17. Abraham Lincoln, "The Perpetuation of Our Political Institutions" (1838), address before the Springfield Young Men's Lyceum, in *The Political Thought of Abraham Lincoln*, ed. Richard N. Current (Indianapolis: Bobbs-Merrill, 1967), 17.

18. Id., 11, 16–17.

19. James Madison to Martin Van Buren, June 3, 1830, in *The Writings of James Madison*, vol. 9, *1819–1836*, ed. Gaillard Hunt (New York: G. P. Putnam's Sons, 1910), 375; Madison to Van Buren, July 5, 1830, in id., 376; see also Alison LaCroix, "The Constitution of the Second Generation," 2013 *University of Illinois Law Review* 1775 (2013).

20. I am grateful to Mary Cate Hickman for this phrase.

21. For a taxonomy distinguishing between "state sovereignty" and "state rights," see Michael Les Benedict, "Abraham Lincoln and Federalism," 10 *Journal of the Abraham Lincoln Association* 1 (1988). For an account distinguishing between "localized law" and "state law," see Laura F. Edwards, *The People and Their Peace: Legal Culture and the Transformation of Inequality in the Post-Revolutionary South* (Chapel Hill: University of North Carolina Press, 2009), 4.

22. See Quentin Skinner, "Meaning and Understanding in the History of Ideas," in *Meaning and Context: Quentin Skinner and His Critics*, ed. James Tully (Princeton: Princeton University Press, 1988), 29–67.

23. Alexander Hamilton, *The Federalist* No. 32, ed. Jacob E. Cooke (Middletown, Conn.: Wesleyan University Press, 1961).

24. The nineteenth-century conception of concurrent power differed in important ways from modern ideas of cooperative federalism. For particularly notable works discussing and, in some cases, critiquing the concept of cooperative federalism on normative or descriptive grounds, see Heather K. Gerken, "The Supreme Court 2009 Term—Foreword: Federalism All the Way Down," 124 *Harvard Law Review* 4 (2010); Jessica Bulman-Pozen and Heather K. Gerken, "Uncooperative Federalism," 118 *Yale Law Journal* 1256 (2009); Daniel J. Elazar, *American Federalism: A View from the States*, 3rd ed. (New York: Harper and Row, 1984); Abbe R. Gluck, "Our [National] Federalism," 123 *Yale Law Journal* 1626 (2014); Roderick M. Hills, Jr., "The Political Economy

of Cooperative Federalism: Why State Autonomy Makes Sense and 'Dual Sovereignty' Doesn't," 96 *Michigan Law Review* 813 (1998).

25. *Mayor, Aldermen, and Commonalty of the City of New York v. George Miln*, 36 U.S. (11 Pet.) 102 (1837).

26. See David A. Strauss, "Common Law Constitutional Interpretation," 63 *University of Chicago Law Review* 877 (1996).

27. Elizabeth Gaskell, *North and South* (1855; repr., New York: Penguin, 1995), 20 "Are those the Gormans who made their fortunes in trade at Southampton? Oh! I'm glad we don't visit them. I don't like shoppy people."

28. Bruce Ackerman, *The Failure of the Founding Fathers: Jefferson, Marshall, and the Rise of Presidential Democracy* (Cambridge, Mass.: Belknap/Harvard University Press, 2005), 242–43.

29. Akhil Reed Amar, *America's Unwritten Constitution: The Precedents and Principles We Live By* (New York: Basic Books, 2012), 5.

30. Id., 22–31; Amar, *Words That Made Us*, 532–47.

31. See, e.g., Albert J. Beveridge, *The Life of John Marshall*, 4 vols. (Boston: Houghton Mifflin, 1916–19); R. Kent Newmyer; *John Marshall and the Heroic Age of the Supreme Court* (Baton Rouge: Louisiana State University Press, 2001); G. Edward White, *The Marshall Court and Cultural Change, 1815–1835* (New York: Cambridge University Press, 1988). Even critics of the decisions credit Marshall with establishing the Court's institutional role. See, e.g., Michael Klarman, "How Great Were the 'Great' Marshall Court Decisions?," 87 *Virginia Law Review* 1111 (2001).

32. Canonical treatments of the period include Arthur M. Schlesinger, Jr., *The Age of Jackson* (Boston: Little, Brown, 1945); David M. Potter, *The Impending Crisis, 1848–1861* (New York: Harper and Row, 1976); Sellers, *Market Revolution;* Sean Wilentz, *The Rise of American Democracy: Jefferson to Lincoln* (New York: Norton, 2005); Howe, *What Hath God Wrought.*

33. See "Debate between Frederick Douglass and Charles Lenox Remond" (1857), in *The Frederick Douglass Papers*, series 1, ed. John W. Blassingame (New Haven: Yale University Press, 1985), 3:151–62. See also Sean Wilentz, *No Property in Man: Slavery and Antislavery at the Nation's Founding* (Cambridge, Mass.: Harvard University Press, 2018); Don E. Fehrenbacher, *The Slaveholding Republic: An Account of the United States Government's Relations to Slavery*, ed. Ward McAfee, 1st ed. (New York: Oxford, 2002); Leonard Richards, *The Slave Power: The Free North and Southern Domination, 1780–1860* (Baton Rouge: Louisiana State University Press, 2000); Paul Finkelman, "Slavery and the Constitutional Convention: Making a Covenant with Death," in *Beyond Confederation: Origins of the Constitution and American National Identity*, ed. Richard Beeman, Stephen Botein, and Edward C. Carter III (Chapel Hill: University of North Carolina Press, 1987), 188–225; William E. Gienapp, "The Republican Party and the Slave Power," in *New Perspectives on Race and Slavery in America: Essays in Honor of Kenneth M. Stampp*, ed. Robert H. Abzug and Stephen E. Maizlish (Lexington: University Press of Kentucky, 1986), 51–78.

Chapter 1. The Constitutional Lawyer in the Long Founding Moment

Epigraph. William Wirt to Dabney Carr, January 16, 1804, Wirt Letters, Library of Virginia, Richmond (hereafter cited as LVA), Folder 1.

1. Prince George's County Register of Wills (Orphans' Court Proceedings), 1777–1790, "Wirt," 1785, 130, C1275-1, Maryland State Archives, Annapolis.

2. See generally *Historical Research Report for the Market Master's House, Magruder House, and the George Washington House, Bladensburg, Prince George's County, Maryland* (Baltimore: Maryland State Highway Administration, 2009).

3. See "Diary of Edward Hooker, 1805–1808," in *Annual Report of the American Historical Association for the Year 1896* (Washington, D.C.: Government Printing Office, 1897), 1:842, 918: "Saw Mr. Wirt, the famous orator in Col. Burr's case. A most beautiful, fair, elegant man of apparently 32. He is the reputed illegitimate son of old Peter Carns [*sic*] of Georgia"; see also Garnett Andrews, *Reminiscences of an Old Georgia Lawyer* (Atlanta: J. J. Toon, 1870), 44n: "Tom Peter Carnes . . . was a lawyer of reputation in Maryland, intimate with the family of Mr. Wirt, in Virginia, married his sister Elizabeth, and came to Augusta. . . . Mr. Wirt was a great favorite of his (and the old people said of much nearer kin than brother in-law) and, when a lad, visited Mr. C., in Augusta." Wirt's biographer John Pendleton Kennedy states that Wirt's journey to Georgia occurred in 1789, while Joseph C. Robert gives a date of 1790. John Pendleton Kennedy, *Memoirs of the Life of William Wirt, Attorney-General of the United States*, new and rev. ed. (New York: G. P. Putnam's Sons, 1872), 1:54 (hereafter cited as *Memoirs*); Joseph C. Robert, "William Wirt, Virginian," 80 *Virginia Magazine of History and Biography* 387, 394 (1972).

4. An Act for the Benefit of William Wirt, December 27, 1791, in *Laws of Maryland Made and Passed at a Session of Assembly, Begun and Held at the City of Annapolis, on Monday the seventh of November, in the year of our Lord one thousand seven hundred and eighty-five* (Annapolis: Frederick Green, 1791), Ch. XLVIII, 36.

5. For a tally of Wirt's appearances before the Court, see Galen N. Thorp, "William Wirt," 33 *Journal of Supreme Court History* 223, 263 (2008).

6. *Memoirs*, 2:384; [Francis Walker Gilmer], *Sketches of American Orators* (Baltimore: J. Robinson, 1816), 36–37.

7. Richard Beale Davis, "Poe and William Wirt," 16 *American Literature* 212, 217 (1944).

8. William Wirt to Dabney Carr, August 3, 1829, LVA, Folder 14.

9. On dueling and the law in this period, see Alison L. LaCroix, " 'To Gain the Whole World, and Lose His Own Soul': Nineteenth-Century American Dueling as Public Law and Private Code," 33 *Hofstra Law Review* 501 (2004).

10. George Alfred Townsend, *Washington, Outside and Inside* (Hartford: James Betts, 1873), 332.

11. See Bruce Ackerman, *The Failure of the Founding Fathers: Jefferson, Marshall, and the Rise of Presidential Democracy* (Cambridge, Mass.: Belknap/Harvard University Press, 2005), 242–43.

12. William Wirt to Peter Carnes, November 1, 1792, William Wirt Papers, Maryland Historical Society, Baltimore (hereafter cited as MdHS), Reel 1.

13. Id.

14. P. H. Cruse, "Biographical Sketch of William Wirt," in *The Letters of the British Spy*, 10th ed. (New York: Harper and Brothers, 1832), 37.

15. See "Mulberry Row," Monticello, https://www.monticello.org/slavery/the-plantation/organization-of-the-monticello-plantation/mulberry-row/; see also Annette Gordon-Reed, *The Hemingses of Monticello: An American Family* (New York: W. W. Norton, 2008), 28, noting that "the Hemings men who were not in the house were artisans who worked just outside of it on Mulberry Row, which abuts and runs parallel to the main house."

16. Thomas Jefferson to William Short, April 13, 1800, in *Papers of Thomas Jefferson*, ed. Barbara B. Oberg (Princeton: Princeton University Press, 2004), 31:502 (hereafter cited as *PTJ*).

17. "Nailery," Thomas Jefferson Encyclopedia, Monticello, https://www.monticello.org/site/research-and-collections/nailery#footnoteref1_96syecb.

18. William Wirt to Thomas Jefferson, with Jefferson's notes, May 4, 1797, in *PTJ*, 29:358–59.

19. Quoted in *Memoirs*, 1:67.

20. Id., 1:68.

21. Cruse, "Biographical Sketch," 41.

22. *Memoirs*, 1:15.

23. Another Carr brother, Samuel, was also falsely named as the father of Hemings's children; both Carrs were conclusively ruled out by DNA testing in 1998. See Gordon-Reed, *Hemingses of Monticello*, 247, 679n18; Annette Gordon-Reed, *Thomas Jefferson and Sally Hemings: An American Controversy* (Charlottesville: University of Virginia Press, 1997).

24. See Anya Jabour, "Male Friendship and Masculinity in the Early National South: William Wirt and His Friends," 20 *Journal of the Early Republic* 83–111 (2000).

25. William Wirt to Dabney Carr, March 19, 1802, MdHS, Reel 1.

26. *Memoirs*, 1:71–72. Carr's 1838 obituary credited Wirt with a different prediction: " 'I foresee you will one day or other be *Judge of the Court of Appeals*; and as for me,' said [Wirt], laughing, 'I shall not be content with less than the *Presidency*!' " "Dabney Carr," 4 *Southern Literary Messenger* 65 (1838).

27. *Memoirs*, 1:76.

28. See Joanne Freeman, "The Election of 1800: A Study in the Logic of Political Change," 108 *Yale Law Journal* 1959 (1999).

29. See Norman K. Risjord, "The Virginia Federalists," 33 *Journal of Southern History* 486 (1967).

30. See Adrienne Koch and Harry Ammon, "The Virginia and Kentucky Resolutions: An Episode in Jefferson's and Madison's Defense of Civil Liberties," 5 *William and Mary Quarterly* 145 (1948); Wendell Bird, "Reassessing Responses to the Virginia and Kentucky Resolutions: New Evidence from the Tennessee and Georgia Resolutions and from Other States," 35 *Journal of the Early Republic* 519 (2015).

31. See Wendell Bird, *Criminal Dissent: Prosecutions under the Alien and Sedition Acts of 1798* (Cambridge, Mass.: Harvard University Press, 2020); Geoffrey R. Stone, *Perilous Times: Free Speech in Wartime from the Sedition Act of 1798 to the War on Terrorism* (New York: W. W. Norton, 2004); Walter Berns, "Freedom of the Press and the Alien and Sedition Laws: A Reappraisal," 1970 *Supreme Court Review* 109 (1970).

32. Virginia Resolutions, December 21, 1798, in *Papers of James Madison*, ed. J. C. A. Stagg et al. (Charlottesville: University Press of Virginia, 1992), 17:189.

33. Resolutions Adopted by the Kentucky General Assembly, November 10, 1798, in *PTJ*, 30:550.

34. Id.

35. Jefferson's Draft, Kentucky Resolution, before October 4, 1798, in *PTJ*, 30:536.

36. Kentucky Resolution, in *PTJ*, 30:536.

37. Virginia Resolution, in *PTJ*, 17:189.

38. See Bird, "Reassessing Responses," 524; see also Koch and Ammon, "Virginia and Kentucky Resolutions"; Stanley Elkins and Eric McKitrick, *The Age of Federalism* (New York: Oxford University Press, 1993), 720.

39. William Wirt to Dabney Carr, December 14, 1798, MdHS, Reel 1.

40. See *Marbury v. Madison*, 5 U.S. (1 Cranch) 137 (1803); see also Alison L. LaCroix, *The Ideological Origins of American Federalism* (Cambridge, Mass.: Harvard University Press, 2010); William Michael Treanor, "Judicial Review before *Marbury*," 58 *Stanford Law Review* 455 (2005); Mary Sarah Bilder, "Idea or Practice: A Brief Historiography of Judicial Review," 20 *Journal of Policy History* 6 (2008); Charles F. Hobson, "John Marshall, the Mandamus Case, and the Judiciary Crisis, 1801–1803," 72 *George Washington Law Review* 289 (2003).

41. Kentucky Resolution of 1799, November 14, 1799, in *The Debates in the Several State Conventions on the Adoption of the Federal Constitution: As Recommended by the General Convention at Philadelphia in 1787: Together with the Journal of the Federal Convention, Luther Martin's letter, Yates's minutes, Congressional Opinions, Virginia and Kentucky Resolutions of '98-'99, and Other Illustrations of the Constitution*, ed. Jonathan Elliot, 2nd ed. (Washington, D.C.: Printed for the Editor, 1836), 4:544–45.

42. James Madison, "The Report of 1800," January 7, 1800, in *The Papers of James Madison*, vol. 17, *31 March 1797–3 March 1801 with a supplement 22 January 1778–9 August 1795*, ed. David B. Mattern, J. C. A. Stagg, Jeanne K. Cross, and Susan Holbrook Perdue (Charlottesville: University Press of Virginia, 1991), 308–9. In 1787, Madison had endorsed a very different vision of the federal-state relationship. His proposed federal negative would have given the Senate the power to veto state laws. After much

debate, the proposal failed to win the support of the convention. See LaCroix, *Ideological Origins*.

43. Madison, "Report of 1800," 348.

44. Id.

45. See Christian G. Fritz, *Monitoring American Federalism: The History of State Legislative Resistance* (Cambridge: Cambridge University Press, 2023).

46. In 1795–96, Wirt represented Jefferson in a case for which Jefferson paid him five pence. See Robert, "William Wirt, Virginian," 397, citing Jefferson's account book notation: "Pd Mr Wirt 5.D. fee in Cobbs' suit agt me."

47. Robert, "William Wirt, Virginian," 399. Wirt's father's estate had included slaves, who became the subject of a dispute between Peter Carnes and Wirt's uncle, Jasper Wirt. Carnes sought Wirt's assistance in recovering the slaves during the latter's stay with the Carneses in Georgia in 1789. Id., 394.

48. William Wirt to Dabney Carr, February 12, 1802, quoted in *Memoirs*, 1:88.

49. Robert, "William Wirt, Virginian," 401.

50. William Wirt to Benjamin Edwards, March 17, 1805, quoted in *Memoirs*, 1:128: "the first the favorite of Petrarch, the last the christian name of my mother."

51. William Wirt to Dabney Carr, March 28, 1803, LVA, Folder 1; Wirt to Carr, February 13, 1803, quoted in *Memoirs*, 1:93 (beginning "Carissime Currus": "Currus," Latin for "chariot" or "car," was a punning inside joke).

52. William Wirt to Dabney Carr, January 16, 1804, LVA, Folder 1.

53. On the Wirts' household, see Anya Jabour, *Marriage in the Early Republic: Elizabeth and William Wirt and the Companionate Ideal* (Baltimore: Johns Hopkins University Press, 1998).

54. William Wirt to Dabney Carr, June 6, 1803, LVA, Folder 1; William Wirt to William Pope, August 5, 1803, quoted in *Memoirs*, 1:100.

55. William Wirt to Dabney Carr, January 16, 1804, LVA, Folder 1. The letter, longer than Wirt's usual, comprised two sheets of paper folded in half, to make eight pages or sides, plus an additional sheet that was folded to make an envelope.

56. Jabour, *Marriage*, 32.

57. William Wirt to Dabney Carr, January 16, 1804, LVA, Folder 1.

58. William Wirt to Elizabeth Wirt, May 10, 1805, quoted in *Memoirs*, 1:133.

59. [William Wirt], *The Letters of the British Spy*, 10th ed. (New York: Harper and Brothers, 1832), 174, 178, 212.

60. Id., 192, 232.

61. See Jay B. Hubbell, "William Wirt and the Familiar Essay in Virginia," 23 *William and Mary Quarterly* 136 (1943); Michael O'Brien, *Conjectures of Order: Intellectual Life and the American South, 1810–1860* (Chapel Hill: University of North Carolina Press, 2004), 657–66; Alison L. LaCroix, "The Lawyer's Library," in *Subversion and Sympathy: Gender, Law, and the British Novel*, ed. Martha C. Nussbaum and Alison L. LaCroix (New York: Oxford University Press, 2013), 251–73.

62. William Wirt to Elizabeth Wirt, May 10, 1805, quoted in *Memoirs*, 1:133.

63. See R. Kent Newmyer, *The Treason Trial of Aaron Burr: Law, Politics, and the Character Wars of the New Nation* (New York: Cambridge University Press, 2012); James E. Lewis, Jr., *The Burr Conspiracy: Uncovering the Story of an Early American Crisis* (Princeton: Princeton University Press, 2017).

64. *Virginia Argus*, June 17, 1807, quoted in Charles F. Hobson, "The Aaron Burr Treason Trial," *Federal Trials and Great Debates in United States History* (Washington, D.C.: Federal Judicial Center, 2006), 36.

65. See Newmyer, *Treason Trial*, 70, 81.

66. Quoted in id., 70.

67. See id., 79. During this period the U.S. attorneys were typically referred to as "district attorneys." See Susan Low Bloch, "The Early Role of the Attorney General in Our Constitutional Scheme: In the Beginning There Was Pragmatism," 1989 *Duke Law Journal* 561 (1989).

68. William Wirt to Francis Walker Gilmer, July 18, 1807, quoted in Robert, "William Wirt, Virginian," 412.

69. Cited in Lewis, *Burr Conspiracy*, 345. Some members of Elizabeth Wirt's family were Federalists and actively supported Burr. Elizabeth's brother John Grattan Gamble acted as one of Burr's securities, and her mother, Catherine Grattan Gamble, sent fruit and calf's-foot jelly in ice to Burr's alleged co-conspirator, Harman Blennerhassett. See Robert, "William Wirt, Virginian," 412.

70. Jurisdiction lay in the federal court for Virginia based on the island's location in the Ohio River just below Parkersburg.

71. Quoted in *Memoirs*, 1:160.

72. Id., 1:169.

73. *United States v. Burr*, 25 Fed. Cas. 122 (1807).

74. The authorized version was *The Two Principal Arguments of William Wirt, Esquire, on the Trial of Aaron Burr, for High Treason, and on the Motion to Commit Aaron Burr and Others for Trial in Kentucky* (Richmond: Samuel Pleasants, Jr., 1808). Wirt's speech remained popular into the twentieth century. See, e.g., Mayo W. Hazeltine, ed. *Orations from Homer to William McKinley* (New York, P. F. Collier and Son, 1902), 3955.

75. Thomas Jefferson to William Wirt, January 10, 1808, Jefferson Papers, Library of Congress, Washington, D.C.

76. Thomas Jefferson to William Wirt, January 10, 1808, Founders Online, National Archives and Records Administration, https://founders.archives.gov/documents/Jefferson/99-01-02-7178.

77. Id.

78. William Wirt to Thomas Jefferson, January 14, 1808, Jefferson Papers, Library of Congress, Washington, D.C.

79. Thomas Jefferson to William Wirt, July 13, 1812, Jefferson Papers, University of Virginia, Charlottesville.

80. "Will be Sold, Before the door of the Eagle Tavern. At 12 o'clock, on Monday the 24th instant, a number of valuable slaves," announced one typical broadside from 1812. The advertisement described the persons to be auctioned as "An excellent Carpenter, a Brick Moulder, A Tanner, a good Crop Hand, 2 Women, and 5 children." Virginia Memory, "Online Exhibitions," University of Virginia, https://www.virginia-memory.com/online-exhibitions/items/show/378.

81. William Wirt to Dabney Carr, February 10, 1811, quoted in *Memoirs*, 1:270.

82. Robert, "William Wirt, Virginian,"421. On at least one occasion, Wirt asked Gilmer to visit an auctioneer to discuss the sale of slaves. William Wirt to Francis Walker Gilmer, December 29, 1812, quoted in id., 421–22.

83. Jabour, *Marriage*, 66.

84. William Wirt to Dabney Carr, August 23, 1813, LVA, Folder 2.

85. Id.

86. William Wirt to Dabney Carr, October 2, 1813, LVA, Folder 2.

87. William Wirt to Dabney Carr, December 10, 1814, LVA, Folder 2.

88. See Alison L. LaCroix, "A Singular and Awkward War: The Transatlantic Context of the Hartford Convention," 6 *American Nineteenth Century History* 3 (2005); James M. Banner, *To the Hartford Convention: The Federalists and the Origins of Party Politics in Massachusetts, 1789–1815* (New York: Knopf, 1970); J. C. A. Stagg, *Mr. Madison's War: Politics, Diplomacy, and Warfare in the Early American Republic* (Princeton: Princeton University Press, 1983).

89. *Boston Gazette*, December 7, 1814, quoted in Samuel Eliot Morison, *Harrison Gray Otis, 1765–1848: The Urbane Federalist* (Boston: Houghton Mifflin, 1969), 366.

90. Joseph Story to Nathaniel Williams, August 24, 1812, in *Life and Letters of Joseph Story, Associate Justice of the Supreme Court of the United States*, ed. William W. Story (Boston: Little, Brown, 1851), 1:228–29.

91. See "Marshall and the Fairfax Litigation: From the Compromise of 1796 to *Martin v. Hunter's Lessee*," in *Papers of John Marshall*, ed. Charles F. Hobson (Chapel Hill: University of North Carolina Press, 1974–2006) (hereafter cited as *PJM*), 8:108.

92. Id., 112.

93. Id., 118. Charles Hobson notes that real estate was "the principal source of [Marshall's] income apart from his official salary as Chief Justice." Charles F. Hobson, "Review Essay, Paul Finkelman's *Supreme Injustice: Slavery in the Nation's Highest Court*," 43 *Journal of Supreme Court History* 363, 368–69 (2018).

94. As was customary in such suits, the suit was filed in the name of a fictitious plaintiff: "Timothy Trytitle, Lessee of David Hunter." See *Trititle v. Fairfax*, Order Book, Superior Court No. 2, 43, Office of Clerk of Circuit Court, Frederick County, April 24, 1794; see also Stanley Phillips Smith, "The Northern Neck's Role in American Legal History," 77 *Virginia Magazine of History and Biography* 277, 282–83 (1969).

95. John Marshall to Charles Lee, May 7, 1810, in *PJM*, 7:247, and quoted in *PJM*, 8:115, 120n19.

96. See id., 8:115: "In no sense was the appeal contrived to be a test case for determining the extent of the Supreme Court's appellate jurisdiction over the state judiciaries."

97. See David Johnson, *Irreconcilable Founders: Spencer Roane, John Marshall, and the Nature of America's Constitutional Republic* (Baton Rouge: Louisiana State University Press, 2021), 71.

98. In 1807, Congress increased the size of the Court from six to seven justices and added a seventh circuit comprising Ohio, Kentucky, and Tennessee. Act of February 24, 1807, ch. 16, 2 Stat. 420.

99. 11 U.S. (7 Cranch) 603 (1813) (Story, J., for the Court). In resting his opinion on the Jay Treaty of 1794, Story interpreted several Virginia legislative acts. Story's reliance on state law earned criticism from Marshall and likely also increased the Virginia judges' resentment at what they viewed as overreach. See *PJM*, 8:116.

100. Mandate quoted in *Hunter v. Martin, Devisee of Fairfax*, 18 Va. (4 Munf.) 1, 1–3 (1815).

101. *Fairfax's Devisee v. Hunter*, 6 American Law Journal 313, 317 (1817).

102. Id.

103. *Hunter v. Martin, Devisees of Fairfax*, 18 Va. (4 Munf.) 1, 3&n. (1815).

104. 6 American Law Journal 313, 341 (1817).

105. Id., 348, 357.

106. Id., 358.

107. Id.

108. See Johnson, *Irreconcilable Founders*; F. Thornton Miller, "John Marshall versus Spencer Roane: A Reevaluation of *Martin v. Hunter's Lessee*," 96 *Virginia Magazine of History and Biography* 297 (1988); Note, "Judge Spencer Roane of Virginia: Champion of States' Rights—Foe of John Marshall," 66 *Harvard Law Review* 1242 (1953).

109. 6 American Law Journal 313, 368 (1817).

110. Id., 368, 373.

111. Id., 372–73.

112. *Hunter v. Martin*, 18 Va. (4 Munf.) 31.

113. Id., 7 (Cabell, J.) (original parentheses omitted).

114. William Wirt to Dabney Carr, August 23, 1813, LVA, Folder 2.

115. William Wirt to Dabney Carr, May 25, 1819, in William Wirt Letters #798-z, Southern Historical Collection, Wilson Library, University of North Carolina at Chapel Hill (hereafter cited as UNC), Folder 1: "I have never met with but one other man who has come near supplying your place to me and that was Wm H. Cabell."

116. *Hunter v. Martin*, 18 Va. (4 Munf.) at 8–9 (Cabell, J.).

117. I borrow this phrase from Hendrik Hartog, "Pigs and Positivism," 1985 *Wisconsin Law Review* 899, 906 (1985).

118. *Hunter v. Martin*, 18 Va. (4 Munf.) 9 (Cabell, J.).

119. See, e.g., Johnson, *Irreconcilable Founders*; F. Thornton Miller, "John Marshall in Spencer Roane's Virginia: The Southern Constitutional Opposition to the Marshall

Court," 33 *John Marshall Law Review* 1131, 1137 (2000); Miller, "John Marshall Versus Spencer Roane"; Note, "Judge Spencer Roane of Virginia."

120. 18 Va. 26 (Roane, J.).

121. Id.

122. Id., n.(c).

123. The writ of error was likely drafted by Marshall. See G. Edward White, *The Marshall Court and Cultural Change* (New York: Cambridge University Press, 1988). Hobson notes that the Court's records also include a fragmentary document in Marshall's hand that Hobson identifies as "an argument relating to the Hunter and Fairfax dispute." Editorial Note, "Marshall and the Fairfax Litigation," in *PJM*, 8:117.

124. *Martin v. Hunter's Lessee*, 14 U.S. 304, 338 (1816).

125. Id., 362.

126. The Virginia court appears not to have taken further action, leading one commentator to conclude that it "ignored" the Supreme Court. See Miller, "John Marshall in Spencer Roane's Virginia," 1137. But as Hobson notes, the claimant under the now-vindicated Fairfax grant (James Marshall) "did not have to take any further legal steps, since the effect of the decision was to confirm possession in those who had purchased from him years earlier." Editorial Note, "Marshall and the Fairfax Litigation," in *PJM*, 8:119.

127. See, e.g., Donald G. Morgan, *Justice William Johnson, The First Dissenter: The Career and Constitutional Philosophy of a Jeffersonian Judge* (Columbia: University of South Carolina Press, 1954). See also Irwin F. Greenberg, "Justice William Johnson: South Carolina Unionist, 1823–1830," 36 *Pennsylvania History* 307 (1969); Herbert A. Johnson, "The Constitutional Thought of William Johnson," 89 *South Carolina Historical Magazine* 132 (1988).

128. See Mark R. Killenbeck, "William Johnson, The Dog That Did Not Bark?," 62 *Vanderbilt Law Review* 407 (2009); Mark R. Killenbeck, "No Bed of Roses: William Johnson, Thomas Jefferson, and the Supreme Court, 1822–23," 37 *Journal of Supreme Court History* 95 (2012).

129. Killenbeck, "Dog That Did Not Bark?," 408.

130. *Martin*, 14 U.S. (1 Wheat.) 363 (Johnson, J., concurring).

131. Id., 372.

132. Id., 373.

133. Id., 380.

134. Id., 382. Johnson had dissented in the previous round before the Court, *Fairfax's Devisee v. Hunter's Lessee*, which ended with the issuance of the mandate to the Virginia Court of Appeals.

135. Id., 379.

136. William Wirt to Dabney Carr, December 10, 1814, LVA, Folder 2.

137. On Jefferson as a "republican patriarch," see Annette Gordon-Reed and Peter S. Onuf, *"Most Blessed of the Patriarchs": Thomas Jefferson and the Empire of the Imagination* (New York: W. W. Norton, 2017).

138. See Erwin C. Surrency, *A History of the Federal Courts*, 2nd ed. (Dobbs Ferry, N.Y.: Oceana, 2002), 376, 378–80. Surrency notes that "[f]or most of the first century of the Court's existence, no time limit on the oral argument was imposed"; in 1812, the Court limited the number of lawyers for each side to two, and an 1848 rule limited the argument to two hours per lawyer. An 1821 rule required printed briefs containing "the substance of all the material pleadings, facts, and documents on which the parties relied and the points of law and the facts intended to be presented at the argument."

139. Thorp, "William Wirt," 245.

140. The courtroom is now known as the "Old Supreme Court Chamber." The Court met there from 1810 to 1860, when it moved one floor upstairs to the former Senate chamber. See Architect of the Capitol, "Old Supreme Court Chamber," https://www.aoc.gov/explore-capitol-campus/buildings-grounds/capitol-building/senate-wing/old-supreme-court-chamber.

141. Charles Warren, *The Supreme Court in United States History*, rev. ed. (Boston: Little, Brown, 1926), 1:466–67 (quoting New York correspondent); G. Edward White, "The Working Life of the Marshall Court," 70 *Virginia Law Review* 1, 6 (1984) (quoting observer).

142. Quoted in Warren, *Supreme Court*, 1:467.

143. William Wirt to Francis Walker Gilmer, April 1, 1816, quoted in *Memoirs*, 1:358. The case was *Jones v. Shore's Executor*, 14 U.S. 462 (1816).

144. William Wirt to Dabney Carr, April 7, 1816, quoted in *Memoirs*, 1:359.

145. The near-duel arose out of an unspecified insult of Wirt by Pinkney in open court while the two were opposing counsel in a high-profile piracy trial in Baltimore late in 1818. Wirt felt that he had no choice but to demand satisfaction. The confrontation was averted by the intervention of "friends"—seconds—who coaxed an apology from Pinkney. William refrained from mentioning the incident to his wife, Elizabeth, until after it had been resolved. He then attempted to justify his actions, saying, "I was driven to the unchristian necessity of exacting from him the reparation due to my honor." Elizabeth was horrified: "Oh my Husband, my Husband, what shall I say or do," she chastised him. "Can it be that you the Father of ten children could have forsaken them, and rushed unbidden before your creator and this for a rash word spoken by reptile man." But William, a self-made gentleman, was resolute in his adherence to the code of gentlemanly behavior: "Your letter recd. To day disappoints me a little—How would you have recd. An insulted & disgraced husband?" A day later, Elizabeth's remonstrance was still on his mind: "Your husband's honor should be left in his own hands." William could not help noting that the non-duel had advanced his professional standing: "Pinkney has injured his personal popularity by his treatment of me—and my conduct has carried mine" to its "summit." See William Wirt to Elizabeth Wirt, December 2, 1818; Elizabeth Wirt to William Wirt, December 3, 1818; and William Wirt to Elizabeth Wirt, December 4, 1818, MdHS, Reel 3.

146. See *Memoirs*, 1:354.

147. William Wirt to Dabney Carr, February 27, 1817, UNC, Folder 1. The case was *The Fortuna*, 15 U.S. (2 Wheat.) 161 (1817).

148. Id.

149. William Wirt to Dabney Carr, March 24, 1817, UNC, Folder 1.

150. On the strains in the Wirts' marriage during this period, see Jabour, *Marriage*, 96–99. William cited "the pressure of business" as the reason for his brief letters from Washington: "Console yourself by remembering that any hour which I take from you to devote to business, contributes, so far to hasten my return to your arms." Elizabeth Wirt, at home with eight children and pregnant with another, was unmollified. She replied, "So it is with merit in this bad world. It is always slighted, and made to bear more than others—when your next wife comes, she'll make you know how a woman ought to be treated, who has half as much to recommend her as your humble servant." William Wirt to Elizabeth Wirt, January 6, 1816, MdHS; Elizabeth Wirt to William Wirt, January 7, 1816, MdHS, both quoted in Jabour, *Marriage*, 98–99. Another letter from the fed-up Elizabeth finished, "So take that, with your silk stockings, & your levees." Elizabeth Wirt to William Wirt, January 7, 1816, MdHS. Wirt was far from the only busy lawyer of the era who received from home pointed references to his absence. The wife of one of Wirt's colleagues, John Coalter, wrote to her husband that their small son had encountered Wirt in the street in Williamsburg and embraced him, mistaking Wirt for his own father. See Phillip Hamilton, *The Making and Unmaking of a Revolutionary Family: The Tuckers of Virginia, 1752–1830* (Charlottesville: University of Virginia Press, 2008), 128–29.

151. William Wirt to Dabney Carr, September 13, 1817, UNC, Folder 1.

152. William Wirt to Dabney Carr, August 20, 1815, LVA, Folder 2.

153. Id.; Thomas Jefferson to William Wirt, November 12, 1816, Jefferson Papers, University of Virginia.

154. William Wirt, *Sketches of the Life and Character of Patrick Henry* (Philadelphia: James Webster, 1817), xii–xiv.

155. John Adams to William Wirt, January 5, 1818; Wirt to Adams, January 12, 1818, both quoted in *Memoirs*, 2:44–46.

156. James Monroe to William Wirt, October 29, 1817, quoted in *Memoirs*, 2:29.

157. William Wirt to Elizabeth Wirt, November 13, 1817, MdHS.

158. Id.

159. *City of Washington Gazette*, November 21, 1817.

160. Jabour, *Marriage*, 101.

161. The Wirts' household during their early years in Washington appears to have included three enslaved women, Mary, Celia, and Hannah; at least one enslaved man, Frederick; possibly other enslaved men, some of whom had been with the family in Richmond, including James, Omai, and Billy; a hired white manservant, Stephen; and a hired white housekeeper, Mrs. Lane. See Jabour, *Marriage*, 103–4, 107.

162. William Wirt to William Pope, January 18, 1818, quoted in *Memoirs*, 2:62.

163. See Bloch, "Early Role of the Attorney General"; Jed Handelsman Shugerman, "Professionals, Politicos, and Crony Attorneys General: A Historical Sketch of the U.S. Attorney General as a Case for Structural Independence," 87 *Fordham Law Review* 1965 (2019).

164. Quoted in Henry Barrett Learned, "The Attorney-General and the Cabinet," 24 *Political Science Quarterly* 444 (1909).

165. The solicitor general's office was established in 1870, and the Office of Legal Counsel in 1934.

166. William Wirt to Hugh Nelson, March 27, 1818, quoted in *Memoirs*, 2:58.

167. Id., 2:60.

168. Id., 2:60–61.

169. The following year, Congress provided a fund of five hundred dollars for stationery, fuel, and "a boy to attend the menial duties." Act of March 3, 1819, ch. 54, 3 Stat. 496, 500.

170. All conversions in this paragraph are taken from the CPI Inflation Calculator, Official Inflation Data, https://www.officialdata.org/.

171. See Joseph C. Burke, *William Wirt: Attorney General and Constitutional Lawyer* (unpub. Ph.D. diss., Indiana University, 1965), 84–85. This amount for 1824 would be roughly $317,000 today. Not until 1853 did Congress make the attorney general's salary comparable to those of other Cabinet officials.

172. William Wirt to William Pope, January 18, 1818, quoted in *Memoirs*, 2:64–65.

173. William Wirt to Major Samuel Miller, June 12, 1818, in *Official Opinions of the Attorneys General of the United States* (Washington, D.C.: Robert Farnham, 1852), 1:211–12.

174. Id., 1:215.

175. William Wirt to Dabney Carr, January 21, 1818, UNC, Folder 1.

176. William Wirt to William Pope, January 18, 1818, quoted in *Memoirs*, 2:62.

177. William Wirt to Elizabeth Wirt, May 7, 1818, MdHS, Reel 3.

178. William Wirt to Dabney Carr, February 1, 1824, LVA, Folder 3.

179. See, e.g., Burke, *William Wirt*, 85.

180. William Wirt to Dabney Carr, October 12, 1819, in *Memoirs* 2:84.

181. William Wirt to Dabney Carr, December 29/30/31, 1819, UNC, Folder 1.

182. Id.

183. John Quincy Adams, "January 2, 1820," in *John Quincy Adams: Diaries* (New York: Library of America, 2017), 1:516.

184. See *Osborn v. Bank of the United States*, 22 U.S. 738 (1824).

185. See John Lauritz Larson, *Internal Improvement: National Public Works and the Promise of Popular Government in the Early United States* (Chapel Hill: University of North Carolina Press, 2002); Alison L. LaCroix, "The Interbellum Constitution: Federalism in the Long Founding Moment," 67 *Stanford Law Review* 397 (2015).

186. James Monroe, *Message From the President of the United States With His Objections to the Bill for the Preservation and Repair of the Cumberland Road; Also, a Paper Containing His Views on the Subject of Internal Improvements* (Washington, D.C.: Gales and Seaton, 1822).

187. See Robert Pierce Forbes, *The Missouri Crisis and Its Aftermath: Slavery and the Meaning of America* (Chapel Hill: University of North Carolina Press, 2007); Sean Wilentz, "Jeffersonian Democracy and the Origins of Political Antislavery in the United States: The Missouri Crisis Revisited," 4 *Journal of the Historical Society* 375 (2004).

188. Adams, *Diaries*, 1:537–38.

189. "To the President of the United States," March 4, 1820, JQA Letter-book, 28 September 1817–19 May 1831, "Public," Microfilms of The Adams Papers, Part II, Massachusetts Historical Society, 1955, Reel 146.

190. Id.

191. Id.

192. Adams, *Diaries*, 1:517.

193. Id., 2:11–12.

194. Id., 2:12.

195. Id., 2:12–13.

196. Id., 2:29–30.

197. Id., 2:31.

198. Adams, Diaries, 2:29–30; To the President [James Monroe], November 20, 1821, *Official Opinions of the Attorneys General of the United States* (Washington: Robert Farnham, 1852), 1:519; To the Secretary of State [John Quincy Adams], September 27, 1822, in id., 1:569–70.

199. Id.

Chapter 2. The Many Directions of Federal Power

1. Index Deaths 1810–1848, vol. G–O, Massachusetts, U.S., Town and Vital Records, 1620–1988, Ancestry.com, https://www.ancestry.com/discoveryui-content/view/43721660:2495?tid=&pid=&queryId=e1f3ed53d2c9fc4d7a6bef7a0dd53d42&_phsrc=qHY49&_phstart=successSource.

2. "List of Piracies, Taken from the Boston Daily Advertiser, since January 1, 1819," *Baltimore Patriot and Mercantile Advertiser*, January 3, 1820; see also "To the Public," *American Beacon and Norfolk and Portsmouth Daily Advertiser*, November 13, 1819. Facts from 1 Brockenbrough's Reports. Almeida's attacks led Spain's consul general in the United States to file libels against both the *Wilson* and the *Almeida* on behalf of his government. See Jeffrey Orenstein, "Joseph Almeida: Portrait of a Privateer, Pirate and Plaintiff," pt. 1 and 2, *Green Bag* 2d (2007 and 2008).

3. Deposition of Bush, quoted in *Case of the Brig Wilson*, Brockenbrough 423, 424, 426 (1820).

4. The ordeals of the vessel under its various *noms de guerre* ended in 1822, when the Supreme Court invalidated the Venezuelan prize court's 1819 condemnation order, under which Almeida claimed title, and ordered the vessel's restitution to its original Spanish owners. *The Arrogante Barcelones*, 20 U.S. 496 (1822). Almeida's decades-long career of piracy ended in 1832 with his execution by Spanish authorities. See Orenstein "Joseph Almeida," pt. 1, 307.

5. Newspapers in Norfolk and far beyond followed the sagas of intercepted privateersmen, including the exploits of the *Wilson*. See, e.g., the Norwich, Connecticut, *Courier*, November 17, 1819.

6. "Notes of Cases in the Courts of the United States in Virginia, 1813–1833," Notebook 3, in St. George Tucker, *St. George Tucker's Law Reports and Selected Papers*, ed. Charles F. Hobson (Chapel Hill: University of North Carolina Press, 2013), 1:1715 (hereafter cited as *SGTLR*).

7. Federal jurisdiction lay under the Judiciary Act of 1789, sec. 9 (exclusive for proceedings *in rem*).

8. See "Plan of the Edition," in *SGTLR*, 1:xix.

9. See, e.g., a notebook entry from spring 1820, in *SGTLR*, 3:1719.

10. "Tucker's *Blackstone*," as it was known, was the most frequently cited American legal authority until 1827, when it was overtaken by James Kent's *Commentaries on American Law* (1826), and subsequently by Joseph Story's *Commentaries on the Constitution of the United States* (1833). Paul Finkelman and David Cobin, introduction to *St. George Tucker's Blackstone's Commentaries* (1803; repr., Union, N.J.: Lawbook Exchange, 1996).

11. Federal circuit courts of the era did not typically function as appellate courts, but they had jurisdiction to hear appeals of admiralty and maritime cases where the amount in controversy exceeded three hundred dollars. See Judiciary Act of 1789, sec. 21.

12. *The Records of the Federal Convention of 1787*, rev. ed., ed. Max Farrand (New Haven: Yale University Press, 1937), 1:164.

13. See Alison L. LaCroix, *The Ideological Origins of American Federalism* (Cambridge, Mass.: Harvard University Press, 2010).

14. See, e.g., James Madison to William C. Rives, October 21, 1833, Founders Online, National Archives and Records Administration, https://founders.archives.gov/documents/Madison/99-02-02-2852.

15. U.S. Const., Art. VI, cl. 2.

16. See LaCroix, *Ideological Origins*.

17. 14 U.S. 304 (1816).

18. See, e.g., Albert O. Hirschman, *The Passions and the Interests: Political Arguments for Capitalism before Its Triumph* (Princeton: Princeton University Press, 1977); Emma Rothschild, *Economic Sentiments: Adam Smith, Condorcet, and the Enlightenment* (Cambridge, Mass.: Harvard University Press, 2002); Paul Cheney, *Revolutionary Commerce: Globalization and the French Monarchy* (Cambridge, Mass.: Harvard

University Press, 2010); Joyce Appleby, *Capitalism and a New Social Order: The Republican Vision of the 1790s* (New York: New York University Press, 1984).

19. Huntress's petition, reprinted in *American Beacon and Norfolk and Portsmouth Daily Advertiser*, November 27, 1819; see also Admiralty Case Files of the U.S. District Court for the Eastern District of Virginia, 1801–1861, M1300, Records of the District Courts of the United States, R.G. 21, National Archives and Records Service, Washington, D.C. (hereafter cited as Admiralty Case Files), microfilm roll 9.

20. Order, November 24, 1819, reprinted in *American Beacon and Norfolk and Portsmouth Daily Advertiser*, November 27, 1819; "Memorandum of An Agreement made the thirtieth day of August 1798, between St George Tucker and Jeremiah Satterwhite, both of Williamsburg," appendix to "St. George Tucker House Architectural Report" (1990), Block 29, Building 2, Lot 163–164–169, Colonial Williamsburg Foundation Library Research Report Series—1569, Williamsburg, Va.

21. Huntress appears to have incurred this debt to Thomas K. Jones in the prior year, when Huntress was in debtors' prison in Boston. Huntress noted in a letter to Jones that the amount was "for the sum you paid for me at the time I accidentially [*sic*] broke my bond last year which you was good enough to sign for the limits of the gaoal [*sic*] at Boston." See Ivory Huntress to Thomas K. Jones, December 14, 1819, in the author's collection. The amount Huntress paid to clear his debt to Jones was around $21,300 in today's dollars; conversion made with the CPI Inflation Calculator, Official Inflation Data, https://www.officialdata.org/us/inflation/1819?amount=882. On "prison limits," see Bruce H. Mann, *Republic of Debtors: Bankruptcy in the Age of American Independence* (Cambridge, Mass.: Harvard University Press, 2002), 293–94n42.

22. Libel, *The United States v. Brig Wilson*, reprinted in *SGTLR*, Notebook 3, 3:1715.

23. The charge listed in count three, unloading goods without permit from collector, carried the penalty of forfeiture of both goods and vessel. See *SGTLR*, Notebook 3, 3:1715n31, citing the Act to Regulate the Collection of Duties on Imports and Tonnage, March 2, 1799, sec. 50, U.S. Statutes at Large 1:665.

24. Libel, in id., 3:1715–16.

25. Brockenbrough, 427.

26. *SGTLR*, Notebook 3, 3:1718.

27. See Peter Linebaugh and Marcus Rediker, *The Many-Headed Hydra: Sailors, Slaves, Commoners, and the Hidden History of the Revolutionary Atlantic* (Boston: Beacon Press, 2000); Sharon Block, *Colonial Complexions: Race and Bodies in Eighteenth-Century America* (Philadelphia: University of Pennsylvania Press, 2018).

28. Quoted by Marshall in Brockenbrough, 439 (italics removed).

29. An Act to Prevent the Migration of Free Negroes and Mulattoes into This Commonwealth, December 12, 1793, in *Statutes at Large of Virginia* (Richmond: Samuel Shepherd, 1835), 1:239.

30. Act of February 28, 1803, ch. 10, 2 Stat. 205 (1803).

31. Id.

32. Id., sec. 2.

33. Id., sec. 3.

34. Another Virginia law passed in 1793 required that free Black persons in the state register with local authorities.

35. U.S. Const., Art. I, sec. 9: "The migration or importation of such persons as any of the states now existing shall think proper to admit, shall not be prohibited by the Congress prior to the year one thousand eight hundred and eight." Article V made the prohibition unamendable: "no Amendment which may be made prior to the Year One thousand eight hundred and eight shall in any Manner affect the first and fourth Clauses in the Ninth Section of the first Article." U.S. Const., Art. V.

36. See Mary Sarah Bilder, "The Struggle over Immigration: Indentured Servants, Slaves, and Articles of Commerce," 61 *Missouri Law Review* 743, 674–75 (1996). Bilder documents uses of the terms "imported" and "importers" in reference to "indentured servants and their transport to the colonies" during the seventeenth and eighteenth centuries. Id., 674–75.

37. Id., 787.

38. See Paul Finkelman, "Slavery and the Constitutional Convention: Making a Covenant with Death," in *Beyond Confederation: Origins of the Constitution and American National Identity*, ed. Richard Beeman et al. (Chapel Hill: University of North Carolina Press, 1987), 188–225; William Wiecek, "Slavery in the Making of the Constitution," in *The Sources of Anti-Slavery Constitutionalism in America, 1760–1848* (Ithaca: Cornell University Press, 1977), 62–83; David Waldstreicher, *Slavery's Constitution: From Revolution to Ratification* (New York: Hill and Wang, 2009); George William Van Cleve, *A Slaveholders' Union: Slavery, Politics, and the Constitution in the Early American Republic* (Chicago: University of Chicago Press, 2010); Sean Wilentz, *No Property in Man: Slavery and Antislavery at the Nation's Founding* (Cambridge, Mass.: Harvard University Press, 2018).

39. See Max Farrand, *Records of the Federal Convention* (New Haven: Yale University Press, 1966), 2:414–15: "Genl Pin[c]kney moved to strike out the words 'the year eighteen hundred' [as the year limiting the importation of slaves], and to insert the words 'the year eighteen hundred and eight.' "

40. Paul Finkelman, "Regulating the African Slave Trade," 54 *Civil War History* 379, 383 (2008). During the 1780s and early 1790s, South Carolina and North Carolina at times permitted the international trade.

41. See Jed Handelsman Shugerman, "The Louisiana Purchase and South Carolina's Reopening of the Slave Trade in 1803," 22 *Journal of the Early Republic* 263 (2002); Finkelman, "Regulating the African Slave Trade."

42. On the Haitian Revolution, see Julius S. Scott, *The Common Wind: Afro-American Currents in the Age of the Haitian Revolution* (New York: Verso, 2018); Laurent Dubois, *Avengers of the New World: The Story of the Haitian Revolution*

(Cambridge, Mass.: Belknap/Harvard University Press, 2005); C. L. R. James, *The Black Jacobins: Toussaint L'Ouverture and the San Domingo Revolution* (London: Secker and Warburg, 1938).

43. 12 *Annals of the Congress of the United States* 9–10 (hereafter cited as *Annals*), House of Reps., February 2, 1803, 459–60.

44. Id., 472.

45. On the 1803 act, see Don E. Fehrenbacher, *The Slaveholding Republic: An Account of the United States Government's Relations to Slavery*, ed. Ward McAfee, 1st ed. (New York: Oxford, 2002), 141–42; Nicholas P. Wood, "A 'Class of Citizens': The Earliest Black Petitioners to Congress and Their Quaker Allies," 74 *William and Mary Quarterly* 109 (2017); Padraig Griffin Riley, *Northern Republicans and Southern Slavery: Democracy in the Age of Jefferson, 1800–1819* (Ph.D. diss., University of California, Berkeley, 2007), 365–68; Howard Albert Ohline, *Politics and Slavery: The Issue of Slavery in National Politics, 1787–1815* (Ph.D. diss., University of Missouri, 1969), 342–48.

46. U.S. Const., Art. IV, sec. 2 ("The Citizens of each State shall be entitled to all Privileges and immunities of Citizens in the several States"); Remarks of Mr. Bacon, *Annals*, February 7, 1803, 467–68. The debate surrounding the act is discussed in Ohline, *Politics and Slavery*, 342–48. The final version of the bill excepted "native[s] . . . citizen[s] . . . or registered seam[e]n of the United States."

47. "Remarks of Mr. Bacon," in *Annals*, 467–68.

48. 60 U.S. (19 How.) 393, 403, 404 (1857): "[T]hat class of persons" whose "ancestors were negroes of the African race, and imported into this country and sold and held as slaves" were "not included, and were not intended to be included, under the word 'citizens' in the Constitution."

49. See Martha S. Jones, *Birthright Citizens: A History of Race and Rights in Antebellum America* (Cambridge: Cambridge University Press, 2018); Kate Masur, *Until Justice Be Done: American's First Civil Rights Movement, from the Revolution to Reconstruction* (New York: W. W. Norton, 2021).

50. Thomas Jefferson to Jared Sparks, February 4, 1824, in *Thomas Jefferson: Writings*, ed. Merrill D. Peterson (New York: Library of America, 1984), 1485; see also Peter S. Onuf, "To Declare Them a Free and Independent People': Race, Slavery, and National Identity in Jefferson's Thought," 18 *Journal of the Early Republic* 1 (1998).

51. William Wirt, "Opinion," November 7, 1821, in *Opinions of the Attorneys General of the United States, from the Beginning of the Government to March 1st, 1841 . . . Published under the Inspection of Henry D. Gilpin* (Washington, D.C.: Blair and Rives, 1841), 383.

52. See Masur, *Until Justice Be Done*, 60, noting that New York's 1821 constitutional convention "restricted Black men's right to vote while also explicitly recognizing African Americans as New York citizens."

53. "Remarks of Mr. Bacon."

54. *Annals*, February 1803, 469–70.

55. Id., 470.

56. "Remarks of Mr. Mitchill," in id. Mitchill and fourteen other members—not including Bacon—voted against the bill, while a number of others abstained. The final vote in the House was 48–15. See *Annals*, 533–34.

57. See Gautham Rao, *National Duties: Custom Houses and the Making of the American State* (Chicago: University of Chicago Press, 2016).

58. In *Brigantine Amiable Lucy v. United States*, Attorney General Caesar Rodney argued that the 1803 act required forfeiture of a vessel that "imports a slave into a state where such importation is prohibited" (italics omitted). 10 U.S. (6 Cranch) 330, 332 (1810).

59. See generally Shugerman, "Louisiana Purchase."

60. *SGTLR*, Notebook 3, 3:1717–18.

61. Id., 3:1718.

62. Id. Taylor's honorific, like those of many of his contemporaries, stemmed from his state militia service.

63. Bill of Sale, July 1, 1817, *United States v. Schooner Louisa*, U.S. Dist. Ct. E.D. Va. (1819), Admiralty Case Files of the U.S. District Court for the Eastern District of Virginia, Norfolk Division, R.G. 21, National Archives, roll 7.

64. *United States v. Schooner Louisa*, U.S. Dist. Ct. E.D. Va., November 15, 1819, in *SGTLR*, Notebook 3, 3:1713; see also Peter Graham Fish, *Federal Justice in the Mid-Atlantic South: United States Courts from Maryland to the Carolinas, 1789–1835* (Washington, D.C.: Administrative Office of the United States Courts, 2002), 286–87.

65. An Act to Prohibit the Importation of Slaves into Any Port or Place within the Jurisdiction of the United States, from and after the First Day of January, in the Year of Our Lord One Thousand Eight Hundred and Eight, March 2, 1807. The act of 1807 thus took effect immediately upon the expiration of the time period set forth in Article I, sec. 9.

66. *United States v. Schooner Louisa*, in *SGTLR*, Notebook 3, 3:1714; see also Fish, *Federal Justice*, 286–87.

67. *SGTLR*, Notebook 3, 3:1714. Tucker may have had insight into the content of the convention debates: his former law teacher, George Wythe, had been a delegate to the convention, and in 1790, Tucker succeeded Wythe as professor of law and police at William and Mary.

68. Fish, *Federal Justice*, 287n86, citing Admiralty Case Files, microfilm reel 7; see also "Voyage of Deception: Captain Rasmyne and the Schooner *Louisa*," Norfolk Historical Society *Courier*, Spring 2006, https://www.historicforrest.com/norfolkHistoricalSociety/insights/2006_spring/Rasmyne.html.

69. See *United States v. La Jeune Eugenie*, 26 F. Cas. 832 (C. C. Mass. 1822) (Story, J.), declaring the slave trade "repugnant to the great principles of Christian duty, the dictates of natural religion, the obligations of good faith and morality, and the eternal maxims of social justice" and inconsistent with "any system of law that purports to

rest on the authority of reason or revelation." See also Note, "International Norms and Politics in the Marshall Court's Slave Trade Cases," 128 *Harvard Law Review* 1184 (2015).

70. *Annals*, 472.

71. An Act to Prohibit the Importation of Slaves, into Any Port or Place within the Jurisdiction of the United States, from and after the First Day of January, in the Year of Our Lord, One Thousand Eight Hundred and Eight, 2 Stat. 426, Ch. 22 (March 2, 1807).

72. In 1815, Tucker's Williamsburg household included fifteen slaves: "2. Males over fifty years of Age; 5. Males between twelve & fifty; 1. Female over fifty; 4. Females between twelve & fifty; 3. Females under twelve years of age, valued At $3,000. Dollars." See "List of Lands, Lots of Ground, with their Improvements, dwelling houses & Slaves, owned by St. George Tucker . . .," "List of Taxable Property 1815 of St. George Tucker," Tucker-Coleman Papers, appendix to Tucker House Architectural Report, Block 29, Building 2, Lot 163–164–169, Colonial Williamsburg Foundation Library Research Report Series—1569, Williamsburg, Va., 1990.

73. See Alan Taylor, *The Internal Enemy: Slavery and War in Virginia, 1772–1832* (New York: W. W. Norton, 2013), 87–89, 106–10; Paul Finkelman, "The Dragon St. George Could Not Slay: Tucker's Plan to End Slavery," 47 *William and Mary Law Review* 1213 (2006); Phillip Hamilton, *The Making and Unmaking of a Revolutionary Family: The Tuckers of Virginia, 1752–1830* (Charlottesville: University of Virginia Press, 2008).

74. See David Thomas Konig, "St. George Tucker and the Limits of States' Rights Constitutionalism: Understanding the Federal Compact in the Early Republic," 47 *William and Mary Law Review* 1279 (2006).

75. The Judiciary Act of 1802 was part of the newly elected Jeffersonian Republicans' reversal of the Federalists' expansion of the federal judiciary following the election of 1800. See Alison L. LaCroix, "Federalists, Federalism, and Federal Jurisdiction," 30 *Law and History Review* 205 (2012).

76. See John Marshall to St. George Tucker, June 2, 1820, in *Papers of John Marshall*, ed. Charles F. Hobson (Chapel Hill: University of North Carolina Press, 1974–2006) (hereafter cited as *PJM*), 9:47.

77. Jefferson visited the original in 1787, while serving as minister to France: "Here I am, Madam, gazing whole hours at the Maison quarrée, like a lover at his mistress. . . . From Lyons to Nismes I have been nourished with the remains of Roman grandeur." Thomas Jefferson to Madame de Tessé, March 20, 1787, Founders Online, National Archives and Records Administration, https://founders.archives. gov/documents/Jefferson/01-11-02-0229. That grandeur was not republican but imperial, however: the structure is estimated to date from approximately 12 B.C.E., and its architrave bore a dedication to the adopted sons of the emperor Augustus.

78. Marshall evidently did not share the view of the virtues of a walking commute held by his colleague Dabney Carr, who chose, after "a severe attack of gravel" (kidney

stones), to live more than mile and a half from the Richmond courthouse in order to ensure a healthful daily constitutional. Carr called the house "Elba," a joking reference to Napoleon's brief exile. See "Dabney Carr," 4 *Southern Literary Messenger* 65, 67 (1838); F. Thornton Miller, "Dabney Carr (1773–1837)," in *Dictionary of Virginia Biography* (Richmond: Library of Virginia, 1998).

79. See Paul Finkelman, *Supreme Injustice: Slavery in the Nation's Highest Court* (Cambridge, Mass.: Harvard University Press, 2018), 31.

80. The *Papers of John Marshall* list the date of decision as "ca. May 22," while the notes to *Tucker's Law Reports* give a date of June 8. *PJM*, 9:31; *SGTLR*, 3:1719.

81. The record stated that the *Wilson* was commissioned by the United Provinces of Venezuela and New Grenada; Marshall referred to it as having been commissioned by "the government of Buenos Ayres." Brockenbrough, 424, 433.

82. *The Brig Wilson. Huntress vs. The United States.* John Marshall, *Opinions Delivered in the Circuit Court of the United States, 1803–1831*, American Philosophical Society, Philadelphia.

83. U.S. Const., Art. I, sec. 8, cl. 3.

84. *United States v. The William*, 28 Fed. Cas. 614 (D. Mass. 1808).

85. Id., 621.

86. The argument that the 1808 clause was a temporary exception to an otherwise broad commerce power found support in the debates of the Constitutional Convention. See David L. Lightner, *Slavery and the Commerce Power: How the Struggle against the Interstate Slave Trade Led to the Civil War* (New Haven: Yale University Press, 2006), 17.

87. *McCulloch v. Maryland*, 17 U.S. 316 (1819).

88. Brockenbrough, 431–32.

89. During the Confederation period, several members of Congress—including Virginians Monroe and Madison—advocated giving Congress exclusive power over interstate commerce. In 1785, Monroe chaired a congressional committee that recommended amending the Articles to give Congress the "sole and exclusive right" of "regulating the trade of the states, as well with foreign nations, as with each other." See *The Committee Consisting of ___, to whom was referred the motion of Mr. Monroe, submit the following report . . .* (New York, 1785), Library of Congress.

90. See *McCulloch*; see also Alison L. LaCroix, "The Shadow Powers of Article I," 123 *Yale Law Journal* 2044 (2014).

91. Brockenbrough, 432–33.

92. Id., 435–36.

93. Id., 436.

94. Id., 437.

95. Id., 438.

96. See Lightner, *Slavery and the Commerce Power*, 19, 30.

97. National Park Service, John Marshall House, Richmond, Va.; see also Finkelman, *Supreme Injustice*.

98. Brockenbrough, 438.

99. Id., 439.

100. *SGTLR*, Notebook 3, 3:1719.

101. *Niles' Weekly Register*, July 22, 1820.

102. *Niles' Weekly Register*, July 29, 1820.

103. *United States vs. Officers and Crew of the Brigantine Wilson, lying in port of Norfolk*, June 15, 1820, in *SGTLR*, Notebook 3, 3:1733–34 and nn.

104. *Niles' Weekly Register*, July 1, 1820.

105. *La Jeune Eugenie*, 26 Fed. Cas. 832, 837. See also Note, "International Norms and Politics in the Marshall Court's Slave Trade Cases," 128 *Harvard Law Review* 1184 (2015).

106. 8 Fed. Cas. 493 (No. 4366) (C.C.D.S.C. 1823).

107. John Marshall to Joseph Story, September 26, 1823, Joseph Story Papers, Massachusetts Historical Society. The original is torn, causing a few letters to be missing.

108. Brockenbrough, 431. Marshall's handwritten draft shows that the phrase "& Congress is unable their entry" was an emendation, added above a carat. Brockenbrough presumably added "to prevent." Marshall, *Opinions*.

109. Brockenbrough, 431. The phrase "for the sake of argument" was also an emendation. Marshall, *Opinions*.

110. Cf. Finkelman, *Supreme Injustice*, 30 and 232n7, inaccurately describing *The Brig Wilson* as a case that "involved the African slave trade" and in which "no federalism issue actually arose."

111. Charles Warren, *The Supreme Court in United States History*, rev. ed. (Boston: Little, Brown, 1926), 1:627.

Chapter 3. The Steamboat and the Commerce of the Union

1. Felix Frankfurter, *The Commerce Clause under Marshall, Taney, and White* (Chapel Hill: University of North Carolina Press, 1937), 1.

2. Edward S. Corwin, *The Commerce Power versus States' Rights* (Princeton: Princeton University Press, 1936).

3. G. Edward White, *The Marshall Court and Cultural Change, 1815–1835* (New York: Cambridge University Press, 1988), 575.

4. 22 U.S. 1 (1824).

5. John Marshall to Joseph Story, September 26, 1823, in Joseph Story Papers, Massachusetts Historical Society.

6. Albert J. Beveridge, *The Life of John Marshall* (Boston: Houghton Mifflin, 1916–19), 4:429–30.

7. See, e.g., Richard Primus, "The *Gibbons* Fallacy," 19 *University of Pennsylvania Journal of Constitutional Law* 567 (2017); Norman R. Williams, "Gibbons," 79 *New York University Law Review* 1398 (2004); Michael J. Klarman, "How Great Were the 'Great' Marshall Court Decisions?," 87 *Virginia Law Review* 1111 (2001); George Lee Haskins, "John Marshall and the Commerce Clause of the Constitution," 104 *University of Pennsylvania Law Review* 23 (1955); Frederick H. Cooke, "The *Gibbons v. Ogden* Fetish," 9 *Michigan Law Review* 324 (1910–11). On the commerce power generally, see Jack M. Balkin, "Commerce," 109 *Michigan Law Review* 1 (2010); William N. Eskridge, Jr., and John Ferejohn, "The Elastic Commerce Clause: A Political Theory of American Federalism," 47 *Vanderbilt Law Review* 1355 (1994); Richard A. Epstein, "The Proper Scope of the Commerce Power," 73 *Virginia Law Review* 1387 (1987). Histories of the case include Herbert A. Johnson, Gibbons v. Ogden: *John Marshall, Steamboats, and the Commerce Clause* (Lawrence: University Press of Kansas, 2010); Thomas H. Cox, Gibbons v. Ogden, *Law, and Society in the Early Republic* (Athens: Ohio University Press, 2009); Maurice G. Baxter, *The Steamboat Monopoly: Gibbons v. Ogden, 1824* (New York, Knopf: 1972).

8. See *National Federation of Independent Business v. Sebelius*, 567 U.S. 519 (2012), citing *Gibbons* to rebut the proposition that "the Framers had . . . an obscure meaning in mind when they used the word 'regulate.' "

9. Johnson, *Gibbons*, 50.

10. See Robert O. Woods, "The Genesis of the Steamboat," 131 *Mechanical Engineering* 44–47 (2009); see also Walter Johnson, *River of Dark Dreams: Slavery and Empire in the Cotton Kingdom* (Cambridge, Mass.: Harvard University Press, 2013).

11. *Corfield v. Coryell*, 6 Fed. Cas. 546 (C.C. E.D. Pa. 1825) (argued in 1823). On Washington's life and jurisprudence, see Gerard N. Magliocca, *Washington's Heir: The Life of Bushrod Washington* (New York: Oxford University Press, 2022).

12. See William Winslow Crosskey, "Mr. Chief Justice Marshall," in *Mr. Justice*, ed. Allison Dunham and Philip B. Kurland (Chicago: University of Chicago Press, 1956), critiquing this view.

13. Corwin, *Commerce Power*.

14. Details in this and the following paragraph are drawn from Johnson, *Gibbons*, 26–29. On the history and culture of steamboat travel, see Johnson, *River of Dark Dreams*.

15. Burr counseled Gibbons that any suit Ogden might commence in New York state court could be removed by Gibbons, as the defendant, to federal court, based on diversity of citizenship between the Georgian Gibbons and the New Jerseyite Ogden. Both Burr and Gibbons believed that federal court would provide a friendlier forum than the courts of the state that had issued the monopoly. Burr's advice was correct, but when Ogden sued Gibbons in 1818, Gibbons's lawyers failed to observe a new New York rule requiring that a notice of removal be filed prior to the lawyers' appearance in state court. Johnson, *Gibbons*, 56–58.

16. *Ogden v. Gibbons*, 4 Johns. Ch. 150, 153 (N.Y. Ch. 1819).

17. Id., 164–65.

18. See Daniel J. Hulsebosch, "An Empire of Law: Chancellor Kent and the Revolution in Books in the Early Republic," 60 *Alabama Law Review* 377, 380 (2009).

19. Paul Finkelman and David Cobin, introduction to *St. George Tucker's Blackstone's Commentaries* (1803; repr., Union, N.J.: Lawbook Exchange, 1996).

20. *Ogden*, 4 Johns. Ch. 152–53.

21. Id., 153–54.

22. Id., 154.

23. Act of February 18, 1793, ch. 8, sec. 6, 1 Stat. 305.

24. Gautham Rao, *National Duties: Custom Houses and the Making of the American State* (Chicago: University of Chicago Press, 2016), 75: "By 1793 the customs houses were the federal government's sole reliable and significant stream of revenue."

25. That is, between around eight and thirty-two dollars in 2023 dollars. See the CPI Inflation Calculator, Official Inflation Data, https://www.officialdata.org/us/inflation/1824?amount=1.

26. Act of February 18, 1793, ch. 8, sec. 6, 1 Stat. 305.

27. 4 Johns. Ch. 157.

28. Id.

29. Id., 158–59.

30. Id., 158.

31. 9 Johns. 507 (N.Y. 1812). The court was known as the "Court of Errors."

32. See William J. Novak, *The People's Welfare: Law and Regulation in Nineteenth-Century America* (Chapel Hill: University of North Carolina Press, 1996); see also Laura F. Edwards, *The People and Their Peace: Legal Culture and the Transformation of Inequality in the Post-Revolutionary South* (Chapel Hill: University of North Carolina Press, 2009); Christopher L. Tomlins, *Law, Labor, and Ideology in the Early American Republic* (Cambridge: Cambridge University Press, 1993).

33. *Livingston v. Van Ingen*, 9 Johns. 548, 554 (argument of Emmet).

34. Id., 577–78 (Kent, C. J.).

35. Id., 576.

36. Id., 576, 578.

37. Id., 578.

38. The Court of Errors at that time included the president of the New York senate, the senators, and the judges of the Supreme Court or the chancellor, whichever was not the court that had heard the case below.

39. *Gibbons v. Ogden*, 17 Johns. 488, 504 (N.Y. 1820) (argument of Hoffman).

40. See Robert Pierce Forbes, *The Missouri Compromise and Its Aftermath: Slavery and the Meaning of America* (Chapel Hill: University of North Carolina Press, 2007); Merrill D. Peterson, *The Great Triumvirate: Webster, Clay, and Calhoun* (New York: Oxford University Press, 1987); Sean Wilentz, "Jeffersonian Democracy and the Origins

of Political Antislavery in the United States: The Missouri Crisis Revisited," 4 *Journal of the Historical Society* 375 (2004).

41. *Gibbons v. Ogden*, 19 U.S. (6 Wheat.) 448 (1821). The report of the dismissal of Gibbons's appeal immediately followed Wheaton's report of *Cohens v. Virginia* (1821), in which the Court held that it had jurisdiction to review the state criminal conviction of the Cohen brothers for unlawfully selling lottery tickets; 19 U.S. (6 Wheat.) 264 (1821).

42. See Gerald T. Dunne, "Smith Thompson," in Leon Friedman and Fred L. Israel, *Justices of the Supreme Court: Their Lives and Major Opinions*, 4th ed. (New York: Infobase, 2013), 1:185–86.

43. William Wirt to James Monroe, May 5, 1823, James Monroe Papers, Manuscript Division, New York Public Library; see also H. Jefferson Powell, "William Wirt and the Invention of the Public Lawyer," 4 *Green Bag 2d* 297 (2001).

44. William Wirt to James Monroe, May 5, 1823.

45. Quoted in Dunne, "Smith Thompson," 187.

46. William Wirt to Francis Walker Gilmer, January 26, 1817, quoted in John Pendleton Kennedy, *Memoirs of the Life of William Wirt, Attorney-General of the United States*, new and rev. ed. (New York: G. P. Putnam's Sons, 1872) (hereafter cited as *Memoirs*), 2:17.

47. William Wirt to Dabney Carr, February 1, 1824, Wirt Letters, Library of Virginia, Richmond, Folder 3. Kennedy's version of the letter replaced "Lucifer" with "Caesar."

48. A. Oakey Hall, "Thomas Addis Emmet," 8 *Green Bag* 273, 275–76 (1896).

49. See *The Papers of Daniel Webster, Legal Papers*, vol. 3, *The Federal Practice*, pt. 1, ed. Andrew J. King (Hanover, N.H.: University Press of New England, 1989), 153–54. The peroration is not mentioned in Wheaton's reports, but the editors of *The Papers of Daniel Webster* find "strong evidence" that Webster "said something along the lines of this reported peroration," which stemmed from firsthand recollections recorded in 1852. The speech's effects were reported in contemporaneous accounts. Id., 154.

50. Salma Hale to William Allen, March 12, 1818, in *The Papers of Daniel Webster Digital Edition*, ed. Charles M. Wiltse (Charlottesville: University of Virginia Press, Rotunda, 2018) (hereafter cited as *PDWDE*). Hale was a New Hampshire congressman and a trustee of the newly created entity, Dartmouth University. Hale also deemed Webster's arguments "very disingenuous" and noted "it cost me almost the nights labor to furnish Mr. Wirt with facts & authority to put him down." Salma Hale to William Allen, March 11, 1818, in id.

51. See appendix in Galen N. Thorp, "William Wirt," 33 *Journal of Supreme Court History* 223, 263 (2008).

52. Daniel Webster to Jeremiah Mason, February 22, 1818, in *PDWDE*.

53. Thomas Gibbons to Daniel Webster, December 13, 1819, in *PDWDE*.

54. "Receipt," February 28, 1821, in *PDWDE*. See also Robert Remini, *Daniel Webster: The Man and His Time* (New York: W. W. Norton, 1997), 201.

55. William Wirt and Daniel Webster to William Gibbons, February 18, 1824, in *PDWDE*. Wirt and Webster thus each earned a total of roughly $48,000 in today's money ($16,000 for the retainer plus $32,000 for the remaining payment). See the CPI Inflation Calculator, Official Inflation Data, https://www.officialdata.org/us/inflation/1824?amount=500.

56. A sense of the spectacle that accompanied the Court's proceedings is evident in this report regarding William Pinkney, considered by many observers to be the most brilliant advocate who practiced before the Marshall Court, but also a divisive figure. An essayist in the Washington *Gazette* lampooned Pinkney's performance: he "enters a la dandy, makes his bow to the audience and then to the Court, who sit as kind of managers of the farce. Five or six hours are consumed, part in traversing the bar, part in argument, part in rhodomontade [a bragging speech]. The ladies go home marvelously delighted." As Pinkney's fellow Marylander Roger Brooke Taney observed, "[A] man who, at the age of fifty, spoke in amber-colored doeskin gloves, could hardly be expected to have a taste for simple or natural elocution." Quoted in White, *Marshall Court and Cultural Change*, 247, 251; see also Robert M. Ireland, *The Legal Career of William Pinkney* (Ph.D. diss, University of Nebraska, 1967), 329.

57. Act of March 3, 1837, ch. 34, 5 Stat. 176.

58. Margaret Bayard Smith, *The First Forty Years of Washington Society*, ed. Gaillard Hunt (New York: Charles Scribner's Sons, 1906), 96; see also Catherine Allgor, *A Perfect Union: Dolley Madison and the Creation of American Nationhood* (New York: Henry Holt, 2006), 152.

59. William Wirt to Agnes Wirt, February 4, 1830, William Wirt Papers, Maryland Historical Society, Baltimore, Reel 13. The microfilmed version of the letter is a copy, and the copyist emended "Webster" to "W___." The case was *Carver v. Jackson ex dem. Astor*, 29 U.S. 172 (1830). A few days later, Elizabeth Wirt reported to William Wirt that his client, the mighty John Jacob Astor, had called on the family in Baltimore: "Mr Aster appeared indeed to be delighted with your management of his case—and seemed not to have a doubt of his success. Said that you had far transcended his highest expectations, although they had been very great—that you studied your causes thoroughly—that indeed he fears you [?] of your health by such intense application &c. &c. . . . All this was a delightful hearing to your affectionate wife." Elizabeth Wirt to William Wirt, February 7, 1830, id.

60. See Charles Warren, *The Supreme Court in United States History*, rev. ed. (Boston: Little, Brown, 1926), 1:467–68.

61. See Johnson, Gibbons v. Ogden, 61.

62. Webster quoted in Warren, *Supreme Court*, 1:603.

63. Felix Frankfurter, *The Commerce Clause under Marshall, Taney, and Waite* (Chapel Hill: University of North Carolina Press, 1937), 12–14.

64. *Gibbons v. Ogden*, 22 U.S. (9 Wheat.) 1, 4–5 (1824).

65. 9 Wheat. 9. Notably, throughout the arguments, the lawyers referred simply to "the power of Congress to regulate commerce"—not "interstate commerce" or "commerce among the states."

66. Id.

67. Id., 13.

68. Id., 9.

69. Id., 14.

70. Id., 14, 24.

71. Id., 15–17; see also Daniel J. Hulsebosch, *Constituting Empire: New York and the Transformation of Constitutionalism in the Atlantic World, 1664–1830* (Chapel Hill: University of North Carolina Press, 2005), 88; Alison L. LaCroix, "Rhetoric and Reality in Early American Legal History: A Reply to Gordon Wood," 78 *University of Chicago Law Review* 757–78 (2011).

72. 9 Wheat. 18–20.

73. To give but one example, following the argument in *Dartmouth College*, while Wheaton was preparing his reports, he shared the notes of all the lawyers in the case with Webster. Webster in turn assured his co-counsel Joseph Hopkinson, "I can easily so arrange your notes, as not to suffer by comparison." Daniel Webster to Joseph Hopkinson, April 23, 1819, in *PDWDE*.

74. 9 Wheat. 27, 28, 31. Webster's first reference to the coasting statute does not appear until page 27.

75. 17 Johns. 507.

76. 9 Wheat. 20.

77. See David L. Lightner, *Slavery and the Commerce Power: How the Struggle against the Interstate Slave Trade Led to the Civil War* (New Haven: Yale University Press, 2006).

78. John Marshall to Joseph Story, September 26, 1823, in Joseph Story Papers, Massachusetts Historical Society.

79. 9 Wheat. 34.

80. Id., 34, 65.

81. Id., 65.

82. Id., 62–63.

83. Id., 63.

84. Id., 88. Emmet owed his life to Robert Fulton, who had died in 1815 as a result of pneumonia contracted when he saved Emmet from drowning in the frozen Hudson River. Thomas Addis Emmet, *Memoirs of Thomas Addis and Robert Emmet* (New York: Emmet Press, 1915), 1:427–28.

85. 9 Wheat. 91–92.

86. Id., 99–100.

87. Id., 100. Note again the scrambled nature of interbellum views on federal power: Tucker the Virginian plantation owner advocating exclusive federal authority over commerce, and Kent the New York Federalist promoting concurrent power.

88. Id., 106.

89. Id., 106–7.

90. Id., 107.

91. Id., 107, 110–12.

92. *New-York Evening Post*, February 12, 1824.

93. *Richmond Enquirer*, March 2, 1824.

94. *New-York Evening Post*, February 12, 1824. Reports of the case were reprinted throughout the nation while it was being argued. See, e.g., *Charleston Courier*, February 24, 1824 (leading with "Steam-Boat Cause, from the New-York Statesman").

95. 9 Wheat. 4–5.

96. Cf. David Armitage, *Civil Wars: A History in Ideas* (New York: Alfred A. Knopf, 2017).

97. 9 Wheat. 185.

98. 9 Wheat. 184–85.

99. 9 Wheat. 181.

100. Validity of the South Carolina Police Bill, May 8, 1824, in *Official Opinions of the Attorneys General of the United States* (Washington, D.C.: Robert Farnham, 1852), 1:659–61.

101. 9 Wheat. 180–81.

102. Id., 181, 182.

103. Id., 162.

104. Id., 183.

105. *Livingston v. Van Ingen*, 580.

106. 9 Wheat. 182–83.

107. Samuel Johnson, *A Dictionary of the English Language; in which the words are deduced from their originals and illustrated in their different significations by examples from the best writers. To which are prefixed, a history of the language, and an English grammare*, 2 vols., s.v. "Commerce" (London: W. Strahan, 1755). On the connections between the terms "commerce" and "intercourse," see Balkin, "Commerce"; Mark R. Killenbeck, "The Original (?) Public (?) Meaning of 'Commerce,' " 16 *University of Pennsylvania Journal of Constitutional Law* 289 (2013).

108. Henry Seawell to Thomas Ruffin, February 12, 1824, quoted in Warren, *Supreme Court*, 1:606. Ruffin later became chief justice of North Carolina.

109. 22 U.S. 189–90.

110. *Charleston Courier*, February 24, 1824 (from *New-York Statesman*) (italics omitted).

111. Id.

112. Virgil, *Eclogues. Georgics. Aeneid: Books 1–6*, trans. H. Rushton Fairclough, Loeb Classical Library 63 (Cambridge, Mass.: Harvard University Press, 1916), 294–95.

113. Quoted in *Memoirs*, 2:145–45.

114. *Richmond Enquirer*, March 2, 1824.

115. 9 Wheat. 185.

116. Id., 209.

117. Id., 229 (Johnson, J., concurring).

118. See, e.g., *Mayor of New York v. Miln* (1837); *License Cases* (1847); *Passenger Cases* (1849). The Court held in *Cooley v. Board of Wardens* (1851) that states could regulate commerce that was "local and not national." As Chapter 8 discusses, that line proved difficult to draw.

119. 9 Wheat. 210–11 (Marshall, C.J.).

120. See, e.g., id., 210 ("collision" and "supremacy").

121. Id., 230, 238 (Johnson, J., concurring).

122. *Memoirs*, 2:142.

123. William Wirt to Elizabeth Wirt, February 11, 1824, William Wirt Papers, Maryland Historical Society, Baltimore, Reel 5.

124. John Quincy Adams, *Memoirs of John Quincy Adams, Comprising Portions of His Diary from 1795 to 1848*, ed. Charles Francis Adams (Philadelphia: J. B. Lippincott, 1874–77), 6:252.

125. The day before the Wirts' party, William Gibbons wrote to Webster from Elizabethtown: "I am authorized to say that your wishes as expressed in your Letter of the 18th of February," in which Webster and Wirt had delivered their additional bill for one thousand dollars each, "will be complied with." William Gibbons to Daniel Webster, March 8, 1824, in *PDWDE*.

126. *Memoirs*, 2:145.

127. Id.; 9 Wheat. 158.

128. Peter Harvey, *Reminiscences and Anecdotes of Daniel Webster* (Boston: Little, Brown, 1877), 142–43.

129. See *Cooley v. Board of Wardens*, 53 U.S. (12 How.) 299 (1852).

130. [James Kent], Handwritten Notes, *Wheaton's Reports*, vol. 9, James Kent Law Library Collection, New York State Library.

Chapter 4. The Justice, the Sailors, and the Founders' Legacy

1. *South Carolina Gazette*, November 21, 1774.

2. See Lorri Glover, *Eliza Lucas Pinckney: An Independent Woman in the Age of Revolution* (New Haven: Yale University Press, 2020); Margaret F. Pickett, *Eliza Lucas Pinckney: Colonial Plantation Manager and Mother of American Patriots, 1722–1793* (Jefferson, N.C.: McFarland, 2016); Darcy R. Fryer, "The Mind of Eliza Pinckney: An Eighteenth-Century Woman's Construction of Herself," 99 *South Carolina Historical Magazine* 215 (1998); Harriet Simons Williams, "Eliza Lucas Pinckney and Her Family: Before the Letterbook," 99 *South Carolina Historical Magazine* 259 (1998); Anne Firor Scott, "Self-Portraits: Three Women," in *Uprooted Americans: Essays to Honor Oscar Handlin*, ed. Richard L. Bushman et al. (Boston: Little, Brown,

1979), 43–76; Adam Nicolson, "Courage," in *The Gentry* (London: Harper, 2011), 243; Elise Pinckney and Marvin R. Zahniser, eds. *The Letterbook of Eliza Lucas Pinckney* (Columbia: University of South Carolina Press, 1997); Harriet Horry Ravenel, *Eliza Pinckney* (New York: Charles Scribner's Sons, 1896). On the Pinckney family, see Frances Leigh Williams, *A Founding Family: The Pinckneys of South Carolina* (New York: Harcourt Brace Jovanovich, 1978); Marvin R. Zahniser, *Charles Cotesworth Pinckney, Founding Father* (Chapel Hill: University of North Carolina Press, 1967); George C. Rogers, *Charleston in the Age of the Pinckneys* (Columbia: University of South Carolina Press, 1980).

3. Glover, *Eliza Lucas Pinckney*, 2.

4. Tiffany Momon, "John 'Quash' Williams, Charleston Builder," *Journal of Southern Decorative Arts* (2020), https://www.mesdajournal.org/2020/john-quash-williams-charleston-builder/.

5. Gene Waddell, "Charles Pinckney's Double House," in *Charleston Architecture, 1670–1860* (Charleston: Wyrick, 2003), 1:79, 93.

6. Id., 93. Williams advertised in the *South Carolina Gazette*, noting that "as he is a free man, he promises, that whosoever shall please to employ him, shall find not only their work well done and handsomely finish'd, but with great fidelity, justice, and dispatch." Quoted in id.; see also Momon, "John 'Quash' Williams."

7. See Waddell, "Charles Pinckney's Double House," 79.

8. See Thomas Pinckney to Charles Cotesworth Pinckney, October 1, [1774], in *The Papers of the Revolutionary Era Pinckney Statesmen Digital Edition*, ed. Constance B. Schulz (Charlottesville: University of Virginia Press, Rotunda, 2016) (hereafter cited as *PPSDE*). Thomas Pinckney, studying law at the Middle Temple in London, wrote to his brother Charles Cotesworth Pinckney in Charles Town, "I expect to find my Neice [*sic*] grown a stout young Woman by the Time I arrive."

9. The city's name was changed from "Charles Town" to "Charleston" in 1783, when the city was incorporated following the end of the Revolution.

10. See Donald G. Morgan, *Justice William Johnson, The First Dissenter: The Career and Constitutional Philosophy of a Jeffersonian Judge* (Columbia: University of South Carolina Press, 1954). Johnson has received surprisingly little attention from modern scholars. Notable exceptions include Mark R. Killenbeck, "No Bed of Roses: William Johnson, Thomas Jefferson, and the Supreme Court, 1822–23," 37 *Journal of Supreme Court History* 95 (2012); Mark R. Killenbeck, "William Johnson, The Dog That Did Not Bark?," 62 *Vanderbilt Law Review* 407 (2009); Sandra F. VanBurkleo, "In Defense of 'Public Reason': Supreme Court Justice William Johnson," 32 *Journal of Supreme Court History* 115 (2007); Irwin F. Greenberg, "Justice William Johnson: South Carolina Unionist, 1823–1830," 36 *Pennsylvania History* 307 (1969); Herbert A. Johnson, "The Constitutional Thought of William Johnson," 89 *South Carolina Historical Magazine* 132 (1988); "William Johnson, Jr.," in *Princetonians, 1784–1790: A Biographical Dictionary*, ed. Ruth L. Woodward and Wesley Frank Craven (Princeton: Princeton

University Press, 1991), 494. Older works include Oliver Schroeder, Jr., "Life and Judicial Work of Justice William Johnson, Jr.," 95 *University of Pennsylvania Law Review* 164 (1946–47); see also A. J. Levin's series of seven articles in the *Michigan Law Review* between 1944 and 1949.

11. Johnson's fellow members of the Princeton class of 1790 included two cousins of Thomas Gibbons, later the appellee in *Gibbons v. Ogden*. See "Barach Gibbons" and "Joseph Gibbons," in Woodward and Craven, *Princetonians*, 477.

12. See Charles Cotesworth Pinckney, "Return of Taxable Property, 1808–1811," a note regarding 1801 tax return, in *PPSDE*. The return for 1808 lists several numbers of enslaved people under the categories of "in Town" and "in the Country"—twenty-eight or thirty-two "Negroes in Town," and 162 or 151 "Negroes in the Country."

13. The history of the Revolution told by Joseph Johnson, the brother of William Johnson, describes the family's return to Charleston after the war: "My father . . . proceeded to his own house, on East Bay, opposite to Guignard-street, No. 140, and found it in the care of his own servants, and in a habitable condition, but the fences had all been torn down and burnt." Joseph Johnson, *Traditions and Reminiscences, Chiefly of the American Revolution in the South* (Charleston: Walker and James, 1851), 385. According to the 1816 and 1819 city directories, the blacksmith shop was located one block west, at the corner of Anson and Guignard streets. James W. Hagy, ed., *Charleston, South Carolina City Directories for the Years 1816, 1819, 1822, 1825, and 1829* (1996; repr., Baltimore: Genealogical Publishing, 2002) (hereafter *Charleston Directories*).

14. Alice R. Huger Smith and D. E. Huger Smith, *The Dwelling Houses of Charleston, South Carolina* (Philadelphia: J. B. Lippincott, 1917), 367–68; Ravenel, *Eliza Pinckney*, 112; see also Momon, "John 'Quash' Williams."

15. See Waddell, "Charles Pinckney's Double House," 88.

16. According to Pinckney descendant Harriet Horry Ravenel's 1896 account, "The lot occupied the whole square from Market to Guignard Streets, on the western side of the East Bay. The house stood in the centre, facing east to the water, and the ground across the street, down to the water's edge, also belonging to the family, was never built upon, but kept open for air and for the view." See Ravenel, *Eliza Pinckney*, 110.

17. Also in the audience for Blackstone's lectures during this period was Jeremy Bentham. See Zahniser, *Charles Cotesworth Pinckney*, 17n42.

18. Ravenel, *Eliza Pinckney*, 111–12.

19. See, e.g., Morgan, *Justice William Johnson, The First Dissenter*.

20. William Johnson, dated September 16, 1830, *Charleston Courier*, October 1, 1830; reprinted in *Niles' Weekly Register*, October 16, 1830, 132.

21. On the complex political environment of South Carolina in this period, see Manisha Sinha, *The Counterrevolution of Slavery: Politics and Ideology in Antebellum South Carolina* (Chapel Hill: University of North Carolina Press, 2000); Lacy K. Ford, *Origins of Southern Radicalism: The South Carolina Upcountry, 1800–1860* (New York:

Oxford, 1988); William W. Freehling, *Prelude to Civil War: The Nullification Controversy in South Carolina, 1816–1833* (New York: Oxford, 1966); George C. Rogers, Jr., "South Carolina Federalists and the Origins of the Nullification Movement," 101 *South Carolina Historical Magazine* 53 (2000); James M. Banner, Jr., "The Problem of South Carolina," in *The Hofstadter Aegis: A Memorial*, ed. Stanley Elkins and Eric McKitrick (New York: Knopf, 1974), 60–93; James Haw, " 'The Problem of South Carolina' Reexamined: A Review Essay," 107 *South Carolina Historical Magazine* 9 (2006).

22. Two centuries later, pluff mud featured in Pinckney's novelistic description of "the whole complex of smells that was summer in Charleston—heavy salt, pluff mud, oleanders, and drains." Josephine Pinckney, *Three O'Clock Dinner* (1945; repr., Columbia: University of South Carolina Press, 2001), 5.

23. *Miller's Planters' and Merchants' Almanac for the Year of Our Lord 1826, Calculated for the States of Carolina and Georgia* (Charleston: A. E. Miller, 1826), 34.

24. A Member, "The Association," *Charleston Courier*, July 24, 1823. See also Alan F. January, "The South Carolina Association: An Agency for Race Control in Antebellum Charleston," 78 *South Carolina Historical Magazine* 191, 195 (1977); Ryan A. Quintana, "Planners, Planters, and Slaves: Producing the State in Early National South Carolina," 81 *Journal of Southern History* 79 (2015).

25. This chapter will use these terms to follow early-nineteenth-century usage, which distinguished between the categories of "Black" and "person of color" in ways that combined assumptions about race, ancestry, and free versus slave status. See Bernard Powers, *Black Charlestonians: A Social History, 1822–1885* (Fayetteville: University of Arkansas Press, 1994), 38: "[I]n South Carolina and throughout the Lower South, free Negroes were usually designated free persons of color. According to a South Carolina jurist, this term was 'of as settled significance and import as any to be found in our laws . . . and is never applied to any persons but those of mixed blood and who are descended from negroes.' "

26. Peter A. Coclanis, *The Shadow of a Dream: Economic Life and Death in the South Carolina Low Country, 1670–1920* (New York: Oxford University Press, 1991), 115, cited in Maurie Dee McInnis, *The Politics of Taste in Antebellum Charleston* (Chapel Hill: University of North Carolina Press, 2005), 20.

27. See, e.g., Douglas R. Egerton et al., *The Denmark Vesey Affair: A Documentary History* (Gainesville: University Press of Florida, 2017), xv; Michael P. Johnson, "Denmark Vesey and His Co-Conspirators," 58 *William and Mary Quarterly*, 3rd ser. 915 (2001).

28. The Neck was an area north of Boundary Street (today's Calhoun Street) that was outside the city limits. In the late eighteenth century, it had included "numerous small farms, a few larger plantations, pastures, and a small number of suburban residences." In the early nineteenth century, when the Johnsons built their house, it was a developing area, with "the rise of new farms, houses, and shops, as well as the creation of some new suburban boroughs." Charleston County Public Library,

"Squeezing Charleston Neck," https://www.ccpl.org/charleston-time-machine/ squeezing-charleston-neck-1783-present. William Johnson and his father, William Johnson, Sr., developed property around the city, including a row of stuccoed brick houses on Queen Street, "Johnson's Row," that still stands today. "Johnson's Row," Archive Record, Historic Charleston Foundation.

29. See *Charleston Directories*.

30. See "Plan of the City and Neck of Charleston, S.C. Reduced from Authentic Documents and Engraved By W. Keenan," pub. September 1844, David Rumsey Map Collection, Stanford University, https://searchworks.stanford.edu/view/10450942.

31. See Pamela Durkin Gabriel, *The Unique Charleston Single House: A Brief Guide to Charleston Architecture* (2009; repr., Charleston: n.p., 2016).

32. Kitty Ravenel, "Do You Know Your Charleston? 156 Rutledge Avenue," *Charleston News and Courier*, October 7, 1940, 10.

33. Morgan, *Justice William Johnson*, 99n21, citing 1820 census schedules.

34. The twentieth-century novelist Madeline L'Engle was a descendant of Johnson, through both the adopted L'Engle children and Johnson's biological daughter Anna Hayes Johnson Saunders. See Madeline L'Engle, *The Summer of the Great-Grandmother* (New York: Harper, 1974), 192.

35. [William Johnson], "Communication: Melancholy Effect of Popular Excitement," *Charleston Courier*, June 21, 1822.

36. The court of magistrates and freeholders dated from South Carolina's colonial period. It had "nearly exclusive jurisdiction over criminal cases involving slaves and free persons of color and was the court of trial for violations of vagrancy laws." A quorum of the court consisted of two magistrates and three freeholders; there was no jury. Sentences were carried out immediately by constables or marshals. See Social Networks and Archival Context, "South Carolina: Court of Magistrates and Freeholders," http://n2t.net/ark:/99166/w63r6x5l.

37. See Lacy K. Ford, *Deliver Us from Evil: The Slavery Question in the Old South* (New York: Oxford, 2011), 212–13.

38. See Egerton et al., *Denmark Vesey Affair*, xx–xxi.

39. Johnson, *Charleston Courier*, June 29, 1822. See Morgan, *Justice William Johnson*, 131–32; Timothy S. Huebner, "Divided Loyalties: Justice William Johnson and the Rise of Disunion in South Carolina, 1822–1834," 1995 *Journal of Supreme Court History* 21–22 (1995).

40. William Johnson, *To the Public of Charleston* (Charleston: C. C. Sebring, 1822).

41. Id., 5, 12.

42. On the centrality of honor to white southern men in the period, see Bertram Wyatt-Brown, *Southern Honor: Ethics and Behavior in the Old South* (New York: Oxford University Press, 1982, 2007).

43. Johnson, *To the Public of Charleston*, 12.

44. Quoted in Morgan, *Justice William Johnson*, 131–32.

45. Johnson, "To the Public of Charleston," 15–16.

46. See "Forms of Prayer to Be Used in Families, Morning Prayer," in *The Book of Common Prayer and Administration of the Sacraments, and Other Rites and Ceremonies of the Church, According to the Use of the Protestant Episcopal Church in the United States of America, Together With the Psalter, or Psalms of David* (Philadelphia: Hall and Sellers, 1790): "Almighty and everlasting God, in whom we live and move and have our being." Johnson applied the sonorous phrase to the issue of federal jurisdiction in his 1824 dissent in *Osborn v. Bank of the United States*, writing, "An action may 'live, move, and have its being' in a law of the United States." 9 Wheat. (22 U.S.) 738, 887–88.

47. *Charleston Directories.*

48. Memoir of Jane Claudia Johnson, 29 *Southern Historical Society Papers* 34, 35 (1901).

49. See William Johnson, *Sketches of the Life and Correspondence of Nathanael Greene, Major General of the Armies of the United States, in the War of the Revolution, Compiled Chiefly from Original Materials* (Charleston: A. E. Miller, 1822). The title page listed the author as "William Johnson, of Charleston, South-Carolina."

50. William Johnson to Thomas Jefferson, March 4, 1817, Thomas Jefferson Papers at the Library of Congress, Series 1: General Correspondence, 1651–1827, quoted in Nic Butler, "Remembering Charleston's Liberty Tree, Part 2," 2020, Charleston County Public Library, https://www.ccpl.org/charleston-time-machine/remembering-charlestons-liberty-tree-part-2#_edn15.

51. Anna Hayes Johnson to Elizabeth Haywood, July 24, 1822, Ernest Haywood Papers, Southern Historical Collection, Wilson Library, University of North Carolina at Chapel Hill. Anna seems to have been close to her father. She ended another letter to her cousin by noting that "my day must be devoted to my father for whom I have a great deal of copying to do." Anna Hayes Johnson to Elizabeth Haywood, June 23, 1833, id.

52. *Martin v. Hunter's Lessee*, 14 U.S. 373 (1816) (Johnson, J., concurring).

53. See Killenbeck, "No Bed of Roses." In Johnson's first term on the Court, he was scolded by his fellow justices for issuing a separate concurrence. He lamented to Jefferson: "[D]uring the rest of that Session I heard nothing but Lectures on the Indecency of Judges cutting at each other, and the Loss of Reputation which the Virginia appellate Court had sustained by pursuing such a Course." William Johnson to Thomas Jefferson, December 10, 1822, cited in Meredith Kolsky Lewis, "Justice William Johnson and the History of Dissent," 83 *Georgetown Law Journal* 2069, 2078 (1995). The case was *Huidekoper's Lessee v. Douglass*, 7 U.S. (3 Cranch) 1 (1805).

54. Of Johnson's 172 opinions, 112 were for the majority; twenty-one were concurrences; thirty-four were dissents; and five were *per curiam*. See "William Johnson," in *Biographical Encyclopedia of the Supreme Court*, ed. Melvin I. Urofsky (Washington, D.C.: CQ Press, 2006), 303.

55. William Johnson to Thomas Jefferson, April 11, 1823, in "Letters from Judge William Johnson to Thomas Jefferson," 1 *South Carolina Historical and Genealogical Magazine* 207 (1900) (emphasis added).

56. Thomas Jefferson to William Johnson, June 12, 1823, in id.

57. A Member, "The Association."

58. Act of December 21, 1822, ch. 3, sec. 1, 2, 7, in *Acts and Resolutions of the General Assembly of the State of South Carolina, Passed in December, 1822* (Columbia, S.C., 1823), 11–14 (hereafter cited as Seamen Act).

59. See Michael A. Schoeppner, *Moral Contagion: Black Atlantic Sailors, Citizenship, and Diplomacy in Antebellum America* (Cambridge: Cambridge University Press, 2019), 27.

60. See id., 23–30. On Black sailors during the period, see W. Jeffrey Bolster, *Black Jacks: African American Seamen in the Age of Sail* (Cambridge, Mass.: Harvard University Press, 1997); see also Peter Linebaugh and Marcus Rediker, *The Many-Headed Hydra: Sailors, Slaves, Commoners, and the Hidden History of the Revolutionary Atlantic* (Boston: Beacon Press, 2000).

61. Seamen Act, §§ 2, 7. See CPI Inflation Calculator, Official Inflation Data, https://www.officialdata.org/.

62. Achates [Thomas Pinckney], *Reflections, Occasioned by the Late Disturbances in Charleston* (Charleston: A. E. Miller, 1822), 6–7.

63. Eliza Lucas Pinckney to Mary Bartlett, [1742], in *The Papers of Eliza Lucas Pinckney and Harriott Pinckney Horry Digital Edition*, ed. Constance Schulz (Charlottesville: University of Virginia Press, Rotunda, 2012): "I devote the rest of the time till I dress for dinner to our little polly and two black girls who I teach to read, and if I have my papa's approbation (my Mamas I have got) I intend them for school mistress's for the rest of the Negroe children."

64. Achates [Pinckney], *Reflections*, 13–16.

65. See Schoeppner, *Moral Contagion*, 35; January, "South Carolina Association," 195.

66. "Petition of Thomas Paine, Harbor Master of Charleston," November 19, 1823, General Assembly Petitions 1823 No. 39, Box 83, South Carolina Department of Archives and History, Columbia (hereafter cited as SCDAH).

67. Id.

68. "Report on Petition of Thomas Paine, Harbor Master of Charleston," General Assembly Committee Reports 1823, Box 54, SCDAH.

69. See Schoeppner, *Moral Contagion*, 35.

70. William Johnson to Thomas Jefferson, December 10, 1822, Founders Online, National Archives and Records Administration, https://founders.archives.gov/documents/Jefferson/98-01-02-3203.

71. Robert Hayne to C. C. Pinckney, Jr., December 21, 1824, in Theodore Dehon Jervey, *Robert Y. Hayne and His Times* (New York: Macmillan, 1909), 181.

72. *Charleston Courier*, July 28, 1823.

73. A Member, "The Association."

74. "Vindex," *Charleston Courier*, August 15, 1823, cited in January, "South Carolina Association," 194.

75. A Member, "The Association."

76. "Memorial of the South Carolina Association," [November] 1823, Legislative Papers, SCDAH.

77. Stratford Canning to John Quincy Adams, February 15, 1823, in *Correspondence Relative to the Prohibition against the Admission of Free Persons of Colour into Certain Ports of the United States, 1823–1850*, vol. 579, Ser. 5, Foreign Office Papers [UK], n.p., n.d.

78. John Quincy Adams to Stratford Canning, quoted in *Elkison v. Deliesseline*, 8 Fed. Cas. 493 (No. 4,366) (C.C.D. S.C., August 1823); see Philip M. Hamer, "Great Britain, the United States, and the Negro Seamen Acts, 1822–1848," 1 *Journal of Southern History* 3, 4 (1935).

79. See Hamer, "Great Britain," 5.

80. Schoeppner expresses skepticism that Adams's interventions, rather than the local dispute between harbormaster and sheriff, caused the hiatus in enforcement. But Adams conveyed to Canning that the administration had had some role. See *Moral Contagion*, 36 and n9.

81. "Memorial of the South Carolina Association," [November] 1823, quoted in January, "South Carolina Association," 195.

82. *Charleston Courier*, August 11, 1823. A "coppered" hull was sheathed in copper to protect it from rot.

83. Kerr's name was sometimes spelled "Ker." See James Risk, "Seven Flags over Charleston Harbor: James M. Elford and the Quest for a Universal Maritime Signal Code," 118 *South Carolina Historical Magazine* 132 (154).

84. *Charleston City Gazette*, March 27 and April 7, 1823.

85. *Charleston Courier*, July 11, 1823.

86. Katherine Drayton Simons, *Stories of Charleston Harbor* (Columbia, S.C.: State Co.), 36.

87. John R. Parker, *American Signal Book, or, The United States Telegraph Vocabulary, Being an Appendix to Elford's Marine Telegraph Signal Book* (Boston: Steam Power Press Office, W. L. Lewis, printer, 1832), 7, 124.

88. *J. M. Elford's Marine Telegraph; or, Universal Signal Book* (Charleston: James M. Elford, 1823), vii, quoted in Risk, "Seven Flags over Charleston Harbor," 134. Elford's code appears to have assigned the *Homer* the signal "12." See Parker, *American Signal Book*, Appendix, 149 (listing "12" for "Brig [sic] Homer, Greenock").

89. *Charleston Courier*, July 25, 1823.

90. See Thomas Ellison, *The Cotton Trade of Great Britain: Including a History of the Liverpool Cotton Market and of the Liverpool Cotton Brokers' Association* (London: Effingham Wilson, 1886), 237; Mary Gallant, "Recollections of a Charleston Childhood, 1822–1836," 98 *South Carolina Historical Magazine* 56, 64 (1997).

91. *Charleston Courier*, July 25, 1823.

92. *Elkison v. Deliesseline*, 8 Fed. Cas. 493 (1823). The sole contemporary report of the case was published by Jacob D. Wheeler in 1824 and reprinted in Jacob D. Wheeler, ed., *Reports of Criminal Law Cases* (Albany: Gould, Banks and Gould, 1851), 2:56, 57.

93. See Schoeppner, *Moral Contagion*, 39.

94. King later became a city-court judge and a philanthropist. See "Biographical Information," Mitchell King Papers, 1801–1862, #400, Southern Historical Collection, The Wilson Library, University of North Carolina at Chapel Hill.

95. 8 Fed. Cas. 493.

96. Wheeler, *Reports*, 2:56.

97. During this period, with the exception of 1801–2, there were no federal circuit-court judges per se. The U.S. circuit courts were staffed by the designated Supreme Court justice, riding circuit, and the federal district judge of that judicial district. The U.S. district judge in South Carolina at this time was Thomas Lee, who had been appointed by Monroe earlier in 1823. Contemporary accounts of *Elkison* refer to Johnson alone as the presiding judge. The Judiciary Act of 1802 permitted a single judge to preside over the circuit court: "when only one of the judges hereby directed to hold the circuit courts, shall attend, such circuit court may be held by the judge so attending." Judiciary Act of 1802, 2 Stat. 156, sec. 4. B. F. Hunt, one of the lawyers representing the South Carolina Association, characterized the proceeding as "a Circuit Judge at Chambers." *The Argument of Benjamin Faneuil Hunt, in the Case of the Arrest of the Person Claiming to Be a British Seaman, Under the 3d Section of the State Act of December 1822 . . .* (Charleston: A. E. Miller, 1823), 18.

98. "Free People of Color: Memorial of Sundry Masters of American Vessels Lying in the Port of Charleston, S.C., in the House of Representatives," February 19, *Niles' Weekly Register*, March 15, 1823.

99. Gallant, "Recollections of a Charleston Childhood," 64. By 1838, the Calder family had returned to Liverpool.

100. See Michael A. Schoeppner, "Peculiar Quarantines: The Seamen Acts and Regulatory Authority in the Antebellum South," 31 *Law and History Review* 559 (2013); see also Sven A. Beckert, *Empire of Cotton: A Global History* (New York: Alfred A. Knopf. 2013); Hamer, "Negro Seamen Acts."

101. See Schoeppner, *Moral Contagion*, 32.

102. *Calder v. Deliesseline*, in William Harper, ed., *Report of Cases Decided in the Constitutional Court of South Carolina* (Charleston: McCarter and Dawson, 1824), 186. In *Elkison*, Johnson noted that the Seamen Act prescribed jailing "without the intervention of a court of justice." *Elkison*, 8 Fed. Cas. 496.

103. *Calder v. Deliesseline*.

104. James Calder to Benjamin Moodie, January 15, 1823, in *Correspondence*, n.p. This document was a "statement of facts," which Calder apparently prepared at Moodie's request. Moodie forwarded Calder's letter to British Ambassador Stratford

Canning in Washington. Canning sent these letters, with a copy of his own letter to Adams demanding federal intercession, to his cousin George Canning, the British foreign secretary (and future prime minister). Id., 1–3.

105. *Calder v. Deliesseline.* Calder cited a different amount—$17.31—in his statement to Moodie. He also noted that he had paid twenty dollars in fees to his lawyer. James Calder to Benjamin Moodie, January 15, 1823, in *Correspondence*, 3.

106. *Calder v. Deliesseline.*

107. James Calder to Benjamin Moodie, January 15, 1823, in *Correspondence*, 3.

108. Schoeppner, *Moral Contagion*, 33.

109. Cf. id., 34.

110. According to the report of the constitutional court's decision in *Calder v. Deliesseline*, Calder's attorney had raised the issue of the act's unconstitutionality, insofar as it conflicted with international treaties, before the trial and appeals courts. But the argument failed in both courts, and the constitutional court declined to take it up again. *Calder v. Deliesseline.* My reading of the case thus differs from Schoeppner's. See Schoeppner, *Moral Contagion*, 34: "What was never raised, at least at this juncture, was the constitutionality of the law."

111. William Johnson, "To the Editor of the Mercury," *Charleston Mercury*, August 20, 1823.

112. See Jonathan H. Poston, *Buildings of Charleston: A Guide to the City's Architecture* (Columbia: University of South Carolina Press, 1997), 184.

113. See Carl R. Lounsbury, *From Statehouse to Courthouse: An Architectural History of South Carolina's Colonial Capitol and Charleston County Courthouse* (Columbia: University of South Carolina Press, 2001), 23.

114. Id., 57.

115. *Elkison*, 8 Fed. Cas. 493.

116. Id., 494; see also Schoeppner, *Moral Contagion*, 40–41; William H. Pease and Jane H. Pease, *James Louis Petigru: Southern Conservative, Southern Dissenter* (Columbia: University of South Carolina Press, 2002), 29, 139. Petigru, who served as South Carolina's attorney general from 1822 to 1830, is today memorialized in the James L. Petigru Law Library on the second floor of the Charleston County Courthouse, across the hall from the courtroom where the *Elkison* hearing was held.

117. See, e.g., *McCulloch v. Maryland* (1819); *Cohens v. Virginia* (1821).

118. *The Brig Wilson v. the United States*, 1 Brockenbrough's Reports 423, 424, 426 (C.C.D. Va. 1820).

119. *Argument of Benjamin Faneuil Hunt*, 18–19.

120. Id., 19–20.

121. See id. (title and caption used by Hunt in pamphlet).

122. Id., 20.

123. Id., 8.

124. Id., 11–12.

125. Id., 7–8.

126. The best surviving evidence of King's arguments comes from Johnson's opinion.

127. Id., 12–13; see Schoeppner, *Moral Contagion*, 42 and *passim*.

128. See William J. Novak, *The People's Welfare: Law and Regulation in Nineteenth-Century America* (Chapel Hill: University of North Carolina Press, 1996); Kathleen Sullivan, "Charleston, the Vesey Conspiracy, and the Development of the State Police Power," in *Race and American Political Development*, ed. Joseph Lowndes, Jule Novkov, and Dorian T. Warren (New York: Routledge, 2008), 59.

129. *Argument of Benjamin Faneuil Hunt*, 6.

130. William M. Wiecek, *The Sources of Antislavery Constitutionalism in America, 1760–1848* (Ithaca: Cornell University Press, 1977), 134.

131. *Elkison*, 8 Fed. Cas. 493–94.

132. Moodie had apparently sought out Johnson, who "lamented so improper an Act had been passed in this State, and assured me that previous to his departure for Washington to meet the Supreme Court, he would leave such instructions with the District [U.S.] Attorney as would prevent any similar outrage during his absence." Benjamin Moodie to Stratford Canning, January 20, 1823, in *Correspondence*, 2.

133. 8 Fed. Cas. 494.

134. Id., 494–95.

135. Id., 495.

136. Id.

137. See Huebner, "Divided Loyalties," 23.

138. 8 Fed. Cas. 494.

139. [Isaac Holmes and Robert J. Turnbull], "Caroliniensis," no. 4, in *Caroliniensis* (Charleston: A. E. Miller, 1824), 18–19 (characterizing Holmes's remark as "altogether *hypothetical*" and then criticizing Johnson for "seiz[ing] hold of a sentiment expressed by Counsel, irrelevant to the point . . . and not censured at the moment" and "mak[ing] it the subject of a judicial remark, in a written opinion"); William Johnson, "To the Editor of the Mercury," *Charleston Mercury*, August 20, 1823. The "Caroliniensis" essays were originally published in the *Mercury* between August 15 and September 11, 1823, and were subsequently issued in a single pamphlet.

140. "Provided, That writs of habeas corpus shall in no case extend to prisoners in gaol, unless where they are in custody, under or by colour of the authority of the United States, or are committed for trial before some court of the same, or are necessary to be brought into court to testify." Judiciary Act of 1789. sec. 14.

141. *Elkison*, 8 Fed. Cas. 496.

142. Id., 497.

143. Id. In fact Fitzherbert cited examples of cases in which the writ *de homine replegiando* issued to officials such as sheriffs. I thank R. H. Helmholz for bringing this point to my attention.

144. *Elkison*, 8 Fed. Cas. 497–98. Some northern courts recast the writ as an action for "personal replevin," with an avowedly antislavery purpose. See Dallin H. Oaks, "Habeas Corpus in the States: 1776–1865," 32 *University of Chicago Law Review* 243, 284–87 (1965).

145. 8 Fed. Cas. 498. The references to the "ship-master" and the "captain" suggest that Kerr had also been charged with violating the act, for failing both to remove Elkison from the state and to pay the expenses of jailing him.

146. Wiecek, *Sources of Antislavery Constitutionalism*, 134; see also Hamer, "Negro Seamen Acts," 8.

147. Charleston *City Gazette and Commercial Daily Advertiser*, August 15, 1823.

148. See Morgan, *Justice William Johnson*, 195.

149. See also Schoeppner, *Moral Contagion*, 41.

150. See Wiecek, *Sources of Antislavery Constitutionalism*, 128.

151. *Free Colored Seamen—Majority and Minority Reports*, House of Representatives Rep. No. 80, January 20, 1843, 27th Congress, 3d Session; see also Schoeppner, *Moral Contagion*, ch. 6, discussing Massachusetts commissioner Samuel Hoar; Kate Masur, *Until Justice Be Done: American's First Civil Rights Movement, from the Revolution to Reconstruction* (New York: W. W. Norton, 2021); Maeve Glass, "Citizens of the State," 85 *University of Chicago Law Review* 865 (2018).

152. Wiecek, *Sources of Antislavery Constitutionalism*, 136–37; Schoeppner, *Moral Contagion*, 186–90.

153. *Roberts v. Yates*, 20 Fed. Cas. 937 (C.C. D.S.C. 1853).

154. Id., 938.

155. Id.

156. See Schoeppner, *Moral Contagion*, 187–91.

157. John Quincy Adams, *Memoirs of John Quincy Adams, Comprising Portions of His Diary from 1795 to 1848*, ed. Charles Francis Adams (Philadelphia: J. B. Lippincott, 1874–77), August 19, 1823, 6:175; William Johnson to [unknown], August 11, 1823, Simon Gratz Collection, Historical Society of Pennsylvania; Irwin F. Greenberg, "Justice William Johnson: South Carolina Unionist, 1823–1830," 36 *Pennsylvania History* 307, 311 (1969).

158. Id., September 4, 1823, 6:176.

159. Id., April 3, 1824, 6:279.

160. Id., April 19, 1824, 6:295.

161. Id., April 20, 1824, 6:297.

162. Id., April 24, 1824, 6:307.

163. "Validity of the South Carolina Police Bill," May 8, 1824, in *Official Opinions of the Attorneys General of the United States* (Washington, D.C.: Robert Farnham, 1852), 1:659.

164. Id., 1:659–60.

165. Id., 1:660.

166. See Adams, *Memoirs*, 6:376; "South Carolina's Reply to Ohio and the Federal Government," in *State Documents on Federal Relations: The States and the United States*, ed. Herman V. Ames (1906; repr. New York: Da Capo Press, 1970), 12. See also Scott Wallace Stucky, "*Elkison v. Deliesseline*: Race and the Constitution in South Carolina, 1823," 14 *North Carolina Central Law Review* 361, 395–96 (1984).

167. Message of Governor John L. Wilson of South Carolina, December 1, 1824, in Ames, *State Documents on Federal Relations*, 14.

168. Id., 14–16.

169. Wirt and Berrien first crossed swords in 1825. The context was the case of *The Antelope*, in which Wirt—representing the United States—argued that the African slave trade violated the law of nations. Based on Berrien's reports, Georgia governor George Troup erroneously told the state legislature that "[t]he Attorney General, representing the United States, says before the Supreme Court, in a ripe and splendid argument, that slavery, being inconsistent with the laws of God and nature, cannot exist." Troup's comments led to attacks on Wirt from many in the South. Quoted in Jonathan M. Bryant, *Dark Places of the Earth: The Voyage of the Slave Ship* Antelope (New York: Liveright, 2015), 245.

170. "Opinion of the Attorney General," April 23, 1821, in *Opinions of the Attorneys General of the United States, From the Beginning of the Government to March 1st, 1841*, ed. Henry D. Gilpin (Washington, D.C.: Blair and Rives, 1841), 343: "My duty to my clients is discharged, and the cause is in the hands of the court. In the private practice of my profession, I have nothing more to do with it. Since the argument, however, I have been reflecting on it *officially*; and . . . I should have considered myself as failing, criminally, in my duty to the Government whose officer I am, to have omitted the communication I have made to you [President Monroe]."

171. William Wirt to John Calhoun, February 3, 1820, quoted in Homer Cummings and Carl McFarland, *Federal Justice: Chapters in the History of Justice and the Federal Executive* (New York: Macmillan, 1937), 90; *Papers of John C. Calhoun*, ed. Clyde N. Wilson and W. Edwin Hemphill (Columbia: University of South Carolina Press, 1977), 4:633.

172. Schoeppner identifies "Caroliniensis" and "Philo-Caroliniensis" as noms de plume of Holmes and Turnbull; *Moral Contagion*, 47n32, 50n37.

173. See Brutus [Robert J. Turnbull], *The Crisis: or, Essays on the Usurpation of the Federal Government* (Charleston: A. E. Miller, 1827).

174. Brutus [Turnbull], *Crisis*, no. 4, 12.

175. [Holmes and Turnbull], "Caroliniensis," no. 6, in *Caroliniensis*, 30.

176. William Johnson, "To the Editor of the Mercury," *Charleston Mercury*, August 20, 1823.

177. [Holmes and Turnbull], "Philo-Caroliniensis," nos. 2 and 3, in *Caroliniensis*, 69–73.

178. Id., 72.

179. [William Johnson], "Philonimus," September 26 and October 7, 1823, *Charleston Mercury.*

180. [Johnson], "Philonimus," October 7, 1823.

181. William Johnson to Thomas Jefferson, August 11, 1823, in 1 *South Carolina Historical and Genealogical Magazine* 211–12 (1900).

182. Adams, *Memoirs*, September 1823, 6:175.

183. William Johnson to John Quincy Adams, July 3, 1824, in *Free Colored Seamen—Majority and Minority Reports*, 27th Congress, 3d Session, January 20, 1843.

184. John Marshall to Joseph Story, September 26, 1823, in Joseph Story Papers, Massachusetts Historical Society.

185. Id.

186. Robert Y. Hayne, *An Oration, Delivered in the Independent or Congregational Church, Charleston, Before the State Rights and Free Trade Party, the Society of Cincinnati, the Revolution Society, the '76 Association, and Several Volunteer Companies of Militia, on the 4th of July 1831, Being the 55th Anniversary of American Independence* (Charleston: A. E. Miller, 1831), 31.

187. *U.S. v. Holmes and Mazyck* (Dist. of SC, 1831); *Charleston Courier*, September 24, 1831, reprinted in *Niles' Weekly Register*, October 8, 1831; aff'd *Holmes v. U.S.* (C.C. Dist. of SC, 1832), reprinted in *City Gazette*, June 9, 1832.

188. *New York Evening Star*, August 5, 1834, quoted in Morgan, *Justice William Johnson*, 281.

189. An obelisk honoring Johnson stands near the graves of his father, mother, wife, and other family members, but some doubt exists as to whether Johnson was in fact buried there rather than in New York. See George A. Christensen, "Here Lies the Supreme Court: Gravesites of the Justices," 17 *Yearbook: Supreme Court Historical Society* 23–24 (1983).

190. I thank Gabriel Lear and Fran Spaltro for this translation.

191. Johnson, "To the Public of Charleston," 15–16.

192. See Morgan, *Justice William Johnson*, 282n10.

Chapter 5. The Revolutionary Daughter

1. Harriet Horry Ravenel, *Eliza Pinckney* (New York: Charles Scribner's Sons, 1896), 320.

2. Caroline Elliott Pinckney to Reverend Charles Cotesworth Pinckney, December 26, 1832, Pinckney-Means Family Papers, 1701–1983 (208.00), South Carolina Historical Society (hereafter cited as PMFP), Box 3.

3. See Jane H. Pease and William H. Pease, *Ladies, Women, and Wenches: Choice and Constraint in Antebellum Charleston and Boston* (Chapel Hill: University of North Carolina Press, 1990), 168; Pinckney's treatise "became a standard nullifier text."

4. *Charleston Mercury*, May 14, 1836.

5. On women's political activities in this period, see Catherine Allgor, *Parlor Politics: In Which the Ladies of Washington Help Build a City and a Government* (Charlottesville: University of Virginia Press, 2000); David S. Shields and Fredrika J. Teute, "The Republican Court and the Historiography of Women's Domain in the Public Sphere," 35 *Journal of the Early Republic* 169 (2015); Jan Lewis, "Politics and the Ambivalence of the Private Sphere: Women in Early Washington, D.C.," in *A Republic for the Ages: The United States Capitol and the Political Culture of the Early Republic*, ed. Donald R. Kennon (Charlottesville: University Press of Virginia, 1999), 122–51; Elizabeth R. Varon, "Tippecanoe and the Ladies, Too: White Women and Party Politics in Antebellum Virginia," 82 *Journal of American History* 494 (1995).

6. See also Joyce Appleby, *Inheriting the Revolution: The First Generation of Americans* (Cambridge, Mass.: Harvard University Press, 2000).

7. Eliza Lucas Pinckney, *The Letterbook of Eliza Lucas Pinckney, 1739–1762*, ed. Elise Pinckney (1972; repr., Columbia: University of South Carolina Press, 1997).

8. See Lorri Glover, *Eliza Lucas Pinckney: An Independent Woman in the Age of Revolution* (New Haven: Yale University Press, 2020), 216, describing Maria Henrietta's father Charles Cotesworth, his brother Thomas, and his sister Harriott as "a fiercely unified team" in family matters.

9. Quoted in id., 221.

10. Darcy R. Fryer, "The Mind of Eliza Pinckney: An Eighteenth-Century Woman's Construction of Herself," 99 *South Carolina Historical Magazine* 215, 232 (1998).

11. Pinckney, *Letterbook*, 25, 37.

12. Glover, *Eliza Lucas Pinckney*, 3.

13. "Pinckney, Maria," in *Biographical Dictionary of Authors*, vol. 15 of *Library of Southern Literature*, eds. Edwin Anderson Alderman and Joel Chandler Harris (Atlanta: Martin and Hoyt, 1910), 345. Maria Henrietta Pinckney's second cousin twice removed, Henry Laurens Pinckney (1794–1863), gained fame as a South Carolina congressman and mayor of Charleston. An ardent defender of states' rights, he was also founder and editor of the *Charleston Mercury*.

14. The dress, of peach-hued English silk brocade with a climbing floral print, is in the collection of the Charleston Museum, of which Charles Cotesworth Pinckney was a founder. See Marvin R. Zahniser, *Charles Cotesworth Pinckney, Founding Father* (Chapel Hill: University of North Carolina Press, 1967), 28.

15. [Maria Henrietta Pinckney], *The Quintessence of Long Speeches, Arranged as a Political Catechism: By a Lady, for Her God-Daughter* (Charleston: A. E. Miller, 1830); [Maria Henrietta Pinckney], *A Notice of the Pinckneys* (Charleston: Evans and Cogswell, 1860). Three plays published in a volume titled *Essays, Religious, Moral, Etc. by a Lady* that was published in Charleston in 1818 were for many years mistakenly attributed to Pinckney. See William S. Kable, "South Carolina District Copyrights: 1794–1820," in *Proof: The Yearbook of American Bibliographical and Textual Studies* (Columbia: University of South Carolina Press, 1971), 1:181, 196.

16. See "Charles Cotesworth Pinckney and His Family," in *The Papers of the Revolutionary Era Pinckney Statesmen Digital Edition*, ed. Constance B. Schulz (Charlottesville: University of Virginia Press, Rotunda, 2016) (hereafter cited as *PPSDE*).

17. Glover, *Eliza Lucas Pinckney*, 215.

18. Id., citing 1790 census data.

19. Id., 223; see also Zara Anishanslin, *Portrait of a Woman in Silk: Hidden Histories of the British Atlantic World* (New Haven: Yale University Press, 2016), 160, 308, 310–11.

20. Archibald Henderson, *Washington's Southern Tour* (1791; repr., Boston: Houghton, Mifflin, 1923), 139.

21. See also Glover, *Eliza Lucas Pinckney*, 226, calling all three "planters and entrepreneurs"; Anishanslin, *Portrait of a Woman in Silk*, 311, where Horry is described as "a slaveholder greeting another slaveholder."

22. [Pinckney], *Notice of the Pinckneys*, 20.

23. Id., 3.

24. Id., 8.

25. Id., 7.

26. Id., 7–8.

27. Id., 8.

28. Id., 12.

29. Glover, *Eliza Lucas Pinckney*, 230.

30. Id., 233.

31. Charles Cotesworth Pinckney to Thomas Pinckney, April 16, 1793, in *The Papers of Eliza Lucas Pinckney and Harriott Pinckney Horry Digital Edition*, ed. Constance Schulz (Charlottesville: University of Virginia Press, Rotunda, 2012) (hereafter cited as *PPHDE*).

32. Glover, *Eliza Lucas Pinckney*, 232.

33. Harriott Pinckney Horry, 1793 journal, May 7, 1793, in *PPHDE*.

34. See Fryer, "Mind of Eliza Pinckney," 222.

35. Glover, *Eliza Lucas Pinckney*, 244.

36. Id., 245.

37. Charles Cotesworth Pinckney, "Instructions for His Attorneys," September 26, 1796, in *PPSDE*.

38. Marshall's staff included eighteen-year-old John Grattan Gamble, whose sister Elizabeth later married William Wirt. In 1807, Gamble posted bond for Aaron Burr during Burr's treason trial in Richmond, in which Wirt (by then Gamble's brother-in-law) was a prosecutor. See John G. Gamble to Thomas Jefferson, July 20, 1813, and Editorial Note, Founders Online, National Archives and Records Administration, https://founders.archives.gov/documents/Jefferson/03-06-02-0252.

39. See William Stinchcombe, "The Diplomacy of the WXYZ Affair," 34 *William and Mary Quarterly* 590 (1977); also William Stinchcombe, *The XYZ Affair* (Westport, Conn.: Greenwood Press, 1980), 598.

40. See Stinchcombe, "Diplomacy," 600. According to one contemporary account, Pinckney insisted throughout his life that he had said, "Not a sixpence, sir." When asked why he had not corrected other versions, he replied, "The nation adopted the expression, and I always thought there would have been more ostentation in denying than submitting to the report. The nation adopted it." Quoted in "Notes and Queries," 1 *South Carolina Historical and Genealogical Magazine* 98, 100–101 (1900).

41. Thomas Pinckney, Jr., to Maria Henrietta Pinckney, December 17, 1799, in *PPSDE*.

42. Cotesworth, who was born in 1789, was the godson of his first cousin Maria Henrietta Pinckney, who was fifteen when he was born. See Thomas Pinckney to Harriott Pinckney Horry and Maria Henrietta Pinckney, June 29, 1790, in *PPSDE*. Cotesworth is sometimes referred to as "Charles Cotesworth Pinckney, Jr." and sometimes as "Charles Cotesworth Pinckney III." He had a son, also named Charles Cotesworth Pinckney, who was born in 1812; that Charles Cotesworth Pinckney, who was ordained as an Episcopal priest in 1836, is often referred to in family records as "Rev. Charles Pinckney." See "Notes and Queries," 98, 104, quoting the epitaph.

43. Thomas Pinckney to Harriott Pinckney Horry, March 29, 1823, in *PPHDE*.

44. See William M. Wiecek, *The Sources of Antislavery Constitutionalism in America, 1760–1848* (Ithaca: Cornell University Press, 1977), 63.

45. Quoted in id., 70 (Iredell), 71 (G. Morris).

46. Id., 70.

47. Id.

48. Quoted in Wiecek, *Sources of Antislavery Constitutionalism*, 73.

49. Jonathan Elliot, ed., *Debates in the Several State Conventions, on the Adoption of the Federal Constitution*, 2nd ed. (Washington, D.C.: Printed for the Editor 1836), 4:285.

50. U.S. Const., Art. I, sec. 9.

51. Wiecek, *Sources of Antislavery Constitutionalism*, 16, 82.

52. U.S. Const., Art. IV, sec. 2.

53. Max Farrand, ed., *Records of the Federal Convention* (New Haven: Yale University Press, 1966), 2:443. Later that day (August 28, 1787), the convention rejected a proposal requiring a two-thirds majority for navigation acts—i.e., acts regulating international or interstate commerce. The South Carolinians had supported the supermajority requirement for fear of "oppressive regulation" by commercial interests in other states. But now C. C. Pinckney was willing to accept a simple majority rule. Although "it was the true interest of the S. States to have no regulation of commerce," given "the loss brought on the commerce of the Eastern States by the revolution, their liberal conduct toward the views of South Carolina, and the interest the weak Southn. [sic] States had in being united with the strong Eastern States, he thought it proper that no fetters should be imposed on the power of making commercial regulations." Farrand, *Records*, 2:449–50. In a footnote to this report of Pinckney's com-

ments, Madison noted, "He meant the permission to import slaves. An understanding on the two subjects of *navigation* and *slavery*, had taken place between those parts of the Union, which explains the Motion depending, as well as the language of Genl. Pinkney [*sic*] & others." On Madison's notes, see Mary Sarah Bilder, *Madison's Hand: Revising the Constitutional Convention* (Cambridge, Mass.: Harvard University Press, 2015).

54. Elliot, *Debates*, 4:286.

55. Glover, *Eliza Lucas Pinckney*, 219.

56. See Charles Cotesworth Pinckney, "Return of Taxable Property, 1808–1811," with a note detailing a 1801 tax return, in *PPSDE*.

57. See William Johnson, *Sketches of the Life and Correspondence of Nathanael Greene, Major General of the Armies of the United States, in the War of the Revolution* (Charleston: A. E. Miller, 1822), 2:345.

58. Charles Cotesworth Pinckney, "Transfer of Enslaved People to His Daughter," October 1, 1807, in *PPSDE*.

59. Charles Cotesworth Pinckney, "Will," October 8, 1807, in *PPSDE*. One of the witnesses to the will was John Faucheraud Grimké, associate justice of the South Carolina Court of Common Pleas and General Sessions. A longtime friend of the Pinckneys, Grimké was the father of the abolitionists Sarah and Angelina Grimké.

60. The other executors were their stepmother, aunt, and uncle, all of whom predeceased the sisters.

61. After C. C. Pinckney's death, in 1825, his siblings renounced their interests in his estate, leaving his three daughters as heirs. See "Estate Document of Charles C. Pinckney," Pinckney-Lowndes Family Papers, 1825–1847, Letters, 1825–1847, in Harriott Horry Ravenel Family Papers, 1694–ca.1935 (1086.00), South Carolina Historical Society, Charleston.

62. See Harriott Pinckney Horry to Eliza Lucas Pinckney (Mrs. Ralph) Izard, August 23, 1826, in *PPHDE*.

63. See Christine Leigh Heyrman, *Southern Cross: The Beginnings of the Bible Belt* (Chapel Hill: University of North Carolina, 1998); Nancy Cott, *The Bonds of Womanhood*, 2nd ed. (New Haven: Yale University Press, 1997).

64. See [Maria Henrietta Pinckney], *Political Catechism*, Pinckney Family Papers, South Carolina Historical Society, Charleston.

65. One chronicler called Belvidere the gift of "those exemplars of patriotism and beneficence, the daughters of the late Gen. Charles Cotesworth Pinckney." John B. Irving, *A Day on Cooper River* (Charleston: A. E. Miller, 1842), 3.

66. See Harriott Horry Rutledge and Harriet R. Holman, "Charleston in the Summer of 1841: The Letters of Harriott Horry Rutledge," 46 *South Carolina Historical and Genealogical Magazine* 1, 4n9 (1945); "Belmont Plantation," glossary entry, in *PPSDE*.

67. Rebecca Motte Lowndes Rutledge to Edward Cotesworth Rutledge, September 6, 1832, Rutledge Family Papers, South Caroliniana Library, University of South Carolina (hereafter cited as RFP).

68. Rebecca Motte Lowndes Rutledge to Edward Cotesworth Rutledge, October 5–6, 1832, RFP.

69. Id.

70. Harriott Pinckney Rutledge Holbrook to Edward Cotesworth Rutledge, October 13, 1832, RFP.

71. Rebecca Motte Lowndes Rutledge to Edward Cotesworth Rutledge, November 19, 1832, RFP.

72. Rebecca Motte Lowndes Rutledge to Edward Cotesworth Rutledge, January 4, 1833, RFP.

73. See Rebecca Lamar, "The Loss of the Steamer Pulaski," 3 *Georgia Historical Quarterly* 63 (1919); James P. Beckwith, Jr., and Thomas Pinckney Rutledge, " 'A Short History of the A.O.C.': By Thomas Pinckney Rutledge," 77 *South Carolina Historical Magazine* 97 (1976). A note on the back of the manuscript of the *Political Catechism* in the Harriott Horry Ravenel Family Papers reads: "Harriott Horrÿ Rutledge—Ravenel/ from H.P. 1859/Written by Miss Maria Henrietta Pinckney for her Gd. daughter Maria P. Rutledge/(lost in the Pulaski steamer)." Harriot Horry Rutledge Ravenel, in whose collection the manuscript resides, was the daughter of Edward Cotesworth Rutledge and Rebecca Motte Lowndes Rutledge. She was another formidable family record-keeper. The notation states that the manuscript of the *Political Catechism* was given to Harriot Horry Rutledge Ravenel by "H. P." in 1859. "H. P." is almost certainly Harriott Pinckney, sister of Maria Henrietta. On female Pinckney family members' authorship of cookbooks and involvement in the creation of a particular antebellum Lowcountry culture, see Donna Gabaccia and Jane Aldrich, "Recipes in Context: Solving a Small Mystery in Charleston's Culinary History," 15 *Food, Culture and Society* 197 (2012).

74. See Manisha Sinha, *The Counterrevolution of Slavery: Politics and Ideology in Antebellum South Carolina* (Chapel Hill: University of North Carolina Press, 2000); William W. Freehling, *Prelude to Civil War: The Nullification Controversy in South Carolina, 1816–1833* (New York: Oxford, 1966); William W. Freehling, *The Road to Disunion: Secessionists at Bay, 1776–1854* (New York: Oxford University Press, 1990): Richard Ellis, *The Union at Risk* (New York: Oxford, 1987); Lacy K. Ford, Jr., "Inventing the Concurrent Majority: Madison, Calhoun, and the Problem of Majoritarianism in American Political Thought," 60 *Journal of Southern History* 19 (1994); Merrill D. Peterson, *Olive Branch and Sword: The Compromise of 1833* (Baton Rouge: Louisiana State University Press, 1982); Donald Ratcliffe, "The Nullification Crisis, Southern Discontents, and the American Political Process," 1 *American Nineteenth-Century History* 1 (2000); Keith Whittington, "The Political Constitution of Federalism in Antebellum America: The Nullification Debate as an Illustration of Informal Mechanisms of Constitutional Change," 26 *Publius* 1 (1996).

75. "South Carolina Exposition and Protest," in *Papers of John C. Calhoun*, ed. Clyde N. Wilson and W. Edwin Hemphill (Columbia: University of South Carolina Press, 1977), 10:445.

76. See Merrill D. Peterson, *The Great Triumvirate: Webster, Clay, and Calhoun* (New York: Oxford University Press, 1987); Robert Elder, *Calhoun: American Heretic* (New York: Basic Books, 2021); John G. Grove, "Binding the Republic Together: The Early Political Thought of John C. Calhoun," 115 *South Carolina Historical Magazine* 100 (2014); Lacy K. Ford, Jr., "Republican Ideology in a Slave Society: The Political Economy of John C. Calhoun," 54 *Journal of Southern History* 405 (1988); Pauline Maier, "The Road Not Taken: Nullification, John C. Calhoun, and the Revolutionary Tradition in South Carolina," 82 *South Carolina Historical Magazine* 1 (1981).

77. See Harry L. Watson, *Liberty and Power: The Politics of Jacksonian America* (1990; repr., New York: Hill and Wang, 2006), 116–27; Sean Wilentz, *The Rise of American Democracy: Jefferson to Lincoln* (New York: W. W. Norton, 2005), 376; see also Richard R. Stenberg, "The Jefferson Birthday Dinner, 1830," 4 *Journal of Southern History* 334, 341 (1938): "Calhoun from 1828 until his death sought to restrain the South Carolina fire-eaters, though this fact was not altogether evident at all times to his contemporaries."

78. John C. Calhoun, "Address on the Relation Which the States and General Government Bear to Each Other" (Fort Hill Address), July 26, 1831, in *Reports and Public Letters of John C. Calhoun*, ed. Richard K. Crallé (New York: D. Appleton, 1855), 6: 60–61, 73. The address first appeared in print in the *Pendleton Messenger* on August 3, 1831. Calhoun's Fort Hill plantation was located in Pickens County, known prior to 1826 as "Pendleton District," in the northwestern corner of the state. The essay took up nearly three full pages of the four-page newspaper; it was dated July 26 and signed "John C. Calhoun." See *Pendleton Messenger*, August 3, 1831; see also Peterson, *Great Triumvirate*, 193 and 522n43.

79. John C. Calhoun, "Speech on the Reception of Abolition Petitions, February 1837," February 6, 1837, in *Speeches of John C. Calhoun: Delivered in the Congress of the United States from 1811 to the Present Time* (New York: Harper and Bros., 1843), 225.

80. Harriott Pinckney to [Reverend] Charles Cotesworth Pinckney, Jr., August 1, 1831, Spared and Shared 11, https://sparedshared11.wordpress.com/2016/01/02/1831-harriott-pinckney-to-charles-cotesworth-pinckney-jun/.

81. Peterson, *Great Triumvirate*, 192.

82. [Pinckney], *Political Catechism*, 3.

83. *Martin v. Hunter's Lessee*, 14 U.S. 373 (Johnson, J., concurring).

84. [Pinckney], *Political Catechism*, 4.

85. Id., 6.

86. Jean-Jacques Rousseau, *The Social Contract*, trans. Christopher Betts (1762; repr., Oxford: Oxford University Press, 1999), bk. IV, Ch. 1, para. 1, 134.

87. See Pinckney, *Letterbook*, 19, 48.

88. In 1745, Eliza wrote to a friend in London: "Shall I give you the trouble my dear Mad[a]m to buy him the new toy (a description of w[hi]ch I inclose) to teach him according to Mr. Lock's method (which I have carefully studied) to play himself into

learning. Mr Pinckney himself has been contriving a set tof toys to teach him his letters by the time he can speak." See Ravenel, *Eliza Pinckney*, 113. According to Maria Henrietta, her father later disapproved of such methods, "saying that from an over-anxiety to make him a clever fellow he had run the risk of being a very stupid one." [Pinckney], *Notice of the Pinckneys*, 9.

89. *McCulloch v. Maryland*, 17 U.S. 316 (1819); [Pinckney], *Political Catechism*, 13.

90. Id., 408; see also Alison L. LaCroix, "The Shadow Powers of Article I," 123 *Yale Law Journal* 2047–48 (2014).

91. See Daniel Webster, Second Reply to Hayne [published version], January 26–27, 1830, in *The Papers of Daniel Webster Digital Edition*, ed. Charles M. Wiltse (Charlottesville: University of Virginia Press, Rotunda, 2018).

92. [Pinckney], *Political Catechism*, 13.

93. Id.

94. *Martin v. Hunter's Lessee*, 14 U.S. 304 (1816).

95. See id.

96. [Pinckney], *Political Catechism*, 18.

97. 5 U.S. 137 (1803).

98. Introduction to Maria Henrietta Pinckney, "The Quintessence of Long Speeches Arranged as a Political Catechism . . .," in *Southern Pamphlets on Secession, November 1860–April 1861*, ed. Jon L. Wakelyn (Chapel Hill: University of North Carolina Press, 1996), 3.

99. Phoebe Caroline Elliott Pinckney to Charles Cotesworth Pinckney, Jr., December 26, 1832, in *PMFP*. For "Nullification Castle," see Barbara L. Bellows, "Of Time and the City: Charleston in 1860," 112 *South Carolina Historical Magazine* 157, 164 (2011); Maurie D. McInnis, *The Politics of Taste in Antebellum Charleston* (Chapel Hill: University of North Carolina, 2005), 80.

100. James Louis Petigru to Hugh S. Legaré, February 5, 1833, in *Life, Letters, and Speeches of James Louis Petigru: The Union Man of South Carolina*, ed. James Petigru Carson (Washington, D.C.: W. H. Lowdermilk, 1920), 118n. The footnote may have been added by Petigru's grandson, the volume's editor.

101. Id., 117–18.

102. Harriott Pinckney to Charles Cotesworth Pinckney, Jr., August 1, 1831, Spared and Shared 11, https://sparedshared11.wordpress.com/2016/01/02/1831-harriott-pinckney-to-charles-cotesworth-pinckney-jun/.

103. *Proceedings of the Celebration of the 4th July, 1831, at Charleston, S.C. by the State Rights and Free Trade Party* (Charleston: Archibald E. Miller, 1831).

104. [Pinckney], *Political Catechism*, 24.

105. "A Member," *Charleston Courier*, July 24, 1823.

106. A third Pinckney, distant cousin William Cotesworth Pinckney, was also present. See *Journal of the Conventions of the People of South Carolina, Held in 1832, 1833, and 1852* (Columbia, S.C.: R. W. Gibbes, 1860), 8.

107. Harriet Martineau, *Harriet Martineau's Autobiography, With Memorials by Maria Weston Chapman*, 2nd ed. (London: Smith, Elder, 1877), 2:9.

108. Harriet Martineau, *Retrospect of Western Travel* (1838; repr., Cambridge: Cambridge University Press, 2010), 2:73–74.

109. An Act Further to Provide for the Collection of Duties on Imports, 4 Stat. 632 (1833).

110. Martineau, *Retrospect*, 74.

111. There were two arsenals in Charleston at the time. One had been built by the federal government between 1825 and 1832 and was located on Ashley Avenue, less than a block west of Justice Johnson's house. The other, the "Old Citadel" on Marion Square, was built in 1822 in the aftermath of the Vesey conspiracy.

112. Martineau, *Retrospect*, 75.

113. *Charleston Mercury*, May 14, 1836.

114. Id.

115. *Charleston Mercury*, May 16, 1836.

116. Ravenel, *Eliza Pinckney*, 320.

117. Mrs. St. Julien [Harriott Horry Rutledge] Ravenel, *Charleston: The Place and the People* (New York: Macmillan, 1906), 453.

118. Mary Boykin Chesnut, April 8, 1861, in *A Diary from Dixie* (New York: Peter Smith, 1929), 32.

119. See Marie Ferrara, "Moses Henry Nathan and the Great Charleston Fire of 1861," 104 *South Carolina Historical Magazine* 258 (2003).

120. "The Condition of Charleston," *New York Times*, December 29, 1861.

121. Ravenel, *Eliza Pinckney*, 497.

122. "Condition of Charleston."

Chapter 6. The Editor and the Faithful Ally

1. Elias Boudinot and Harriett Gold Boudinot to Herman and Flora Gold Vaill, July 1, 1831, Herman Landon Vaill Collection, Manuscripts and Archives, Yale University Library, New Haven (hereafter cited as VC). This and other Boudinot letters are reprinted in Theresa Strouth Gaul, ed., *To Marry an Indian: The Marriage of Harriett Gold and Elias Boudinot in Letters, 1823–1839* (Chapel Hill: University of North Carolina Press, 2005), 176–77. The brackets here are Gaul's.

2. The romanized version of the newspaper's name in Cherokee is *Tsalagi Tsulehisanvhi*.

3. As with many names in this period, spellings of Harriett's name varied.

4. Sequoyah was also known by his English name, "George Gist" (sometimes spelled "Guist" or "Guess"). See Elias Boudinot, "To the Editor of the Annals of Education," *American Annals of Education*, April 1, 1832, reprinted in *Cherokee Editor: The Writings of Elias Boudinot*, ed. Theda Perdue (1983; repr., Athens: University of Georgia Press, 1996), 50 and 62n23.

5. See *Oxford English Dictionary*, s.v. "papoose," citing English-language attestations of the Narragansett "*papoòs*" and Pequot "*pouppous*" in the 1670s. The Cherokee language is classified as part of the Iroquoian language family.

6. See newspaper report of the Gold-Boudinot marriage: "It appears that the *orthodox fair ones* at Cornwall, have an overweening attachment to the *Indian dandies*, educated at that Mission School. Their love-smitten hearts are probably overcome by the *celestial charms*, which their *spiritual eyes* discover in those tawny sons of the forest." Quoted in Gaul, *To Marry an Indian*, 14. But cf. the Methodist minister and member of the Pequot nation William Apess, whose 1829 memoir was titled *A Son of the Forest*.

7. Quoted in John Demos, *The Heathen School: A Story of Hope and Betrayal in the Age of the Early Republic* (New York: Vintage, 2014), 177; see also id., 244, quoting Catharine Beecher in 1831 noting Boudinot's "pleasing and gentlemanly manners" and that he "speaks English as fluently as tho a native."

8. Elias Boudinot, *An Address to the Whites. Delivered in the First Presbyterian Church, on the 26th of May, 1826, by Elias Boudinott, a Cherokee Indian* (Philadelphia: William F. Geddes, 1826), 3–4, 13, 9.

9. Id., 6.

10. Elias Boudinot, "To the Editor of the Cherokee Phoenix," August 4, 1832, quoted in Perdue, *Cherokee Editor*, 172.

11. Id.

12. Cf. Perdue, introduction to *Cherokee Editor*, 10–11. Perdue is critical of Boudinot as an assimilationist, characterizing him as having "no doubt . . . absorbed White attitudes toward aboriginal Cherokee culture," based on "a hierarchical view of human cultures and societies." Theda Perdue, "Rising from the Ashes: The Cherokee Phoenix as an Ethnohistorical Source," 24 *Ethnohistory* 207, 215–16 (1977).

13. Elias Boudinot and Harriett Gold Boudinot to Herman Vaill and Flora Gold Vaill, July 1, 1831, VC.

14. See Nancy J. Parezo and Angelina R. Jones, "What's in a Name?: The 1940s–1950s 'Squaw Dress,' " 33 *American Indian Quarterly* 373, 376 (2009).

15. Cf. Gaul, *To Marry an Indian*, 178.

16. Elias Boudinot and Harriett Gold Boudinot to Herman Vaill and Flora Gold Vaill, January 7, 1831, VC.

17. Elias Boudinot to Herman Vaill and Flora Gold Vaill, July 1, 1831, VC.

18. Id.

19. "My health has been poor for two months past. I shall write Mother more particularly about it." Harriett Gold Boudinot to Herman Vaill and Flora Gold Vaill, July 1, 1831, VC. Sarah Parkhill Boudinot was born on February 24, 1832, suggesting that Harriett was approximately two months pregnant at the time of this letter.

20. On the framing of Native polities as nations, by themselves and others, during this period, see Gregory Ablavsky, *Federal Ground: Governing Property and Violence in*

the First U.S. Territories (New York: Oxford University Press, 2021); Ned Blackhawk, The Rediscovery of America: Native Peoples and the Unmaking of U.S. History (New Haven: Yale University Press, 2023); Ned Blackhawk, Violence over the Land: Indians and Empires in the Early American West (Cambridge, Mass.: Harvard University Press, 2006); Steven C. Hahn, The Invention of the Creek Nation, 1670–1763 (Lincoln: University of Nebraska Press, 2004); Pekka Hämäläinen, Lakota America: A New History of Indigenous Power (New Haven: Yale University Press, 2019); Peter Cozzens, Tecumseh and the Prophet: The Shawnee Brothers Who Defied a Nation (New York: Knopf, 2020); Claudio Saunt, Unworthy Republic: The Dispossession of Native Americans and the Road to Indian Territory (New York: W. W. Norton, 2020); Stuart Banner, How the Indians Lost Their Land: Law and Power on the Frontier (Cambridge, Mass.: Harvard University Press, 2007); Gregory Ablavsky, "Sovereign Metaphors in Indian Law," 80 Montana Law Review 11 (2019).

21. Rachel Caroline Eaton, John Ross and the Cherokee Indians (Menasha, Wis.: George Banta, 1914), 7.

22. Perdue, Cherokee Editor, 147n20.

23. The historical literature on the Cherokee Nation in this period, culminating in the Cherokees' forced removal west of the Mississippi, is vast. See especially Theda Perdue and Michael D. Green, The Cherokee Nation and the Trail of Tears (New York: Penguin, 2007); Theda Perdue and Michael D. Green, The Cherokee Removal: A Brief History with Documents, 3rd ed. (Boston: Bedford/St. Martin's, 2016); Thurman Wilkins, Cherokee Tragedy: The Ridge Family and the Decimation of a People, 2nd. ed. (Norman: University of Oklahoma Press, 1986); William G. McLoughlin, Cherokees and Missionaries, 1789–1839 (Norman: University of Oklahoma Press, 1995).

24. In addition to sources cited in the previous note, see Tim Alan Garrison, The Legal Ideology of Removal: The Southern Judiciary and the Sovereignty of Native American Nations (Athens: University of Georgia Press, 2002); Lisa Ford, Settler Sovereignty (Cambridge, Mass.: Harvard University Press, 2010); Jill Norgren, The Cherokee Cases: Two Landmark Federal Decisions in the Fight for Sovereignty (Norman: University of Oklahoma Press, 2004); Gregory Ablavsky, "The Savage Constitution," 63 Duke Law Journal 999 (2014). For treatments that discuss the cases in the context of modern federal Indian law, see Maggie Blackhawk, "Federal Indian Law as Paradigm within Public Law," 132 Harvard Law Review 1787 (2019); Wenona T. Singel, "The First Federalists," 62 Drake Law Review 775 (2014).

25. Boudinot, Address to the Whites, 14.

26. The Cherokee Nation was not the first Indigenous polity to use the courts of a would-be superior government to challenge the authority of an intermediate power. In 1706, a dispute between the Mohegan Nation and Connecticut colony was appealed to the Privy Council, which held that "the Mohegan Indians are a Nation with whom frequent Treatys have been made." As a result of the decision, "the colony's ability to take Indian land was legally limited and subject to the higher

authority of the Privy Council." Craig Yirush, *Settlers, Liberty, and Empire: The Roots of Early American Political Theory, 1675–1775* (New York: Cambridge University Press, 2011), 124–25.

27. Cf. Elizabeth A. Reese, "The Other American Law," 73 *Stanford Law Review* 555, 557 (2021), arguing that "[t]ribal law is American law, and as such it ought to occupy an equally prominent place alongside federal, state, and local law."

28. See Alison L. LaCroix, *The Ideological Origins of American Federalism* (Cambridge, Mass.: Harvard University Press, 2010).

29. *Chisholm v. Georgia*, 2 U.S. (2 Dall.) 419, 456 (1793) (Wilson, J.).

30. My view thus differs from that of Greg Ablavsky, who argues that the late eighteenth century—specifically, the drafting and ratification of the U.S. Constitution—effectively foreclosed arguments for multiple layers of sovereignty. See Gregory Ablavsky, "Empire States: The Coming of Dual Federalism," 128 *Yale Law Journal* 1792, 1796 (2019).

31. See Gregory Ablavsky, "Species of Sovereignty: Native Nationhood, the United States, and International Law," 106 *Journal of American History* 591 (2019).

32. Boudinot, *Address to the Whites*, 14.

33. Interview with Tuxie Miller, March 15, 16, and 17, 1937, in Grant Foreman, *Indian-Pioneer Papers Collection*, Works Progress Administration, Western History Collection, University of Oklahoma, 277.

34. See Perdue and Green, *Cherokee Removal*, 156. The Trail of Tears is also known as the "Trail Where They Cried," or, in Cherokee, "Nunahi-Duna-Dlo-Hilu-I."

35. See Perdue and Green, *Cherokee Nation*, 17.

36. See Tyler Boulware, "The Effect of the Seven Years' War on the Cherokee Nation," 5 *Early American Studies* 395, 401–4 (2007); Tyler Boulware, *Deconstructing the Cherokee Nation: Town, Region, and Nation among Eighteenth-Century Cherokees* (Gainesville: University Press of Florida, 2011).

37. See Julie L. Reed, *Serving the Nation: Cherokee Sovereignty and Social Welfare, 1800–1907* (Norman: University of Oklahoma Press, 2016), 7.

38. Boulware, "Effect of the Seven Years' War," 398; see also William G. McLoughlin, *Cherokee Renascence in the New Republic* (Princeton: Princeton University Press, 1986).

39. See LaCroix, *Ideological Origins*; see also Eric Nelson, *The Royalist Revolution: Monarchy and the American Founding* (Cambridge, Mass.: Belknap/Harvard University Press, 2014); Brendan McConville, *The King's Three Faces: The Rise and Fall of Royal America, 1688–1776* (Chapel Hill: University of North Carolina Press, 2006)); Jack P. Greene, "The Glorious Revolution and the British Empire, 1688–1783," in *The Revolution of 1688–1689: Changing Perspectives*, ed. Lois G. Schwoerer (Cambridge: Cambridge University Press, 1992), 260–71.

40. The fear was not hypothetical: in 1742, Spain invaded Georgia as part of the War of Jenkins' Ear.

41. See Lisa Ford, *Settler Sovereignty: Jurisdiction and Indigenous People in America and Australia, 1788–1836* (Cambridge, Mass.: Harvard University Press, 2010), 7, 22.

42. See Ablavsky, "Savage Constitution," 1005; see also Peter Onuf, *The Origins of the Federal Republic: Jurisdictional Controversies in the United States, 1775–1787* (Philadelphia: University of Pennsylvania Press, 1983).

43. See Ford, *Settler Sovereignty*, 24.

44. Ablavsky, "Savage Constitution," 1071.

45. Id., 1075.

46. An Act to Ratify and Confirm Certain Articles of Agreement and Cession Entered into on the 24th Day of April 1802, between the Commissioners of the State of Georgia on the one part, and the Commissioners of the United States on the other part, ratified June 16, 1802, Acts of the General Assembly of the State of Georgia Passed in June and November 1802, Georgia Legislative Documents, in *Compilation of the Laws of the State of Georgia, Passed by the Legislature since the Political Year 1800, to the Year 1810, Inclusive*, ed. Augustin Smith Clayton (Augusta: Adams and Duyckinck, 1812).

47. See Daniel J. Hulsebosch, "Being Seen Like a State: How Americans (and Britons) Built the Constitutional Infrastructure of a Developing Nation," 59 *William and Mary Law Review* 1239 (2018); Eliga H. Gould, *Among the Powers of the Earth: The American Revolution and the Making of a New World Empire* (Cambridge, Mass.: Harvard University Press, 2012).

48. See generally Gregory Ablavsky, *Federal Ground: Governing Property and Violence in the First U.S. Territories* (New York: Oxford, 2021); see also Henry Knox to George Washington, July 7, 1789, Founders Online, National Archives and Records Administration, https://founders.archives.gov/documents/Washington/05-03-02-0067: "The independent nations and tribes of indians ought to be considered as foreign nations, not as the subjects of any particular state."

49. An Act to Regulate Trade and Intercourse with the Indian Tribes, and to Preserve Peace on the Frontiers, Act of March 30, 1802, Pub. L. No. 7–13, § 12, 2 Stat. 139, 143. Prior acts dated from 1790, 1793, 1796, and 1799.

50. Id.

51. Perdue and Green, *Cherokee Nation*, 38–39; Norgren, *Cherokee Cases*, 42–43.

52. See Norgren, *Cherokee Cases*, 42; McLoughlin, *Cherokee Renascence*, 225.

53. McLoughlin, *Cherokee Renascence*, 226–27.

54. Perdue and Green, *Cherokee Nation*, 52; see also McLoughlin, *Cherokee Renascence*; Michael D. Green, *The Politics of Indian Removal: Creek Government and Society in Crisis* (Lincoln: University of Nebraska Press, 1982).

55. See Trade and Intercourse Act of 1793, sec. 9; see also Theda Perdue, *"Mixed Blood" Indians: Racial Construction in the Early South* (Athens: University of Georgia Press, 2003), ch. 3.

56. See Garrison, *Legal Ideology of Removal*, 24.

57. See Perdue and Green, *Cherokee Nation*, 52.

58. Quoted in Garrison, *Legal Ideology of Removal*, 25. As Garrison and other scholars note, this particular racialized view of the United States, and the consequent racial dimension of American expansion, were relatively new developments in the early nineteenth century. See also Perdue, *"Mixed-Blood" Indians*, 80.

59. Note that the terms "remove" and "removal" were employed differently from the ways in which they are used today. The word "remove" was often used intransitively, to mean to move one's location. See, e.g., Jane Austen, *Pride and Prejudice* (1813; repr., Oxford: Oxford University Press, 1990), 30: " 'She is a great deal too ill to be moved. Mr. Jones says we must not think of moving her. We must trespass a little longer on your kindness.' 'Removed!' cried Bingley. 'It must not be thought of. My sister, I am sure, will not hear of her removal.' " See also Banner, *How the Indians Lost Their Land*, 192–93.

60. Charles R. Hicks and John Ross to Joseph McMinn, July 22, 1823, quoted in Gary E. Moulton, *John Ross: Cherokee Chief* (Athens: University of Georgia Press, 1978), 25.

61. Id., 26–27; Wilkins, *Cherokee Tragedy*, 95, 158.

62. Ridge's Cherokee name was "Kah-nung-da-tla-geh," according to the spelling used by his son John Ridge, which loosely translates as "the man who walks on the mountaintop." In English, his name was "The Ridge"; after serving alongside Jackson in the Battle of Horseshoe Bend in 1814, he took the name "Major Ridge." See Wilkins, *Cherokee Tragedy*, 6.

63. See id., 186–88; see also Oklahoma Historical Society, "Major Ridge," https://www.okhistory.org/publications/enc/entry.php?entryname=MAJOR%20RIDGE, for the number of slaves. On slaveholding in the Cherokee Nation, see Tiya Miles, *Ties That Bind: The Story of an Afro-Cherokee Family in Slavery and Freedom*, 2nd ed. (Oakland: University of California Press, 2015); Tiya Miles, *The House on Diamond Hill: A Cherokee Plantation Story* (Chapel Hill: University of North Carolina Press, 2010).

64. See Moulton, *John Ross*; Eaton, *John Ross*.

65. See generally Theda Perdue, *Cherokee Women: Gender and Cultural Change, 1700–1835* (Lincoln: University of Nebraska Press, 1998), 41.

66. See Wilkins, *Cherokee Tragedy*, 4n.

67. See Theda Perdue, "John Ross and the Cherokees," 70 *Georgia Historical Quarterly* 456, 457 (1986); see also Fay A. Yarbrough, *Race and the Cherokee Nation: Sovereignty in the Nineteenth Century* (Philadelphia: University of Pennsylvania Press, 2008).

68. Moulton, *John Ross*, 2.

69. Moulton, *John Ross*, 6; Wilkins, *Cherokee Tragedy*, 206 ("backwoods aristocrats").

70. Tennison's Hotel, the precursor of the Willard Hotel, comprised six houses that Joshua Tennison began operating as a hotel in 1816. See G. Martin Moeller, Jr., *AIA Guide to the Architecture of Washington*, 4th ed. (Baltimore: Johns Hopkins University Press, 2006), 133.

71. John Quincy Adams, *Memoirs of John Quincy Adams, Comprising Portions of His Diary from 1795 to 1848*, ed. Charles Francis Adams (Philadelphia: J. B. Lippincott, 1874–77), June 3, 1824, 6:373 (hereafter cited as JQA *Memoirs*). "Purfled" in this case referred to a "border of threadwork or embroidery." See *Oxford English Dictionary*, s.v. "purfle" (noting archaic usage). The exceedingly well-read Adams might have been consciously echoing the phrase "purfled scarf" from Milton's 1634 masque *Comus*. John Milton, *Poems upon Several Occasions* (London: James Dodsley, 1785), 259, ll. 992–95: "Iris there with humid bow / Waters the odorous banks, that blow / Flowers of more mingled hue / Than her purfled scarf can shew."

72. JQA *Memoirs*, March 29, 1824, 6:272.

73. See Moulton, *John Ross*, 26; John Calhoun to John Ross et al., January 30, 1824, "Extinguishment of Cherokee Indian Title to Land in Georgia," in *American State Papers: Indian Affairs* (Washington, D.C.: Gales and Seaton, 1832–34), 2:473.

74. John Ross et al. to John Calhoun, February 11, 1824, in id., 474.

75. JQA *Memoirs*, March 29, 1824, 6:272.

76. See Joanne B. Freeman, *The Field of Blood: Violence in Congress and the Road to Civil War* (New York: Farrar, Straus and Giroux, 2018), 5–6.

77. JQA *Memoirs*, March 12, 1824, 6:255.

78. Id., 6:256.

79. Id.; see also See Harry L. Watson, *Liberty and Power: The Politics of Jacksonian America* (1990; repr., New York: Hill and Wang, 2006), 107, noting that the lottery, "a gesture to republican equality" for "struggling farmers," gave "every white family in Georgia a personal stake in Indian removal."

80. JQA *Memoirs*, March 12, 1824, 6:256.

81. Id., March 29, 1824, 6:271.

82. Id., 6:271–72.

83. James Monroe, "Message to the Senate and House of Representatives of the United States," March 30, 1824, in *Compilation of the Messages and Papers of the Presidents* (Washington, D.C.: Bureau of National Literature, 1917), 2:235–37.

84. See Wilkins, *Cherokee Tragedy*, 156, citing 18th Cong. 1st sess., House Doc. 133 (Serial 102).

85. *Illinois Intelligencer* (Vandalia), August 20, 1824, quoted in Wilkins, *Cherokee Tragedy*, 158.

86. Wilkins, *Cherokee Tragedy*, 158.

87. JQA *Memoirs*, 6:272.

88. "Oo-watie" can be translated as "the Ancient One." See Wilkins, *Cherokee Tragedy*, 7.

89. Susannah Reese's father, Charles T. Reese, was a North Carolinian of Welsh extraction who fought in the Continental Line during the Revolution and became known as "Fighting Charles Reese." See "Payroll Record Rev War," Charles T. Reese, 1792, WikiTree, https://www.wikitree.com/photo/jpg/Reese-2125. Boudinot family

legend held that Oo-watie was descended from a member of the expedition led by Hernando de Soto of Spain in 1539–43. See Mary B. Church, "Elias Boudinot," 17 *Magazine of History with Notes and Queries* 209, 210 (1913), written by a granddaughter of Elias and Harriett Boudinot.

90. Perdue, *Cherokee Editor*, 5.

91. Id., 6.

92. The Cherokee Elias Boudinot occasionally spelled his name with two final *T*s: Boudinott. This orthographic difference likely reflected the pronunciation of the final consonant in his surname. See Gaul, *To Marry an Indian*, 68n8.

93. Adam Hodgson, quoted in Ralph Henry Gabriel, *Elias Boudinot, Cherokee, and His America* (Norman: University of Oklahoma Press, 1941), 55–56.

94. Quoted in Perdue, *Cherokee Editor*, 8.

95. Quoted in Demos, *Heathen School*, 176.

96. Quoted in id., 177.

97. Elias Boudinot to Jeremiah Evarts, November 12, 1822, American Board of Commissioners for Foreign Missions Papers 12.1, Houghton Library, Harvard University, Cambridge, Mass. By permission of the Houghton Library, Harvard University.

98. Wilkins, *Cherokee Tragedy*, 136.

99. See Ann McGrath, *Illicit Love: Interracial Sex and Marriage in the United States and Australia* (Lincoln: University of Nebraska Press, 2015), 35–39.

100. Quoted in Gabriel, *Elias Boudinot*, 63.

101. Isaac Bunce quoted in Demos, *Heathen School*, 154.

102. John F. Wheeler quoted in Wilkins, *Cherokee Tragedy*, 146. On Cherokee views on intermarriage, see Perdue, *"Mixed Blood" Indians*, 94–95.

103. Stephen Gold to Herman Vaill and Flora Gold Vaill and Catharine Gold, June 11, 1825, VC.

104. Mary Gold Brinsmade to Herman Vaill and Flora Gold Vaill and Catharine Gold, July 14, 1825, VC.

105. Gaul, *To Marry an Indian*, 14; Gabriel, *Elias Boudinot*, 80.

106. Harriett Gold to Herman Vaill and Flora Gold Vaill, June 25, 1825, VC.

107. Gabriel, *Elias Boudinot*, 78.

108. Daniel Brinsmade to Herman Vaill and Flora Gold Vaill, June 29, 1825, VC. Brother-in-law Herman Vaill struck a similar note: "better to die on the side of Xtian honour & Gospel sincerity than to pine away with satisfied love, & its consequences, on the bed of Love." Herman Vaill to Mary Gold Brinsmade, August 2, 1825, id. On the repeated accusations of lust and "animal" passions leveled at Harriett by her family, especially her brothers-in-law, see McGrath, *Illicit Love*, 47.

109. Daniel Brinsmade to Herman Vaill and Flora Gold Vaill, June 29, 1825, VC.

110. Quoted in Gaul, *To Marry an Indian*, 44.

111. Benjamin Gold to Herman Vaill, September 1, 1825, VC.

112. See Demos, *Heathen School*, 186.

113. See Gaul, *To Marry an Indian*, 19, describing ball plays as "a traditional Cherokee sport combining preparation for battle with ritual"; missionaries regarded them as unwholesome because "the players are literally *naked* and yet a large proportion of the spectators are females" (quotation from McLoughlin, *Cherokees and Missionaries*, 208).

114. Quoted in Gaul, *To Marry an Indian*, 19.

115. Wilkins, *Cherokee Tragedy*, 152.

116. *Niles' Weekly Register*, July 9, 1825, 298; see also Perdue, *"Mixed Blood" Indians*, 75.

117. See Gabriel, *Elias Boudinot*, 71.

118. Quoted in Gaul, *To Marry an Indian*, 22.

119. Harriett Gold to Herman Vaill and Flora Gold Vaill, January 2, 1826, VC.

120. Church, "Elias Boudinot," 215.

121. Gaul, *To Marry an Indian*, 44.

122. Boudinot, *Address to the Whites*, 8.

123. See Gaul, *To Marry an Indian*; Wilkins, *Cherokee Tragedy*.

124. Boudinot, *Address to the Whites*, 9.

125. Resolution, "Convention to Draft a Constitution for the Cherokee Nation," November 13, 1826, John Howard Payne Papers (hereafter cited as JHPP), Newberry Library, Chicago, Box 7, Folder 6.

126. Wilkins, *Cherokee Tragedy*, 201.

127. Perdue and Green, *Cherokee Removal*, 58.

128. Id.

129. Constitution of the Cherokee Nation, Art. I, sec. 1 and 2.

130. Constitution of the Cherokee Nation (1827), Art. II, sec. 1; Art. III, sec. 1, 7; Art. IV, sec. 1, 18; Art. V, sec. 1.

131. Id., Art. III, sec. 4, 7. See also Miles, *Ties That Bind*; Miles, *House on Diamond Hill*; R. Halliburton, *Red over Black: Black Slavery among the Cherokee Indians* (Westport: Greenwood, 1977); Natalie Joy, "Cherokee Slaveholders and Radical Abolitionists," 10 *Common-place* (2010), http://commonplace.online/article/cherokee-slaveholders-radical-abolitionists/.

132. Resolution that an editor be appointed to edit a weekly newspaper at New Echota to be styled the *Cherokee Phoenix*, JHPP, Folder 6. The close connection between government and newspaper distinguished the *Phoenix* from non-Indigenous American newspapers of the period. See Mary Young, "The Cherokee Nation: Mirror of the Republic," 33 *American Quarterly* 502, 509 (1981).

133. "Cherokee Newspaper—Prospectus," *Religious Intelligencer* (New Haven, Conn.), January 5, 1828.

134. Elias Boudinot to Herman Vaill and Flora Gold Vaill, November 21, 1827, VC. On the "competing yet overlapping demands" of Boudinot's Cherokee and non-Cherokee "network of readers," see Ellen Cushman, "Elias Boudinot and the *Cherokee*

Phoenix: The Sponsors of Literacy They Were and Were Not," in *Literacy, Economy, and Power: Writing and Research after "Literacy in American Lives,"* ed. John Duffy, Julie Nelson Christoph et al. (Carbondale: Southern Illinois University Press, 2013), 17, 21; see also Daniel Heath Justice, *Our Fire Survives the Storm: A Cherokee Literary History* (Minneapolis: University of Minnesota Press, 2006); Ellen Cushman, *The Cherokee Syllabary: Writing the People's Perseverance* (Norman: University of Oklahoma Press, 2011).

135. Ellen Cushman notes the significance of Boudinot's decision to lay out the page with the Cherokee and U.S. constitutions side by side, "visually equal systems of government." Cushman, "Elias Boudinot," 23.

136. Elias Boudinot to Council, November 3, 1829, JHPP, Folder 7, Box 7.

137. Perdue, *Cherokee Editor*, 87.

138. Elias Boudinot and Harriett Gold Boudinot to Herman Vaill and Flora Gold Vaill, January 23, 1829, VC.

139. See Mary Ann Littlefield, "John Foster Wheeler of Fort Smith: Pioneer Printer and Publisher," 44 *Arkansas Historical Quarterly* 260 (1985).

140. Perdue, "Rising from the Ashes," 216; see also Benedict Anderson, *Imagined Communities: Reflections on the Origin and Spread of Nationalism*, rev. ed. (London: Verso, 2006).

141. *Cherokee Phoenix*, January 21, 1829, in Perdue, *Cherokee Editor*, 103.

142. Elias Boudinot to Reverend Elias Cornelius, March 11, 1829, in *Journal of Humanity; and Herald of the American Temperance Society*, July 1, 1829, reprinted in Perdue, *Cherokee Editor*, 48.

143. See Perdue, *Cherokee Editor*, 11.

144. *Cherokee Phoenix*, March 13, 1828, reprinted in Perdue, *Cherokee Editor*, 95–96.

145. See Perdue, *Mixed-Blood Indians*, 93–95.

146. Elias Boudinot and Harriett Gold Boudinot to Herman Vaill and Flora Gold Vaill, January 5, 1827, VC; Church, "Elias Boudinot," 216–17.

147. See Church, "Elias Boudinot," 216–17.

148. See Elias Boudinot and Harriett Gold Boudinot to Herman Vaill and Flora Gold Vaill, January 5, 1827, VC; Elias Boudinot to Stand Watie, March 7, 1832, in Edward Everett Dale and Gaston Litton, *Cherokee Cavaliers: Forty Years of Cherokee History as Told in the Correspondence of the Ridge-Watie-Boudinot Family* (1939; repr., Norman: University of Oklahoma Press, 1995), 5–6.

149. Elias Boudinot and Harriett Gold Boudinot to Herman Vaill and Flora Gold Vaill, January 23, 1829, VC.

150. The difficulty of Worcester's undertaking is captured in this comment from Boudinot:

> I presume the Cherokee verbs are the most complicated in the world—nothing like it in any language, whether learned or Savage, unless we except those spo-

ken by the Indians generally. You will form a slight idea of the almost infinite forms in the Cherokee verbs, when I tell you that we have discovered 29 Tenses in the indicative more, in all the verbs, & 30 in some; & that in the verb *To tie*, there are not less than 178 forms, only in the present Tense indicative mode. Mr. Worcester however proceeds rapidly in acquiring the language—he intends to preach in it—the blessing of God attend him.

Elias Boudinot and Harriett Gold Boudinot to Herman Vaill and Flora Gold Vaill, January 5, 1827, VC. On Boudinot and Worcester's linguistic collaboration, see Jack Frederick Kilpatrick and Anna Gritts Kilpatrick, eds., *New Echota Letters: Contributions of Samuel A. Worcester to the Cherokee Phoenix* (Dallas: Southern Methodist University Press 1968); Althea Bass, *Cherokee Messenger* (Norman: University of Oklahoma Press, 1936); Willard Walker, "The Roles of Samuel A. Worcester and Elias Boudinot in the Emergence of a Printed Cherokee Syllabic Literature," 51 *International Journal of American Linguistics* 610 (1985).

151. Harriett Gold Boudinot to Herman Vaill and Flora Gold Vaill, January 7, 1831, VC: "Our coffee sugar & Tea amounts to about 50_ dollars a year." The Boudinots obtained staples such as sugar, molasses, and flour from Augusta, some two hundred miles away.

152. Harriett Gold Boudinot to Flora Gold Vaill, April 14, 1830, VC.

153. Benjamin Gold to Herman Vaill and Flora Gold Vaill, October 29, 1829, VC.

154. Benjamin Gold to Hezekiah Gold, December 8, 1829, quoted in Church, "Elias Boudinot," 217–18.

155. Benjamin Gold to Herman Vaill and Flora Gold Vaill, April 14, 1830, VC.

156. Quoted in Church, "Elias Boudinot," 218.

157. See Elias Boudinot and Harriett Gold Boudinot to Herman Vaill and Flora Gold Vaill, January 23, 1829, VC.

158. Benjamin Gold to Herman Vaill and Flora Gold Vaill, October 29, 1829, VC.

159. Norgren, *Cherokee Cases* 46–47.

160. *Cherokee Phoenix*, February 28, 1828, quoted in Perdue, *Cherokee Editor*, 146.

161. Jackson's nationalism explicitly aimed to "maintain white supremacy and expand the white empire, to evict the Indian tribes, [and] to support and extend slavery." Daniel Walker Howe, *What Hath God Wrought: The Transformation of America, 1815–1848* (New York: Oxford, 2007), 280. See also Watson, *Liberty and Power*; Richard E. Ellis, *The Union at Risk: Jacksonian Democracy, States' Rights, and the Nullification Crisis* (New York: Oxford, 1987); Ronald N. Satz, *American Indian Policy in the Jacksonian Era* (Lincoln: University of Nebraska Press, 1975).

162. Andrew Jackson to James Monroe, March 4, 1817, in *Papers of Andrew Jackson Digital Edition*, ed. Daniel Feller (Charlottesville: University of Virginia Press, 2015–), 4:93.

163. Andrew Jackson to John C. Calhoun, September 2, 1820, in id., 4:388.

164. Andrew Jackson, "First Annual Message to Congress," December 8, 1829, in *A Compilation of the Messages and Papers of the Presidents, 1789–1897*, ed. James D. Richardson (Washington, D.C.: Government Printing Office, 1896), 2:457 (emphasis added).

165. Id. at 2:458.

166. Howe, *What Hath God Wrought*, 352. Some of these congressmen viewed the bill as reneging on existing treaties, and others feared its fiscal impact on their agenda of federally funded internal improvements. Howe notes the many political and ideological currents that underlay the vote: "Without the three-fifths clause jacking up the power of the slaveholding interest, Indian Removal would not have passed. Yet sectionalism did not determine positions so much as political loyalties and moral values."

167. David Crockett, *Narrative of the Life of David Crockett, Written by Himself*, 6th ed. (Philadelphia: E. L. Carey and A. Hart, 1834), 206. Two years after publishing his memoir, Crockett died at the Battle of the Alamo.

168. *Cherokee Phoenix*, December 10, 1828, quoted in McLoughlin, *Cherokee Renascence*, 425.

169. *Cherokee Phoenix*, June 17, 1829.

170. *Cherokee Phoenix*, February 19, 1831, quoted in Perdue and Green, *Cherokee Removal*, 133.

Chapter 7. *The Cherokee Nation v. Georgia v. United States*

1. See Jeremiah Evarts to William Wirt, June 12, 1830, Letters to Domestic Correspondents, ABC 1, American Board of Commissioners for Foreign Missions Papers (hereafter cited as ABCFM), Houghton Library, Harvard University, Cambridge, Mass.

2. To the Secretary of War (John C. Calhoun), in *Official Opinions of the Attorneys General of the United States* (Washington, D.C.: Robert Farnham, 1852), April 2, 1824, 1:645.

3. William Wirt to Dabney Carr, June 21, 1830, Wirt Letters, Library of Virginia, Richmond (hereafter cited as LVA), Folder 4.

4. William Wirt to George R. Gilmer, June 4, 1830, reprinted in *Niles' Weekly Register*, September 18, 1830.

5. Id.

6. Id.

7. Georgia had a long history with sovereign immunity: the state lost the Supreme Court case that spawned, and was abrogated by, the Eleventh Amendment. See *Chisholm v. Georgia*, 2 U.S. (2 Dall.) 419 (1793).

8. U.S. Const., 11th Am.

9. William Wirt, "To the Editor of the Baltimore Gazette," September 9, 1830, repr. in *Niles' Weekly Register*, September 18, 1830; *McCulloch v. Maryland*, 17 U.S. (4 Wheat.) 316 (1819); *Brown v. Maryland*, 25 U.S. (12 Wheat.) 419 (1827).

10. Wirt, "To the Editor of the Baltimore Gazette." These cases were not collusive but rather highly adversarial. The significance of the consent was that the issues were

presented in stripped-down form, such that the central question—the constitutionality of a state law—could be decided. As James Pfander notes, such cases resemble the modern declaratory judgment suit. See James E. Pfander and Daniel D. Birk, "Article III Judicial Power, the Adverse-Party Requirement, and Non-Contentious Jurisdiction," 124 *Yale Law Journal* 1346 (2015).

11. George R. Gilmer to William Wirt, June 19, 1830, reprinted in *Niles' Weekly Register*, September 18, 1830; *Georgia Journal*, "Mr. Wirt and the Cherokees," August 28, 1830, repr. in *Niles' Weekly Register*, September 18, 1830.

12. George R. Gilmer to William Wirt, June 19, 1830, reprinted in *Niles' Weekly Register*, September 18, 1830.

13. *Georgia Journal*, "Mr. Wirt and the Cherokees."

14. Gilmer later stated that he had "never felt so indignant as I did upon reading Mr. Wirt's letter." The multiple familial connections between Wirt and himself "induced me to believe that Mr. Wirt expected that his age, high-standing, and intimate relationship with my family friends, would induce me to do at his request what I would refuse to another." Elsewhere in the same memoir, however, Gilmer's indignation gave way to almost-fawning admiration, with Gilmer praising Wirt's "glossy curling hair, fine person, and expressive features" and his "talents, learning, and graceful address." George R. Gilmer, *Sketches of Some of the First Settlers of Upper Georgia* (New York: D. Appleton, 1855), 354, 28.

15. William Wirt to Dabney Carr, June 21, 1830, LVA, Folder 4.

16. William Wirt to Dabney Carr, September 29, 1830, LVA, Folder 4; Wirt to Carr, May 23, 1832, University of North Carolina.

17. William Wirt, *Opinion on the Right of the State of Georgia to Extend Her Laws over the Cherokee Nation* (New Echota: John Wheeler for the Cherokee Nation, 1830).

18. Id., 14, 18–19.

19. See Galen N. Thorp, "William Wirt," 33 *Journal of Supreme Court History* 223, 263 (2008).

20. William Wirt to William H. Underwood, September 10, 1830, Gilcrease Collection, Tulsa. The handwriting of the letters suggests that Wirt dictated his letters to Underwood, while he personally penned his letters to Ross. Local counsel and clients evidently received different degrees of attention from the former attorney general of the United States.

21. Judiciary Act of 1789, sec. 25.

22. William Wirt to Dabney Carr, June 21, 1830, LVA. On Berrien, see Thomas P. Govan, "John M. Berrien and the Administration of Andrew Jackson," 5 *Journal of Southern History* 447 (1939).

23. *State v. George Tassel*, 1 Dudley 229 (1830); Jill Norgren, *The Cherokee Cases: Two Landmark Federal Decisions in the Fight for Sovereignty* (Norman: University of Oklahoma Press, 2004), 97–98.

24. See Gilmer, *Sketches*, 357.

25. *Cherokee Phoenix*, January 8, 1831, quoted in Theda Perdue and Michael D. Green, *The Cherokee Removal: A Brief History with Documents*, 3rd ed. (Boston: Bedford/St. Martin's, 2016), 132.

26. 14 U.S. (1 Wheat.) 304 (1816).

27. 6 *American Law Journal* 313, 368 (1817).

28. Id.

29. John Quincy Adams, *Memoirs of John Quincy Adams, Comprising Portions of His Diary from 1795 to 1848*, ed. Charles Francis Adams (Philadelphia: J. B. Lippincott, 1874–77), May 16, 1828, 7:437 (hereafter cited as JQA *Memoirs*).

30. Wirt also considered commencing a suit in federal circuit court, under the lower courts' original jurisdiction. He discussed this strategy in his correspondence with Kent, contemplating a suit on behalf of an individual Cherokee plaintiff against Georgia. Ross, for his part, reportedly met with Justice Johnson, the circuit justice for Georgia and South Carolina, to discuss the possibility of a circuit-court suit. Ultimately, Wirt concluded that the Supreme Court offered a more favorable forum, and that the best plaintiff was the Nation itself. See Joseph C. Burke, "Cherokee Cases," 21 *Stanford Law Review* 500, 511–12 (1969); "Mr. Wirt and the Cherokees," *Richmond Enquirer*, September 10, 1830 (reprinting report from the *Georgia Journal*).

31. U.S. Const., Art. III, sec. 2, cl. 1 and 2.

32. William Wirt to Dabney Carr, June 21, 1830, LVA.

33. William Wirt to James Kent, December 3, 1830, James Kent Papers, Library of Congress, Reel 3/Box 6.

34. William Wirt to Dabney Carr, June 21, 1830, LVA.

35. Id.

36. John Marshall to Dabney Carr, June 26, 1830, in *Papers of John Marshall*, ed. Charles F. Hobson (Chapel Hill: University of North Carolina Press, 1974–2006) (hereafter cited as *PJM*), 11:380–81; Editorial Note, in id., 12:45.

37. Gary E. Moulton, *John Ross: Cherokee Chief* (Athens: University of Georgia Press, 1978), 44; Editorial Note, in *PJM*, 12:47.

38. John Ross to William Wirt, January 1, 1831, Gilcrease Collection, Tulsa. Wirt obtained a retainer of $500 (nearly $14,000 in today's money) from the Nation. His usual fee for arguing a case of this magnitude before the Supreme Court was $3,000 (nearly $84,000 today), but he offered Ross a reduced fee of $1,000 prior to the argument, stating, "if we succeed, I shall expect from your justice a farther and most liberal compensation." Wirt to Ross, November 15, 1830, id.

39. See, e.g., John McLean Papers, 1817–1861, Library of Congress, Manuscript Division, Washington, D.C.

40. See Anya Jabour, *Marriage in the Early Republic: Elizabeth and William Wirt and the Companionate Ideal* (Baltimore: Johns Hopkins University Press, 1998), 145.

41. William Wirt to Elizabeth Wirt, March 12, 1831, William Wirt Papers, Maryland Historical Society, Baltimore (hereafter cited as MdHS), Reel 14.

42. JQA *Memoirs*, 8:276.

43. Elizabeth Wirt to William Wirt, March 13, 1831, MdHS, Reel 14.

44. Id.

45. Id.; Catharine Wirt to Elizabeth Wirt, March 14, 1831, MdHS, Reel 14. On George Beltzhoover's "Phoenix line" coach service between Baltimore and Washington, see James M. Goode, *The Evolution of Washington, D.C.: Historical Selections from the Albert H. Small Washingtoniana Collection at George Washington University* (Washington, D.C.: Smithsonian, 2015), 64.

46. See Jabour, *Marriage in the Early Republic*, 152.

47. Catharine Wirt to Elizabeth Wirt, March 14, 1831, MdHS, Reel 14.

48. Richard Peters, *The Case of the Cherokee Nation against the State of Georgia* (Philadelphia: J. Grigg, 1831), 157–58.

49. *Daily National Intelligencer*, March 18, 1831, quoted in Editorial Note, in *PJM*, 12:51.

50. JQA *Memoirs*, 8:345.

51. Catharine Wirt to Elizabeth Wirt, March 14, 1831, MdHS, Reel 14.

52. Thurman Wilkins, *Cherokee Tragedy: The Ridge Family and the Decimation of a People*, 2nd. ed. (Norman: University of Oklahoma Press, 1986), 220–21. Wilkins gives an erroneous date for the decision (July 18); the actual date was March 18.

53. *Cherokee Nation v. Georgia*, 30 U.S. (5 Peters) 1 (1831).

54. 30 U.S. 17.

55. Id., 15.

56. Id., 20.

57. Id., 20; see also Editorial Note, in *PJM*, 12:51.

58. Baldwin and Johnson wrote separate concurrences; McLean concurred silently; and Duvall was absent. Editorial Note, in *PJM*, 12:52.

59. Joseph Story to Richard Peters, May 17, 1831, quoted in Burke, "Cherokee Cases," 516; see also Editorial Note, in *PJM*, 12:53.

60. "Cherokee Nation vs. The State of Georgia," *Cherokee Phoenix*, April 16, 1831.

61. Id.

62. 30 U.S. 20.

63. *McCulloch*, 17 U.S. (4 Wheat.) 436 (1816); *Cohens v. Virginia*, 19 U.S. (6 Wheat.) 264.

64. Jeremiah Evarts and David Greene to Samuel Worcester, February 1, 1831, Letters to Domestic Correspondents, ABC 1, ABCFM.

65. Samuel Worcester to Jeremiah Evarts, January 28, 1831, LFCM, VII, ABCFM, quoted in Edwin A. Miles, "After John Marshall's Decision: *Worcester v. Georgia* and the Nullification Crisis," 39 *Journal of Southern History* 519, 522 (1973).

66. Editorial Note, *Worcester v. Georgia*, in *PJM*, 12:151.

67. Id.

68. Gilmer's letter to Worcester was reprinted in "Affairs of the Cherokees: From the Cherokee Phoenix of May 28, 1831," *Niles' Weekly Register*, June 25, 1831.

69. Miles, "After John Marshall's Decision," 523.

70. "Affairs of the Cherokees."

71. Id.

72. William Wirt to Samuel Worcester, July 19, 1831, LFCM VII, ABCFM, quoted in Miles, "After John Marshall's Decision," 525.

73. David Greene to William Wirt, July 12, 1831, ABC 1, ABCFM.

74. See *Worcester v. Georgia*, 31 U.S. (6 Pet.) 515–16 (1832).

75. See David Greene to William Wirt, July 12, 1831; Greene to Wirt, March 9, 1832, ABC 1, ABCFM: enclosing "a draft for $500, being his fee for arguing the case of Messrs. Worcester & Butler before the Supreme Court of the U.S."; Editorial Note, in *PJM*, 12:152.

76. David Greene to Elias Boudinot, December 13, 1831, ABC 1, ABCFM.

77. See *The Proceedings of the Second United States Anti-Masonic Convention, Held at Baltimore, September 1831* (Boston: Boston Type and Stereotype Foundry, 1832); William Preston Vaughan, *The Anti-Masonic Party in the United States, 1826–1843* (Lexington: University Press of Kentucky, 1983); Michael Holt, "The Anti-Masonic and Know-Nothing Parties," in *Political Parties and American Political Development from the Age of Jackson to the Age of Lincoln*, ed. Michael Holt (Baton Rouge: Louisiana State University Press, 1992), 115.

78. William Wirt to Dabney Carr, January 22, 1832, UNC.

79. William Wirt to Dabney Carr, May 23, 1832, UNC.

80. JQA *Memoirs*, 8:477.

81. Editorial Note, in *PJM* 12:153, 158; see also Joseph Story, *Memoranda on Arguments before the Supreme Court, 1831–1832*, Special Collections, Harvard Law School Library, Cambridge, Mass.

82. Charles R. Williams I, *Life of Rutherford Birchard Hayes* (1914), quoted in Charles Warren, *The Supreme Court in United States History*, rev. ed. (Boston: Little, Brown, 1926), 1:756n1.

83. Joseph Story to Sarah Wetmore Story, February 26, 1832, in *Life and Letters of Joseph Story: Associate Justice of the Supreme Court of the United States* (Boston: C. C. Little and J. Brown, 1851), 2:84.

84. Id.

85. "Georgia and Missionaries," *New York Daily Advertiser*, March 7, 1832.

86. See R. Kent Newmyer, *John Marshall and the Heroic Age of the Supreme Court* (Baton Rouge: Louisiana State University Press, 2001), 451.

87. Upon hearing from Physick that the mortality rate following the procedure was around 50 percent, Marshall replied that he would "die rather than live in agony." William Jeffery Klein and J. Patrick O'Leary, "Judicial Lithiasis," 67 *American Surgeon* 813, 814 (2001); see also Alexander Randall, "Philip Syng Physick's Last Major Operation," 9 *Annals of Medical History* 133 (1937); Editorial Note, in *PJM*, 12:105.

88. Klein and O'Leary, "Judicial Lithiasis," 814; Editorial Note, in *PJM*, 12:109.

89. Editorial Note, in *PJM*, 12:109.

90. 31 U.S. 519.

91. 31 U.S. 562–63, 596–97.

92. See Miles, "After John Marshall's Decision," 528; Washington *Daily National Intelligencer*, quoted in Editorial Note, in *PJM*, 12:155.

93. Judiciary Act of 1789, sec. 25. The writ of error in *Worcester* asserted that the Gwinnett County Superior Court was such a court, and Marshall's opinion adopted this assertion without comment. 31 U.S. 532.

94. See, e.g., *Weston v. City Council of Charleston*, 27 U.S. (2 Pet.) 449, 457 (1829) (argument of counsel).

95. Judiciary Act of 1789, sec. 25.

96. Editorial Note, in *PJM*, 12:155.

97. Burke, "Cherokee Cases," 525.

98. William Wirt to Lewis Williams, April 28, 1832, Wirt Papers, Manuscript Division, Library of Congress, Box 9, Reel 4; see also Burke, "Cherokee Cases," 526–27. The following month, Representative Edmund Pendleton of New York presented a petition "praying Congress to adopt the most speedy and effectual measures to enforce the judgment of the Supreme Court of the United States, in the case of the missionaries Worcester and Butler." After some debate, the House voted 106 to 57 to table the petition. "Indian Missionaries," May 28, 1832, and "Georgia and the Missionaries," June 11, 1832, in *Register of Debates in Congress* 8 (1833): 3105–19, 3400–20.

99. The Force Act of 1833 expanded the scope of the federal courts' habeas powers, but the majority of Wirt's proposed statutory reforms did not come to pass until Congress passed the Habeas Corpus Act of 1867. Act of February 5, 1867, Ch, 28, *Statutes at Large of the United States*, XIV (1868), 385.

100. Peters, *Case of the Cherokee Nation*, 155.

101. See Andrew Jackson, "First Annual Message to Congress," December 8, 1829, in *A Compilation of the Messages and Papers of the Presidents, 1789–1897*, ed. James D. Richardson (Washington, D.C: Government Printing Office, 1896), 2:457.

102. See Burke, "Cherokee Cases," 525; see also Miles, "After John Marshall's Decision"; *PJM*, 12:156. Jackson called the decision "still born" upon hearing of Georgia's refusal to order execution of the judgment. Quoted in Miles, "After John Marshall's Decision," 528.

103. Lewis Williams to William Lenoir, April 9, 1832, quoted in Miles, "After John Marshall's Decision," 533n33.

104. William Wirt to Lewis Williams, April 28, 1832, William Wirt Papers, Library of Congress, Reel 4; quoted in Burke, "Cherokee Cases," 527.

105. Joseph Story to George Ticknor, March 8, 1832, in *Life and Letters of Joseph Story, Associate Justice of the Supreme Court of the United States*, ed. William W. Story (Boston: Little, Brown, 1851), 2:83.

106. See Alan Taylor, *The Internal Enemy: Slavery and War in Virginia, 1772–1832* (New York: W. W. Norton, 2013).

107. Ellen Cushman, "Elias Boudinot and the *Cherokee Phoenix*: The Sponsors of Literacy They Were and Were Not," in *Literacy, Economy, and Power: Writing and Research After "Literacy in American Lives,"* ed. John Duffy, Julie Nelson Christoph et al. (Carbondale: Southern Illinois University Press, 2013), 25.

108. Elias Boudinot to Stand Watie, March 7, 1832, in *Cherokee Cavaliers: Forty Years of Cherokee History as Told in the Correspondence of the Ridge-Watie-Boudinot Family*, ed. Edward Everett Dale and Gaston Litton (1939; repr., Norman: University of Oklahoma Press, 1995), 5–6.

109. Id., 6.

110. Id., 4–5.

111. Id., 7.

112. John Ridge to Stand Watie, April 6, 1832, in id., 7–8.

113. Id.

114. Andrew Jackson to John Coffee, April 7, 1832, in *Papers of Andrew Jackson Digital Edition*, ed. Daniel Feller (Charlottesville: University of Virginia Press, 2015–).

115. David Greene to John Ridge, April 25, 1832, ABC 1, ABCFM.

116. See Miles, "After John Marshall's Decision," 526.

117. David Greene to Samuel Worcester, April 25, 1832, ABC 1, ABCFM.

118. 31 U.S. 589–90, 593 (McLean, concurring).

119. Quoted in Editorial Note, in *PJM*, 12:156.

120. Copy of Letter from John McLean to Chief John Ross. 4026.107-a.1, John Ross Papers, May 23, 1832, Gilcrease Collection, Tulsa.

121. Id.

122. See Gregory Ablavsky, "Beyond the Indian Commerce Clause," 124 *Yale Law Journal* 1012 (2015).

123. John McLean to John Ross, May 23, 1832, Gilcrease Collection, Tulsa.

124. Elias Boudinot to John Ross, August 1, 1832; "To the Readers of the Cherokee Phoenix," *Cherokee Phoenix*, August 11, 1832, reprinted in Elias Boudinot, *Letters and Other Papers Relating to Cherokee Affairs; Being a Reply to Sundry Publications Authorized by John Ross* (Athens, Ga., 1837), 6–7 (emphasis added).

125. John Ross to the Committee and Council in General Council Convened, August 4, 1832, reprinted in Boudinot, *Letters and Other Papers*, 8. It is unclear whether the italics were Ross's or Boudinot's.

126. Id., 8.

127. See Wilkins, *Cherokee Tragedy*, 251–52; Perdue and Green, *Cherokee Nation*, 105; Act of June 9, 1825 (authorizing the 1827 drawing); see, e.g., Henry G. Clauder to Elizur Butler, January 23, 1836 (reporting an offer from "the so called Fortunate drawers" to permit Clauder, a Moravian missionary, to rent back his premises for "150$ per annum"), John Howard Payne Papers (hereafter cited as JHPP), Newberry Library, Chicago, Box 5, Folder 1a.

128. "To the Cherokee Citizens of Amokee District," May 8, 1832, Box 7, Folder 11, JHPP.

129. Editorial Note, in *PJM*, 12:157; Miles, "After John Marshall's Decision," 533–35.

130. Miles, "After John Marshall's Decision," 535–39. ABCFM secretary Greene "raised the lone dissenting voice against the recommendation." Id., 539.

131. Id., 540–41.

132. See id., 543–44; Burke, "Cherokee Cases," 531; Merrill D. Peterson, *Olive Branch and Sword: The Compromise of 1833* (Baton Rouge: Louisiana State University Press, 1982).

133. Peterson, *Olive Branch*, 87–88.

134. See Jabour, *Marriage in the Early Republic*, 154–60. The plantation— "Wirtland"—was located in Monticello, twenty-five miles east of Tallahassee. By 1834, it was growing corn and cotton. Labor was to be provided by a "German Colony" of contract workers and their families, with supplemental labor from enslaved workers. Both Elizabeth and William Wirt declared themselves to view with "repugnance" the prospect of becoming large-scale slaveowners. But difficulties with the German workers led William to purchase more slaves, even as Elizabeth urged him to reduce their slaveholding. "Oh! I do so wish to have nothing more to do with such property," she wrote. Daughter Catharine wrote to her father, "Mother says that instead of . . . incurring this great debt, she wishes you wd. have the negroes sold again as soon as possible." Catharine reported that her mother, Elizabeth, "hates the idea of having such a plantation of *negroes*, as every body else has—she so greatly prefers the white Germans." Quoted in id., 156–57.

135. Catharine Wirt to Eliza Clayton, February 22, 1834, "The Last Days of William Wirt, Esq., Late Attorney General of the United States, By His Daughter," *Christian Advocate* (Philadelphia), 1834, 12.

136. "Last Days of William Wirt."

137. Jabour, *Marriage in the Early Republic*, 162.

138. "Last Days of William Wirt."

139. Id.

140. JQA *Memoirs*, 9:97, 99.

141. Id., 9:99–100.

142. Id., 6:518.

143. Id., 9:100.

144. Id., 9:100–101. See Thursday, February 20, 1834, in *Journal of the House of Representatives of the United States*, 23rd Congress, 1st Sess. (Washington, D.C.: Gales and Seaton, 1833), 348–49.

145. William Wirt to Elizabeth Wirt, May 10, 1805, in John Pendleton Kennedy, *Memoirs of the Life of William Wirt, Attorney-General of the United States*, new and rev. ed. (New York: G. P. Putnam's Sons, 1872), 1:133.

146. See chart in appendix to Thorp, "William Wirt," 279–80.

147. John Ross, message to General Council, Red Clay, October 13, 1834, Box 7, JHPP, Folder 11.

148. Lewis Cass to John Ross and delegation, February 16, 1835, Box 7, JHPP, Folder 11.

149. Elias Boudinot to the editor of the *Phoenix*, October 2, 1832, in Boudinot, *Letters and Other Papers*, 15.

150. Elias Boudinot to John Ross, November 25, 1836, in Boudinot, *Letters and Other Papers*, 64–65.

151. See Norgren, *Cherokee Cases*, 124.

152. Boudinot, *Letters and Other Papers*, 57, 65.

153. Wilkins, *Cherokee Tragedy*, 285–86.

154. Quoted in J. W. H. Underwood, "Reminiscences of the Cherokees," *Cartersville (Ga.) Courant*, March 26, 1885.

155. Id.

156. The undated letter is quoted in Gaul, *To Marry an Indian*, 60. Cf. Rebecca Nagle, "This Land" podcast in which Nagle—a descendant of John Ridge—distinguishes between Ross's plan to keep the land but lose the Nation, versus the Treaty Party plan to move west, lose the land, but retain the Nation. See Rebecca Nagle, "The Treaty," in *This Land*, podcast, Season 1, Episode 4, https://crooked.com/podcast-series/this-land/.

157. Treaty with the Cherokee, 1835, December 29, 1835, 7 Stat. 478, in *Indian Affairs: Laws and Treaties* (Washington, D.C.: Government Printing Office, 1904), 2:439.

158. Underwood, "Reminiscences"; Wilkins, *Cherokee Tragedy*, 289.

159. *Laws of the Cherokee Nation* (Tahlequah, C.N.: Cherokee Advocate, 1852), 136–37; see also Mary Young, "The Cherokee Nation: Mirror of the Republic," 33 *American Quarterly* 520 (1981).

160. See Julie L. Reed, "An Absolute and Unconditional Pardon: Nineteenth-Century Cherokee Indigenous Justice," in *The Native South: New Histories and Enduring Legacies*, ed. Tim Alan Garrison and Greg O'Brien (Carbondale: Southern Illinois University Press, 2013); Michelle Daniel, "From Blood Feud to Jury System: The Metamorphosis of Cherokee Law from 1750 to 1840," 11 *American Indian Quarterly* 97 (1987).

161. Quoted in Wilkins, *Cherokee Tragedy*, 289.

162. Id.

163. Quoted in id., 292–93.

164. Perdue and Green, *Cherokee Nation*, 113.

165. Elias Boudinot to Benjamin and Eleanor Gold, August 16, 1836, quoted in Theresa Strouth Gaul, ed., *To Marry an Indian: The Marriage of Harriett Gold and Elias Boudinot in Letters, 1823–1839* (Chapel Hill: University of North Carolina Press, 2005), 183. See also id. at xiv–xv (discussing source of the letter and accompanying newspaper piece).

166. Id., 183, 188.

167. Id., 189–90.

168. Id., 190–93, quoting *New York Observer*, November 26, 1836.

169. Sophia Sawyer to David Greene, 1836, quoted in id., 197–98. Frank Brinsmade Boudinot, the youngest of Elias and Harriett's children, had been born on May 15, 1836, three months before Harriett's death.

170. Elias Boudinot to Benjamin and Eleanor Gold, March 22, 1837, in id., 198.

171. Id., 200.

172. See Wilkins, *Cherokee Tragedy*, 309.

173. Perdue and Green, *Cherokee Nation*, 121; Wilkins, *Cherokee Tragedy*, 309; James W. Parins, *Elias Cornelius Boudinot: A Life on the Cherokee Border* (Lincoln: University of Nebraska Press, 2005), 13.

174. Wilkins, *Cherokee Tragedy*, 312.

175. The literature on the Trail of Tears is voluminous. Among many sources, see Wilkins, *Cherokee Tragedy*; Perdue and Green, *Cherokee Nation*, from which the material in the next two paragraphs is drawn.

176. Quoted in Ralph Henry Gabriel, *Elias Boudinot, Cherokee, and His America* (Norman: University of Oklahoma Press, 1941), 170–71. Ross's Landing was renamed Chattanooga in 1839.

177. Perdue and Green, *Cherokee Nation*, 130–32.

178. Quoted in Wilkins, *Cherokee Tragedy*, 328.

179. Daniel Butrick to John Howard Payne, January 19, 1841, JHPP, Box 9.

180. Daniel Butrick to Elias Boudinot, June 9, 1839 (copy), id.

181. See Wilkins, *Cherokee Tragedy*, 334; Young, "Cherokee Nation," 520; Reed, "Absolute and Unconditional Pardon," 126–27; Daniel, "From Blood Feud to Jury System," 115.

182. Quoted in Grant Foreman, ed., "The Murder of Elias Boudinot," 12 *Chronicles of Oklahoma* 23 (1934).

183. Quoted in Wilkins, *Cherokee Tragedy*, 335.

184. Sarah Fitzjarrald, "John Foster Wheeler: Mayor of Fort Smith in 1854," 13 *Journal of the Fort Smith Historical Society* 3, 5 (1989).

185. Samuel Worcester to Daniel Brinsmade, June 26, 1839, in Gaul, *To Marry an Indian*, 202.

186. Quoted in Wilkins, *Cherokee Tragedy*, 336. See account in id., 334–39. Cf. the slightly different account from Interview with J. F. Weaver, "General Stand Watie—An Act in His Early Career That Showed the Stuff of Which He Was Made," February 25, 1938, in Grant Foreman, *Indian-Pioneer Papers Collection*, Works Progress Administration, Western History Collection, University of Oklahoma, 47–48.

187. Wilkins, *Cherokee Tragedy*, 338.

188. Quoted in id., 340; see also Carolyn Thomas Foreman, *Park Hill* (Muskogee, Okla.: Star Printery, 1948), 36.

189. Wilkins, *Cherokee Tragedy*, 340.

190. Quoted in Edward C. Starr, *History of Cornwall, Connecticut, A Typical New England Town* (New Haven: Tuttle, Morehouse and Taylor, 1926), 278.

191. Samuel Worcester to Daniel Brinsmade, June 26, 1839, in Gaul, *To Marry an Indian*, 202–3.

192. Id., 203.

193. Id.

194. Wilkins, *Cherokee Tragedy*, 338–41.

195. Id., 342.

196. Official records list E. C. Boudinot as having resigned from the Confederate Army as a major, but he used the title "Colonel" throughout his life, likely having been brevetted to that rank through a battlefield promotion that was never formalized. Parins, *Elias Cornelius Boudinot*, 51. Cornelius's younger brother Frank Brinsmade Boudinot also served in the Civil War—on the Union side, as a captain in the New York Mounted Rifles. He was killed in Virginia in May 1864.

197. See the obituary of Boudinot's wife, Clara Minear Boudinot, *Evening Star* (Washington, D.C.), September 25, 1911; see also Clare Cushman, "Women Advocates before the Supreme Court," 26 *Journal of Supreme Court History* 67, 71 (2001). The case was *The Cherokee Tobacco Case*, 78 U.S. (11 Wall.) 616, 618 (1871).

Chapter 8. The Customs of Commerce

Epigraph. Abel P. Upshur, *A Brief Enquiry into the True Nature and Character of Our Federal Government: Being a Review of Judge Story's Commentaries on the Constitution of the United States* (1840; repr., Philadelphia: J. Campbell, 1863), 6.

1. *Gibbons v. Ogden*, 22 U.S. (9 Wheat.) 1, 158–59, 183–86 (1824) (arguments of Emmet and Wirt, respectively, as reported by Henry Wheaton); *Charleston Courier*, February 24, 1824 (from *New-York Statesman*) (Emmet, as reported by newspaper); William Wirt, *Memoirs of the Life of William Wirt, Attorney-General of the United States*, ed. John Pendleton Kennedy (1849; repr., New York: G. P. Putnam and Sons, 1872), 2:145 (Emmet, as reported by Wirt's biographer).

2. Gibbons, 22 U.S. (9 Wheat.) at 209–10 (1824) (Marshall, C. J., for the Court).

3. Upshur, *Brief Enquiry*, 6.

4. "U.S., Atlantic Ports Arriving and Departing Passenger and Crew Lists, 1820–1959," records from Record Group 287, Publications of the U.S. Government; Record Group 85, Records of the Immigration and Naturalization Service; and Record Group 36, Records of the United States Customs Service. National Archives and Records Administration, reproduced on Ancestry.com, https://www.ancestry.com/discoveryui-content/view/7103734:8758?tid=&pid=&queryId=e3433ccb7ba6be9eeccdd699ccecb2aa&_phsrc=qHY41&_phstart=successSource (hereafter cited as Ship Emily Passenger List).

5. The average time for a trip from Liverpool to New York by sail was around forty-four days. See Raymond L. Cohn, *Mass Migration under Sail: European Immigration to the Antebellum United States* (Cambridge: Cambridge University Press, 2009), 137.

6. Between the early 1830s and the early 1840s, approximately 650,000 people immigrated to the United States. The numbers spiked in the subsequent decade, with more than 2.5 million people immigrating to the United States between 1845 and 1855. See Kunal Parker, *Making Foreigners: Immigration and Citizenship Law in America, 1600–2000* (Cambridge: Cambridge University Press, 2015), 83. Most of the migrants hailed from areas of northern Europe ravaged by famine, political turmoil, and economic hardship. By 1861, "approximately 70 percent of the foreign-born nationwide were of Irish or German descent." Id.

7. An Act Concerning Passengers in Vessels Coming to the Port of New-York, 47th Sess., Ch. XXXVII, § 1 (February 11, 1824), in *Laws of the State of New-York, Passed at the Forty-Seventh Session of the Legislature, Begun and Held at the City of Albany, the Sixth Day of January, 1824* (Albany: Leake and Croswell, 1824). Other sections of the act required the master or commander of the ship to obtain sureties and to remove any passenger whom the mayor or recorder "deemed likely to become chargeable to the said city." See id. §§ 2, 3.

8. All conversions taken from the CPI Inflation Calculator, Official Inflation Data, https://www.officialdata.org/us/inflation/1829?amount=75.

9. See Hendrik Hartog, *Public Property and Private Power: The Corporation of the City of New York in American Law, 1730–1870* (Ithaca: Cornell University Press, 1989); Gautham Rao, *National Duties: Custom Houses and the Making of the American State* (Chicago: University of Chicago Press, 2016); Harry L. Watson, *Liberty and Power: The Politics of Jacksonian America* (1990; repr., New York: Hill and Wang, 2006); Daniel Walker Howe, *What Hath God Wrought: The Transformation of America, 1815–1848* (New York: Oxford, 2007).

10. 22 U.S. (9 Wheat.) 1 (1824).

11. An Act for Enrolling and Licensing Ships or Vessels to Be Employed in the Coasting Trade and Fisheries, and for Regulating the Same, 2nd Congress, Sess. II, Ch. 8 (February 18, 1793).

12. 9 Wheat. 182–83.

13. See Thomas Addis Emmet in *Gibbons v. Ogden*, 22 U.S. (9 Wheat). 1, 107 (1824).

14. Cf. Akhil Amar's reframing of the Commerce Clause as the "With-and-Among Clause." Akhil Reed Amar, *America's Constitution: A Biography* (New York: Random House, 2005), 108.

15. Cf. *United States v. Lopez*, 514 U.S. 549, 615 (1995): "Not every epochal case has come in epochal trappings" (Souter, J., dissenting).

16. Marshall declined to distinguish between steamboats transporting passengers and those carrying merchandise. See 22 U.S. 220; see also Mary Sarah Bilder, "The

Struggle over Immigration: Indentured Servants, Slaves, and Articles of Commerce," 61 *Missouri Law Review* 743, 797–98 (1996).

17. 22 U.S. 195. Marshall had also used water imagery five years previously in *McCulloch v. Maryland,* drawing a parallel between the federal government's powers and the nation's riverine borders. See 17 U.S. (4 Wheat.) 316, 408 (1819).

18. 25 U.S. (12 Wheat.) 419 (1827).

19. 27 U.S. (2 Pet.) 245 (1829). The "sluggish, reptile stream" characterization comes from the argument of William Wirt, representing the dam company. 27 U.S. 249.

20. *Elkison v. Deliesseline,* 8 F. Cas. 493 (C.C.D.S.C. 1823) (No. 4,366).

21. *Worcester v. Georgia,* 31 U.S. (6 Pet.) 515, 520 (1832); see also Gregory Ablavsky, "Beyond the Indian Commerce Clause," 124 *Yale Law Journal* 1012 (2015).

22. See Alison L. LaCroix, *The Ideological Origins of American Federalism* (Cambridge, Mass.: Harvard University Press, 2010); Daniel J. Hulsebosch, *Constituting Empire: New York and the Transformation of Constitutionalism in the Atlantic World, 1664–1830* (Chapel Hill: University of North Carolina Press, 2005).

23. *Gibbons,* 22 U.S. 209: "It has been contended by the counsel for the appellant that, as the word 'to regulate' implies in its nature *full power over the thing to be regulated,* it excludes necessarily the action of all others that would perform *the same operation on the same thing.* There is great force in this argument, and the Court is not satisfied that it has been refuted" (emphasis added).

24. Cf. Albert S. Abel, "The Commerce Clause in the Constitutional Convention and in Contemporary Comment," 25 *Minnesota Law Review* 432, 432 (1941), distinguishing between "*a* power of regulating commerce" versus "*the* power to regulate commerce."

25. See Bilder, "Struggle over Immigration," tracing "articles of commerce" as a legal category originating in colonial and early republican regulation of migrants, poor persons, indentured servants, and slaves. On the significance of textiles to this "layered federal system," see Laura F. Edwards, *Only the Clothes on Her Back: Clothing and the Hidden History of Power in the Nineteenth-Century United States* (New York: Oxford University Press, 2022), 40.

26. For influential accounts of the Taney Court, see Austin Allen, *Origins of the Dred Scott Case: Jacksonian Jurisprudence and the Supreme Court* (Athens: University of Georgia Press, 2006); Tony Allan Freyer, *The Passenger Cases and the Commerce Clause: Immigrants, Blacks, and States' Rights in Antebellum America* (Lawrence: University Press of Kansas, 2014); Harold Hyman and William Wiecek, *Equal Justice under Law: Constitutional Development, 1835–1875* (New York: Harper and Row, 1982); Carl Brent Swisher, *The Taney Period, 1836–64,* History of the Supreme Court of the United States (New York: Macmillan, 1974); H. H. Walker Lewis, *Without Fear or Favor: A Biography of Chief Justice Roger Brooke Taney* (Boston: Houghton Mifflin, 1965); Felix Frankfurter, *The Commerce Clause under Marshall, Taney, and White* (Chapel Hill: University of North Carolina Press, 1937); Carl Brent Swisher, *Roger B. Taney* (New York: Macmillan, 1935). On the lively political culture of the capital during this period, see Rachel A.

Shelden, *Washington Brotherhood: Politics, Social Life, and the Coming of the Civil War* (Chapel Hill: University of North Carolina Press, 2013).

27. See, e.g., David S. Schwartz, *The Spirit of the Constitution* (New York: Oxford, 2019), 109–10.

28. 60 U.S. (19 How.) 393 (1857); see, e.g., Don Fehrenbacher, *The Dred Scott Case: Its Significance in American Law and Politics* (New York: Oxford, 1978); Mark Graber, *Dred Scott and the Problem of Constitutional Evil* (New York: Cambridge University Press, 2006); Lea VanderVelde, *Mrs. Dred Scott: A Life on Slavery's Frontier* (New York: Oxford University Press, 2009).

29. See generally Sean Wilentz, *No Property in Man: Slavery and Antislavery at the Nation's Founding* (Cambridge, Mass.: Harvard University Press, 2018); Paul Finkelman, *Slavery and the Founders: Race and Liberty in the Age of Jefferson*, 3rd ed. (London: Taylor and Francis, 2014); William Van Cleve, *A Slaveholders' Union: Slavery, Politics, and the Constitution in the Early American Republic* (Chicago: University of Chicago Press, 2010); David Waldstreicher, *Slavery's Constitution: From Revolution to Ratification* (New York: Hill and Wang, 2009); Robin L. Einhorn, *American Taxation, American Slavery* (Chicago: University of Chicago Press, 2006); Leonard Richards, *The Slave Power: The Free North and Southern Domination, 1780–1860* (Baton Rouge: Louisiana State University Press, 2000); David Brion Davis, *The Problem of Slavery in the Age of Revolution, 1770–1823* (Ithaca: Cornell University Press, 1975).

30. See, e.g., David L. Lightner, *Slavery and the Commerce Power: How the Struggle against the Interstate Slave Trade Led to the Civil War* (New Haven: Yale University Press, 2006).

31. See Allen, *Origins of the Dred Scott Case*, 92.

32. Cf. Quentin Skinner, "Meaning and Understanding in the History of Ideas," in *Meaning and Context: Quentin Skinner and His Critics*, ed. James Tully (Princeton: Princeton University Press, 1988), 29–67.

33. 52 U.S. (12 How.) 299 (1852); see also R. Kent Newmyer, "History over Law: The Taney Court," reviewing Swisher, *Taney Period*, 27 *Stanford Law Review* 1373, 1378 (1975), terming *Cooley* "less a doctrinal clarification than it was an agreement to stop looking for one."

34. See Rao, *National Duties*, 176.

35. Id., 171.

36. Id.; see also Jane Manners, " 'Storehouse of the Industry of the Nation': Fire and Federalism in the Age of Jackson" (unpublished ms.).

37. See Rao, *National Duties*, 173–76.

38. See Bilder, "Struggle over Immigration," 784.

39. Redemptioners, who in this period were typically from the German states and often traveled as families, "migrated without paying the entire passage fare or signing an indenture." See Bilder, "Struggle over Immigration," 755–56.

40. See, e.g., U.S. Const., Art. I, sec. 9. As Bilder notes, the meaning of the terms "migration" and "importation" was unsettled in this period: "To some, 'importation,'

and perhaps 'commerce,' referred to immigrants, indentured servants, and slaves. To others, 'imported' could refer only to slaves—or, at the most, involuntary imported convicts." Bilder, "Struggle over Immigration," 787.

41. See Bilder, "Struggle over Immigration," 791; Parker, *Making Foreigners*; Hidetaka Hirota, *Expelling the Poor: Atlantic Seaboard States and the Nineteenth-Century Origins of American Immigration Policy* (New York: Oxford University Press, 2017); Michael A. Schoeppner, *Moral Contagion: Black Atlantic Sailors, Citizenship, and Diplomacy in Antebellum America* (Cambridge: Cambridge University Press, 2019); Mae M. Ngai, *Impossible Subjects: Illegal Aliens and the Making of Modern America* (Princeton: Princeton University Press, 2004); Kristin Collins, "Illegitimate Borders: *Jus Sanguinis* Citizenship and the Legal Construction of Family, Race, and Nation," 123 *Yale Law Journal* 2134 (2014).

42. An Act Regulating Passenger Ships and Vessels, ch. XLVI (March 1819), 3 Stat. 488–89 (1819).

43. Ship Emily Passenger List.

44. See, e.g., an 1820 New York law requiring ship captains to continue to provide passenger reports to local officials: An Act to Amend the Act, entitled "An Act to reduce several laws, relating particularly to the city of New-York into one act," so far as it relates to the importation of Passengers. In *Laws of the State of New-York, Passed at the Forty-Third Session of the Legislature, Begun and Held at the City of Albany, the Fourth day of January, 1820*. Ch. CCXXII. Albany: J. Buel, 1820. Passed April 14, 1820; cited in Bilder, "Struggle over Immigration," 792.

45. On the police power, see William Novak, *The People's Welfare: Law and Regulation in Nineteenth-Century America* (Chapel Hill: University of North Carolina Press, 1996); William Novak, *New Democracy: The Creation of the Modern American State* (Cambridge, Mass.: Harvard University Press, 2022); Christopher L. Tomlins, *Law, Labor, and Ideology in the Early American Republic* (Cambridge: Cambridge University Press, 1993); Laura F. Edwards, *The People and Their Peace: Legal Culture and the Transformation of Inequality in the Post-Revolutionary South* (Chapel Hill: University of North Carolina Press, 2009); Kate Masur, *Until Justice Be Done: American's First Civil Rights Movement, from the Revolution to Reconstruction* (New York: W. W. Norton, 2021); Markus Dirk Dubber, *The Police Power: Patriarchy and the Foundations of American Government* (New York: Columbia University Press, 2005).

46. See Kate Masur, "State Sovereignty and Migration before Reconstruction," 9 *Journal of the Civil War Era* 588, 591 (2019); see also Masur, *Until Justice Be Done*, 8.

47. Ernst Freund, *The Police Power: Public Policy and Constitutional Rights* (Chicago: Callaghan, 1904), 2.

48. Id., n2.

49. Existing records suggest that Thompson also failed to file a federal manifest in New York, despite the 1819 act. See silence in Elizabeth Petty Bentley, *Passenger Arrivals at the Port of New York, 1820–29* (Baltimore: Genealogical Publishing, 1999).

50. *Mayor of New York v. Miln*, Transcript of Record, December 31, 1832, Making of Modern Law: U.S. Supreme Court Records and Briefs, 1823–1978, Gale, https://www.gale.com/c/making-of-modern-law-us-supreme-court-records-and-briefs-1832-1978 (hereafter cited as *Miln* Transcript, MML).

51. *Longworth's American Almanac, New-York Register*, and *City Directory* for 1829/30 and 1832/33 (New York: Thos. Longsworth), New York Public Library Digital Collections, https://digitalcollections.nypl.org/items/a04bd020-973c-0136-7750-65cfeac8b95c and https://digitalcollections.nypl.org/items/98d51340-9feb-0136-297b-017ad4a87d14.

52. P. William Filby, ed. *Passenger and Immigration Lists Index, 1500s–1900s* (Farmington Hills, Mich.: Gale Research, 2012), reproduced on Ancestry.com, https://www.ancestry.com/search/collections/7486/; "Registers of Vessels Arriving at the Port of New York from Foreign Ports, 1789–1919," Microfilm Publication M237, rolls 1–95, National Archives and Records Administration, Records of the U.S. Customs Service, 1745–1997, Record Group 36, National Archives at New York, reproduced on Ancestry.com, https://www.ancestry.com/search/collections/7485.

53. Traces of Miln recur in later records. The 1850 census contains what is likely an entry for the same George Miln, age fifty-five, born around 1795 in Scotland; occupation: merchant; residence, New York City; wife, Isabella; six children ranging in age from twenty-one years to seven months. It is likely also the same George Miln who died in October 1876 and is buried in Green-Wood Cemetery in Brooklyn. 1850 U.S. Federal Census Records, Ancestry.com, https://www.ancestry.com/sharing/3219178?mark=7b22746f6b656e223a22265766e49396e61307471434b5a6648654d3467756361 46767a54306b636d6974422f4645715a424d4c4d453d222c22746f6b656e5f-76657273696f6e223a2225632227d.

54. See Judiciary Act of 1789, sec. 12. An Act to Establish the Judicial Courts of the United States, 1 Stat. 73.

55. Alison L. LaCroix, "Federalists, Federalism, and Federal Jurisdiction," 30 *Law and History Review* 205 (2012).

56. On Betts, see Georgina Betts Wells, *Life and Career of George Rossiter Betts* (New York: Maurice Sloog, 1934). On Thompson, see Donald Roper, *Mr. Justice Thompson and the Constitution* (New York: Garland, 1987).

57. *Miln* Transcript, MML, 4. The circuit-court transcript was kept by the clerk of the circuit court, Frederick J. Betts, who was the half-brother of Judge Betts. Wells, *Life and Career*, 30.

58. *Miln* Transcript, MML, 4.

59. After the initial hearing in October 1829, the case was called and the attorneys appeared in May 1830, October 1830, May 1831, October 1831, April 1832, and October 1832. Id., 4–5.

60. Id.

61. Id., 5.

62. Id. The date of F. J. Betts's minutes was December 31, 1832. On the certificate of division procedure, see Erwin C. Surrency, *A History of the Federal Courts*, 2nd ed. (Dobbs Ferry, N.Y.: Oceana, 2002), 368–69; Jonathan Remy Nash and Michael G. Collins, "The Certificate of Division and the Early Supreme Court," 94 *Southern California Law Review* 733 (2021).

63. 33 U.S. (8 Pet.) 120, 122 (1834).

64. Id.

65. 34 U.S. (9 Pet.) 85 (1835).

66. 36 U.S. 106.

67. Id., 114–15.

68. Id., 110.

69. As Novak notes, "despite being a 'state' power, the police power was usually exercised by local officials." Novak, *People's Welfare*, 13.

70. See Peter Linebaugh and Marcus Rediker, *The Many-Headed Hydra: Sailors, Slaves, Commoners, and the Hidden History of the Revolutionary Atlantic* (Boston: Beacon Press, 2000); C. L. R. James, *The Black Jacobins: Toussaint L'Ouverture and the San Domingo Revolution* (London: Secker and Warburg, 1938).

71. 36 U.S. 127.

72. Id., 121.

73. Id., 116.

74. Id., 118.

75. Id., 120.

76. Id., 133.

77. Id., 132. But see Kent's skepticism toward the *Miln* decision: "[I]t is rather difficult, as I apprehend, to exempt the New York law from the character of a regulation of commerce, or to withdraw the case out of the reach of the former doctrines of the court, that the power to regulate commerce with foreign nations is, and necessarily must be, *exclusive* in the government of the United States." James Kent, *Commentaries on American Law* (Philadelphia: Blackstone, 1889), 439 n.(c).

78. 36 U.S. 136–37.

79. See W. Stephen Belko, *Philip Pendleton Barbour in Jacksonian America: An Old Republican in King Andrew's Court* (Tuscaloosa: University of Alabama Press, 2016).

80. See Bilder, "Struggle over Immigration," 799.

81. 36 U.S. 151. Wayne later stated that Taney had originally asked Thompson to write the majority opinion but changed to Barbour because several justices disagreed with Thompson's view. *The Passenger Cases*, 48 U.S. (7 How.) 282, 430–31 (Wayne, J.); see also Maurice G. Baxter, *The Steamboat Monopoly: Gibbons v. Ogden, 1824* (New York, Knopf: 1972), 92.

82. Id., 144–45.

83. 36 U.S. 159 (Story, J. dissenting).

84. Id., 161.

85. Id.

86. *Passenger Cases*, 48 U.S. 428–32 (Wayne, J.).

87. Id., 432.

88. See Hirota, *Expelling the Poor*; Parker, *Making Foreigners*.

89. See Amy Greenberg, *A Wicked War: Polk, Clay, Lincoln, and the 1846 U.S. Invasion of Mexico* (New York: Alfred A. Knopf, 2012); Thomas R. Hietala, *Manifest Design: Anxious Aggrandizement in Late Jacksonian America* (Ithaca: Cornell University Press, 1985).

90. Webster's celebrity was not limited to his own era. See, e.g., "The Godlike Black Dan, A Selection of Portraits from Life in Commemoration of the Two Hundredth Anniversary of the Birth of Daniel Webster," National Portrait Gallery, Washington, D.C., June 4–November 28, 1982; see also Stephen Vincent Benét, *The Devil and Daniel Webster* (1937; repr., New York: Holt, Rinehart and Winston, 1965), originally published in the *Saturday Evening Post* and later issued as a freestanding book, broadcast as a radio play, and adapted into a folk opera.

91. Daniel Webster, "Second Reply to Hayne [Published Version]," January 26–27, 1830, in *The Papers of Daniel Webster Digital Edition* (Charlottesville: University of Virginia Press, Rotunda, 2018), https://rotunda-upress-virginia-edu.proxy.uchicago.edu/founders/WBST-04-01-02-0015-0002.

92. See William M. Wiecek, "Slavery and Abolition before the United States Supreme Court, 1820–1860," 65 *Journal of American History* 34, 50 (1978), characterizing Webster, Marshall, and Story as "[c]onservative nationalists."

93. Abraham Lincoln, "The Perpetuation of Our Political Institutions," address before the Springfield Young Men's Lyceum, 1838, in *The Political Thought of Abraham Lincoln*, ed. Richard N. Current (Indianapolis: Bobbs-Merrill, 1967), 17.

94. Cf. Scott M. Reznick, "On Liberty and Union: Moral Imagination and Its Limits in Daniel Webster's Seventh of March Speech," 6 *American Political Thought* 371, 373–74 (2017).

95. Daniel Webster, "The Constitution and the Union," *Congressional Globe*, 31st Cong., 1st sess., Appendix, 269–76.

96. See Daniel Webster to [George Ticknor], June 1, 1850, *in The Papers of Daniel Webster Digital Edition*, ed. Charles M. Wiltse (Charlottesville: University of Virginia Press, Rotunda, 2018) (hereafter cited as *PDWDE*); Webster, "The Constitution and the Union," *Congressional Globe*, 31st Cong., 1st sess., Appendix, 269–76.

97. Daniel Webster to Richard Milford Blatchford, February 27, 1849, in *Writings and Speeches of Daniel Webster* (Boston: Little, Brown, 1903) (hereafter cited as *WSDW*), 16:508.

98. *Groves v. Slaughter*, 40 U.S. (15 Pet.) 449 (1841).

99. Cf. William Faulkner, *Requiem for a Nun* (1951; repr., New York: Vintage, 2012), 73: "The past is never dead. It's not even past."

100. See, e.g., *Martin v. Hunter's Lessee* (1815); *Cohens v. Virginia* (1821); see also Mark Graber, "James Buchanan as Savior? Judicial Power, Political Fragmentation,

and the Failed 1831 Repeal of Section 25," 88 *Oregon Law Review* 1 (2009); James W. Ely, Jr., review of *The Papers of Daniel Webster, Legal Papers*, vol. 3, *The Federal Practice*, ed. Andrew J. King Hanover, N.H.: University Press of New England, 1989), 8 *Constitutional Commentary* 246, discussing Webster's role in fending off attacks on sec. 25.

101. See statutes as set forth in *Passenger Cases*, 7 How. (48 U.S.) 283, 283–85 (1849).

102. The 1789 Massachusetts passenger law excluded foreign convicts and required shipmasters to post bond for certain categories of migrants (the poor) and to submit passenger manifests setting forth each passenger's "character and condition." As Gerald Neuman notes, "Massachusetts integrated its convict statute with its poor laws," which were bolstered by a 1794 poor law. In 1820, the legislature passed a new statute that "returned to the colonial system of demanding security from masters of vessels when their passengers seemed likely to become paupers." This was likely the law to which Marshall referred in his 1823 letter to Story. Gerald L. Neuman, "The Lost Century of American Immigration Law (1776–1875)," 93 *Columbia Law Review* 1833, 1842–43, 1849 (1993). See also Anna O. Law, "Lunatics, Idiots, Paupers, and Negro Seamen—Immigration Federalism and the Early American State," 28 *Studies in American Political Development* 107, 114 (2014).

103. Baxter characterizes the New York and Massachusetts passenger tax laws as responses to *Miln*. See Maurice G. Baxter, *Daniel Webster and the Supreme Court* (Amherst: University of Massachusetts Press, 1966), 218.

104. John Marshall to Joseph Story, September 26, 1823, in Joseph Story Papers, Massachusetts Historical Society. The case in which Marshall "escaped on construction of the act" was *Brig Wilson*, 1 Brockenbrough's Reports 423, 424, 426 (1820).

105. An Act to Prevent the Introduction of Paupers, from Foreign Ports or Places, ch. 165 (February 25, 1820), in *The General Laws of Massachusetts, From the Adoption of the Constitution, to February, 1822* (Boston: Wells and Lilly, and Cummings and Hilliard, 1823), 2:531; see also Neuman, "Lost Century," 1849; Parker, *Making Foreigners*, 75.

106. See Philip M. Hamer, "Great Britain, the United States, and the Negro Seamen Acts, 1822–1848," 1 *Journal of Southern History* 3, 4 (1935); Philip M. Hamer, "British Consuls and the Negro Seamen Acts, 1850–1860," 1 *Journal of Southern History* 138 (1935); Schoeppner, *Moral Contagion*.

107. See also *Roberts v. Yates*, 20 Fed. Cas. 937 (C.C. D.S.C. 1853), discussed in Chapter 4.

108. "Statement of Hon. Samuel Hoar, The Agent of the State of Massachusetts to South Carolina" December 20, 1844, reprinted in *Christian Register*, January 18, 1854. "Foreign agent" quoted in Schoeppner, *Moral Contagion*, 150. See also *Free Colored Seamen—Majority and Minority Reports*, House of Representatives Rep. No. 80, January 20, 1843, 27th Congress, 3d Session.

109. Daniel Webster to John Plummer Healy, February 18, 1845, in *WSDW*, 16:432. On Healy, see id., 691n.

110. *Passenger Cases*, 7 How. 298 (hereafter cited as *PC*) (argument of David B. Ogden).

111. *PC*, 7 How. 287.

112. Id., 284–85, 287.

113. See *Norris v. City of Boston*, 45 Mass. 282, 296–97 (Supreme Judicial Court of Massachusetts, 1842).

114. See T. Sheppard, "The *Sirius*: The First Steamer to Cross the Atlantic," 23 *Mariner's Mirror* 84 (1937).

115. See Raymond L. Cohn, "The Transition from Sail to Steam in Immigration to the United States," 65 *Journal of Economic History* 469, 460–70 (2005).

116. New York law, sec. 9, *PC*, 7 How. 283.

117. Daniel Webster to Edward Everett, January 17, 1839, in *WSDW*, 18:42: "My dear Sir,—Enclosed is my receipt for 500 dollars." Ed. footnote: "Fee as counsel for the Commonwealth."

118. Oliver Wendell Holmes, Sr., "The Autocrat of the Breakfast-Table," *Atlantic Monthly*, April 1858.

119. See Carl E. Prince and Seth Taylor, "Daniel Webster, the Boston Associates, and the U.S. Government's Role in the Industrializing Process, 1815–1830," 2 *Journal of the Early Republic* 283 (1982).

120. See, e.g., Webster, List of Debts, [April, 1845?], in *PDWDE;* the total amount owed was in excess of $41,000.

121. The number and schedule of the Court's terms changed several times between the founding and interbellum eras. In 1802, the Court shifted to a single annual term beginning the first Monday in February. In 1827, the start was moved to the first Monday in January; in 1844, to the first Monday in December. See National Constitution Center, "Constitution Daily: Why the Supreme Court Starts on the First Monday in October," https://constitutioncenter.org/blog/why-the-supreme-court-starts-on-the-first-monday-in-october.

122. Choate (Dartmouth '19) served in Congress and then the Senate, taking Webster's seat in 1841 when Webster became secretary of state.

123. "The Alien Passenger Tax," *Niles' National Register*, March 28, 1849, citing *New York Journal of Commerce* for original report.

124. Id.

125. Id.

126. Fee Agreement, January 8, 1849, in *The Papers of Daniel Webster: Legal Papers*, vol. 3, *The Federal Practice*, pt. 2, ed. Andrew J. King (Hanover, N.H.: University Press of New England, 1989) (hereafter cited as *PDWLP*), 725–26.

127. See, e.g., Chapter 3's discussion of Wirt's annoyance at the version of Emmet's peroration that appeared in Wheaton's reports, which robbed Wirt's extensive *Aeneid* quotation of the sting it had delivered in the courtroom.

128. Daniel Webster to Daniel Fletcher Webster, February 7, 1847, in *PDWLP*, 56.

129. See *Mayor of New York v. Miln*, 36 U.S. (11 Pet.) 102, 161 (1837) (Story, J. dissenting); John Marshall to Joseph Story, September 26, 1823, September 26, 1823, Joseph Story Papers, Massachusetts Historical Society.

130. Daniel Webster to Robert Bowne Minturn, December 24, 1847, in *PDWLP*, 718–19.

131. Daniel Webster to William Thomas Carroll, December 17, 1847, in *PDWLP*, 716.

132. Daniel Webster to Daniel Fletcher Webster, December 29, 1847, in *PDWLP*, 716.

133. "Argument in the Passenger Tax Case," December 23, 1847, in *WSDW*, 15:403–4.

134. "The Alien State Tax Case," February 9, 1847, in *PDWLP*, 712–13 (emphasis added).

135. Id., 714.

136. *Gibbons*, 9 Wheat. (22 U.S.) 209.

137. See Webster, "The Alien State Tax Case," in *PDWLP*, 714 ("This court has decided that Congress possesses the exclusive power to regulate commerce—15 *Peters*, 504, 511"); *Groves v. Slaughter*, 40 U.S. (15 Pet.) 449 (1841). As Wiecek notes, *Groves* was "the only significant case involving the interstate slave trade ever decided by the United States Supreme Court." Wiecek, "Slavery and Abolition," 49. The case immediately following *Groves* in Peters's reports was the case of the schooner *Amistad*, the Court's most significant case involving the international slave trade. *United States v. Amistad*, 40 U.S. (15 Pet.) 518 (1841). The two cases overlapped in the Court's calendar: *Amistad* was argued between February 20 and March 2 and decided on March 9; *Groves* was argued between February 12 and February 19 and decided on March 10.

138. See Wiecek, "Slavery and Abolition," 50, noting the "variety of motives" leading to the amendment.

139. See William G. Thomas III, *A Question of Freedom* (New Haven: Yale University Press, 2020); see also Sven Beckert and Seth Rockman, *Slavery's Capitalism* (Philadelphia: University of Pennsylvania Press, 2016).

140. 40 U.S. 502.

141. See, e.g., Francis P. Weisenburger, *The Life of John McLean: A Politician on the United States Supreme Court* (Columbus: Ohio State University Press, 1937); Paul Finkelman, "John McLean: Moderate Abolitionist and Supreme Court Politician," 62 *Vanderbilt Law Review* 519 (2009); Justin Buckley Dyer, "Lincolnian Natural Right, Dred Scott, and the Jurisprudence of John McLean," 41 *Polity* 63 (2009); Thomas E. Carney, "The Political Judge: Justice John McLean's Pursuit of the Presidency," 111 *Ohio History* 121 (2002).

142. 40 U.S. 504 (citation omitted).

143. Id., 508.

144. Id., 507–8.

145. Id., 504.

146. Id., 489 (argument of Clay) (emphasis added).

147. Id., 488 (argument of Clay).

148. Id., 488–89 (argument of Clay); see also Davis, *Problem of Slavery*, 128–30; Walter Berns, "The Constitution and the Migration of Slaves," 78 *Yale Law Journal* 198 (1968).

149. "The Alien State Tax Case," February 9, 1847, in *PDWLP*, 712–14.

150. Id., 710–11.

151. U.S. Const., Art. I, sec. 10, cl. 2.

152. "Alien State Tax Case," 711.

153. Daniel Webster to Daniel Fletcher Webster, December 26, 1848, in *PDWLP*, 724n87.

154. Daniel Webster to John McLean, December 27, 1848, in *PDWLP*, 724.

155. John McLean to Daniel Webster, January 3, 1849, in *PDWLP*, 724.

156. Daniel Webster to [Edward Curtis], January 3, 1849, in *PDWLP*, 724–25.

157. Id.

158. Daniel Webster to John Plummer Healy, January 24, 1849, in *PDWLP*, 726.

159. See Freyer, *Passenger Cases*.

160. See, e.g., Lightner, *Slavery and the Commerce Power*; Freyer, *Passenger Cases*; David P. Currie, *The Constitution in the Supreme Court: The First Hundred Years, 1789–1888* (Chicago: University of Chicago Press, 1985); Newmyer, "History over Law."

161. 53 U.S. (12 How.) 299 (1852).

162. Roger Taney to J. Mason Campbell, February 22, 1850, cited in Swisher, *Taney Period*, 389.

163. John Greenleaf Whittier, "Ichabod" (1850), in John Greenleaf Whittier, *The Poetical Works of John Greenleaf Whittier* (Boston: Ticknor and Fields, 1864), 2:99–100.

Chapter 9. The Fugitive Slave Laws, States' Rights, and Northern Nullification

Epigraph 1. Charles Sumner to Byron Paine, January 18 and August 8, 1856, Byron Paine Papers, Wisconsin Historical Society, Madison.

Epigraph 2. Frederick Douglass, "Speech on John Brown," Tremont Temple, Boston, December 3, 1860, in *Frederick Douglass: Selected Speeches and Writings*, ed. Philip S. Foner and Yuval Taylor (Chicago: Chicago Review Press, 1999), 420.

1. Argument of Byron Paine, Esq., in *Unconstitutionality of the Fugitive Act: Argument of Byron Paine, Esq., and Opinion of Hon. A. D. Smith, Associate Justice of the Supreme Court of Wisconsin* (Milwaukee: Free Democrat, 1854), 1.

2. Opinion of Hon. A. D. Smith, in id., 27.

3. 21 How. (62 U.S.) 506 (1859).

4. William Henry Seward, "The Irrepressible Conflict: A Speech by William H. Seward, Delivered at Rochester, Monday, Oct 25 1858" (New York: New York Tribune, 1860).

5. See Paul Finkelman, "The Appeasement of 1850," in *Congress and the Crisis of the 1850s*, ed. Finkelman and Donald R. Kennon (Athens: Ohio University Press, 2012); R. J. M. Blackett, *The Captive's Quest for Freedom: Fugitive Slaves, the 1850*

Fugitive Slave Law, and the Politics of Slavery (New York: Cambridge, 2018); Andrew Delbanco, *The War before the War: Fugitive Slaves and the Struggle for America's Soul from the Revolution to the Civil War* (New York: Penguin, 2018); Mark A. Graber, "The Nonmajoritarian Difficulty: Legislative Deference to the Judiciary," 7 *Studies in American Political Development* 35, 46–49 (1993).

6. "There shall be neither slavery nor involuntary servitude in this State otherwise than for the punishment of crime, whereof the party shall have been duly convicted." Wisconsin Constitution, Art. I, sec. 2. The 1848 constitution, with 102 amendments, is still in force. Besides five New England states, Wisconsin's is the oldest state constitution in the United States.

7. Cf. Robert M. Cover, *Justice Accused: Antislavery and the Judicial Process* (New Haven: Yale University Press, 1975), 190: "Because neutral principles of constitutional lines of authority had to be violated to effectuate the result in the *Booth* cases, they became not a showcase for the legal denouement of slavery, but a battle over the structure of federalism." Unlike Cover, I do not attribute the Wisconsin crisis to the breakdown of neutral principles of constitutional law.

8. This opposition has a long and storied pedigree in twentieth-century constitutional law. See, e.g., Felix Frankfurter, *The Commerce Clause under Marshall, Taney, and White* (Chapel Hill: University of North Carolina Press, 1937); Edward S. Corwin, *The Commerce Power versus States' Rights* (Princeton: Princeton University Press, 1936).

9. See Leonard Richards, The Slave Power: The Free North and Southern Domination, 1780–1860 (Baton Rouge: Louisiana State University Press, 2000); William Van Cleve, A Slaveholders' Union: Slavery, Politics, and the Constitution in the Early American Republic (Chicago: University of Chicago Press, 2010); Don E. Fehrenbacher, The Slaveholding Republic: An Account of the United States Government's Relations to Slavery, ed. Ward McAfee, 1st ed. (New York: Oxford, 2002); Matthew Karp, This Vast Southern Empire: Slaveholders at the Helm of American Foreign Policy (Cambridge, Mass: Harvard University Press, 2016).

10. "Anti-Slave-Catchers' Mass Convention!," 1854, Wisconsin Historical Society, Madison, Image ID 1928.

11. See Ruby West Jackson and Walter T. McDonald, *Finding Freedom: The Untold Story of Joshua Glover, Runaway Slave* (Madison: Wisconsin Historical Society Press, 2007), 25–27.

12. Id., 31, 37.

13. See *History of Milwaukee, Wisconsin, from Pre-Historic Times to the Present Date* (Chicago: Western Historical Company, 1881), 1:224, calling Wisconsin "the foremost State in the West in the Anti-Slavery movement."

14. See H. Robert Baker, *The Rescue of Joshua Glover: A Fugitive Slave, the Constitution, and the Coming of the Civil War* (Athens: Ohio University Press, 2006), 2. Baker highlights the importance that Glover's status and character took on during the course of the crisis. The *Racine Advocate*, an antislavery newspaper, described Glover

as "one of our most industrious and worthy colored citizens. He has been frequently in the city with articles, the product of his labor, for sale, and is well known and esteemed by most of our business men." *Racine Advocate*, March 12, 1854, quoted in id., 70–71. In contrast, the Democratic press described Glover as a drunkard and adulterer who had a "notoriously bad" and "dissipated" character. *Milwaukee News* and *Daily Wisconsin*, quoted in id., 71. Baker also notes that "[t]he standard by which both friend and foe measured Glover relied on an evaluation of stereotypes derived from popular culture," in particular Harriet Beecher Stowe's novel *Uncle Tom's Cabin*, which had been published in 1852 and was dramatized for the stage shortly thereafter. A production of the play debuted in Milwaukee on the night of Glover's capture, March 10, 1854. See Jackson and McDonald, *Finding Freedom*, 39.

15. The door was opened by Nelson Turner, a freed slave who contemporary reports claimed had provided information to Garland and his associates. Glover's other companion, William Alby, fled during the struggle. See Jackson and McDonald, *Finding Freedom*, 39.

16. Id., 39–40; see also James I. Clark, *Wisconsin Defies the Fugitive Slave Law: The Case of Sherman M. Booth* (Madison: Wisconsin Historical Society, 1955), 4.

17. 9 Statutes at Large 462 (1850).

18. 41 U.S. (16 Pet.) 539 (1842).

19. See Paul Finkelman, "Story Telling on the Supreme Court: *Prigg v. Pennsylvania* and Justice Joseph Story's Judicial Nationalism," 1994 *Supreme Court Review* 247 (1994).

20. Those states included Massachusetts (1843), Pennsylvania (1847), and Rhode Island (1848). See Baker, *Rescue of Joshua Glover*, 178 ("noncooperation laws"); see also Thomas Morris, *Free Men All: The Personal Liberty Laws of the North, 1780–1861* (Baltimore: Johns Hopkins, 1974).

21. See Finkelman, "Appeasement of 1850"; Blackett, *Captive's Quest for Freedom*; Delbanco, *War before the War*; Merrill D. Peterson, *The Great Triumvirate: Webster, Clay, and Calhoun* (New York: Oxford University Press, 1987).

22. Webster's embrace of compromise was viewed by many of his fellow New Englanders as a betrayal. The excoriation from Ralph Waldo Emerson, while florid, was not atypical: " 'Liberty! liberty!' Pho! Let Mr. Webster, for decency's sake, shut his lips once and forever on this word. The word *liberty* in the mouth of Mr. Webster sounds like the word *love* in the mouth of a courtezan." Ralph Waldo Emerson, 1851, in *Journals of Ralph Waldo Emerson, with Annotations*, ed. Edward Waldo Emerson and Waldo Emerson Forbes (Boston: Houghton, Mifflin, Co., 1912), 8:182.

23. Millard Fillmore, "First Annual Message," December 2, 1850, in *A Compilation of the Messages and Papers of the Presidents, 1789–1897*, ed. James D. Richardson (Washington, D.C.: Government Printing Office, 1897), 5:138-39.

24. See Sean Wilentz, *The Rise of American Democracy: Jefferson to Lincoln* (New York: Norton, 2005), characterizing the compromise as "the evasive truce of 1850"; see also Finkelman, "Appeasement of 1850."

25. See A. J. Beitzinger, "Federal Law Enforcement and the Booth Cases," 41 *Marquette Law Review* 7 (1957).

26. See Charles A. Lindquist, "The Origin and Development of the U.S. Commissioner System," 14 *American Journal of Legal History* 1, 1 (1970).

27. Fugitive Slave Act, sec. 3: "*And be it further enacted*, That the Circuit Courts of the United States shall from time to time enlarge the number of the commissioners, with a view to afford reasonable facilities to reclaim fugitives from labor, and to the prompt discharge of the duties imposed by this act."

28. Gary Collison, *Shadrach Minkins: From Fugitive Slave to Citizen* (Cambridge, Mass.: Harvard University Press, 1997); see also Gordon S. Barker, *Fugitive Slaves and the Unfinished American Revolution: Eight Cases* (Jefferson, N.C.: McFarland, 2013). On the subsequent arrest and trial of Robert Morris, one of Minkins's lawyers and one of the first Black attorneys in the United States, who was charged with treason for allegedly aiding Minkins's escape, see John D. Gordan, *The Fugitive Slave Rescue Trial of Robert Morris: Benjamin Robbins Curtis on the Road to* Dred Scott (Clark, N.J.: Talbot, 2013).

29. The courthouse, which had been built in 1836, stood at what is now 26 Court Street. See WBUR Boston, "From Boston's First Jail to Fugitive Slave Trials, 26 Court St. Has History," April 8, 2015, https://www.wbur.org/news/2015/04/08/boston-old-courthouse-jail-court-street. It housed municipal, state, and federal courts, as well as federal marshals. See Isaac Smith Homans, *Sketches of Boston Past and Present: And of Some Few Places in Its Vicinity* (Boston: Phillips, Sampson, 1851), 169. The federal government paid an annual rent of three thousand dollars to the city "for the use of their apartments in the building." Id., 170. By 1855, the federal court had moved to new quarters. The Court Street building was demolished in 1909.

30. Collison, *Shadrach Minkins*, 126–27.

31. Several city officers, including at least one police constable on duty at the courthouse, expressed doubts about the lawfulness of their participation in the federal rendition process. Massachusetts's personal liberty law of 1843, like the law the Court had struck down in *Prigg* in 1842, prohibited state officials from enforcing the federal Fugitive Slave Act. See Collison, *Shadrach Minkins*, 122.

32. Quoted in Barker, *Fugitive Slaves*, 40.

33. Quoted in Collison, *Shadrach Minkins*, 127; see Richard Henry, Jr., *The Journal of Richard Henry Dana, Jr.*, ed. Robert F. Lucid (Cambridge, Mass.: Belknap/Harvard University Press, 1968), 410.

34. On the activities of Black abolitionists in Boston, see Gordan, *Trial of Robert Morris*; Jeffrey L. Amestoy, *The Slavish Shore: The Odyssey of Richard Henry Dana, Jr.* (Cambridge, Mass.: Harvard University Press, 2015).

35. Collison, *Shadrach Minkins*, 201.

36. William Henry Seward, *The Works of William H. Seward*, ed. George E. Baker (New York: Redfield, 1853), 1:74.

37. See Amestoy, *Slavish Shore*; Alexandra D. Lahav and Kent Newmyer, "The Law Wars in Massachusetts, 1830–1860," 58 *American Journal of Legal History* 326 (2018); Daniel Farbman, "Resistance Lawyering," 107 *California Law Review* 1878 (2019); Gordan, *Trial of Robert Morris*.

38. *Milwaukee Sentinel*, March 13, 1854, cited in Jackson and McDonald, *Finding Freedom*, 38.

39. Wisconsin Street has since been renamed Wisconsin Avenue.

40. Jackson and McDonald, *Finding Freedom*, 38.

41. Baker, *Rescue of Joshua Glover*, 2–3.

42. Clark, "Wisconsin Defies the Fugitive Slave Law," 4; Jackson and McDonald, *Finding Freedom*, 42.

43. Id., 42; Baker, *Rescue of Joshua Glover*, 3.

44. Jackson and McDonald, *Finding Freedom*, 42.

45. *Racine Advocate*, March 11, 1854. The brief notice, headlined "Kidnapping," reported that at "[a]bout 10 o'clock last evening," the editors had received "intelligence that a negro had been kidnapped about four miles north of the city, by two persons who left in the direction of Racine."

46. See Encyclopedia of Milwaukee (University of Wisconsin–Milwaukee), "Telecommunications," https://emke.uwm.edu/entry/telecommunications/.

47. The Old Settlers' Club of Milwaukee County was founded in 1869 by a group of men who had "settled in Milwaukee County previous to January, 1839." A 1916 history of the club makes explicit its connection to the Glover events. The founding meeting, with Judge Andrew G. Miller presiding, was held in the courthouse, and "adjoining it on the east was the old county jail, the scene in 1854 of the Glover rescue, one of the conspicuous incidents illustrating the conflict of sentiment on the subject of slavery which brought on the Civil War." *Early Milwaukee: Papers from the Archives of the Old Settlers' Club of Milwaukee County, Published by the Club* (Milwaukee, 1916), 3–4.

48. The facts in this and the following two paragraphs draw on Diane S. Butler, "The Public Life and Private Affairs of Sherman M. Booth," 82 *Wisconsin Magazine of History* 166, 168 (1999).

49. William Lloyd Garrison to Reverend Samuel J. May, July 17, 1845, in *The Letters of William Lloyd Garrison*, ed. Walter M. Merrill (Cambridge, Mass.: Belknap/Harvard University Press, 1973), 3:303; *The Liberator*, May 6, 1842.

50. See William E. Gienapp, *The Origins of the Republican Party, 1852–1856* (New York: Oxford University Press, 1987); Eric Foner, *Free Soil, Free Labor, Free Men: The Ideology of the Republican Party before the Civil War* (1970; repr., New York: Oxford, 1995).

51. Quoted in Baker, *Rescue of Joshua Glover*, 5.

52. Quoted in id., 6.

53. Jackson and McDonald, *Finding Freedom*, 45.

54. Baker, *Rescue of Joshua Glover*, 8.

55. But in a different building: the offices of J. H. Paine and Sons were located in the Juneau Block, on Water Street near the intersection with Wisconsin Street, while Arnold and Hamilton's offices were in Ludington's Block on the corner. See J. M. Van Slyck, *Milwaukee City Directory and Business Advertiser, 1856–57* (Milwaukee: Daily Wisconsin Print, 1856).

56. Foner, *Free Soil*, 77; see Baker, *Rescue of Joshua Glover*, 8. On Chase, see William M. Wiecek, *The Sources of Antislavery Constitutionalism in America, 1760–1848* (Ithaca: Cornell University Press, 1977); Randy E. Barnett, "From Antislavery Lawyer to Chief Justice: The Remarkable but Forgotten Career of Salmon P. Chase," 63 *Case Western Reserve Law Review* 653 (2013); Michael Les Benedict, "Salmon P. Chase and Constitutional Politics," 22 *Law and Social Inquiry* 459 (1997). On antislavery lawyers, see Cover, *Justice Accused*; Lahav and Newmyer, "Law Wars in Massachusetts"; Farbman, "Resistance Lawyering"; Gordan, *Trial of Robert Morris*; Manisha Sinha, *The Slave's Cause: A History of Abolition* (New Haven: Yale University Press, 2016); Peter Karsten, "Revisiting the Critiques of Those Who Upheld the Fugitive Slave Acts in the 1840s and '50s," 58 *American Journal of Legal History* 291 (2018); James Turner, "Use of the Courts in the Movement to Abolish Slavery," 31 *Ohio State Law Journal* 304 (1970).

57. Baker, *Rescue of Joshua Glover*, 9.

58. Id.

59. Quoted in id. Versions of the handbill were printed in Booth's newspaper and in the *Milwaukee Sentinel*, edited by Rufus King, one of Milwaukee's leading citizens and a grandson of a signer of the Constitution (with whom he shared a name). They also became evidence in subsequent trials involving Booth. See id., 190n17.

60. Quoted in id., 10; Chauncey C. Olin, "Reminiscences of the Busy Life of C. C. Olin," in *The Olin Album, 1893* (Indianapolis: Baker Randolph, 1893), 55.

61. Fugitive Slave Act, sec. 7.

62. See Jackson and McDonald, *Finding Freedom*, 46; Baker, *Rescue of Joshua Glover*, 191n20.

63. Beginning in the 1850s, Milwaukee became known as the "German Athens" of America. See Kathleen Neils Conzen, *Immigrant Milwaukee, 1836–1860: Accommodation and Community in a Frontier City* (Cambridge, Mass.: Harvard University Press, 1976).

64. Baker, *Rescue of Joshua Glover*, 18.

65. Olin, "Reminiscences," 56.

66. Id.

67. Id.

68. See Eva Slye Alexander, "Recollections of Ableman in the Early Days, Written for the Sauk County Historical Society" (1917), Sauk County Historical Society, Baraboo, Wisconsin, https://saukcountyhistory.org/recollections-of-ableman-in-the-early-days, which describes "Col. Ableman's home."

69. See Baker, *Rescue of Joshua Glover*, 22; Jackson and McDonald, *Finding Freedom*, 48.

70. See Gordon S. Wood, *The Creation of the American Republic, 1776–1787* (Chapel Hill: University of North Carolina Press, 1969), 319–20, describing America's "long tradition of extra-legislative action by the people"; Larry D. Kramer, *The People Themselves: Popular Constitutionalism and Judicial Review* (New York: Oxford University Press, 2004), 35.

71. Olin, "Reminiscences," 57. It is reasonable to conclude that much of Olin's account came from conversations with Glover while they traveled from Waukesha to Racine.

72. "Helped Save Glover," *Milwaukee Sentinel*, June 10, 1900.

73. See National Register of Historic Places Inventory, Nomination Form, St. John's Cathedral, https://npgallery.nps.gov/NRHP/GetAsset/NRHP/74000108_text.

74. Olin, "Reminiscences," 57.

75. Baker, *Rescue of Joshua Glover*, 23.

76. Olin, "Reminiscences," 57.

77. Jackson and McDonald, *Finding Freedom*, 90, 103.

78. Id., 106–8, 110.

79. Id., 117.

80. Id., 122.

81. See Wilentz, *Rise of American Democracy*, 671–75.

82. On the convention as an institution of popular will, see James T. Kloppenberg, *Toward Democracy: The Struggle for Self-Rule in European and American Thought* (New York: Oxford, 2016).

83. See, e.g., Richard R. Stenberg, "The Jefferson Birthday Dinner, 1830," 4 *Journal of Southern History* 334 (1938).

84. "Anti-Slave-Catchers' Mass Convention!" handbill, 1854, Wisconsin Historical Society, Madison.

85. See Official Statement of the Committee, *Milwaukee Daily Sentinel*, April 14 and 15, 1854.

86. Id.

87. James Madison, Virginia Resolution, December 24, 1798, cl. 2; see also Madison's "Report of 1800": states may take actions such as "declaring the unconstitutionality of proceedings in the Federal Government, . . . communicating the declaration to other states, and inviting their concurrence in a like declaration." James Madison, "The Report of 1800," January 7, 1800, in *The Papers of James Madison*, vol. 17, *31 March 1797–3 March 1801 with a supplement 22 January 1778–9 August 1795*, ed. David B. Mattern, J. C. A. Stagg, Jeanne K. Cross, and Susan Holbrook Perdue (Charlottesville: University Press of Virginia, 1991), 348.

88. John C. Calhoun, "On the Relation Which the States and General Government Bear to Each Other" (Fort Hill Address), July 26, 1831, in *Reports and Public Letters of John C. Calhoun*, ed. Richard K. Crallé (New York: D. Appleton, 1864), 6:59.

89. *Congressional Globe*, 31st Congress, 1st Session, vol. 22, pt. 1 (1850), 451–55.

90. "Official Statement of the Committee," *Milwaukee Sentinel*, April 14–15, 1854.

91. The phrase "Declaration of Sentiments" was also used by the women's rights activists who met at the Seneca Falls Convention in New York in July 1848. Given the many connections between the women's rights and abolition movements—including overlapping members such as Frederick Douglass—the use of the phrase by the Milwaukee convention was likely intentional.

92. "Declaration of Sentiments of the Convention," *Milwaukee Sentinel*, April 14–15, 1854.

93. Id.

94. Quoted in Baker, *Rescue of Joshua Glover*, 85. Section 7 of the act authorized a fine of up to one thousand dollars and imprisonment of up to six months for "any person who any person who shall aid, abet, or assist such person so owing service or labor as aforesaid, directly or indirectly, to escape from such claimant, his agent or attorney, or other person or persons legally authorized as aforesaid."

95. The office of solicitor of the Treasury was created in 1830 and was charged with overseeing the work of district (U.S.) attorneys. See Susan Low Bloch, "The Early Role of the Attorney General in Our Constitutional Scheme: In the Beginning There Was Pragmatism," 1989 *Duke Law Journal* 561 (1989); Jed Handelsman Shugerman, "The Creation of the Department of Justice: Professionalization without Civil Rights or Civil Service," 66 *Stanford Law Review* 121 (2014).

96. See John R. Berryman, *History of the Bench and Bar of Wisconsin* (Chicago: H. C. Cooper, 1898), 1:552. Smith, who like many men of his generation was named after General Winfield Scott, under whom his father had served in the Mexican-American War, went on to serve as attorney general of Wisconsin from 1862–66.

97. Baker, *Rescue of Joshua Glover*, 86.

98. Or $7,300 in 2023 dollars. See CPI Inflation Calculator, Official Inflation Data, https://www.officialdata.org/us/inflation/1854?amount=200.

99. In today's dollars, Garland claimed $65,800 as the value of Glover, and $146,000 in total damages. See id.

100. Argument of Byron Paine, in *Unconstitutionality of the Fugitive Act*, 1, 3, 6.

101. Argument of District Attorney John Sharpstein, in id., 23.

102. Opinion of the Honorable A. D. Smith, in id., 31; see also *In re Booth*, 3 Wis. 1 (1854). The case is also cited as 3 *Smith and Dixon* 13 (1854).

103. Opinion of Honorable A. D. Smith, in *Unconstitutionality of the Fugitive Act*, 27, 29, 31.

104. Some reports give the caption of the case at this stage as *Ableman v. State of Wisconsin ex rel. Booth*. See *Unconstitutionality of the Fugitive Act*, 31. Chief Justice Edward V. Whiton delivered the opinion of the court; Justice Smith concurred; and Justice Crawford dissented. Rufus King, editor of the *Milwaukee Sentinel* and an ally of Booth, published a compendium of the reports of the Booth decisions before the Wisconsin Supreme Court. See *Unconstitutionality of the Fugitive Slave Act: Decisions of the*

Supreme Court of Wisconsin in the Cases of Booth and Rycraft (Milwaukee: Rufus King, 1855). The arguments of Sharpstein, "the able Counsel for the United States," before the Wisconsin Supreme Court found a friendly conduit in the columns of the Madison *Daily Argus and Democrat*, June 30, 1854. While praising Sharpstein, Beriah Brown, editor of the *Argus and Democrat* and a staunch supporter of Stephen A. Douglas, lamented the "unfortunate idiosyncrasies of opinion" that Paine put forward on behalf of Booth. Id.

105. *Ex parte Booth*, 3 Wis. 145, 148–49 (1854).

106. *U.S. v. Rycraft*, 27 Fed. Cas. 918 (D.C. D. Wis., 1854) (No. 16,211). Charge language is from *In re Booth and Rycraft*, 3 Wis. 157, 182.

107. *In re Booth and Rycraft*, 3 Wis. 157, 182 (1855) (Crawford, J.).

108. See Beitzinger, "Federal Law Enforcement," 18.

109. See *U.S. v. Booth* and *Ableman v. Booth*, 59 U.S. (18 How.) 476, 476–77 (1855) (affidavit of Sharpstein). The writ of error was returned in the earlier of the two cases, *In re Booth*, which the Supreme Court referred to as *Ableman v. Booth*. The state court did not respond to the writ of error for the later habeas case, *In re Booth and Rycraft*, which the Supreme Court referred to as *U.S. v. Booth*, perhaps because that was the caption for the underlying federal prosecution that the Wisconsin court had purported to have the power to review via habeas. See also Beitzinger, "Federal Law Enforcement," 17–20.

110. *U.S. v. Booth* and *Ableman v. Booth*, 59 U.S. 476, 477.

111. Id., 478–79.

112. Booth submitted to the Court a copy of Byron Paine's argument in Booth's initial hearing before Justice Smith. See Beitzinger, "Federal Law Enforcement," 20.

113. *Ableman v. Booth and U.S. v. Booth*, 62 U.S. (21 How.) 525.

114. Id., 526.

115. Id., 514.

116. See Francis P. Weisenburger, *The Life of John McLean: A Politician on the United States Supreme Court* (Columbus: Ohio State University Press, 1937), 195–210.

117. See Michael Les Benedict, "Abraham Lincoln and Federalism," 10 *Journal of the Abraham Lincoln Association* 1, 11 (1988).

118. *Hunter v. Martin*, 18 Va. (4 Munf.) (1815) 1, 9 (Cabell, J.).

119. *Fairfax's Devisee v. Hunter*, 6 *American Law Journal* 313, 373 (1817).

120. *Ableman*, 62 U.S. (21 How.) 516.

121. Id., 515.

122. Id., 526.

123. See Beitzinger, "Federal Law Enforcement," 24–26.

124. Id., 27.

125. 60 U.S. (19 How.) 393 (1857).

126. An Act Relating to the Writ of Habeas Corpus to Persons Claimed as Fugitive Slaves, Wisconsin—10th Session, General Acts 12 (published February 23, 1857).

127. Id., sec. 6.

128. Joint Resolution No. IV (1859), quoted in *Journal of the Senate of Wisconsin, 14th Annual Session* (Madison: Smith and Cullaton, 1862), 138, reporting proceedings on the 1862 joint resolution.

129. Joint Resolution No. IV, in *General Laws Passed by the Legislature of Wisconsin, in the Year 1859, Together with Joint Resolutions and Memorials* (Madison: James Ross, 1859) (13th Legislature), 248.

130. Memorandum of William T. Carroll, Transcript of Record, *Ableman v. Booth* and *U.S. v. Booth*, Record Group 267: Records of the Supreme Court of the United States, Entry 21: Appellate Jurisdiction Case Files, Case Nos. 3202 and 3550, National Archives and Records Administration.

131. James Buchanan, Message of the President [Fourth Annual Message], December 3, 1860, in Appendix, *Congressional Globe*, 36th Congress, 2nd Session, 1.

132. Id., 2.

133. An Act to Provide for the Collection of Duties on Imports, Ch. 57, 22nd Congress, Session 2. U.S. Statutes at Large 4:632 (1833).

134. Argument of Byron Paine, in *Unconstitutionality of the Fugitive Act*, 3.

135. See David W. Blight, *Frederick Douglass: Prophet of Freedom* (New York: Simon and Schuster, 2018), 328–30.

136. Quoted in id., 329. Another account stated that Douglass was "thrown 'down the staircase to the floor of the hall.' " Foner and Taylor, *Frederick Douglass*, 417.

137. Frederick Douglass, "Speech on John Brown, Delivered in Tremont Temple, Boston, December 3, 1860," in Foner and Taylor, *Frederick Douglass*, 417, 419.

138. Id., 421.

139. Id., 420.

140. Id. Douglass had spent decades considering and discussing the question whether the Constitution was inherently pro-slavery, antislavery, or agnostic. At one particularly notable meeting, in New York in May 1857, he and his fellow Black abolitionist Charles Lenox Remond conducted a lengthy disputation on the issue. Douglass had taken the view that the Constitution was an antislavery document, while Remond argued that it was proslavery. This view represented a change from some of Douglass's earlier public statements, when he had allied himself with the Garrisonian abolitionists, who rejected the Constitution as a "covenant with death." See "Is the Plan of the American Union under the Constitution, Anti-Slavery or Not?: A Debate between Frederick Douglass and Charles Lenox Remond in New York, New York, on 20, 21 May 1857," in *The Frederick Douglass Papers, Series One: Speeches, Debates, and Interviews*, ed. John W. Blassingame (New Haven: Yale University Press, 1985), 3:151.

141. Douglass, "Speech on John Brown," 420.

142. "Dissolution of the American Union," January 1861, in Foner and Taylor, *Frederick Douglass*, 425.

143. Id.

144. Id., 425–26.

145. Id., 426.

146. Id.

147. Id.

148. Frederick Douglass, "The Union and How to Save It" (February 1861), in Foner and Taylor, *Frederick Douglass*, 429.

149. Id., 431.

150. U.S. district judge Miller had written to Buchanan and Attorney General Black in the spring of 1860 to request that Booth's fines be remitted. On March 23, 1860, Booth completed his one-month sentence, but he continued to be held in federal custody because he refused to pay the fine and costs levied by the federal court ($1,250, or $46,200 today). See the CPI Inflation Calculator, Official Inflation Data, https://www.officialdata.org/us/inflation/1860?amount=1250. In his letters to Buchanan and Black requesting Booth's release, Miller noted that Booth's state-court suits against Ableman and himself for false imprisonment had been "discontinued"; that "a pardon of the fine and costs would be approved by the people"; and that Booth's "imprisonment in a room of the custom house is attended with daily expenses, as a guard has to be constantly on duty, and it is also inconvenient, as the room occupied is the jury room, which is needed for that purpose." Andrew G. Miller to James Buchanan, April 20, 1860, and Andrew G. Miller to Jeremiah Black, May 2, 1860, in Alexander McDonald Thomson, *A Political History of Wisconsin* (Milwaukee: E. C. Williams, 1900), 102–4.

151. David M. Potter, *The Impending Crisis, 1848–1861*, completed by and ed. Don E. Fehrenbacher (New York: Harper and Row, 1976), 295.

152. Id., 295–96.

153. Michael J. C. Taylor, " 'A More Perfect Union: *Ableman v. Booth* and the Culmination of Federal Sovereignty," 28 *Journal of Supreme Court History* 101, 113 (2003).

154. On notions of union and disunion, see Elizabeth Varon, *Disunion! The Coming of the American Civil War* (Chapel Hill: University of North Carolina Press, 2010).

Epilogue

1. Ulysses S. Grant, *The Personal Memoirs of Ulysses S. Grant: The Complete Annotated Edition* (Cambridge, Mass.: Harvard University Press, 2017), 756.

2. Id.

3. Id.

4. Id.

5. Id., 757 (emphasis added).

6. Cf. Anne Twitty, *Before* Dred Scott: *Slavery and Legal Culture in the American Confluence, 1787–1857* (Cambridge: Cambridge University Press, 2016), discussing this "American Confluence" region.

7. See Eric Foner, *Free Soil, Free Labor, Free Men: The Ideology of the Republican Party before the Civil War* (1970; repr., New York: Oxford University Press, 1995).

8. Grant, *Personal Memoirs*, 757 (emphasis added).

9. See, e.g., Harriet Martineau, "Transport and Markets," in *Society in America* (London: Saunders and Otley, 1837), 2:171–72, 208; Daniel Walker Howe, *What Hath God Wrought: The Transformation of America, 1815–1848* (New York: Oxford, 2007).

10. A related but distinct part-whole dynamic, in the opposite direction, moved some in the southern states to support the Confederacy. One notable example was Robert E. Lee's decision to resign his commission in the U.S. Army and stand with Virginia when it joined the Confederacy in April 1861. "Lee had never expressed an interest in states' rights, much less state sovereignty. Secession, he thought, was 'nothing but revolution.' . . . The real choice, however, wasn't between region and nation but between region and anti-slavery nation. For Lee it was Northern political agitators, not Southern secessionists, who had disrupted the Union." Matthew Karp, "His Whiskers Trimmed," review of Allen Guelzo, *Robert E. Lee: A Life*, by Allen Guelzo, *London Review of Books*, April 7, 2022. It should be noted, however, that the South was demanding more, in structural terms, from the North. Southerners demanded that their putatively local institution be protected in the North, despite indifference or outright opposition from many northerners. Northerners, meanwhile, were arguing only that they should not have to enforce a southern institution, not that a northern institution should be affirmatively extended into the South. In 1861, Lincoln and other moderate Republicans made clear that they did not seek to extend freedom into the South. Emancipation became a war aim only later, and at first only to the limited degree set forth in the Emancipation Proclamation, which took effect on January 1, 1863.

11. "Dissolution of the American Union," January 1861, in *Frederick Douglass: Selected Speeches and Writings*, ed. Philip S. Foner and Yuval Taylor (Chicago: Chicago Review Press, 1999), 426.

12. William Johnson, *To the Public of Charleston* (Charleston: C. C. Sebring, 1822), 15; *John Quincy Adams: Diaries* (New York: Library of America, 2017), 2:12.

13. Abraham Lincoln, "The Old Policy of the Fathers," address at the Cooper Union, February 27, 1860, in *The Political Thought of Abraham Lincoln*, ed. Richard N. Current (Indianapolis: Bobbs-Merrill, 1967), 159–61.

14. Id., 161.

15. Id., 141.

SELECTED BIBLIOGRAPHY

Primary Sources

Manuscript and Archival Sources

American Philosophical Society, Manuscript Collection, Philadelphia
> John Marshall, Opinions Delivered in the Circuit Court of the United States

D'Angelo Law Library, University of Chicago
> United States Supreme Court Portraits and Autographs, Silver Collection

Gilcrease Museum, Tulsa
> John Ross Papers

Harvard Law School Library, Historical and Special Collections, Cambridge, Mass.
> Joseph Story, Memoranda on Arguments before the Supreme Court, 1831–1832

Historical Society of Pennsylvania, Philadelphia
> Autograph Collection
> Cadwalader Family Papers
> Ferdinand Dreer Collection
> Frank C. Etting Collection
> George M. Conarroe Collection
> Gilpin Family Papers
> James Wilson Papers
> Joel Roberts Poinsett Papers
> Simon Gratz Collection

Houghton Library, Harvard University, Cambridge
> American Board of Commissioners for Foreign Missions Archives

Library of Congress, Manuscript Division, Washington, D.C.
> Benjamin Robbins Curtis Papers
> Carl Brent Swisher Papers
> James Kent Papers

John McLean Papers
Read Family Papers
Roger Taney Papers
Thomas Jefferson Papers
William Wirt Papers
Library of Virginia, Richmond
William Wirt Letters
Maryland Historical Society, Baltimore
William Wirt Letterbooks (microfilm)
William Wirt Papers (microfilm)
Maryland State Archives, Annapolis
Prince George's County Register of Wills (Orphans' Court Proceedings), 1777–1790
Massachusetts Historical Society, Boston
Adams Papers (microfilm)
Joseph Story Papers
Morgan Library and Museum, New York, N.Y.
Henry Wheaton Papers
National Archives and Records Administration, Washington, D.C.
Admiralty Case Files of the U.S. District Court for the Eastern District of Virginia, 1801–1861 (microfilm)
Criminal Case Files of the U.S. Circuit Court for the District of Maryland, 1795–1860 (microfilm)
Minutes of the U.S. Circuit Court for the District of Maryland, 1790–1911 (microfilm)
Records of the Supreme Court of the United States, Record Group 267 (microfilm)
Appellate Case Files of the Supreme Court
Minutes of the Supreme Court
Newberry Library, Chicago
John Howard Payne Papers
New-York Historical Society, Manuscript Department, New York, N.Y.
Smith Thompson Collection
New York Public Library, Manuscript Division, New York, N.Y.
James Monroe Papers
New York State Library, Manuscripts and Special Collections, Albany
James Kent Law Library Collection
Regenstein Library, University of Chicago, Special Collections
Miscellaneous Manuscripts Collection
Stephen A. Douglas Papers
South Carolina Department of Archives and History, Columbia
General Assembly Records

South Carolina Historical Society, Charleston
    Harriott Horry Ravenel Papers
    Pamphlet Collection
    Pinckney Family Papers
    Pinckney Means Family Papers
South Caroliniana Library, University of South Carolina, Columbia
    Rutledge Family Papers
Stanford University Library, Department of Special Collections and University
Archives, Stanford
    Gerald Gunther Papers
University of North Carolina, Southern Historical Collection, Wilson Special Collections
Library, Chapel Hill
    Ernest Haywood Papers
    Mitchell King Papers
    William Wirt Letters
University of Oklahoma Libraries, Western History Collections, Norman
    Indian-Pioneer Papers Collection
University of Virginia Library, Albert and Shirley Small Special Collections Library,
Charlottesville
    Thomas Jefferson Papers
Wisconsin Historical Society, Madison
    Byron Paine Papers
Yale University Library, Manuscripts and Archives, New Haven
    Herman Landon Vaill Collection (microfilm)

Published Primary Sources (Including Modern Editions)

Books, Pamphlets, Speeches, and Essays

"1850 United States Census Records, New York." Digital image s.v. "George Miln."
    Ancestry.com, https://www.ancestry.com/sharing/3219178?mark=7b22746f6b
    656e223a22265766e49396e61307471434b5a6648654d346775636146767a5430
    6b636d6974422f4645715a424d4c4d453d222c22746f-
    6b656e5f76657273696f6e22
    3a225632227d.
Achates [Thomas Pinckney]. *Reflections, Occasioned by the Late Disturbances in Charles-*
    ton. Charleston: A. E. Miller, 1822.
Adams, John Quincy. *John Quincy Adams: Diaries.* New York: Library of America,
    2017.
————. *Memoirs of John Quincy Adams, Comprising Portions of His Diary from 1795 to*
    1848. Edited by Charles Francis Adams. 12 vols. Philadelphia: J. B. Lippincott,
    1874–77.

Ames, Herman Vandenburg. *State Documents on Federal Relations: The States and the United States. 1900–1906.* Reprint, New York: Da Capo Press, 1970.

Apes[s], William. *A Son of the Forest: The Experience of William Apes, A Native of the Forest.* 2nd ed. New York: The Author, 1831.

The Book of Common Prayer and Administration of the Sacraments, and Other Rites and Ceremonies of the Church, According to the Use of the Protestant Episcopal Church in the United States of America. Philadelphia: Hall and Sellers, 1790.

Boudinot, Elias. *An Address to the Whites. Delivered in the First Presbyterian Church, on the 26th of May, 1826, by Elias Boudinott, a Cherokee Indian.* Philadelphia: William F. Geddes, 1826.

———. *Cherokee Editor: The Writings of Elias Boudinot.* Edited by Theda Perdue. Athens: University of Georgia Press, 1996.

———. *Letters and Other Papers Relating to Cherokee Affairs; Being a Reply to Sundry Publications Authorized by John Ross.* Athens, Ga.: Southern Banner, 1837.

Brutus [Robert James Turnbull]. *The Crisis: or, Essays on the Usurpation of the Federal Government.* Charleston: A. E. Miller, 1827.

C. Keenan's Baltimore Directory for 1822 and 1823. Baltimore: R. J. Matchett, 1822.

Calhoun, John C. "Address on the Relation Which the States and General Government Bear to Each Other" (Fort Hill Address). In *Reports and Public Letters of John C. Calhoun.* Vol. 6, edited by Richard K. Crallé. New York: D. Appleton, 1855.

———. *The Papers of John C. Calhoun.* Edited by Robert L. Meriwether. 28 vols. Columbia: University of South Carolina Press, 1959–2003.

———. *Speeches of John C. Calhoun: Delivered in the Congress of the United States from 1811 to the Present Time.* New York: Harper and Brothers, 1843.

———. *Union and Liberty: The Political Philosophy of John C. Calhoun.* Edited by Ross M. Lence. Indianapolis: Liberty Fund, 1992.

Chesnut, Mary Boykin. *A Diary from Dixie.* New York: Peter Smith, 1929.

The Committee Consisting of ___, to Whom Was Referred the Motion of Mr. Monroe, Submit the Following Report. . . . New York, 1785.

Cooke, Jacob E., ed. *The Federalist.* Middletown, Conn.: Wesleyan University Press, 1961.

Correspondence Relative to the Prohibition against the Admission of Free Persons of Colour into Certain Ports of the United States, 1823–1850. Vol. 579, Ser. 5. Foreign Office [UK] Papers, n.d.

Crockett, David. *Narrative of the Life of David Crockett, Written by Himself.* 6th ed. Philadelphia: E. L. Carey and A. Hart, 1834.

Cruse, P. H. "Biographical Sketch of William Wirt." In *The Letters of the British Spy.* 10th ed. New York: Harper and Brothers, 1832.

Dana, Jr., Richard Henry. *The Journal of Richard Henry Dana, Jr.* Edited by Robert F. Lucid. 3 vols. Cambridge, Mass.: Belknap/Harvard University Press, 1968.

Douglass, Frederick. *Frederick Douglass: Selected Speeches and Writings.* Edited by Philip S. Foner and Yuval Taylor. Chicago: Chicago Review Press, 1999.

———. *The Frederick Douglass Papers.* Series 1, *Speeches, Debates, and Interviews.* Edited by John W. Blassingame. New Haven: Yale University Press, 1985.

Elford, James M. *J. M. Elford's Marine Telegraph; or, Universal Signal Book.* Charleston: James M. Elford, 1823.

Elliot, Jonathan, ed. *The Debates in the Several State Conventions on the Adoption of the Federal Constitution: As Recommended by the General Convention at Philadelphia in 1787: Together with the Journal of the Federal Convention, Luther Martin's Letter, Yate's Minutes, Congressional Opinions, Virginia and Kentucky Resolutions of '98–'99, and Other Illustrations of the Constitution.* 2nd ed. 5 vols. Washington, D.C.: Printed for the Editor, 1836–45.

Emerson, Ralph Waldo. *Journals of Ralph Waldo Emerson, with Annotations.* Vol. 8, edited by Edward Waldo Emerson and Waldo Emerson Forbes. Boston: Houghton, Mifflin, 1912.

Farrand, Max, ed. *The Records of the Federal Convention of 1787.* 3 vols. New Haven: Yale University Press, 1937.

Filby, P. William, ed. *Passenger and Immigration Lists Index, 1500s–1900s.* Farmington Hills, Mich.: Gale Research, 2012. Reproduced on Ancestry.com, https://www.ancestry.com/search/collections/7486/.

Founders Online. National Archives and Records Administration. https://founders.archives.gov.

Garrison, William Lloyd. *The Letters of William Lloyd Garrison.* Vol. 3, edited by Walter M. Merrill. Cambridge, Mass.: Belknap/Harvard University Press, 1973.

Gilmer, George R. *Sketches of Some of the First Settlers of Upper Georgia, of the Cherokees, and the Author.* New York: D. Appleton, 1855.

Grant, Ulysses S. *The Personal Memoirs of Ulysses S. Grant: The Complete Annotated Edition.* Cambridge, Mass.: Harvard University Press, 2017.

Hagy, James W., ed. *Charleston, South Carolina City Directories for the Years 1816, 1819, 1822, 1825, and 1829.* Baltimore: Clearfield, 1996.

Harper, William, ed. *Report of Cases Decided in the Constitutional Court of South Carolina.* Charleston: McCarter and Dawson, 1824.

Harvey, Peter. *Reminiscences and Anecdotes of Daniel Webster.* Boston: Little, Brown, 1877.

Hayne, Robert Y. *An Oration, Delivered in the Independent or Congregational Church, Charleston, before the State Rights and Free Trade Party, the Society of Cincinnati, the Revolution Society, the '76 Association, and Several Volunteer Companies of Militia, on the 4th of July 1831, Being the 55th Anniversary of American Independence.* Charleston: A. E. Miller, 1831.

[Holmes, Isaac, and Robert Turnbull]. *Caroliniensis.* Charleston: A. E. Miller, 1824.

Holmes, Sr., Oliver Wendell. "The Autocrat of the Breakfast-Table." *Atlantic Monthly,* April 1858.

Homans, Isaac Smith. *Sketches of Boston Past and Present: And of Some Few Places in Its Vicinity.* Boston: Phillips, Sampson, 1851.

Hone, Philip. *The Diary of Philip Hone.* Edited by Bayard Tuckerman. 2 vols. New York: Dodd, Mead, 1889.

Hunt, Benjamin Faneuil. *The Argument of Benjamin Faneuil Hunt, in the Case of the Arrest of the Person Claiming to Be a British Seaman, Under the 3d Section of the State Act of Dec. 1822. . . . .* Charleston: A. E. Miller, 1823.

Irving, John B. *A Day on Cooper River.* Charleston: A. E. Miller, 1842.

Jackson, Andrew. *The Papers of Andrew Jackson: Digital Edition.* Edited by Michael E. Woods. Charlottesville: University of Virginia Press, Rotunda, 2015. https://rotunda.upress.virginia.edu/founders/JKSN.

Jefferson, Thomas. "Letter from Thomas Jefferson to Judge William Johnson." 1 *South Carolina Historical and Genealogical Magazine* 7 (1900).

———. *The Papers of Thomas Jefferson.* Vols. 29 and 31, edited by Barbara B. Oberg. Princeton: Princeton University Press, 2002 and 2004.

———. *The Papers of Thomas Jefferson: Digital Edition.* Edited by James P. McClure and J. Jefferson Looney. Charlottesville: University of Virginia Press, Rotunda, 2009. https://rotunda.upress.virginia.edu/founders/TSJN.

———. *Thomas Jefferson: Writings.* Edited by Merrill D. Peterson. New York: Library of America, 1984.

Johnson, Joseph. *Traditions and Reminiscences, Chiefly of the American Revolution in the South: Including Biographical Sketches, Incidents, and Anecdotes.* Charleston: Walker and James, 1851.

Johnson, Samuel. *A Dictionary of the English Language.* London: J. and P. Knapton, 1755.

Johnson, William. "Letters from Judge William Johnson to Thomas Jefferson." 1 *South Carolina Historical and Genealogical Magazine* 207 (1900).

———. "Memoire on the Strawberry." 5 *Southern Agriculturalist* 568 (1832).

———. *Sketches of the Life and Correspondence of Nathanael Greene, Major General of the Armies of the United States, in the War of the Revolution, Compiled Chiefly from Original Materials.* 2 vols. Charleston: A. E. Miller, 1822.

Journal of the Conventions of the People of South Carolina, Held in 1832, 1833, and 1852. Columbia, S.C.: R. W. Gibbes, 1860.

Kennedy, John Pendleton. *Memoirs of the Life of William Wirt, Attorney-General of the United States.* 2 vols. 1849. Reprint, New York: G. P. Putnam's Sons, 1872.

Kent, James. *Commentaries on American Law.* 4 vols. Philadelphia: Blackstone, 1889.

Lincoln, Abraham. *The Political Thought of Abraham Lincoln.* Edited by Richard N. Current. New York: Macmillan, 1967.

Longworth's American Almanac, New-York Register, and City Directory for 1829 and 1832. New York: Thos. Longsworth.

Madison, James. *The Papers of James Madison: Digital Edition*. Edited by J. C. A. Stagg. Charlottesville: University of Virginia Press, Rotunda, 2010. https://rotunda. upress.virginia.edu/founders/JSMN.

———. *The Writings of James Madison, 1819–1836*. Vol. 9, edited by Gaillard Hunt. New York: G. P. Putnam's Sons, 1910.

Marshall, John. *The Papers of John Marshall*. Edited by Herbert A. Johnson, Charles T. Cullen, and Charles F. Hobson. 12 vols. Chapel Hill: University of North Carolina Press, 1974–2006.

Martineau, Harriet. *Harriet Martineau's Autobiography, with Memorials by Maria Weston Chapman*. 2nd ed. 3 vols. London: Smith, Elder, 1877.

———. *Retrospect of Western Travel*. 3 vols. London: Saunders and Otley, 1838.

———. *Society in America*. 3 vols. London: Saunders and Otley, 1837.

Mayor, Aldermen and Commonalty of City of New York v. Miln, 36 U.S. 102. *Transcript of Record*. December 31, 1832. *The Making of Modern Law: U.S. Supreme Court Records and Briefs, 1832–1978*. https://www.gale.com/c/making-of-modern-law-us-supreme-court-records-and-briefs-1832-1978.

Miller's Planters' and Merchants' Almanac for the Year of Our Lord 1826, Calculated for the States of Carolina and Georgia. Charleston: A. E. Miller, 1826.

Monroe, James. *Message from the President of the United States with His Objections to the Bill for the Preservation and Repair of the Cumberland Road; Also, a Paper Containing His Views on the Subject of Internal Improvements*. Washington, D.C.: Gales and Seaton, 1822.

Olin, Chauncey C. "Reminiscences of the Busy Life of C. C. Olin." In *The Olin Album, 1893*. Indianapolis: Baker Randolph, 1893.

Parker, John R. *American Signal Book, or, The United States Telegraph Vocabulary, Being an Appendix to Elford's Marine Telegraph Signal Book*. Boston: Steam Power Press Office, W. L. Lewis, printer, 1832.

Peters, Richard. *The Case of the Cherokee Nation against the State of Georgia, Argued and Determined at the Supreme Court of the United States, January Term 1831*. Philadelphia: J. Grigg, 1831.

Petigru, James Louis. *Life, Letters, and Speeches of James Louis Petigru: The Union Man of South Carolina*. Washington, D.C.: W. H. Lowdermilk, 1920.

Pinckney, Eliza Lucas. *The Letterbook of Eliza Lucas Pinckney*. Edited by Elise Pinckney and Marvin R. Zahniser. Columbia: University of South Carolina Press, 1997.

Pinckney, Eliza Lucas, and Harriott Pinckney Horry. *The Papers of Eliza Lucas Pinckney and Harriott Pinckney Horry: Digital Edition*. Edited by Constance Schulz. Charlottesville: University of Virginia Press, Rotunda, 2012. https://rotunda. upress.virginia.edu/founders/PIHO.

Pinckney, Harriott. Harriott Pinckney to Charles Cotesworth Pinckney, Jr., August 1, 1831. Spared and Shared 11. https://sparedshared11.wordpress. com/2016/01/02/1831-harriott-pinckney-to-charles-cotesworth-pinckney-jun/.

[Pinckney, Maria Henrietta]. *A Notice of the Pinckneys*. Charleston: Evans and Cogswell, 1860.

———. *The Quintessence of Long Speeches, Arranged as a Political Catechism: By a Lady, for Her God-Daughter*. Charleston: A. E. Miller, 1830.

Plan of the City and Neck of Charleston, S.C. Reduced from Authentic Documents and Engraved by W. Keenan. Charleston, 1844.

Proceedings of the Celebration of the 4th July, 1831, at Charleston, S.C. by the State Rights and Free Trade Party. Charleston: Archibald E. Miller, 1831.

Proceedings of the Second United States Anti-Masonic Convention, Held at Baltimore, September 1831. Boston: Boston Type and Stereotype Foundry, 1832.

Proceedings of the State Rights Celebration, at Charleston, S.C., July 1st, 1830. Charleston: A. E. Miller, 1830.

"Records from Record Group 287, Publications of the U.S. Government; Record Group 85, Records of the Immigration and Naturalization Service [INS] and Record Group 36, Records of the United States Customs Service." National Archives, Washington, D.C. Reproduced on Ancestry.com, https://www.ancestry.com/search/collections/8758/.

"Registers of Vessels Arriving at the Port of New York from Foreign Ports, 1789–1919." Microfilm publication M237, rolls 1–95. National Archives and Records Administration, Records of the U.S. Customs Service, 1745–1997, Record Group 36, National Archives at New York. Reproduced on Ancestry.com, https://www.ancestry.com/search/collections/7485/.

Rousseau, Jean-Jacques. *The Social Contract*. Translated by Christopher Betts. Oxford: Oxford University Press, 1999.

Schulz, Constance, ed. *The Papers of the Revolutionary Era Pinckney Statesmen: Digital Edition*. Charlottesville: University of Virginia Press, Rotunda, 2016. https://rotunda.upress.virginia.edu/founders/PNKY.

Seward, William Henry. *The Irrepressible Conflict: A Speech by William H. Seward*. New York: New York Tribune, 1858.

———. *The Works of William H. Seward*. Volume 1, ed. George E. Baker. New York: Redfield, 1853.

Smith, Margaret Bayard. *The First Forty Years of Washington Society*. Edited by Gaillard Hunt. New York: Charles Scribner's Sons, 1906.

Story, Joseph. *Life and Letters of Joseph Story: Associate Justice of the Supreme Court of the United States*. Edited by William Wetmore Story. 2 vols. Boston: Charles C. Little and James Brown, 1851.

Trollope, Frances. *Domestic Manners of the Americans*. 1832. Reprint, Oxford: Oxford University Press, 2014.

Tucker, St. George. *St. George Tucker's Law Reports and Selected Papers, 1782–1825*. Edited by Charles F. Hobson. 3 vols. Chapel Hill: University of North Carolina Press, 2013.

Unconstitutionality of the Fugitive Act: Argument of Byron Paine, Esq., and Opinion of Hon. A. D. Smith, Associate Justice of the Supreme Court of Wisconsin. Milwaukee: Free Democrat, 1854.

Unconstitutionality of the Fugitive Slave Act: Decisions of the Supreme Court of Wisconsin in the Cases of Booth and Rycraft. Milwaukee: Rufus King, 1855.

Upshur, Abel P. *Brief Enquiry into the True Nature and Character of Our Federal Government: Being a Review of Judge Story's* Commentaries on the Constitution of the United States. 1840. Reprint, Philadelphia: J. Campbell, 1863.

Van Slyck, J. M. *Milwaukee City Directory and Business Advertiser, 1856–57.* Milwaukee: Daily Wisconsin Print, 1856.

Wakelyn, Jon L., ed. *Southern Pamphlets on Secession, November 1860–April 1861.* Chapel Hill: University of North Carolina Press, 1996.

Webster, Daniel. *The Papers of Daniel Webster.* Series 2, *Legal Papers.* Vol. 3, *The Federal Practice,* pts. 1 and 2, edited by Andrew J. King. Hanover, N.H.: University Press of New England, 1989.

———. *The Papers of Daniel Webster: Digital Edition.* Edited by Charles M. Wiltse. Charlottesville: University of Virginia Press, Rotunda, 2018. https://rotunda. upress.virginia.edu/founders/WBST.

———. *Writings and Speeches of Daniel Webster.* Edited by Edward Everett. 18 vols. Boston: Little, Brown, 1903.

Wheeler, Jacob D., ed. *Reports of Criminal Law Cases with Notes and References; Containing Also a View of the Criminal Laws of the United States.* Vol. 2. Albany: Gould, Banks and Gould, 1851.

Wirt, William. *An Address, Delivered before the Peithessophian and Philoclean Societies of Rutgers College.* 2nd ed. New Brunswick, N.J.: Terhune and Letson, 1830.

———. *Opinion on the Right of the State of Georgia to Extend Her Laws over the Cherokee Nation.* New Echota: John Wheeler for the Cherokee Nation, 1830.

———. *Sketches of the Life and Character of Patrick Henry.* Philadelphia: James Webster, 1817.

———. *The Two Principal Arguments of William Wirt, Esquire, on the Trial of Aaron Burr, for High Treason, and on the Motion to Commit Aaron Burr and Others for Trial in Kentucky.* Richmond: Samuel Pleasants, Jr., 1808.

[Wirt, William]. *The Letters of the British Spy.* 10th ed. New York: Harper and Brothers, 1832.

———. *The Old Bachelor.* 2 vols. Baltimore: Fielding Lucas, Jr., 1810.

Statutes

State Statutes

Georgia. An Act to Ratify and Confirm Certain Articles of Agreement and Cession Entered into on the 24th Day of April 1802, between the Commissioners of the

State of Georgia on the One Part, and the Commissioners of the United States on the Other Part. In Acts of the General Assembly of the State of Georgia Passed in June and November 1802, Georgia Legislative Documents, in *Compilation of the Laws of the State of Georgia, Passed by the Legislature since the Political Year 1800, to the Year 1810, Inclusive*. Edited by Augustin Smith Clayton. Augusta: Adams and Duyckinck, 1812. Passed June 16, 1802.

Maryland. An Act for the Benefit of William Wirt. In *Laws of Maryland Made and Passed at a Session of Assembly, Begun and Held at the City of Annapolis, on Monday the seventh of November, in the year of our Lord one thousand seven hundred and eighty-five*. Ch. XLVIII, 36. Annapolis: Frederick Green [1791]). Passed December 27, 1791.

———. An Act Laying Duties on Licenses to Retailers of Dry Goods, and for Other Purposes. Ch. 184. In *Laws Made and Passed by the General Assembly of the State of Maryland*. Annapolis: Jonas Green, 1820. Passed February 14, 1820.

Massachusetts. An Act to Prevent the Introduction of Paupers, from Foreign Ports or Places. Ch. 165. In *The General Laws of Massachusetts, from the Adoption of the Constitution, to February, 1822*. Boston: Wells and Lilly, and Cummings and Hilliard, 1823. Vol. 2. Passed February 25, 1820.

New York. An Act to Amend the Act, entitled "An Act to reduce several laws, relating particularly to the city of New-York into one act," so far as it relates to the importation of Passengers." In *Laws of the State of New-York, Passed at the Forty-Third Session of the Legislature, Begun and Held at the City of Albany, the Fourth day of January, 1820*. Ch. CCXXII. Albany: J. Buel, 1820. Passed April 14, 1820.

———. An Act Concerning Passengers in Vessels Coming to the Port of New-York. Ch. XXXVII. In *Laws of the State of New-York, Passed at the Forty-Seventh Session of the Legislature, Begun and Held at the City of Albany, the Sixth Day of January, 1824*. Albany, Leake and Croswell, 1824. Passed February 11, 1824.

South Carolina. An Act for the Better Regulation and Government of Free Negroes and Persons of Colour; and for other purposes. 3, sec. 1, 2, 7, in *Acts and Resolutions of the General Assembly of the State of South Carolina*. Columbia: Daniel Faust, 1823. Passed December 21, 1822.

Virginia. An Act to Prevent the Migration of Free Negroes and Mulattoes into This Commonwealth. In *Statutes at Large of Virginia*. Richmond: Samuel Shepherd, 1835. Passed December 12, 1793.

Wisconsin. An Act Relating to the Writ of Habeas Corpus to Persons Claimed as Fugitive Slaves. Wisconsin—10th Session, General Acts 12. Madison: Atwood and Rublee, 1857. Passed February 19, 1857.

———. Joint Resolution No. IV (1859). In *General Laws Passed by the Legislature of Wisconsin, in the Year 1859, Together with Joint Resolutions and Memorials*. Madison: James Ross, 1859, 248. 13th legislature. Passed March 19, 1859.

———. *Journal of the Senate of Wisconsin, 14th Annual Session*. Madison: Smith and Cullaton, 1862.

U.S. Statutes, Congressional Documents, and Tribal Laws

Statutes

An Act to Establish the Judicial Courts of the United States (Judiciary Act of 1789). Ch. 20, 1 Stat. 73 (September 24, 1789).

An Act for Enrolling and Licensing Ships or Vessels to Be Employed in the Coasting Trade and Fisheries, and for Regulating the Same. Ch. 8, sec. 1 Stat. 305 (February 18, 1793).

An Act to Provide for the More Convenient Organization of the Courts of the United States (Judiciary Act of 1801). 2 Stat. 89 (1801).

An Act to Repeal Certain Acts Respecting the Organization of the Courts of the United States; and for Other Purposes (Judiciary Act of 1802). 2 Stat. 132 (March 8, 1801).

An Act to Regulate Trade and Intercourse with the Indian Tribes, and to Preserve Peace on the Frontiers. Pub. L. No. 7–13, § 12. 2 Stat. 139, 143 (March 30, 1802).

An Act to Prevent the Importation of Certain Persons into Certain States, Where, by the Laws Thereof, Their Admission Is Prohibited. Ch. 10, 2 Stat. 205 (February 28, 1803).

An Act Establishing Circuit Courts, and Abridging the Jurisdiction of the District Courts in the Districts of Kentucky, Tennessee and Ohio. Ch. 16, 2 Stat. 420 (February 24, 1807).

An Act to Prohibit the Importation of Slaves, into Any Port or Place within the Jurisdiction of the United States, from and after the First Day of January, in the Year of Our Lord, One Thousand Eight Hundred and Eight. Ch. 22, 2 Stat. 426 (March 2, 1807).

An Act Regulating Passenger Ships and Vessels. Ch. 46, 3 Stat. 488–89 (March 1819).

An Act Further to Provide for the Collection of Duties on Imports (Force Act). 4 Stat. 632 (1833).

Eighth and Ninth Circuits Act. Ch. 34, 5 Stat. 176 (March 3, 1837).

An Act to Amend, and Supplementary to, the Act Entitled "An Act Respecting Fugitives from Justice, and Persons Escaping from the Service of Their Masters, Approved February Twelfth, One Thousand Seven Hundred and Ninety-Three" (Fugitive Slave Act of 1850). 9 Stat. 462 (September 18, 1850).

An Act to Amend "An Act to Establish the Judicial Courts of the United States, Approved September Twenty-Fourth, Seventeen Hundred and Eighty-Nine" (Habeas Corpus Act of 1867). 14 Stat. 385 (February 5, 1867).

Congressional Documents

American State Papers: Indian Affairs. 2 vols. Washington, D.C.: Gales and Seaton, 1832–34.

Annals of the Congress of the United States, Seventh Congress—Second Session. In *The Debates and Proceedings in the Congress of the United States; with an Appendix, Containing Important State Papers and Public Documents, and All the Laws of a Public Nature; With a Copious Index.* Vol. 12, 1802–3. Washington, D.C.: Gales and Seaton, 1851.

Committee on Commerce, House of Representatives. *Free Colored Seamen—Majority and Minority Reports.* 27th Congress, 3d Session. January 20, 1843. Washington, D.C.: [s.n.], 1843.

Congressional Globe. 31st Congress, 1st Session (1850).

Journal of the Senate of the United States of America (1803).

Journal of the House of Representatives of the United States (1803).

Executive-Branch Materials

Buchanan, James. "Message of the President" [Fourth Annual Message]. December 3, 1860. In *Congressional Globe*, 36th Congress, 2nd Session, Appendix, 1.

Fillmore, Millard. "First Annual Message." December 2, 1850. In *A Compilation of the Messages and Papers of the Presidents, 1789–1897.* Edited by James D. Richardson. Washington, D.C.: Government Printing Office, 1897, 5:138–39.

Jackson, Andrew. "First Annual Message." December 8, 1829. In *A Compilation of the Messages and Papers of the Presidents, 1789–1897.* Edited by James D. Richardson. Washington, D.C.: Government Printing Office, 1896, 2:457.

Monroe, James. "Message to the Senate and House of Representatives of the United States," March 30, 1824. In *Compilation of the Messages and Papers of the Presidents.* Washington, D.C.: Government Printing Office, 1896, 2:234–37.

Official Opinions of the Attorneys General of the United States. Vols. 1–12. Washington, D.C.: R. Farnham, 1852–70.

Opinions of the Attorneys General of the United States, from the Beginning of the Government to March 1st, 1841 . . . Published under the Inspection of Henry D. Gilpin. Washington, D.C.: Blair and Rives, 1841.

Tribal Laws

Laws of the Cherokee Nation: Adopted by the Council at Various Periods. Tahlequah, C.N.: Cherokee Advocate, 1852.

Cases

Ableman v. Booth, 59 U.S. (18 How.) 476 (1855).

Ableman v. Booth, 62 U.S. (21 How.) 506 (1859).

The Antelope, 23 U.S. (10 Wheat.) 66 (1825).

The Arrogante Barcelones, 20 U.S. 496 (1822).

The Brig Wilson v. the United States, 1 Brockenbrough's Reports 423 (C.C.D. Va. 1820).

The Brigantine Amiable Lucy v. United States, 10 U.S. (6 Cranch) 330 (1810).

Brown v. Maryland, 25 U.S. (12 Wheat.) 419 (1827).

C&A Carbone, Inc. v. Town of Clarkstown, 511 U.S. 383 (1994).

Calder v. Deliesseline, 16 S.C.L. (Harp.) 186 (1824).

Cherokee Nation v. Georgia, 30 U.S. (5 Pet.) 1 (1831).

The Cherokee Tobacco Case, 78 U.S. (11 Wall.) 616 (1871).

Chisholm v. Georgia, 2 U.S. (2 Dall.) 419, 456 (1793).

Cohens v. Virginia, 19 U.S. (6 Wheat.) 264 (1821).

Comptroller of the Treasury of Maryland v. Wynne, 575 U.S. 542 (2015).

Cooley v. Board of Wardens of Port of Philadelphia, 52 U.S. (12 How.) 299 (1852).

Corfield v. Coryell, 6 Fed. Cas. 546 (C.C. E.D. Pa. 1825).

Dred Scott v. Sandford, 60 U.S. (19 How.) 393 (1857).

Elkison v. Deliesseline, 8 Fed. Cas. 493 (No. 4366) (C.C. D.S.C. 1823).

Ex parte Booth, 3 Wis. 145, 148–49 (1854).

Fairfax's Devisee v. Hunter, 6 American Law Journal 313 (1817).

Fairfax's Devisee v. Hunter's Lessee, 11 U.S. (7 Cranch) 603 (1813).

The Fortuna, 15 U.S. (2 Wheat.) 161 (1817).

Gibbons v. Ogden, 19 U.S. (6 Wheat.) 448 (1821).

Gibbons v. Ogden, 22 U.S. (Wheat.) 1 (1824).

Groves v. Slaughter, 40 U.S. (15 Pet.) 449 (1841).

Holmes v. U.S. (C.C.D.S.C. 1832).

Huidekoper's Lessee v. Douglass, 7 U.S. (3 Cranch) 1 (1805).

Hunter v. Martin, Devisee of Fairfax, 18 Va. (4 Munf.) 1 (1815).

In re Booth, 3 Wis. 1 (1854).

In re Booth and Rycraft, 3 Wis. 157, 182 (1855).

Jones v. Shore's Executor, 14 U.S. 462 (1816).

The License Cases, 46 U.S. (5 How.) 504 (1847).

Livingston v. Van Ingen, 9 Johns. 507 (N.Y. 1812).

Marbury v. Madison, 5 U.S. (1 Cranch) 137 (1803).

Martin v. Hunter's Lessee, 14 U.S. 304 (1816).

Mayor, Aldermen, and Commonalty of the City of New York v. George Miln, 33 U.S. (8 Pet.) 120 (1834).

Mayor, Aldermen, and Commonalty of the City of New York v. George Miln, 34 U.S. (9 Pet.) 85 (1835).

Mayor, Aldermen, and Commonalty of the City of New York v. George Miln, 36 U.S. (11 Pet.) 102 (1837).

McCulloch v. Maryland, 17 U.S. 316 (1819).

Michelin Tire Corp. v. Wages, 423 U.S. 276 (1976).

National Federation of Independent Business v. Sebelius, 567 U.S. 519 (2012).

Ogden v. Gibbons, 4 Johns. Ch. 150 (N.Y. Ch. 1819).

Osborn v. Bank of the United States, 22 U.S. 738 (1824).

The Passenger Cases, 48 U.S. (7 How.) 283 (1849).

Prigg v. Pennsylvania, 41 U.S. (16 Pet.) 539 (1842).

Roberts v. Yates, 20 Fed. Cas. 937 (C.C. D.S.C. 1853).

State v. George Tassels, 1 Dudley 229 (1830).

Trititle v. Fairfax, Order Book, Superior Court No. 2, 43, Office of Clerk of Circuit Court, Frederick County (April 24, 1794).

United States v. Amistad, 40 U.S. (15 Pet.) 518 (1841).

United States v. Booth, 59 U.S. (18 How.) 476 (1855).

United States v. Burr, 25 Fed. Cas. 122 (1807).

United States v. Holmes and Mazyck (D.C. D.S.C. 1831).

United States v. La Jeune Eugenie, 26 Fed. Cas. 832 (C.C. Mass. 1822).

United States v. Lopez, 514 U.S. 549, 615 (1995).

United States. v. Rycraft, 27 Fed. Cas. 918 (D.C. D. Wis., 1854) (No. 16,211).

United States v. Schooner Louisa, U.S. Dist. Ct. E.D. Va. (November 15, 1819).

United States v. The William, 28 Fed. Cas. 614 (D. Mass.) (1808).

Weston v. City Council of Charleston, 27 U.S. (2 Pet.) 449 (1829).

Willson v. Black Bird Creek Marsh Company, 27 U.S. (2 Pet.) 245 (1829).

Worcester v. Georgia, 31 U.S. (6 Pet.) 515 (1832).

Periodicals

American Beacon and Norfolk and Portsmouth Daily Advertiser

Baltimore Patriot and Mercantile Advertiser

Boston Courier

Boston Gazette

Cartersville (Georgia) Courant

Charleston City Gazette and Commercial Daily Advertiser

Charleston Courier

Charleston Mercury

Charleston News and Courier

Cherokee Phoenix

Christian Advocate

Christian Register

City of Washington Gazette

Daily Argus and Democrat (Madison, Wisc.)

Daily Missouri Republican (St. Louis)

Daily National Intelligencer (Washington, D.C.)

Daily Wisconsin

Delaware Gazette and Peninsula Advertiser

Illinois Intelligencer

The Liberator

Milwaukee Sentinel

New-York Evening Post

New York Evening Star
New York Times
Niles' National Register
Niles' Weekly Register
Norwich (Conn.) Courier
Pendleton Messenger
Racine Advocate
Religious Intelligencer
Richmond Enquirer
South Carolina Gazette
Southern Banner
Virginia Argus

ACKNOWLEDGMENTS

When I began working in 2013 on the project that became this book, I had two firm yet inchoate ideas in mind. First, I wanted to write a book about the period between the founding era and the Civil War that was neither an "after the founding" nor a "before the war" book, and I wanted to give that period a name. Second, I wanted the book to have a story that was driven by historical actors whom I could portray as characters living in specific times and places, facing a particular set of concerns, and with their own views on law and politics. Friends and colleagues offered encouraging words such as "symphonic" and "chronothematic" that helped me conceptualize what it was that I was trying to do. And I also hoped there would be some room for creativity—not constitutional creativity in the early-nineteenth-century sense, but in the sense of the great Tudor historian G. R. Elton's exhortation on the historian's writerly craft, in his 1967 book *The Practice of History*: "Imagination, controlled by learning and scholarship, learning and scholarship rendered meaningful by imagination—those are the tools of enquiry possessed by the historian."

Along the way, I learned that imagination, learning, and scholarship are just some of the tools that make the historian's enquiry possible. A fortunate historian also comes to rely on well-timed advice, hard questions, archival and research assistance, serendipitous hallway and workshop conversations, collegial bonhomie, reading suggestions, and willing listeners. I count myself fortunate on all these fronts. Now, with the book complete, I consider myself even luckier to be able to acknowledge these debts and offer thanks.

I have had the opportunity to present drafts of parts of the book at workshops, colloquia, conferences, and seminars around the country. I have benefited enormously from conversations at the Yale Center for Historical Enquiry and the Social Sciences; Harvard Law School; the American Bar Foundation; the University of Notre Dame in London; the University of Arizona; the University of Chicago History and Social Sciences Forum; the University of Wisconsin and the University of Maryland Carey Law

School Discussion Groups on Constitutionalism (also known collectively as "the Schmooze"); Georgetown University Law Center; Stanford Law School; New York University Law School; the University of Michigan Law School; Brooklyn Law School; the University of Virginia Law School; Columbia Law School; the University of California, Berkeley, School of Law; the University of Toronto Faculty of Law; the University of Chicago Graham School; and the incomparable University of Chicago Law School Faculty Work-in-Progress Workshop. The annual meeting of the American Society for Legal History, including but not limited to formal panel presentations, has been a reliably generative forum for discussing the book. I was also honored to be able to present portions of the book as the Philip Pro Lecture in Legal History at the William S. Boyd School of Law, University of Nevada, Las Vegas, in 2014, at the kind invitation of Dan Hamilton and David Tanenhaus; and the Judge Robert A. Ainsworth, Jr., Memorial Lecture at Loyola University New Orleans College of Law in 2019, where Jim Viator was an extraordinarily gracious host.

I am grateful to the many outstanding research assistants who have eagerly dived into primary sources, phoned and emailed archives around the country, battled microfilm readers, struggled with nineteenth-century cursive, and assisted in cite-checking. Thank you, Patty Herold, Abbey Molitor, Charlie Zagnoli, Aasiya Mirza Glover, Evelyn Atkinson, Katy Cummings, Rebecca Boorstein, Rachel Zemil, Michael Sanders, Clare Downing, Ryan Clark, Alex Hale, Patrick Berning-O'Neill, James Sowerby, Angela Peterson, Samara Arain, and Ivy Truong. I have also been fortunate to teach a seminar titled "The Interbellum Constitution" several times, each time enjoying rigorous and nuanced discussions with stellar students, including Caroline Veniero, Ryne Cannon, Juan Wilson, and Mary Cate Hickman, who gave unvarnished opinions on the sources we read and helped me to hone my arguments.

I am indebted to librarians and archivists at the collections that I have visited or consulted for the book, including the Library of Congress; the National Archives and Records Administration; the Library of Virginia; the Houghton Library of Harvard University; Stanford Special Collections; the Newberry Library; the New York Public Library; the Wilson Special Collections Library of the University of North Carolina; the Albert and Shirley Small Special Collections Library of the University of Virginia; the Maryland Historical Society; the Maryland State Archives; the Morgan Library; the American Philosophical Society; the New York State Library; the New-York Historical Society; the Oklahoma Historical Society; the Western History Collections at the University of Oklahoma Libraries; the Cherokee Heritage Center; the Gilcrease Museum; the Maryland State Archives; the Yale University Library; the Harvard Law School Library; and the Regenstein Library of the University of Chicago. For their willingness to answer a series of research queries, I particularly thank Patrick Kerwin at the Manuscript Division of the Library of Congress; Molly Silliman at the South Carolina Historical Society; Dan Preston at the Papers of James Monroe; Susan Pearl at the Prince George's County Historical Society; David Haugaard at the Historical Society of Pennsylvania; David Gomez at the New Echota State Historic Site; Jeff Briley at the Oklahoma History Center; McKenzie Lemhouse at the South Caroliniana Library; Jennifer McCormick at the Charleston Museum; Karen Brickman Emmons at the Historic Charleston Foundation; Brianne Barrett at the American Antiquarian Society; and Lisa Marine and Lee Grady at the Wisconsin Historical Society.

The indefatigable staff of the D'Angelo Law Library at the University of Chicago have been tireless, knowledgeable, and good humored as they have fielded my countless and sometimes rushed requests for National Archives and Records Administration microfilm reels, obscure antebellum newspapers and pamphlets, and assistance on contacting other repositories. Connie Fleischer, Sheri Lewis, Margaret Schilt, Bill Schwesig, James Patterson, and the late Greg Nimmo are experts in their fields, and I am deeply grateful to them for their help.

Steve Livengood of the U.S. Capitol Historical Society escorted me on a fascinating private tour of the Old Supreme Court Chamber. At the Anacostia Watershed Society in Bladensburg, Maryland, Simon Plog and Erin Borgeson Castelli very kindly allowed me to wander through their headquarters, formerly the Brick Store, the sale of which funded William Wirt's legal education. My brother David LaCroix accompanied me on the expedition, not only retracing Wirt's steps but also hunting for the locations of the dueling ground and the August 1814 "Bladensburg Races," all amid a period-appropriate onslaught by late-summer mosquitoes. My sister-in-law Helen LaCroix has shared my enthusiasm for field research and characterful nineteenth-century portraits.

I am grateful to the National Endowment for the Humanities, which awarded me a fellowship for the project in 2018–19. The Mayer Brown Faculty Research Fund at the University of Chicago Law School also provided financial support.

I have been fortunate to have the benefit of comments on parts of the manuscript from many friends and colleagues at the University of Chicago. I especially thank Emily Buss, Aziz Huq, Matthew Kruer, Jon Levy, Martha Nussbaum, Farah Peterson, Randy Picker, Steve Pincus, Jim Sparrow, and David Strauss. Dick Helmholz has been a source of wisdom on a variety of questions ranging from English equity practice to the nuances of the writ *de homine replegiando*. He also supplied an original treatise just when it was needed to clarify what Justice Johnson might have been up to in *Elkison*.

I am extremely grateful to have had rich discussions about the book with fartherflung friends and colleagues, including Tanner Allread, Adam Cox, Justin Driver, Dan Ernst, Yonatan Eyal, Lisa Ford, Mark Graber, Dan Hulsebosch, Amalia Kessler, Michael McConnell, Gerard Magliocca, Ioana Marinescu, John Mikhail, Cynthia Nicoletti, Nick Parrillo, Richard Primus, Jack Rakove, Liz Reese, Adam Samaha, David S. Schwartz, Rachel Shelden, Brad Snyder, and Anne Twitty. Rivka Weill posed usefully provocative queries in a conversation after a workshop presentation. Gerry Leonard asked a key question at a key moment in the project at the American Society for Legal History conference in Las Vegas in 2017. Chris Schmidt graciously organized a manuscript workshop *nonpareil* at a crucial stage, at which Laura Edwards, Jonathan Gienapp,

Joanna Grisinger, Bill Novak, and Allison Tirres asked important questions and offered trenchant comments that improved the book immeasurably.

I am indebted to Sandy Levinson and Greg Ablavsky, who each provided thoughtful and engaged reader's reports on the manuscript at a key stage. At an earlier point, two anonymous readers reviewed the proposal for Yale University Press and offered helpful comments on framing and argument.

I continue to benefit from the intellectual generosity and unstinting support of many of my teachers over the years, from my undergraduate professors in the Yale History Department, to my professors at Yale Law School, to my Ph.D. advisors and committee members in the Harvard History Department and at Harvard Law School. I thank Diane Kunz, Jay Gitlin, Bob Gordon, Morton Horwitz, Christine Desan, and especially the late Bill Gienapp, who shepherded my first foray into writing on the nullification crisis and introduced me to a host of foundational texts, many of which are cited in these pages. Jim Kloppenberg and David Armitage have offered inspiration, encouragement, and enthusiasm, over meals as well as by email, and provide models of scholarly excellence and rigorous intellectual history to which I continue to aspire.

For friendship, solidarity, and intellectual and moral support, I thank Emily Buss, Gabriel Lear, Emily Osborn, and Jennifer Pitts. Josephine Bradley supplied essential and much-appreciated aid throughout the research and writing process.

My family has lived with this book since its beginning and has helped me in innumerable ways along its path, offering both internal and external improvements. My parents, Terri and David LaCroix, could not have known when they moved to the Milwaukee suburbs in 1970 that they had seeded a future chapter, as well as providing welcome opportunities for research trips even amid a global pandemic. My daughters, Elspeth, Isolde, and Alana, have gamely listened to recordings of "Tippecanoe and Tyler Too!," endured discourses on early-nineteenth-century politics, and learned to recognize Wirt, Webster, and Marshall from their portraits (or, as appropriate, bobbleheads). They have eagerly accompanied me on research travels, always ready to inhale the scent of old buildings and to try to absorb the ancient essence of a place. (Sweet tea, biscuits, and carriage rides have offered additional means of site-specific immersion.) Finally, I thank my husband, William Birdthistle, with whom I share my love of writing, my hopes, and my life. *Ad astra*.

Alison L. LaCroix
Hyde Park, Chicago, Illinois

INDEX